DATE DUE

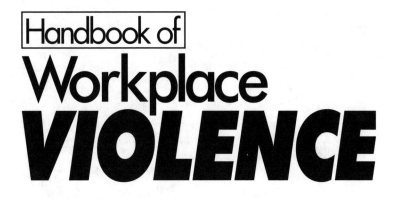

Handbook of
Workplace
VIOLENCE

Handbook of
Workplace
VIOLENCE

E. KEVIN
KELLOWAY

Saint Mary's University, Halifax, Canada

JULIAN
BARLING

Queen's University, Kingston, Canada

JOSEPH J.
HURRELL, JR.

National Institute for Occupational Safety and Health, U.S.

SAGE Publications
Thousand Oaks ■ London ■ New Delhi

For information:

Sage Publications, Inc.
2455 Teller Road
Thousand Oaks, California 91320
E-mail: order@sagepub.com

Sage Publications Ltd.
1 Oliver's Yard
55 City Road
London EC1Y 1SP
United Kingdom

Sage Publications India Pvt. Ltd.
B-42, Panchsheel Enclave
Post Box 4109
New Delhi 110 017 India

Printed in the United States of America

Library of Congress Cataloging-in-Publication Data

Handbook of workplace violence / editors: E. Kevin Kelloway, Julian Barling,
Joseph J. Hurrell, Jr.
      p. cm.
Includes bibliographical references and index.
ISBN 0-7619-3062-0 (cloth)
   1. Violence in the workplace. 2. Violence in the workplace—Prevention.
I. Kelloway, E. Kevin. II. Barling, Julian. III. Hurrell, Joseph J.

HF5549.5.E43H36 2006
363.32—dc22   2005023062

This book is printed on acid-free paper.

05   06   07   08   09   10   9   8   7   6   5   4   3   2   1

Acquisitions Editor:	Al Bruckner
Editorial Assistant:	MaryAnn Vail
Production Editor:	Diane S. Foster
Copy Editor:	Robert Holm
Typesetter:	C&M Digitals (P) Ltd.
Proofreader:	Scott Oney
Indexer:	Will Ragsdale
Cover Designer:	Candice Harman

Contents

Part III: Prevention and Intervention   **489**

PART I

Perspectives on Workplace Violence

1

Editors'
Introduction to Part I

> *Work is, by its very nature, about violence—to the spirit as well as to the body. It is about ulcers as well as accidents, about shouting matches as well as fistfights, about nervous breakdowns as well as kicking the dog around. It is, above all (or beneath all), about daily humiliations. To survive the day is triumph enough for the walking wounded among the great many of us.*
>
> —Studs Terkel, *Working* (1974), p. xi

In his classic book *Working*, the American journalist Studs Terkel gave a prescient analysis of work in the 20th and 21st centuries. In the last 10 to 15 years, research on workplace violence and aggression has proliferated, and as constructs and measures are developed and refined, the fundamental soundness of Terkel's analysis has become apparent. For many employees, work is fundamentally about violence. The postal shootings of the mid-1990s (see U.S. Postal Service Commission on a Safe and Secure Workplace, 2000) and the resulting popularization of the phrase *going postal* to describe an enraged state were, arguably, the defining moments that focused organizational and research attention on the notion of workplace violence and aggression. This is not to say that the postal shootings were the first incident of this kind. As Terkel's observations and those of numerous others attest (e.g., Grinker & Spiegel, 1945; Loo, 1986; Stouffer et al., 1949; Southard, 1919), the problem and consequences of workplace violence have been known for some time.

The timing of the postal shootings, however, was coincident with the APA-NIOSH initiative on occupational health psychology (Sauter & Hurrell, 1999) and the inauguration of the APA-NIOSH Work, Stress, and Health Conferences. Media attention highlighted the problem at the same time as researchers concerned with health and safety in the workplace were beginning to come together in a more organized fashion. Perhaps not surprisingly, workplace violence emerged as an issue at the first such conference (e.g., Braverman, 1992) and became a focus at the second Work, Stress, and Health Conference leading to the publication of a seminal collection of papers on the topic (VandenBos & Bulatao, 1996).

As this volume attests, research on workplace violence and aggression has proliferated since that time. To some extent, research has followed the path originally described by Terkel. From an initial focus on physical violence (the fistfights noted by Terkel), researchers have moved on to consider a wider variety of aggressive behaviors (Terkel's shouting matches) under various rubrics (see Schat & Kelloway, 2004, for a review). Research has explored the connections between various forms of aggression and violence in the workplace (e.g., Barling, Rogers, & Kelloway, 2001). More recently, empirical attention has focused on the "violence to the spirit" and "daily humiliations" associated with workplace bullying (e.g., Rayner, Hoel, & Cooper, 2002) or emotional abuse (e.g., Keashly, 1998; Keashly & Jagatic, 2003). As our understanding of the range of behaviors constituting workplace violence and aggression grows, so does our appreciation of the enormity of the problem.

Like work, this handbook is fundamentally about violence. Our intent was to bring together the leading researchers to summarize the current state of knowledge and to begin to chart the course for future research. The chapters in this first section provide an appropriate foundation for this endeavor.

The study of aggression and violence is characterized by two fundamental theoretical orientations: the *rational choice model* and the *frustration-aggression hypothesis*. It is not clear that these are competing, as much as complementary, approaches that have something to tell us about the causes of workplace violence and aggression.

In the first chapter, Felson presents an argument in favor of a rational choice understanding of violence and aggression. Essentially he argues that the key to understanding violence and aggression is to recognize that individuals engage in such behaviors because "they can (a) force others to comply, (b) restore justice when they believe they have been wronged, (c) achieve a desired image or reputation, and (d) entertain themselves with a potentially risky activity" (Felson, this volume, p. 16). Felson's focus is on violence in general rather than on workplace violence. Thus, his analysis avoids the balkanization that is apparent in many studies of workplace violence and provides a context in which workplace violence can be understood.

Spector, Fox, and Domagalski begin with a focus on "frustration-aggression" but expand this analysis in two major ways. First, as they note, current research has moved beyond *frustration* to consider a range of negative emotional states. Their approach draws on previously developed models that posit emotions as resulting from organizational stressors and influencing responses such as violence and aggression (e.g., Spector & Fox, 2002, 2004). Like Felson, Spector et al. offer an expanded context for understanding workplace violence and aggression. Rather than go beyond the workplace, however, Spector et al. suggest that workplace violence and aggression be understood within a broader framework of counterproductive work behaviors, again a perspective that is likely to add to our understanding of the phenomenon.

Schat, Frone, and Kelloway also offer a foundation for understanding workplace violence and aggression. Drawing on a national probability sample, the authors go beyond the media hype and the widespread use of convenience samples to generate accurate prevalence estimates for workplace violence and aggression. Schat et al. note the need for consistent operationalization and rigorous sampling methodology in generating accurate prevalence estimates. They use their data to examine the impact of demographic and occupational factors on workplace violence and aggression. The results of their analyses show that approximately 47 million U.S. employees (41.4%) are exposed to psychological aggression, and 15 million (13%) are exposed to physical aggression in the workplace.

For many employees, then, work is fundamentally about violence. Changing this situation requires an understanding of how violence occurs as well as its effects on individuals. Change also requires understanding who is affected by workplace violence and aggression and what interventions are available to organizations and individuals. Facilitating such understanding is the goal of this handbook.

References

Barling, J., Rogers, G., & Kelloway, E. K. (2001). Behind closed doors: In-home workers' experience of sexual harassment and workplace violence. *Journal of Occupational Health Psychology, 6*, 255–269.

Braverman, M. (1992). Post-trauma crisis intervention in the workplace. In J. C. Quick, L. R. Murphy, & J. J. Hurrell (Eds.), *Stress and well-being at work* (pp. 299–316). Washington, DC: American Psychological Association.

Grinker, R. R., & Spiegel, J. P. (1945). *Men under stress.* New York: McGraw-Hill.

Keashly, L. (1998). Emotional abuse in the workplace: Conceptual and empirical issues. *Journal of Emotional Abuse, 1*(1), 85–117.

Keashly, L., & Jagatic, K. (2003). By any other name: American perspectives on workplace bullying. In S. Einarsen, H. Hoel, D. Zapf, & C. Cooper (Eds.), *Bullying and emotional abuse in the workplace: International research and practice perspectives* (pp. 31–61). London: Taylor Francis.

Loo, R. (1986). Post-shooting reactions among police officers. *Journal of Human Stress, 2*, 27–31.

Rayner, C., Hoel, H., & Cooper, C. L. (2002). *Bullying at work: What we know, who is to blame and what can we do?* London: Taylor Francis.

Sauter, S. L., & Hurrell, J. J. (1999). Occupational health psychology: Origins, content and direction. *Professional Psychology: Research and Practice, 30*, 117–122.

Schat, A., & Kelloway, E. K. (2004). Workplace violence. In J. Barling, E. K. Kelloway, & M. Frone (Eds.), *Handbook of workplace stress.* Thousand Oaks, CA: Sage.

Southard, E. E. (1919). *Shell-shock and other neuropsychiatric problems*. Boston: Leonard.

Spector, P. E., & Fox, S. (2002). An emotion-centered model of voluntary work behavior: Some parallels between counterproductive work behavior (CWB) and organizational citizenship behavior (OCB). *Human Resource Management Review, 12,* 269–292.

Spector, P. E., & Fox, S. (2004). The stressor-emotion model of counterproductive work behavior (CWB). In S. Fox & P. E. Spector (Eds.), *Counterproductive work behavior: Investigations of actors and targets* (pp. 151–174). Washington, DC: American Psychological Association.

Stouffer, S. A., Lumsdaine, A. A., Lumsdaine, M. J., Williams, R. M., Smith, M. B., Janis, I. L., et al. (1949). *The American soldier: Combat and its aftermath* (Vol. 2). Princeton, NJ: Princeton University Press.

Terkel, S. (1974). *Working: People talk about what they do all day and how they feel about what they do*. New York: Pantheon.

U.S. Postal Service Commission on a Safe and Secure Workplace. (2000). *Report of the United States Postal Service Commission on a Safe and Secure Workplace*. New York: National Center on Addiction and Substance Abuse at Columbia University.

VandenBos, G. R., & Bulatao, E. Q. (Eds.). (1996). *Violence on the job: Identifying risks and developing solutions*. Washington, DC: American Psychological Association.

2   Violence as Instrumental Behavior

Richard B. Felson

Violence is violence, whether it occurs in the home, on the street, or in the workplace. Although there may be some differences between violent events in different settings, there are likely to be many similarities. For example, the motivation to assault a coworker should not be all that different from the motivation to assault a family member or stranger. Some of the causal factors implicated in robberies of commercial establishments are similar to those that that are implicated street robberies. Unfortunately, the field of violence has been balkanized, and separate research literatures have developed. It is sometimes useful to examine violence in particular settings against different types of targets, but we should not ignore the larger picture. Scholars need to communicate with each other in the "spirit of parsimony," if for no other reason.

In this essay, I present a rational choice perspective to aggression and violence that, it is hoped, applies to any setting.[1] I attempt to show why rational choice is preferable to the frustration-aggression approaches that are more dominant in the field. I use some evidence and examples from the workplace, but for the most part I leave the application to others. I begin by distinguishing a rational choice approach from frustration-aggression approaches and review some evidence that supports it. Then I deal with conceptual issues. I develop an alternative typology of aggression and then distinguish aggression from deviant behavior. Later on, I consider the decision-making process and review the various motives for aggression and violence. Finally, I discuss the factors that create or reduce the opportunity to engage in violence.

Rational Choice Versus Frustration-Aggression

The rational choice perspective assumes that aggressive behavior has a purpose or goal. People harm others if it will help them achieve some outcome that they value (the reward) and if the costs are not too high. From this perspective, all aggression is instrumental behavior. Rational choice theorists use the name reluctantly because they know that rationality is "bounded," that is, that behavior reflects subjective judgments about payoffs and that individuals often make careless decisions with outcomes that are disastrous for themselves as well as their victims. In the case of aggression, actors may be in a state of mind in which they do not even consider the costs at the time. But the behavior is still goal-oriented, and the actor is still making decisions.

From a rational choice approach, the use of violence is related to basic human desires. People want to influence others because many of our rewards are provided by other people. They want to be treated fairly, and they think that those who fail to do so should be punished. They want the esteem of others and to think favorably of themselves. Finally, some people enjoy activities that are exciting and entail some risk. These basic goals of human behavior are also the goals of aggression and violence. People engage in aggression because they can (a) force others to comply, (b) restore justice when they believe they have been wronged, (c) achieve a desired image or reputation, and (d) entertain themselves with a potentially risky activity.

Frustration-aggression approaches, on the other hand, treat most violence as an irrational response to aversive stimuli. According to the most recent version of the theory, aversive stimuli cause a person to experience negative affect, which instigates *reactive* or *expressive aggression* (Berkowitz, 1989; see also Dollard, Doob, Miller, Mowrer, & Sears, 1939). People lash out after experiencing stress, pain, failure, or suffering of any sort. Although some aggression is instrumental (a means to an end), expressive aggression is more common. From a frustration-aggression perspective, a rational choice perspective can only explain the motivation for instrumental aggression.

The frustration-aggression approach is basically a biological approach because the instigation for expressive aggression is a biological urge, not a reward. Aggression satisfies an innate desire to harm others when one is feeling bad or frustrated. A biologically based frustration-aggression mechanism is necessary to explain expressive aggression. Without the biological connection, expressive aggression is difficult to explain because it is difficult to argue that people are rewarded for aggression following exposure to most aversive stimuli. The rational choice approach, on the other hand, emphasizes social psychological factors in the instigation of aggression. The effects of biology are more indirect (see below).

Both approaches emphasize the role of costs as an inhibitory factor for aggression. *Costs* include the inhibiting effects of internalized moral beliefs and negative external consequences (e.g., punishment and retaliation). Thus, frustration-aggression approaches treat expressive aggression as, to some extent, a rational choice—a decision affected by cost considerations. Both theories predict that the actor may use indirect forms of aggression if the costs of direct aggression are high. In addition, both theories acknowledge that people fail to consider costs in the heat of the moment if the instigation is strong. The theories differ, however, in their claim of how a person motivated to use aggression responds when the costs are high, and indirect aggression is not a possibility. Frustration-aggression approaches claim that the person displaces the aggression onto an innocent third party. From a rational choice perspective, if the costs are too high, there is no incentive to engage in displaced aggression.

Do Aversive Stimuli Instigate Aggression?

From a frustration-aggression perspective, any type of aversive stimuli leads to aggression. From a rational choice perspective, only personal attacks and other behavior the person finds offensive instigate aggression. There must be an attribution of blame, a loss of face, or a concern for deterrence. Aversive stimuli produced by nonhuman sources or accidental behavior should not instigate aggression, unless the person attributes negligence or intent to harm to someone. Other forms of aversive stimuli may facilitate an aggressive response, but they are not instigators. They are neither necessary nor sufficient to produce aggression, and if they have any effect, it is likely to be weak.

It seems clear that most aversive stimuli do not instigate aggressive responses. For example, death is considerably more aversive than a verbal insult. Yet a person is likely to respond with aggression when insulted, not when they are told that they have a terminal illness or a loved one has died. If aversive stimuli were important, homicides would be more common at funerals and hospitals than during recreational activities, and of course, they are not (Luckenbill, 1977). In addition, we feel worse when we blame ourselves for a problem, not the other person, but blaming others, not self-blame, leads to aggression. Finally, it seems unlikely that aversive stimuli have a biological link to aggression from an evolutionary perspective. If such a link exists, it must have contributed to the survival of the species at some point in human history; it must have been instrumental aggression in the past. It is difficult to imagine how attacking people when one is in a bad mood would have contributed to human survival.

In testing the rational choice approach, it is unnecessary to show that incentives and costs can affect aggressive behavior because everyone agrees that some violence is instrumental and that perceived costs inhibit all forms of aggression. The challenge for a rational choice perspective is to show that only aversive stimuli stemming from disputes, not aversive stimuli generally, instigate aggression. In other words, it is important to show that instances that appear to be expressive aggression are really instrumental aggression. In addition, it is necessary for the rational choice approach to explain what appears to be displaced aggression; frustration-aggression has a simple, straightforward explanation for why people sometimes attack innocent third parties. If the empirical basis of frustration-aggression approaches is undermined, rational choice is all that is left standing.

Laboratory studies show that the key determinant of aggressive behavior is an intentional attack by a confederate, not generally aversive stimuli. Participants will not deliver shock or cause harm to a confederate unless they have been shocked or insulted themselves (Tedeschi & Felson, 1994). Some studies do show small effects of physical pain, or losing contests, if the participant is also attacked, but an aversive stimulus has no effect by itself. Berkowitz (1993) argues that aversive stimuli do instigate aggression in laboratory studies but that the attack is necessary to overcome inhibitions; however, a more likely explanation is that aversive stimuli are a weak facilitator and not an instigator of aggression.

Laboratory research also shows that the attribution of blame is critical in determining whether a negative experience leads to aggression. It is primarily negative experiences that are perceived as unjustifiable that lead to aggression. Berkowitz (1989) explains this well-known finding by claiming that unjustifiable frustrations are more aversive than justifiable frustrations; however, research also shows that participants retaliate for intended shocks, even when they do not actually receive the shock (Epstein & Taylor, 1967; Geen, 1968; Gentry, 1970; Nickel, 1974; Pisano & Taylor, 1971). The results suggest that "bad intentions," not bad experiences, lead to aggression, because they imply blame. Other laboratory studies show that participants are more likely to retaliate when a person shocks them than when a machine shocks them (Sermat, 1967). The pain is the same, but the meaning differs. When someone zaps them, and participants think that they have been wronged, they retaliate.

Research on the sequence of events leading to homicide and assault suggests that they begin when someone believes they have been wronged or personally attacked (Felson, 1984; Luckenbill, 1977). When someone provides an excuse or justification for his or her behavior—reducing the level of blame assigned—the conflict is less likely to escalate to violence (Felson, 1982). Aversive stimuli of a general sort are never mentioned in descriptions of actual violent events, nor is displaced aggression; the motive almost always has something to do with the victim. That is why the police are able to catch offenders and prosecutors "establish motive" and get convictions. They show that the defendant had a grievance with the victim.

Research showing a relationship between the experience of stressful life events and violence appears to provide support for the frustration-aggression approach; however, stress also interferes with competent performance and the tendency to be polite and friendly. That may anger others. Thus evidence shows that individuals who experience stressful life events are more likely to be the victims of violence (Felson, 1992; see also Silver, 2002). The relationship between a person's stress and their aggressive behavior disappears when the victimization measure is controlled. This finding suggests that the relationship between stress and violence generally reported in the literature may be due to the fact that people under stress are more likely to generate grievances, get into conflicts, and then engage in aggression themselves. Stress may also facilitate an aggressive response if it affects the decision-making process.

Frustration-aggression implies that work settings that generate more aversive stimuli are likely to have higher rates of violence. It would predict that those who work in the hot sun or under difficult conditions of any sort are more likely to use violence. From a rational choice approach, on the other hand, work settings that generate grievances are likely to have higher rates of violence. Employees may be physically comfortable, but if they believe they have been treated unfairly by their employers or coworkers, they are likely to be angry; and some of them may become aggressive or even violent. Research on workplace violence focuses on these factors (e.g., Folger & Skarlicki, 1998; Greenberg & Barling, 1999).

The frustration-aggression approach appears to be supported by evidence of displaced aggression in laboratory studies; however, there are alternative social psychological explanations. Attacks on "innocent" third parties may be an attempt to salvage some face or an attempt to restore equity when people think someone else has been unfairly rewarded (i.e., jealousy), or they may be an attack on someone who is a member of a group with whom one feels aggrieved (see Tedeschi & Felson, 1994, for a review). Outside the laboratory, many acts of what appear to be displaced aggression are not: The person is irritable but has no intent to harm, or the person does in fact have some grievance with the victim.

Studies of workplace aggression suggest that people attack the person with whom they have a grievance, not innocent third parties. Thus, Greenberg and Barling (1999) found that employees who felt they were unjustly treated by a supervisor were more likely to be aggressive toward their supervisors but not their coworkers (see also Hershcovis & Barling, 2003). They attributed a transgression to a particular person and were aggressive against that person. In addition, Inness, Barling, and Turner (in press) found that hostile supervision predicted aggression against the supervisor only in the job in which it occurred.

_____ Predatory Versus Dispute-Related Aggression

Interpersonal aggression is typically defined as any behavior intended to harm another person (Berkowitz, 1962). The definition includes behaviors that are intended to harm but are unsuccessful and intended harm that is viewed as socially desirable. It excludes behaviors that involve accidental harm and expressions of emotional upset directed at no one that are sometimes described as *anger*. *Violence* refers to aggression that involves the use or threat of physical force.

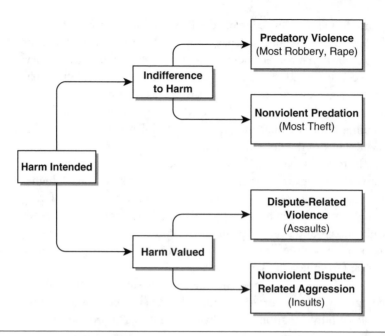

Figure 2.1   The Relationship Between Harm Doing, Aggression, and Violence With Typical
Cases

In Figure 2.1, I attempt to categorize acts of aggression according to the actor's attitude toward harming the victim. The figure indicates that for some acts of aggression, harm is incidental to the actor, but for others, harm is desired or specifically valued. Those who engage in predatory behavior deliberately harm victims but do not have a particular desire to harm them. For them, victims are substitutable, although they may prefer some victims over others because of reward/cost considerations. Harm is incidental to them, not their goal, but they are willing to harm the victim in order to achieve some other goal.[2] For example, robbery and rape typically involve predatory violence because most robbers and rapists are indifferent to the victim's suffering. They use violence to force the victim to comply because compliance will allow them to get something else they want (e.g., money or sex).[3] Other predatory behavior involves nonviolent methods, such as theft without confrontation.[4] Harm is incidental to most thieves; they desire the stolen object but do not care whether the victim's insurance can replace it. Note that those scholars who take a frustration-aggression approach treat offenses in which harm is deliberate but incidental to the offender as instrumental aggression.

For other acts of aggression, harm is the actor's desired outcome and the proximate goal. One might refer to these behaviors as judgmental rather than incidental aggression. The behavior stems from a dispute, and actors have a particular target or targets in mind. They have a grievance with their victim; they are angry; and they want to see their victim suffer in some way. Most homicides and assaults stem from disputes, but so do some robberies, rapes, thefts, arsons, and frauds (Black, 1983). For example, Greenberg (1993) found that employees who were unfairly underpaid punished their employer through theft.[5] Thus actors have a variety of ways of harming their victims; violence is relatively rare. The most common method is a verbal attack, but they may also use indirect methods.

Rational choice and frustration-aggression perspectives differ in their interpretation of the motivation for dispute-related aggression; this is their battleground. From a frustration-aggression perspective, these behaviors involve expressive aggression: Harm has intrinsic value for a person who has experienced negative affect for any reason. From a rational choice perspective, dispute-related aggression is instrumental behavior, and harm has extrinsic value: The aggressor values harm to the victim because it achieves some other purpose. Disputes are a critical source of aggression from a rational choice perspective, whereas they are just one of many sources of aversive stimuli from the point of view of frustration-aggression.

Frustration-aggression posits a special mechanism for one type of behavior, expressive aggression. The rational choice approach, on the other hand, treats expressive aggression as similar to any other human behavior. It is therefore more parsimonious. The question is whether this general theory of human behavior, so central in the social sciences, can explain dispute-related aggression and violence. In addition, one might consider dispute-related violence as the last frontier for a rational choice approach to human behavior: "If one can take it there, one can take it anywhere."

Aggression and Deviance

Aggression and deviance (or norm violations) are overlapping domains. Some aggressive behavior is deviant behavior, and some deviant behavior involves aggression. If the rule that is violated is codified in law, its violation is considered criminal.[6] Sometimes the failure to use aggression is considered deviant. For example, failing to harm someone who deserves to be punished is a violation of the rule of retributive justice. On the other hand, sometimes an aggressive response is perceived as appropriate, but the offender's overreaction or disproportionate response is perceived as deviant. For example, we might view an insult as appropriate response to a verbal attack, but not violent retaliation. Although groups vary in what they consider deviant, there is considerable consensus about most deviant acts, particularly those involving intentional harm doing (Rossi, Waite, Bose, & Berk, 1974).

Violent crime involves both deviance and aggression. Thus, an offender's proclivity to commit illegal violence may reflect both a willingness to violate norms or laws and a willingness or desire to harm others. As a result, theories of conformity and theories of harm doing may be needed to understand why an offender uses violence.[7] One problem in the study of violent crime is that we are not certain what should be our dependent variable: Is it rule breaking or harm doing?

Gottfredson and Hirschi (1990, 1993) suggest that we should be studying why people conform, not why they use violence. Violence is just a serious form of deviance. They cite evidence that most violent offenders commit a variety of offenses; they are not specialists. The evidence on the versatility of offenders suggests that some individual characteristics are common to all offending, whether it involves deliberate harm or not. Gottfredson and Hirschi (1990) attribute versatility to individual differences in self-control. They cite evidence that offenders believe that their behaviors are wrong but do not act on their beliefs. They also point out that offenders tend to engage in a variety of behaviors indicating low self-control (e.g., they tend get into accidents, drive too fast, drink too much, and perform poorly in school and at work).

Offenders do specialize to some extent, however. Although those who commit more serious offenses usually commit less serious crimes, the reverse is not necessarily true. Thus, serious crimes occur much less frequently than minor crimes. In addition, some offenders commit property or drug offenses but avoid violence unless they are strongly provoked. Some may use illegal drugs but would prefer not to harm others. Most offenders are inhibited, at least to some extent, in the crimes they are willing to commit. They may take a "cafeteria style" approach to crime, but they won't put everything on their plate.

Clearly, the individual characteristics that produce violence and other crime are sometimes similar and sometimes different. Low self-control or any characteristic that makes a person more willing to violate laws or less likely to conform should lead to criminal behavior generally, not just violations involving harm doing. Low empathy, hostility biases, punitiveness, selfishness, or any characteristic that increases a person's desire or indifference to harming others is likely to lead to crimes involving deliberate harm. In addition, there may be individual difference factors that are associated with violence but not other forms of aggression or crime. Physical strength, fighting skills, and attitudes about the efficacy and morality of violence should be associated primarily with violence, not other crime.

The distinction between deviance and aggression is also relevant to the study of biological effects. Testosterone and pubertal development are associated with male criminal behavior generally, not just violent behavior (Booth & Osgood, 1993; Felson & Haynie, 2002). Adolescent boys who are physically mature are more likely than physically immature boys of the same age to use illegal drugs and steal, as well as fight. We do not understand the mechanism, but it is apparently explained by processes related to conformity, not harm doing.

The Decision to Harm Someone

According to a rational choice approach, it is important to examine the decision-making process that precedes an aggressive act. The rationality of decision makers is particularly limited because violent encounters often involve quick decisions, strong emotions, and alcohol. People who are angry, hurried, lacking in self-control, and drunk often fail to consider costs, morals, or alternative approaches. Those who are upset after experiencing aversive stimuli may also make careless or impulsive decisions. Thus, aversive stimuli facilitate rather than instigate aggression, a much more limited role. In addition, people may strike out habitually in certain circumstances, based on past rewards rather than the anticipation of future ones. In general, ill-considered decisions rather than inner compulsions result in behaviors that seem irrational (i.e., costly and immoral) to the objective observer.

People's inhibitions may be overwhelmed when they are angry and have a strong desire to hurt someone, but the source of that desire is not a biological urge caused by aversive stimuli. Anger can be a strong emotion, but it is a response to being mistreated and humiliated, not a response to all types of aversive stimuli (Averill, 1983). Of course, people respond emotionally when they have other bad experiences, but they respond with sadness and other emotions, not anger.

Although offenders may behave impulsively in the sense that they fail to consider long-range consequences, they are still making decisions. Even when people use violence in a rage, they must still decide how and when to attack and how to respond to their adversary's counterattack. The hockey player, no matter how angry, remembers to drop his gloves and stick. He is more effective without his gloves and with stick in hand, but the use of the stick would get him into serious trouble.

A rational choice perspective has also been described as a social interactionist approach because it emphasizes the social interaction between antagonists and third parties in disputes that culminate in violence (Tedeschi & Felson, 1994). When people express their grievances or exchange insults, they often do not anticipate that the conflict will escalate to physical violence. Verbal conflicts sometimes spiral out of control when adversaries fail to anticipate how each other will respond. Almost all violent incidents stemming from disputes are preceded by verbal aggression. Thus, to understand the violent outcome, it is important to understand the interim decisions that lead up to it.

Getting One's Way

People often attempt to influence the behavior of others. They use persuasion; they promise rewards; or they threaten or administer punishment. Aggression is a social influence tactic, sometimes used as a last resort, sometimes as a first resort. It can compel targets to do something they would otherwise not do. For example, predatory offenders such as robbers and rapists often use contingent threats to compel their victims to comply. Aggression can also be used to deter targets from what they are already doing. For example, parents use threats and punishment as a deterrent when their children misbehave or disobey them, and judges sentence criminals to prison in order to deter them. Thus, aggression can be considered a form of informal social control (Black, 1983; see also Greenberg & Barling, 1999).

Sometimes threats and punishment are successful. For example, an employer threatens to fire a tardy employee (a contingent threat), and the employee starts coming in on time. At other times, threats and punishment are not a deterrent. The target resists or retaliates and the conflict escalates (see below). Disputes involve an interaction between at least two parties, and the cooperation of both is required for a peaceful solution. Unilateral behavior, whether aggressive or cooperative, is unlikely to work. This basic dilemma is the subject of game theory and the basis for strategic thinking in international relations.

Unfortunately, many discussions of aggression ignore the central role of interpersonal conflict. Conflict is a ubiquitous aspect of social life and an important source of aggression and violence. The most violent people may be cordial and polite until they have a conflict or think they have been mistreated. For example, in work settings, the divergent interests of employers and employees create conflict, which may lead to aggression. Employees may get along fine until their interests diverge.

The inherent conflict between social control agents and the people they are supposed to control create opportunities for violence. Thus, the interaction between the police and suspects and other citizens creates opportunities for violence (Westley, 1970). Many violent conflicts in bars are between bartenders and patrons when the bartender refuses to serve underage or extremely intoxicated patrons (Felson, Baccaglini, & Gmelch, 1986). Child abuse typically occurs in disciplinary situations when parents have difficulties controlling their children (Tedeschi & Felson, 1994). Finally, supervisors and managers serve as social control agents, so conflicts with employees are inevitable sources of aggression.

Getting Justice

The desire to punish someone who does wrong reflects a belief in retributive justice as well as a concern for deterrence. The person who believes he or she has been wronged has a grievance and believes that justice will only be restored if there is appropriate punishment. The belief in retributive justice can also lead third parties to advocate punishment or carry it out themselves. Note that the motive for justice can be described using the language of rational choice, but it can also be described as normative behavior. Either way, people are choosing to behave in a way that achieves something they value.

It is ironic that people who engage in dispute-related violence often feel self-righteous and view their behavior as an act of justice (see Black, 1983). To fail to punish the misdeeds of others would be morally wrong. Whereas pacifists view violence as a clear moral evil, for most people moral values regarding the use of violence are ambiguous and context-dependent. They describe harm doing as just punishment when they approve of it and as aggression or violence when they do not (e.g., Kane, Joseph, & Tedeschi, 1976).

The tendency for observers to weigh negative information about an actor more heavily than positive information is likely to lead to grievances (Kanouse & Hanson, 1971). One nasty remark from an employer or coworker may override numerous compliments. The explanation of the negativity bias is unclear. It may have an evolutionary basis. It could be due to the tendency to assume that positive behaviors are attributable to social norms and other external factors. Negative information is more difficult to explain in terms of external factors and is therefore likely to be perceived as internally caused and therefore more blameworthy. It may be related to the general tendency to attribute unexpected behavior to internal causes (Jones & McGillis, 1976). Whatever the explanation, the negativity bias helps explain why people hold grudges. They never forget the misdeed, and they believe that it shows the actor's "true colors."

Mikula, Petri, and Tanzer (1989) identified three basic types of justice: distributive, procedural, and interactional. *Distributive justice* refers to a fair allocation of outcomes. For example, if employees believe they are under-paid or overworked by an employer, they are more likely to be angry and aggressive. *Procedural justice* refers to the use of just methods to determine outcomes. For example, employees may be angry and aggressive if they believe the procedures for deciding raises are unfair or if they have no oppor-tunity to have their views heard by management. Finally, *interactional justice* involves showing respect for others (i.e., following rules of polite-ness). For example, employees may be angry if a supervisor or colleague gives harsh criticism. Violations of interactional justice were by far the most important category of unjust events reported by respondents in the data collected by Mikula et al. (1989). Research has shown evidence of aggres-sive responses in work settings stemming from all three types of justice (e.g., Baron, 1988; Greenberg, 1993; Greenberg & Barling, 1999; Klein & Bierhoff, 1992).

Biases in Assigning Blame

If justice restoration is important in dispute-related aggression and violence, then the attribution of blame is critical. We punish people when we blame them for negative outcomes. We assign blame when we think that they have misbehaved intentionally or recklessly. We wish to harm people when we believe that they have wronged us, not when we believe that they have harmed us through no fault of their own.

People are often careless and excessive in their attributions of blame—sometimes they can be described as "blame mongers." That is, they tend to assign blame even when it is undeserved. They may fail to understand their adversary's perspective, or they may ignore exonerating circumstances, committing the fundamental attribution error (Ross, 1977). Sometimes they blame others to avoid self-blame. People working together on a task are motivated to blame the other person in cases of failure. Sometimes blaming others can help explain traumatic events that are otherwise difficult to understand. In addition, some people have a "hostility bias" and are quick to assign blame and respond with aggression (Dodge & Coie, 1987). Finally, an aggrieved party may blame an organization or group for the misbehavior of one its members (Tedeschi & Norman, 1985). Aggression is then directed at targets who share some social category with the person with whom the offender has a grievance. For example, an employee may seek retribution against management for mistreatment by one supervisor. Here there is some notion of collective liability, or guilt by association.

Expectations

People evaluate negative outcomes in terms of their expectations (Folger, 1986; Homans, 1961; Thibaut & Kelley, 1959). Those with high expectations will be disappointed with outcomes that people with lower expectations experience as satisfying. For example, Best and Andreasen (1977) found that middle-class consumers reported greater dissatisfaction with goods and services than did lower-class consumers. Presumably they had higher expectations. Also, evidence suggests that parents with unrealistically high standards for their children are more likely to engage in child abuse (Parke & Collmer, 1975). The use of violence in response to violation of expectations in a work setting was demonstrated in Homans's (1950) classic study of a bank wiring observation room. Men would ridicule or punch in the arm ("bing") coworkers who were "ratebusters."

Expectations are based on both temporal and social comparison. In the case of temporal comparison, people compare a present outcome with outcomes they have experienced in the past. For example, if a tough supervisor replaces an easygoing supervisor, the employee is likely to develop grievances. In the case of social comparison, reference groups provide standards or levels for expectations. When the outcomes people receive are less than those of other members of their reference group, they experience relative deprivation (Runciman, 1966). Thus, an employee who gets a raise might be pleased (using temporal comparison), but if a colleague gets a larger raise, social comparison will lead to a grievance. The classic study of relative deprivation found that Air Force personnel in the U.S. Army were more dissatisfied than military police with the promotion system, although promotions were more frequent for Air Force personnel (Stouffer, Suchman, DeVinney, Star, & Williams, 1949). The feeling of greater relative deprivation among Air Force personnel was attributed to the fact that the higher rate of promotions created higher expectations for promotion and paradoxically increased the level of dissatisfaction. Unfortunately, relative deprivation theory does not provide a basis for predicting who a person will choose as a comparison other (Schruijer, 1990). In addition, it is not clear when people use social comparison rather than temporal comparison.

Expressing Grievances

Grievances are common in social life because people frequently break rules and offend each other; however, people often do not express their grievances to the offending party (Averill, 1983; Goffman, 1959). They do not confront the person either because they want to avoid an embarrassing scene or they want to avoid damaging their relationship. Rules of politeness help regulate interpersonal relations by preventing aggression.

Evidence suggests that inhibitions about expressing grievances and getting into altercations are particularly strong in work settings. Felson, Ackerman, and Yeon (2003) found that people are particularly unlikely to become involved in verbal altercations when they are angry with someone at work. For example, a verbal attack is more than four times as likely to occur in conflicts involving strangers as it is in conflicts involving work relationships. The study found that there is also reluctance to become involved in altercations with in-laws and extended family.

We suspect that the reluctance to become involved in verbal altercations with coworkers is attributable to its greater costs. For example, open conflict with people at work, particularly those in superordinate positions, interferes with occupational success. For these reasons, social interaction at work may be more likely to involve proper behavior, polite conversation, and the inhibition of grievance expression and aggression.

Inhibitions about expressing grievance, however, can sometimes lead to more aggression and violence; they are a double-edged sword. First, grievances accumulate, and the offended person may be particularly angry when he or she finally responds. Note, however, that from a rational choice perspective, the accumulation involves a cognitive summing of grievances, not a buildup of aggressive energy, drive, or arousal. Second, inhibitions sometimes prevent conflicts from being resolved and targets from knowing when their behavior is offensive or their performance substandard. Finally, when the grievance is finally expressed, the accused may feel aggrieved because the criticism is unexpected. For example, employees may be angry when they get fired after having received consistently positive evaluations from their supervisor. They may then perceive that they have been victims of procedural injustice.

Self-Image and Reputation

People also use aggression to enhance or protect their identities (their self or social image). For example, by using violence, a young man demonstrates that he is powerful, tough, and courageous. By showing skill with his fists, he can increase his status among his friends. If winning is impossible, standing up to the antagonist maintains some level of honor and provides a measure of satisfaction.

An insult or "put-down" dishonors the target and makes him appear weak and ineffectual, but a counterattack nullifies that image. Retaliation is a form of defensive self-presentation, a way of "saving face" or maintaining one's honor when one has been attacked; however, the counterattack puts down the adversary, who may retaliate in turn, creating a "conflict spiral." When these face-saving contests occur, adversaries try to win rather than limit their punishments to fit the offense. Sometimes small disputes escalate into physical violence.

Escalation is particularly likely to occur when an audience is watching because the threat to face is greater. Thus, an employer who criticizes an employee in front of other employees is more likely to get an aggressive response. In other settings, third parties egg on the adversaries, making it difficult for them to back down without losing face. Sometimes third parties act as mediators, allowing both sides to back down without losing face (Felson, 1978). The response of third parties is a key factor in the escalation of aggressive interactions.

It is apparent that the manner in which criticism is given is important in determining whether identities are attacked. This is demonstrated in a study of the response of participants to constructive criticism versus destructive criticism from subordinates, peers, or supervisors (Baron, 1988). All groups received identical, negative ratings of their performance, but participants in the destructive criticism condition received additional criticisms that were general and inconsiderate in tone and that attributed poor performance to internal causes. The results showed that destructive criticism made the participants angry, particularly when it came from a subordinate; however, in the negotiation session that immediately followed, participants were apparently intimidated by the confederates who gave destructive criticism, because they made more concessions to them. Aggression in this instance increased both compliance and anger.

Bullies are typically attempting to promote or assert an identity rather than defend one. Their behavior is typically predatory rather than dispute-related. Bullies prey on vulnerable targets, usually in the presence of third parties, in order to show how tough they are (see Olweus, 1978). For the bully, dominating the victim is an accomplishment, a way of demonstrating power to himself and others.

In the case of jealousy, a person may intentionally harm another person who has not attacked them or wronged them in any way. Both justice and self-image concerns can produce an aggressive response when someone is jealous. When people think that someone has received an unfair share of some reward, they may attempt to restore equity by harming the person, even when that person is not held responsible for the injustice. We have referred to this behavior as "redistributive justice" (to distinguish it from "retributive justice"). Thus, an employee may blame the supervisor who gives a raise to someone else but attempt to produce unfavorable outcomes for the coworker who received a raise. Jealous people may also attempt to harm the object of jealousy for purposes of downward comparison (Wills, 1981). They may engage in aggressive behavior that lowers the standing of the target on some dimension, thereby providing a favorable comparison for the actor. They put themselves "up" by putting the other "down." Wills (1981) suggested that downward comparison was an alternative explanation for the displacement effects obtained in experiments testing frustration-aggression theory. He noted that investigations of displaced aggression, scapegoating, and hostility generalization all involve some challenge to the participants' identities.

Those in superordinate positions may engage in aggression in order to demonstrate their authority in response to insubordination. They may believe that any attempt to placate or accommodate a dissident may be perceived by the dissident or the audience as weakness and may legitimate the disruptive behavior. A public display of aggression serves the purpose of showing that the authority cannot be disobeyed without costs, and it may influence the insubordinate person and others to submit to the authority. Challenges to the authority of participants acting as supervisors were manipulated in simulated work settings by Kipnis and Consentino (1969). Supervisors were more likely to use coercive means against workers who refused to work than against those who lacked the skill to do a good job. Presumably, they viewed the refusal to work as a challenge to their authority.

Threats have strong implications for social identities because they can imply weakness for either of the parties in a conflict. Targets of threats give an appearance of weakness if they comply. As a result, threats often fail or even lead to retaliation (Deutsch, 1960). Those who make threats feel it necessary to carry out the threat if the target is defiant. Failure to do so would reveal the source as bluffing, weak, and lacking in credibility and undermine the effectiveness of future influence. These considerations provide strong motivation for the source to deliver the threatened punishment, even when it is costly to do so (Tedeschi, Horai, Lindskold, & Faley, 1970).

Thrill Seeking

Many people enjoy activities that involve or appear to involve risk. They like to gamble, play competitive sports, and ride roller coasters. Many prefer to avoid taking real risks themselves but enjoy watching others do so. Thus, viewing violence on television and film is a popular activity in most parts of the world.

The desire for thrills and the enjoyment of risk provide an incentive for predatory violence, particularly among young men (see Katz, 1988). They may enjoy a certain degree of physical danger or the risk of being caught by the police. From this perspective, individuals view risk itself as a value rather than as a reflection of potential costs. They seek it rather than avoid it. Note that individual differences in thrill seeking provide an alternative explanation for the versatility of offenders. Versatility is not necessarily due to low self-control or careless thinking.

Research suggests that individual differences in sensation seeking reflect, at least in part, biological differences (see Raine, Brennan, Farrington, & Mednick, 1997). People who engage in antisocial behavior tend to be physiologically underaroused, as indicated by lower resting heart rate levels. These persons may seek out exciting activities to compensate for their physiological underarousal and bring some physiological balance to their systems. Resting heart rates have also been shown to be lower for violent offenders than for nonviolent offenders (e.g., Farrington, 1987), suggesting that thrill seeking may be a more important motive for violence than for other criminal behavior.

Opportunities for Violence

One of the most influential theoretical applications of the rational choice approach in the field of criminology is the *routine-activity approach* (M. Felson, 1994; Cohen & M. Felson, 1979). According to this approach, crime is more likely to occur (and crime rates are likely to be high) when there are more opportunities to commit crime. A situation that provides an opportunity for a crime requires three elements: a motivated offender, a suitable target, and the absence of capable guardians. Crime is more likely to occur when routine activities, such as those associated with leisure and work, bring together offenders and victims in the absence of effective guardians. For example, Cohen and M. Felson (1979) provided evidence that the increase in crime from the 1960s to the 1980s was due to increases in rates of travel outside the home, single-person households, college attendance, labor force participation among women, and the percentage of households left unattended during the day. They show that the dispersion of activity away from households over time rather than cultural change or poverty explained changes in crime rates over time.

The applied side of the routine-activity approach is referred to as *situational crime prevention* (e.g., Clarke, 1992). This approach refers to strategies that make targets less vulnerable or that increase guardianship by altering people's activities or the physical environment (see also Brantingham & Brantingham, 1990). A prominent example is Crime Prevention Through Environmental Design (CPTED; Jeffery, 1971). This involves methods that attempt to "design out" crime in commercial establishments (see Poyner & Fawcett, 1995). For example, convenience stores and other small stores are vulnerable to robbery. On the advice of researchers, the owners of a convenience store chain moved cash registers to the front of the store and removed display advertising that covered windows so that robberies could be seen from the street. They eliminated all alley exits so that access was restricted to the front of the store. They encouraged taxis to use premises by providing free coffee and restrooms. Using these methods, they were able to achieve a 30% decline in the number or robberies (Duffala, 1976). Another study showed a decline in robberies of convenience stores when at least two clerks were on duty late at night (Hunter & Jeffery, 1997). Finally, recent work is applying the routine-activities/situational crime–prevention approach to crimes committed in work settings that involve violations of trust (Friedrichs, 2004). Many of these white-collar crimes are predatory, but some stem from disputes.

Situational crime–prevention strategies have also been successful in reducing violence in bars. Bars generate high levels of violence because they bring young, intoxicated men together in a single location (Felson et al., 1986). Thus, the key predictor of the frequency of violence in bars is the age of the clientele. It is possible to reduce the number of violent confrontations by changing the physical design of the bar or nightclub, for example, by changing traffic patterns (e.g., MacIntyre & Homel, 1997). Methods of lowering alcohol consumption have also been used, such as the reduction of time for happy hour and the serving of more food and smaller and weaker drinks. Another recommendation is the use of safer bar glasses that are less effective weapons when broken (M. Felson, 1994).

Although the routine-activity approach has been applied most often to predatory crime, it is also relevant to dispute-related crime. It would predict that violence is more likely to occur in settings that generate conflict situations and thus produce motivated offenders. For example, Baron (1988) identified sources of conflict among white-collar employees in a food-processing plant. The most important sources of conflict were poor communication, interdependence, feelings of being treated unfairly, ambiguity of responsibility, and poor use of criticism. When sources of conflict are reduced, when grievances are addressed, and when threats to identity are minimized, then the likelihood of dispute-related violence in the workplace should be lower.

Conclusion

A rational choice perspective suggests that it is important to consider incentives and costs when studying any type of violence. Violence has a purpose, whether the offender commits the act at work, on the street, or at home. Differences between workplace and other violence should be demonstrated, not assumed.

In studying individual differences in the propensity to use violence, it is important to understand that violent crime involves crime and aggression. We need to understand why people violate laws rather than conform and why they deliberately harm others. Although some of the causes of violence and other crime are similar, some are different. The versatility of many offenders implies that common causes, such as low self-control and thrill seeking, are important; however, the reluctance of some offenders to commit violent crimes implies that inhibitions about harming others or using physical violence are also important.

My focus has been on motives and other situational factors involved in aggression (or deliberate harm doing). I have challenged the distinction between instrumental and expressive aggression, arguing that all aggression is instrumental. Motives include effecting compliance, retribution, producing favorable identities, and thrill seeking. These motives can explain why people engage in what is sometimes called expressive aggression. They can explain why only certain types of aversive stimuli—perceived wrongdoing and intentional attack—lead to anger and dispute-related aggression. Pain, illness, and death, the most aversive stimuli in the human experience, do not have this effect. They do make people unhappy, which may facilitate aggression if mood affects decision making; however, a strong biological link between aversive stimuli and aggression has not been demonstrated. Even if a rational choice perspective proves to be an inadequate explanation of all forms of aggression, it seems unlikely that frustration-aggression approaches can fill the gap.

From a rational choice perspective, the distinction between predatory and dispute-related aggression is useful. In predatory aggression, offenders intentionally harm their victims, but that is not their goal. They want to force compliance, promote an identity, or entertain themselves at the victim's expense. In dispute-related aggression, the proximate goal of offenders is to harm, but their motives are deterrence, retribution, and saving face. A special frustration-aggression mechanism is not necessary to explain why participants in social conflicts want to see their adversaries suffer.

Notes

1. This chapter borrows material from Felson (2004) and Tedeschi and Felson (1994).

2. Behavior has multiple consequences; some of these consequences are goals but others are incidental outcomes. In addition, a consequence that is incidental to the offender may be quite costly for the victim. The victim's experience of harm should be the focus in treating the victim, but it is irrelevant to an understanding of the offender's behavior.

3. Evidence suggests that rapists are sexually motivated, not power motivated (Felson, 2002).

4. Behaviors involving deception or stealth are not generally treated as examples of aggression, although they fit the definition.

5. However, it may be that they were financially motivated but that they were disinhibited by the fact that they were underpaid.

6. Crime involves behaviors that are harmful according to the judgment of lawmakers; many crimes, however, do not involve intentional harm doing. For example, thieves and violent offenders deliberately harm their victims, although no harm is intended by drunken drivers, prostitutes, and users of illegal drugs.

7. To some extent, individual differences in the proclivity to break laws, do harm, or use violence may reflect differences in the willingness to commit serious crime; however, violence and aggression are only considered serious violations when they are perceived as unprovoked or disproportionate to the provocation (e.g., Kane et al., 1976).

References

Averill, J. R. (1983). Studies on anger and aggression: Implications for theories of emotion. *American Psychologist, 38,* 1145–1160.

Baron, R. A. (1988). Negative effects of destructive criticism: Impact on conflict, self-efficacy, and task performance. *Journal of Applied Psychology, 73,* 199–207.

Berkowitz, L. (1962). *Aggression: A social psychological analysis.* New York: McGraw-Hill.

Berkowitz, L. (1989). The frustration-aggression hypothesis: An examination and reformulation. *Psychological Bulletin, 106,* 59–73.

Berkowitz, L. (1993). *Aggression: Its causes, consequences, and control.* New York: McGraw-Hill.

Best, A., & Andreasen, A. R. (1977). Consumer responses to unsatisfactory purchases: A survey of perceiving defects, voicing complaints, and obtaining redress. *Law and Society Review, 11,* 701–742.

Black, D. J. (1983). Crime as social control. *American Sociological Review, 48,* 34–45.

Booth, A., & Osgood, D. W. (1993). The influence of testosterone on deviance in adulthood: Assessing and explaining the relationship. *Criminology, 31,* 93–117.

Brantingham, P. J., & Brantingham, P. L. (1990). *Environmental criminology.* Prospect Heights, IL: Waveland.

Clarke, R. V. (1992). *Situational crime prevention: Successful case studies.* New York: Harrow and Heston.

Cohen, L. E., & Felson, M. (1979). Social change and crime rate trends: A routine activity approach. *American Sociological Review, 44,* 588–608.

Deutsch, M. (1960). Trust, trustworthiness, and the *F* scale. *Journal of Abnormal and Social Psychology, 61,* 138–140.

Dodge, K. A., & Coie, J. D. (1987). Social-information-processing factors in reactive and proactive aggression in children's peer groups. *Journal of Personality and Social Psychology, 53,* 1146–1158.

Dollard, J., Doob, L. W., Miller, N., Mowrer, O. H., & Sears, R. R. (1939). *Frustration and aggression.* New Haven, CT: Yale University Press.

Duffala, D. C. (1976). Convenience stores, robbery, and physical environmental features. *American Behavioral Scientist, 20,* 227–246.

Epstein, S., & Taylor, S. P. (1967). Instigation to aggression as a function of degree of defeat and perceived aggressive intent of the opponent. *Journal of Personality, 35,* 265–289.

Farrington, D. P. (1987). Implications of biological findings for criminological research. In S. A. Mednick, T. E. Moffitt, & S. A. Stack (Eds.), *The causes of crime: New biological approaches* (pp. 42–64). New York: Cambridge University Press.

Felson, M. (1994). *Crime and everyday life: Insights and implications for society.* Thousand Oaks, CA: Pine Forge.

Felson, R. B. (1978). Aggression as impression management. *Social Psychology, 41,* 205–213.

Felson, R. B. (1982). Impression management and the escalation of aggression and violence. *Social Psychology Quarterly, 45,* 245–254.

Felson, R. B. (1984). Patterns of aggressive social interaction. In A. Mummendey (Ed.), *Social psychology of aggression: From individual behavior to social interaction* (pp. 107–126). New York: Springer-Verlag.

Felson, R. B. (1992). Kick 'em when they're down: Explanations of the relationship between stress and interpersonal aggression and violence. *Sociological Quarterly, 33,* 1–16.

Felson, R. B. (2002). *Violence and gender reexamined.* Washington, DC: American Psychological Association.

Felson, R. B. (2004). A rational choice approach to violence. In M. A. Zahn, H. H. Brownstein, & S. L. Jackson (Eds.), *Violence: From theory to research* (pp. 71–90). Cincinnati, OH: Anderson.

Felson, R. B., Ackerman, J., & Yeon, S. (2003). The (in)frequency of family violence. *Journal of Marriage and Family, 65*(3), 622–634.

Felson, R. B., Baccaglini, W., & Gmelch, G. (1986). Bar-room brawls: Aggression and violence in Irish and American bars. In A. Campbell & J. J. Gibbs (Eds.), *Violent transactions* (pp. 153–166). Oxford, UK: Basil Blackwell.

Felson, R. B., & Haynie, D. L. (2002). Pubertal development, social factors, and delinquency among adolescent boys. *Criminology, 40,* 967–988.

Folger, R. (1986). A referent cognitions theory of relative deprivation. In J. M. Olson, C. P. Herman, & M. P. Zanna (Eds.), *Relative deprivation and social comparison: The Ontario Symposium* (Vol. 4. pp. 33–55). Hillsdale, NJ: Lawrence Erlbaum.

Folger, R., & Skarlicki, D. P. (1998). A popcorn metaphor for workplace violence. In R. W. Griffin, A. O'Leary-Kelly, & J. Collins (Eds.), *Dysfunctional behavior in organizations: Violent and deviant behavior* (Monographs in Organizational Behavior and Relations, Vol. 23, pp. 43–81). Greenwich, CT: JAI.

Friedrichs, D. O. (2004). *Trusted criminals: White collar crime in contemporary society.* Belmont, CA: Wadsworth.

Geen, R. G. (1968). Effects of frustration, attack, and prior training in aggressiveness upon aggressive behavior. *Journal of Personality and Social Psychology, 9,* 316–321.

Gentry, W. D. (1970). Effects of frustration, attack, and prior aggressive training on overt aggression and vascular processes. *Journal of Personality and Social Psychology, 16,* 718–725.

Goffman, E. (1959). *The presentation of self in everyday life.* New York: Doubleday Anchor.

Gottfredson, M. R., & Hirschi, T. (1990). *A general theory of crime.* Stanford, CA: Stanford University Press.

Gottfredson, M. R., & Hirschi, T. (1993). A control theory interpretation of psychological research on aggression. In R. B. Felson & J. T. Tedeschi (Eds.), *Aggression and violence* (pp. 47–68). Washington, DC: American Psychological Association.

Greenberg, J. (1993). Stealing in the name of justice: Informational and interpersonal moderators of theft reactions to underpayment inequity. *Organizational Behavior and Human Decision Processes, 54,* 81–103.

Greenberg, L., & Barling, J. (1999). Predicting employee aggression against coworkers, subordinates and supervisors: The roles of person behaviors and perceived workplace factors. *Journal of Organizational Behavior, 20,* 897–913.

Hershcovis, M. S., & Barling, J. (2003). *Preventing workplace violence.* Unpublished manuscript.

Homans, G. C. (1950). *The human group.* New York: Harcourt, Brace, and Jovanovich.

Homans, G. C. (1961). *Social behavior: Its elementary forms.* New York: Harcourt, Brace and World.

Hunter, R. D., & Jeffery, C. R. (1997). Preventing convenience store robbery through environmental design. In R. V. Clarke (Ed.), *Situational crime prevention: Successful case studies* (pp. 194–204). New York: Harrow and Heston.

Inness, M., Barling, J., & Turner, N. (in press). Situational specificity, individual differences and workplace aggression. *Journal of Applied Psychology.*

Jeffery, C. R. (1971). *Crime prevention through environmental design.* Beverly Hills, CA: Sage.

Jones, E. E., & McGillis, D. (1976). Correspondent inferences and the attribution cube: A comparative reappraisal. In J. H. Harvey, W. J. Ickes, & R. F. Kidd (Eds.), *New directions in attribution research* (Vol. 1, pp. 389–420). Hillsdale, NJ: Lawrence Erlbaum.

Kane, T. R., Joseph, J. M., & Tedeschi, J. T. (1976). Person perception and an evaluation of the Berkowitz paradigm for the study of aggression. *Journal of Personality and Social Psychology, 33,* 663–673.

Kanouse, D. E., & Hanson, L. R. (1971). Negativity in evaluations. In E. E. Jones, D. E. Kanouse, H. H. Kelley, R. E. Nisbett, S. Valins, & B. Weiner (Eds.), *Attribution: Perceiving the causes of behavior* (pp. 47–62). Morristown, NJ: General Learning Press.

Katz, J. (1988). *Seductions of crime: Moral and sensual attractions of doing evil.* New York: Basic Books.

Kipnis, D., & Consentino, J. (1969). Use of leadership powers in industry. *Journal of Applied Psychology, 53,* 460–466.

Klein, R., & Bierhoff, H. W. (1992). *Responses to achievement situations: The mediating function of perceived fairness.* Unpublished manuscript.

Luckenbill, D. F. (1977). Criminal homicide as a situated transaction. *Social Problems, 25,* 176–186.

MacIntyre, S., & Homel, R. (1997). Danger on the dance floor: A study of interior design, crowding, and aggression in nightclubs. In R. Homel (Ed.), *Policing for prevention: reducing crime, public intoxication and injury* (Crime Prevention Studies, Vol. 7, pp. 91–114). Monsey, NY: Criminal Justice Press.

Mikula, G., Petri, B., & Tanzer, N. (1989). What people regard as unjust: Types and structures of everyday experiences of injustice. *European Journal of Social Psychology, 20,* 133–149.

Nickel, T. W. (1974). The attribution of intention as a critical factor in the relation between frustration and aggression. *Journal of Personality, 42,* 482–492.

Olweus, D. (1978). *Aggression in the schools: Bullies and whipping boys.* Washington, DC: Hemisphere.

Parke, R. D., & Collmer, C. W. (1975). Child abuse: An interdisciplinary analysis. In E. M. Hetherington (Ed.), *Review of child development research* (Vol. 5, pp. 509–590). Chicago: University of Chicago Press.

Pisano, R., & Taylor, S. P. (1971). Reduction in physical aggression: The effects of four different strategies. *Journal of Personality and Social Psychology, 19,* 237–242.

Poyner, B., & Fawcett, W. H. (1995). *Design for inherent security: Guidance for nonresidential buildings.* London: Construction Industry Research and Information Association.

Raine, A., Brennan, P. A., Farrington, D. P., & Mednick, S. A. (1997). *Biosocial bases of violence.* New York: Plenum.

Ross, L. (1977). The intuitive psychologist and his shortcomings: Distortions in the attribution process. In L. Berkowitz (Ed.), *Advances in experimental social psychology* (Vol. 10, pp. 174–221). New York Academic.

Rossi, P. H., Waite, E., Bose, C. E., & Berk, R. E. (1974). The seriousness of crime: Normative structure and individual differences. *American Sociological Review, 39,* 224–237.

Runciman, W. G. (1966). *Relative deprivation and social justice.* London: Routledge & Kegan Paul.

Schruijer, S. G. L. (1990). *Norm violation, attribution and attitudes in intergroup relations.* Tilburg, The Netherlands: Tilburg University Press.

Sermat, V. (1967). The possibility of influencing the other's behavior and cooperation: Chicken vs. prisoner's dilemma. *Canadian Journal of Psychology, 21,* 204–219.

Silver, E. (2002). Mental disorder and violent victimization: The mediating effect of involvement in conflicted social relationships. *Criminology, 40,* 191–212.

Stouffer, S. A., Suchman, E. A., DeVinney, L. C., Star, S. A., & Williams, R. M., Jr. (1949). *The American soldier: Adjustment during army life* (Vol. 1, pp. 97–125). Hillsdale, NJ: Lawrence Erlbaum.

Tedeschi, J. T., & Felson, R. B. (1994). *Violence, aggression, and coercive actions.* Washington, DC: American Psychological Association.

Tedeschi, J. T., Horai, J., Lindskold, S., & Faley, T. E. (1970). The effects of opportunity costs and target compliance on the behavior of a threatening source. *Journal of Experimental Social Psychology, 6,* 205–213.

Tedeschi, J. T., & Norman, N. (1985). Social mechanisms of displaced aggression. In E. J. Lawler (Ed.), *Advances in group processes: Theory and research* (Vol. 2, pp. 29–56). Greenwich, CT: JAI.

Thibaut, J., & Kelley, H. H. (1959). *The social psychology of groups.* New York: John Wiley.

Westley, W. A. (1970). *Violence and the police: A sociological study of law, custom, and morality.* Cambridge: MIT Press.

Wills, T. A. (1981). Downward comparison principles in social psychology. *Psychological Bulletin, 90,* 245–271.

3 Emotions, Violence, and Counterproductive Work Behavior

Paul E. Spector
Suzy Fox
Theresa Domagalski

E motion has long played a central role in research and theory concerning human aggression and violence. Thinking in experimental and social psychology has evolved from an initial focus on frustration mainly as a situational condition (Dollard, Doob, Miller, Mowrer, & Sears, 1939) to more modern theories that incorporate a variety of negative emotional states in response to situational frustration and other environmental conditions and events (Anderson & Bushman, 2002; Berkowitz, 1998). Parallel to the social psychology work on human aggression, emotion has also been central in much organizational work on workplace aggression and the broader concept of counterproductive work behavior (CWB). Injustice and stressful conditions have been specifically linked to negative emotions and both aggression and CWB (e.g., Fox, Spector, & Miles, 2001).

It has been recognized that aggressive acts can occur for a variety of reasons, and a distinction has been made between affective aggression that is associated with negative emotion and instrumental aggression that is not (Neuman & Baron, 1997). Affective, or "hot," aggression has as its primary goal the injury of a target, whether physical or psychological, at times impulsively and immediately during the experience of negative emotion in response to provocation. With instrumental, or "cold," aggression, harm of another may be a means to desired ends. In work organizations, instrumental aggression may be the chosen path toward status, power, perks, assignments, bonuses, promotions, and reputation, that is, "getting ahead" (Neuman & Baron, 2005). Our focus in this chapter will be on affective aggression and CWB, in which harm of another person or an organization is the primary goal.

Merchant and Lundell (2001) distinguished four types of workplace violence, depending on the relationship between actor and recipient. Type 1 is *criminal intent* that consists mainly of instrumental acts of violence in the commission of a crime such as robbery, which is not the focus of this chapter. Type 2 is *customer or client violence,* which is most likely affective in nature. LeBlanc and Barling (2005) discuss the greater risk faced by employees who deal directly with customers, clients, or patients experiencing frustration and anger. This might occur when the employee is in a position to deny requests or services, for example. The underlying psychological process in this sort of violence is very similar to coworker violence, although the acts are more immediate and impulsive and may be more likely to be physical. Type 3 is *coworker violence,* which also can be affective in nature. A variety of models have been provided in the literature to explain this sort of violence, and a number of both individual and situational variables have been linked to it. Most of the research on workplace violence has involved this type, which will be the major focus of this chapter. Type 4 is *relationship violence* that falls mainly outside of the models and research in the organizational realm.

Counterproductive Work Behavior and Violence

Counterproductive work behavior consists of intentional acts by employees that harm organizations or their stakeholders. Included under CWB are acts of physical violence against people (Type 3 violence), as well as milder forms of aggressive behavior such as verbal aggression and other forms of mistreatment directed toward people. CWB also includes acts directed toward organizations rather than people (although people are often indirect targets). This includes destruction and misuse of organizational property, doing work incorrectly, or failing to notify superiors about mistakes and work problems (e.g., a machine malfunction), and withdrawal (e.g., calling in sick when not ill). CWB has been studied from a variety of perspectives, using different terms to refer to a partially overlapping set of harmful acts. This includes *aggression* (Neuman & Baron, 1997; Spector, 1978), *deviance* (Hollinger, 1986; Robinson & Bennett, 1995), *retaliation* (Skarlicki & Folger, 1997), and *revenge* (Bies, Tripp, & Kramer, 1997). Acts directed specifically at people have been studied as *bullying* (Hoel, Rayner, & Cooper, 1999), *emotional abuse* (Keashly, 1998), and *mobbing* (Zapf, Knorz, & Kulla, 1996).

Researchers who have studied these various related phenomena have taken a variety of theoretical positions that give different emphasis to emotions. Neuman and Baron's (1997, 1998, 2005) work, based on the human aggression literature, considers the role of negative emotions in affective aggression. They provided an integrated model of aggression (Neuman & Baron, 2005) in which negative emotion (hostility, anger, and shame) plays a central role. According to this model, aggression is triggered by environmental conditions and stressors, including situational frustration, injustice, insults, and presence of things associated with aggression. These lead to negative emotions and aggressive cognitions that together lead to appraisal of the situation and decisions about whether or not to respond aggressively. Their model draws upon a cognitive-neoassociationistic analysis of aggression (Anderson, Anderson, & Deuser, 1996; Anderson, Deuser, & DeNeve, 1995; Berkowitz, 1990). Situational variables (such as perceived threat, mistreatment, or frustration resulting from thwarted goals) may lead to primary and secondary appraisal and on to aggressive behavioral choices by one or more of three paths: *cognition* (excitation of hostile thoughts, memories, or aggression scripts), *affect* (priming hostile or angry feelings), and/or *arousal* (excitation transfer). Through accessible hostile schemata, these paths may lead to more hostile interpretation of ambiguous events and ambiguous affective states. It is noteworthy that anger can play several causal roles in this process (Anderson & Bushman, 2002). Anger may reduce inhibitions against aggression by providing a justification when aggressive retaliation is part of the decision rule in the aggression script. Anger may interfere with higher-level cognitive processes in the appraisal stages, such as moral reasoning. Anger may prime memory of and processing of the provoking events, enabling a person to maintain aggressive intentions over time; may be used as an information cue in the interpretation of ambiguous events; and may prime aggressive scripts and associated behaviors. Finally, anger may energize behavior by increasing arousal levels. Thus, anger plays a role in all three paths to aggressive behavior: cognition, affect, and arousal. Negative emotions besides anger, such as sadness, grief, or depression, may lead into the process as well.

O'Leary-Kelly, Griffin, and Glew (1996) note that aggression in organizations may be triggered by negative affect, even when the adverse environment or outcomes cannot be blamed on a specific person. In that case, emotional arousal may be general, and aggression may target any object that is available and perceived to be appropriate.

Bies and Tripp (2005; see also Bies et al., 1997) posit a clear role for emotions in their concept of revenge. They suggest that an act of revenge is a response to certain situations in organizations that involve goal obstruction; violations of rules, norms, and promises; or attacks on power and status. *Goal obstruction* is similar to situational frustration that has been a central feature of human aggression work (e.g., Dollard et al., 1939). *Violations* can involve injustice but can consist of other acts, such as poor etiquette (e.g., betraying a confidence). *Attacks on power and status* are often harsh criticisms that hold a person up to ridicule. All these situations can trigger anger, a sense of violation, and feelings of helplessness, as well as revenge cognitions and thoughts. Both emotions and cognitions can endure over time, perhaps building in intensity until an act of revenge occurs. At other times they may dissipate. This suggests that revenge is not always an immediate and impulsive reaction to a situation but rather involves a complex interplay of cognition and emotion over time. Furthermore, intervening situations may either increase or decrease the likelihood that an act of revenge will occur.

Retaliation theory, like revenge theory, also considers harmful acts conducted in response to feelings of having been wrongly treated, but in this case the focus is specifically on injustice. Skarlicki and Folger (1997) noted how anger and outrage are emotions experienced in response to injustice. Although their initial work focused on the reactions of those affected by injustice, more recent work has explored vicarious reactions to the injustice experienced by others (Folger & Skarlicki, 2005). According to this view, *deontic anger* occurs when one witnesses injustice against others, and this can be associated with overt or covert retaliation against the perceived cause of the injustice.

The specific negative emotion experienced in response to negative events or outcomes may depend upon the individual's causal attributions for the precipitating event. Martinko, Gundlach, and Douglas (2002) suggest that although internal attributions for negative events (my fault) are likely to lead to negative emotions (e.g., self-deprecation or helplessness) and behaviors (e.g., learned helplessness or substance abuse) directed toward self, external attributions, coupled with perceived intentionality, are likely to lead to negative emotions (such as anger) and behaviors (such as aggression, revenge, or sabotage) directed toward others.

Spector and Fox (2002, 2005) developed a model of CWB that gives central importance to emotions as a response to workplace stressors. Conditions and events at work are perceived and appraised by employees. Those perceived to be stressors induce negative emotions, including anger, anxiety, and depression. Such emotions contribute to CWB that can occur immediately and impulsively or at a later time. In many cases, emotions help motivate intentions to engage in later CWB. This model includes an important role for perceived control that affects both the appraisal of situations and the decision to engage in CWB or some alternative constructive act. Those who perceive control in a situation will be less likely to perceive a stressor, experience negative emotion, and engage in CWB. Personality (particularly affective dispositions that will be discussed later) is also an important element that can affect both appraisal and the decision to act. Individuals who have a tendency to experience negative emotions will be more sensitive to stressors and will be more likely to exhibit emotional reactions to the environment, as well as CWB.

Emotional Experience Versus Affective Dispositions _____

It is important to distinguish emotional states from affective dispositions and the impact of momentary states from more chronic and long-term emotional experiences. An emotional state refers to a moment in time during which an individual experiences an emotion. Although emotional states certainly last for some period of time, the assessment is generally of a particular instance, and states are relatively short-lived. Thus an event occurs at work (a coworker makes a sarcastic comment), and the employee becomes angry.

That anger may dissipate in a few minutes or hours. Of course, a particular pattern of events that elicit emotional responses might occur; for example, a coworker might periodically make nasty comments, which elicit angry reactions repeatedly over time.

Models of CWB do not explicitly deal with this time distinction, although much of the writing about these models seems to describe particular events. Tests of models, however, tend to assess conditions and emotions more on a chronic or periodic level. The typical questionnaire study asks employees to indicate how often certain events occur (e.g., arguments with coworkers) and how often they experience negative emotions such as anger. Inferences are drawn from relations among frequencies of conditions and emotions to processes suggesting emotions are a response to particular conditions.

Emotion can also be assessed at the trait level as affective dispositions. Such traits reflect that certain individuals are more likely to experience negative emotions than others. Distinctions have been made among different discrete emotions, such as *trait anger* (tendency to experience anger) and *trait anxiety* (tendency to experience anxiety). It is assumed that affective dispositions are personality variables that arise at least partially from genetic predispositions, and although it is beyond our scope here, there are data suggesting that these dispositions are clearly different from emotional states or even the frequency of states over time within a particular setting (Spector, Chen, & O'Connell, 2000).

Empirical Evidence of Linkages Between Emotional States and CWB

Given the central role of experienced emotions in theories of aggression, it is surprising how few empirical studies have been published linking emotional states to both organizational stressors and counterproductive behavioral responses. Much of the empirical work consists of laboratory studies in the domain of general discomfort-anger-aggression processes (e.g., Anderson et al., 1995; Anderson et al., 1996; Asmus & Bell, 1999; Bell & Baron, 1976; Berkowitz, 1990).

Among the exceptions, Skarlicki and Folger (1997) summarize research linking employees' perceptions of unfair treatment with negative emotions such as anger, outrage, and resentment and in turn to behavioral responses that we would call CWB and they call ORB (organizational retaliatory behavior). Cropanzano and Baron (1991) also link injustice to emotions and workplace conflict, and Cropanzano, Howes, Grandey, and Toth (1997) relate CWB to high levels of job tension, somatic tension, fatigue, and burnout.

Spector (1997) presents a meta-analysis of 12 early studies reporting correlations between experienced frustration (defined as state emotion) and other work variables. Antecedents were defined as *frustrators,* or what the current stressor-emotion model of CWB calls stressors. Frustrators that related to experienced frustration included lack of autonomy, interpersonal conflict, organizational constraints, role ambiguity, role conflict, and workload. Behavioral and other outcomes that were correlated with experienced frustration included job satisfaction, work anxiety, physical health symptoms, employee withdrawal behavior (e.g., intention to quit, but not absence), aggression, hostility, and sabotage. Chen and Spector (1992) found a measure of anger but not experienced frustration correlated with theft, and anger correlated more strongly than experienced frustration with aggression, hostility, and sabotage. It is noteworthy that most of the studies reported in this meta-analysis were self-report, except for Spector, Dwyer, and Jex (1988) in which incumbent-reported experienced frustration was correlated with supervisor-reported constraints, conflict, role ambiguity, and workload.

In a meta-analysis, Spector and Goh (2001) found anger and anxiety to be related to a variety of stressors, with mean correlations ranging from .29 (anxiety and role conflict) to .49 (anger and organizational constraints). Similarly, linkages between negative emotion (measured by the Job-Related Affective Well-Being Scale, or JAWS; Van Katwyk, Fox, Spector, & Kelloway, 2000) and CWB were reported in a number of studies (Fox et al., 2001; Goh, Bruursema, Fox, & Spector, 2003; Miles, Borman, Spector, & Fox, 2002). Correlations were significant for all cases of negative emotions and CWB, with correlations as high as .45. Fox et al. (2001) found negative emotions, as measured by the JAWS, to be related to both organizational stressors (conflict, $r = .49$; organizational constraints, $r = .47$; distributive justice, $r = .38$; and procedural justice, $r = .44$) and to CWB (targeting organizations, $r = .45$; targeting people in organizations, $r = .30$). Furthermore, everysignificant relationship between stressors and CWB was mediated by negative emotion. Fox and Spector (1999) also found that both experienced frustration and job satisfaction mediated the positive relation between employees' experience of situational constraints (events frustrating their achievement of organizational and personal goals) and CWB (both personal and organizational).

Lee and Allen (2002) examined the relative contributions of cognition and affect on different types of "workplace deviance behavior" (WDB). They proposed that some behaviors (such as voluntary turnover) would best be explained by instrumental motives and would be primarily influenced by cognitive evaluations of work, whereas other behaviors (such as unexcused absence) were derived from expressive motives, primarily influenced by affective experiences at work. They thus predicted that job cognitions would have a stronger impact on WDBO (behaviors targeting the organization), whereas job affect would more strongly affect WDBI (behaviors targeting individuals in the organization). In addition, they pointed out that discrete emotions may exert different effects on peoples' behavior: guilt may reduce WDB while anger may increase it. Unfortunately, they were not able to test the distinct antecedents of WDBO versus WDBI, as they were unable to obtain a factor structure justifying the distinction. The higher-order negative affect variable only marginally predicted WDB, but the discrete emotion of hostility significantly increased predictability beyond negative affect. Similarly, when comparing cognition with higher-order negative affect, cognition was a stronger predictor of WDB, but when the discrete emotion of hostility replaced negative affect, it was as important a predictor of WDB as cognition. This strongly reinforces the need to investigate the effects of discrete emotions in the stressor-emotion model of counterproductive work behavior.

Finally, Glomb (2002) collected in-depth data about specific incidents of workplace aggression, demonstrating linkages among various antecedent, individual difference, and behavioral variables; however, she incorporated the experience of anger in her definition of aggression itself rather than demonstrating exogenous linkages between emotional state and aggression. Her results suggest an escalatory pattern, in which less severe incidents often lead to more severe incidents, with both parties experiencing anger as outcome as well as antecedent of the incident.

The results of existing workplace research clearly support the central role of emotional experience in violence and CWB. Most of these studies assessed more chronic exposure to stressors and negative emotional states rather than investigating specific incidents. Clearly more needs to be done to link emotion to cognition in CWB, particularly at the level of specific stressful antecedents, discrete emotional reactions, and specific behavioral incidents. Innovative research designs are needed to tap into the dynamic, reciprocal, and iterative stressor-emotion-CWB processes.

Affective Traits and CWB

Together, the organizational and social psychology literatures demonstrate that individual differences constitute an important explanation for workplace aggression, violence, and other CWB. Numerous personality traits have been examined for their association with CWB and include trait anger (Domagalski & Steelman, 2004; Douglas & Martinko, 2001; Fox & Spector, 1999; Hepworth & Towler, 2004), negative affectivity (Douglas & Martinko, 2001; Hepworth & Towler, 2004; Skarlicki, Folger, & Tesluk, 1999), self-control (Douglas & Martinko, 2001; Hepworth & Towler, 2004; Marcus & Schuler, 2004), emotional stability (Colbert, Mount, Harter, Witt, & Barrick, 2004; Salgado, 2002), narcissism (Penney & Spector, 2002), agreeableness (Skarlicki et al., 1999), self-esteem (Harvey & Keashley, 2003), and trait anxiety (Fox & Spector, 1999). Those that have demonstrated the greatest explanatory power in our understanding of CWB are trait anger and self-control.

In separate studies by Douglas and Martinko (2001) and Hepworth and Towler (2004), trait anger emerged as a prominent predictor of workplace aggression. *Trait anger,* as noted earlier, is described as an individual affective disposition to experience chronic feelings of anger over time and across situations (Spielberger, Jacobs, Russell, & Crane, 1983). Individuals high in trait anger are prone to experience anger more intensely across situations because of an angry temperament and also, more frequently, as a result of negative appraisals across various situations (Fox & Spector, 1999; Spielberger et al., 1983). *State anger,* by contrast, describes the experience of negative emotions that vary in intensity ranging from mild irritation to outrage, which are generally of limited duration in response to specific events (Spielberger, Ritterband, Sydeman, Reheiser, & Unger, 1995). The time distinction between anger as a momentary state and anger as an affective trait is important to an understanding of aggressive and violent behaviors at work. Individuals with high trait anger have the tendency to perceive a broad range of situations negatively and to react with intense anger (Spielberger et al., 1983; Gibson & Barsade, 1999). Those with higher levels of trait anger have reported engaging in a greater incidence of aggressive and antisocial behaviors such as doing or saying things to purposely harm others (Douglas & Martinko, 2001; Hepworth & Towler, 2004), striking out at the source of their anger, slamming doors, and using sarcasm (Domagalski & Steelman, 2004).

Although employees who possess angry dispositions are inclined to display CWB more so than those who are low in trait anger, the observed relationship becomes more complex when self-control is introduced. *Self-control* is the individual tendency to assess the long-term consequences of one's behavior (Marcus & Schuler, 2004). When self-control is low, individuals lack the ability to effectively manage their frustrations. Instead, they lose their inhibitions by reacting impulsively or aggressively to provocations (Douglas & Martinko, 2001).

Megargee and colleagues (Megargee, 1966; Megargee, Cook, & Mendelsohn, 1967) developed a typology of control to theorize the relationship between aggression and personality. Their classification posits the existence of three control-related personality types: chronically overcontrolled, undercontrolled, and appropriately controlled. Chronically *overcontrolled* individuals are prone to rigidly inhibit their reactions to provocations, whereas *appropriately controlled* types are generally restrained, except when assertiveness is perceived to be justifiable. *Undercontrolled* individuals lack the ability to inhibit aggressive and antisocial impulses. According to their framework, undercontrolled personalities will engage in frequent acts of aggressive and counterproductive behavior; however, more extreme acts of violence may be exhibited instead by those classified as chronically overcontrolled when their emotionless demeanor and rigid inhibitions break down. Thus, brutality and violence are not enacted as a culmination of frequent mild displays of aggression by undercontrolled personality types but rather by otherwise mild-mannered, highly controlled individuals.

The Megargee classification theorizes the relationship between an individual disposition and aggression but does not consider situational influences. Yet, as we have earlier stated, the literature demonstrates that violent, aggressive, and counterproductive behaviors are best explained when both individual differences and situational factors are examined. Although our focus in this chapter precludes discussion of environmental antecedents and correlates of CWB, it is important to consider the context in which these behaviors are examined, such as criminal behavior or work environments, because explanatory models may vary.

An affective disposition characterized by low self-control—what the Megargee typology refers to as undercontrolled types—has been identified as a strong predictor of counterproductive behavior among employees (Hepworth & Towler, 2004; Marcus & Schuler, 2004). The impulsive and uninhibited tendencies of individuals who lack self-control in the face of potentially detrimental consequences figure prominently in the display of CWB such as theft, fraud, sabotage, and aggression. In addition, aggressive and counterproductive workplace behaviors occur more readily when individuals with low self-control also possess high levels of trait anger (Douglas & Martinko, 2001). Thus, the combined effects of two distinct dispositional tendencies, trait anger and self-control, have been found to jointly influence negative work behavior; however, the distinction between low self-control and overcontrol has not been examined in the organizational literature and thus limits the ability to establish whether workplace violence and highly aggressive acts are performed by overcontrolled personalities rather than individuals with low self-control. It is possible that external constraints imposed by organizations will mitigate the dispositional effects of low self-control (Marcus & Schuler, 2004). Company policies that communicate negative sanctions associated with rule violations or inform employees of surveillance measures may induce employees with low self-control to otherwise restrain themselves. It is unclear, however, whether such measures would be effective in preventing highly aggressive and violent acts by employees with overcontrolled personalities who reach a breaking point.

The important role of trait anger in combination with other affective dispositions is further reinforced by an investigation of narcissistic personalities (Penney & Spector, 2002). *Narcissism* may be described as an individual desire to perceive oneself as superior to others. Narcissistic individuals possess a tenuous sense of self-esteem in which they are highly vigilant and emotionally sensitive to information that might threaten their desired superior self-appraisals. Penney and Spector (2002) found evidence of an indirect relationship between narcissism and CWB that was mediated by trait anger. They concluded that employees who are narcissistic experience more anger than others because of the tendency to maintain constant vigilance to ego threats, and when threats to their egos surface, they are likely to respond by engaging in CWB.

Other personality traits have been empirically tested in relationship to counterproductive workplace behaviors, among them the Big Five personality factors of Agreeableness, Conscientiousness, and Emotional Stability. All three share the common feature of being stable, enduring, individual level characteristics, although Emotional Stability is arguably the sole trait among these with an affective orientation. Nonetheless, the importance of dispositional characteristics as predictors of CWB is supported by several studies. Colbert and her colleagues (2004) found that Agreeableness moderates the relationship between perceived organizational support and interpersonal deviance, whereas Conscientiousness moderates the relationship between perceptions of an organization's developmental environment and the behavioral outcome of withholding effort. Furthermore, individuals who lack Emotional Stability, meaning those with a tendency to experience stable feelings of insecurity, depression, despair, and fearfulness, are significantly more likely to withhold work effort when they perceive an organizational environment lacking in encouragement, feedback, and support needed for employee development.

In a meta-analysis conducted by Salgado (2002), the association between the Big Five personality factors and CWB—defined as absenteeism, accident rate, deviant behavior, and turnover—also supported the influence of personality characteristics as predictors of CWB. Conscientiousness and Agreeableness both predicted deviant behavior such as theft and substance use, whereas employee turnover was explained by all five personality traits, with Emotional Stability showing the strongest negative relationship to turnover.

The value of specifying theoretical models that explore the interactive relationship between situational and dispositional variables has been addressed in a study by Skarlicki et al. (1999). They found that for individuals with antagonistic personalities (those who are low in agreeableness), there was an interaction between interactional and distributive justice in predicting *organizational retaliatory behavior* (ORB). ORB was operationalized as behavior that includes purposely damaging company equipment and taking company supplies home without permission.

Negative affectivity was also examined as a possible predictor of retaliation (Skarlicki et al., 1999). A similar three-way interaction was found which demonstrated that individuals who may be characterized by the trait of *negative affectivity* (feelings of discomfort, dissatisfaction, and distress, with a generally negative orientation toward life) are more likely to retaliate when both distributive and interactional justice are low. Interestingly, those with a negative affect have not been shown to directly engage in workplace aggression (Douglas & Martinko, 2001; Hepworth & Towler, 2004). These seemingly contradictory empirical findings suggest that individual differences do not necessarily independently explain acts of workplace violence or aggression but instead require theoretical frameworks to model the joint effects of situational factors and individual differences in order to understand CWB.

One final affective disposition that has been examined in relation to workplace aggression is trait anxiety (Fox & Spector, 1999). Individuals prone to trait anxiety are those with a stable tendency to experience elevated feelings of tension and apprehension across a multitude of situations. Highly anxious employees respond to work events with heightened feelings of frustration and job dissatisfaction, and these negative emotional responses lead to counterproductive behavioral responses such as CWB directed at the organization and CWB directed toward others. Although trait anxiety indirectly predicts CWB through its association with experienced negative emotional states, these findings attest to the complex interrelationships among experienced emotional states and affective personality traits in influencing CWB. Moreover, as the foregoing discussion suggests, theoretical models of workplace violence and other undesirable behaviors such as aggression, deviance, and retaliation would be incomplete without the inclusion of individual personality differences, particularly trait anger and self-control. In light of the potentially detrimental implications of counterproductive work behavior to organizations and those employed by them, continued research that integrates environmental and individual level variables is warranted.

Implications for Practice, Policy, and Intervention

The centrality of emotion's role in CWB and violence in the workplace should inform how this important social issue is addressed. This means considering both the precipitating individual and organizational factors that lead to negative emotions at work and factors that trigger aggressive and violent responses to emotional experiences. A dual focus on reducing unnecessary emotional provocation and providing productive outlets for emotional experience that is inevitable would prove most effective. These goals can be accomplished using a variety of strategies.

Dispositional Approach

As summarized in this chapter, clear evidence shows that some people are more dispositionally inclined to engage in CWB and violence than others. Trait anger and self-control in particular have been linked to these behaviors. Thus, one approach to addressing CWB would be through selection by screening out from hiring those individuals who are high on these personality traits. Although this approach may well identify some individuals with aggressive tendencies who would have engaged in these behaviors, there are limitations that make it insufficient as a complete strategy to control CWB. First, although research has linked these traits to CWB, studies combine a large variety of discrete acts into behavioral indexes, and it is unclear to what extent personality predicts the more serious aggressive and violent acts that are rarely reported. Thus personality may predict milder acts, such as spreading rumors or CWBs that are not really aggressive, such as taking a longer break than entitled. Furthermore, behavior is a complex interplay of both personality and environment so that in many organizations where provocation is rare, CWB may not often occur, and therefore, screening out those so inclined may not accomplish much.

Second, the mechanisms by which personality relates to CWB are not well understood. It might be tempting to assume that these individuals are merely aggressive by their nature and thus likely to by hyperreactive. As we discuss in this chapter, emotional states are precursors to aggression and CWB and likely mediate the relationship between personality traits, especially affective dispositions, and CWB. Thus, for example, the high trait anger individuals are more likely to respond to environmental conditions with anger and thereby engage in CWB. On the other hand, it is possible that the relation between personality and CWB is mediated by the environment. For example, those high in affective traits might find themselves in worse jobs that may be more stressful. Spector, Zapf, Chen, and Frese (2000) discussed evidence for mechanisms whereby those high in negative affectivity (NA) tended to be selected into higher-stress jobs and tended to create more stressful conditions for themselves. The selection mechanism is particularly troublesome for the efficacy of affective traits as a selection device, as it implies that the reason high-NA individuals are aggressive is that they are in jobs that are more provoking and not just because they have a tendency to engage in such behavior.

Finally, personality measures can be subject to applicant faking, and measures of affective dispositions in particular can be influenced by social desirability (Chen, Dai, Spector, & Jex, 1997). Thus, these measures might be particularly prone to bias in a situation in which applicants are highly motivated to appear in a desirable way on the test, and thus they will score low on these dispositions. The reduced accuracy of measurement would reduce the predictive validity of these tests as selection devices.

Clearly, before these tests could be used for selection, validation studies would have to be conducted with the specific target behaviors as criteria. Whereas the research studies done to date are suggestive that measures of affective dispositions can predict CWB, this needs to be verified. Furthermore, although most of the research done to date has looked at individual personality traits, interactions among some traits might be important. As noted earlier, undercontrolled individuals respond impulsively. Such individuals, if also high in affective traits, will likely be hyperreactive to the environment, frequently experiencing negative emotion without effective control mechanisms to inhibit aggressive responses. Interactions among personality variables should be explored to see if they enhance prediction of aggression and CWB.

Environmental Approach

The research on CWB clearly shows that these acts are precipitated by conditions and situations in the work environment. Although some individuals are more inclined to experience negative emotion and engage in CWB, there is some provocation that triggers a reaction. Efforts to manage such provocations can short-circuit the processes that lead to CWB. Of course, one cannot eliminate all such conditions from the workplace, so efforts to do so would certainly be counterproductive and wasteful. Furthermore, it is likely that some individuals are hypersensitive to either anger- or anxiety-provoking situations, and one cannot design the work environment to the lowest common denominator in terms of assuring that no action ever distresses anyone.

On the other hand, the emotions and reactions of employees should be considered in the design and administration of organizations and their policies. Quite often this means just adopting sound management practices that promote organizational effectiveness through employee performance and well-being, creating a healthy work organization (Sauter, Lim, & Murphy, 1996). Joint facilitation of employee performance and well-being can be accomplished by reducing impediments and unnecessary stress. First, proper selection and training should be used to achieve a good match between employee skills and job requirements. Second, organizational constraints that interfere with performance (Peters & O'Connor, 1980) should be reduced when possible by providing needed resources and removing impediments. Third, fairness can be accomplished by adopting, communicating, and following reasonable policies for salaries, rewards, promotions, and organizational actions. Fourth, workloads should be kept within reason so as not to produce excessive fatigue and require working hours that allow little time for nonwork and family activities. Finally, organization leaders should develop organizational cultures in which employees are treated with respect by managers, and managers should require employees to treat one another with respect.

Of course, even with the best run organizations, problems arise that are stressful for employees, and employees may get into conflicts with one another and supervisors that result in aggression and violence. Supervisors should be trained to recognize and deal with negative emotional reactions by subordinates, if for no other reason than that such reactions are detrimental to job performance and can interfere with employees' ability to cooperate and collaborate with one another. The idea is not to turn managers into clinicians who can deal with personal problems but to have managers help their subordinates cope with workplace issues relevant to their jobs. This might mean helping employees devise strategies to improve task efficiency, more effectively manage time, or serve as mediators in disputes between subordinates. Ignoring such issues will likely have detrimental effects, not only by increasing the likelihood of CWB and violence but also by reducing performance and job satisfaction.

Finally, organizations need clear policies to deal with cases in which employees are caught engaging in CWBs. Such policies are likely to be complex because there are a wide variety of behaviors that might occur, and certainly punching a coworker is quite different from making a nasty comment. Management action is needed for many such behaviors because lack of action may be interpreted as encouragement, which might lead to escalation, with even fairly minor acts of rudeness spiraling into overt aggression (Pearson, Andersson, & Porath, 2005). In the long run, this can produce a negative climate in which escalating nastiness produces frequent negative emotion and detrimental effects on organizations and people. Actions can range from supervisor requests that certain behaviors be stopped to disciplinary actions and even termination. Extreme cases, such as physical assault, might result in legal action and calling the police. A clearly articulated and enforced set of policies can go a long way toward minimizing CWB, particularly in combination with the other actions we have discussed.

So far we have discussed actions taken to handle Type 3 violence and CWB. Many of these approaches would be appropriate for Type 2 violence as well, given that client or customer violence can occur for similar reasons. Organizations should evaluate their approach to dealing with clients or customers and reduce situations that might be unnecessarily stressful. This means, for example, reducing waiting times through efficient appointment scheduling and assuring that employees who engage clients or customers are competent, courteous, and well trained. In hospitals and other medical settings where violence is relatively frequent, direct-care employees should be trained to recognize and deal appropriately with patient and family anger and anxiety. Employees who deal with the public should receive training in handling angry clients or customers so they can defuse a potentially violent situation. Supervisors should serve as backup to employees who are unable to manage an escalating situation and might serve to mediate a disagreement between a client or customer and employee. Finally, organizations need clear policies that empower employees to deal with clients or customers who engage in certain behaviors. Although clients or customers should be given some latitude, there comes a point when the behavior has become harmful and potentially violent and employees might have to ask the person to leave or call security or even the police.

Summary and Conclusions

Negative emotion plays an important role in much CWB and violence at work, particularly acts committed by clients, customers, and employees. As we have shown, work stressors can trigger anger, anxiety, and other emotions that under some circumstances might lead to CWB and violence. Personality serves an important function as well, as the interplay of individual differences and the work environment combine to induce emotion and produce behavior. We have suggested several actions that organizations can take to minimize negative emotion and CWB, including selection, minimizing stressors, training supervisors to recognize and handle emotional reactions of subordinates, developing a civil organizational culture, and enforcing policies to deal with employee CWB. These approaches can be modified to deal with client or customer CWB and violence, as well.

Violence at work and milder forms of CWB are a major problem for employees and their employers. Both reduce employee effectiveness, which has detrimental effects on organizational functioning. They also have adverse effects on employee health and well-being (LeBlanc & Kelloway, 2002), particularly when employees have to endure both physical and verbal abuse. Policies and practices that can reduce CWB and violence will go a long way toward enhancing the well-being of both employees and organizations.

References

Anderson, C. A., Anderson, K. B., & Deuser, W. E. (1996). Examining an affective aggression framework: Weapon and temperature effects on aggressive thoughts, affect, and attitudes. *Personality and Social Psychology Bulletin, 22,* 366–376.

Anderson, C. A., & Bushman, B. J. (2002). Human aggression. *Annual Review of Psychology, 53,* 27–51.

Anderson, C. A., Deuser, W. E., & DeNeve, K. M. (1995). Hot temperatures, hostile affect, hostile cognition, and arousal: Tests of a general model of affective aggression. *Personality and Social Psychology Bulletin, 21,* 434–448.

Asmus, C. L., & Bell, P. A. (1999). Effects of environmental odor and coping style on negative affect, anger, and arousal. *Journal of Applied Social Psychology, 29,* 245–260.

Bell, P. A., & Baron, R. A. (1976). Aggression and heat: The mediating role of negative affect. *Journal of Applied Social Psychology, 6,* 18–30.

Berkowitz, L. (1990). On the formulation and regulation of anger and aggression: A cognitive neo-associationistic approach. *American Psychologist, 45,* 494–503.

Berkowitz, L. (1998). Affective aggression: The role of stress, pain, and negative affect. In R. G. Geen & E. Donnerstein (Eds.), *Human aggression: Theories, research and implications for social policy* (pp. 49–72). San Diego, CA: Academic.

Bies, R. J., & Tripp, T. M. (2005). The study of revenge in the workplace: Conceptual, ideological, and empirical issues. In S. Fox & P. E. Spector (Eds.), *Counterproductive work behavior: Investigations of actors and targets* (pp. 65–81). Washington, DC: American Psychological Association.

Bies, R. J., Tripp, T. M., & Kramer, R. M. (1997). At the breaking point: Cognitive and social dynamics of revenge in organizations. In R. A. Giacalone & J. Greenberg (Eds.), *Antisocial behavior in organizations* (p. 43). Thousand Oaks, CA: Sage.

Chen, P. Y., Dai, T., Spector, P. E., & Jex, S. M. (1997). Relationship between negative affectivity and positive affectivity: Effects of judged desirability of scale items and respondent's social desirability. *Journal of Personality Assessment, 69,* 183–198.

Chen, P. Y., & Spector, P. E. (1992). Relationships of work stressors with aggression, withdrawal, theft and substance use: An exploratory study. *Journal of Occupational and Organizational Psychology, 65,* 177–184.

Colbert, A. E., Mount, M. K., Harter, J. K., Witt, L. A., & Barrick, M. R. (2004). Interactive effects of personality and perception of the work situation on workplace deviance. *Journal of Applied Psychology, 89,* 599–609.

Cropanzano, R., & Baron, R. (1991). Injustice and organizational conflict: The moderating role of power restoration. *International Journal of Conflict Management, 2,* 5–26.

Cropanzano, R., Howes, J. C., Grandey, A. A., & Toth, P. (1997). The relationship of organizational politics and support to work behaviors, attitudes, and stress. *Journal of Organizational Behavior, 18,* 159–180.

Dollard, D., Doob, L., Miller, N., Mowrer, O., & Sears, R. (1939). *Frustration and aggression.* New Haven, CT: Yale University Press.

Domagalski, T., & Steelman, L. (2004. August). *The impact of work events and disposition on the experience and expression of employee anger.* Paper presented at the annual meeting of the Academy of Management Conference, New Orleans.

Douglas, S. C., & Martinko, M. J. (2001). Exploring the role of individual differences in the prediction of workplace aggression. *Journal of Applied Psychology, 86,* 547–559.

Folger, R., & Skarlicki, D. P. (2005). Beyond counterproductive work behavior: Moral emotions and deontic retaliation vs. reconciliation. In S. Fox & P. E. Spector (Eds.), *Counterproductive work behavior: Investigations of actors and targets* (p. 44). Washington, DC: American Psychological Association.

Fox, S., & Spector, P. E. (1999). A model of work frustration-aggression. *Journal of Organizational Behavior, 20,* 915–931.

Fox, S., Spector, P. E., & Miles, D. (2001). Counterproductive work behavior (CWB) in response to job stressors and organizational justice: Some mediator and moderator tests for autonomy and emotions. *Journal of Vocational Behavior, 59,* 291–309.

Gibson, D. E., & Barsade, S. G. (1999, August). The experience of anger at work: Lessons from the chronically angry. In R. R. Callister (Chair), *Anger in organizations: Its causes and consequences.* Symposium presented at the annual meeting of the Academy of Management Conference, Chicago.

Glomb, T. (2002). Workplace anger and aggression: Informing conceptual models with data from specific encounters. *Journal of Occupational Health Psychology, 7,* 20–36.

Goh, A., Bruursema, K., Fox, S., & Spector, P. E. (2003, April). *Comparisons of self and co-worker reports of counterproductive work behavior.* Paper presented at the Society for Industrial/Organizational Psychology Conference, Orlando, FL.

Harvey, S., & Keashly, L. (2003). Predicting the risk for aggression in the workplace: Risk factors, self-esteem and time at work. *Social Behavior and Personality, 31,* 807–814.

Hepworth, W., & Towler, A. (2004). The effects of individual differences and charismatic leadership on workplace aggression. *Journal of Occupational Health Psychology, 9,* 176–185.

Hoel, H., Rayner, C., & Cooper, C. L. (1999). Workplace bullying. In C. L. Cooper & I. T. Robertson (Eds.), *International Review of Industrial and Organizational Psychology 1999* (pp. 195–230). Chichester, UK: John Wiley.

Hollinger, R. C. (1986). Acts against the workplace: Social bonding and employee deviance. *Deviant Behavior, 7,* 53–75.

Keashly, L. (1998). Emotional abuse in the workplace: Conceptual and empirical issues. *Journal of Emotional Abuse, 1,* 85–117.

LeBlanc, M. M., & Barling, J. (2005). Understanding the many faces of workplace violence. In S. Fox & P. E. Spector (Eds.), *Counterproductive work behavior: Investigations of actors and targets* (p. 44). Washington, DC: American Psychological Association.

LeBlanc, M. M., & Kelloway, E. K. (2002). Predictors and outcomes of workplace violence and aggression. *Journal of Applied Psychology, 87,* 444–453.

Lee, K., & Allen, N. J. (2002). Organizational citizenship behavior and workplace deviance: The role of affect and cognition. *Journal of Applied Psychology, 87,* 131–142.

Marcus, B., & Schuler, H. (2004). Antecedents of counterproductive behavior at work: A general perspective. *Journal of Applied Psychology, 89,* 647–660.

Martinko, M. J., Gundlach, M. J., & Douglas, S. C. (2002). Toward an integrative theory of counterproductive workplace behavior: A causal reasoning perspective. *International Journal of Selection and Assessment, 10,* 36–50.

Megargee, E. I. (1966). Undercontrolled and overcontrolled personality types in extreme antisocial aggression. *Psychological Monographs, 80,* 1–29.

Megargee, E. I., Cook P. E., & Mendelsohn, G. A. (1967). Development and validation of an MMPI scale of assaultiveness in overcontrolled individuals. *Journal of Abnormal Psychology, 72,* 519–528.

Merchant, J. A., & Lundell, J. A. (2001). *Workplace violence: A report to the nation.* Iowa City: University of Iowa.

Miles, D. E., Borman, W. E., Spector, P. E., & Fox, S. (2002). Building an integrative model of extra role work behaviors: A comparison of counterproductive work behavior with organizational citizenship behavior. *International Journal of Selection and Assessment, 10,* 51–57.

Neuman, J. H., & Baron, R. A. (1997). Aggression in the workplace. In R. A. Giacalone & J. Greenberg (Eds.), *Antisocial behavior in organizations* (pp. 37–67). Thousand Oaks, CA: Sage.

Neuman, J. H., & Baron, R. A. (1998). Workplace violence and workplace aggression: Evidence concerning specific forms, potential causes, and preferred targets. *Journal of Management, 24,* 391–419.

Neuman, J. H., & Baron, R. A. (2005). Aggression in the workplace: A social-psychological perspective. In S. Fox & P. E. Spector (Eds.), *Counterproductive work behavior: Investigations of actors and targets* (p. 45). Washington, DC: American Psychological Association.

O'Leary-Kelly, A. M., Griffin, R. W., & Glew, D. J. (1996) Organization-motivated aggression: A research framework. *Academy of Management Review, 21,* 225–253.

Pearson, C. M., Andersson, L. M., & Porath, C. L. (2005). Workplace incivility. In S. Fox & P. E. Spector (Eds.), *Counterproductive work behavior: Investigations of actors and targets* (p. 45). Washington, DC: American Psychological Association.

Penney, L. M., & Spector, P. E. (2002). Narcissism and counterproductive work behavior: Do bigger egos mean bigger problems? *International Journal of Selection and Assessment, 10,* 126–134.

Peters, L. H., & O'Connor, E. J. (1980). Situational constraints and work outcomes: The influences of a frequently overlooked construct. *Academy of Management Review, 5,* 391–397.

Robinson, S. L., & Bennett, R. J. (1995). A typology of deviant workplace behaviors: A multidimensional scaling study. *Academy of Management Journal, 38,* 555–572.

Salgado, J. F. (2002). The Big Five personality dimensions and counterproductive behaviors. *International Journal of Selection and Assessment, 10,* 117–125.

Sauter, S. L., Lim, S. Y., & Murphy, L. R. (1996). Organizational health: A new paradigm for occupational stress research at NIOSH. *Japanese Journal of Occupational Mental Health, 4,* 248–254.

Skarlicki, D. P., & Folger, R. (1997). Retaliation in the workplace: The roles of distributive, procedural, and interactional justice. *Journal of Applied Psychology, 82,* 434–443.

Skarlicki, D. P., Folger, R., & Tesluk, P. (1999). Personality as a moderator in the relationship between fairness and retaliation. *Academy of Management Journal, 42,* 100–108.

Spector, P. E. (1978). Organizational frustration: A model and review of the literature. *Personnel Psychology, 31,* 815–829.

Spector, P. E. (1997). The role of frustration in antisocial behavior at work. In R. A. Giacalone & J. Greenberg (Eds.), *Antisocial behavior in organizations* (pp. 1–17). Thousand Oaks, CA: Sage.

Spector, P. E., Chen, P. Y., & O'Connell, B. J. (2000). A longitudinal study of relations between job stressors and job strains while controlling for prior negative affectivity and strains. *Journal of Applied Psychology, 85,* 211–218.

Spector, P. E., Dwyer, D. J., & Jex, S. M. (1988). The relationship of job stressors to affective, health, and performance outcomes: A comparison of multiple data sources. *Journal of Applied Psychology, 73,* 11–19.

Spector, P. E., & Fox, S. (2002). An emotion-centered model of voluntary work behavior: Some parallels between counterproductive work behavior (CWB) and organizational citizenship behavior (OCB). *Human Resource Management Review, 12,* 269–292.

Spector, P. E., & Fox, S. (2005). The stressor-emotion model of counterproductive work behavior (CWB). In S. Fox & P. E. Spector (Eds.), *Counterproductive work behavior: Investigations of actors and targets* (p. 46). Washington, DC: American Psychological Association.

Spector, P. E., & Goh, A. (2001). The role of emotions in the occupational stress process. In P. L. Perrewé & D. C. Ganster (Eds.), *Research in occupational stress and well-being* (Vol. 1, pp. 195–232). Greenwich, CT: JAI.

Spector, P. E., Zapf, D., Chen, P. Y., & Frese, M. (2000). Why negative affectivity should not be controlled in job stress research: Don't throw out the baby with the bath water. *Journal of Organizational Behavior, 21,* 79–95.

Spielberger, C. D., Jacobs, G., Russell, S., & Crane, R. S. (1983). Assessment of anger: The state-trait anger scale. In J. N. Butcher & C. D. Spielberger (Eds.), *Advances in personality assessment* (Vol. 2, pp. 161–189). Hillsdale, NJ: Lawrence Erlbaum.

Spielberger, C. D., Ritterband, L. M., Sydeman, S. J., Reheiser, E. C., & Unger, K. K. (1995). Assessment of emotional states and personality traits: Measuring psychological vital signs. In J. N. Butcher (Ed.), *Clinical personality assessment: Practical approaches.* New York: Oxford University Press.

Van Katwyk, P. T., Fox, S., Spector, P. E., & Kelloway, E. K. (2000). Using the Job-Related Affective Well-Being Scale (JAWS) to investigate affective responses to work stressors. *Journal of Occupational Health Psychology, 5,* 219–230.

Zapf, D., Knorz, C., & Kulla, M. (1996). On the relationship between mobbing factors, and job content, social work environment, and health outcomes. *European Journal of Work and Organizational Psychology, 5,* 215–237.

4
Prevalence of Workplace Aggression in the U.S. Workforce

Findings From a National Study

Aaron C. H. Schat
Michael R. Frone
E. Kevin Kelloway

Aggression, whether harmful to life and limb or merely painful to the ego, seems to be a real and important part of the human condition.

(Geen, 2001, p. 1)

Workplace aggression and violence have garnered a great deal of public attention due to the media exposure given to serious acts of workplace violence. The phrase "going postal," referring to an act of vengeful violence carried out by a disgruntled fired employee on his former boss and coworkers, has become part of our vernacular. Although these acts are extremely serious and call for action to understand their causes and prevent their occurrence, the available evidence suggests that they are actually quite rare and represent only the "tip of the iceberg" of workplace aggression (Baron & Neuman, 1998).

There has been remarkable growth in the amount of research that has been conducted to investigate workplace aggression and related constructs such as abuse, harassment, bullying, and victimization. This body of work has made

Authors' Note: Data collection was supported by the National Institute on Alcohol Abuse and Alcoholism through a grant (R01-AA12412) to Michael R. Frone. Preparation of this chapter was supported by grants from the Arts Research Board of McMaster University to Aaron Schat and the Nova Scotia Health Research Foundation and Social Sciences Research Council of Canada to E. Kevin Kelloway.

numerous contributions to our understanding of the causes and consequences of workplace aggression; however, although many studies report estimated frequencies of aggressive behavior, data are lacking that reflect the prevalence rates and demographic predictors of exposure to various types (e.g., physical and psychological) and sources (e.g., coworkers, supervisors, members of the public) of workplace aggression across a broad spectrum of the workforce.

Purpose of the Chapter

This chapter has several goals. First, we define *workplace aggression* and describe the behaviors that constitute the construct. Second, we review the existing literature on the prevalence of workplace aggression and discuss its limitations. Third, we review research related to demographic and occupational predictors of aggression. Fourth, we report prevalence rates and demographic predictors of exposure to workplace aggression based on data from a nationally representative survey of more than 2,500 U.S. workers. Our presentation of the results of this survey will focus on three issues: (a) the overall prevalence of exposure to physical violence and psychological aggression at work; (b) the prevalence of exposure to these behaviors from three different sources: one's supervisor or boss, coworkers (employees other than one's supervisor or boss), and members of the public (customers, clients, or patients); and (c) the extent to which various general (e.g., gender, age) and occupational (e.g., job type, industry classification) demographic variables predict exposure to the two types and three sources of workplace aggression. Finally, we discuss the implications of these results for future research on workplace aggression and intervention strategies aimed at preventing workplace aggression.

Conceptualizing Workplace Aggression

There are a variety of behaviors that constitute the construct domain of workplace aggression, including seemingly minor, nonphysical behaviors such as being glared at, more serious nonphysical behaviors such as verbal threats, and actual physical assaults with or without the use of a weapon. Given this range of behavior, it is not surprising to find inconsistencies in the literature regarding how workplace aggression has been conceptualized and operationalized. Some researchers, for example, have narrowly operationalized aggression by considering only physically aggressive behaviors such as assaults (e.g., Kraus, Blander, & McArthur, 1995), whereas others also have included threats of assault (e.g., Jenkins, 1996) and behaviors reflecting psychological aggression, such as being yelled at or cursed (e.g., Baron & Neuman, 1998; Rogers & Kelloway, 1997; Schat & Kelloway, 2000, 2003).

The broad conceptualization of workplace aggression is reflected in Schat and Kelloway's (2005) definition in which *workplace aggression* is defined as "behavior by an individual or individuals within or outside an organization that is intended to physically or psychologically harm a worker or workers and occurs in a work-related context" (p. 191). This definition has several important features. First, it is consistent with definitions of aggression used in the general human aggression literature (e.g., Baron & Richardson, 1994; Berkowitz, 1993; Geen, 2001), which is appropriate given the extent to which this literature has informed the study of workplace aggression (e.g., Neuman & Baron, 1997). Second, it is general enough to include a wide range of physical and psychological behaviors that constitute the construct of workplace aggression. Third, it encompasses aggressive behavior enacted by a variety of sources within (e.g., supervisors, coworkers) and outside (e.g., clients, customers, and patients) the organization. Although few studies have distinguished between sources, the available evidence demonstrates that there are different antecedents and consequences of aggression from different sources (e.g., Greenberg & Barling, 1999; LeBlanc & Kelloway, 2002), suggesting the importance of making this distinction.

Before moving on, it is important to discuss our use of the term *workplace aggression* and how it relates to other similar constructs such as *workplace abuse, victimization, harassment,* and *bullying.* First, although there may be variations in how some of these constructs are defined, the behaviors that constitute workplace aggression are generally consistent with the behaviors that constitute these related constructs. That is, we would make no distinction between *abusive behavior* and *aggressive behavior.* We use the latter terminology simply because it is more widely used and makes more explicit the conceptual link between research on workplace aggression and the large body of work on human aggression in general. Second, although the terms *workplace aggression* and *workplace violence* are sometimes treated interchangeably, it is appropriate to distinguish between them. We suggest that *workplace aggression* is a higher-order construct that includes *workplace violence,* which is a specific type of aggression consisting of behaviors that are intended to cause physical harm, and *workplace psychological aggression,* which consists of behaviors that are intended to cause psychological harm. This distinction is consistent with much of the general human aggression literature (e.g., Anderson & Bushman, 2002) and has also been made by a number of workplace aggression researchers (e.g., Greenberg & Barling, 1999; Neuman & Baron, 1998; Schat & Kelloway, 2005).

Prevalence of Workplace Aggression

There is a dearth of valid data available on the prevalence of workplace aggression. Although there are data available related to workplace homicide, rates of physical assault or injuries due to physical assault, and frequency of exposure to various forms of psychological aggression (e.g., verbal abuse, threats), there are a number of limitations associated with these data. Before discussing the limitations, we first review what past studies suggest about the prevalence of workplace aggression.

Fatal Workplace Violence: Workplace Homicide

A number of agencies in the United States collect information about the rates of death and physical injury due to work-related assaults. The Census of Fatal Occupational Injuries (CFOI) data collected by the Bureau of Labor Statistics (BLS; 2004) show that workplace homicide, the most severe form of workplace aggression, is the third leading cause of work-related death and accounted for 631 deaths in the year 2003. This represents an incidence rate of approximately 4.6 homicides per 1 million workers. The data also suggested that between 1992 and 2000, the workplace homicide rate dropped nearly 40%. During this period, the highest number of workplace homicides occurred in 1994 (1,080 homicides) and the lowest number in 2002 (609 homicides). Therefore, there has been a general downward trend over this period, despite the small increases that occurred between 1999 and 2000 and between 2002 and 2003. Although media reports imply that the prototypical case of workplace homicide is committed by a "disgruntled ex-employee," the data do not support this. In a review of earlier CFOI data, Sygnatur and Toscano (2000) found that in cases for which the victim-perpetrator association was identifiable, employees or former employees accounted for 15% of the homicides, whereas 67% occurred during robberies and other crimes perpetrated by organizational outsiders. Customers or clients (8%), acquaintances (7%), and relatives (4%) accounted for the remaining homicides for which the victim-perpetrator association was known. Sygnatur and Toscano also state that the workplace homicides for which the victim-perpetrator associations are not known likely occurred during robberies or attempted robberies, suggesting the 67% may be an underestimate.

Nonfatal Workplace Violence

Data are also available on the frequencies and injury rates of nonfatal violence. A survey conducted by the Northwestern National Life Insurance Company (NNLIC; 1993) found that 15% of workers reported being physically attacked at some point during their working life, and 2.5% reported being physically attacked during the previous year. A more recent U.S. national survey conducted by the National Center on Addiction and Substance Abuse at Columbia University (NCASA; 2000) found that 5%[1] of respondents reported having been assaulted at work during the previous year.

According to data from the National Crime Victimization Survey (NCVS) conducted by the Bureau of Justice Statistics (Duhart, 2001), an average of 11.7 out of every 1,000 employees were victims of assault (including either simple or aggravated assault) between 1993 and 1999, which represents slightly more than 1.6 million workers and a prevalence rate of 1.27%. When sexual assault, rape, and robberies are included, these numbers are somewhat higher (1.744 million workers). According to these data, men are about 56% more likely to be the victims of workplace violence than women, and workers aged 20 to 34 experienced the highest rates of violence, with the rates of those aged 12 to 19 and 35 to 49 being comparable with one another and somewhat less than the 20 to 34 age group.

In Canada, the Public Service Employment Survey (PSES; Public Service Commission [PSC], 2002) was based on approximately 94,000 responses. Although the term *physical violence* was not defined for participants, approximately 2% of respondents reported being the victim of physical violence at work in the last 2 years. Data from the Bureau of Justice Statistics (Duhart, 2001) shows that workplace violence accounted for 18% of all violent crime reported between 1993 and 1999. Interestingly, when the rates are disaggregated by year during this 7-year period, the data suggest that nonfatal victimization rates decreased by about 44% over this time period, which is consistent with the 40% decrease in overall violent crime victimization rates (at work and elsewhere) during the same period. Therefore, the data contradict the belief that workplace violence is on the rise, a belief that is likely perpetuated by the media attention given to serious acts of workplace violence.

Psychological Workplace Aggression

Numerous estimates of the frequency with which workers experience nonphysical forms of aggression (e.g., bullying, generalized harassment) are available. Many of these come from surveys carried out by industry and employee groups or by researchers conducting empirical studies. Einarsen and Skogstad (1996) summarize the results of 14 Norwegian studies of bullying and report an average prevalence rate of 8.6% during a 6-month reporting period. Because the definition of *bullying* used in that study included reference to prolonged duration of exposure to negative acts that were associated with feelings of powerlessness,[2] the resulting prevalence rate likely represents very serious cases of victimization and an underestimate of the prevalence of workplace victimization that is not characterized by these definitional constraints. In fact, at the other extreme, Einarsen and Raknes (1997) found that 75% of Norwegian engineering employees reported experiencing at least one incident of general harassment during the previous 6 months. Similarly, a survey of public sector employees in the United States found that 71% of respondents reported at least some experience of workplace incivility during the previous 5 years, and 6% reported experiencing such behavior many times (Cortina, Magley, Williams, & Langhout, 2001). In one study of Canadian public employees, 69% of respondents reported experiencing verbal aggression at work (Pizzino, 2002). The PSES (2002) found that 21% of respondents reported being the victim of "harassment" in the previous 2 years.[3]

These data—and many other estimates of the prevalence of workplace aggression—are not representative of well-defined populations and are characterized by other limitations (which we discuss below). Therefore, it is impossible to discern the degree to which they are generally representative. In addition to these data, however, data are also available from two surveys based on more representative samples of the U.S. workforce. In the U.S. national survey conducted by the NCASA (2000), 33% of the respondents reported experiencing verbal abuse at work.[4] In the NNLIC (1993) survey, 19% of respondents reported experiencing work-related harassment, and 7% reported experiencing threats of physical harm during the previous year. As we discuss below, differences in definitions and operationalizations may account for the differences in prevalence that emerged from these two surveys.

Demographic and Occupational Predictors of Workplace Aggression

The vast majority of incidents of workplace violence and aggression originate with individuals external to the workplace. For example, 67% of workplace homicides occur during a robbery (Sygnatur & Toscano, 2000). Respondents to the Canadian PSES reported that violence was most likely from clients, residents, or other members of the public (approximately 71% of those reporting workplace violence) rather than from coworkers (approximately 34% of those reporting workplace violences;[5] PSC, 2002).

Given these observations, it is not surprising that occupation is a predictor of workplace violence and aggression. Although there are data identifying specific occupations at risk (e.g., retail workers, service employees, taxi drivers; Casteel & Peek-Asa, 2000; Castillo & Jenkins, 1994; Peek-Asa, Runyan, & Zwerling, 2001), a more detailed approach has been to focus on the characteristics of occupations that place individuals at risk. A number of these have been documented in the literature.

For example, working alone, at night, or around money or valuables places individuals at risk for violence associated with robbery and violent crime (Canadian Centre for Occupational Health and Safety [CCOHS], 1999; LeBlanc & Kelloway, 2002). Having custodial responsibility for others, particularly those who are under stress, is a risk factor for occupational violence (PSC, 2002), as is being in a position to deny a service or refuse a request (LeBlanc & Kelloway, 2002; National Institute for Occupational Safety and Health [NIOSH], 2002).

Although most of the available data have focused on occupational characteristics as predictors of physical violence, LeBlanc and Kelloway (2002) found that a measure of occupational risk based on these characteristics predicted exposure to both physical violence and psychological aggression. Moreover, the measure of risk predicted respondents' perceived likelihood of experiencing future violence, suggesting that individuals base their subjective estimates of risk on these occupational characteristics.

Although the literature on occupational characteristics has been reasonably consistent, there are mixed data on demographic predictors of workplace violence and aggression. Below we focus our attention on gender and age because they are the most commonly examined demographic predictors of workplace violence and aggression.

Gender

Most of the available data suggest that men are more likely than women to both experience (Duhart, 2001) and commit (Geen, 2001; McFarlin, Fals-Stewart, Major, & Justice, 2001) violence. Hurrell, Worthington, and Driscoll (1996) surveyed 2,525 women and 2,324 men about their experiences of workplace violence. Approximately 17% of the men reported that they had been physically assaulted at work in the preceding year. In contrast, approximately 9% of the women reported being assaulted during the same time period. Guterman, Jayaratne, and Bargal (1996) found that male social workers were more likely to report both assaults and physical threats than were female social workers in an American sample. They found no differences between genders, however, in an Israeli sample of social workers. Safran and Tartaglini (1996) also found that males were more at risk of physical assault than females in their study of workers in an urban jail setting.

Although these data are reasonably consistent in suggesting that men are more at risk for workplace violence than are women, at least two observations would suggest that other factors may be obscuring the relationship. First, occupational differences in violence are well established, and it is clear that the workforce is gender segregated. For example, nurses and those who work in health care settings are at greater risk of workplace violence than are members of other occupations (see Lanza, Chapter 8, this volume) and are more likely to be female than male. Second, it is clear that partner violence or domestic violence can be expressed in, or has consequences for, the workplace (Friedman, Brown-Tucker, Neville, & Imperial, 1996; see also Swanberg, Logan, & Macke, Chapter 16, this volume) and is more likely to occur among women than men (Tjaden & Thoennes, 2000).

Based on their review, Hewitt and Levin (1997) concluded that women were more at risk for nonfatal workplace assaults but that men were more at risk for workplace homicide. Based on his analysis of data from the NCVS, Warchol (1998) concluded that men were more likely than women to experience violence at work but that women were more likely than men to experience sexual assaults and assaults perpetrated by acquaintances (as opposed to strangers) outside of work. Results from the NNLIC (1993) study suggested that women were more likely than men to experience verbal harassment at work, whereas men were more likely than women to experience physical threats at work. Thus, although the general conclusion is that men are more at risk for violence, this observation is conditioned by the type and source of violence and may be confounded with occupational characteristics.

Age

When it comes to the risk of experiencing workplace violence, the general conclusion is that younger adult workers are at greater risk. For example, Hurrell et al. (1996) found that for both women and men, assault victims were younger than nonvictims. In contrast, Guterman et al. (1996) found no effect of age but reported a significant effect of work experience such that less experienced workers were more likely to report receiving threats and being assaulted. As with gender, the risk for violence experienced by younger workers may be related to occupational characteristics. For example, younger workers are more likely to be employed in the fast-food industry and may experience a high rate of workplace aggression as a result (see, for example, Mayhew & Quinlan, 2002).

Together, these findings suggest that there is considerable variation in the frequency of exposure to workplace violence and aggression across occupational and demographic groups. As noted above, these are not independent groupings. The workforce is both gender and age segregated such that these groups are disproportionately represented in high-risk occupations (e.g., youth in retail and fast-food services, women in nursing). Moreover, demographic and occupational characteristics may combine to place individuals at risk. For example, although denying a service may place individuals at risk for workplace violence, the risk may be heightened when the worker is obviously young or inexperienced. These observations suggest the need to examine the prevalence of workplace violence and aggression across occupational and demographic groups.

Evaluation of Existing Prevalence Estimates of Workplace Aggression

Accurate surveillance of the forms and frequency of workplace aggression requires representative sampling procedures and standardized definitions, measures, and reporting mechanisms (Peek-Asa, Schaffer, Kraus, & Howard, 1998). Although the literature contains numerous estimates of the prevalence of workplace aggression, the data on which these estimates are based have a number of methodological limitations, precluding the drawing of valid conclusions about the degree to which members of the workforce are exposed to aggressive work-related behavior. These methodological limitations include data sources that contain inaccuracies, small and convenience samples that are not representative of a broad or specific population, reporting periods that vary across studies, and inconsistent definitions and operationalizations of workplace aggression. In addition, few of the estimates provide data related to demographic, occupational, or other predictors of exposure to the various forms and sources of workplace aggression, information that is critical to identifying the workers at greatest risk and developing intervention programs to address and prevent their exposure to such behavior.

Data Source Limitations

The data on workplace homicide are taken from the CFOI (BLS, 2004), which is compiled from a variety of sources, including death certificates, workers' compensation claims, and police and medical examiner reports. Various sources are used because individual sources are limited and do not capture all work-related homicides. The results of one review suggested that death certificates identified 81% of occupational fatalities, medical examiner records identified 61%, workers' compensation reports identified 57%, and Occupational Safety and Health Administration reports identified 32% (Stout & Bell, 1991). When these records are compiled, steps are taken to verify their accuracy, although limitations of the original sources adversely affect the accuracy of the resulting estimates (BLS, 2004), likely yielding underestimates (Horan & Mallonee, 2003; Stout & Bell, 1991). Stout and Bell suggest that of all work-related deaths, homicides are among the least accurately identified as work-related. Therefore, although the range of sources from which these data are compiled and the care taken in their compilation would make them more valid than estimates based on fewer or narrower sources, the prevalence rates of work-related homicide derived from the CFOI data are likely underestimates of its true prevalence.

Sampling Limitations

Much of the data on the prevalence of workplace aggression comes from survey data. Ideally, these surveys would be based on probability samples to ensure that the prevalence rates derived from the data accurately represent a well-defined population of workers (e.g., all construction workers in a country, all customer service representatives in the financial industry, or all paid workers in a country). Most surveys of workplace aggression and related constructs, however, are conducted to empirically test specific theoretical propositions and not necessarily to provide population level information about prevalence. Many such surveys are based on convenience or purposive samples that are limited with respect to their geographical location, occupational characteristics, organizational setting, and other variables. As a result, such findings are not generalizable beyond the sample at hand, and their utility for providing information concerning the wider prevalence of exposure to workplace aggression is limited.

The NCASA (2000) and NNLIC (1993) surveys were designed to be representative of the U.S. workforce; however, both have several methodological limitations. For example, the NNLIC study used a small sample ($N = 600$), did not include part-time workers, and had a low response rate of about 29%. Moreover, although each study drew a probability sample from the U.S. workforce, neither study used fully developed sampling weights to adequately adjust for differential probability of selection, nonresponse, and poststratification to known population totals.

Inconsistent Definitions and Operationalizations

One of the major limitations of the workplace aggression literature is the considerable variation that exists regarding terminology, definitions, and operationalizations. Numerous constructs have emerged in this literature that are conceptually similar to and could be encompassed by the general definition of *workplace aggression*. Some of these constructs are interchangeable with one another and others have unique characteristics. For example, behaviors that constitute *work-related psychological and emotional abuse* are the same as those that constitute *work-related psychological aggression*. Similarly, workplace *physical abuse* and *violence* are interchangeable with one another. On the other hand, as we noted earlier in this chapter, the terms *workplace aggression* and *workplace violence*, which have in some cases been treated interchangeably, are most appropriately distinguished from one another.

In addition to differences in terminology, the types of aggressive behavior that researchers examine tend to differ across studies, even studies that purport to measure similar constructs. For example, threats with a weapon are included in the physical assault category in the survey report of the NCASA (2000) but are treated independently of actual assault in other survey reports (e.g., NNLIC, 1993). We believe that including threats of assault in a measure of assault creates a potential confound that only serves to artificially inflate estimates of exposure to physical assault. In fact, we suggest that it is more appropriate to treat threats of assault as *psychological aggression* rather than *physical violence*. Consistent with the definitions of *aggression* and *violence* that we presented earlier, threats of assault would constitute *psychological aggression* and enacted assault would constitute *violence*.

In addition to the conceptual challenges introduced by the use of different constructs and operational definitions of *workplace aggression*, the data suggest that differences in operational definitions may influence the resultant prevalence rates. For example, the NCASA (2000) survey yielded a higher prevalence estimate of physical assault (5%) than the other two large-scale surveys we discussed (NNLIC and BJS NCVS surveys: 2.5% and 1.2% respectively). This survey included a number of questions representing a wide range of physically abusive behaviors (e.g., thrown something at you that could hurt you; pushed, grabbed, slapped, hit, kicked you) that were comparable with the other two surveys. Although direct comparisons between these surveys cannot be made because they are nonequivalent in a number of ways, it is interesting to note that the higher overall prevalence rate for physical assault emerged in the survey that included a larger number of questions tapping a number of specific, concrete behaviors. It may be that in surveys of this nature, the use of a large number of behaviorally specific questions increases the likelihood that respondents will recall such behavior if it occurred, yielding higher prevalence rates than surveys that use few questions and/or broad behavioral categories. Alternative explanations for the difference in prevalence rates may exist. For example, as we noted earlier, the NCASA (2000) survey included threats with a weapon in its physical assault category, whereas other surveys have treated actual assaults and threats of assault independently.

Inconsistencies in the prevalence of workplace psychological aggression also emerged in the data from the NCASA (2000) and NNLIC (1993) surveys. The former found that 33% of respondents reported experiencing verbal abuse at work, and the latter found that 19% of respondents reported experiencing work-related harassment and 7% reported threats of physical harm. These differences may be a function of the cognitive dynamics associated with how respondents were queried about their exposure to harassment and abuse. The NNLIC survey used one item, in which respondents were asked to indicate whether they had been harassed on the job in the last 12 months. In contrast, the NCASA survey used six items, which asked respondents to indicate whether they had experienced six discrete abusive behaviors during the past year, with the overall prevalence rate being a composite score across these items. Although harassment and abusive behaviors are generally considered to be similar, respondents may have different interpretations of what they comprise. As a result, when respondents are asked to indicate how often they have been harassed, with no reference to the specific behaviors this might entail, they may not report or recall the full range of potential harassment behaviors. What they report may be limited by what they are able to recall from memory or what they interpret to be "harassment" behavior and may be different from what they would report if asked about their frequency of exposure to a number of discrete behaviors, as was the case with the NCASA survey. With this latter approach, the specificity of the question should contribute to more accurate recall. This may explain why the NNLIC survey yielded a lower prevalence rate (19%) than the NCASA survey (33%) and shows how question type and response format can influence prevalence rates yielded by surveys (see Schwarz, 1999, for a review), even when other methodological characteristics (e.g., random sampling) are similar.

In addition to variation in the types of aggressive behavior, the reporting period is another important factor to consider when assessing and interpreting the prevalence of exposure to workplace aggression. Although a 1-year time frame appears to be used in the majority of studies (e.g., NCASA, 2000; NNLIC, 1993), some studies have asked respondents to report their experience of aggression over shorter (e.g., 6 months; Einarsen & Skogstad, 1996) and longer (5 years; Cortina et al., 2001) periods. Two issues are particularly important to consider in this regard. First and most obvious, a survey that uses a longer reporting period will yield a higher prevalence rate than an otherwise equivalent survey using a shorter reporting period. Second, a longer reporting period increases the likelihood that memory decay will adversely affect the accuracy of participants' responses. This is particularly likely to occur with certain psychologically aggressive behaviors that are less salient—and perhaps more susceptible to memory decay—than more serious acts of aggression such as assault. Such memory decay could produce either over- or underestimates, the nature of which may be influenced by survey characteristics such as the response formats that are employed (Schwarz, 1999).

Summary of Previous Estimates of Workplace Aggression Prevalence

Based on our review, a number of data sources exist that provide information regarding the prevalence of workplace aggression; however, these data sources vary widely with respect to the type(s) of workplace aggression considered, the prevalence of exposure suggested by the data, and the quality of the methods that were used to collect the data. Before presenting the results of the present study, we attempt to distill from the available data the most accurate summary to date of the prevalence of three types of workplace aggression: physical violence causing death (workplace homicide), nonfatal physical violence, and psychological aggression. In addition, we summarize important gaps in our knowledge that the survey data we present later in the chapter will help to fill.

The CFOI data collected by the BLS (2004) represents the most valid workplace homicide data available in the United States, although limitations in the records on which these data are based likely lead to underestimates of the number of workplace homicides. These data suggest that physical violence at work has accounted for between 600 and 700 deaths per year in the United States during the most recent 5 years for which data were available (1999–2003), that the workplace homicide rate has exhibited a general decrease over the past 10 years (with 2 minor year-to-year increases), and that most workplace homicides occur during robberies perpetrated by individuals outside the workplace with no prior relationship to the victims.

The available data suggest that the percentage of workers who experience nonfatal assault ranges between 1.2% and 5%. The Bureau of Justice Statistics NCVS data (Duhart, 2001) represents the lower end of this range (1.2%; 11.7 out of 1,000 workers), the NCASA (2000) survey data represents the higher end (5%), and the NNLIC (1993) survey data and the Canadian Public Service Employment Survey (PSC, 2002) data fall in between (at 2.5% and 2%, respectively). The variance in these estimates is likely due to methodological differences between the surveys, such as differences in the specific types of aggressive behavior queried. Interestingly, in a pattern similar to the workplace homicide data collected by the BLS (2004), the NCVS data (collected from 1993 to 1999) suggest that rates of nonfatal workplace assault have also decreased over this time period. (Duhart, 2001).

Prevalence rates of psychological workplace aggression and harassment suggested by previous research vary widely, depending on a number of methodological characteristics (e.g., type of behavior, reporting period). The most representative data to date come from the studies conducted by the NNLIC (1993) and the NCASA (2000) surveys, which yielded prevalence rates of 19% and 33%, respectively. Although the NNLIC study used a single question to query about exposure to the general behavioral category of harassment, the NCASA study used a number of questions referring to specific behaviors. The latter approach is likely to result in more accurate responses than the former. Therefore, we suggest that the 33% rate represents the best available estimate to date on the prevalence of nonphysical aggression in the U.S. workforce.

Despite certain limitations in these data, three general observations can be made. First, rates of workplace homicide and nonfatal violence appear to be decreasing over time. Second, members of the public entering workplaces to commit theft or other crimes—rather than employees or former employees—are the primary perpetrators of workplace violence. It is notable that these two conclusions are at odds with two prevailing beliefs about workplace violence: that it is occurring with greater frequency and that it is mostly perpetrated by disgruntled employees (or former employees). Third, rates of psychological workplace aggression are significantly higher than rates of physical violence, and the data suggest that about a third of workers experience such acts in a given year (some estimates are much higher than this). In light of these data, and the evidence suggesting the negative consequences of such behavior for individuals and organizations (for a review, see Schat & Kelloway, 2005), continued research is needed toward understanding and preventing work-related psychological aggression.

Due to limitations in the scope and methodology of the existing studies of the prevalence of workplace aggression, there are a number of issues that warrant replication and, in some cases, initial investigation. First, relatively little is known about the prevalence of exposure to workplace aggression from different sources (e.g., coworkers, supervisors, and members of the public). The available data suggest that exposure to workplace aggression varies across potential perpetrators of aggression and that exposure to aggression from different sources is associated with different patterns of consequences (Frone, 2000; LeBlanc & Kelloway, 2002). One implication of this is the need to distinguish between and assess the different sources of aggression in future research. A second implication is the need to incorporate source-specific considerations into the design of intervention strategies.

Second, additional research is needed that explores the distribution of exposure to workplace aggression (by type and source) across important general demographic and occupational characteristics. Such research can provide a better understanding of which workers are at greatest risk of exposure to workplace aggression and lay the foundation for more precisely tailored—and likely more effective—interventions to prevent workplace aggression. In the remainder of the chapter, we report the results of a national survey that assessed exposure to workplace aggression in the U.S. workforce based on a representative sample of 2,508 wage and salary workers. This study represents a step toward addressing the limitations of prior research.

Results

An extensive description of the survey methodology is provided in the chapter's appendix. Below we present the results of the survey in two sections. In the first section, we present data regarding the degree to which U.S. wage and salary employees are exposed to the two major types of workplace aggression: psychological aggression and physical violence. We begin by presenting data on the frequency of exposure to these two broad categories of workplace aggression as well as to specific behaviors within these broad categories. Then we report the results of a series of bivariate and multivariate logistic regression analyses that were conducted to examine whether or not general and occupational demographic characteristics predict exposure to psychological aggression and physical violence at work. In the second section, we report results related to the frequency of employees' exposure to any type of aggression (psychological or physical) from three sources: one's supervisor or boss, one's coworkers (employees other than one's supervisor or boss), and members of the public (customers, clients, or patients). Then we describe the results of bivariate and multivariate logistic regression analyses that were conducted to examine the general and occupational demographic predictors of exposure to aggression from these three sources.

Prevalence and Frequency of Exposure to Psychological and Physical Workplace Aggression

Data regarding the overall percentage and estimated numbers of U.S. wage and salary workers who are exposed to psychological aggression and physical violence are presented in Tables 4.1 and 4.2. As shown in Table 4.1, 41.4%

Table 4.1   Overall Prevalence and Frequency of Psychological Aggression Experienced at Work

Type of Aggression	Prevalence (%) / Estimated Population Total					
	Never	Less Than Monthly	Monthly	Weekly	Overall Prevalence
Any psychological aggression	58.6 66,274,483	19.4 21,910,110	9.1 10,292,826	13.0 14,699,531	41.4 46,902,467
Shouted obscenities at you or screamed at you in anger	65.0 73,591,311	17.0 19,192,083	7.5 8,542,656	10.5 11,850,900	35.0 39,585,639
Insulted you or called you names in front of other people	75.6 85,552,561	10.9 12,368,633	5.8 6,617,410	7.6 8,638,345	24.4 27,624,388
Made an indirect or hidden threat, such as saying that "something bad" would happen to you	87.8 99,394,214	7.1 8,067,771	2.3 2,647,448	2.7 3,067,517	12.2 13,782,736
Threatened to hit you or throw something at you	92.4 104,573,504	3.9 4,362,460	1.3 1,414,795	2.5 2,826,190	7.6 8,603,446
Threatened you with a knife, gun, or another weapon	98.1 111,056,494	1.3 1,481,061	0.4 437,003	0.2 202,392	1.9 2,120,455

NOTE: N = 2,508

61

Table 4.2 Overall Prevalence and Frequency of Physical Violence Experienced at Work

Type of Aggression	Prevalence (%) / Estimated Population Total				
	Never	Less Than Monthly	Monthly	Weekly	Overall Prevalence
Any physical violence	94.0 106,331,552	3.6 4,090,823	1.2 1,323,388	1.3 1,431,188	6.0 6,845,398
Pushed you, grabbed you, or slapped you in anger	96.1 108,793,962	2.4 2,724,424	0.7 801,045	0.8 857,518	3.9 4,382,987
Kicked you, bit you, or hit you with a fist	97.0 109,826,516	1.6 1,827,854	0.7 836,850	0.6 685,730	3.0 3,350,434
Hit you with an object, tried to hit you with an object, or threw an object at you in anger	95.8 108,472,515	2.3 2,599,061	1.0 1,100,781	0.9 1,004,593	4.2 4,704,435
Attacked you with a knife, gun, or another weapon	99.3 112,391,363	0.6 733,013	0.1 52,575	0.0 0	0.7 785,586

NOTE: N = 2,508.

of respondents—representing nearly 47 million U.S. workers—report having experienced psychological aggression at work during the past 12 months. Moreover, 13%, or nearly 15 million workers, report experiencing psychological aggression on a weekly basis. These workers represent nearly a third of all workers reporting exposure to psychological aggression at work during the past 12 months (13% / 41.4% = 31.4%). Turning to the five specific psychologically aggressive behaviors examined in the survey, being the target of "shouted obscenities" or being "screamed at in anger" represented the most common forms of psychological aggression, being reported by 35% of respondents. Nearly a quarter of respondents (24.4%) reported being insulted or called names; 12.2% reported being threatened indirectly; 7.6% reported being threatened with being hit or having something thrown at them; and 1.9% reported being threatened with a knife, gun, or other weapon.

As shown in Table 4.2, 6% of respondents—representing nearly 7 million U.S. workers—experienced workplace violence during the previous year. About 1.3%, or nearly 1.5 million workers, reported experiencing acts of violence on a weekly basis. These workers represent about 22% of all workers reporting exposure to physical violence at work during the 12 months preceding the survey. Turning to the four specific physically aggressive behaviors examined in the survey, assault with an object was the most common, being reported by 4.2% of respondents. Being pushed, grabbed, or slapped in anger was reported by 3.9% of respondents; being kicked, hit, or bitten was reported by 3%; and being attacked with a knife, gun, or other weapon was reported by 0.7%.

Predictors of Exposure to Psychological and Physical Workplace Aggression

In addition to examining bivariate relationships with psychological aggression and physical violence, we also carried out multivariate logistic regression analyses in which the predictive power of all general and occupational demographic variables was simultaneously examined. This is a particularly conservative strategy, because a significant relationship that emerges for a specific predictor represents a unique relationship, controlling for other predictor variables in the model. The multivariate regression results include both p values and odds ratios for each predictor in the model. Recall that an odds ratio that is less than 1 indicates a negative relationship between the predictor and outcome variables; an odds ratio equal to 1 indicates no relationship; and an odds ratio greater than 1 indicates a positive relationship.

The results of the bivariate logistic regression analyses regarding the general and occupational demographic predictors of exposure to workplace aggression are provided in Tables 4.3 and 4.4, respectively, and the results of the multivariate logistic regression analyses are provided in Table 4.5. The general demographic predictor variables that were included in these analyses were gender, race, age, and education level, and the occupational demographic predictors were occupation type, industry class, job tenure, weekly work hours, work shift, whether or not the respondent worked in a seasonal job, and union membership.

As shown in Table 4.3, gender was a significant predictor of exposure to psychological aggression, with men (43.3%) being more likely than women (39.4%) to report experiencing psychological aggression; however, this effect did not remain in the multivariate analyses (see Table 4.5), after controlling for all other variables in the model. In contrast, the bivariate relation between gender and physical violence was not statistically significant, with 6.9% of women and 5.3% of men reporting exposure to acts of physical violence at work.

Age was a significant predictor of exposure to both psychological aggression and physical violence. Because some nonlinearity appeared to be present in this relationship, the regressions were rerun to include a quadratic term involving age (age squared). The quadratic term was significant for psychological aggression but not physical violence. The results suggest that there was a negative linear relationship between age and exposure to physical violence. To show the quadratic relationship of age and psychological aggression, age was categorized into six groups. As shown in Table 4.3, exposure to aggression initially increases (until about age 30) and then decreases with age.

Neither race nor level of educational attainment was significantly associated with exposure to work-related psychological aggression or physical violence in either the bivariate or multivariate analyses.

The results of the bivariate logistic regression analyses examining occupational demographic variables as predictors of workplace aggression (see Table 4.4) showed that occupation was significantly associated with exposure to both psychological aggression and physical violence. Both the professional (9.1%) and service (12.4%) groups experienced significantly more physical violence than the reference group (management/business/financial, 2.1%). Similar findings emerged in the multivariate analyses (see Table 4.5), with odds ratios of 3.50 and 3.72 for the professional and service occupations, respectively. Interestingly, a significant multivariate effect for installation, maintenance, and production jobs also emerged. Although the percentage of respondents in this occupational category that reported exposure to physical violence at work (4.5%) was not as high as the percentage of respondents in professional or service occupations that reported pysical violence, after controlling for other variables in the model, it was a significant predictor and had an odds ratio similar to these other occupations (odds ratio [OR] = 3.55). For exposure to psychological aggression, although a significant omnibus test was found for occupation in both the bivariate and multivariate regression analyses, no reliable occupational differences emerged in the analyses that used management occupations as the reference category. Table 4.5 suggests, however, that the significant omnibus test for occupation occurred because sales workers (OR = 1.42) reported higher levels of exposure to psychological aggression than did workers in transportation/material moving occupations (OR = 0.66) and in professional occupations (OR = 0.75). These differences can also be observed in the prevalence rates reported for these occupations in Table 4.4.

Table 4.3   Prevalence of Any Psychological Aggression and Physical Violence
at Work by General Demographic Characteristics

General Demographic Characteristic	Prevalence (%) / Estimated Population Total	
	Psychological Aggression at Work	Physical Violence at Work
Gender		
Male	43.3*	5.3
	25,768,820	3,146,417
Female	39.4	6.9
	21,133,647	3,698,981
Race		
White	41.6	5.5
	34,022,700	4,494,038
Minority	40.9	7.5
	12,879,767	2,351,360
Age		
18–25	40.0***	6.9**
	8,165,233	1,411,776
26–30	49.3	8.1
	6,573,024	1,083,073
31–35	47.0	7.0
	5,706,424	848,714
36–40	42.6	7.7
	6,251,455	1,136,291
41–50	41.3	4.3
	12,697,668	1,326,131
51–65	34.3	4.7
	7,508,662	1,039,413
Education		
Less than high school graduate	38.8	6.2
	1,878,426	302,475
High school graduate	39.2	3.7
	10,465,469	989,810
Some College	44.8	7.7
	18,829,619	3,240,990
Bachelor's degree	40.3	5.7
	10,327,910	1,459,407
Graduate degree	38.8	6.1
	5,401,042	852,715

NOTES: $N = 2,508$. Significance levels for the bivariate relations were based on bivariate logistic regression analyses. For significance testing, all variables were entered in their original form. Thus, age, education, job tenure, and weekly work hours were entered as continuous predictors. All other predictors were naturally dichotomous or polytomous.

*$p < .10$; **$p < .05$; ***$p < .001$.

Table 4.4   Prevalence of Any Psychological Aggression or Physical Violence
at Work by Occupational Demographic Characteristics

	Prevalence (%) / Estimated Population Total	
Occupational Demographic Characteristic	Psychological Aggression at Work	Physical Violence at Work
Occupation		
Management/business/	42.9*	2.1****
financial	5,493,092	275,510
Professional	36.9	9.1
	10,489,389	2,603,669
Service	46.8	12.4
	8,446,346	2,244,309
Sales	46.5	2.7
	4,563,044	265,666
Office/administrative support	40.7	2.8
	7,873,273	535,664
Construction/extraction/	45.7	3.7
Farming/fishing/forestry	2,477,747	199,383
Installation/maintenance/	42.2	4.5
production	5,101,516	539,157
Transportation/material	34.2	2.5
moving	2,458,060	182,040
Industry		
Construction/mining/	42.0**	2.6****
forestry/agriculture	2,572,850	158,006
Manufacturing	33.7	0.7
	5,149,519	100,191
Transportation/communication/	45.0	4.9
public utilities	3,686,504	403,982
Wholesale/retail trade	43.1	5.4
	6,033,362	757,998
Finance/insurance/real estate	36.6	0.4
	2,313,323	23,467
Services	41.5	8.4
	23,505,032	4,729,061
Public administration	54.6	10.1
	3,641,877	672,695
Job Tenure		
1 year or less	36.0*	5.2
	13,178,507	1,901,536
GT 1 year and LE 2 years	44.3	5.9
	7,897,399	1,056,104
GT 2 years and LE 3 years	46.9	6.8
	6,394,919	932,408

(Continued)

Table 4.4 (Continued)

Occupational Demographic Characteristic	Prevalence (%) / Estimated Population Total	
	Psychological Aggression at Work	Physical Violence at Work
GT 3 years and LE 5 years	42.9	5.4
	6,291,497	795,859
GT 5 years	43.1	7.1
	13,140,145	2,159,491
Weekly Work Hours		
LT 35 hours	31.6****	4.5
	5,586,142	797,072
GE 35 hours and LE 40 hours	39.4	5.9
	17,657,669	2,656,550
GT 40 hours	46.7	6.7
	23,658,656	3,391,777
Work Shift		
Days (1st shift)	40.2*	4.8****
	35,222,560	4,192,777
Evenings (2nd shift)	42.6	11.2
	3,800,640	1,001,574
Nights (3rd shift)	56.8	15.1
	2,391,357	634,255
Rotating shift	38.8	6.7
	1,624,296	287,039
Nonstandard (irregular/flexible) shift	47.0	8.9
	3,863,613	729,752
Seasonal Job		
No	41.6	6.0
	44,705,679	6,461,703
Yes	38.0	6.6
	2,196,787	383,695
Union Member		
No	40.0***	5.5**
	37,367,279	5,137,026
Yes	48.0	8.6
	9,535,188	1,708,372

NOTES:

LT = less than; LE = equal to or less than; GE = equal to or greater than; GT = greater than; N = 2,508. Significance levels for the bivariate relations were based on bivariate logistic regression analyses. For significance testing, all variables were entered in their original form. Thus, age, education, job tenure, and weekly work hours were entered as continuous predictors. All other predictors were naturally dichotomous or polytomous.

*$p < .10$; **$p < .05$; ***$p < .01$; ****$p < .001$.

The bivariate and multivariate results showed that industry was significantly associated with exposure to both types of aggression. Of the industry categories, public administration employees reported the highest levels of both psychological (54.6%) and physical (10.1%) aggression. Service industry employees had the second highest level of exposure to physical violence at 8.4%. Employees in the manufacturing and finance industries reported the lowest degree of exposure to both psychological (33.7% and 36.6%, respectively) and physical (0.7% and 0.4%, respectively) aggression. However, of these findings, the only effect that emerged in the multivariate analyses was the higher prevalence of psychological aggression in the public administration industry class ($OR = 1.86$). Although the omnibus test for industry differences in exposure to physical violence was significant, no significant dummy variables were observed. Because of the low base rate of physical violence and the relatively small numbers of respondents in some of the industry categories, the multivariate results probably had low statistical power. Supporting this possibility is the relatively large odds ratios (large deviations from a null effect of 1.0 in either direction) in Table 4.5 that were not statistically significant. If we take this into account, the results in Tables 4.4 and 4.5 suggest that compared with the construction industry, exposure to physical violence is lower among workers in manufacturing ($OR = 0.21$) and finance/insurance/real estate ($OR = 0.30$) and higher in the remaining four industry groups (ORs ranging from 2.49 to 4.62).

Job tenure was significantly associated with exposure to both types of aggression, and, as with age, there was some evidence for nonlinear relations. Although not significant in the bivariate regression analysis for exposure to physical abuse, the multivariate results revealed a positive linear relation for job tenure. The bivariate and multivariate results for psychological aggression revealed a quadratic relationship with job tenure. The cross-tabulations in Table 4.4 illustrate the nature of the quadratic relationship, suggesting a sharp increase in exposure between the first and third year of employment (from 36% to 46.9%), after which it decreases marginally and stabilizes.

In both the bivariate and multivariate analyses, weekly work hours significantly predicted exposure to psychological aggression, with more hours worked associated with higher exposure to psychological aggression. The number of hours worked was also significantly and positively associated with exposure to physical violence in the multivariate results, although this effect was not significant in the bivariate analyses.

The type of work shift was a predictor of both types of aggression. Both the bivariate and multivariate results indicated that those working evening (11.2%) and night (15.1%) shifts were more likely to experience violence than those working day shifts (4.8%). Night shift workers were also more likely to experience psychological aggression (56.8%) than day shift workers (40.2%). Those working nonstandard shifts reported somewhat higher levels of exposure to both types of aggression than day shift workers, although these effects were not significant.

Whether or not workers were employed in a seasonal job did not significantly predict exposure to workplace aggression in either the bivariate or multivariate analyses.

Table 4.5 Multivariate Logistic Regression Results Predicting Psychological and Physical Violence From General and Occupational Demographic Characteristics

Predictor	Psychological Aggression at Work		Physical Violence at Work	
	Odds Ratio	p Value	Odds Ratio	p Value
Gender (male)	1.10	.370	.74	.152
Race (minority)	.92	.454	1.27	.313
Age	**1.05**	**.119**	**.97**	**.011**
Age squared	**.99**	**.022**	—	—
Education	1.00	.890	1.02	.791
Occupation		**.022**		**.001**
Management/business/ financial	RG	RG	RG	RG
Professional	.75	.101	**3.50**	**.008**
Service	1.17	.462	**3.72**	**.012**
Sales	1.42	.142	.64	.533
Office/administrative support	1.09	.638	1.10	.869
Construction/extraction/ farming/fishing/forestry	1.17	.656	2.51	.376
Insallation/maintenance/ production	1.19	.471	**3.55**	**.042**
Transportation/material moving	.66	.144	.77	.698
Industry		**.032**		**.001**
Construction/mining/ forestry/agriculture	RG	RG	RG	RG
Manufacturing	.78	.468	.21	.159
Transportation/ communication/ public utilities	1.32	.441	2.49	.410
Wholesale/retail trade	1.28	.470	4.62	.127
Finance/insurance/real estate	1.06	.874	.30	.373
Services	1.36	.337	2.73	.276
Public administration	**1.86**	**.093**	3.34	.198
Job tenure	**1.06**	**.010**	**1.04**	**.033**
Job tenure squared	**.99**	**.046**	—	—
Weekly work hours	**1.03**	**.000**	**1.03**	**.001**

(Continued)

Table 4.5 (Continued)

Predictor	Psychological Aggression at Work		Physical Violence at Work	
	Odds Ratio	p Value	Odds Ratio	p Value
Work Shift		**.097**		**.005**
Days **(1st shift)**	RG	RG	RG	RG
Evenings (2nd shift)	1.18	.405	**2.67**	**.003**
Nights (3rd shift)	**1.88**	**.028**	**2.87**	**.006**
Rotating shift	.76	.326	1.02	.973
Nonstandard (irregular/flexible) shift	1.26	.222	1.67	.162
Seasonal job (yes)	.97	.909	1.33	.500
Union member (yes)	**1.35**	**.027**	1.23	.407

NOTES: $N = 2,508$. Because of the complex sample design, significance levels (p values) reported in the table were based on adjusted Wald F tests. Relations with $p < .10$ are in bold. RG = reference group.

In the bivariate analyses, union membership was found to be associated with higher exposure to both psychological aggression and physical violence, with 48% of union members reporting exposure to psychological aggression, compared with 40% of nonunion members, and 8.6% of union members reporting exposure to physical violence, compared with 5.5% of nonunion members. After controlling for the effects of all other demographic variables in the model, however, the association between union membership and exposure to physical violence became nonsignificant (see Table 4.5). The positive association between union membership and exposure to psychological aggression remained significant, however.

Prevalence and Frequency of Exposure to Workplace Aggression by Supervisors, Coworkers, and Members of the Public

Data regarding the overall percentage and estimated numbers of U.S. wage and salary workers who are exposed to aggression (either psychological or physical) from their supervisors, other employees, and members of the public (customers, clients, patients) are presented in Table 4.6. As shown, 13.5% (approximately 15 million workers) experience aggression from their supervisors, 15% (approximately 17 million workers) from their coworkers, and 23.4% (approximately 26.5 million workers) from members of the public. When one looks at the specific frequencies of aggression from these sources, an interesting pattern emerges. The discrepancy in the degree of exposure to public and insider-initiated (coworkers and supervisors) aggression becomes larger with increasing frequency of exposure. Among workers who report

Table 4.6 Overall Prevalence and Frequency of Any Aggression Experienced at Work by Source

Source of Aggression	Never	Less Than Monthly	Monthly	Weekly	Overall Prevalence
		Prevalence (%) / Estimated Population Total			
Supervisor or boss	86.5	8.0	3.0	2.5	13.5
	97,856,814	8,999,662	3,382,854	2,937,620	15,320,136
Coworkers (i.e., other employees at work)	85.0	8.8	3.5	2.7	15.0
	96,197,708	9,922,101	4,003,677	3,053,464	16,979,242
Members of the public (i.e., customers, clients, or patients)	76.6	9.7	5.6	8.2	23.4
	86,649,262	10,962,300	6,340,318	9,225,070	26,527,688

NOTE: $N = 2,508$.

relatively infrequent exposure (less than monthly) to workplace aggression, approximately the same percentage of workers report experiencing aggression from the three sources (between 8% and 9.7%); however, among workers who report frequent exposure (weekly) to workplace aggression, the percentage of workers reporting aggression from members of the public (8.2%) is substantially higher than the percentage reporting aggression from either supervisors (2.5%) or coworkers (2.7%).

Although the prevalence rates reported in Table 4.6 refer to any type of aggression, supplemental analyses revealed that only a small proportion of these prevalence rates represent physical violence, which is expected based on the data presented in Tables 4.1 and 4.2. Less than 1% of respondents reported experiencing physical violence from their supervisors (0.4%) and other employees (0.8%), whereas 3.6% reported experiencing physical violence from members of the public.[6] Compared with the overall rates that suggest workers are about 1.5 times more likely to experience aggression from members of the public than from supervisors or other employees, the data regarding physical violence in particular indicate that respondents are more than 4 times more likely to experience physical violence from members of the public than from supervisors and other employees.

Predictors of Workplace Aggression by Supervisors, Coworkers, and Members of the Public

The results of the bivariate logistic regression analyses regarding the general and occupational demographic predictors of supervisor, coworker, and public aggression are provided in Tables 4.7 and 4.8, respectively, and the results of the multivariate logistic regression analyses are provided in Table 4.9. As shown in Table 4.7, gender was not a significant predictor of exposure to public aggression but was a significant predictor of exposure to supervisor and coworker aggression, with men being more likely than women to experience aggression from these sources (14.9% vs. 12.1% and 17.4% vs. 12.4%). As shown in Table 4.9, however, gender did not remain a significant predictor in the multivariate results after controlling for all other demographic variables in the model.

There was no evidence of racial differences in exposure to aggression from any of the three sources in either the bivariate or multivariate logistic regressions.

Age was a significant predictor of aggression from all three sources in both the bivariate and multivariate models. As with the regression models predicting the types of aggression, there was evidence of nonlinear relations involving age. For the relationship between age and coworker aggression, the bivariate and multivariate analyses (see Tables 4.7 and 4.9) converged in suggesting a quadratic relationship. For the relationship between age and supervisor aggression, the bivariate results suggested a quadratic relationship; however, in the multivariate regression, the quadratic effect was dropped

(Text continues on page 77)

Table 4.7 Prevalence of the Aggression at Work From Different Sources by Occupational Demographic Characteristics

General Demographic Characteristic	Prevalence (%) / Estimated Population Total		
	Supervisor or Boss	Coworkers	Members of the Public
Gender			
male	14.9*	17.4***	22.1
	8,844,654	10,332,742	13,148,524
female	12.1	12.4	24.9
	6,475,481	6,646,501	13,379,164
Race			
White	13.0	15.4	23.4
	10,640,745	12,599,341	19,167,555
Minority	14.9	13.9	23.4
	4,679,390	4,379,901	7,360,133
Age			
18–25	13.6***	11.9****	24.6***
	2,785,213	2,428,921	5,032,090
26–30	21.8	23.5	28.3
	2,907,489	3,128,518	3,767,526
31–35	13.1	17.1	29.4
	1,597,414	2,080,162	3,574,731
36–40	12.0	14.3	23.3
	1,764,111	2,102,271	3,416,574
41–50	12.5	16.0	21.3
	3,831,110	4,908,321	6,541,318
51–65	11.3	10.7	19.2
	2,434,800	2,331,049	4,195,449
Education			
Less than high school graduate	22.7	13.5	12.1*
	1,100,566	655,503	584,232
High school graduate	12.0	14.0	18.9
	3,215,724	3,742,065	5,051,898
Some college	14.4	15.9	27.9
	6,054,894	6,710,696	11,746,976
Bachelor's degree	12.1	16.0	23.4
	3,100,130	4,112,305	5,995,859
Graduate degree	13.3	12.6	22.6
	1,848,821	1,758,673	3,148,724

NOTES: $N = 2,508$. Significance levels for the bivariate relations were based on bivariate logistic regression analyses. For significance testing, all variables were entered in their original form. Thus, age education, job tenure, and weekly work hours were entered as continuous predictors. All other predictors were naturally dichotomous or polytomous.

*$p < .10$; ***$p < .01$; ****$p < .001$.

Table 4.8   Prevalence of Aggression at Work From Different Sources by
                  Occupational Demographic Characteristics

Occupational Demographic Characteristic	Prevalence (%) / Estimated Population Total		
	Supervisor or Boss	Coworkers	Members of the Public
Occupation			
Management/business/ financial	15.5 1,983,163	16.6* 2,131,964	24.1**** 3,093,587
Professional	10.4 2,962,741	12.3 3,496,995	23.2 6,608,345
Service	15.2 2,737,896	15.2 2,742,233	33.4 6,030,932
Sales	12.3 1,208,033	10.0 981,869	29.8 2,923,452
Office/administrative support	14.0 2,714,409	14.9 2,887,525	24.8 4,801,593
Construction/extraction/ farming/fishing/forestry	16.5 896,448	22.8 1,236,734	9.0 488,356
Installation/maintenance/ production	16.1 1,951,141	18.9 2,283,712	13.9 1,680,671
Transportation/material moving	12.0 866,304	16.9 1,218,210	12.5 900,752
Industry			
Construction/mining/ forestry/agriculture	16.0 978,679	23.6* 1,447,880	9.2**** 566,126
Manufacturing	13.8 2,104,981	15.9 2,433,367	8.9 1,361,622
Transportation/ communication/ public utilities	17.2 1,412,352	18.0 1,476,961	24.6 2,017,000
Wholesale/retail trade	11.2 1,563,217	13.7 1,913,594	22.9 3,214,176
Finance/insurance/real estate	11.0 694,376	8.5 537,938	22.7 1,434,137
Services	13.0 7,360,399	14.4 8,164,315	26.9 15,219,625
Public administration	18.1 1,206,132	15.1 1,005,187	40.7 2,715,003
Job Tenure			
1 year or less	13.1 4,811,234	12.9 4,729,823	20.9* 7,638,284
GT 1 year and LE 2 years	15.5 2,752,465	19.8 3,517,765	24.9 4,437,740
GT 2 years and LE 3 years	13.5 1,843,069	15.5 2,113,256	27.0 3,682,349

(Continued)

Table 4.8 (Continued)

Occupational Demographic Characteristic	Prevalence (%) / Estimated Population Total		
	Supervisor or Boss	Coworkers	Members of the Public
GT 3 years and LE 5 years	14.5	15.7	23.0
	2,132,036	2,296,411	3,369,612
GT 5 years	12.4	14.2	24.3
	3,781,332	4,321,988	7,399,703
Weekly Work Hours			
LT 35 hours	7.8****	7.4****	19.2**
	1,373,571	1,307,651	3,391,733
GE 35 hours and LE 40 hours	12.6	14.4	22.8
	5,661,821	6,471,824	10,215,050
GT 40 hours	16.3	18.2	25.5
	8,284,744	9,199,767	12,920,905
Work Shift			
Days (1st shift)	13.7	14.2***	22.3
	11,987,064	12,442,578	19,567,935
Evenings (2nd shift)	12.6	12.8	24.1
	1,126,581	1,145,012	2,148,947
Nights (3rd shift)	12.8	33.6	29.2
	541,514	1,413,805	1,232,244
Rotating shift	14.3	16.6	23.8
	597,446	692,777	996,540
Nonstandard (irregular/ flexible) shift	13.0	15.6	31.4
	1,067,530	1,285,070	2,582,023
Seasonal Job			
No	13.5	14.9	23.8*
	14,488,546	16,009,954	25,567,855
Yes	14.4	16.8	16.7
	831,590	969,289	959,833
Union Member			
No	13.0	14.3*	22.4**
	12,146,066	13,328,562	20,918,557
Yes	16.0	18.4	28.2
	3,174,070	3,650,680	5,609,131

NOTES: LT = less than; LE = equal to or less than; GE = equal to or greater than; GT = greater than; $N = 2,508$. Significance levels for the bivariate relations were based on bivariate logistic regression analyses. For significance testing, all variables were entered in their original form. Thus, age, education, job tenure, and weekly work hours were entered as continuous predictors. All other predictors were naturally dichotomous or polytomous.

$*p < .10$; $**p < .05$; $***p < .01$; $****p < .001$.

Table 4.9   Multivariate Logistic Regression Results Predicting Sources of Aggression From General and Occupational Demographic Characteristics

Predictor	Supervisor or Boss		Coworkers		Members of the Public	
	Odds Ratio	p Value	Odds Ratio	p Value	Odds Ratio	p Value
Gender (male)	1.07	.666	1.22	.191	1.00	.981
Race (minority)	1.14	.398	.80	.193	.91	.491
Age	**.98**	**.001**	**1.09**	**.026**	**.98**	**.000**
Age squared	—	—	**.99**	**.009**	—	—
Education	.98	.668	1.03	.398	1.01	.838
Occupation		.451		.203		**.001**
Management/ business/financial	RG	RG	RG	RG	RG	RG
Professional	.66	.108	.68	.114	.82	.336
Service	1.01	.985	1.00	.995	1.31	.233
Sales	1.04	.905	.67	.231	**1.73**	**.040**
Office/administrative support	1.07	.796	1.25	.391	1.08	.716
Construction/ extraction/farming/ fishing/forestry	.90	.838	1.08	.868	.46	.180
Installation/ maintenance/ production	1.11	.743	1.18	.560	.78	.411
Transportation/ material moving	.70	.353	.97	.931	**.44**	**.014**
Industry		.800		.453		**.000**
Construction/mining/ forestry/agriculture	RG	RG	RG	RG	RG	RG
Manufacturing	.95	.912	.67	.367	.76	.583
Transportation/ communication/ public utilities	1.35	.516	.71	.479	**2.60**	**.035**
Wholesale/retail trade	.84	.722	.821	.662	1.72	.233
Finance/insurance/ real estate	.83	.724	**.434**	**.099**	1.97	.151
Services	1.14	.778	.810	.613	**2.47**	**.034**
Public administration	1.34	.573	.587	.276	**3.79**	**.005**
Job tenurem	1.02	.442	1.00	.907	**1.07**	**.012**
Job tenure squared	1.00	.292	1.00	.869	**.99**	**.022**

(Continued)

Table 4.9 (Continued)

Predictor	Supervisor or Boss		Coworkers		Members of the Public	
	Odds Ratio	p Value	Odds Ratio	p Value	Odds Ratio	p Value
Weekly work hours	**1.04**	**.000**	**1.03**	**.000**	**1.02**	**.000**
Work shift		.947		**.022**		.313
Days (1st shift)	RG	RG	RG	RG	RG	RG
Evenings (2nd shift)	.91	.714	1.04	.904	1.04	.854
Nights (3rd shift)	.78	.563	**2.99**	**.001**	1.36	.302
Rotating shift	.89	.763	1.26	.471	.77	.375
Nonstandard (irregular/flexible) shift	.87	.568	1.08	.754	**1.42**	**.097**
Seasonal Job (yes)	1.12	.708	1.13	.680	.85	.552
Union Member (yes)	1.32	.152	1.33	.123	**1.45**	**.020**

NOTES: $N = 2,508$. Because of the complex sample design, significance levels (p values) reported in the table were based on adjusted Wald F tests. Relations with $p < .10$ are in bold. RG = reference group.

because it was not significant, though a negative linear relation between age and exposure to supervisor aggression was found. Both the bivariate and multivariate regression results supported a negative linear relationship between age and exposure to public aggression.

Education level did not predict supervisor or coworker aggression in either the bivariate or multivariate analyses. It did predict public aggression in the bivariate analyses (those with less than high school education are least likely to experience public aggression, and those with some college are most likely). This effect disappears, however, in the multivariate analyses, suggesting that as a predictor of public aggression, education level is confounded with other demographic variables (such as occupation type).

The results of the bivariate regressions indicated that occupation predicted exposure to coworker and public aggression. For coworker aggression, the effect was quite marginal and disappeared in the multivariate regressions. For public aggression, inspection of the cross-tabulations in Table 4.8 suggest that service employees (33.4%) and sales employees (29.8%) experienced the highest levels of public aggression, whereas employees in transportation and material moving (12.5%), as well as those in construction, extraction, farming, fishing, and forestry (9%), experienced the lowest levels. Two of these emerged as significant in the multivariate analyses: compared with the management reference group, sales employees had significantly higher levels of exposure, and transportation and material-moving employees experienced lower levels of exposure to public aggression.

Industry type was a significant predictor of exposure to both coworker and public aggression in the bivariate analyses. For coworker aggression, the effect was marginal and disappeared in the multivariate regressions. For public aggression, employees from three industries—public administration (40.7%), services (26.9%), and transportation (24.6%)—reported the highest prevalence rates. In the multivariate analyses, employees from these three industries were significantly more likely than the management reference group to experience public aggression.

Turning to job tenure, the bivariate and multivariate results suggest that tenure was not associated with supervisor or coworker aggression but was associated with public aggression. For public aggression, the significant relation is quadratic, with the degree of exposure increasing between year 1 and 3 and decreasing thereafter.

The relationship between weekly work hours and exposure to aggression was significant and positive for all three sources. This finding was consistent across the bivariate and multivariate regression analyses.

Work shift was a significant predictor of exposure to coworker aggression in both the bivariate and multivariate results. Specifically, as shown in Table 4.8, night shift workers were more likely to report exposure to coworker aggression than workers of other shifts (33.6%, compared with a range of 12.8% to 16.6% for the other shifts). This observation was supported in the multivariate analyses, which produced a significant odds ratio of 2.99 for the night shift. Thus, the odds of experiencing aggression from coworkers are nearly three times higher among workers on the night shift than workers on the day shift. Although the omnibus multivariate test for the effect of shift work on exposure to public aggression was not significant, a specific effect emerged indicating that those with nonstandard shifts were more likely to experience aggression from members of the public than were day shift workers.

There was a small bivariate effect for holding a seasonal job, indicating that those working in a seasonal job were less likely to experience public aggression than were those in a nonseasonal job; however, this effect disappeared in the multivariate results, suggesting it was not unique but explained by other variables in the model.

Union membership significantly predicted coworker and public aggression in the bivariate analyses. The effect for coworker aggression was not significant in the multivariate results, but the effect for public aggression remained. The odds ratio suggests that the odds of being exposed to aggression from the public were 1.45 times higher among workers belonging to a union than workers not belonging to a union.

Discussion

The purpose of this chapter was to (a) review the available data regarding the prevalence of worker exposure to workplace aggression and (b) provide comprehensive and representative data regarding the prevalence and demographic predictors of workplace aggression from a national sample of wage and salary workers in the United States. In particular, the results of the survey provide data regarding the prevalence of two general types of workplace aggression (psychological aggression and physical violence), the prevalence of workplace aggression from three different sources (supervisors, coworkers, and members of the public), and the extent to which general demographic (e.g., gender, age) and occupational demographic (e.g., industry type, work shift) variables are associated with exposure to the aforementioned types and sources of workplace aggression.

The results of the survey, which was conducted from January 2002 to June 2003, revealed that 41.4% of U.S. wage and salary workers—nearly 47 million people—experienced psychological acts of aggression at work during the 12-month reporting period. The results also indicate that 6% of this population—nearly 7 million people—experienced acts of physical violence at work. These prevalence rates are higher than the comparable rates reported in NCASA (2000) data, which indicated prevalence rates of 33% for psychological aggression (referred to as "verbal abuse") and 5% for physical violence (referred to as "assault"). The present survey also examined the prevalence of aggression by various sources and found that during the 12-month reporting period, 23.4% of respondents experienced aggression from members of the public (e.g., customers, clients, or patients), 15% from other employees at work, and 13.5% from their supervisors or bosses. For physical violence in particular, 3.6% of respondents experienced violence from members of the public, compared with 0.8% from other employees and 0.4% from supervisors.

Together, these data indicate that work-related psychological aggression is far more prevalent than work-related physical violence. In addition, the results by source indicate that the most common source of both psychological aggression and physical violence at work is members of the public. The higher rates of aggression from members of the public are notable because they go against the popular media-driven myth that the prototypical—and most common—form of workplace violence is an act perpetrated by a disgruntled (ex-)employee. Although aggression from supervisors and coworkers remains a significant problem, we hope these data will contribute to the debunking of this widely held myth that runs the risk of directing attention—and prevention efforts—away from more common types (psychological aggression) and sources (members of the public) of workplace aggression.

The results of logistic regression analyses revealed a number of predictors of the two types and three sources of workplace aggression. The results derived from the multivariate logistic regression analyses are particularly conservative, as the significant relationships that emerge from these analyses represent unique risk factors (controlling for all other variables in the model). Below we present and discuss some of the main findings from these analyses.

Although the bivariate regression results showed gender differences in exposure to aggression, these differences did not emerge in the multivariate regression results, suggesting that gender is confounded with other demographic variables. This suggests that the gender differences that have been observed in previous studies can be explained by variables other than gender, such as occupation or industry.

The relationships between exposure to workplace aggression and both age and job tenure were consistent and similar. In general, the results suggest that exposure to aggression exhibits an early peak (between the ages of 18 and 30 and for job tenure, between year 1 and 3) and thereafter decreases over time. This suggests that younger workers are more likely to experience workplace aggression, controlling for other variables that would normally be considered to explain a potential age effect, such as occupation type. The explanation for these findings may relate to work experience. One possibility is that as work experience increases, one's job level also likely increases. This may be coupled with increases which in work-related discretion and control, may help workers be better able to address potentially aggressive situations, thereby limiting their exposure to aggression. An alternative explanation emphasizes skill development rather than job level. In particular, it is possible that the knowledge and skills employees develop during their first several years of work accumulate to make them better able to deal with potentially aggressive situations, thereby reducing their exposure to aggressive behavior. Research is needed to help explain these results and provide the basis for interventions aimed at younger and less experienced workers to reduce their degree of exposure to workplace aggression.

A number of notable effects also emerged for occupation. Employees in professional and service occupations reported the highest exposure to physical violence at work. The professional occupation group includes social workers, therapists, and doctors. The nature of these jobs, particularly with respect to contact with patients and clients, would put them at increased risk of violence (LeBlanc & Kelloway, 2002). The service occupation group includes police and security officers and health care workers, such as nursing aides and orderlies, all occupations that have been found to be at increased risk for aggression because of certain job characteristics (e.g., exposure to people who are under the influence of drugs or medication or experiencing psychiatric symptoms; LeBlanc & Kelloway, 2002).

Another finding that emerged is that employees in sales-related occupations were more likely to experience aggression from members of the public. This likely reflects the customer-focused nature of many of these occupations (e.g., sales representatives, telemarketers). With the mantra "the customer is always right" being so prevalent, it may be that aggression from customers is tolerated in sales and customer service settings, increasing the extent to which individuals working in these occupations are exposed to such behavior (Grandey, Dickter, & Sin, 2004).

The type of work shift is also a predictor of exposure to workplace aggression. Working the night shift is a significant risk factor for both psychological aggression and physical violence. Working the evening shift is also associated with exposure to physical violence, although not to the same degree as the night shift. The data by source revealed that night shift employees are much more likely than employees of other shifts to experience aggression from coworkers. Research is needed to examine what is unique about the night shift that increases workers' exposure to coworker aggression. For example, does the type of work done during night shifts, which may differ from day shifts (Parkes, 1999), increase the likelihood of aggressive interactions between coworkers? Do reduced staffing levels that often accompany night shifts increase the rate of interpersonal conflict among coworkers? Is there less supervision of workers during night shifts, and does the reduction of this common constraint on employee behavior increase the rate of aggression that occurs? Past research suggests that shift work, particularly when it involves night shifts, is associated with emotional distress, sleep disturbances, and physical symptoms (Smith, Folkard, & Fuller, 2003). Whether these or other variables may explain the higher prevalence of aggression from coworkers or other sources during night shifts remains to be investigated.

Being a union member is also associated with higher exposure to psychological aggression, particularly from members of the public. These findings emerged in the multivariate analyses that controlled for occupational or industry characteristics, suggesting that this effect cannot be explained by these characteristics. It is possible, however, that the aggregate occupation and industry groupings failed to fully adjust for occupation and industry differences between union and nonunion employees. Another potential explanation is that members of the public may hold negative attitudes about unions and their members that may in some cases lead to hostile behavior toward union members. Related to this, strikes and other job actions can at times increase tensions between unionized workers and members of the public, particularly when the strike inconveniences or otherwise adversely affects members of the public. For example, strikes by teachers, health care workers, and workers in other contexts that serve important public needs can arouse public hostility, which may result in aggressive behavior being directed toward the striking workers. Future research is needed to examine this explanation or other potential explanations for the elevated risk of public aggression faced by union members.

Implications for Research

The wide variance in the prevalence rates derived from previous studies made it difficult to determine the extent of the U.S. workforce's exposure to aggressive behavior at work. The prevalence rates we report in this chapter, based as they are on nationally representative data, make an important contribution by clarifying the scope of the problem of workplace aggression. Furthermore, these results should stimulate future research that seeks to explain the demographic differences in exposure to workplace aggression that we found. For example, what are the psychosocial job characteristics that might explain exposure to the different types and sources of aggression at work? In addition, research is also needed to examine whether the different types and sources of aggression are associated with different outcomes and to investigate whether the outcomes of exposure to workplace aggression vary by demographic or other relevant variables.

Implications for Practice

Understanding the scope and predictors of exposure to workplace aggression is an important basis for the development of intervention strategies to prevent workplace aggression. In particular, intervention strategies can be tailored to address specific manifestations (e.g., related to types and sources) of workplace aggression in particular contexts (e.g., occupations), which should increase their effectiveness. For example, these data suggest that employees in sales-related occupations are at increased risk of exposure to aggression from members of the public. Therefore, an intervention aimed at training these employees to respond to acts of aggression from members of the public may help to minimize the occurrence—and negative consequences— of such acts. It is important that interventions include rigorous assessments of their effectiveness to facilitate their continuous improvement and to contribute to the research literature related to the prevention of workplace aggression, an area of the literature that has to date been underdeveloped.

Limitations

As comprehensive as these data are, they represent wage and salary workers in the United States and, therefore, may not generalize beyond this population. Research is needed to directly examine the prevalence and predictors of workplace aggression in other countries. A report by the International Labour Office (Chappell & Di Martino, 1998) provides some international data regarding the prevalence of workplace aggression, but methodological and other limitations preclude direct country-by-country comparisons. Nevertheless, readers are referred to this source for information regarding rates of workplace victimization in countries besides the United States.

Earlier in this chapter, we suggested that the types of workplace aggression that are asked about in surveys may influence the prevalence rates obtained. Therefore, the results we report should be considered in light of this possibility as well. That is, had we included additional examples of aggressive behavior (e.g., having rumors spread about you; having your work interfered with), the overall prevalence rates may have been somewhat higher. On the other hand, had we used fewer examples of aggressive behavior, the overall prevalence rates may have been lower.

_____**Conclusion**

In this chapter, we report the results from a survey of wage and salary workers in the United States regarding the prevalence of exposure to workplace aggression. These results have a number of important implications. First, they provide information regarding the scope of the problem of workplace aggression by indicating the frequency with which workers are exposed to different manifestations of aggressive behavior at work. Second, they shed light on demographic characteristics that place employees at greater risk of exposure to workplace aggression. Third, they can provide a basis for developing interventions that are specifically tailored to address aggression, which should contribute to a reduction in its incidence. Finally, by illuminating the scope and risk factors of workplace aggression, these results can stimulate additional research aimed at understanding and ultimately preventing workplace aggression. We hope that such research—and its translation into action to address workplace aggression—will result in future studies showing a decrease in the proportion of employees exposed to workplace aggression.

_____ **Notes**

1. The definition of *physical assault* used in this survey included throwing something, pushing, grabbing, slapping, hitting or kicking, hitting with an object, beating, rape or attempted rape, and the threat or use of weapons.

2. In this study, a person was defined as *bullied* "if he or she was repeatedly subjected to negative acts in the workplace . . . [and felt] inferiority in defending oneself in the actual situation" (Einarsen & Skogstad, 1996, p. 187).

3. In this study, *harassment* was defined as "any improper conduct by an individual, that is directed at and offensive to another person or persons in the workplace, and that the individual knew or ought reasonably to have known would cause offense or harm. It comprises any objectionable act, comment or display that demeans, belittles, or causes personal humiliation or embarrassment, and any act of intimidation or threat. It includes harassment within the meaning of the Canadian Human Rights Act."

4. The definition of *verbal abuse* used in this survey included provoking arguments, calling names or putting people down in front of others, making people feel inadequate, shouting or swearing, frightening people, and making intimidating and threatening gestures.

5. Note that participants could report violence from both sources.

6. Readers may notice that the percentages of respondents reporting physical violence from the three specific sources (i.e., 0.4%, 0.8%, and 3.6% from supervisors, coworkers, and members of the public, respectively) do not add up to the total percentage reporting physical violence that is reported in Table 4.2 (4.8%, compared with 6.0%). The results reported in Table 4.2 are based on the survey items in which respondents were asked to indicate how often they experienced various physically abusive behaviors from someone at work, whereas the source-specific percentages

are based on the survey items in which respondents were asked to indicate how often they experienced physical abuse from their supervisor or boss, other employees, or clients, customers, or patients. Thus, the discrepancy may be accounted for by other sources of work-related aggression that were not specifically asked about in the survey (e.g., senior managers, subordinates, or outside vendors).

References

Anderson, C. A., & Bushman, B. J. (2002). Human aggression. *Annual Review of Psychology, 53,* 27–51.

Baron, R. A., & Neuman, J. H. (1998, Winter). Workplace aggression—the iceberg beneath the tip of workplace violence: Evidence on its forms, frequency, and targets. *Public Administration Quarterly,* 446–464.

Baron, R. A., & Richardson, D. R. (1994). *Human aggression* (2nd ed.). New York: Plenum.

Berkowitz, L. (1993). *Aggression: Its causes, consequences, and control.* Philadelphia: Temple University Press.

Bureau of Labor Statistics. (2004). *National census of fatal occupational injuries in 2003.* Washington, DC: Author.

Canadian Centre for Occupational Health and Safety. (1999). *Violence in the workplace.* Retrieved December 23, 2004, from www.ccohs.ca/oshanswers/psychosocial/violence.html

Casteel, C., & Peek-Asa, C. (2000). Effectiveness of Crime Prevention Through Environmental Design (CPTED) in reducing robberies. *American Journal of Preventive Medicine, 18,* 99–115.

Castillo, D. N., & Jenkins, E. L. (1994). Industries and occupations at high risk for work-related homicide. *Journal of Occupational Medicine, 36,* 125–132.

Chappell, D., & Di Martino, V. (1998). *Violence at work.* Geneva: International Labour Office.

Cortina, L. M., Magley, V. J., Williams, J. H., & Langhout, R. D. (2001). Incivility in the workplace: Incidence and impact. *Journal of Occupational Health Psychology, 6,* 64–80.

Duhart, D. T. (2001). *Bureau of Justice Statistics special report: Violence in the workplace, 1993–1999* (NCJ 190076). Washington, DC: U.S. Bureau of Justice Statistics.

Einarsen, S., & Raknes, B. I. (1997). Harassment at work and the victimization of men. *Violence and Victims, 12,* 247–263.

Einarsen, S., & Skogstad, A. (1996). Bullying at work: Epidemiological findings in public and private organizations. *European Journal of Work and Organizational Psychology, 5,* 185–201.

Friedman, L. N., Brown-Tucker, S., Neville, P. R., & Imperial, M. (1996). The impact of domestic violence on the workplace. In G. R. VandenBos & E. Q. Bulatao (Eds.), *Violence on the job: Identifying risks and developing solutions* (pp. 153–161). Washington, DC: American Psychological Association.

Frone, M. R. (2000). Interpersonal conflict at work and psychological outcomes: Testing a model among young workers. *Journal of Occupational Health Psychology, 5,* 246–255.

Geen, R. G. (2001). *Human aggression* (2nd ed.). Buckingham, UK: Open University Press.

Grandey, A. A., Dickter, D. N., & Sin, H. P. (2004). The customer is not always right: Customer aggression and emotion regulation of service employees. *Journal of Organizational Behavior, 25,* 397–418.

Greenberg, L., & Barling, J. (1999). Predicting employee aggression against co-workers, subordinates and supervisors: The roles of person behaviors and perceived workplace factors. *Journal of Organizational Behavior, 20,* 897–913.

Guterman, N. B., Jayaratne, S., & Bargal, D. (1996). Workplace violence and victimization experienced by social workers: A cross-national study of Americans and Israelis. In G. R. VandenBos & E. Q. Bulateo (Eds.), *Violence on the job: Identifying risks and developing solutions.* Washington, DC: American Psychological Association.

Hewitt, J. B., & Levin, P. F. (1997). Violence in the workplace. *Annual Review of Nursing Research, 15,* 81–99.

Horan, J. M., & Mallonee, S. (2003). Injury surveillance. *Epidemiologic Reviews, 25,* 24–42.

Hurrell, J. J., Worthington, K. A., & Driscoll, R. J. (1996). Job stress, gender, and workplace violence: Analysis of assault experiences of state employees. In G. R. VandenBos & E. Q. Bulateo (Eds.), *Violence on the job: Identifying risks and developing solutions.* Washington, DC: American Psychological Association.

Jenkins, E. L. (1996). *Violence in the workplace: Risk factors and prevention strategies.* (DHHS [NIOSH] Publication Number 96–100). Washington, DC: Government Printing Office.

Korn, E., & Graubard, B. (1999). *Analysis of health surveys.* New York: John Wiley.

Kraus, J. F., Blander, B., & McArthur, D. L. (1995). Incidence, risk factors, and prevention strategies for work-related assault injuries: A review of what is known, what needs to be known, and countermeasures for intervention. *Annual Review of Public Health, 16,* 355–379.

LeBlanc, M. M., & Kelloway, E. K. (2002). Predictors and outcomes of workplace violence and aggression. *Journal of Applied Psychology, 87,* 444–453.

Levy, P. S., & Lemeshow, S. (1999). *Sampling of populations: Methods and applications.* New York: John Wiley.

Mayhew, C., & Quinlan, M. (2002). Fordism in the fast food industry: Pervasive management control and occupational health and safety for young temporary workers. *Sociology of Health and Illness, 24*(3), 261–284.

McFarlin, S. K., Fals-Stewart, W., Major, D., & Justice, E. M. (2001). Alcohol use and workplace aggression: An examination of perpetration and victimization. *Journal of Substance Abuse, 13,* 303–321.

National Center on Addiction and Substance Abuse at Columbia University. (2000). *Report of the United States Postal Service Commission on a Safe and Secure Workplace.* New York: Author.

National Institute for Occupational Safety and Health. (2002). *Violence: Occupational hazards in hospitals* (DHHS Publication No. 2002–101). Retrieved December 22, 2004, from www.cdc.gov/niosh/2002-101.html#intro

Neuman, J. H., & Baron, R. A. (1997). Aggression in the workplace. In R. A. Giacalone & J. Greenberg (Eds.), *Antisocial behavior in organizations* (pp. 37–67). Thousand Oaks, CA: Sage.

Neuman, J. H., & Baron, R. A. (1998). Workplace violence and workplace aggression: Evidence concerning specific forms, potential causes, and preferred targets. *Journal of Management, 24,* 391–419.

Northwestern National Life Insurance Company. (1993). *Fear and violence in the workplace: A survey documenting the experience of American workers.* Minneapolis, MN: Author.

Parkes, K. R. (1999). Shiftwork, job type, and the work environment as joint predictors of health-related outcomes. *Journal of Occupational Health Psychology, 4,* 256–268.

Peek-Asa, C., Runyan, C. W., & Zwerling, C. (2001). The role of surveillance and evaluation research in the reduction of violence against workers. *American Journal of Preventive Medicine, 20,* 141–148.

Peek-Asa, C., Schaffer, K. B., Kraus, J. F., & Howard, J. (1998). Surveillance of non-fatal workplace assault injuries, using police and employers' reports. *Journal of Occupational and Environmental Medicine, 40,* 707–713.

Pizzino, A. (2002). Dealing with violence in the workplace: The experience of Canadian unions. In M. Gill, B. Fisher, & V. Bowie (Eds.), *Violence at work: Causes, patterns, and prevention* (pp. 165–179). Cullompton, UK: Willan.

Potthoff, R. F. (1994). Telephone sampling in epidemiologic research: To reap the benefits, avoid the pitfalls. *American Journal of Epidemiology, 139,* 967–978.

Public Service Commission. (2002). *2002 Public Service Employment Survey.* Retrieved February 27, 2005, from www.survey-sondage.gc.ca/2002/results-resultats/index-e.htm

Rogers, K., & Kelloway, E. K. (1997). Violence at work: Personal and organizational outcomes. *Journal of Occupational Health Psychology, 2,* 63–71.

Safran, D., & Tartaglini, A. J. (1996). Workplace violence in an urban jail setting. In G. R. VandenBos & E. Q. Bulatao (Eds.), *Violence on the job: Identifying risks and developing solutions.* Washington, DC: American Psychological Association.

Schat, A. C. H., & Kelloway, E. K. (2000). The effects of perceived control on the outcomes of workplace aggression and violence. *Journal of Occupational Health Psychology, 4,* 386–402.

Schat, A. C. H., & Kelloway, E. K. (2003). Reducing the adverse consequences of workplace aggression and violence: The buffering effects of organizational support. *Journal of Occupational Health Psychology, 8,* 110–122.

Schat, A. C. H., & Kelloway, E. K. (2005). Workplace aggression. In J. Barling, E. K. Kelloway, & M. R. Frone (Eds.), *Handbook of work stress* (pp. 189–218). Thousand Oaks, CA: Sage.

Schwarz, N. (1999). Self-reports: How the questions shape the answers. *American Psychologist, 54,* 93–105.

Smith, C. S., Folkard, S., & Fuller, J. A. (2003). Shiftwork and working hours. In J. C. Quick & L. E. Tetrick (Eds.), *Handbook of occupational health psychology* (pp. 163–183). Washington, DC: American Psychological Association.

Stout, N., & Bell, C. (1991). Effectiveness of source documents for identifying fatal occupational injuries: A synthesis of studies. *American Journal of Public Health, 81,* 725–728.

Sygnatur, E. F., & Toscano, G. A. (2000, Spring). Work-related homicides: The facts. *Compensation and Working Conditions,* 3–8.

Tjaden, P., & Thoennes, N. (2000). *Extent, nature, and consequences of intimate partner violence.* Washington, DC: U.S. Department of Justice, National Institute of Justice.

Tucker, C., Lepkowski, J. M., & Piekarski, L. (2002). The current efficiency of list-assisted telephone sampling designs. *Public Opinion Quarterly, 66,* 321–338.

Warchol, G. (1998). *Workplace violence, 1992–1996.* Retrieved February 27, 2005, from www.ojp.usdoj.gov/bjs/pub/pdf/wv96.pdf

Appendix 4.1

Methodology for the National
Survey of Workplace Health and Safety

Study Design

The 2,829 study participants took part in the National Survey of Workplace Health and Safety. They were sampled from a population of noninstitutionalized adults aged 18 to 65 who were employed in the civilian labor force and residing in households in the 48 contiguous United States and the District of Columbia. The sample of 34,000 telephone numbers was generated by Survey Sampling International. A list-assisted, two-stratum, truncated design (e.g., Levy & Lemeshow, 1999; Tucker, Lepkowski, & Piekarski, 2002) was used to identify the sampling frame of telephone numbers. The numbers in the sampling frame were then stratified by county, and the actual sample of telephone numbers was selected from the sampling frame using systematic sampling. These procedures result in an approximately equal probability sample at the household level with a proportional spread of telephone numbers across the country that is more efficient than simple random digit dialing methods. Data were collected by 19 extensively trained interviewers using computer-assisted telephone interviewing (CATI) stations from January 2002 to June 2003. Each number was called up to 20 times in an attempt to determine eligibility of the household and select an eligible respondent. Numbers from which an eligible individual was selected to participate were each called up to an additional 20 times in an effort to secure an interview with the selected respondent. Within a household with more than one eligible individual, the most recent birthday method was used to select at random one individual for participation in the study (e.g., Potthoff, 1994). Of all selected eligible individuals, 57% participated in the study. Before being interviewed, informed consent was obtained from all participants. Also, each participant was informed that a Certificate of Confidentiality was obtained from the U.S. National Institutes of Health in order to assure the confidentiality and privacy of study participants. This certificate assures confidentiality and privacy to study participants by allowing the investigator and others who have access to research records to refuse to disclose identifying information on research participants in any civil, criminal, administrative, legislative, or other proceeding, whether at the federal, state, or local level. On average, the interview lasted 45 minutes and participants were paid $25.00 for their time.

Sampling Weights

In all analyses, the 2,829 interviewees are weighted according to standard procedures for sample survey data in order to make inference to the target population defined earlier (e.g., Korn & Graubard, 1999; Levy &

Lemeshow, 1999). Several steps went into the computation of the sampling weights. In step 1, the initial base weight for each interviewee in each of five independent batches of telephone numbers was a function of the selection probability for the reached telephone number, the number of different telephone lines (top-coded to 3) through which the household could be reached (i.e., excluding lines devoted exclusively for business, fax machines, or computers), and the number of eligible adults in the household (top-coded to 4). In step 2, the five independent batches of sample telephone numbers were combined to form one sample of interviewees using the procedure presented by Korn and Graubard (1999). In step 3, the initial base weight was adjusted for differential nonresponse by U.S. Census division. In step 4, the nonresponse-adjusted sampling weights were poststratified to the average population totals obtained from the Current Population Survey for the months during which the present study was in the field (January 2002 to June 2003). The Current Population Survey is a monthly survey conducted by the BLS and is the basis for all official labor force statistics in the United States. Poststratification cells were defined by the cross-classification of gender (2 levels), region of the country (4 levels), race/ethnicity (2 levels, non-Hispanic White and others), and age (either two or three age-groups, depending on race or ethnicity). Poststratification adjusts for known differences between the sample and population on key variables that may be due to sampling error, undercoverage, or nonresponse. Consistent with most random digit dial telephone surveys, poststratification was to all eligible household residents, not just eligible residents who reside in a telephone household. In step 5, weight trimming was performed on the final poststratified sampling weight for five interviewees whose value of their poststratified weight exceeded four times the median value of the poststratified weight.

Respondent Characteristics

Of the 2,829 study participants, the present analyses were restricted to the 2,508 wage and salary workers who had complete data on all of the variables used in this report. Of the 321 individuals excluded from the analyses, 294 were participants who owned and operated their own business and 27 were wage and salary workers who did not have complete data. Fifty-three percent of the respondents were male; 72% were White, 13% African American, 8% Hispanic, and 7% other racial or ethnic makeup. Sixty-seven percent were married or living as married. Average total family income was $60,455. In terms of occupations, 11.3% were in management occupations; 25.1% were in professional occupations; 15.9% were in service occupations; 8.7% were in sales occupations; 17.1% were in office or administrative support occupations; 0.5% were in farming, fishing, or forestry occupations; 4.3%

were in construction and extraction occupations; 4.9% were in installation, maintenance, or repair occupations; 5.8% were in production occupations; and 6.4% were in transportation or material-moving occupations. The participants worked on average 42 hours per week and held their present job for an average of 5 years. Seventy-seven percent worked a day shift; 8% worked an evening shift; 4% worked a night shift; 4% worked a rotating shift; and 7% worked a nonstandard (irregular or flexible) shift. Five percent of the participants held seasonal jobs, and 18% reported belonging to a union.

Measures

General demographic characteristics. The following five general demographic characteristics were assessed: gender (male vs. female), race (White vs. minority), age (in years), years of formal education, and marital status (not married vs. married or living as married).

Occupational demographic characteristics. The following seven occupational demographic characteristics were assessed: occupation (eight categories based on the Standard Occupational Classification codes), industry (seven categories based on the North American Industry Classification System), job tenure (in years), number of weekly work hours, work shift (five categories), seasonal job (yes, no), and union membership (yes, no).

Workplace abuse. Five items assessed the frequency of exposure to psychological abuse. Participants were asked how frequently someone at work did the following: shouted obscenities at you or screamed at you in anger; insulted you or called you names in front of other people; made an indirect or hidden threat, such as saying that "something bad" would happen to you; threatened to hit you or throw something at you; and threatened you with a knife, gun, or another weapon. Four items assessed the frequency of exposure to physical abuse. Participants were asked how frequently someone at work did the following: pushed you, grabbed you, or slapped you in anger; kicked you, bit you, or hit you with a fist; hit you with an object, tried to hit you with an object, or threw an object at you in anger; and attacked you with a knife, gun, or another weapon. Six items assessed the source of the abuse. For both psychological abuse and physical abuse, participants were asked if the source of that abuse was the following: a supervisor or boss; other employees; or clients, customers, or patients. The items assessing the type of abuse were adapted from McFarlin, Fals-Stewart, Major, and Justice (2001), and the items assessing the source of abuse were developed for this study. All 15 items used the following response anchors: 1 = *never*, 2 = *less than once a month*, 3 = *1 to 3 days a month*, 4 = *1 to 2 days a week*, 5 = *3 to 5 days a week*, 6 = *6 to 7 days a week*.

PART II

Sources and Forms of Workplace Violence

5

Editors' Introduction to Part II

No doubt as a result of several highly publicized events over the past two decades, workplace aggression and violence has captured the attention of the lay public. It is not surprising, therefore, to find that pervasive stereotypes now exist about workplace aggression and violence in which it is viewed as primarily a function of employees who beat up on their supervisors; however, although widely held, such stereotypes simply do not do justice to the wide scope of the problem. In this section, researchers who are experts in the full range of workplace violence redress this stereotype with numerous stimulating chapters. In doing so, the authors of these chapters focus on topics that have received and will continue to receive considerable research, policy, and public attention; but in addition, they examine several new aspects of workplace aggression.

Emotional abuse and bullying in the workplace, two topics that have each attracted considerable attention, are dealt with separately by Keashly and Harvey (emotional abuse) and Rayner and Cooper (bullying)—and it is certainly interesting to note that more research on these two topics has appeared in European than North American venues.

Several sectors in which aggression has historically received very prominent attention are the hospital or health care sector, the educational and police environments, and the field of labor relations. Lanza discusses the research on aggression and violence in the health care environment. Schonfeld then focuses on school violence—on the nature and amount of violence within this environment and on school employees as victims of workplace aggression and violence. Next, Perrott and Kelloway examine violence in the workplace of police, an occupation in which violence is virtually a defining feature of the role. Finally, although picket line violence is by no means a new phenomenon, Francis, Cameron, and Kelloway apply a novel perspective in their chapter addressing the issue of aggression and violence in the industrial and labor relations process; and LeBlanc, Dupré, and Barling provide a review of the vexing issue of aggression and violence perpetrated by customers on employees doing their normal duty.

On an almost daily basis, news coverage of world events during and since the last decade of the 20th century has shown us soldiers exposed to workplace aggression and violence. Farley and Catano address the issue of battlefield stress, which is of considerable relevance given the increasing reliance placed on child soldiers and private contractors to fight modern wars. In a similar vein, Inness and Barling address the unique nature of workplace violence encountered by soldiers serving in the role of peacekeepers.

Three chapters focus attention on the notion that workplace aggression and violence do not take place in isolation. First, given continuing wars throughout the past decade or so, Dietz and Gill appropriately address the extent to which workplace violence is influenced by community levels of aggression and violence. Second, Swanberg, Logan, and Macke discuss how being the victim of partner or marital violence spills over into the workplace with negative effects for the employees themselves, their colleagues, and the organization. Finally, Bates, Bowes-Sperry, and O'Leary-Kelly examine the interrelationships of workplace violence and sexual harassment.

Young workers have largely escaped empirical attention in the literature of workplace violence, despite their increasing workplace presence over the past two decades in many countries, often in high-risk jobs (Barling & Kelloway, 1999). Tucker and Loughlin go a long way toward providing a framework within which research on the meaning of workplace aggression for young workers can be initiated.

Last, Weatherbee by and Kelloway examine cyberviolence and aggression in the new world of workplaces revolutionized by computerization.

Reference

Barling, J., & Kelloway, E. K. (Eds.). (1999). *Young workers*. Washington, DC: American Psychological Association.

6

Workplace
Emotional Abuse

Loraleigh Keashly
Steve Harvey

Just before leaving for the weekend, George answers a call on the help line and quickly realizes it's from Mr. French, who's always got a problem late in the day. His computer's crashed again, he informs George, and this time he demands to talk to somebody competent!

George has had his share of problems with Mr. French, the sales department manager. On several occasions in management meetings, he's questioned George's competence. He just ignores George anytime he meets him in the hall, and George has heard he bad-mouths him to his staff.

When it becomes clear that Mr. French has no one but George to turn to this late in the day, he gets even more insulting about George's inability to fix his problem. Just before he slams the phone down, Mr. French lets loose one final attack: "I should come down there and knock some sense into you overpaid, underperforming college kids!"

George is barely able to speak to Mr. French, let alone find a solution to his problem before he hangs up. He sits and wonders what nice things Mr. French will be saying about him at the next management meeting. George tries to understand why his manager never seems to defend him at these meetings. He's also insulted about being called an incompetent college kid and annoyed that Mr. French would have the gall to suggest that he could smack him into compliance. That just infuriates George, particularly because he sees no alternative than to suck it up. Another weekend wasted worrying about this joker, he thinks. Why do I put up with this treatment?

Unfortunately, the scenario above is common in many organizations. It depicts employee experience with persistent psychological aggression. In fact, the majority of workplace aggression acts are nonphysical (Chappel & Di Martino, 1998; Keashly & Harvey, 2004; Neuman & Baron, 1997). One recent statewide survey by Jagatic and Keashly (2000) found that 24% of respondents report being exposed to psychologically aggressive behavior on a frequent basis. Although there has been some resistance to including the more "psychological" forms of aggression under the rubric of *workplace violence,* traditionally defined as physical (Di Martino, Hoel, & Cooper, 2003), recent occupational health and safety guidelines recognizing the extent and impact of nonphysical aggression do incorporate verbal abuse and harassment in their definitions of workplace violence (e.g., Canadian Centre for Occupational Health and Safety, 2003, www.ccohs.ca/oshanswers/psychosocial/violence.html). Accordingly, in this chapter we elaborate on emotional abuse as a nonphysical form of workplace violence.

Our first goal in this chapter will be to provide some conceptual clarity on what we intend by the term *emotional abuse.* Several constructs of nonphysical harassment have been introduced to the literature, and we need to understand how emotional abuse is proposed as a way of integrating these seemingly distinct phenomena (Keashly & Harvey, 2004). We then articulate our current thinking on emotional abuse as a workplace phenomenon; illustrate its various and far-reaching effects individually, organizationally, and socially; and discuss what we know and what is still to be known about its sources. Once we have laid out this landscape, we will identify and prioritize needed areas of research. We conclude with discussion about the implications for action by organizations concerned with emotional abuse in the workplace.

Emotional Abuse: Meaning, Measurement, and Prevalence

Discussion of the prevalence and impact of emotional abuse at work must be preceded by a discussion of its nature, one that delimits the construct with respect to a variety of phenomena that have recently been articulated in the research literatures on workplace hostility, harassment, aggression, and conflict. A central defining element of emotional abuse is that it involves repeated or persistent hostility over an extended period of time. Thus, we exclude from this conceptual domain the *occasional* aggressive acts or lack of decorum that arise out of everyday encounters. We view research on abusive supervision (Tepper, 2000), social undermining (Duffy, Ganster, & Pagon, 2002), bullying and mobbing (e.g., Einarsen, 1999; Leymann, 1990; Namie, 2000), harassment (Brodsky, 1976), petty tyranny (Ashforth, 1997), and generalized workplace abuse (Richman, Flaherty, & Rospenda, 1996) as examples of repeated and enduring hostility. Further, all these forms of persistent hostility have been demonstrated to undermine the target's sense of competence as a worker and a person, which is a second defining feature of emotional abuse (Keashly, 2001). A particularly unique feature of these types of hostility is that they occur in an ongoing relationship between the target and actor(s) rather than from "strangers or acquaintances." These forms of mistreatment are about hostile relationships rather than hostile events. In contrast to most occasional aggression, exposure to persistent hostility within an ongoing relationship creates a psychological work environment akin to being under siege (Waldron, 2000). Thus, the individual who is repeatedly exposed to fellow workers' verbal or nonverbal, but *nonphysical*, aggressive behaviors attacking their person is said to be undergoing emotional abuse at work.

This conceptualization of emotional abuse as a chronic state of existence has implications for measurement and hence for the determination of prevalence. The research on workplace aggression generally, and persistent hostility in particular, has typically measured constructs in terms of frequency of a variety of behaviors over a specified period of time (ranging from 6 months to 5 years) presented on a checklist. Further, with the exception of European workplace bullying research and recent North American research (e.g., Keashly & Neuman, 2002), even the indicators of frequency of occurrence that could in a limited fashion be equated to an assessment of degree of repetition have been vague and ill defined (e.g., *never* to *very often*). Moreover, until recently, the relationship of the actor to the target was also not part of the assessment (Keashly & Neuman, 2002). Such measurement does permit a picture of employees' degree of exposure to hostility at work but does not truly capture a state of emotional abuse—when a situation moves from being difficult or abrasive to being abusive (Ryan & Oestreich, 1991). A complementary measurement approach that reflects this concern is seen in the workplace bullying and sexual harassment literatures, which utilizes detailed definitions to which respondents identify as reflective of their experience (or not). Several workplace bullying studies (see Hoel, Rayner, & Cooper, 1999, for review) have also included behavioral checklists and defined respondents as bullied or not based on whether they endorse experiencing at least one behavior at least weekly for a specified period of time, often 6 months (Saline, 2001). As with the sexual harassment literature, the two methods produce different victimization rates but allow the opportunity to explore the thresholds of when hostility becomes abuse.

Acknowledging these different measurement perspectives and applying the criteria of persistence and impact, we share the following statistics to give the reader a sense of the extent of emotional abuse at work. Based on data from a 2004 statewide survey ($N = 438$), approximately 10% of a representative sample of working adults self-identified as having been persistently mistreated by someone with whom they worked in the previous 12 months. Ninety percent of those indicated that they were notably bothered by it, for a rate of 1 in 10 respondents being treated abusively (Burnazi, Keashly, & Neuman, 2005). A study of workplace stress and aggression with the U.S. Department of Veterans Affairs ($N = 4,790$) reported a higher rate with 36% of workers exposed to persistent hostility, with persistence defined as experiencing at least one aggressive behavior at least weekly for a period of a year (Keashly & Neuman, 2002). Almost 7% of the respondents reported being exposed to at least five or more different aggressive behaviors persistently. When the additional criterion of impact was applied (i.e., bothered them *moderately to a great deal*), 19% of all respondents would be described as experiencing abuse at work. To paint the picture even more starkly, data from a Web-based survey of self-identified targets of workplace bullying in the United States (Namie, 2000) revealed the average length of such abuse was 16.5 months. These figures reveal to us that a significant proportion of working adults can be considered to be undergoing emotional abuse at work.

Effects of Emotional Abuse

Now that we know emotional abuse is indeed part of many workers' working experience, what does it cost them, their organizations, and others with whom they are connected? Although the literature on occasional aggression has tended to focus more on antecedents than effects, research on persistent interpersonal hostility such as emotional abuse has been primarily focused on documenting the effects of exposure. Table 6.1 provides a listing of the well-established effects of *persistent aggression* along psychological, behavioral, and organizational dimensions (Keashly & Harvey, 2004; Keashly & Jagatic, 2003).

In viewing Table 6.1, it is important to indicate that research on emotional abuse and aggression at work has drawn on occupational stress models as an organizing framework (e.g., Keashly & Harvey, 2004; Schat & Kelloway, 2003). These frameworks represent aggression as an environmental stressor, and that which follows is represented as the personal stress experience and the psychological, physical, and behavioral strain that develop through ongoing or extreme exposure. These frameworks also specify several moderating and mediating variables that are also common to stress research. Many of these outcomes are, in fact, predicted to be causally associated with one another through various mediating mechanisms. These issues and the relevant processes have been discussed elsewhere (e.g., Harvey & Keashly, 2003b; Keashly & Harvey, 2004; Schat & Kelloway, 2003), so we reserve our comments to six observations regarding the collective import of these outcomes:

First and perhaps most powerful about this list is how extensive and comprehensive the impact of undergoing emotional abuse at work can be. Psychological effects ranging from anxiety and negative mood to depression, as well as behavioral impacts related to problem drinking and substance abuse, are clearly suggestive of the potential for a broad spectrum of generalized effects. These effects seem to cover the full range of effects typically noted within stress research generally (Jex & Beehr, 1991). Indeed, so pervasive are the effects that one can presume that they affect individuals' functioning in several aspects of their lives.

A second factor relates to the retaliatory behavioral effects that can emerge from such treatment. Prolonged exposure to abuse can result in the target behaving in a hostile and aggressive manner, both actively (e.g., verbal

Table 6.1   Some Effects of Emotionally Abusive Behaviors on Targets

Category	Effect	Source
Direct		
Negative mood	Anger, resentment	Ashforth (1997); Richman et al. (1999); Richman et al. (2001)
	Anxiety	Keashly et al. (1994); Richman et al. (1999); Richman et al. (2001); Tepper (2000)
	Depressed mood	Richman et al. (1999); Richman et al. (2001)
Cognitive distraction	Concentration	Brodsky (1976)
Indirect		
Decreased psychological well-being	Lowered self-esteem	Ashforth (1997); Cortina et al. (2001); Price Spratlen (1995)
	Problem drinking	Richman et al. (1999); Richman et al. (2001); Rospenda et al. (2000)
	Depression	Tepper (2000)
	Overall emotional health	Jagatic & Keashly (2000); Rospenda (2002)
	Self-efficacy	Duffy et al. (2002)
	Life satisfaction	Tepper (2000)
Poor psychosomatic function	Physical ill health (general)	Duffy et al. (2002); Price Spratlen (1995); Richman et al. (1999)
Reduced organizational	Decreased job satisfaction	Burnazi et al. (2005); Cortina et al. (2001); Harvey et al. (2005); (1996); functioning Jagatic & Keashly (2000); Keashly & Neuman (2002); Keashly et al. (1994); Keashly et al. (1997); Price Spratlen (1995); Sinclair et al. (2002); Tepper (2000)
	Job tension	Harvey (1996); Keashly et al. (1997)
	Greater turnover	Keashly et al. (1994); Sinclair et al. (2002); Tepper (2000)
	Work withdrawal behaviors	Cortina et al. (2001)
	Greater intention to leave	Ashforth (1997); Burnazi et al. (2005); Cortina et al. (2001); Harvey (1996); Jagatic & Keashly (2000); Keashly & Neuman (2002); Keashly et al. (1994); Keashly et al. (1997); Tepper (2000)
	Increased absenteeism	Price Spratlen (1995)
	Decreased productivity	Ashforth (1997); Price Spratlen (1995)
	Organizational Commitment	Duffy et al. (2002); Keashly & Neuman (2002); Tepper (2000)
	Family-work conflict	Tepper (2000)
	Leadership endorsement	Ashforth (1997)
	Work unit cohesiveness	Ashforth (1997)
	Organizational citizenship behaviors	Zellars et al. (2002)
	Counterproductive behaviors	Duffy et al. (2002)

outbursts, physical assault) and passively (withholding organizational citizenship behaviors, silent treatment). Such responses may fuel escalatory spirals that may lead to physical violence (e.g., Folger & Baron, 1996; Glomb, 2002) or the spreading of hostility to initially uninvolved others (Andersson & Pearson, 1999). This has clear implications for organizations and effective functioning, but it can also contribute to the misdiagnosis of these situations as conflicts to be resolved between parties when, in fact, there are harmful elements of one party abusing the other.

Third, the effect of alcohol use and abuse is revealing for its potentially exceptional relationship to prolonged exposure to workplace hostility. Many of the other effects noted are fairly characteristic of exposure to any workplace stressor, including occasional aggression (Barling, 1996). However, Richman and her colleagues (1996, 1999) and Rospenda, Richman, Wislar, and Flaherty (2000) argue that chronic *social or relational* stressors like emotional abuse are more predictive of disorders or diseases that develop slowly over time, such as alcohol abuse. In their 2-year longitudinal study of generalized workplace abuse, individuals exposed to chronic abuse were more likely to manifest drinking problems than those who had been exposed to it on a more time-limited basis (Richman, Rospenda, Flaherty, & Freels, 2001).

Fourth, the overall nature of the effects indicates deterioration or disabling of the target, the people around him or her, and the organization. In fact, several of these effects (e.g., hypervigilance, intrusive imagery, avoidance behaviors) are considered symptomatic of posttraumatic stress disorder (PTSD). Although PTSD has been defined as a response to a single, overwhelming event (e.g., workplace shooting, natural disaster), it has been argued to apply to targets that experience prolonged hostile interactions (e.g., Namie & Namie, 2000). For example, Namie (2000) reports that 31% of women and 21% of men responding to his survey on workplace bullying reported exhibiting all three trauma symptoms. Similar arguments are made in the European literature on workplace bullying (e.g., Hoel et al, 1999) and have been supported in psychological harassment research in Canada (Soares, 2002). These are alarming mental health correlates that clearly warrant more data and long-term monitoring.

Our fifth observation is that the research has tended to focus on the link between exposure and these measured effects without distinguishing between direct (immediate) effects and indirect (medium to long-term) effects (Barling, 1996; Rospenda et al, 2000; Tepper, 2000). As our observations above would indicate, there are likely more specific linking mechanisms to consider. For example, Barling (1996) has argued that the direct effects of the psychological experience of hostile behaviors are negative mood, cognitive distraction, and fear of violence. If these immediate effects are not alleviated, they will result in the more long-term and extensive effects, such as decreased psychological well-being, poor psychosomatic functioning, reduced organizational functioning, emotional exhaustion, poor job performance, and accidents. In addition to explicating the evolution of these effects, this approach identifies places for tertiary action in helping targets deal with even limited experience of emotional abuse before the damage becomes more extensive.

The final observation regards the focus of the impact. Most research on emotional abuse has tended to focus on the individual and, to a more limited extent, the organization; however, there is evidence that the victim net needs to be cast more broadly to include third parties, described as covictimization (Glomb, 2002) and vicarious victims (Rogers & Kelloway, 1997). This net includes family and friends who act as support for the target, as well as coworkers who either see or hear of the mistreatment. In addition to spawning secondary incivility spirals, hostility directed at others has been shown to cause similar negative effects in witnesses, such as fear they will be next, frustration over not being able to intervene, poorer teamwork and a diminished sense of empowerment, and anger at the organization for not controlling the actors (e.g., Andersson & Pearson, 1999; Bennett & Lehman, 1999; Neuman & Baron, 1997; Rogers & Kelloway, 1997; Schneider, 1996). Glomb (2002) extends the net even further with evidence that similar negative effects can be expected for the actors themselves. Broadening the notion of victimization enables a more detailed accounting of the human and organizational costs of emotional abuse and forms the basis for building the "business case" for the economic and social value of intervention (secondary and tertiary). Preventive action requires an understanding of the sources of emotional abuse, to which we now turn our attention.

Sources of Emotional Abuse

The literature on persistent hostility has focused primarily on effects rather than antecedents of emotional abuse. A notable exception is the more mature literature on sexual harassment in the workplace, wherein the antecedents have been drawn out and studied more carefully (e.g., Pryor & Fitzgerald, 2003). Accordingly, we will necessarily be drawing on the broader workplace aggression literature to explore the sources of emotional abuse. We do this cautiously, understanding that explaining how someone will behave aggressively (occasional aggression) does not necessarily extend to predicting when someone will engage in persistent hostility toward another person (emotional abuse).

A major assumption of and theoretical force for conceptualizing emotional abuse has been to cast the problem from an interactionist perspective (Keashly & Harvey, 2004; Keashly & Jagatic, 2003). The belief is that emotional abuse arises from a complex interaction of individual actor, target, and situational forces. The notion is that emotional abuse is a hostile relationship that *occurs* and is *maintained* through a variety of mechanisms that we can identify as sources of the condition. In this section, we will focus initially on the actor, move to discussion of target vulnerability, and then step back to consider broader situational forces in the form of organizational culture and workplace norms. It will be argued through empirical work and relevant theory where applicable that emotional abuse is a condition that arises and is maintained through these interactive forces.

Individual Influences: Actor Factors

The popular literature on abusive bosses and coworkers describes them as psychopathological, often with roots in their experiences as abused children or as schoolyard bullies (e.g. Namie & Namie, 2000; Wyatt & Hare, 1997). The empirical literature has examined more specific personality characteristics and provides some support that an individual's personality does play an important role in subsequent behavior. A basic premise of trait theories of personality is that traits represent a relatively stable set of characteristics about a person that predisposes the individual to behaving in predictable ways. Not surprisingly, personality characteristics associated with anxiety or anger and hostility, such as trait anger and self-control (Douglas & Martinko, 2001), depression (Tepper, Duffy, & Henle, 2002), type A personality (Neuman & Baron, 1998), negative affectivity (Neuman & Baron, 1998), neuroticism (Jockin, Arvey, & McGue, 2001), emotional susceptibility and irritability (Caprara, Rnezi, Alcini, D'Imperio, & Travaglia, 1983), and attributional style (Douglas & Martinko, 2001) have all been linked to increased aggressive behavior. Traits such as tolerance for ambiguity (Ashforth, 1997), agreeableness, conscientiousness (Jockin et al. 2001), and high self-monitoring (Neuman & Baron, 1998) similarly are predictive of reduced likelihood of aggression. In a related vein, Ashforth (1997) found that managers who hold Theory X beliefs (workers need to be forced to work) were more likely to behave aggressively toward subordinates. Thus, the personality and cognitive biases of actors seem to have an influence on engaging in aggressive behaviors. Whether certain personality types are predictive of tendencies to show *persistent* aggression is as yet an unexplored question.

Positional characteristics may also have an important influence on engaging in aggressive behavior. In terms of the actor-target relationships, the research is suggesting that there may be differences worth investigating further. For example, Keashly and Neuman (2002) report that superiors and coworkers are more often actors than subordinates or clients, and LeBlanc and Kelloway (2002) found that aggression is more likely from the public than from organizational insiders. These varied findings are likely a result of the nature of occupations and types of behaviors categorized as workplace aggression. Schat and Kelloway (2000), for example, included a variety of occupations, some of which are considered at high risk for workplace violence from customers or strangers (e.g., bank tellers, taxi drivers, home care workers). Keashly and Neuman (2002) were able to demonstrate that different actors (superiors, coworkers, subordinates, and customers) engaged in different forms of aggression, concluding that physical aggression is more likely from organizational outsiders than insiders, whereas the reverse is true for nonphysical aggression. These findings are interesting when examined in the light of LeBlanc and Kelloway's (2002) conclusions that factors that predicted violence from a member of the public were different from those that predicted violence from an organizational insider. It is possible that factors may vary because they are predicting or explaining different types of aggressive behavior. This interpretation has interesting implications for the emotional abuse literature. If, indeed, it is the issue of type of aggression that is key, and the distinction between occasional and persistent aggression that we have drawn is valid, then it is likely that there are unique predictors for emotional abuse. Regardless, although evidence is slowly gathering about an actor-behavior link, it is still unclear whether such differences are due to variation in or a combination of issues related to definitions of aggression, opportunity to aggress, occupations studied, and other situational factors to be considered later.

In regard to actor gender, there have been mixed results regarding whether men or women are more likely to be the aggressor (Keashly & Jagatic, 2003). Again, this appears to be linked to the type of aggression examined. For example, men are more often perpetrators of physical aggression than women (Eagly & Steffen, 1986). Drawing on the social psychological literature on gender and aggression, Bowes-Sperry, Tata, and Luthar (2003) have argued that the nature of workplace aggression (primarily psychological and often provoked) suggests that there would be no gender differences. We have consistently found no gender differences in the reported actors of emotionally abusive behaviors (see Keashly & Jagatic, 2003, for review). The studies we reviewed, however, did not examine the issue of motive for the aggression. Bettencourt and Miller (1996) note that gender differences in aggression are more likely when aggression is unprovoked, that is, when aggression is proactive. It may be that persistent aggression, such as emotional abuse, reflects a more proactive or instrumental aggression, and if so, gender may be expected to account for some variability in this form of aggression, with men being more aggressive. Data from a Web-based survey of self-reported victims of workplace bullying (Namie, 2000) found that contrary to Bettencourt and Miller's (1996) conclusions, women were more frequently identified as actors. Such differences may reflect the limited types of aggressive behaviors included in the studies reviewed. Specifically, they note that more indirect aggression, which Bjorkqvist, Osterman, and Hjelt-Back (1994) suggest women are more likely to engage in, was not well represented in these studies. Such mixed results are provocative, and the identification of motive and type of aggression as important influences should fuel future research to continue examining potential effects of gender.

Moving a step away from positional and personal characteristics to more person behaviors, two factors have received some empirical support: abuse history and alcohol use. Alcohol use and abuse and past aggressive or antisocial behavior have both been found to predict self-reports of engaging in primarily psychologically aggressive behavior at work (Greenberg &

Barling, 1999; Jockin et al., 2001). Alcohol use has been well established as a precursor to aggressive behavior. For example, the family violence literature consistently reports an association between family alcohol abuse and various forms of aggression in the home (e.g., O'Farrell & Murphy, 1995; Pan, Neidig, & O'Leary, 1994). By extension, this suggests that there is reason to expect a comparable link to the more persistent forms of aggressive behavior in the workplace, such as emotional abuse. Abuse history has also been found to be important in target's appraisal of emotionally abusive behavior. In both a scenario study (Keashly, Welstead, & Delaney, 1996) and an interview study of targets (Keashly, 2001), we found that previous hostile history with the actor was linked to judgments of the behaviors as abusive. Taken together, these studies provide strong support for the relationship of person behaviors to subsequent emotionally abusive behavior and the need for such behaviors to be explored more systematically.

Individual Influences: Target Factors

It may seem odd to discuss target characteristics as sources of emotional abuse. It seems suggestive of blaming the victim; however, because emotional abuse has been characterized as a hostile relationship, it is important to consider both members. Two different lines of research are of interest here. The first line of research focuses on the target's personality or interpersonal style. The premise is that a person may be at risk for being selected as a target of someone else's aggressive behavior because of how he or she interacts in the workplace. Olweus's (1993) work on schoolyard bullying identifies provocative and submissive victims. Provocative victims were characterized as obnoxious and somewhat aggressive in style. Submissive victims were characterized as anxious and socially awkward. And it would appear that the results may generalize to the workplace. Target negative affectivity has been linked to reports of being a target of aggressive behavior (Aquino, Grover, Bradfield, & Allen, 1999). Tepper et al. (2002) demonstrated that this was also true for persistent forms of hostility. Specifically, a supervisor who was depressed or felt he or she had been treated unfairly was more likely to become emotionally abusive to a subordinate who was high in negative affectivity.

The second line of research is exemplified by the work of Zapf and Gross (2001) on workplace bullying focusing on the conflict management behaviors of targets. They argue and demonstrate that targets may contribute to the escalation of hostilities because of their responses to the actor. Work by Aquino and Byron (2002) also finds similar results in relation to both high and low dominating conflict styles: targets possessing these styles were more likely to report being victimized at work. Such findings are consistent with various social psychological theories. For example, based on the frustration-aggression principle (e.g., Fox & Spector, 1999), it is possible that certain competitive styles may be perceived by actors to frustrate their goals and thus encourage retaliation through aggression. One can also invoke justice constructs to illustrate that perceived injustices predict workplace aggression (Baron, Neuman, & Geddes, 1999). Although we believe that targets are not responsible for an actor's abusive treatment, studies like these identify additional places where primary intervention can be undertaken. Thus, recognizing that a target's response or typical way of handling difficult situations may have some impact on the direction in which an initially hostile situation may go suggests that enhancing employee skills in dealing with potentially difficult situations, as well as stress management, may be helpful (Schat & Kelloway, 2000).

Situational Forces

Situational forces that facilitate (or mitigate) the likelihood of aggression have been discussed within the workplace (e.g., Neuman & Baron, 1998) and general societal contexts (e.g., Anderson & Bushman, 2002). Our focus here is to examine those situational factors we believe may be responsible for *persistent* hostility in the workplace.

Actors and targets exist within the broader social context of an organization and its environment. Thus, their behaviors are guided by and evaluated based on social norms of what is and is not appropriate. The characterization by a number of researchers of emotional abuse specifically and workplace aggression more generally as socially or organizationally deviant (e.g., Andersson & Pearson, 1999; Neuman & Baron, 1997; O'Leary-Kelly, Griffin, & Glew, 1996) assumes that social norms exist that discourage such behavior. Yet research described here indicates that such persistent and enduring hostility characterizes many people's work environments. In contrast to occasional aggression, the existence of persistent hostility suggests either that there has been a weakening or failure of social norms (Neuman & Baron, 2003; Richman et al. 1996) or that unspoken norms exist that at their worst support such behavior and at their best tolerate it (Douglas & Martinko, 2001; Keashly, 2001).

Although broader societal concerns, issues, and, thus, norms are imported into organizations (Donnellon & Kolb, 1994), organizations have their own unique influence on the behavior of their members. Together these factors contribute to the organization's culture, which is a shared system of beliefs, values, and behaviors that determines the kind of workplace behaviors that are rewarded and punished (Schein, 1990; Sperry, 1998). That is, organizations may vary in the extent to which they sanction aggression through the culture that prevails (Douglas, 2000). This thinking is consistent with social learning theory (Bandura, 1973), which stresses the importance of modeling and of rewards in learning and expression of aggressive behavior. Within work teams, Glomb and Liao (2003) have demonstrated the impact of coworker modeling of aggression on increased likelihood of an individual's aggression. At the broader organizational culture level, the organization through its actions (or inactions) signals its perspective on aggression. The notion that organizational tolerance of various abusive behaviors plays an enabling role has been well supported in the sexual harassment literature (see Pryor & Fitzgerald, 2003, for review). Similar findings of organizational influence are found in the research on emotionally abusive behaviors through studies looking at facets of organizational culture (Douglas, 2000; Jagatic, 2001; Keashly & Jagatic, 2000) and at perceptions of unjust treatment by the organization (Tepper et al., 2002). Regarding organizational culture, the more negatively employees (Keashly & Jagatic, 2000) and professionals in training (Jagatic, 2001) perceived their organization in terms of morale, quality of supervision and teamwork, and employee involvement, the more frequently they reported experiencing emotionally abusive behaviors. Taking a person X situation perspective, Douglas (2000) found that the impact of organizational culture on engaging in aggressive behavior was more dramatic for those employees who were low in self-control. Although we have noted actor proclivities for aggressive behavior, this finding is supportive of the enabling (and potentially mitigating) role that an organization can have on aggressive expression by its members.

This effect can also be noted through the lens of organizational justice theory. Perceived organizational injustice can be viewed as an indicator of a hostile work culture and has been consistently found to be linked to reports of behaving aggressively at work (Greenberg & Barling, 1999; Neuman & Baron, 1997; Tepper et al. 2002). Because of their enduring nature, these situational factors would seem to be of particular importance to an understanding of emotional abuse as *persistent* hostility and be less important as a triggering mechanism for *occasional* aggression. Thus, norms represented within the organization's culture, whether imported and tolerated or internally generated, may surreptitiously function to maintain the psychological hostility.

Although intriguing, the current challenge with most organizational culture-behavior research is that the data are correlational. This opens up the question of the causal nature of this link. Does a negative workplace environment result in more hostile employee behavior, as the European literature on workplace bullying (e.g., Einarsen, 1999; Hoel et al. 1999) and the American literature on toxic work environment (Harmon et al. 2003; Neuman & Baron, 1997; Wright & Smye, 1996) suggest? Or does hostile behavior left unchecked result in a toxic work environment, as suggested by Andersson and Pearson's (1999) discussion of the development of "uncivil" workplaces? The relationship is likely bidirectional, the dynamics of which can be more fully explored only through longitudinal research.

A Comment: Emotional Abuse as Proactive or Reactive Aggression?

Having reviewed the sources of emotional abuse, it is important that we acknowledge the distinction between reactive (affective) and proactive (instrumental) aggression in discussions of workplace aggression (Anderson & Bushman, 2002; Duffy et al. 2002; Keashly & Jagatic, 2003; Neuman & Baron, 1997; Tepper et al., 2002). In the discussion of gender and workplace aggression, we suggested that emotional abuse might be reflective of instrumental aggression. The workplace aggression literature appears to have an implicit assumption that such aggression is reactive or "emotional" in nature as evidenced by work on the aspects of a hostile or aggressive personality (e.g., Neuman & Baron, 1997) and work looking at actors also being targets (e.g., Glomb, 2002). But aggression can also be instrumental or predatory (Felson, 1993), wherein the actor is not simply reacting to some hurt or frustration (also referred to as dispute-related aggression; Felson, 1993) but may view treating another in this manner as instrumental to the achievement of some desired end, such as gaining compliance. References to these hostile behaviors as exercises of power (e.g., Cortina, Magley, Williams, & Langhout, 2001; Lewis & Zare, 1999; Namie & Namie, 2000) and as efforts to control and create target dependency (e.g., Bassman, 1992; Hornstein, 1996) or hinder a person's reputation and success on the job (Duffy et al. 2002) are consistent with an instrumental aggression perspective. Thus, although both types of aggression *intend* harm by definition, the ultimate goal for behavior is different (e.g., harm or injury vs. compliance; Anderson & Bushman, 2002). Accordingly, the goal of behavior becomes a central question and one that has been assumed rather than explicitly examined in either the emotional abuse or workplace aggression literatures (Neuman & Keashly, 2004). O'Leary-Kelly, Paetzold, and Griffin (2000) have explicitly surfaced the notion of emotional and instrumental goals in their discussion of an actor-based perspective on sexual harassment, and perhaps it is time we do the same with respect to other forms of aggression in the workplace.

Major Empirical Studies

A variety of qualitative and descriptive studies can be identified as instrumental to later work on emotional abuse. These were pioneering inquiries that provided the rich descriptions of a workplace problem that researchers had until that point generally overlooked. Among these are Brodsky's (1976) examination of workers' compensation claims revealing generalized forms of harassment, Ryan and Oestreich's (1991) qualitative interview study describing sources of fear in the organization and the "undiscussable" of abusive managerial behavior, Bassman's (1992) depiction of the sources of abusive practices and behaviors in organizations, and the nursing and medical literatures' quantitative descriptions of abusive treatment of nurses and medical students (e.g., Cox, 1991; Diaz & McMillin, 1991; Rosenberg & Silver, 1984; Silver & Glicken, 1990). This early literature painted a picture of hostile interpersonal relationships in North American organizations that was seemingly generalized and went well beyond the traditional sexual and racial lines that were at that time familiar to organizational researchers. The sexual harassment research that began in earnest in the 1980s (see Pryor & Fitzgerald, 2003, for review) has provided models and perspectives that have guided some of the work on emotional abuse. In the late 1980s and into the 1900s, Leymann's (1990) work on mobbing in the workplace fueled an incredible burst of empirical research in the European Community that was and continues to be influential in thinking about and examining workplace emotional abuse in the United States and Canada. It is out of this context that a number of research studies related to emotional abuse emerged. We highlight three of them in this section: (a) the earlier work of Keashly and her colleagues in assessing the existence and parameters of emotional abuse as a workplace phenomenon; (b) the longitudinal work of Richman, Rospenda, and their colleagues that has revealed the impact of chronic or persistent exposure to hostility in the workplace; and (c) the work of Tepper and his colleagues on abusive supervision and links to organizational justice.

In 1994, Keashly, Trott, and MacLean introduced to the organizational and violence literatures the notion of emotional abuse as a significant part of workers' experience. Taking an exploratory approach, Keashly et al. (1994) had undergraduate students with work experience indicate the frequency with which they had experienced a number of different behaviors in the workplace (both positive and negative), the degree of negative or positive impact of each of the behaviors on them, characteristics of the actor, their responses to the actor, and the impact of those responses on the overall situation. Several facets of job satisfaction were examined as outcome variables. Although the methodology of this study is simple, the results were quite revealing and sparked further research related to key findings.

First, this study found that a significant proportion of respondents were dealing with ongoing hostility from people with whom they worked. Specifically, 14% of the sample reported being exposed to 10 or more behaviors (out of a possible 28). This was evidence of the existence of nonsexual, nonphysical persistent hostility (i.e., emotional abuse). Second, these seemingly minor behaviors were rated as having moderate to extremely negative impact on the respondents and were significantly related to job satisfaction. Further, 14% of the sample left the organization as a result of the treatment. That is, these behaviors were harmful to both the individual and the organization (i.e., turnover) and thus needed to be included in assessments of hostility at work. Third, bosses and coworkers were reported to be the main actors, which highlighted the organizational insider aspect of emotional abuse (in contrast to physical violence in which actors are typically organizational outsiders) and introduced the notion of power differential to the discussion. Finally, the study provided evidence of the nature of target responses and the impact of those responses on changing the situation. Targets tended to use indirect, emotion-focused strategies that did not alter the situation notably. This finding drew attention to the need to look at target coping and more broadly the types of responses both individually and organizationally that would alter such hostile situations (i.e., secondary intervention).

Utilizing a similar behavioral indicator of abusive behaviors, Keashly and her colleagues (Harvey, 1996; Keashly, Harvey, & Hunter, 1997) extended their findings of impact to include turnover intention, job commitment, and job-related tension with different working populations. Perhaps most important for the development of the construct of emotional abuse, this study demonstrated the unique and significant contribution of emotional abuse to these outcomes over and above that accounted for by the classic role state stressors of role conflict, role ambiguity, and role overload (Keashly et al., 1997). Thus, emotional abuse was demonstrated to be a unique *sociorelational* stressor that is qualitatively a different from the more structurally linked role state stressors. This led to the expectation that it may have different effects on targets and perhaps a different process dynamic (e.g., coping mechanism effectiveness may vary). This theme has been resoundingly supported in the work of Richman, Rospenda, and their colleagues, to which our attention now turns.

What is particularly notable about the work of Richman and her colleagues (e.g., Richman et al., 1999; Richman et al., 2001; Rospenda et al., 2000) is the longitudinal nature of their research. Framing hostile treatment as a sociorelational stressor (i.e., one grounded in working relationships rather than work structure), they have collected four waves of data on faculty and staff of a midwestern university and are in the process of gathering a fifth wave. Data on over 1,500 employees and former employees over this time period have been gathered. The published literature reflects results from the first three waves of data (1996, 1997, 2001), with fourth-wave data (1 year later) beginning to be presented and discussed. This study is a mail survey that, among other things, included a measure of generalized workplace abuse (a similar measure to emotional abuse), as well as sexual harassment. Outcome variables of interest were the proximal indicators of mental and physical health and more distal, long-term effects of indicators of alcohol use and abuse. Further, indicators of coping with exposure to hostile behaviors were also included and their impact on outcomes examined. Overall findings are that generalized workplace abuse is more frequent than sexual harassment and that physical violence was less frequent than all other forms, confirming the significance of emotional abuse as frequent and therefore an important form of workplace violence and hostility.

Of particular interest to this discussion is the published work on the first two waves of data (Richman et al, 2001) that permitted the identification of employees who were exposed to chronic abuse (reporting exposure at each of the first two waves of data, reflecting 2 years of abusive treatment), those who had not previously been mistreated but now were, those who had been mistreated according to the first wave but were no longer being abused in the second wave, and those people who had not been exposed to such hostility. Such comparisons directly address a core element of emotional abuse, that is, persistence (frequency and duration). The results are telling. Those exposed to chronic abuse show greater evidence of negative health outcomes and negative drinking behaviors compared with the experience of all three other groups. Highlighting the unique impact of this sociorelational stressor, even those for whom abuse had desisted continued to show negative drinking outcomes long past the end of the abuse. Richman et al. (2001) argue that such findings support the distinction between stressors of an interpersonal nature and those of a more structural nature. When the latter end, the effects tend to diminish with time. Such was not the case for abusive treatment, suggestive of the impact of such treatment for undermining and disabling the target (Keashly, 1998). The findings with regard to coping are also troubling. Efforts at active coping (confronting the actor, reporting it to the supervisor, or filing a grievance) often failed, and when they did, the effects on targets were intensified. Richman and her colleagues take this as additional evidence that persistent hostile mistreatment (emotional abuse) is a profoundly different kind of stressor, the effects of which are more extensive and enduring. Indeed, she argues that such persistence and the failure of individual coping to alter the situation are characteristic of a sociostructural rather than a strictly interpersonal phenomenon, directing attention to the organization as a key source of, and resource for challenging, abusive treatment (Keashly & Harvey, 2004; Richman et al., 1999).

Tepper and his colleagues' work on abusive supervision picks up on this organizational connection in their studies examining the role of perceived organizational injustice as an antecedent in supervisor's abusive treatment of subordinates (Tepper et al., 2002) and as a mediator of its impact on subordinates (Tepper, 2000) and of subordinates' responses to the mistreatment (Zellers, Tepper, & Duffy, 2002). Tepper (2000) introduced his notion of abusive supervision in a study focused on subordinates' perceptions of abusive supervision on the part of their direct superior. Reflecting that the effects of abusive supervision may be lagged, Tepper gathered his data at two points in time, 6 months apart. In Time 1, 712 residents (53% response rate) of a midwestern city who were employed and were formally supervised returned usable surveys with questions about abusive supervision, perceived job mobility, and organizational justice (distributive, procedural, and interactional). At Time 2, individuals who completed the first survey and who still had the same supervisors ($n = 362$) were invited to complete this follow-up survey, consisting of items on job and life satisfaction, organizational commitment, conflict between work and family, and psychological distress. Those Time 1 respondents who did not have the same supervisors at Time 2 were asked to describe how the relationships had ended. These responses were coded as either *voluntarily quit* ($n = 119$) or those whose *supervisors left or were fired*. This group was contrasted with the group who still had the same supervisors. They found that subordinates who perceived their supervisors as more abusive were more likely to quit their jobs or positions.

Of those who stayed in their jobs, abusive supervision was associated with poorer outcomes. The role of organizational justice was shown to be important in mediating these effects. Tepper argued that the existence of abusive supervision fundamentally violated subordinates' sense of (a) being treated in a fair and respectful manner (interactional justice), (b) the organization developing and enforcing procedures that discipline abusers (procedural justice), and (c) receiving the same amount and type of positive input from supervisors that other coworkers do (distributive justice). These results speak directly to the significance of the organization and its norms for defining employees' experiences.

This selective set of studies paints a clear picture that emotional abuse is a distinctive stressor in the workplace and that it seems to be maintained through interplay of the actor(s), the situation, and the organizational environment. These studies also demonstrate that methodological improvements are being made regularly in the area, so the type of data being reported is increasingly providing actionable information. Nevertheless, the emotional abuse construct is still nascent; much has to be examined in future research.

Future Research Directions

As research on emotional abuse evolves, new directions for research and scholarship have become evident. We have explored some specific directions in other writing (Keashly, 1998; Keashly & Harvey, 2004; Keashly & Jagatic, 2003), so we will focus here on three meta-themes for such research. Research and scholarship are needed to address (a) the "black box" of the emotional abuse experience, (b) the notion of persistent hostility as a defining feature of emotional abuse, and (c) the bridging of cross-specialty and disciplinary findings.

We invoke the black box analogy in emotional abuse research to suggest that limited work has focused on the psychological and cognitive mechanisms involved in victims' experience of emotional abuse. Emotional abuse is as much a psychological experience as it is a study of external events and outcomes. Most research has focused on the more easily accessible elements of the concept, and we have yet to appreciably explore the psychological processes relating to the human affective and cognitive experience that can be associated with the phenomenon (Harvey, 2003; Harvey & Keashly, 2003b). There are studies examining these types of psychological variables as part of a more general investigation (e.g., fear; Harvey, 1996; Schat & Kelloway, 2000); however, there is limited research that has an explicit focus on understanding these experiences (cf. Harlos & Pinder, 2000; Keashly, 2001). There are numerous potential approaches to studying the psychological processes involved in the experience of emotional abuse. For example, researchers can look at several affective and cognitive issues regarding the role of target's emotional reactions (Weiss & Cropanzano, 1996), ruminations (Harvey & Keashly, 2003b), worry (Harvey, 2003), and posttraumatic symptoms (Soares, 2002). The case can also be made for personality as a psychological process variable, and some research is now beginning to emerge that is also likely to be revealing (e.g., Tepper, Duffy, & Shaw, 2001). It is clear that much is to be done in understanding those psychological processes most relevant to understanding emotional abuse and health at work.

It is apparent from extant research that aggression can be conceptualized as varying from the more occasional exposures to the chronic forms we labeled as emotional abuse. The premise of emotional abuse is that this persistence is an important element in the conditions and outcomes that targets report. There are likely important differences in these experiences that are critical to understand. Indeed, research on stress more generally has noted that acute and chronic stressors are different and potentially have different forms of impact on the individual (Kahn & Byosiere, 1992). It is our belief that the research aim of understanding the impact of persistent hostility will be best achieved through a pluralistic research agenda. Longitudinal research such as that by Richman and her colleagues (e.g., Richman et al., 2001) is an example of the type of research that gives us compelling information on the problem and its effects. Continued research along these lines is highly desirable; however, other research methodologies can also contribute through in-depth analysis of fewer cases. Understanding the experience of emotional abuse will benefit from an ongoing dialogue with those who have undergone the ordeal. This almost certainly involves research methodologies such as diary studies, case studies, and detailed interviews that are geared toward collecting rich information.

Although it may sound trite, it is nonetheless true that cross-disciplinary research would be advantageous. Much can be gained by exploring the work on emotional abuse and related concepts in other disciplines. The workplace is a relatively new context to be examining the emotional abuse construct. We have drawn on the concept of sexual harassment due to its related context and because it is proximal to our knowledge and experience with organizations; however, other areas as diverse as organizational communication (e.g., Lutgen-Sandvik, 2003; Meares, Oetzel, Torres, Derkacs, & Ginossar, 2004), child sexual abuse (e.g., Spaccarelli, 1994), spousal psychological abuse (e.g., Follingstad & DeHart, 2000), and aggression more generally (Anderson & Bushman, 2002) are among examples of several areas from which we can draw insights for model building and research. In some cases (e.g., Spaccarelli, 1994), the specified models identify psychological variables and other processes that generalize well to the experience within the context of work. The failure to draw on and work with a variety of literatures leads to reinvention of the wheel and reduced progress in addressing this very costly workplace phenomenon (Keashly & Jagatic, 2003).

Implications for Practice

To comprehensively address the wide range of factors that contribute to the development and maintenance of abuse and to deal with the impact, a multipronged approach is necessary (Di Martino et al., 2003; Glomb & Liao, 2003). Most fundamentally, people in the organization need to recognize the importance and centrality of work and working relationships to people's identities and sense of self (Harlos & Pinder, 2000). Acknowledging this allows for the development and implementation of effective action. Effective response to the problem will entail not only risk assessments, preventative measures, and policies but also effective leadership and role modeling to inculcate the needed culture. These are primary and secondary forms of intervention that we must engage. Tertiary interventions must also be considered in regard to the needs of the target of emotional abuse, for changing or removing the source of the problem may not deal fully with the scars that remain and continue to impede the individual. We briefly outline some implications for practice that our current knowledge of emotional abuse allows.

A risk management approach would suggest the need for a comprehensive assessment of risk factors (e.g., Harvey & Keashly, 2003a; LeBlanc & Kelloway, 2002) as well as protective mechanisms. Although the research literature and theorizing on sources of emotional abuse are still developing, there are some directions that can be fruitfully pursued in terms of reducing the risk. The earlier discussion of organizational culture suggests the need for clear policies against persistent forms of aggression. Moreover, evidence of the co-occurrence of various forms of harassment and abuse (Keashly & Rogers, 2001; Lim & Cortina, 2005; Richman et al., 1999) suggest that policies need to be conceived broadly to promote respectful treatment and at the same time define and proscribe certain types of aggressive behaviors, such as sexual and racial harassment, intimidation, and exclusion (Meares et al., 2004). The organization needs to indicate clearly what constitutes abusive treatment and to identify the procedures for notifying appropriate persons of the situation and for investigating the concerns raised. Further, the range of consequences associated with engaging in such treatment of other employees needs to be clearly spelled out (Glomb & Liao, 2003).

The existence of these policies is not enough, however. How these policies are implemented and controlled is most critical for success, including how leaders are seen to respond. As Offerman and Malamut (2002) note with respect to sexual harassment, "Paper policy isn't enough—leaders need to walk the talk" (p. 892). The notion of leadership giving life and substance to policies speaks to the different levels of messages communicated to employees. If the choice is between what is said in policy and how the leadership behaves with respect to that policy, employees will go with behavior. Prevention work must involve organizational leadership (management and union) working together to develop a shared vision of a healthy workplace and communicate it in writing and action.

A similar logic applies to employees who are at risk for being actors and dealing with them through clear policy and action. Research provides support for the notion that individual characteristics and circumstances at work are key determinants of aggressive behaviors in the workplace. Thus, in addition to organizational culture and policy changes, those individual characteristics that can be changed through training should be (e.g., skills in stress management and dealing with difficult situations, as well as adequate job training), but when characteristics are resistant to change, removal of the person may be required. Indeed, the group influences literature indicates the need to "eliminate aggressive role model," (people who persist in treating others in a hostile manner). Screening during hiring has been suggested by some, but we feel the nascent state of the research on traits and emotional abuse prevents such a recommendation.

Even committed leadership and proactive polices implemented consistently and fairly may not be able to prevent all mistreatment. Organizations need to be prepared with a variety of actions to intervene when the situations arise. Assuming that the reporting mechanisms are viewed as accessible and effective, actions that focus on supporting targets in their efforts to cope and to deal with the aftermath of such treatment become critical. Some suggestions come from the developing coping and social support literature regarding aggressive treatment. As noted by Richman et al. (2001), social support that arises from within the organization (as opposed to extraorganizationally in the form of friends and family) and that directly addresses the situation will be more effective than more emotion- or internally focused coping. As an example, Schat and Kelloway (2003) examined the moderating impact of two types of intraorganizational support. Instrumental support (direct help and assistance from coworkers and supervisors in dealing with the events) buffered the impact of aggressive treatment on emotional and physical health as well as job-related affect. Such findings highlight the importance of developing an organizational culture that does not tolerate aggression and behaviorally supports employees in dealing with it. Informational support in the form of training in how to deal with aggressive or violent behavior also buffered impact but only on emotional well-being. Although limited in its impact, training is a standard organizational response to dealing with issues. The question remains as to what such training could or should involve. Training in conflict management skills (e.g., Glomb & Liao, 2003; Zapf & Gross, 2001) has been proposed for all employees including actors. Such thinking is based on the premise that most aggression is reactive and the result of mishandled conflict. As we have argued, however, emotional abuse has a more one-sided or nonreciprocal quality to it, which may militate against conflict management skills as an effective tool for targets in dealing with an abusive actor. Indeed, some conflict management processes can effectively suppress public recognition and hence response to these kinds of hostile relationships (see Keashly & Nowell, 2003, for further discussion). Nevertheless, training all employees in alternative responses, besides aggression, to these situations can provide the space and time for other organizational actions to come into play.

For those who have been harmed, the provision of counseling and recovery time, as well as rehabilitation (e.g., job retraining or relocation to take on a new position), is an important part of a systemwide approach to dealing with emotional abuse. It is hoped that such remedial actions would not be necessary for any well-designed system, but it is a naive hope that researchers can ill afford to entertain. As with any other form of hazard to which the organization might inadvertently expose its employees, the effects of emotional abuse, should they occur, must be understood and dealt with in their entirety. Tertiary care that is most effective and to be recommended is difficult to stipulate at this stage due to the lack of systematic research; however, action is clearly needed here if what some authors suggest is confirmed

through continued research—that serious psychological damage in the form of posttraumatic stress disorder can result from certain lengths of exposure (Leymann & Gustafsson, 1996). These types of outcomes go well beyond the everyday risk and stress that are an expected part of working life.

References

Anderson, C. A., & Bushman, B. J. (2002). Human aggression. *Annual Review of Psychology, 53,* 27–51.

Andersson, L. M., & Pearson, C. M. (1999). Tit for tat? The spiraling effect of incivility in the workplace. *Academy of Management Review, 24,* 452–471.

Aquino, K., & Bryon, K. (2002). Dominating interpersonal behavior and perceived victimization in groups: Evidence for a curvilinear relationship. *Journal of Management, 28,* 69–87.

Aquino, K., Grover, S. L., Bradfield, M., & Allen, D. G. (1999). The effects of negative affectivity, hierarchical status, and self-determination on workplace victimization. *Academy of Management Journal, 42,* 260–272.

Ashforth, B. E. (1997). Petty tyranny in organizations: A preliminary examination of antecedents and consequences. *Canadian Journal of Administrative Sciences, 14,* 126–140.

Bandura, A. (1973). *Aggression: A social learning analysis.* Oxford, UK: Prentice Hall.

Barling, J. (1996). The prediction, psychological experience, and consequences of workplace violence. In C. VandenBos & E. Q. Bulatao (Eds.), *Violence on the job: Identifying risks and developing solutions.* Washington, DC: American Psychological Association.

Baron, R. A., Neuman, J. H., & Geddes, D. (1999). Social and personal determinants of workplace aggression: Evidence for the impact of perceived injustice and the Type A behavior pattern. *Aggressive Behavior, 25,* 281–296.

Bassman, E. S. (1992). *Abuse in the workplace.* Westport, CT: Quorum.

Bennett, J. B., & Lehman, W. E. (1999). The relationship of problem co-workers and quality of work practices: A case study of exposure to sexual harassment, substance abuse, violence and job stress. *Work & Stress, 13,* 299–311.

Bettencourt, B. A., & Miller, N. (1996). Gender differences in aggression as a function of provocation: A meta-analysis. *Psychological Bulletin, 119,* 422–447.

Bjorkqvist, K., Osterman, L., & Hjelt-Back, M. (1994). Aggression among university employees. *Aggressive Behavior, 20,* 173–184.

Bowes-Sperry, L., Tata, J., & Luthar, H. K. (2003). Comparing sexual harassment to other forms of workplace aggression. In M. Sagie, M. Koslowsky, & S. Stashevsky (Eds.), *Misbehavior and dysfunctional attitudes in organizations* (pp. 33–56). New York: Palgrave/Macmillan.

Brodsky, C. M. (1976). *The harassed worker.* Toronto: D.C. Heath.

Burnazi, L., Keashly, L., & Neuman, J. H. (2005, August). *Aggression revisited: Prevalence, antecedents, and outcomes.* Paper presented at the Academy of Management Annual Conference, Honolulu.

Canadian Centre for Occupational Health and Safety (2005). *What Is Workplace Violence?* Retrieved on December 7, 2005 from: www.ccohs.ca/oshanswers/psychosocial/violence.html

Caprara, G. V., Rnezi, P., Alcini, P., D'Imperio, G., & Travaglia, G. (1983). Instigation to aggress and escalation of aggression examined from a psychological perspective: The role of irritability and of emotional susceptibility. *Aggressive Behavior, 9,* 345–351.

Chappel, D., & Di Martino, V. (1998). *Violence at work.* Geneva: ILO.

Cortina, L. M., Magley, V. J., Williams, J. H., & Langhout, R. D. (2001). Incivility in the workplace: Incidence and impact. *Journal of Occupational Health Psychology, 6,* 64–80.

Cox, H. (1991). Verbal abuse nationwide, Pt. 2: Impact and modifications. *Nursing Management, 22,* 66–69.

Diaz, A. L., & McMillin, J. D. (1991). A definition and description of nurse abuse. *Western Journal of Nursing Research, 13,* 97–109.

Di Martino, V., Hoel, H., & Cooper, C. (2003). *Prevention of violence and harassment in the workplace.* Dublin: European Foundation for the Improvement of Living and Working Conditions.

Donnellon, A., & Kolb, D. M. (1994). Constructive for whom? The fate of diversity disputes in organizations. *Journal of Social Issues, 50,* 139–155.

Douglas, S. C. (2000). *Individual and situational workplace antecedents to workplace aggression: A model and test.* Unpublished dissertation, Florida State University.

Douglas, S. C., & Martinko, M. J. (2001). Exploring the role of individual differences in the prediction of workplace aggression. *Journal of Applied Psychology, 86*(4), 547–559.

Duffy, M. K., Ganster, D. C., & Pagon, M. (2002). Social undermining in the workplace. *Academy of Management Journal, 45,* 331–351.

Eagly, A. H., & Steffen, J. (1986). Gender and aggressive behavior: A meta-analytic review of the social psychological literature. *Psychological Bulletin, 100,* 309–330.

Einarsen, S. (1999). The nature and causes of bullying at work. *International Journal of Manpower, 20*(1/2), 16–27.

Felson, R. B. (1993). Predatory and dispute-related violence: A social interactionist approach. In R. V. Clarke & M. Felson (Eds.), *Routine activity and rational choice* (Chap. 5). New Brunswick, NJ: Transaction.

Folger, R., & Baron, R. A. (1996). Violence and hostility at work: A model of reactions to perceived injustice. In G. R. VandenBos & E. Q. Bulatao (Eds.), *Violence on the job: Identifying risks and developing solutions* (pp. 51–85). Washington, DC: American Psychological Association.

Follingstad, D. R., & DeHart, D. D. (2000). Defining psychological abuse of husbands toward wives: Contexts, behaviors, and typologies. *Journal of Interpersonal Violence, 15,* 891–920.

Fox, S., & Spector, P. E. (1999). A model of work frustration-aggression. *Journal of Organizational Behavior, 20,* 915–931.

Glomb, T. M. (2002). Workplace aggression: Informing conceptual models with data from specific encounters. *Journal of Occupational Health Psychology, 7,* 20–36.

Glomb, T. M., & Liao, H. (2003). Interpersonal aggression in work groups: Social influence, reciprocal, and individual effects. *Academy of Management Journal, 46,* 486–496.

Greenberg, L., & Barling, J. (1999). Predicting employee aggression against coworkers, subordinates, and supervisors: The roles of person behaviors and perceived workplace factors. *Journal of Organizational Behavior, 20,* 897–913.

Harlos, K., & Pinder, C. (2000). Emotion and injustice in the workplace. In S. Fineman (Ed.), *Emotion in organizations.* Thousand Oaks, CA: Sage.

Harmon, J., Scotti, D. J., Behson, S., Farias, G., Petzel, R., Neuman, J. H., & Keashly, L. (2003). Effects of high-involvement work practices on employee satisfaction and service costs in the Veterans Health Administration. *Journal of Healthcare Management, 48*(6), 393–406.

Harvey, S. (1996). *Bosses' negative interpersonal behaviors: A latent variable test of personal and organizational outcomes.* Unpublished doctoral dissertation, University of Guelph, Ontario.

Harvey, S. (2003, June). Some thoughts on the targets' experience of aggression in the workplace: Beyond the concept of fear. In E. K. Kelloway (Chair), *Symposium on workplace violence and aggression: Risk and responses.* Paper presented at the Annual Meeting of the Canadian Psychological Association, Hamilton, Ontario.

Harvey, S., & Keashly, L. (2003a). Predicting the risk for aggression in the workplace: Risk factors, self-esteem and time at work. *Social Behavior and Personality, 31,* 807–814.

Harvey, S., & Keashly, L. (2003b). Rumination: A psychological mechanism for transmitting and maintaining the effect of emotional abuse at work. *Proceedings of the American Society for Business and the Behavioral Sciences, 10,* 593–601.

Hoel, H., Rayner, C., & Cooper, C. L. (1999). Workplace bullying. In C. L. Cooper & I. T. Robertson (Eds.), *International review of industrial and organizational psychology.* Chichester, UK: John Wiley.

Hornstein, H. (1996). *Brutal bosses and their prey.* New York: Riverhead.

Jagatic, K. (2001). *The influence of educational culture on experienced and witnessed hostility by faculty toward professionals-in-training.* Unpublished doctoral dissertation, Wayne State University, Detroit.

Jagatic, K., Keashly, L. (2000, September). *The nature, extent, and impact of emotional abuse in the workplace: Results of a statewide survey.* Paper presented at the Academy of Management Conference, Toronto.

Jex, S., & Beehr, T. A. (1991). Emerging theoretical and methodological issues in the study of work-related stress. *Research in Personnel and Human Resource Management, 9,* 311–365.

Jockin, V., Arvey, R. D., & McGue, M. (2001). Perceived victimization moderates self-reports of workplace aggression and conflict. *Journal of Applied Psychology, 86*(6), 1262–1269.

Kahn, R. L., & Byosiere, P. (1992). Stress in organizations. In M. D. Dunnette & L. M. Hough (Eds.), *Handbook of industrial and organizational psychology* (2nd ed., Vol. 3, pp. 571–650). Palo Alto, CA: Consulting Psychologists.

Keashly, L. (1998). Emotional abuse in the workplace: Conceptual and empirical issues. *Journal of Emotional Abuse, 1,* 85–117.

Keashly, L. (2001). Interpersonal and systemic aspects of emotional abuse at work: The target's perspective. *Violence & Victims, 16*(3), 233–268.

Keashly, L., & Harvey, S. (2004). Emotional abuse at work. In P. Spector & S. Fox (Eds.), *Counterproductive workplace behavior: An integration of both actor and recipient perspectives on causes and consequences* (pp. 201–236). Washington, DC: American Psychological Association.

Keashly, L., Harvey, S. R., & Hunter, S. (1997). Abusive interaction and role state stressors: Relative impact on student residence assistant stress and work attitudes. *Work & Stress, 11,* 175–185.

Keashly, L., & Jagatic, K. (2003). By any other name: American perspectives on workplace bullying. In S. Einarsen, H. Hoel, D. Zapf, & C. Cooper (Eds.),

Bullying and emotional abuse in the workplace: International perspectives in research and practice (pp. 31–61). London: Taylor Francis.

Keashly, L., & Neuman, J. H. (2002, August). *Exploring persistent patterns of workplace aggression.* Paper presented at the Annual Meeting of the Academy of Management, Denver, CO.

Keashly, L., & Nowell, B. (2003). Workplace bullying and conflict resolution. In S. Einarsen, H. Hoel, D. Zapf, & C. Cooper (Eds.), *Bullying and emotional abuse in the workplace: International research and practice perspectives* (pp. 339–358). London: Taylor Francis.

Keashly, L., & Rogers, K. A. (2001). *Aggressive behaviors at work: The role of context in appraisals of threat.* Unpublished manuscript.

Keashly, L., Trott, V., & MacLean, L. M. (1994). Abusive behavior in the workplace: A preliminary investigation. *Violence & Victims, 9,* 125–141.

Keashly, L., Welstead, S., & Delaney, C. (1996). *Perceptions of abusive behaviors in the workplace: Role of history, emotional impact and intent.* Unpublished manuscript, University of Guelph, Ontario.

LeBlanc, M. M., & Kelloway, E. K. (2002). Predictors and outcomes of workplace violence and aggression. *Journal of Applied Psychology, 87,* 444–453.

Lewis, G. W., & Zare, N. C. (1999). *Workplace hostility: Myth and reality.* Philadelphia: Accelerated Development.

Leymann, H. (1990). Mobbing and psychological terror at workplaces. *Violence & Victims, 5,* 119–126.

Leymann, H., & Gustafsson, A. (1996). Mobbing at work and the development of post-traumatic stress disorders. *European Journal of Work and Organizational Psychology, 5,* 251–275.

Lim, S., & Cortina, L. M. (2005). Interpersonal mistreatment in the workplace: The interface and impact of general incivility and sexual harassment. *Journal of Applied Psychology, 90,* 483–496.

Lutgen-Sandvik, P. (2003). The communicative cycle of employee emotional abuse: Generation and regeneration of workplace mistreatment. *Management Communication Quarterly, 16,* 471–501.

Meares, M. M., Oetzel, J. G., Torres, A., Derkacs, D., & Ginossar, T. (2004). Employee mistreatment and muted voices in the culturally diverse workplace. *Journal of Applied Communication Research, 32,* 4–27.

Namie, G. (2000, October). *U.S. Hostile Workplace Survey 2000.* Paper presented at the New England Conference on Workplace Bullying, Suffolk University Law School, Boston.

Namie, G., & Namie, R. (2000). *The bully at work: What you can do to stop the hurt and reclaim your dignity on the job.* Naperville, IL: Sourcebooks.

Neuman, J. H., & Baron, R. A. (1997). Aggression in the workplace. In R. A. Giacalone & J. Greenberg (Eds.), *Antisocial behavior in organizations.* Thousand Oaks, CA: Sage.

Neuman, J. H., & Baron, R. A. (1998). Workplace violence and workplace aggression: Evidence concerning specific forms, potential causes, and preferred targets. *Journal of Management, 24,* 391–411.

Neuman, J. H., & Baron, R. A. (2003). Social antecedents of bullying: A social interactionist perspective. In S. Einarsen, H. Hoel, D. Zapf, & C. Cooper (Eds.), *Bullying and emotional abuse in the workplace: International perspectives in research and practice* (pp. 185–202). London: Taylor Francis.

Neuman, J. H., & Keashly, L. (2004, August). *Means, motive, opportunity and abusive workplace behavior*. Paper presented at the Annual Meeting of the Academy of Management, New Orleans.

O'Farrell, T. J., & Murphy, C. M. (1995). Marital violence before and after alcoholism treatment. *Journal of Consulting and Clinical Psychology, 63*, 256–262.

Offerman, L. R., & Malamut, A. B. (2002). When leaders harass: The impact of target perceptions of organizational leadership and climate on harassment reporting and outcomes. *Journal of Applied Psychology, 87*(5), 885–893.

O'Leary-Kelly, A. M., Griffin, R. W., & Glew, D. J. (1996). Organization-motivated aggression: A research framework. *Academy of Management Review, 21*, 225–253.

O'Leary-Kelly, A. M., Paetzold, R. L., & Griffin, R. W. (2000). Sexual harassment as aggressive behavior: An actor-based perspective. *Academy of Management Review, 25*, 372–388.

Olweus, D. (1993). Victimization by peers: Antecedents and long-term outcomes. In K. H. Rubin & J. B. Asendorf (Eds.), *Social withdrawal, inhibition, and shyness in childhood* (pp. 315–341). Chicago: University of Chicago Press.

Pan, H. S., Neidig, P. H., & O'Leary, K. D. (1994). Predicting mild and severe husband-to-wife physical aggression. *Journal of Consulting and Clinical Psychology, 62*, 975–981.

Price Spratlen, L. (1995). Interpersonal conflict which includes mistreatment in a university workplace. *Violence & Victims, 10*, 285–297.

Pryor, J. B., & Fitzgerald, L. F. (2003). Sexual harassment research in the U.S. In S. Einarsen, H. Hoel, D. Zapf, & C. Cooper (Eds.), *Bullying and emotional abuse in the workplace: International perspectives in research and practice* (pp. 79–100). London: Taylor Francis.

Richman, J. A., Flaherty, J. A., & Rospenda, K. M. (1996). Perceived workplace harassment experiences and problem drinking among physicians: Broadening the stress/alienation paradigm. *Addiction, 91*, 391–403.

Richman, J. A., Rospenda, K. M., Flaherty, J. A., & Freels, S. (2001). Workplace harassment, active coping, and alcohol-related outcomes. *Journal of Substance Abuse, 13*, 347–366.

Richman, J. A., Rospenda, K. M., Nawyn, S. J., Flaherty, J. A., Fendrich, M., Drum, M. L., et al. (1999). Sexual harassment and generalized workplace abuse among university employees: Prevalence and mental health correlates. *American Journal of Public Health, 89*, 358–364.

Rogers, K. A., & Kelloway, E. K. (1997). Violence at work: Personal and organizational outcomes. *Journal of Occupational Health Psychology, 12*, 63–71.

Rosenberg, D. A., & Silver, H. K. (1984). Medical student abuse: An unnecessary and preventable cause of stress. *Journal of the American Medical Association, 251*, 739–742.

Rospenda, K. M. (2002). Workplace harassment, service utilization, and drinking outcomes. *Journal of Occupational Health Psychology, 2*, 141–155.

Rospenda, K. M., Richman, J. A., Wislar, J. S., & Flaherty, J. A. (2000). Chronicity of sexual harassment and generalized workplace abuse: Effects on drinking outcomes. *Addiction, 95*(12), 1805–1820.

Ryan, K. D., & Oestreich, D. K. (1991). *Driving fear out of the workplace*. San Francisco: Jossey-Bass.

Saline, D. (2001). Prevalence and forms of bullying among business professionals: A comparison of two different strategies for measuring bullying. *European Journal of Work and Organizational Psychology, 10,* 425–441.

Schat, A. C. H., & Kelloway, E. K. (2000). Effects of perceived control on the outcomes of workplace aggression and violence. *Journal of Occupational Health Psychology, 5*(3), 386–402.

Schat, A. C. H., & Kelloway, E. K. (2003). Reducing the adverse consequences of workplace aggression and violence: The buffering effects of organizational support. *Journal of Organizational Health Psychology, 8,* 110–122.

Schein, E. H. (1990). Organizational culture. *American Psychologist, 45,* 109–119.

Schneider, K. T. (1996, August). *Bystander stress: Effects of sexual harassment on victims' co-workers.* Paper presented at the Annual Convention of the American Psychological Association, Toronto.

Silver, H. K., & Glicken, A. D. (1990). Medical student abuse: Incidence, severity, and significance. *Journal of the American Medical Association, 263,* 527–532.

Sinclair, R. R., Martin, J. E., & Croll, L. W. (2002). A threat-appraisal perspective on employees' fears about antisocial workplace behavior. *Journal of Occupational Health Psychology, 7,* 37–56.

Soares, A. (2002). *Bullying: When work becomes indecent.* Unpublished manuscrpt, Université du Québec à Montréal.

Spaccarelli, S. (1994). Stress, appraisal, and coping in child sexual abuse: A theoretical and empirical review. *Psychological Bulletin, 116,* 340–362.

Sperry, L. (1998). Organizations that foster inappropriate aggression. *Psychiatric Annals, 28*(5), 279–284.

Tepper, B. J. (2000). Consequences of abusive supervision. *Academy of Management Journal, 43*(2), 178–190.

Tepper, B. J., Duffy, M. K., & Henle, C. A. (2002). *Development and test of an interactional model of abusive supervision.* Unpublished manuscript, University of North Carolina, Charlotte.

Tepper, B. J., Duffy, M. K., & Shaw, J. D. (2001). Personality moderators of the relationship between abusive supervision and subordinates' resistance. *Journal of Applied Psychology, 86,* 974–983.

Waldron, V. R. (2000). Relational experiences and emotion at work. In S. Fineman (Ed.), *Emotion in organizations* (2nd ed., pp. 25–45). Thousand Oaks, CA: Sage.

Weiss, H. M., & Cropanzano, R. (1996). Affective events theory: A theoretical discussion of the structure, causes and consequences of affective experiences at work. *Research in Organizational Behavior, 18,* 1–74.

Wright, L., & Smye, M. (1996). *Corporate abuse: How lean and mean robs people and profits.* New York: Macmillan.

Wyatt, J., & Hare, C. (1997). *Work abuse: How to recognize and survive it.* Rochester, VT: Scheming.

Zapf, D., & Gross, C. (2001). Conflict escalation and coping with workplace bullying: A replication and extension. *European Journal of Work and Organizational Psychology, 10,* 497–522.

Zellers, K. L., Tepper, B. J., & Duffy, M. K. (2002). Abusive supervision and subordinates' organizational citizenship behavior. *Journal of Applied Psychology, 87,* 1068–1076.

7

Workplace Bullying

Charlotte Rayner
Cary L. Cooper

This chapter sets out to examine a phenomenon that has been studied relatively recently: that of workplace bullying. Bullying has been established as a feature of schools and playgrounds for many years (e.g., Burk, 1897) and as such has received considerable attention (e.g., Bernstein & Watson, 1997; Besag, 1989; Olweus, 1983). Contemporary studies of bullying at work have drawn from the original conceptual base in childhood studies and have developed the topic to be applicable to modern-day working situations. Within a decade, research in this topic has grown to a point that it is well established in several countries. Currently, we perceive a turning point at which other more established areas of academic endeavor are now looking at workplace bullying as a phenomenon in order to understand linkages and contribute as a broader academic community to our sense making in this area. The very appearance of this chapter in this text is evidence of such progression and one that we would welcome.

We begin the first section of this chapter by describing the emergence of the academic study of workplace bullying, which will lead us into a section covering contemporary definitions. After a summary of issues relating to the measurement of bullying at work, we will conclude by discussing the interaction of measurement and definitional issues.

In the second section, we will provide an overview of key findings from research into bullying at work and a selection of the new links with related fields of study. In the final section, we will attempt to shed light on the task that faces organizations when tackling bullying within their workplaces and conclude with prevention aspects.

Section One: The Development, Definition, and Measurement of Bullying at Work

Development

Arguably, bullying has existed since ordered work patterns were established (e.g., Ashforth, 1994; Baumeister, Smart, & Boden, 1996; Christie & Geiss, 1970), although its systematic study is a recent event. Carroll Brodsky, a senior clinician processing compensation claims in the United States, described bullying in his seminal text *The Harassed Worker* in 1976. Largely ignored at the time, this text was rediscovered by Scandinavian researchers who have since provided the initial impetus for contemporary studies into childhood bullying (e.g., Olweus, 1983) and adult bullying in the workplace (e.g., Einarsen, Raknes, & Matthiesen, 1994; Leymann, 1990). Olweus originally used the term *mobbing* when he saw a child being mobbed by other children in the playground (akin to birds mobbing each other), although the UK term *bullying* is now the common descriptor in the field.

Heinz Leymann provided the first systematic deconstruction of the problem through analysis of several hundred "critical-incident" interviews with targets of bullying in Sweden. From this work came a description of common behaviors experienced by people through which he developed the LIPT (Leymann Inventory of Personal Terror), which has formed the basis of most quantitative investigation in the field (Leymann, 1996). He also suggested a cycle of escalation in which organizational aspects contribute to the victimization of the target (e.g., Leymann, 1996). Although the specific patterns that Leymann suggested have not received support, the existence of negative organizational measures to potentially exacerbate the experience of a target of bullying is acknowledged by most researchers in the field (e.g., Bassman, 1992). Indeed, this latter aspect is a topic of considerable discussion in which some writers have found that organizational measures in themselves can be experienced as bullying (e.g., Harlos & Pinder, 1999; Liefooghe & Mackenzie Davey, 2001). We will return to this aspect later in the chapter.

Leymann's work generated significant attention and was closely followed by other Scandinavian academics, most of whom had occupational or clinical psychology training. Replication and extension of investigations were conducted in Norway (e.g., Einarsen & Raknes, 1995) in the public sector (Einarsen & Skogstad, 1996) and in Finland (e.g., Bjorkqvist, Osterman, & Hjelt-Back, 1994; Vartia, 1993) and Germany (e.g., Zapf, Knorz, & Kulla, 1996).

Research into bullying in the United Kingdom and Australia began in parallel from work-based studies (as opposed to much Scandinavian investigation that used clinical samples of targets of bullying). A study in Australia (McCarthy, Sheehan, & Kearns, 1995) painted a pressurized and tough environment on restructuring where many staff felt bullied. In the United Kingdom, a study sponsored by the BBC found that around half the working population described themselves as having been bullied in their working lives (Rayner, 1997). The scale of the reports of negative experience in these studies attracted significant press attention in their respective countries, fueling interest among a variety of legal and occupational health practitioners, trade unions, and academics alike (e.g., Lewis, 1999). Considerable research has been published since the late 1990s, and a recent publication series provided helpful texts for counselors and advisers (Tehrani, 2001), practitioners in the workplace (Rayner, Hoel, & Cooper, 2002), and academics (Einarsen, Hoel, Zapf, & Cooper 2003).

In North America, a far less cohesive picture has emerged. No doubt the struggle of this topic to gain attention in the United States will also be a focus for future business historians. Loraleigh Keashly has been a key player, with a paper of analysis (Keashly, 1998) and further empirical work (e.g., Jagatic & Keashly, 2000). Arguably, an acceptance of the issue has been held back by other competing topics and a confusion of contemporary emerging constructs. It is instructive to observe that this confusion is coagulating into a more systematized picture in which a multiplicity of approaches are being valued for their individual contribution to a holistic attempt in order to find clear representation.

Key North American studies include Blake Ashforth's paper (1994) on abusive bosses perpetrating "petty tyranny," which can be applied to the bully; and Bennett and Robinson's (2000) study of deviance that highlighted several aspects of verbal and other abuse perpetrated by actors. More mainstream work (from a European perspective) has continued through studies of interpersonal conflict (e.g., Baron & Neuman, 1996), although most do not reflect the breadth of workplace bullying but focus on verbal aggression. Further, studies into antisocial behavior (e.g., Robinson & O'Leary-Kelly, 1998) and revenge (e.g., Aquino, Tripp, & Bies, 2001) have been largely ignored in European circles but would contribute to the development of the target becoming the actor and contributing to the "cycle of violence" (Andersson & Pearson, 1999; Einarsen, 2000). As our investigations continue, the challenge will be as much to absorb and place these and others' contributions in the field as to conduct further work.

Definition

This section will start by emphasizing that different definitions of bullying at work are used by different people (Rayner, 2002), depending on their actor perspective or their professional interest in the area. For example, lawyers will need someone who has been bullied to have experienced "damage" before they can take a claim and be defined as "bullied" (Yamada, 2003), whereas those looking to judge prevention measures may seek far lower levels of distress when evaluating their endeavors (e.g., Bassman, 1992).

Workplace policies need to use definitions to provide a basis for anyone making a complaint, and these definitions will form the backbone of this section. In the United Kingdom, many organizations have used others' work to inform their approach, and thus an evolution of definition has taken place. An early mover in the United Kingdom was the Industrial Society (now the Work Foundation), on whose definition many UK corporate definitions were based. A contemporary example would be the Andrea Adams Trust, a charity set up to assist targets of bullying and their employers. Its definition is as follows:

> [Workplace bullying is] unwarranted humiliating offensive behavior toward an individual or groups of employees. Such . . . attacks are typically unpredictable, unfair . . . and often unseen. [It is] an abuse of power or position that can cause such anxiety that people gradually lose all belief in themselves, suffering physical ill health or mental distress as a direct result. (Andrea Adams Trust, *Factsheet on Workplace Bullying,* http://www.andreaadamstrust.org/factsheet.pdf)

Fundamental to all definitions is that bullying at work is about the experience of behaviors. All UK definitions suggest that bullying at work is about interpersonal abuse in which another individual is the source of negative actions. This section will return to the issue of corporate bullying (or "negative *organizational* behavior," Rayner, 2005) but will meanwhile take its focus on negative interpersonal behavior (Rayner, 2005).

Bullying Behaviors

There is no definitive list of behaviors that are considered to be bullying at work, and definitions will normally include examples of types of behaviors. Leymann's original work on the LIPT (1996) was tested by Zapf et al. (1996), who found seven constructs from empirical results using the LIPT. These were organizational measures, social relationships with social isolation, attacking the target's private life, physical violence, and verbal aggression and rumors.

Rayner and Hoel (1997) conducted a content analysis of Andrea Adams's (1992) descriptive text on bullying and surmised five categories: threat to professional status, threat to personal standing, isolation, overwork, and destabilization. Analysis by Rayner and Dick (2005) of two large, previously collected data sets found four sets of behaviors: task attack, personal attack, isolation, and physical attack.

Keashly and Jagatic used an adapted version of the Buss (1961) typology of aggression—covert/overt, verbal/nonverbal, physical/nonphysical—to review other studies (2003). This provides a framework to describe behaviors in terms of the nature of how the attack is made. This framework, however, does not provide any insight into what is attacked. All studies have shown an uneven distribution of negative acts experienced, however they are classified.

Physical aggression has apparently a very low incidence in the United Kingdom (Rayner, 1997) and Australian (McCarthy et al., 1995) workplaces (around 1–2%) and even less in Scandinavia (e.g., Einarsen & Skogstad, 1996).

In the United States, Glomb found 3% incidence (2002) for reports of physical aggression, and for all countries this is the lowest category of incidence.

The most common category of bullying behavior reported is that of covert nonverbal attack on task, perhaps best exemplified by withholding of information to do the job. This might be through noninclusion in e-mail communication, not being circulated relevant minutes (paper noncommunication), or not being included in formal and informal briefings (verbal noncommunication). We can begin to see why bullying at work has been so hard to identify. These behaviors are all what people do *not* do. As such, they are very difficult to identify and analyze. Equally, such voids are much harder to complain about than tangible behaviors that are inherently offensive or abusive.

Attacks on task can, however, also include active behaviors, such as unreasonable requests as to the quality or quantity of work demanded in the time available. Here we must pause to note that employees seem to be able to distinguish overwork (which most people experience) from this type of bullying demand, which is seen as being different in quality (it is an *unreasonable* attack) (Ishmael, 1999). Included in this area would be micromanagement, in which a person's work is examined repeatedly to the point of undermining the individual's confidence in his or her professional competency. All of these tactics can be completed in reasonable tones and without verbal abuse.

Perhaps the most common stereotype of the bully is the yelling and screaming "tyrant" that Blake Ashforth includes in his 1994 paper on abusive managers. Verbal abuse is also the most common technique that links studies of bullying at work to others such as deviance (Bennett & Robinson, 2000) and uncivil behavior (Andersson & Pearson, 1999). Although easily identifiable by actors and researchers, Rayner and Dick's (2005) analysis of data sets revealed that this was not as common as other bullying behaviors in UK workplaces. A concern is that if this stereotype is used in training and awareness- raising activities, it will present an inaccurate reflection of bullying behaviors employees are likely to experience. Instead, targets of bullying are much more likely to encounter subversive and passive undermining.

A very strong association was found between task attack and personal attack in the Rayner and Dick analysis. It is possible that as someone's work (task) is persistently criticized, the recipient takes this as a personal attack; however, it is common for employees to describe personal criticism that is unwarranted and personally offensive in its own right. Examples might include making comments about someone's physical appearance (e.g., "they called me piggy because I am overweight") or interests outside work ("I had to wash up my mug with a dirty cloth because I supported Manchester United" [a UK soccer team]; UNISON, 1997). It is perhaps within this area of personal attack that commonality with racial and sexual harassment and discrimination can sometimes be found. What is different about bullying is that it can happen to anyone and is rarely personal or about gender or race, per se. If alleged bullies do appear to be racist or sexist, then we would suggest that conventional and specific routes be taken for those individuals in racism and gender training or disciplinary action.

Isolation is an aspect of bullying that has had a continual presence in European and Australian work and is largely absent in North American work, except for that which is focused on bullying (e.g., Jagatic & Keashly, 2000). Isolation is often in the realm of what people do not do rather than what they do. For example, *isolation* would include not being invited to meetings, social events, or other activities that should be inclusive. It might go further into work itself and include being excluded from training or even advancement opportunities. Being ignored is a phenomenon that most people find deeply disturbing, arguably a deep evolutionary trigger for a social species such as man and one that most people will have experienced in childhood (Besag, 1989). The Rayner and Dick (2005) analysis found a strong link between isolation and personal attack—perhaps isolation is hard not to take personally. Isolation might be reported reasonably frequently in surveys, but one can imagine the difficulties a staff member will have in raising it as an issue. Once again, reverberations from childhood experiences might make complaining a shameful (and thus avoided) prospect for employees.

For all of these behaviors, perception will be key. What one of us might find to be personally attacking is not what another would label as such (Painter, 1991). Thus workplace bullying is to some extent in the eye of the beholder. Value judgments are often being made by professionals and demanded by researchers so that individuals who might experience behaviors are asked whether they found these "abusive" or "negative." In a study among education workers, Rayner (1999a) tested whether behaviors did actually "bother" people and indeed discovered that what researchers into bullying have termed "negative" are, in fact, seen as such by respondents (Rayner & Cooper, 2003). In a parallel study, Keashly used the same terminology and confirmed the same result in a U.S. population (Jagatic & Keashly, 2000).

Persistency

During the 1990s, it was stressed that bullying was not a one-off situation but rather behavior that was repeated over a period of time (for a full discussion see Hoel, Rayner, & Cooper, 1999); however, recent years have seen feedback from human resource (HR) and personnel practitioners. Their concern is that if persistency is stressed, then it "disempowers" investigations in which a single event is reported. At the extreme, insisting on persistency gives a perpetrator permission to continue. Contemporary applied definitions now state that serious one-off events may be seen as bullying, or they simply fail to refer to persistency, thus obviating it from inclusion as a parameter.

Persistency has been an important issue for researchers, partly because the politics of an emerging topic often mean that very rigorous (and tough) definitions are used in incidence studies in an attempt to preclude critical commentary. Consequently, in early studies, only respondents who had experienced weekly negative behaviors for many months and labeled themselves as bullied were counted as being bullied (e.g., UNISON, 1997). However, there is also a need to establish common parameters between studies when judging if someone has been bullied; thus measuring persistency does have utility for the academic. Typically, the experience of weekly behaviors in the last 6 months is judged to be bullying in academic studies (Rayner et al., 2002).

Most studies will now have an item list of behaviors and for each item ask the frequency of experience in the last 6 months. Thus anyone who has reported a single behavior weekly would be counted, as would someone who has reported four monthly behaviors, and so on (Rayner & Dick, 2005).

When comparing studies, it is always worth examining carefully the parameters of persistency actually used. In some studies, behaviors that occur at a rate of less than once weekly are used, as otherwise the researchers will not have sufficiently large subsamples of "bullied" for further analysis. In addition, some early studies (including the LIPT) asked respondents to check against behaviors (in a simple yes or no fashion) before asking how often they had experienced these behaviors *overall* (e.g., Leymann, 1996). Clearly, this crude assessment does not provide any delineating information about the behaviors themselves and differences between them.

Finally, some studies use item frequencies that are termed very loosely, such as "now and then." We would argue that, although respondents' memories maybe inaccurate representations of reality, there would be a stronger convergence with concrete, time-bound constructs such as "weekly" and "monthly" rather than the vaguer terms like "every so often," in which an extra layer of interpretation is needed on the respondents' parts.

As the field becomes better established, we suspect that interest in this aspect of measurement will change. In the United Kingdom, less and less interest is shown in the parameter of persistency by practitioners, except as it contributes to estimates of incidence of bullying at work (which is of great importance). The exception is physical abuse, which, understandably, most organization-based staff are anxious to see at zero for health and safety reasons. As programs of intervention and prevention begin, however, practitioners would be well advised to attend to this aspect of measurement. We would expect differences in *patterns* of frequency of behaviors to be shown over time as an intervention program takes effect. We have so little data connected to achievement of intervention and prevention programs that we cannot suggest how those patterns might emerge and develop, but it is an exciting and worthwhile area for future research.

Labeling

Whether or not someone should label themselves bullied against a definition in order to be counted as bullied has also seen some discussion (see Rayner et al., 2002, for a review). This has been a point of contention between practitioners and researchers in the large U.S. study into sexual harassment in the military (Munson, Miner, & Hulin, 2001), in which there was contention about "counting" and paying attention to those who did not label themselves as sexually harassed. One can see this point from the practitioner's perspective, who may only be concerned with those who do label themselves. Indeed, the same might be said for bullying at work: Why should a practitioner be concerned if people are experiencing negative behaviors but not labeling themselves as bullied?

There are two arguments to be made for considering those who not label themselves. As will be seen in section two of this chapter, people who experience bullying behaviors suffer negative health consequences (Hoel, Faragher, & Cooper, 2004), regardless of whether or not they label themselves. Of concern is that witnesses are also affected (Hoel et al., 2004). As bullying at work falls within health and safety remits (the employer has a duty of care to provide an environment that is both physically and psychologically safe), this finding militates against using labeling because damage is likely to be experienced regardless. Second, we would suggest that those who experience but do not label today are likely to label tomorrow or at some stage in the future; time and persistency often enable individuals to make sense of their situation and call it bullying (Adams, 1992).

Examination of some data from a UK study shows how the patterns actually fall in real numbers (Rayner, 1999b). This conference paper compared two methods for counting bullying: Leymann's method, in which he counted those who had weekly behaviors but did not use the label *bullying* (Leymann, 1996), and the method employed by Einarsen et al. (1994), which considered a label as important but used much looser time frequencies. The data collected by Rayner for UNISON (the largest trade union in the United Kingdom servicing public sector workers, usually nonmanagerial) enabled a comparison of the two methods (UNISON, 1997). Table 7.1 shows the number of people labeling themselves as being bullied on the vertical axis and the frequency of behaviors they experienced on the horizontal axis. Maximum frequency of behaviors experienced is shown against respondents labeling themselves as bullied or not ($N = 737$) (Rayner, 1999b).

Leymann (1990) would ignore the yes/no label but be concerned with frequency, counting those in cells *Bullied "Yes"* and *"No"* on at least a weekly basis (i.e., $103 + 111 = 214$). The Einarsen et al. (1994) method uses only those on the *Bullied "Yes"* line but would include all frequencies to

Table 7.1

Experience of Behaviors	Daily and Weekly	Every Month	Less Than Monthly	Never
Bullied? "Yes"	103	18	14	4
Bullied? "No"	111	79	160	248

provide a total of 135 (103 + 18 + 14). "Not only are the numbers different, but *so are the people* included in the sets" (Rayner, 1999b, p. 88). This illustration demonstrates to any researcher and practitioner the importance of ensuring commonalities in measuring regimes.

Other Definitional Aspects

Intention of the bully has long been disregarded as a definitional and measurable parameter. Obviously, if intent to bully is included as a definitional parameter and the bully denies intent, then the definition is not met and no bullying would have taken place. One must ask which bullies would not deny!

Another aspect that has become of minor importance is a parameter that was originally used to differentiate bullying at work from conflict at work: *conflict* is between those of equal power and *bullying* is between those of unequal power (Leymann, 1996). We would suggest that this distinction is now beyond usefulness, serving to provide artificial boundaries between two topics that are surely entwined, with many parallels and a great deal to offer each other. We know of no studies into bullying in which the target felt as powerful as his or her "apparent" abuser; however, stories of targets being negative to their abusers are present in the literature, as are stories of revenge (e.g., Adams, 1992).

Summary of Definitional Parameters

Bullying involves a wide range of behaviors. Those who have conducted studies in this area have restricted their study to the behaviors that people experience, as opposed to behaviors that they do themselves; however, it is the range of behaviors that bullying at work encompasses that makes this area of study unique. They may be undertaken in an overt or covert way (and often it is covert), verbal or nonverbal (verbal abuse being less likely), and physically or nonphysically aggressive (with physical aggression being very rare), as shown by Keashly and Jagatic's (2003) review of bullying attacks. In terms of what is attacked, the task is the most common focus, as reported by targets (e.g., Zapf et al., 1996). Personal attacks are also common; isolation and verbal attacks are less common; and physical abuse is rarely reported.

For practitioners at work, the point that bullying affects the mental health of people, regardless of whether or not they label themselves as bullied, has meant that labeling tends to be ignored rather than used as part of definitions, given that the behaviors are present. Similarly, the intent of the bully and the imbalance of power between the parties have now been dropped from definitions used in workplaces. Thus occupational parameters have contracted in recent years to being connected to the experience of behaviors that can be construed as bullying (Rayner & Keashly, 2005).

Other professionals need more tangible aspects to be present, and these depend on their needs. Lawyers would require someone to have experienced damage as a direct result of bullying. Academic researchers have also employed a variety of definitions for measurement when conducting incidence surveys, and these are connected to measurement (see below).

The previous discussion demonstrates a recent evolution in definition in those countries where bullying as a phenomenon is accepted as a negative aspect of work to be addressed, such as the United Kingdom. Workplace practitioners have mediated the more stringent operational definitions from both lawyers and academics. We see this as a healthy product of an ongoing debate in those countries, and although well worth keeping abreast of, we would not anticipate many further changes in the future.

Summary of Measurement Parameters

The previous discussion on definitions examined the issue of measurement, and this section will provide a summary only. As definitions revolve around them, the experience of negative behaviors at work is at the center of studies into bullying at work. The investigation of a wide range of behaviors is fundamental to effective study. Frequency of experience is measured, but increasingly as a way to understand how the patterns coalesce rather than as a definitional parameter in itself. That said, for academic purposes, the simplest form of measurement is to count any respondent who reports behaviors experienced (either as an individual or as a member of a group) that average a weekly experience for the last 6 months as *bullied* from an incidence point of view.

To date, very little work that examines organizational bullying has been undertaken. Often, as in this section, it is an irritant left flapping in the breeze; however, as every qualitative study in the area has shown (e.g., Harlos & Pinder, 1999; Liefooghe & Mackenzie Davey, 2001), people do feel bullied by organizational measures. Both Leymann (e.g., Leymann, 1996) and Brodsky (1976) also deal with this in a descriptive pattern, but neither has presented an operational typology for use in contemporary workplaces. This represents an area for further investigation and one that will challenge the most adroit employer. Examples from the aforementioned studies would include appraisal systems that completely fail to appraise, justice systems that do not (in the eyes of their users) deliver justice, and promotion and reward systems that are systematically kept out of reach of employees.

A developing area for U.S. researchers is that of negative behavior toward the organization (e.g., Andersson & Pearson, 1999; Bennett & Robinson, 2000). These studies and their accompanying analysis may be of great assistance in the field of bullying at work, as they work from the perpetrator perspective. No doubt, as this area develops, considerable light might be shed on the full dimensions of bullying at work, including negative organizational behavior.

Multiple Realities of Workplace Bullying

In common with forensic situations, which are also complex, differing versions of events are construed by different actors involved in the process. Practitioners and researchers undertaking case investigations are likely to expose a variety of "stories" in which people have perceived differently, interpreted differently, and, as a result, report the same incident in various ways. Attribution theory has been invoked to explain this (e.g., Hoel et al., 1999). In a study on reports of "angry" situations, Baumeister, Stillwell, and Wotman (1990) found that actors reporting on situations when they were perpetrators of the anger provided commentary that was very different from that of the same people reporting on situations when they were recipients of the anger. The scant data available for workplace settings all point to the potential for very different views of incidents.

Einarsen considers bullying to be a spiral of conflict (Einarsen, 1999). Excepting the single events, most practitioners would probably agree with this (e.g., Ishmael, 1999). Adams (1992) details many cases of bullying in which she describes a series of events that build on one another, which fits Einarsen's spiral notion very well. Of very current interest is the potential link that can be made to studies on revenge and incivility (e.g., Andersson & Pearson, 1999). In these studies, people describe how they "get back" at others through overt and covert means, which effectively winds the spiral up.

Section Two: Overview of Key
_____ Findings in the Study of Bullying at Work

Prevalence of Bullying at Work

In the United Kingdom, between 10 and 20% of employees will label themselves as bullied for the last 6 months (e.g., Hoel et al., 2004; Lewis, 1999; Quine, 1999; UNISON, 1997, 2000). Incidence measured in this way (labeling) in the Scandinavian countries is less than half this number (Zapf, Einarsen, Hoel, & Vartia, 2003, have useful tables: pp. 105–108). Studies in Australia have findings similar to those done in the United Kingdom (e.g., McCarthy et al., 1995). In the United States, there is not an acceptance of the term *bullying*, and thus Keashly, for example, has used the term *mistreated* and found slightly higher incidence (Keashly & Jagatic, 2003) than in the United Kingdom.

If one uses just the experience of weekly behaviors to identify targets of bullying, then incidence doubles in the United Kingdom and Australia, with similar but less strong effects in Scandinavia (e.g., McCarthy et al., 1995; UNISON, 2000; Zapf et al., 2003). Why only half those who experience weekly negative behaviors also label themselves bullied is not known. It is possible that those who experience negative interpersonal behaviors but do not label have yet to make sense of their situation: Often targets initially blame themselves (Adams, 1992; Brodsky, 1976). They may, of course, genuinely not feel *bullied,* according to their own understanding of the word. As will be seen in the sections on outcomes that follow, regardless of whether or not people label, their health is likely to be affected (Hoel et al., 2004).

Who Is Bullied?

In all countries studied, the striking aspect is the absence of data from which to form a profile of targets from a demographic point of view. Differences are unlikely to be found in terms of age, gender, length of employment, or position in the hierarchy (e.g., Hoel & Cooper, 2000, described in Rayner et al., 2002). That is not to say that demographic factors may not be useful in research; for example, it is possible that a young worker might be bullied for reasons different from those of someone approaching retirement; however, overall incidence is rarely informed by demographic differences.

Coyne, Seigne, and Randall (2000) used a paired-sample approach for bullied and nonbullied within the same organization in an attempt to profile targets. Their pairs, matched on gender, age, and home-life situation, among other variables, were then tested for personality differences. They did find significant differences between the bullied and nonbullied groups on their personality scores, with a profile for the targets emerging similar to "victim" studies in forensic science; however, as this work was undertaken after the bulling events, we would suggest a very cautious approach toward the predictive value of such profiling.

Who Bullies?

In the United Kingdom and Australia, it would appear that many people are bullied by someone in authority above them, often their boss. The UNISON studies (1997, 2000) found that 80% of bullying was hierarchical. In contrast, Scandinavian studies have found that this figure is only 50% for authority figures. In all instances, the vast majority of the remainder is accounted for by peer bullying. "Upwards" bullying, in which the boss is bullied by subordinates, is very seldom reported. Recent data from a large study in the Veterans Administration (2005) in the United States found the sources of aggression were coworkers (44%) and supervisors (35%), with supervisors more likely to engage in passive forms of aggression; but stress was reported as being mainly connected to aggression from bosses.

We therefore have a reasonable grasp of who are the reported bullies in interpersonal bullying; however, it is a very tricky issue when individuals feel bullied by their organization. A maxim used in HR management is "Organizations don't do things; people do." However, when one turns to cases of organizational bullying, this becomes a difficult argument to pursue.

Liefooghe and Mackenzie Davey (2001) reported on call center staff who felt bullied. In one instance, the failure to finish calls within the specified time meant that employees were precluded from overtime opportunities. The staff wanted to provide more time to callers in order to be able to solve their problems and found difficulty in reconciling their concern for callers with their own desires for overtime, which would require ending the call on some pretext or passing the caller on in order to comply with "the statistics."

The staff did not hold supervisors responsible for "the system," as they understood the decisions regarding working rules had been made elsewhere. But where exactly? The study implied that the system had been in place for some time and that the operators' problems with it had not been addressed. Many staff would have been approached, such as line management, personnel, union representatives, and health and safety professionals. Nebulous and undefined responsibility is likely to result in unresolved complaints in which everyone but no one is responsible. One can understand why these staff felt bullied by the organization (Rayner, 1999c).

Why Do People Bully?

We will return to interpersonal bullying in order to understand the reasons people bully, and there are likely to be many. Those who run charities to assist targets of bullying (such as the Andrea Adams Trust in the United Kingdom) find that the overwhelming number of their clients claim that bullying occurs because they are too good at their job and they think that they threaten the bully (usually their boss). In addition, these people are often singled out and victimized as individuals.

Surveys have shown repeatedly that in the United Kingdom and Australia, 15% to 20% of bullied respondents report being bullied on their own, with the rest bullied alongside coworkers. In roughly one third of situations, the whole work-group is bullied (UNISON, 2000). This allows us to see that those who use help lines are from a minority group of targets. It may be the case that the users of the charities are correct in their judgment; however, it also highlights the problems of studies constantly working with data from a single source not corroborated by third parties.

Predatory and Dispute-Related Bullying

Einarsen (1999) has postulated that there are two broad categories of bullying with concomitant motivations and patterns. The first, *predatory bullying*, focuses on the bully, who might be an individual or a group of people who appear to single out people for consistent focus of attention (see Zapf et al., 2003, p. 114, for a review of Scandinavian studies). There may be no apparent reason for this, or it may link into other prejudicial reasons, such as hostility to a particular group (e.g., gay, single parent, race, social class) of which the target is a member (Allport, 1954). Whatever the target may do in terms of attempts to defuse or de-escalate the situation, the bullying will continue. As the name suggests, the bully (or bullies) are out to get the target. Einarsen (1999) suggests these situations are not particularly common.

In contrast, he sees the other category, *dispute bullying,* as much more common. This is when the bully or bullies and the target get into a spiral of conflict, with each party annoying the other and (in each of their eyes) provoking ever more drastic measures against each other. Zapf and Gross (2001) found the concept useful in their analysis of qualitative data from in-depth interviews with targets. This analysis finds resonance from John Sutton's study of schoolchildren bullying, in which he found many children engaged as both target and bully but also many who had nothing to do with bullying at all (Sutton, 1998). These he described as "involved" or "not-involved," and this could be a useful concept to bring into the adult domain. Possibly those who are not involved will be able to avoid dispute-related bullying (but will not be able to avoid predatory bullying), whereas those who are involved would be fodder for predatory bullying, engaging and remonstrating as an active member of the spiral.

The delineation between dispute bullying and regular workplace conflict is difficult to identify, and several authors have attempted to draw this line (e.g., Einarsen et al., 2003). Clearly, the two fields overlap, but *all* bullying should not be seen as contained within the academic tradition of conflict, and much in conflict studies will not be applicable in this area. Texts such as this volume can help us understand how topics overlap rather than provide the specification for turf wars between older and newer academic areas of study. In this way, one might be able to use concepts present in the conflict literature (e.g., Zapf & Gross, 2001) to understand bullying.

Theories of Social Dynamics

Equally, it is possible for us to invoke in-group or out-group concepts to attempt to explain situations in which the target appears to be simply the wrong person in the wrong place at the wrong time (e.g., Tajfel & Turner, 2001). This might be especially the case when someone is bullied by more than one person. One can link across to well-established areas of research that include mechanisms for in-group and out-group establishment, such as social identity theory and self-categorization theory. Within these concepts, bullying is part of the process of establishing dominance of a particular set of group norms (Tajfel & Turner, 2001).

The Role of the Organization

Clearly, there is also a role for the organization in explaining why people bully. From Brodsky onward, many writers have commented on the role of the organization in contributing to allowing people to bully. One aspect is to think of the organization as giving permission in a positive sense (e.g., Brodsky, 1976) or, through its apparent inaction, supporting the belief that bullying will not be tackled (e.g., Rayner, 1999c).

Bullying can also be seen as a symptom of other organizationwide problems (Rayner, 2000). Here the underlying organizational causes could be quite different. For example, it might be lack of control (when the bullies are unchecked) or overcontrol (when the stresses and tensions build up to a pressure cooker; Crawford, 1999) so that bullying is one blow-off point. When incidence is high and across the organizational spectrum, such organization-wide analysis might be very effective. Rather like the discrimination issue cited earlier, direct action against bullying might not be the most effective intervention, but looking at the underlying cause (to tighten or loosen control mechanisms) might be more appropriate.

The Unthinking Worker?

Simpler explanations can be derived from staff not knowing the effect of their actions and bullying from ignorance and low social skills. According to Richards and Daley (2003) some people may still bully unintentionally. If staff are either surrounded by others who fail to give them feedback (as may be especially true for those in high positions) or are in an environment where bullying is acceptable, they might not see their actions as anything other than normal. These situations (in which someone acts without much conscious thought) remain largely unrecorded and lack direct research, but probably all readers can think of a situation when this has been the case. One suggestion for academic links in this situation would be the "Johari window," which has recently been adapted beyond its original use (Drejer, 2000) for use at individual, group, and organizational levels. One might think that bullying behavior is in the window "unknown to self" for these individuals.

Units and Levels of Analysis

In understanding what causes bullying, one needs to work through at what level this should be dealt with, rather like deciding whether there is a bad apple or a bad barrel. Bad apples would involve understanding (and then dealing with) people who are bullies through conscious or unconscious mechanisms. Rarely do studies focus on the bully, and this is a clear area for future activity. The few that do (e.g., Rayner & Cooper, 2003) have no clear evidence to assist profiling. In itself, this suggests multiple reasons and complexity at all stages. Group bullying is likely to be best understood at that level and invoke explanations around group affirmation. Finally, the organization level would be appropriate to use if bullying is rife in any organization.

Considerable scope exists for seeing bullying as a symptom of other problems rather than a problem in itself (Rayner, 2000) with many potential patterns and forms. The forms will be present in other literature, and one needs to identify carefully such situations and examine the overlap. Bullying is an area that is rich in providing potential confluence of thinking with other areas of study in the field of behavior at work.

Outcomes of Bullying for the Target

The main effect for targets is a negative impact on their psychological health. At the extreme, bullying can lead to complete breakdown with symptoms that are akin to posttraumatic stress disorder (PTSD). Leymann and Gustafsson (1996) found over 50% of targets who attended a rehabilitation clinic in Sweden ($n = 64$) could be diagnosed as having PTSD. Several studies have been conducted with severely bullied targets, and their findings can be found summarized in Einarsen and Mikkelsen (2003).

Damage is not restricted to those who report a traumatic experience leading to a full breakdown. Important findings from a large UK study by Hoel and Cooper (2000, cited in Rayner et al., 2002) among a cross section of workers found that regardless of whether or not employees labeled themselves as bullied, those who reported exposure to weekly negative behaviors had a significantly worse mental health profile than those who were not. Furthermore, even those who were witnesses also reported negative mental health effects (a full analysis can be found in Hoel et al., 2004).

These findings provide a strong argument for tackling bullying on health and safety grounds. In most countries, the employer has a legal duty of care to protect employees from both physical and psychological harm. With an emphasis on "protect," there is an implication that the employer should be taking preventative measures, as well as dealing with bullying once it arises (intervention measures).

Outcomes of Bullying for the Organization

Many staff chose to leave their jobs as a reaction to being bullied (around 25% of targets in the United Kingdom: Rayner, 1998; Hoel & Cooper, 2000, cited in Rayner et al., 2002), presenting an overwhelming cost argument for employers to act in this area (Rayner, 1999c). In addition, over 20% of witnesses reported in UK studies decided to leave (Rayner et al., 2002). With skills shortages in most Western economies, the drain of staff can be argued to go beyond the cost of replacement, as shortages reported in skilled occupations might affect the strategic position of the firm (Pfeffer, 1998).

Two qualitative studies with targets of bullying (Niedl, 1996; Zapf & Gross, 2001) have investigated targets' actions and deconstructed the "story" of multiple-event bullying. Both these studies have found the EVLN model effective (Withy & Cooper, 1989), in which four strategies to cope with negative experiences at work are identified. These strategies are *exit* (quitting), *voice* (voicing discontent), *loyalty* (working harder), and *neglect* (just sticking to the job one is supposed to do). Although individuals vary somewhat, the general pattern is that of loyalty, followed by voice, then neglect, and finally exit.

Employees who engage in neglect are a problem for employers (Crabb, 1995). Several studies (e.g., Quine, 1999) have found decrease in motivation and job satisfaction in targets of bullying, which fits alongside neglect. Patterns of neglect that are found in reports from targets of bullying at work fit with another established area of research, psychological contract violation (Rousseau, 1995).

These findings are of concern for those trying to build a positive culture in their organization (Rayner et al., 2002). Disengagement and psychological withdrawal from work are unlikely to provide support for a high-performance workforce (Pfeffer, 1998).

A further link exists to literature that would affect the employer, and that might be termed "retaliation," "retribution," or "revenge" (e.g., Aquino et al., 2001). Although we might (correctly) surmise that neglect sits well alongside these notions, we tend to think of it as it is described in the EVLN model, as a passive mode on the part of employees.

There may, however, be more assertive aspects to targets' revenge behavior that might be of concern for employers. Bennett and Robinson's (2000) study of deviant workplace behavior found a surprising number of U.S. employees willing to take negative action against their employer ranging from overclaiming on travel expenses to destruction of property. An interesting participant-observer study by Analoui (1992) found patterns of theft and pilferage (management stealing) and a retribution subculture in a London nightclub during a 5-year study period. There is a remarkable description of the employees setting fire to a small area for amusement and then not putting it out or calling the emergency services until the fire had grown to such a proportion that a major incident was under way, resulting in the closing of the club and refurbishment.

We suggest that the EVLN model requires amendment to incorporate the active side of revenge and present it as shown in Figure 7.1, depicting *Exit* outside the box and leaving space for active negative action against the organization.

It is of note that in all studies of bullying in which the EVLN model has been used to describe targets' responses to being bullied, those responses begin in the right side (the pro-organization side) of the model and then progress to the left side. What causes this progression? It is likely that a

	Anti-organization (Exit)	Pro-organization
Active (Exit)	Retribution	Voice
Passive	Neglect	Loyalty

Figure 7.1   The Amended EVLN Model: The REVLN Model

principal component is a lowering of trust in the organization. Trust is acknowledged as a fundamental tenet of all relationships (Giacalone & Greenberg, 1997). When asked why bullying occurs, over 90% of all respondents to two large UK surveys agreed with the statements, "Bullies can get away with it" and "Workers are too scared to report it" (UNISON, 1997, 2000).

Trust from employees in the organization to act positively and deal with bullying at work is often low, and for this we draw on three main aspects of research. First, in qualitative studies, all respondents report they have "voiced" to someone. Second, the most common perceived response to that action is "nothing" (Rayner, 1999c). Third, the very high exit rates as a result of bullying imply this drastic action is taken by employees as a response to something deeply disturbing. This, we would suggest, is a destruction of the psychological contract and an irreconcilable breakdown in the relationship. We suggest that destruction of trust is the key variable (Elangovan & Shapiro, 1998) and further that unless action is effective, ineffective action leads to further distrust, and the organization becomes a negative actor (Rayner, 1999c).

Section Three: Dealing With Bullying in the Workplace

Creating the Agenda

The effects on the organization should create a sufficiently strong impetus for organizations to act (Archer, 1999). In addition, the distress experienced by many who are the targets can be a motivator for action (Tehrani, 2003). Finally, the threat of legal action under health and safety or other law, with uncomfortable publicity for the organization, can add impetus for not avoiding the problem. In taking action, the organization should undertake a risk analysis to consider the causes of bullying in their circumstances and at what level they wish to tackle bullying: individual, group, or organization. We would suggest that any strategy employ all three levels.

Putting Bullying on the Organizational Map

A first step must be to make a declaration that bullying is not an acceptable form of behavior. This is likely to be a two-step process: first, decide the definition of *bullying*. Second, create and consistently publicize a statement or policy about it. Focusing on the behaviors is helpful as it makes the message easier to deliver and receive. One can think what one likes, but behavior is only acceptable within a range of actions.

Anecdotal data points to consultation as the most effective process to establishing the definition of *bullying* (Richards & Daley, 2003). Engaging unions and worker-representatives from across the board in this process provides support for the policy and its future implementation. It is likely that those in positions of authority need help to be able to scope the issue from many points of view, and this should be entered into as a two-way process rather than as a politically correct exercise. Some organizations have problems defining what should not be done (i.e., antibullying policies) and instead draw up policies that state what should happen. These are called dignity-at-work statements in the United Kingdom (Rayner & Keashly, 2005).

Policies need to (a) state what will happen if an accusation of bullying is made, (b) stress the use of informal processes, but then (c) outline formal investigation processes with timelines such as those that one would find in normal disciplinary codes. It is crucial that bullying can be a dismissal offense (sometimes termed "gross misconduct") so that individuals can be fired if the situation is sufficiently serious. Employers are also cautioned to provide support and counseling for those accused of bullying as otherwise they may be open to counterclaim at a later stage (Tehrani, 2003).

Hearing About Bullying

As mentioned previously, targets of bullying, when interviewed, invariably claim they have told someone about their situation. Thus one first step is for organizations to sharpen up their hearing. Training managers to become sensitized to the atmosphere in their departments is ideal. Bullying promotes a climate of fear (Adams, 1992), and employees are often unwilling to take risks, such as making suggestions or being critical of the status quo. Exit rates are a strong indicator (when alternative employment can be found), so hearing should be especially sharp in departments where there is evidence of high levels of staff turnover.

Having Systems to Deal With It

Having heard about bullying (or being concerned it might be occurring), managers and staff representatives need to act as quickly as possible to defuse situations before they escalate. We would stress the need for informal action to be effective and fast to achieve the best results so that behavior is changed and the target(s) and witnesses experience low levels of damage and can return to business as usual.

In the case of unconscious bullying, this will invariably involve a third party intervening and telling the bully (or group of bullies) that their behavior is outside of acceptability and having a damaging effect. Apologies would be ideal, but most targets simply want to achieve a positive working environment and keep their jobs.

If dispute-related bullying is going on, the need for early and informal intervention is paramount so that escalation of the conflict can be avoided. Mediation might be possible if action is taken early enough (Vartia, Korppoo, Fallenius, & Mattila, 2003).

Predatory bullying will require a focus on the bully or bullies. In this instance, there is likely to be a history of similar instances, and these could be used to inform the situation of specific patterns and behaviors that are typical. As with unconscious bullying, clarity will need to be given on what is required in terms of either the behavior they should not do (where this is clear) or behavior they are required to do (such as treating all staff equally and with dignity and respect).

Where there is an embedded systematic climate of bullying and the behavior has been tacitly or otherwise accepted, interventions are likely to be painful for those taking actions while new standards of behavior are outlined and enforced. It is likely in these circumstances that firing staff might be needed before anyone takes the new conduct code seriously.

If acceptability extends wider than the organization to the whole industry or society (Marais-Steinman, 2003), then those making interventions will need to have very strong leadership and be prepared for a long battle. Examples of industrywide acceptability can be found in the catering industry and the media. Both reflect high time pressures and high costs of failure to meet deadlines, and typically have easily replaced staff. These three factors we see as constituting the key risk factors at the industry level.

Zero Tolerance

To achieve prevention, then, zero tolerance is crucial. We do not know of any organization that has achieved this; therefore, our understanding of this is theoretical only. We suspect that in a zero-tolerance environment, incidents that might become bullying can be openly discussed and behavior trimmed before it causes any of the damage we typically associate with targets.

Organizational Bullying

Organizational bullying has received little recent attention and is perhaps our current challenge, an area likely to resurrect academic thinking such as labor process theory and many aspects of employment relations (Legge, 2005). Our only awareness of this aspect of workplace bullying currently comes from targets' descriptions of what they experience as negative behavior at work, and considerably more academic research needs to be done to open up this area to typologies and effective action.

Summary

The last 10 years have seen a remarkable growth in the study of bullying at work. We are now able to describe interpersonal bullying well and are currently working to understand and model the process so that we can comprehend how to intervene. Evidence collected in many countries shows that this is an aspect of working life that is present in all societies studied, although incidence varies between countries (Zapf et al., 2003).

That bullying at work has a negative effect on targets and witnesses to incidents is well established. The effects are seen in the mental health, the anxiety levels, and the motivation and propensity to leave of both targets (e.g., Quine, 1999) and witnesses (e.g., Hoel et al., 2004). Staff leaving because they experience bullying or witness it can cause profound damage to organizations (Rayner, 1999c).

Over these years, we have become clearer about the behaviors that are involved in bullying at work, and these can be described in terms of how negative behavior is (e.g., Keashly & Jagatic, 2003) to what is attacked. Bullying involves a wide range of behaviors of which verbal abuse is only one. Often bullying is passive, for example withholding information and excluding staff in some way. These passive acts present a challenge for researchers for modeling and measurement. Also, because a target of workplace bullying experiences a range of different behaviors, research that focuses on single types of behavior will have limited contribution. We suspect that, as in other areas of conflict (e.g., Van de Vliert, Euwema, & Huismans, 1995), it is the conglomerate behavior that is important.

Successful interventions are coming to light and include the need for clear policy and process for dealing with incidents. Prevention means a major emphasis on informal methods of scanning the environment and taking action as early as possible in the interests of the organization.

Without doubt, our understanding of this topic has only just started. We welcome the involvement of academics from other disciplines so that together we can achieve a conglomerate of knowledge; however, we warn that researchers who deal only with the single slice of bullying at work (and often this is a realistic path to take) should keep in mind the bigger picture and moderate their claims accordingly. The future holds great promise for this most worthwhile area of research.

References

Adams, A. (1992). *Bullying at work: How to confront and overcome it.* London: Virago.

Allport, G. (1954). *The nature of prejudice.* Reading, MA: Addison Wesley.

Analoui, F. (1992). Unconventional practices at work. *Journal of Managerial Psychology, 7*(5), 3–31.

Andersson, L. M., & Pearson, C. M. (1999). Tit for tat? The spiraling effect of incivility in the workplace. *Academy of Management Review, 24,* 452–471.

Aquino, K., Tripp, T., & Bies, R. J. (2001). How employees respond to personal offense: The effects of blame attribution, victim status, and offender status on revenge and reconciliation in the workplace. *Journal of Applied Psychology, 86*(1), 52–59.

Archer, D. (1999). Exploring "bullying" culture in the para-military organization. *International Journal of Manpower, 20*(1/2), 94–105.

Ashforth, B. (1994). Petty tyranny in organizations. *Human Relations, 47,* 755–778.

Baron, R. A., & Neuman, J. H. (1996). Workplace violence and workplace aggression: Evidence on their relative frequency and potential causes. *Aggressive Behavior, 22,* 161–173.

Bassman, E. (1992). *Abuse in the workplace.* New York: Quorum.

Baumeister, R. F., Smart, L., & Boden, J. M. (1996). Relation of threatened egotism to violence and aggression: The dark side of self esteem. *Psychological Review, 103*(1), 5–33.

Baumeister, R. F., Stillwell, A., & Wotman, S. R. (1990). Victim and perpetrator accounts of interpersonal conflict: Autobiographical narratives about anger. *Journal of Personality and Social Psychology, 59*(5), 994–1005.

Bennett, R. J., & Robinson, S. L. (2000). Development of a measure of workplace deviance. *Journal of Applied Psychology, 85*(3), 349–360.

Bernstein, J. Y., & Watson, M. W. (1997). Children who are targets of bullying: A victim pattern. *Journal of Interpersonal Violence, 12*(4), 483–498.

Besag, V. (1989). *Bullies and victims in schools.* Philadelphia: Open University Press.

Bjorkqvist, K., Osterman, K., & Hjelt-Back, M. (1994). Aggression among university employees. *Aggressive Behavior, 20,* 173–184.

Brodsky, C. M., (1976). *The harassed worker.* Toronto: Lexington Books/D.C. Heath.

Burk, F. L. (1897, April). Teasing and bullying. *Pedagogical Seminary, 4,* 336–371.

Buss, A. H. (1961). *The psychology of aggression.* New York: Wiley.

Christie, R., & Geiss, F. L. (1970). *Studies in Machiavellianism.* New York: Academic.

Coyne, I., Seigne, E., & Randall, P. (2000) Predicting workplace victim status from personality. *European Journal of Work and Organizational Psychology, 9,* 385–392.

Crabb, S. (1995, July). Violence at work: The brutal truths. *People Management, 27,* 25–27.

Crawford, N. (1999). Conundrums and confusion in organizations: The etymology of the word "bully." *International Journal of Manpower, 20*(1/2), 86–93.

Drejer, A. (2000). Organizational learning and competence development. *Learning Organization, 7*(4), 206–220.

Einarsen, S. (1999). The nature and causes of bullying at work. *International Journal of Manpower, 20*(1/2), 16–27.

Einarsen, S. (2000). Harassment and bullying at work: A review of the Scandinavian approach. *Aggression and Violent Behavior, 4,* 371–401.

Einarsen, S., Hoel, H., Zapf, D., & Cooper, C. (2003). The concept of bullying at work. In S. Einarsen, H. Hoel, D. Zapf, & C. Cooper (Eds.), *Bullying and emotional abuse in the workplace: International research and practice perspectives* (pp. 3–30). London: Taylor Francis.

Einarsen, S., & Mikkelsen, E. G. (2003). Individual effects of exposure to bullying at work. In S. Einarsen, H. Hoel, D. Zapf, & C. Cooper (Eds.), *Bullying and emotional abuse in the workplace: International research and practice perspectives* (pp. 127–144). London: Taylor Francis.

Einarsen, S., & Raknes, B. I. (1995, July). *Harassment in the workplace and the victimization of men.* Paper presented to the 7th European Congress of Work and Organizational Psychology, Tampere, Finland.

Einarsen, S., Raknes, B. I., & Matthiesen, S. B. (1994). Bullying and harassment at work and its relationship with work environment quality: An exploratory study. *European Work and Organizational Psychologist, 4,* 381–401.

Einarsen, S., & Skogstad, A. (1996). Bullying at work: Epidemiological findings in public and private organizations. *European Journal of Work and Organizational Psychology, 5*, 185–202.

Elangovan, A. R., & Shapiro, D. L. (1998). Betrayal of trust in organizations. *Academy of Management Review, 23*, 547–566.

Giacalone, R., & Greenberg, J. (Eds.). (1997). *Antisocial behavior in organizations.* Thousand Oaks, CA: Sage.

Glomb, T. M. (2002). Workplace aggression: Informing conceptual models with data from specific encounters. *Journal of Occupational Health Psychology, 7*(1), 20–36.

Harlos, K., & Pinder, C. C. (1999). Patterns of organizational injustice: A taxonomy of what employees regard as unjust. *Qualitative Organizational Research, 2*, 97–125.

Hoel, H., Faragher, B., & Cooper, C. L. (2004). Bullying is detrimental to health, but all bullying behaviors and not necessarily equally damaging. *British Journal of Guidance and Counselling, 32*, 367–387.

Hoel, H., Rayner, C., & Cooper, C. L. (1999). Workplace bullying. *International Review of Industrial and Organizational Psychology, 14*, 189–230.

Ishmael, A., (1999). *Bullying and harassment at work: A practical guide to combating employee abuse.* London: Industrial Society.

Jagatic, K., & Keashly, L. (2000, August). *The nature, extent, and impact of emotional abuse in the workplace: Results of a statewide survey.* Paper presented at the Academy of Management Conference, Toronto, Canada.

Keashly, L. (1998). Emotional abuse in the workplace: Conceptual and empirical issues. *Journal of Emotional Abuse, 1*(1), 85–117.

Keashly, L., & Jagatic, K. (2003). By any other name: American perspectives on workplace bullying. In S. Einarsen, H. Hoel, D. Zapf, & C. Cooper (Eds.), *Bullying and emotional abuse in the workplace: International research and practice perspectives* (pp. 31–61). London: Taylor Francis.

Legge, K. (2005). *Human resource management: Rhetorics and realities* (Anniversary ed.). Basingstoke, UK: Palgrave MacMillan.

Lewis, D. (1999). Workplace bullying: Interim findings of a study in further and higher education in Wales. *International Journal of Manpower, 20*(1/2), 106–118.

Leymann, H. (1990). Mobbing and psychological terror at workplaces. *Violence and Victims, 5*, 119–125.

Leymann, H. (1996). The content and development of mobbing at work. *European Journal of Work and Organizational Psychology, 5*(2), 165–184.

Leymann, H., & Gustafsson, A. (1996). Mobbing at work and the development of port-traumatic stress disorders. *European Journal of Work and Organizational Psychology, 5*, 251–275.

Liefooghe, A. P. D., & Mackenzie Davey, K. (2001). Accounts of workplace bullying: The role of the organization. *European Journal of Work and Organizational Psychology, 10*(4), 375–393.

Marais-Steinman, S. (2003). Challenging workplace bullying in a developing country. In S. Einarsen, H. Hoel, D. Zapf, & C. Cooper (Eds.), *Bullying and emotional abuse in the workplace: International research and practice perspectives* (pp. 312–323). London: Taylor Francis.

McCarthy, P., Sheehan, M., & Kearns, D. (1995). Managerial styles and their effects on employees. *Health and well-being in organizations undergoing restructuring: Report for worksafe Australia.* Brisbane: Griffith University.

Munson, L. J., Miner, A. G., & Hulin, C. (2001). Labeling and sexual harassment in the military: An extension and replication. *Journal of Applied Psychology, 86*(2), 293–303.

Niedl, K. (1996). Mobbing and wellbeing: Economic and personnel development implications. *European Journal of Work and Organizational Psychology, 5*(2), 239–249.

Olweus, D. (1983). *Bullying at school: What we know and what we can do.* Oxford, UK: Blackwell.

Painter, K. (1991). Violence and vulnerability in the workplace: Psychosocial and legal implications. In M. J. Davidson & J. Earnshaw (Eds.), *Vulnerable workers: Psychosocial and legal issues* (pp. 159–201). New York: Wiley.

Pfeffer, J. (1998). *The human equation: Building profits by putting people first.* Boston: Harvard Business School Press.

Quine, L. (1999). Workplace bullying in an NHS Trust. *British Medical Journal, 318,* 228–232.

Rayner, C. (1997). Incidence of workplace bullying. *Journal of Community and Applied Social Psychology, 7*(3), 199–208.

Rayner, R. C. (1998). Workplace bullying: Do something! *Journal of Occupational Health and Safety* Australia *and New Zealand, 14*(6), 581–585.

Rayner, C. (1999a). Unpublished PhD thesis, University of Manchester, UK.

Rayner, C. (1999b). A comparison of two methods for identifying targets of workplace bullying [Abstracts]. *Ninth European Congress on Work and Organizational Psychology, Finnish Institute of Occupational Health, Helsinki,* 88.

Rayner, C. (1999c). From research to implementation: Finding leverage for prevention. *International Journal of Manpower, 20*(1/2), 28–38.

Rayner, C. (2000, September). *Building a business case for tackling bullying in the workplace: Beyond a basic cost-benefit approach.* Keynote paper to Transcending Boundaries Conference, Griffith University, Brisbane, Australia.

Rayner, C. (2002, August). *Round two: Redefining bullying at work.* Paper presented in joint session—Workplace Abuse, Aggression, Bullying and Incivility: Conceptual Integration and Empirical Insights. American Academy of Management Meeting, Denver, CO.

Rayner, C. (2005). Reforming abusive organizations. In V. Bowie, B. Fisher, & C. L. Cooper (Eds.), *Countering workplace violence.* Devon, UK: Willan.

Rayner, C., & Cooper, C. L. (2003). The black hole in "bullying at work" research. *International Journal of Decision Making, 4*(1), 47–64.

Rayner, C., & Dick, G. (2005). *Re-analysing negative interpersonal behavior at work: An evidence-based approach to construct formation.* Paper submitted for publication.

Rayner, C., & Hoel, H. (1997). A summary review of literature relating to workplace bullying. *Journal of Community and Applied Social Psychology, 7*(3), 181–191.

Rayner, C., Hoel, H., & Cooper, C. L. (2002). *Bullying at work: What we know, who is to blame, and what can we do?* London: Taylor Francis.

Rayner, C., & Keashly, L. (2005). Bullying at work: A perspective from Britain and North America. In S. Fox & P. E. Spector (Eds.), *Counterproductive work behavior: Investigations of actors and targets* (pp. 271–296). Washington, DC: American Psychological Association.

Richards, J., & Daley, H. (2003). Bullying policy: Development, implementation and monitoring. In S. Einarsen, H. Hoel, D. Zapf, & C. Cooper (Eds.), *Bullying and emotional abuse in the workplace: International research and practice perspectives* (pp. 127–144). London: Taylor Francis.

Robinson, S. L., & O'Leary-Kelly, A. M. (1998). Monkey see, monkey do: The influence of work groups on the antisocial behavior of employees. *Academy of Management Journal, 41*(6), 658–672.

Rousseau, D. (1995). *Psychological contracts in organizations.* Thousand Oaks, CA: Sage.

Sutton, J. (1998). *Bullying: Social inadequacy or skilled manipulation?* Unpublished PhD thesis, Goldsmiths College, London.

Tajfel, H., & Turner, J. (2001). An integrative theory of intergroup conflict. In M. A. Hogg & D. Abrahams (Eds.), *Intergroup relations: Essential readings in social psychology* (pp. 94–109). Philadelphia: Psychology Press/Taylor Francis.

Tehrani, N. (2001). *Building a culture of respect: Managing bullying at work.* London: Taylor Francis.

Tehrani, N. (2003). Counselling and rehabilitating employees involved with bullying. In S. Einarsen, H. Hoel, D. Zapf, & C. Cooper (Eds.), *Bullying and emotional abuse in the workplace: International research and practice perspectives* (pp. 270–284). London: Taylor Francis.

UNISON. (1997). *UNISON members experience of bullying at work.* London: Author.

UNISON. (2000). *Police staff bullying report.* London: Author.

Van de Vliert, E., Euwema, M. C., & Huismans, S. E. (1995). Managing conflict with a subordinate or a superior: Effectiveness of conglomerate behavior. *Journal of Applied Psychology, 80*(2), 271–281.

Vartia, M. (1993). *Psychological harassment (bullying, mobbing) at work.* Helsinki: OECD Panel on Women, Work, and Health, Ministry of Social Affairs and Health.

Vartia, M., Korppoo, L., Fallenius, S., & Mattila, M. (2003). Workplace bullying: The role of occupational health services. In S. Einarsen, H. Hoel, D. Zapf, & C. L. Cooper (Eds.), *Bullying and emotional abuse in the workplace: International perspectives in research and practice* (pp. 285–298). London: Taylor Francis.

Veterans Administration. (2005). *The VA workplace stress and aggression project: Final report.* Washington, DC: VA Office of Occupational Safety and Health.

Withy, M., & Cooper, W. (1989). Predicting exit, voice, loyalty and neglect. *Administrative Science Quarterly, 34*, 521–539.

Yamada, D. (2003). Workplace bullying and the law: Towards a transnational consensus? In S. Ep[inarsen, H. Hoel, D. Zapf, & C. L. Cooper (Eds.), *Bullying and emotional abuse in the workplace: International research and practice perspectives* (pp. 399–411). London: Taylor Francis.

Zapf, D., Einarsen, S., Hoel, H., & Vartia, M. (2003). Empirical findings on bullying in the workplace. In S. Einarsen, H. Hoel, D. Zapf, & C. L. Cooper (Eds.), *Bullying and emotional abuse in the workplace: International research and practice perspectives* (pp. 103–126). London: Taylor Francis.

Zapf, D., & Gross, C. (2001). Conflict escalation and coping with workplace bullying: A replication and extension. *European Journal of Work and Organizational Psychology, 10*(4), 497–522.

Zapf, D., Knorz, C., & Kulla, M. (1996). On the relationship between mobbing factors, job content, social work environment, and health outcomes. *European Journal of Work and Organizational Psychology, 5*(2), 215–237.

8

Violence in Nursing

Marilyn Lanza

Patient assault is hardly a new subject. Why then are we writing about it? Because there are some new and unexpected findings. First, rate of assault is higher than previously thought; and second, average age of registered nurses (RNs) is greater now than 10 to 15 years ago. Patient assault frequency is documented as far back as 1983, yet it is still ignored. There is still focus on just the patient. Very little literature on the nurse exists. To make matters worse, there is constant verbal abuse: yelling, swearing, name-calling, or using other words to control or hurt (Gates, 2004; Gerberich et al., 2004; Henderson, 2003; Kingma, 2001). Verbal assault is often ignored; physical assault gets the attention (Lanza, Zeiss, & Rierdan, 2005).

Assault is a serious problem in hospitals and outpatient facilities and is reaching epidemic proportions. The rate of assault in hospitals reflects the increasing violence in society (Duncan et al., 2001; Gates, 2004; Gerberich et. al., 2004; Henderson, 2003; Hesketh et al., 2003; Kingma, 2001; Krug, Dahlberg, Mercy, Zwi, & Lozano, 2002; Peek-Asa, Runyan, & Zwerling, 2001; Poster & Ryan, 1994; Rosen, 2001; Shultz, 2000; Tardiff, 1999; *Under Secretary of Health Letter*, 1997). There are many recent studies about nurses being assaulted (Duncan et al., 2001; Henderson, 2003; Hesketh et al., 2003; Gerberich et al., 2004). In fact, nurses are the most frequently assaulted among health care workers. Numerous studies demonstrate similar conclusions.

The health care providers are often taking care of victims and perpetrators of violence from the communities in which they live. They are our friends, families, and neighbors. Violence occurs in areas of the hospital such as emergency rooms and trauma units that are the symbols of safety and care yet have become battlegrounds where people are maimed and killed rather than cured. The upsetting but basic fact is that violence occurs anywhere in the health care system, not just psychiatric units. In fact, the

---

Author's Note: This material is based on work supported by the Office of Research and Development, Edith Nourse Rogers Memorial Veterans Hospital, Bedford, MA.

general hospital has less control over the environment than does a locked psychiatric ward.

Frequency Data

Work-related violence, including physical assaults and threats of assault, directed toward persons at work or on duty (*Appendix C,* 1996) has been recognized as a major problem. During 2001, 639 work-related homicides occurred in the United States, making homicide the third leading cause overall of occupational fatality and the second leading cause of fatality for women.

The World Health Organization released its first report on violence on a global scale. Each year more than 1.6 million persons die from violence, and many more are injured and suffer from a range of physical, sexual, reproductive, and mental health problems (Krug et al., 2002). It is estimated that the cost of workplace violence to employers is in the billions of dollars. Unfortunately, research into the prevention of violence is still in its infancy. Despite our existing research, there remain significant gaps in our knowledge of its causes and potential solutions. The best data available cover fatal events. In 1998, the U.S. Bureau of Labor Statistics (BLS) reported 709 fatalities as a result of job-related homicide, making it the second leading cause of death on the job (Rosen, 2001). For female workers in 1998, homicide was the leading cause of death on the job (Rosen, 2001).

Homicides can make national headlines, but verbal threats, nonfatal physical assaults, and unwanted sexual advances are often underreported or not reported at all. Part of the problem is nurses' perception that assaults come with the territory (Occupational Safety and Health Administration [OSHA], 1996). Most nurses would not think of reporting a patient with Alzheimer's disease who strikes out as he's being fed. Nor would they report the girlfriend of a young man pronounced dead on arrival, who lashes out because, she believes, "you did nothing to save him."

There is less information available concerning injuries from nonfatal events (Peek-Asa et al., 2001; Injury Prevention Research Center, 2001). Workplace violence accounts for some 2 million nonfatal injuries each year in the United States (Rosen, 2001). In 1996, nonfatal violence resulted in 876,000 lost workdays and $16 million in lost wages (Rosen, 2001).

Following is a sample of a few studies of assault:

Ten percent had one assault in the last year. The problem is that nothing has changed. Erikson and Williams-Evans (2000) found that the assault rate was as high as it was 10 or more years ago and estimated that between 1 and 2 million assaults occur annually. Almost half of these assaults occur in health care institutions.

Increased rates for both physical and nonphysical violence were identified for working in a nursing home, long-term care facility, intensive care unit, emergency room, or psychiatric/behavioral department. Providing patient care and supervising patient care, as well as working with primarily geriatric patients, resulted in increased rates for physical violence (Gerberich et al., 2004; Hesketh et al., 2002).

More than 30% of nurses recently surveyed in seven states reported having been the victim of workplace violence in the previous year. The survey was returned by 586 nurses in Alabama, Colorado, Delaware, Hawaii, Illinois, Kansas, and Missouri. Of these nurses, 93.7% are female, 51% staff nurses, 80% have been nurses for more than 10 years, and 55% have worked more than 10 years at their present agency (Carroll & Morin, 1998). Research shows that 90% of staff nurses experience at least one incident a year of abusive anger, condescension, or being ignored by a physician, and 30% of nurses experience sexual abuse, ranging from lewd remarks to inappropriate touching, every 2 to 3 months (Steadman et al., 1998). Lanza, Zeiss, and Rierdan (2005) are now conducting a national Veterans Administration (VA) survey in which 48% reported at least one verbal or physical assault within a 12-month period.

Lehman, McCormick, and Kizer (1999), in a VA survey, and Cheung, Schweitzer, Tuckwell, and Crowley (1997), in Australia, reported the number and frequency of assaults in 1 year. Lehman et al. reported during the survey year that 24,219 incidents of assaultive behavior were documented by 166 VA facilities. Of these, 8,552 incidents involved battery or physical assaults. Assault-related injuries were most common among nursing personnel, approximately 2,200 out of 4,300 incidents. Cheung et al. found 389 assaults (verbal and physical) per 100 staff per year in Australia.

Also, nurses are on average are older than in the 1980s and 1990s. The average age in violence assessment mitigation and prevention is 48. Many published studies document assaults, but institutions have a long way to go toward implementing findings, especially pertaining to staff working conditions (Lanza et al., 2005).

Violence against nurses is not merely a phenomenon of Western culture. It exists in Europe, China, Japan, India, and Africa, although the type of violence may vary. There are reports of nurses assaulted in Mexico, beaten in Guatemala, imprisoned in Vietnam and Cuba, shot in Liberia, and killed in Peru and Colombia (Amnesty International [AI], 1997).

Countries outside the United States document that violence is a serious problem. New Zealand's Occupational Safety and Health Service of the Department of Labor has guidelines for the provision of facilities and general safety and health in the health care industry. Workers' Compensation Board of British Columbia and the United Kingdom Department of Health define violence as being hit, scratched, wounded with a knife or by gunshot, by gang violence or hostage taking, and death. Nearly all were women (96%); the average age was 46 years ($SD = 10.1$); and 75% were RNs.

The most frequently reported primary work facilities were hospital inpatient, nursing home or long-term care, and clinics or health care provider offices. Most nurses reported their primary facility was privately owned, compared with ownership by city or town, country, state, or federal agency.

The primary departments in which nurses most often worked were medical or surgical, followed by public health/home care, family practice, psychiatric or behavioral, operating or recovery, and intensive care. Primarily, nurses worked with nongeriatric adults or geriatric patients. Most nurses reported their primary professional activity as providing patient care.

By location, the physical assaults identified as specific and ongoing events (respectively by percentages) occurred in patient rooms (61; 72); hallways (20; 37); reception, lobby, or lounge areas (8; 11); nursing stations (4; 13); procedure or exam rooms (5; 0); bathrooms (2; 20); classrooms, meeting rooms, offices, and elevators (each less than 1 for both categories); and other (1; 0). Locations/sources of the behaviors associated with nonphysical violence events, by percentages, were face-to-face (90), telephone (16), email/mail (2), and other (3). Anatomically, physical assaults for specific events and ongoing events (respectively by percentages) primarily involved were arm/elbow/wrist (47; 70); hand/finger/thumb (13; 33); face (13; 26); leg (8; 20); head/skull/brain (5; 7); and external chest (6; 2). The resulting types of physical injuries (specific or ongoing) reported most frequently were bruises/contusions (33; 48); temporary discolorations/slap marks (22; 26); cuts/lacerations/scratches, or abrasions (28; 44); and bites/punctures (5; 20). No overt physical injury was identified for some of the events (19; 11) despite the fact that the events were reported according to the definition of physical assault (Gerberich et al., 2004).

The instruments used in the physical assaults for specific and ongoing events (respectively by percentages) were hands/arms (87; 91), feet/legs (39; 63), teeth (15; 31), body fluids, including spitting (7; 19), knives (<1; 2), genitals (<1 for both categories), and other (<1 for both categories) (Gerberich et al., 2004).

The most commonly reported consequences of both physical and nonphysical violence were frustration, anger, fear/anxiety/stress, and irritability, with much greater proportions reported for nonphysical violence for each of the consequences (Gerberich et al., 2004). Reasons given for not reporting the physical events (both specific and ongoing) and nonphysical events included, respectively, (a) considered it part of the job (45% and 44%), (b) considered it a minor or isolated incident (32% and 8%), (c) perceived it as unnecessary to report (14% and 17%), (d) nonsupportive environment (5% and 30%), and (e) too busy (3% and 2%) (Gerberich et al., 2004). This plays a part in assault being high but not taken seriously.

Violence Toward Nursing Staff

It is difficult to obtain an exact number of nurses who have been assaulted. The best estimate is that it is many. The problem is that there is no standard reporting mechanism; the definition varies; and many are not reported for a multitude of reasons. For example, a study by Coombes (1998) found that 85% of nurses experienced verbal abuse or have been threatened with violence. Multinational data report that 75% of all nurses have been assaulted at least once in their careers (Dehn, 1999; Quintal, 2002). In a study across

Veterans' Health Administration (VHA) facilities of patients who assaulted two times or more in a 2-year period, 83% ($N = 5,959$) of the incidents involved patients assaulting nursing staff (Blow, Barry, Copeland, McCormick, Lehmann, & Ulmann, 1999).

Costs

Violence has become a major public health concern. Health care workers are at substantial risk, with most assaults being perpetrated by patients or clients (Findorff, McGovern, Rozman, & Gerberich, 2000). The average cost per assault of RNs was $33,510 per case in 1999 dollars.

Underreporting

The reported statistics are acknowledged to represent only the tip of the iceberg. As first documented in 1981, the assault rate is underreported by as much as 80% (Lion, Snyder, & Merrill, 1981) and reflects a critical incidence measure at best (Lanza & Campbell, 1991; Silver & Yudofsky, 1999). In the Department of Veterans Affairs context, the majority of assaults are perpetrated by men. Although most concern has been with physical violence, verbal abuse and threats have significant sequelae for the victims and negative consequences for the perpetrator. The operational definition for assaultive behavior includes verbal and physical aggression. The types of assault are verbal (yelling, screaming, or threatening) and physical (hitting with part of the body or a weapon or killing—killing a nurse is the most extreme type of assault and gets the most media attention). The total number of verbal and physical assaults is very large, but because death is not the usual outcome, the tendency of the media has been to ignore the fate of those victims.

Risk Factors

Assaultive behavior resulting in threats or physical injury and possibly in death in the health care system represents a serious threat to the welfare of patients, staff, and visitors. Although a certain amount of assaultive behavior is inevitable and predictable, proper preparation and intervention can significantly reduce the frequency and seriousness of disruptive behavior. Assaultive behavior is not restricted to closed psychiatric wards. It often occurs in admitting and emergency rooms, on units managing substance abusers (particularly during the detoxification stage), and with less frequency in other areas of the health care facility. The prevention and management of such behavior must, therefore, be the concern of all clinical and administrative staff.

Box 8.1 identifies a number of key factors in the health care environment that correlate with the increased risk of violence in health care. Boxes 8.2 and 8.3 provide questions developed by the VA Police Department about safetyprocedures.

Box 8.1   Key Factors in the Health Care Environment That Correlate With the Increased
Risk of Violence

The 24-hour open-door policies for patient access

The decrease in available treatment for the mentally ill and substance abuse patients resulting
in the increasing number of acute and chronically mentally ill being released from hospitals

The availability of drugs and money in the hospital settings

The prevalence of weapons among patients

The current cost-cutting focus and widespread downsizing within the health care industry

Working alone during the night or in the early morning

Traditional staffing patterns—often low staffing levels at times of increased activity

Circumstantial factors such as unrestricted movement of the public in health care settings,
presence of gang members, drug or alcohol abuse, trauma patients, distraught family members,
long waiting periods, and the inability to obtain care

Box 8.2   Interior Work Practices and Access Control

Are all doors, electronic or key operated, properly secured/locked?

Are silver recovery and X-ray file storage rooms locked when not in use?

Are desks clear of potential weapon items (pocketknives, forks, tools, pens, pencils, etc.) in
high-risk areas, for example, mental health, outpatient treatment area, and emergency room?

Are purses, wallets, keys, money, credit cards, and other valuables secured in locked desks
or rooms when not in use?

Are office exits unobstructed, not blocked by chairs, desks, coat racks, etc.?

Are there bare cubicles, unlocked construction areas, bare unsecured offices, etc.?

Is there a reception area for visitor and patient sign in/out?

Is there a separate interview area away from the waiting and treatment area?

Are employees required to wear ID badges?

Are stairwells and landings appropriately secured and/or illuminated?

Is access to storage areas, high-risk areas, and unused patient areas appropriately secured?

Are room offices, labs, and research areas containing high-value items positively secured
when not occupied by authorized personnel?

Are employees knowledgeable on threat, disturbance, and bomb-reporting procedures?

Box 8.3   Exterior Access Controls

Are parking lots used by nighttime employees adequately illuminated?

Is there adequate lighting of those exit door areas and pathways used by employees arriving and departing at night?

Are visiting and business hours posted at main entrances used by patients and visitors?

Are facility gates around the property secured at appropriate times, if applicable, and in good working order?

Assessment

Although the ability to predict future violence or assaultive behavior is limited, staff training and the establishment of effective policies and procedures can maximize the ability to identify persons who, in the very short run (generally a matter of minutes or hours), may be at greater risk for violent behavior. For example, a past history of violent behavior or an attachment to weapons means a patient is a higher risk for causing further violence. The presence of a psychiatric disorder may also increase the risk. Paranoid ideation, intoxication, manic syndromes, or delirium are the most common psychiatric disorders associated with violence.

It is essential that staffing levels be adequate to meet the demands involved in the management of assaultive behavior. In addition to adequate staffing levels in the treatment areas, a working reservoir of staff should be available who can be called on in time of crisis. Adequate levels of well-trained staff increase the confidence of staff in managing these difficult situations and lessen the fear and anxiety inherent in the management of disruptive behavior. I cannot emphasize enough that staff must be well trained.

A coordinated plan must be in place. The layout of the physical environment is crucial. Particularly in high-risk areas, the environment should allow for the easy isolation of the patient into an area that has reduced sensory stimulation.

Verbal intervention may preclude the need for physical intervention. Violent patients may feel helpless, terrified of losing control, or frightened by the intensity of their own emotion. It is important to try to establish rapport by acknowledging these feelings and focusing on verbal intervention. The aggressive person should be encouraged to talk or "get it off his or her chest." It should be made clear that violence is not acceptable, and the consequences should be outlined. Threats should be met with a firm but supportive setting of limits and an enforcement of these limits.

Because violent persons can be paranoid and hostile, adversarial aspects of the encounter should be diminished. Staff members should be overtly courteous and respectful. Encourage cooperation. Staff members should appear calm and controlled and should listen actively and speak softly in a nonprovocative, nonjudgmental manner. Brief summaries of what is happening will help the patient break a crisis down into small sections. Foster nonviolent, problem-solving alternatives. Never make promises that cannot be kept. Explicitly and honestly describe anticipated procedures and plans.

Commonsense Views

Box 8.4 lists commonsense precepts for staff that are often overlooked.

Staff should also be well versed on the indications of a "preassaultive tension state," which includes signs of anxiety, breathlessness, ridged posture, clenching and unclenching of fists and jaw, and visible temporal artery pulsation. Other clues include hyperactivity, pacing, and verbal profanity. In addition, one should be observant for verbal and nonverbal cues of hostility, agitation, suspiciousness, withdrawal, and psychosis.

Some patients do not give the usual cues. These patients often surprise staff with their violence. An example is a very tall man who bursts out of a room, comes down the hall, and is swearing and obviously very angry. Most of the staff step back. They have seen him punch people before. One male nurse approaches him and speaks in a calm, low-toned voice. The patient continues swearing and yelling but is able to focus on the nurse. The patient eventually calms down enough so that he can remain on the ward without seclusion or restraints.

Another example concerns a nurse therapist conducting a group of traumatic brain injury (TBI) patients. It was the second session of the group. One of the patients, a large White male who had a history of domestic violence, kept interrupting the group. The small female leader asked other people for their opinions as a way to try to set limits on this patient. It was only partially effective. It seemed to the nurse therapist that she needed to talk individually to this patient. She told him that he was interrupting the group and wondered how they could help him stay within the group contract. By interrupting so much, the patient could not benefit from the knowledge of others. Also, if he was allowed to continue as he was, the group would most likely fall apart in a few more sessions. The nurse therapist had not known the patient for very long. She was quite afraid to approach him about this. But she was low-keyed and asked how they, not just he, could handle this problem. Surprisingly, the patient said that he had difficulty remaining quiet, that this was a big problem to him. They worked it out in the following groups that the leader, if necessary, would give him a signal when he was going on for too long.

Box 8.4   Commonsense Precepts for Staff

Positioning yourself	Your stance should allow you to be able to stand firmly and move quickly. You should not be threatening in your demeanor.
	Know who and what is around you.
	Keep your arms at your sides and hands outside of your pockets. Folded arms convey the message: "I'm not listening."
	Maintain good eye contact. Know the cultural differences of patients (e.g., Native Americans may become agitated with direct contact). Your tone of voice should be assertive, not aggressive or provocative. Stay at least four arm-lengths away from patient.
Dress for safety	Avoid provocative clothing.
What you intend by a touch	Touch may be sexual or threatening to some patients. If possible, tell the patient you are going to touch and why before you do.
Be aware of your surroundings	Avoid turning your back. You do not know who is behind you.
Be careful when entering wards	If doors are locked, check who may be hiding in the corner. If uncertain, wait for another staff member to accompany you.
Be careful when entering elevators	Stay by the control buttons.
Be careful of locked rooms	Patients and staff members should both be able to leave.
Remove objects	Ties, necklaces, and scarves make a ready means for choking the staff member. Remove pens.
Keys, alarms	Keys should be inconspicuous and worn in such a manner to avoid incidents yet be readily available when needed. Personal alarm systems must be utilized by staff members and tested as scheduled (as in the police station of a hospital).
When interviewing patients	Request permission to ask questions. Give the patient control over the situation by offering solutions or alternatives.
	Take action before anger builds.
	Call the patient by name. Let others know where you are. Take another person with you if necessary. Decide whether an interview room or a dayroom is preferable. Your content is very important. "Are you OK?" or "What's wrong?" is not helpful. If the patient knew the answer to that, he or she would not be anxious. It's better to acknowledge his or her emotions: "You look anxious." Or "Sounds as if you're upset." Such phrases tell that you are listening and that you care.

Relationship With Coworkers

It is important to know and communicate your own strengths and weaknesses to coworkers *before* an assault situation. Your coworkers need to know each other very well. There should not be any surprises in the middle of an emergency, such as, "I cannot restrain him. I have a bad back." You do not have to give all the details of how you acquired a bad back, but you do need to let everyone know that they can and cannot count on you in certain ways. There is no one who does not have a useful role. The point is that when an emergency is called, all must know what they should do.

Discuss your own reactions to assault. Discuss how you and your coworkers usually handle fear, anger, denial, omnipotence, and projection. For example, some staff always avoid assaultive situations.

Important Clinical Points

Fear

If a patient asks if you are afraid, ask if you should be. Put as much responsibility on the patient as you can. This helps him or her to stay in control. Try to help a patient review the choice of losing control and resulting consequences.

Denial

Wishing to work with an appealing patient, staff may deny the risk of violent outburst by overlooking significant clinical and historical data. Staff may deny the risk of violence by working with a patient as if there were no reason for concern, using minimal precautionary measures with the hope that the patient will behave accordingly.

Omnipotence

Staff may deny the risk of being assaulted and feel all-powerful. If they have never been assaulted, they may think they never will be. Assault is not a "reality" for them. We are all vulnerable, however. The main predictor of assault is your position in the administrative hierarchy; that is, the person who is most likely to be assaulted is a nursing assistant who spends most of the day caring for patients.

Projection

Staff may project their own sadistic and rageful impulses on a patient and exaggerate the patient's capacity for assaultive behavior. Staff may reject a patient and provoke him or her to violence. They may allow the patient to act disruptively and not report and/or deal with signs of the patient's decompensation. Staff can become punitive and overrestrictive. Patients can also experience these reactions of denial and projection. Any of the above, such as fear or denial, can result in a dividing line between the staff, with half feeling very fearful of the patient and the other half as though there is nothing to fear. This may result in splits between patients and staff or medical and nursing staff.

Discuss Male-Female Roles

Males may protect women and feel invulnerable. Females may overcompensate and put themselves in dangerous situations. This may also explain why we have a formal system in which there is no difference in male and female roles, but covertly people who work on a ward know the difference. In the more violent situation, the woman may be selectively excused. Assaultive behavior toward others must be stopped promptly. The safety of other patients, staff, and other bystanders needs to be a matter of prime concern. The escalation of violent behavior is minimized when staff clearly know what is expected of them and have experience and training that provide them with confidence in the implementation of procedures for the management of the violent patient. Counterthreats, displays of anger, and brusque treatment are likely to exacerbate the situation. It is essential that staff in high-risk areas, such as psychiatric units, geriatric units, and the emergency or admitting area be particularly skilled in verbal and behavioral interventions for the management of violent behavior. This includes physical containment techniques designed to immobilize the patient in a manner that minimizes the possibility of physical harm coming to the patient or to staff. In such areas, a coordinated plan of action should be clearly formulated and practiced as a team at regular intervals. This team should consist of any and all concerned staff, including security personnel. The layout of the physical environment is also crucial. Particularly in high-risk areas, the environment should allow for the easy isolation of the patient into an area that has reduced sensory stimulation.

Practice Controlling an Assaultive Patient With Physical Restraint

Assess the risk of aggression with the particular patient in question or in the clinical situation of concern. For example, a Veterans' Affairs Medical Center (VAMC) Bedford policy, "Identification and Management of Patients at High Risk for Assaultive Behavior," outlines how to identify such patients through the electronic record. There are many assessment tools. Staff members should be able to think through an assessment of patient aggression in the immediate situation if necessary. The steps of assessment should be memorized and practiced so they can be used in a crisis.

A show of force with several people standing by may be enough to deter some aggressive patients. Uniformed guards are especially effective. Practice restraint techniques on the ward. Be familiar with the functioning of your crisis management team. Effective interventions must be known in advance and steps planned well before the staff is confronted with an assaultive emergency.

Procedure for Managing Psychiatric Emergencies

The single most significant characteristic distinguishing the well-managed from the poorly managed assault incident is the presence or absence of staff teamwork. A team includes the leader, team members, and support staff. Intervention does not imply use of a participative, democratic process. Assaultive emergencies cannot be safely managed by peer negotiations and group consensus. The leader's assessment of the situation directs the activities of all other staff involved in the event. It is the leader who decides what steps will be taken; communicates with the patient prior to, during, and after any physical intervention; and communicates decisions and plans to fellow staff members. He or she assumes ultimate accountability for the outcome of the incident. Sometimes, despite all our precautions, it is time for physical intervention.

A useful outline for managing an emergency (see Box 8.5) in almost any situation is offered by Bell (2000).

Box 8.5   Procedure for Managing Psychiatric Emergencies

Identify crisis leader.

Assemble crisis team.

Notify security officers if necessary.

Remove all other patients from area.

Obtain restraints if appropriate.

Devise a plan to manage crisis and inform team.

Assign securing of patient limbs to crisis team members.

Explain necessity of intervention to patient and attempt to enlist cooperation.

Restrain patient when directed by crisis leader.

Administer medication if ordered.

Maintain calm, consistent approach to patient.

Review crisis management interventions with crisis team.

Process events with other patients and staff as appropriate.

Gradually reintegrate patient into milieu.

After the crisis is over, it is recommended that the team discuss any concern they may have had during the crisis, as this type of intervention can be stressful for both staff and patients. The patient's behavior may have evoked feelings of guilt, anger, or aggression in the staff. These issues should be discussed as a team so that care is consistent; interventions are therapeutic; and staff do not become discouraged, develop a negative attitude about their work, or experience burnout. The final intervention is a reevaluation of the patient's status and gradual reintegration into the milieu. We have discussed intervention in a systems approach.

Establishing a Norm Against Violence

The patients and staff on a given ward make up a community of individuals who are brought and held together by commonalties of purpose. Prevailing social norms within this small but dense community can have either facilitatory or inhibitory influences on a patient's potential for assault. The "community" may be any group in which there is some cohesion among members. The community does not have to be a psychiatric ward. It can, for instance, be a group of visitors to a medical unit.

Certain assumptions can foster an increased level of physical aggression. Inexperienced staff and staff who have trouble dealing with their own aggressive feelings may unwittingly give patients cues that they expect them to behave violently. Patients may exercise less control over aggressive impulses if they assume that a diagnosis of a mental illness is exculpatory and that hospitalization protects them from the consequences of untoward behaviors. Patients who fear attacks from others may strike preemptively. A clearly articulated, strongly supported norm against violence is required to minimize the intensity of these dangerous assumptions. The norm against violence can be promulgated through a variety of means. A patient orientation manual, treatment meetings, or staff contacts with individual patients are a few of the means.

Depending on how the norm is developed and enunciated there is risk that it will create rather than prevent aggression. If the norm against violence is perceived as a heavy-handed approach by staff to maintain absolute control, some patients may feel challenged or provoked to test its strength. If a pronounced split exists between patients and staff, the norm can become a focus for contention. When this occurs, patients will accuse staff of erring regardless of what action they take following a violent episode.

To reduce the risk of backlash and patient-staff splitting, hospital staff should involve patients as much as possible in establishing and maintaining the norm against violence. For example, patients can be directly involved in formulating the patient orientation manual. Discussion of the norm can also take place in patient government meetings and in treatment meetings.

Patient-staff discussion about the norm should not focus narrowly on the issue of control. Discussions should stress the ultimate goal to be served by observing the norm: creation of a living and working ambience that is sufficiently safe and trustworthy to allow patients and staff to work effectively on treatment issues. It is not possible for patients to deal with inner conflicts while they are frightened of being assaulted. Any dangerously aggressive act must be regarded as a community event. Although only one or two individuals may have acted violently, the incident will reverberate with negative reactions. Patients will assume that prevention of violence is the province of staff only.

Limits must be placed on verbal as well as physical abuse. All must be treated with respect. This includes examining paternalism within staff. For example, in some circumstances, when the patients and nursing staff are called by their first name but the doctor is addressed as "Dr. Brown," everyone understands that there is a hierarchical status among staff so that hitting Dr. Brown is much worse than hitting a nurse. The physician can use "Dr. Brown," but with a first and last name. Or everyone can be more formal and use titles (Mr., Miss, Nurse, etc.): your patients and every member of the staff on the unit, including secretaries and housekeepers. The point is that no one should have a higher risk to be assaulted.

What Happens When a Nurse Is Assaulted?

The nurse experiences the reactions summarized in Box 8.6 (Lanza et al., 2005). Short-term response was 1 week or less. Long-term response was greater than 1 week. Reactions of nurse victims included emotional, social, biophysiological, and cognitive responses. There are indications that some

---

Box 8.6   *Victims' Reactions to Assault*

Short-term	Helplessness, Irritability, Fear of returning to the scene of the assault, Feeling of resignation, Anger, Anxiety, Shock, Apathy, Disbelief, Self-blame, Dependency	Change in relationship with coworkers, Difficulty returning to work, Fear of other patients, Feel sorry for the patient who hit them, Should have done something to prevent the assault	Startle response, Sleep pattern disturbance, Soreness, Headaches	Denial of thoughts about the assault, Preoccupation with thinking about the assault, Considering change in lifestyle/job change
Long-term	Fear of patient who hit them	Feel sorry for the patient who hit them	Body tension, Soreness	Anger toward authority, Wanting protection by authority and from authority's condition

staff members felt they would be overwhelmed if they allowed themselves to admit their feelings. Some stated that if they allowed themselves to experience feelings about likelihood of assault, they would not be able to function. Some indicated they expected to be hit, believing it was part of the job. Staff members who received the most severe injuries indicated less fear of the patient who had assaulted them than did staff members who were less severely injured. Numerous studies have reported similar findings about intensity and variety of victim's reactions.

Role Conflict

Nurses who are assaulted report conflict between their role as a professional and a victim (Lanza, 1992). Nurses are not socialized to expect to be assault victims, and most do not receive any education to prepare them for such a fate. Any formal training usually comes through employment in a psychiatric facility. There is intense conflict between conflicting realities when a nurse is assaulted (Lanza, 1992; Lanza et al., 2005). He or she generally believes that nurses are not assaulted, and yet it has occurred. There is also divided loyalty between allegiance to one's professional functioning (putting the patient's needs first) and attention to one's own needs as a victim (Lanza, 1992). For example, the nurse is hit by a patient and required to continue working because staffing is inadequate to permit going home. Children question why their mother or father works in "such a place." The victim often defends the institution to family members and denies his or her own feelings of victimization. Nurses are in the somewhat unique position of needing to provide extensive care for a person who assaulted them. For example, the patient may require continuous observation by the nursing staff after assaulting one of the nursing staff members. In summary, victims experience intense emotional reactions, want someone to speak to about their reactions, yet feel that it is "unprofessional" to do so. Victims do not expect to receive support from hospital administrators despite the victim's loyalty to the institution.

Counseling

Facilitating the victim's return to work is often accomplished by counselor-led meetings between the victim and staff and between victim and assailant. The victim and staff meet to review the assault episode. There is exploration about how each person felt at the time of the assault and afterward. Issues of support for all, as well as preventive measures, are discussed. Coworkers often feel guilty about the assault, regardless of the surrounding circumstances. The victim often experiences underlying anger toward coworkers and feels unsupported by them.

Meetings between the victim and assailant are important because they generally continue to interact on the same unit. Both parties explore their feelings about the assault and discuss parameters of their future relationship. Understanding what precipitated the assault and that violence will not be tolerated are essential outcomes.

Victims are encouraged to deal with family concerns by having open discussions with family members about their fears, sense of responsibility in wanting to protect the victim, and sometimes sense of guilt that the victim had been assaulted.

Blame

The role of blame has even a wider impact. Blame is a particularly important concept when addressing the issue of patient assault. Almost everyone involved attributes blame. Victims often blame themselves and/or those in authority. Coworkers, albeit unwittingly, blame the assaultee. Finally, those in authority or the "system" as a whole often engage in the process of blaming the victim (Lanza, 1992).

This last part of the blaming triangle is particularly important to understand because it has profound effects on increasing the incidence of patient violence. Simply stated, if an institution assumes that fault or responsibility lies with the assaulted staff member, then the institution can deny that there is a more general problem of patient assault. As a result, there is no determination of the extent of the problem of assault or recognition that a problem even exists. The assault of a staff member is seen as a rare occurrence and caused by some unique characteristic in that person. The bottom line is that no prevention strategies are established to cope with the problem of assault, and the mythical reality is maintained that "we do not have a problem."

What Can Be Done

There are many things to be done. One may ask if administrators should not be more public in their acknowledgment that patient assault is a problem. On closer inspection, there may be a conflict for administrators in doing so. If administrators admit that patient assault is a problem at their institution, they may find themselves blamed for the problem. For example, the assumption could be made that patient assault is a problem because of poor administration. It could also be suggested that if patients become violent, it is because they are mistreated. As mentioned earlier, issues of patients' rights and safety measures to prevent violence are often presented as adversarial. That is, to institute safety measures, patients' rights are considered at risk when the more global approach suggests that only when safety exists can anyone (staff or patients) have rights. The last dilemma to be faced in publicizing the existence of patient assault is that such knowledge may arouse fear in the community and inhibit the discharge of nonviolent patients. Any patient with a history of mental illness may then be seen as too dangerous to live outside of the hospital, a long-held belief that mental health professionals have valiantly tried to eradicate.

Given that coming to terms with the problem of patient assault may arouse ambivalent feelings and conflict-laden situations, there are steps administrators can take to support nursing staff in dealing with assaultive situations. Administrators can collectively support the legitimacy of patient assault as a frequent problem with which nursing staff must deal. Publicity can be achieved through meetings, journal articles, and the media. Administrators are in a key position to confront the myth of blaming the victim for the assault, to propose legislative plans to guarantee that nurses have the right to work in safety, to develop strategies to improve nurses' power position, to educate the public concerning assaults on nurses, and to encourage research on different aspects of patient assault in nursing practice. Patient violence is an important and long-standing issue that is only beginning to be studied. An alliance with nursing staff to investigate the problem of patient assault at one's institution is effective. In a collaborative fashion, programs can be developed to cope with and prevent violence. They can support nursing staff assault victims through direct administrative contact as well as nonjudgmental, supportive counseling to help victims cope with their reactions.

A specific protocol for assaulted employees such as that instituted at Edith Nourse Rogers Memorial Veterans Hospital can be developed, which outlines the rights and services available for an employee who is assaulted (Lanza, Keefe, & Henderson, 1996). It is also part of the OSHA Guidelines for Preventing Workplace Violence for Healthcare and Social Service Workers.

As time goes on, there is more attention given to nurses as victims. Adequate documentation of assault occurrences is necessary. Lanza and Campbell (1991) describes a much more comprehensive method of documenting verbal and physical assaults with much less paperwork. The Veterans Administration Task Force on Violence Prevention, for example, has just undertaken a fresh look at assault on nurses and is actively studying the problem and generating recommendations.

Nurses have a particular interest in eliminating violence. As health care professionals, nurses often have first-line contact with the increasing numbers of victims of violence. Regrettably, a small number of nurses have also been known to be perpetrators of violence, committing patient or colleague abuse in violation of nursing's code of conduct. Nurses also suffer from societal tolerance of violence. The legal system has on several occasions refused to grant compensation to nurse victims. This was justified on the principle that to practice nursing was to accept the risk of personal violence. Nurses themselves often feel that they are legitimate targets and that violence is part of the job. Nurses are the health care workers most at risk, with female nurses considered the most vulnerable. Physical assault is mostly perpetrated by patients. Seventy-two percent of nurses do not feel safe from assault in their workplace. A campaign of zero tolerance of violence at the workplace needs to address the contributing factors, namely working in isolation; inadequate staff coverage; lack of staff training; poor interrelationships within the work environment (such as managers' disinterest); and difficulty dealing with people who have been drinking or taking drugs or who are under stress, frustrated, violent, or grief-struck.

National Agencies Provide Guidance to Set Up Safety Programs

The VA, in addition to caring for assaultive patients, has policies that include hostage contingency plans, bomb threat procedures, terrorist threats, and demonstrations.

OSHA Guidelines

OSHA sets up guidelines for institutions, including the following:

- Organizational concern for employee emotional and physical safety and health
- Equal commitment to worker safety and health and patient/client safety
- System of accountability for involved managers and employees
- Creation and dissemination of a clear policy of zero tolerance for workplace violence
- Assurance that no reprisals are taken against employees who report incidents
- Encouragement of employees to promptly report incidents and suggest ways to reduce or eliminate risks
- A comprehensive plan for maintaining security in the workplace
- Assignment of responsibility and authority for the program to individuals with appropriate training and skills
- A firm management commitment to a worker-supportive environment
- Company briefings as part of the initial effort to address safety issues

American Industrial Hygiene Association White Paper on Prevention of Workplace Violence

Industrial hygienists have special expertise in developing safety and health programs that may be brought to bear in establishing workplace violence prevention programs. In particular, industrial hygienists have training and skills in evaluating and controlling environmental hazards and in designing and administering health and safety programs that should be adapted to workplace violence prevention.

State Departments of Labor

A study by the Washington State Department of Labor and Industries of workers' compensation claims for 1992 through 1997 showed that psychiatric hospitals had the highest average rate of claims related to workplace violence of all industries: 872 per 10,000 workers. The second, third, and fourth highest industries were also in health care, as follows: residential care, 417/10,000 workers, skilled nursing care, 254/10,000 workers, and nursing/personal care, 240/10,000 workers.

References

Amnesty International. (1997, October 1). *Liberia: A new peace agreement: An opportunity to introduce human rights protection* (AI index: AFR 34/01/95). Retrieved August 24, 2005, from http://web.amnesty.org/library/Index/engAFR 340051997

Bell, C. C. (2000). Assessment and management of the violent patient. *Journal of the National Medical Association, 92*(5), 247–253.

Blow, F. C., Barry, K. L., Copeland, L. A., McCormick, R. A., Lehmann, L. S., & Ulmann, E. S. (1999). Repeated assaults by patients in VA hospital and clinic settings. *Psychiatric Services, 50*(3), 390–394.

Carroll, V., & Morin, K. H. (1998, September/October). Workplace violence affects one third of nurses. *American Nurse, 15.*

Cheung, P., Schweitzer, I., Tuckwell, V., & Crowley, K. C. (1997). A prospective study of aggression among psychiatric patients in rehabilitation wards. *New Zealand Journal of Psychiatry, 30, 257–262.*

Coombes, R. (1998). Violence against nurses: The facts. *Nursing Times, 94*(43), 5.

Dehn, D. S. (1999). Violence against nurses in outpatient mental health settings. *Journal of Psychosocial Nursing Mental Health Services, 37*(6), 28–33.

Duncan, S., Hyndman, K., Estabrooks, C., Hesketh, K., Humphrey, C., Wong, J., et al. (2001). Nurses experience of violence in Alberta and British Columbia Hospitals. *Canadian Journal of Nursing Research, 32*(4), 57–78.

Erikson, L., & Williams-Evans, A. W. (2000). Research: Attitudes of emergency nurses regarding patient assault. *Journal of Emergency Nursing, 26*(3), 210–215.

Findorff, M. J., McGovern, P. M., Rozman, J. M., & Gerberich, S. G. (2000). The cost of violence to health care workers. *Journal of Healthcare Safety: Compliance and Infection Control, 4, 209–217.*

Gates, D. M. (2004). The epidemic of violence against healthcare workers. *Occupational Environmental Medicine, 61, 649–650.*

Gerberich, S., Church, T., McGovern, P., Hansen, H., Nachreiner, N., Geisser, M. S., et al. (2004). An epidemiological study of the magnitude and consequences of work related violence: The Minnesota Nurses' Study. *Occupational Environmental Medicine, 61, 495–503.*

Henderson, A. (2003). Nurses and workplace violence: Nurses' experiences of verbal and physical abuse at work. *Canadian Journal of Nursing Leadership, 16*(4), 82–98.

Hesketh, K., Duncan, S., Estabrooks, C., Reimer, M., Giovannetti, P., Hyndman, K., et al. (2003). Workplace violence in Alberta and British Columbia hospitals. *Health Policy, 63,* 311–321.

Injury Prevention Research Center. (2001, February). *A report to the nation.* Iowa City: University of Iowa. Retrieved August 25, 2004, from http://72.14.207.104/search?q=cache:Mrp9W7sCX_0J:www.public-health.uiowa.edu/iprc/nation.pdf+Injury+Prevention+Research+Center.+(2001,+February).+Workplace+violence:+A+report+to+the+nation.+Iowa+City:+University+of+Iowa&hl=en&ie=UTF-8

Kingma, M. (2001). Workplace violence in the health sector: A problem of epidemic proportion. *International Nursing Review, 48*(3), 129–130.

Krug, E. G., Dahlberg, L. L., Mercy, J. A., Zwi, A. B., & Lozano, R. (2002). *World report on violence and heath.* Geneva: World Health Organization.

Lanza, M. L. (1992, June). Nurses as patient assault victims: An update, synthesis and recommendations. *Archives in Psychiatric Nursing, 6*(3), 163–171.

Lanza, M. L., & Campbell, D. (1991, May). Patient assault: A comparison study of reporting methods. *Journal of Nursing Quality Assurance, 5*(4), 60–68.

Lanza, M. L., Keefe, J., & Henderson, M. C. (1996). Assaulted and/or battered employee policy. *Guidelines for preventing workplace violence of health care and social service workers* (OSHA 3148, Rev. ed. 1998). OSHA, U.S. Department of Labor.

Lanza, M. L., Zeiss, R., & Rierdan, J. (2005, Nov. 11). *Violence assessment, mediation, and prevention: Factors related to staff violence and implications.* American Nurses Association Conference, Washington, DC.

Lehman, L., McCormick, R. A., & Kizer, K. W. (1999). A survey of assaultive behaviour in Veterans Health Administration facilities. *Psychiatric Services, 50*(3), 384–389.

Lion, J. R., Snyder, W., & Merrill, G. (1981, July). Underreporting of assaults on staff in a state hospital. *Hospital & Community Psychiatry, 32,* 497–498.

Occupational Safety and Health Administration. (1996). *Report on violence in the workplace: Guidelines for preventing workplace violence.* Retrieved August 24, 2005, from http://72.14.207.104/search?q=cache:i5UmYd-wIvMJ:www.osha.gov/Publications/osha3148.pdf+National+Institute+of+Occupational+Safety+and+Health.+(1996).+NIOSH+Report+on+Violence+in+the+Workplace&hl=en&ie=UTF-8

Peek-Asa, C., Runyan, C. W., & Zwerling, C. (2001). The role of surveillance and evaluation research in the reduction of violence against workers. *American Journal of Preventative Medicine, 20,* 141–148.

Poster, E. C., & Ryan, J. A. (1994). A multiregional study of nurses' beliefs and attitudes about work safety and patient assault. *Hospital and Community Psychiatry, 45*(11), 1104–1108.

Quintal, A. S. (2002). Violence against psychiatric nurses: An untreated epidemic? *Journal of Psychosocial Nursing, 40*(1), 46–53.

Rosen, J. (2001). A labor perspective of workplace violence prevention: Identifying research needs. *American Journal of Preventative Medicine, 20*(2), 161–168.

Shultz, M. S. (2000). 1999 International Association for Health Care Security and Safety Healthcare (IAHSS) crime survey. *IAHSS Newsletter, 10*(2), 1–2.

Silver, J. M., & Yudofsky, S. C. (1999) Propranolol treatment of chronically hospitalized aggressive patients. *Journal of Neuropsychiatry and Clinical Neuroscience, 11*(3), 328–335.

Steadman, H., Mulvey, E., Monahan, J., Robbins, P., Applebaum, P., & Grisso, T. (1998). Violence by people discharged from active psychiatric in-patient facilities and by others in the same neighborhoods. *Archives of General Psychiatry, 55,* 393–401.

Tardiff, K. (1999). *Medical management of violence.* Washington, DC: American Psychiatric Press.

Under Secretary of Health Letter. (1997, September 8). Nature and extent of repeat assaults by patients in the Veterans Health Administration, IL 10–97–034.

Appendix 8.1

The general focus is to become aware and eliminate violence, particularly for nurses, in whatever location they may work. In recognition of the magnitude of the health problems related to violence, a number of nursing organizations have issued position statements concerning the various aspects of violence. These organizations to date include the American Nurses' Association in 1991; the National Black Nurses'Association in 1994; the American College of Nurse-Midwives in 1995; the Association of Emergency Room Nurses in 1999; and the National Nursing Summit on Violence Against Women in 1997.

9

School Violence

Irvin Sam Schonfeld

A book on workplace violence requires a chapter on school violence. Schools are where teachers *and* children work. One of the goals of the National Educational Goals Panel (2000), an independent agency of the executive branch of the federal government, is the following:

> Every local educational agency will develop and implement a policy to ensure that all schools are free of violence and the unauthorized presence of weapons.

The goal applies to the safety of students, faculty, and staff. The purpose of this chapter is threefold. First, the chapter summarizes what is known about the prevalence of violence and weapons in U.S. schools. Other problematic behaviors that plague schools, including verbally assaultive behavior and drug use, are not addressed. Second, the chapter examines theories that bear on school violence and the empirical evidence linked to those theories. Third, the chapter looks at attempts to prevent school violence and, consequently, the suffering school violence causes.

Prevalence of Violence and Weapons in the Schools

Before reviewing the literature on the prevalence of violence and weapons in schools (in this section I limit prevalence findings to the 1990s and later), it

Author's Note: I thank Pearl Knopf Schonfeld for her editorial suggestions and Mark Davies and Lynn Mollick for comments on specific sections of the chapter.

is important to note a number of obstacles to accurately ascertaining the occurrence of violence. At the school level, officially recorded crime statistics often undercount crimes because of a lack of candor on the part of administrators doing the counting (Bloch, 1978; Dillon, 1994; Furlong & Morrison, 2000; Schonfeld, 1992). Political pressures, the avoidance of embarrassment, and the administrator's desire to avoid jeopardizing his or her career motivate the lack of candor. Moreover, crime-related surveillance at the school level is rarely audited by external agents (Kingery & Coggeshall, 2001). Kingery and Coggeshall (2001) demonstrated that the states' annual reporting of the numbers of students expelled for carrying firearms to school provides misleadingly low estimates of school-related firearms violations. Reporting problems notwithstanding, during the 1999–2000 academic year, an estimated 71% of public schools, as reported by principals, experienced at least one violent incident, and in 36% of public schools at least one violent incident was reported to police, suggesting that police reports underrepresent the extent of violence in schools. Self-report measures constitute an alternative to official records. Self-report data are not without problems. Studies by Cornell and Loper (1998) and Rosenblatt and Furlong (1997) indicate that students whose self-reports have validity problems (e.g., inconsistent responses) are likely to inflate reports of school-related violence.

Epidemiologic surveys are susceptible to problematic reporting. For example, the Youth Risk Behavior Survey (YRBS; Centers for Disease Control and Prevention [CDCP], 2004) asks students, "During the past 30 days, on how many days did you carry a weapon such as a gun, knife, or club on school property?" Although YRBS violence and other items have at least moderate reliability (kappas > .40; Brener et al., 2002), Furlong and Morrison (2000) underline the problematic nature of the above item and items like it. First, the item does not differentiate a student who brings a knife to school with no intention of hurting anyone and a student with intentions to harm. Second, the item does not distinguish bringing a weapon (a) to the grounds outside of school and (b) into the school building. Third, it is not clear from an affirmative answer which type of weapon was involved. Epidemiologic survey items, like the above YRBS item, are often designed for brevity, with each item covering a good deal of information and thus violating a norm of psychometric practice. In a similar vein, the YRBS item asking how often a student was in a physical fight does not distinguish victim from perpetrator. The reader should bear these methodological caveats in mind when considering the published rates of school-associated violence.

Homicide and Suicide

Although there can be problems in tracking and defining them, homicide and suicide are two types of violent events that are counted relatively accurately. Epidemiologic studies of school-associated violent deaths in the 1990s (Anderson et al., 2001; Kachur et al., 1996; see Table 9.1 for key

Table 9.1   School-Associated Homicide and Suicide

Study	Years Covered	Key Findings
Kachur et al. (1996)	1992–1994	105 school-associated deaths 85 homicides 76 homicides were students 20 student suicides Annualized student mortality rate: 0.09 per 100,000
Anderson et al. (2001)	1994–1999	253 school-associated deaths 172 of whom were students Annualized student mortality rate: 0.068 per 100,000 172 school-associated deaths were single homicides 30 suicides 11 homicide-suicides 5 deaths from legal interventions 2 unintentional gun-related deaths 18 homicides were faculty or staff 12 homicides were members of students' families 30 homicides were community residents 4 homicides were associated with the school in other ways 12 homicides were associated with neither the school nor the community 2 homicides were police officers 3 homicide victims' associations with the school were unknown
DeVoe et al. (2003)	1999–2000	CDCP's School-Associated Violent Death Surveillance System: 16 student homicides, 6 student suicides
	2000–2001 (tentative)	10 student homicides, 5 student suicides
	2001–2002 (tentative)	14 student homicides, 3 student suicides

findings) indicate that homicides and suicides occurring while the victims were in school, on the way to or from school, or traveling to or from or attending off-campus school-related events have been rare. Between 1992 and 1994, 96 students were either homicide or suicide victims. By contrast, during the same period, 6,050 children between 5 and 19 were homicide or suicide victims. Between 1994 and 1999, there were 172 school-associated student deaths. During the same period, 20,541 school-aged children were victims of homicide or suicide. Despite high-profile events in places like Littleton, Colorado, and West Paducah, Kentucky, the findings indicate that for children, school is protective vis-à-vis violent death. School, however, is more protective for some students than for others.

Between 1992 and 1994, 62% of school-related deaths occurred in urban areas and 30%, in suburban areas. Between 1994 and 1999, the figures were

52% and 35%, respectively. During that period, Black students had about five times the risk of becoming homicide victims as White students (the odds ratios were not available for 1992 to 1994); Hispanic students had 3.5 times the risk. Owing to its rarity in schools, no significant ethnic differences for suicide were found. Other findings showed that violent death was extremely rare in the context of elementary school and most frequent in the context of high school. About 48% of the homicides between 1994 and 1999 were related to interpersonal disputes (e.g., romantic entanglements), and about 30% of homicides were gang-related; 46% of homicide perpetrators had a history of criminal charges; 39% were gang members; and 20% had been bullied by peers. Between 1994 and 1999, firearms accounted for 69% of the homicides and 90% of the suicides. Although the rates of school-related violent death are still unacceptable, the data indicate that children are far safer inside schools than out.

Nonfatal Violent Behavior and Weapons-Carrying Among Students: National Samples

This section examines estimates of the prevalence of school violence obtained in studies having large nationally representative samples ($n > 4,600$ each year in the field; participation rates > 77%). In obtaining estimates of the prevalence of school-related nonfatal violent behavior and weapons possession, the caveats described earlier must be borne in mind. The YRBS (CDCP, 2004) has possibly been the best vehicle for providing national estimates because it has been conducted biennially since 1993. Estimates from other national studies are examined with reference to the YRBS.

The YRBS, using three-stage cluster sampling procedures, produced cross-sectional samples of high school students between 1993 and 2003. The YRBS includes an anonymously administered questionnaire that incorporates consistency checks that allow investigators to discount participants with anomalous responses (Brener et al., 2002). As shown in Table 9.2, estimates of the rates at which students carried a weapon on school property at least once during the 30-day period preceding the completion of the survey declined between 1993 and 2003 from about 12% to 6%. In 2003, males (9%) were three times as likely as females to report carrying a weapon; there were no marked differences in weapons possession by ethnicity or grade. The carrying of weapons, however, was more prevalent outside of school than on school property.

The YRBS inquired into physical fighting on school property in the 12 months prior to completing the survey. The decline between 1993 and 2003 was small, from 16% to 13%. Twice as many males as females acknowledged having been in a fight; compared with White youth (10%), Black (17%) and Hispanic youth (17%) were more likely to report fighting. Fighting declined from 9th (7%) to 12th grade (4%), although the dropping out of the most combative students may partially account for the decline.

Table 9.2 Prevalence of Nonfatal Violent Behavior and Weapons-Carrying Among Students: National Samples

Study	Years Covered	Key Findings
CDCP (2004)	1993–2003	YRBS data set; 9–12th graders; items cover a 30-day period Weapons-carrying on school property declined from 12% in 1993 to 6% in 2003 In 2003, rate of weapons-carrying outside school was 17% In 2003, 9% of males and 3% of females carried weapons Trend for not going to school because of safety fears was flat between 1993 (4%) and 2003 (5%) The next items covered a 12-month period: Physical fighting on school property declined from 16% in 1993 to 13% in 2003 Physical fighting outside school declined from 42% in 1993 to 33% in 2003 Threatened or injured on school property by someone having a weapon increased from 7% in 1993 to 9% in 2003
Brener et al. (2002)	1999	YRBS applied to a large national convenience sample in retest reliability study; high school students: 5–6% carried weapons to school in last 30 days 5–5.5% felt unsafe in school in the last 30 days 6–7% threatened with or injured by a weapon on school property in last 12 months
DeVoe et al. (2003)	1995–2001	NCVS data set. Annual rates of nonfatal school-associated violent crime in which students 12–18 were victims; time frame is the preceding 6 months: 1995 – 3.0% 1999 – 2.3% 2001 – 1.8%
Bezilla (1993)	1992	Gallup Organization: Ages 13–17, time frame is ever: Ever physically assaulted in school: 7% Had money stolen: 15% Observed fighting in school: 23% Observed weapons in school: 9%
Coggeshall and Kingery (2001)	1997	MTF: 7.7% weapons-carrying among 10th graders over last 4 weeks
	1997	YRBS: 6.8% weapons-carrying among 10th graders over last 30 days
	1995	NCVS: 3.9% of 10th graders brought something for protection over last 6 months
	1997	MTF: 3.9% of 10th graders did not go to school over last 4 weeks out of fear
	1997	YRBS: 4.0% of 10th graders did not go to school over last 30 days out of fear

(Continued)

Table 9.2 (Continued)

Study	Years Covered	Key Findings
	1995	NCVS: no comparable fear item
Kingery and Coggeshall (2001)	1995	Add Health data: 1.1% of students in Grades 7–12 brought guns to school in the last 30 days; estimated number of gun carriers in schools, given confidence interval, is between 200,000 and 310,000 students
	1998	MTF data on bringing gun to school in last 4 weeks: 3.1% of 8th graders (3.2% in 1997) 3.6% of 10th graders (3.5% in 1997) 2.1% of 12th graders (2.9% in 1997) Estimated number of gun carriers in schools (3 grades combined) is 350,000
Nansel et al. (2003) and personal communication (2004)	1998	Health Behavior of School-Aged Children Survey; Grades 6–10; time frame is the current school term: 10% of respondents were bullied 11% bullied others 4% both

NOTES:

YRBS = Youth Risk Behavior Survey.

MTF = Monitoring the Future Study. Also see O'Malley, Johnston, Bachman, and Schulenberg (2000); Johnston, O'Malley, and Bachman (2001).

NCVS = National Crime Victimization Survey/School Crime Supplement.

Add Health = National Longitudinal Study of Adolescent Health. Also see Resnick et al. (1997); Sieving et al. (2001).

The YRBS data also indicated that considerably more fighting took place outside of school than on school property.

Students also reported on having been threatened or injured on school property by someone holding a weapon in the 12 months prior to completing the survey. The trend from 1993 (7%) to 2003 (9%) was flat. Males were almost twice as likely as females to report having been threatened or injured; ethnic differences were minimal; there was a decline from 9th (12%) to 12th grade (6%). Finally, students' reports of not going to school one or more times in the last 30 days owing to safety concerns were stable between 1993 (4%) and 2003 (5%); males were as likely as females to express this concern; and compared with Whites (3%), Blacks (8%) and Hispanics (9%) were more likely to voice this worry.

A 1999 retest reliability study (Brener et al., 2002) applying the YRBS to a large convenience sample of high school students from 20 states and the District of Columbia obtained prevalence rates for carrying a weapon on school property, feeling unsafe at school, feeling threatened, or having been injured on school property that were highly comparable with the rates obtained in the 1999 round of the YRBS (CDCP, 2003).

Several other studies (Bezilla, 1993; Coggeshall & Kingery, 2001; DeVoe et al., 2003) of nationally representative samples of school-age youth have been conducted since 1990. Although the items employed in the surveys and the time frames applied to the items were not exactly the same as those in the YRBS, the prevalence rates were largely consistent with YRBS findings. For example, Kingery and Coggeshall (2001), employing public-use data files, found that the items in the Monitoring the Future (Johnston, O'Malley, & Bachman, 2001; O'Malley, Johnston, Bachman, & Schulenberg, 2000) data set pertaining to weapons-carrying and fear of victimization, items that were worded similarly to YRBS items, yielded prevalence rates similar to the rates obtained in the YRBS conducted the same year.

A problem related to school violence is bullying. Frequent fighting, being injured in a fight, and carrying weapons to school are associated with bullying and being bullied in (or away from) school (Nansel, Craig, Overpeck, Saluja, & Ruan, 2004; Nansel, Overpeck, Haynie, Ruan, & Scheidt, 2003; Nansel, Overpeck, Pilla, Ruan, Simons-Morton, & Scheidt, 2001). *Bullying* involves aggressive behavior with intent to harm that is carried out repeatedly by one or more students who are more powerful than the victim (Olweus, 1999). Bullying includes physical and/or verbal aggression (e.g., belittling). Nansel and her colleagues found that within U.S. schools, about one tenth of all students engaged in bullying and an equal proportion were bullied (personal communication, Sept. 3, 2004).

Nonfatal Violent Behavior and Weapons Carrying Among Students: Regional Samples

In order to look more closely at the rates of student violence, I examined studies having (a) large representative samples of students ($n > 900$) living in specific geographic areas and (b) high completion rates ($> 70\%$). As shown in Table 9.3, the rates of nonfatal violent behavior and weapons-carrying in regional studies, with one exception (Cornell & Loper, 1998), tend to be higher than the rates found in national samples. Table 9.3 indicates that the rates of weapon-carrying and violent behavior in South Carolina (Valois & McKeown, 1998; Valois, Vincent, McKeown, Garrison, & Kirby, 1993), Los Angeles (O'Keefe, 1997), and Texas (Orpinas, Basen-Engquist, Grunbaum, & Parcel, 1995; Orpinas, Murray, & Kelder, 1999) are striking. The studies, however, may overestimate the rates. For example, the weapon of choice in the South Carolina studies (Valois & McKeown, 1998; Valois et al., 1993) was the knife; it, therefore, would have been helpful if the investigators had differentiated more dangerous knives, such as switchblades, from penknives.

Conducting what was perhaps the methodologically soundest study, Cornell and Loper (1998) examined a large representative sample of

Table 9.3   Prevalence of Nonfatal Violent Behavior and Weapons-Carrying Among Students: Regional Samples

Study	Years Covered	Key Findings
Valois et al. (1993)	1990	YRBS instrument; 9–12th graders in South Carolina; items cover a 30-day period: Weapons-carrying in school: White males, 40%; White females, 11%; Black males, 36%; Black females, 14%
Valois and McKeown (1998)	1992	YRBS instrument; 9–12th graders in South Carolina; items cover a 30-day period: Weapons-carrying anywhere: White males, 54%; White females, 9%; Black males, 38%; Black females, 16%
O'Keefe (1997)	Not clear	Modified version of Physical Aggression subscale of the Conflict Tactics scales; items cover 1 year: Mainly 11–12th graders attending 6 inner-city Los Angeles high schools: 85% of males and 78% of females observed someone in school getting beaten up 62% of males and 46% of females witnessed someone in school being threatened by another person holding a gun or knife 49% of males and 40% of females observed a stabbing in school
Cleary (2000)	1997	YRBS instrument; 9–12th graders in New York State but outside New York City: 21% of students were victimized at school in any or all of the following ways: feeling unsafe in the last 30 days, having been threatened or injured in the last year, having property vandalized or stolen in the last year
Orpinas et al. (1995)	1991	YRBS items; 9th and 11th graders in a predominantly White Texas school district; time frame was 30 days: 20% of students had been in a fight anywhere 10% had carried a weapon anywhere 17% had been in a fight and carried a weapon anywhere
Orpinas et al. (1999)	1994	YRBS items; 7th, 8th, and 9th graders in urban Texas school district; time frame was 30 days: 23% of students had been in a fight on school property, including 28% of the boys and 17% of the girls; 23% Hispanic youth, 24% Black, 17% White, and 18% Asian
Cornell and Loper (1998)	1995	School Safety Survey; 7th, 9th, and 11th graders in all middle and high schools in suburban Virginia school district (62% White; 28% of middle and 13% of high school students registered for free or reduced-price lunch); items cover a 30-day period; items below are associated with school: 8% carried a knife 6% carried a gun 19% involved in physical fight (24% of 7th graders; 13.5% of 9th graders; 11% of 11th graders)

students in a suburban Virginia school district. Survey items were factually oriented (e.g., carrying a gun to school to protect oneself; carrying a knife to school to protect oneself) and contemporaneous (the items cover the 30 days antedating the survey). The survey included validity checks (e.g., the negative endorsement of an item such as "I am reading this survey carefully") and the identification of surveys in which the unlikely event that six high-risk behaviors (carrying a gun, knife, and other weapons) were admitted to. Eight percent of the students carried a knife, 6% carried a gun, and 19% were involved in a physical fight. Fighting was more common among boys. The prevalence of fighting declined from 7th to 11th grade. There was also substantial overlap in the tendency to carry weapons and fight in school and out.

Although it would be unwise to average rates from studies using different methods across different time periods, the preponderance of evidence from the above studies indicates that, nationally and regionally, a substantial number of students carry weapons on school property (e.g., 5% carrying any weapon over a 30-day period in 2003 in the YRBS; 6% carrying a gun over a 30-day period in the Cornell and Loper study; slightly lower rates in the MTF and Add Health studies in Table 9.2). Fighting on school property among students is cause for concern (e.g., 13% of high school students in 2003 over the course of a year in the YRBS; 19% of middle and high school students over 30 days in the Cornell and Loper study). The rates were highest in middle school (Cornell & Loper, 1998; Orpinas et al., 1999). The prevalence of threats or injury on school property (9% in 2003 over a school year in the YRBS) is also cause for concern. Although there is evidence that the rates of exposure to violence can be very high in inner-city schools (e.g., O'Keefe, 1997), the problem of school-related violence and weapons possession transcends geography: School violence is a national problem. The combination of weapons, fighting, and victimization at school constitutes a public health threat.

Teachers and Staff

Bloch (1978) observed more than 250 Los Angeles teachers referred for psychiatric evaluation who showed symptoms of "combat neurosis." The teachers reported that their classes often contained a high proportion of violence-prone students. Studies of unselected samples, however, better put into perspective the relation of teaching to violence (see Table 9.4 for a summary of the findings). Anderson et al. (2001) found that between 1994 and 1999, 18 faculty *and* staff were murdered (see Table 9.1), averaging 3.6 homicides per year. According to the National Center for Education Statistics (NCES; 2004), there were approximately 3,071,000 teachers in the United States in 1996, the midpoint of that period. If one conservatively counts all the above homicide victims as teachers, then the yearly homicide rate would be approximately 0.12 per 100,000. In 1996, there were 927 job-associated homicides in the United States (Bureau of Labor Statistics, 2004a). In January 1996, an estimated 132,616,000 Americans were in the

Table 9.4   Prevalence of Violent Behavior With Teachers as Victims

Study	Years Covered	Key Findings
Bureau of Labor Statistics (2004a)	1994–1999	Nationally, 3.6 homicides per year in which teachers and staff were victims 0.12 homicides per 100,000 teachers per year (est. by author) 0.70 homicides per 100,000 workers per year (est. by author)
DeVoe et al. (2003)	1997–2001	Nationally, teachers were victims of 1.3 million nonfatal crimes, including theft, battery, and rape
Peek-Asa et al. (1997)	1994–1995 (4-month period)	California: 269.7 violent workplace injuries per 100,000 teachers; 518 violent workplace injuries per 100,000 school bus drivers; 72.9 to 82.5 violent workplace injuries per 100,000 workers (all covered CA workers)
LaMar et al., (1998)	1992	Minnesota: 70 injury assaults per 100,000 (compensated injury assault rate in the field of education); 47 injury assaults per 100,000 workers (all covered MN workers)
Islam et al. (2003)	1997–1999	West Virginia: 104.6 assault-related injuries per 1,000 injuries among teachers; The state average = 13.5 assault-related injuries per 1,000 injuries
Hashemi and Webster (1998)	1993–1996	Database of 28,000 workers' compensation claims from 51 jurisdictions: 11.4% of school-related claims were violence-related, highest of all economic sectors (Above fraction was probably an underestimate because the "education" category included college professors and college administrators); 74% of claims were filed by women; In random sample of teacher claims, *all* injuries were student perpetrated
Williams et al. (1989)	1985	Texas school district; 90 of 263 teachers participated; 34% completion rate; items cover the present school year: Rate of theft = 24%; 8% if one, conservatively, places *all* 263 teachers in the denominator; Rate of threats = 51%; 17.5% if one places *all* 263 teachers in the denominator
Chang et al. (2003)	1996–1999	National MTF sample of high school seniors: Self-reported rates of hitting a teacher or supervisor in last 12 months = 1.7 and 1.9% Likely underestimate because students who dropped out likely included violent youth
Meyer (2004) personal communication	2003	National MTF sample of high school seniors: Self-reported rates of hitting a teacher or supervisor = 3.2%; Likely underestimate—see above

Study	Years Covered	Key Findings
MetLife (1999)	1998	National sample but completion rate = 20%; items refer to "ever": Rates of victimization in urban teachers = 19% (14% in 1993); Rates of victimization in suburban and rural teachers = 14% (10% in 1993); Findings similar to 1993 MetLife survey

NOTES:

MTF = Monitoring the Future Study
Also see O'Malley, Johnston, Bachman, and Schulenberg (2000); Johnston, O'Malley, and Bachman (2001).

labor force (Bureau of Labor Statistics, 2004b). Thus the estimated annual job-associated homicide rate was 0.70 per 100,000, considerably higher than that of teachers. Although one work-associated murder is too many, teachers were relatively safer than the average worker.

Using data from a national survey, the U.S. Department of Justice estimated that between 1997 and 2001, teachers were victims of more than 1.3 million nonfatal crimes, ranging from theft to battery to rape (DeVoe et al., 2003). The estimated rate of violent victimization was 21 violent crimes per 1,000 teachers per year, with urban, male, and middle and high school teachers more than twice as likely to be victimized as their suburban or rural, female, and elementary school counterparts.

Other evidence indicates that individuals employed in the education field are relatively vulnerable to assault. Studies of workers' compensation claims and employer injury reports (Hashemi & Webster, 1998; Islam, Edla, Mujuru, Doyle, & Ducatman, 2003; LaMar, Gerberich, Lohman, & Zaidman, 1998; Peek-Asa, Howard, Vargas, & Kraus, 1997) indicate that individuals in the field of education have been assaulted at higher rates than members of most other occupational groups. California workplace injury data collected over 4 consecutive months yielded annualized rates of workplace violence–related injuries (Peek-Asa et al., 1997). The rate for teachers was 269.7 per 100,000, more than three times the state average for all workers. The rate for school bus drivers was 518 per 100,000, more than six times the state average. Students perpetrated more than 80% of the assaults in schools and on school buses. In Minnesota in 1992, the compensated injury assault rate for individuals in the education field was 70 per 100,000, 50% higher than the state average (LaMar et al., 1998). The assailants were overwhelmingly students.

In a West Virginia compensation study covering the years 1997 to 1999, Islam et al. (2003) estimated the proportion of all compensated workplace injuries that resulted from assault. (The authors could not obtain denominators representing the numbers of individuals working in each economic sector in the state work force.) The ratio of the proportion of sector-related compensated injuries that resulted from violence to the statewide proportion served as a proxy for job-related assault risk. Islam et al. found that teachers experienced 104.6 assault-related injuries per 1,000 injuries, almost eight times the state average. Hashemi and Webster (1998) examined more than 28,000 workers compensation claims occurring over 4 years in 51 jurisdictions. Although they too could not obtain denominator information, Hashemi and Webster were able to calculate the proportion of claims that were violence-related. Consistent with the West Virginia study, more than 11% of school-related claims were violence-related, the highest of the economic sectors studied. A substudy of a random sample of claims revealed that in *every* school-related claim the perpetrator was a student. It should be noted that studies based on workers' compensation are not without limitations: Some occupations are not covered by workers' compensation (e.g., federal employees) and not all victims of workplace assault take advantage of worker compensation.

Three other studies found in Table 9.4 (Chang, Chen, & Brownson, 2003; Metropolitan Life Insurance Company, 1999; P. Meyer, personal communication, August 13, 2004; Williams, Winfree, & Clinton, 1989) also provide estimates of the rates of teacher victimization. Study limitations, however, restrict the applicability of the estimates.

The extant evidence from studies of unselected samples of students and teachers, including worker injury reports, indicates that being a teacher carries an excess risk for becoming a victim of violence. Moreover, the very high rate of assault of school bus drivers (Peek-Asa et al., 1997) is especially troubling. Because the great majority of the drivers' assailants attended school, other students and staff were also at risk. The Bloch (1978) study suggests that just being exposed to threats and witnessing student-on-student fighting without actually being assaulted adversely affects teachers. A study of a representative group of newly appointed women teachers found that difficult school environments adversely affected the teachers' job satisfaction, self-esteem, motivation to remain in the profession, and levels of depressive symptoms (Schonfeld, 2001). It is impossible to disentangle the adverse school environments, however, because they include a combination of physically and verbally assaultive students, academically weak students, and ineffectual administrative leadership.

Theoretical Models of School Violence

Rephrasing commentary by Farrington (1998), there are no specific models of school violence; there are, however, models of child and adolescent aggression and delinquency. The violence in which children and adolescents engage transcends the school-community boundary. The models described here attempt to account for a variety of antisocial conduct, including violence, in school and out. This section briefly examines five model types (see Table 9.5 for a summary of the models) and provides a selective reading of the supporting evidence. The

Table 9.5   Summary of Models That Bear on the Occurrence of School Violence

Model	Key Features
Ecological-Contextual	Bronfenbrenner's (1979) Russian dolls model. Environments represent nested structures with processes linking lower- and higher-level environments. Immediate environment the child perceives is nested within a higher-level environment. Activities, roles, etc., that are structured by the context play a role in the development of the child. Neighborhood and school context play roles in the development of youth violence.
Strain	Agnew's (1992) diathesis stress model. Social and other stressors affect child, provoking anger. Anger mediates the relation of the stressor to delinquent activity. Social (supportive others) and personal (mastery) resources mitigate the impact of stressors on anger/delinquency.
Control Theory	According to Hirschi (1969), when the "individual's bond to society is weak or broken" delinquent risk increases. Attachments to parents and schools are important for internalizing conventional norms. Attachments to peers do not play a large role.
Bandura's Social Learning Theory	Attentional, memory/representational, motoric, and incentive/motivational processes affected by anticipated, vicarious, and actual reinforcement. Much of human behavior, including violent and aggressive behavior, is learned through observation: TV, parents, peers, etc.
Akers's Social Learning Theory	Learning of antisocial conduct through reinforcement à la Skinner and observation à la Bandura. Differential association with antisocial peers contributes to the development of antisocial conduct; peers reinforce and model antisocial conduct.
Patterson's Social Interactional Model	Coercive cycle of interaction involving parent and child. Role of escape conditioning. Child's successful aversive response to parent negatively reinforces the child by allowing the child to escape the parent's aversive directives. The parent is successfully "punished" for attempting to direct the child to turn off the TV and do homework. Generalization of aversive responding to other contexts, including school.
Dodge's Social Cognition Model	Encoding social cues; interpreting those cues; drawing from a repertoire of behavioral responses stored in long-term memory; evaluating likely consequences of the accessed responses; selecting and enacting a response.

models include ecological-contextual, strain, control, social learning, and social cognitive models. No single model, however, encompasses all the important risk factors (Loeber, Farrington, Stouthamer-Loeber, Moffitt, & Caspi, 1998).

Ecological-Contextual Model

The ecological-contextual model is associated with Urie Bronfenbrenner (1979) although it dates to the work of Kurt Lewin (1935). According to the model, the individual develops within a context of "nested ecological structures" such that the immediate environment the child perceives is embedded within a larger environment such as the home or the classroom, which in turn is embedded within yet a larger environment such as the neighborhood or the school. The contexts within this hierarchy are interrelated. The child progressively accommodates the contexts within which he or she develops. The activities, roles, and interpersonal relations within contexts play parts in human development. Role transitions contribute to developmental change. A distal context exerts effects on the contexts nested within it, until the most proximal context to affect the child is reached. The studies outlined below provide a glimpse into the effects of biological, community, family, and school contexts as they pertain to violence and aggression.

One context that is an addition to the original ecological model is that of the individual's biology (Bronfenbrenner, 2005; Bronfenbrenner & Ceci, 1994). Although the evidence with regard to the contribution of genes to antisocial conduct is not unambiguous (Gottfredson & Hirschi, 1990), biological factors (Raine, 2002) constitute a context that is likely to come into play, particularly with respect to how biological factors interact with the child's social environment. Raine (1993) found that violent youth tend to manifest low resting heart rates, reflecting low levels of autonomic arousal, which in turn may precipitate sensation seeking and concomitant rule breaking. Moffitt (1990) found that delinquent boys with early problematic motor skills, low IQ before the age of 5, attentional deficits, and reading difficulties at school age were more persistently antisocial and had poorer prognoses than other children, including other delinquents without these neuropsychological problems. In her Dunedin, New Zealand, sample, early attentional deficits interacted with family adversity to predict antisocial conduct at age 11. Pine, Shaffer, Schonfeld, and Davies (1997) found that minor physical anomalies, thought to be markers of neural maldevelopment in the fetus, interacted with environmental disadvantage to predict conduct problems in boys at age 17.

The intensity of antisocial activity in the community in which a school is located is directly related to the extent of antisocial conduct occurring inside the school (Bowen & Bowen, 1999; Campbell & Schwarz, 1996; Cornell & Loper, 1998; Evans, 2004; Gottfredson & Gottfredson, 1985; O'Keefe, 1997; Rutter, 1980). A set of studies (Sampson & Groves, 1989; Stouthamer-Loeber,

Loeber, Wei, Farrington, & Wikström, 2002; Wilson, 1987) indicates that neighborhood contextual factors influence violence in the community that in turn carries over into schools. Community contextual factors include joblessness and disorganization (Wilson, 1987); proximity of informal adult friendship networks, extent of adult participation in voluntary groups, and extent of supervision of teenage groups (Sampson & Groves, 1989); and low-income public housing, which has both a main effect and an interactive effect that can amplify the influence of other risk factors on antisocial conduct in boys (Stouthamer-Loeber et al., 2002). Contextual factors such as low socioeconomic standing (SES) and family stressors (e.g., death of a loved one) set the stage for harsh discipline and physical punishment that in turn influence childhood aggression that carries over into schools (Lansford, Deater-Deckard, Dodge, Bates, & Pettit, 2004; Pettit, Clawson, Dodge, & Bates, 1996).

The context of the school has an important connection to the development of aggression. Schools with metal detectors, security guards, and so forth tend to experience more violence (Mayer & Leone, 1999). The presence of security procedures, however, is more likely to be a consequence of school violence than its cause. Arcus (2002) found an association between school shootings and a policy supporting corporal punishment in the state within which the school is located; the association, however, reflected an ecological correlation (Robinson, 1950). An ecological correlation is a correlation between averages obtained from groups of people (e.g., school districts, states) and therefore reveals little about whether shooters had been exposed to corporal punishment.

Some studies examined the relation of school climate and the prevailing zeitgeist of the school to violence. Using a national sample, Mayer and Leone (1999) found that the amount of consistency in rule enforcement in schools was related to lower levels of school disorder. In large Arab and Jewish Israeli samples ranging from Grade 4 to high school, school climate, as reflected in teacher support and prosocial school policies, predicted extent of in-school victimization (Astor, Benbenishty, Zeira, & Vinokur, 2002; Benbenishty, Astor, Zeira, & Vinokur, 2002). The classroom context exerts similar effects. Aggressive first-grade boys placed in classes marked by high aggression are more likely than comparable first graders placed in classes marked by lower levels of aggression to be persistently aggressive in middle school (Kellam, Ling, Merisca, Brown, & Ialongo, 1998).

Schools having as a background characteristic ongoing "low-level" aggression (e.g., hitting and pushing) provide a context that sets the stage for more aggression (Boxer, Edwards-Leeper, Goldstein, Musher-Eizenman, & Dubow, 2003). Although the data are cross-sectional, Boxer et al. (2003) found that students with greater exposure to low-level aggression (e.g., witnessing it or having been victimized) were more likely to engage in aggressive behavior. Felson, Liska, South, and McNulty (1994) took advantage of longitudinal data collected in 87 high schools and conducted perhaps the best study of the influence of school-level zeitgeist on violence. Felson et al. found that school-level values regarding violence directly influenced interpersonal school violence, adjusting for the individual's commitment to such values.

In some respects the ecological-contextual model is a metamodel. Although Bronfenbrenner (1979) underlined the importance of processes connecting a subcontext to a larger context and the processes connecting the immediate context to the behavior of the individual, the processes themselves are more likely the subject of other theoretical models. Nonetheless, the ecological model emphasizes that schools, which are embedded in communities, accommodate those surroundings for better or for worse. School and classroom contexts in turn influence aggressive behavior in individual children.

The Strain Model

General strain theory is associated with Robert Agnew (1992), although its origins date to the work of Robert Merton (1938). Agnew posited three types of strain or adversity in the individual's social environment: (a) the prevention of the individual "from achieving positively valued goals," (b) the withdrawal or threatened withdrawal of objects the individual values, and (c) the introduction or threatened introduction of "noxious or negatively valued stimuli." The first category of strain includes the disjunction between aspirations and actual achievement in everyday life and the absence of fairness, equity, or respect in everyday interactions. The second category includes the loss or anticipated loss of boyfriend or girlfriend, the death of someone important, and parental separation. The third includes such events as criminal victimization, corporal punishment, parent or teacher criticism, and school failure. An encounter with these types of adversity increases the likelihood that the individual will experience a negative emotion, although anger is "the critical emotional reaction" in strain theory. Anger is disinhibiting. It builds a desire for revenge and supplies the emotional arousal required to fuel action; it ignites aggression. Although an antisocial response to strain can be instrumental (e.g., attempt to regain what one lost) or retaliatory, another response to strain is escapist, with the individual turning to drugs to tamp down disagreeable mood states that strain precipitates (Paternoster & Mazerolle, 1994).

Because only a subgroup of strained individuals resorts to violence and delinquency, the theory includes cognitive, emotional, and behavioral coping strategies that mitigate the impact of strain. Other mitigating factors include personal (e.g., intelligence and mastery) and social resources (e.g., supportive others). Contextual factors, such as the social environment's emphasis on money and status or the nature of the social group to whom the individual's failings are visible, can influence the adolescent's response to strain in the direction of violence. Temperamental factors, learning history, and belief system also play a role in shaping the individual's response to strain. Strain theory has accrued a degree of support.

Agnew and White (1992), Paternoster and Mazerolle (1994), and Brezina (1996) provided partial support for the strain model. Using the first wave of a longitudinal study of New Jersey adolescents, Agnew and White found that strain, reflected in stressful life events (SLEs) and "hassles," was cross-sectionally related to a measure of delinquency that included violence in and out of school. In a longitudinal analysis that controlled for Time-1 delinquency and other confounding factors, Time-1 strain predicted delinquency 3 years later.

Using longitudinal data from a national survey of 11- to 17-year-olds, Paternoster and Mazerolle found that Time-1 strain, controlling for Time-1 delinquency, predicted delinquency 1 year later. Delinquency included violence in school such as hitting a teacher. Other analyses were unsupportive of the view that selected factors buffered (e.g., self-efficacy) or amplified (e.g., delinquent peers) the impact of strain on delinquency. In an analysis of multiwave data on male public high school students, Brezina (1996) found that strain—as reflected in parental punitiveness, "mean teachers," and dissatisfaction with school—predicted negative emotions (i.e., anger, resentment, anxiety, and depression) 1 year later, controlling for Time-1 emotions. Brezina also found that delinquency, which included violence in and out of school, buffered the impact of early strain on later anger; the interaction was specific to anger and did not exert comparable effects on other emotions.

Additional partial support for the strain model comes from longitudinal studies by Hoffmann and Cerbone (1999) and Agnew, Brezina, Wright, and Cullen (2002) and cross-sectional studies by Natvig, Albrektsen, and Qvarnstrøm (2001) and Rosario, Salzinger, Feldman, and Ng-Mak (2003). In a 4-year, four-wave study of participants who were initially ages 11 to 14, Hoffmann and Cerbone (1999) found that the accumulation of SLEs over time predicted "growth" in delinquency, which included violence in and out of school, although there was little evidence that hypothesized moderators (e.g., mastery) reduced the influence of life events on delinquency. Using longitudinal data collected on children who were initially between the ages of 7 and 11, Agnew et al. (2002) found that early family and neighborhood strain and a measure obtained independently from parents bearing on the extent to which they lost control and hurt their child influenced delinquency (which included seriously hurting someone anywhere) 5 years later, adjusting for prior conduct.

Using a Norwegian sample of 13- to 15-year-olds, Natvig et al. (2001) found that school stressors were related to increased risk of bullying behavior, and the supportiveness of teachers and peers was related to decreased risk. Rosario et al. (2003) found that in a sample of Hispanic and Black New York City sixth graders, witnessing community violence or having been victimized was related to elevated levels of delinquency (which included fighting anywhere and hitting teachers). Some types of support from others (guardians for girls in the case of victimization; peers for boys in the case of witnessing) buffered the impact of such exposures on delinquency.

Strain theory is familiar to stress researchers because strain theory posits a diathesis-stress model. In stress research, investigators seek to identify uncontrollable SLEs or job conditions that affect outcomes, such as job satisfaction, depressive symptoms, and blood pressure. Personality (e.g., mastery, negative affectivity) and social variables (e.g., support from others) are hypothesized to mitigate or amplify the impact of the stressors. Alternative models assess the effects personality and social variables exert on outcomes independently of the effects of stressors. Thus Agnew's strain model should appeal to stress researchers because of the similarity in paradigm.

Control Theory

Although control theory is associated with Travis Hirschi (1969), its origins can be traced to the work of Emiles Durkheim (1897/1979). According to Hirschi, acts of delinquency are more likely when the "individual's bond to society is weak or broken" (p. 16). Social bonds underlie the internalization of norms and conscience. Delinquency includes violence and other kinds of anti-social conduct in school and out. The theory emphasizes that the weakening of attachments to conventional others is more important to the development of antisocial conduct than are bonds to delinquent peers. The bond itself comprises four elements: attachment in the form of affectional ties to others, particularly parents and school; commitment to conventional endeavors such as schoolwork and a job; involvement in conventional activities such as extracurriculars, studying, and family; and belief in the values of conventional society.

Gottfredson and Hirschi (1990) later built on the above model, developing a theory in which self-control, a key factor in thwarting the development of crime and delinquency, emerges out of socialization and attachment processes (e.g., parental caring). A problematic aspect of the newer theory is the tautological relation between lack of self-control and the variables such a lack explains (e.g., delinquency and drug use; see Akers, 2000). By contrast, "explanations of deviant behavior based on attachment do not beg the question, since the extent to which a person is attached to others can be measured independently of his deviant behavior" (Hirschi, 1969, p. 19).

Hirschi's (1969) cross-sectional findings involving boys attending public junior and senior high schools in northern California were largely consistent with control theory. Extent of the boys' attachment to their parents, regardless of class and race, was inversely related to delinquency, which included violence in and out of school. The extent of the boys' attachment to their fathers, regardless of the boys' attachment to delinquent friends, was inversely related to delinquency. Hirschi also observed that "the idea that delinquents have comparatively warm, intimate social relations with each other (or with anyone) is a romantic myth" (p. 159).

Hirschi and Hindelang (1977) advanced the view that the well-established, inverse relation between IQ and self-reported and official delinquency is mediated by the effect of IQ on "school performance and adjustment." Hirschi (1969) found that attachment to school and concern about teachers' opinions were inversely related to delinquent behavior. Likewise, attachment to conventional peers was inversely related to delinquency.

A good deal of other cross-sectional research has provided evidence consistent with the social control model (Cretacci, 2003; Kerres Malecki & Demaray, 2003; Minden, Henry, Tolan, & Gorman-Smith, 2000; Resnick et al., 1997; Schreck & Fisher, 2004). Using the Add Health data set, Cretacci (2003) found that in middle and late adolescence, but not early adolescence, attachment to school was related to lower levels of violence; in late adolescence, but not earlier, commitment to school was related to lower levels of violence. In attempting to extend control theory to religion, he found no link between either the student's commitment to religion or parental attachment to religion and adolescent violence. In a study of a largely Hispanic, Illinois middle school sample, Kerres Malecki and Demaray (2003) found that choosing not to carry a weapon to school was highly related to teacher support and, to a lesser extent, the supportiveness of parents, classmates, and close friends. Minden et al. (2000) found that school violence in another largely Hispanic Illinois sample of inner-city fifth and seventh graders was inversely related to the extent to which the adults and peers who knew the student (i.e., the members of the student's adult and peer networks) knew one another (i.e., boundary density). School violence was inversely related to the extent of the students' cumulative involvement in conventional activities such as school, church, and athletics.

Using the Add Health data set, Resnick et al. (1997) found that connectedness to family and school was inversely related to health risk behaviors, including fighting and hurting others regardless of location (also see NCES, 2000; Bonny, Britto, Klostermann, Hornung, & Slap, 2000). Schreck and Fisher (2004) conducted one of the few studies that link social ties to victimization. Using the Add Health data set, they found that parents' nurturing feelings for the child and a family climate variable that reflected the child's positive feelings for his or her family were related to lower risk of violent victimization in or out of school. Two protective processes may underlie the findings: (a) strong ties in parents promote more effective guardianship; and (b) strong ties in the child reduce his or her willingness to take risks.

Two longitudinal studies (Borowsky, Ireland, & Resnick, 2002, and Wiesner & Windle, 2004) support the view that social ties protect the individual from engaging in violence. Borowsky et al. (2002) found that among 11th-grade Add Health boys and girls who had ever repeated a grade (these students are at higher risk for engaging in violent behavior), parent and school connectedness in the 11th grade predicted reduced risk of serious violence in or out of school during the 12th, although multivariate analyses did not control for 11th-grade violence and victimization. Wiesner and Windle (2004), using data collected over a 2-year period in a mainly White, middle-class western New York sample of high school students, found that lack of family support at Time 1 was related to the later delinquent behavior including violence (e.g., hitting a teacher) as were (consistent with strain theory) Time-1 SLEs.

Sampson and Laub (1993) integrated and recast an enormous amount of data that Sheldon and Eleanor Glueck (1950) collected earlier on 1,000 White, Boston-area boys. Multivariate analyses bearing on the cross-sectional and case-control components of the study revealed that number of delinquent acts (which included teacher-reported cruelty) were associated with early temperamental difficulties (e.g., tantrums); parents' use of harsh, erratic discipline; parental rejection; poor maternal supervision (e.g., leaving the boy on his own without care); crowding at home; disconnectedness from school; and attachment to delinquent peers.

Sampson and Laub took Hirschi's original theory as a point of departure by mapping out a network of causal factors that come to the fore and recede at different points in the life course. Different sorts of social bonds exert informal control over the individual, and their presence or absence play a role in the prevention or onset of, or desistance from, delinquency and crime. Moreover, their findings also suggest that antisocial conduct undermines social ties.

Social Learning Models

Theories of social learning (SL) are associated with Albert Bandura and Ronald Akers. Bandura's (1977, 1983) model of observational learning encompasses four interrelated processes: attentional, memory/representational, motoric, and incentive/motivational processes. *Attentional processes* refer to the regulation of perception. *Representational processes* concern the encoding in memory of enduring symbols—verbal or iconic—of what was observed. *Motoric processes* concern the transformation into behavior of mental representations of what was observed. *Motivational processes* manage observationally learned behavior; these processes include the actual and anticipated reinforcement of the individual, as well as models, and include tangible and intangible (e.g., status) rewards. Because a good deal of human behavior is learned by observation, it is a corollary that aggressive behavior is observationally learned. According to Bandura's theory, with the learning that occurs over time, the child increasingly becomes a psychologically self-regulating individual, developing internal standards against which to judge his or her own behavior. Such a self-system can be particularly troubling if the individual's internal standards are ones that value aggression.

Akers's (2000; Akers, Krohn, Lanza-Kaduce, & Radosevich, 1979) version of SL theory holds that children and adolescents learn antisocial behavior through differential reinforcement—à la B. F. Skinner—as well as through elements of Bandura's more cognitive, observational learning. A feature of Akers's (2000; Akers et al., 1979) model is that of differential association, which refers to the extent children become exposed to reference individuals who define, reinforce, and model antisocial or conforming behavior. Association with antisocial peers precedes and paves the way for the individual's becoming engaged in antisocial conduct. A parallel process is thought to underlie conforming behavior. The view of Akers contrasts with that of Hirschi (1969) regarding the role of the peer group in socializing the child.

Gerald Patterson's (1982, 1995) social interactional model is a more behavioristic and less cognitive SL theory than the models associated with Bandura and Akers. At the core of Patterson's theory is the concept of *coercion,* which involves the individual's application and counterapplication of aversive behaviors contingent on target behaviors in another person. Aversive behaviors are ordinarily punishing; in the Skinnerian model, a punishment causes a target behavior to occur less frequently. Patterson identified many aversive behaviors in the parent-child relationship, for example, hitting, yelling, and whining. Sometimes a child resists a mother who attempts to coerce the child into performing certain behaviors (e.g., shutting off the TV and beginning a homework assignment). If the child successfully uses aversive means (e.g., by hitting or screaming) to escape the mother's intrusions, the child learns to apply such behaviors at home and then elsewhere, including the school.

Consistent with SL theory, investigators have documented the impact of exposure to violent television programs (Bushman & Huesmann, 2001; Paik & Comstock, 1994) and, to a lesser extent, violent video games (Anderson & Bushman, 2001) on childhood violence. SL theory also holds that children learn from live models they observe. Considerable research has linked exposure to physical punishment by parents to aggressive behavior in children (e.g., Sampson & Laub, 1993; Straus, 1991). Exemplary research involving a large, diverse urban sample that was followed longitudinally revealed that the extent to which first through third graders initially witnessed violence in their communities was related to aggression, as reflected by the judgments of classmates and teachers, in Grades 4 through 6, controlling for initial aggression (Guerra, Huesmann, & Spindler, 2003). The effects of exposure to community violence on later aggression also affected the extent to which the children cognized about aggression, analyses suggesting that children's cognitions mediate the relation of early exposure to later aggression.

There is evidence supporting Akers's view regarding the influence of peers on an individual's propensity to engage in antisocial conduct, although there is some support for the view that similarity in attributes such as minor delinquency precedes friendship pairing and guides such pairing (Kandel, 1978). Wright, Caspi, Moffitt, and Silva (2001) found that children with low self-control (a construct that includes antisocial conduct) through age 11 become more antisocial in adolescence to the extent that they are exposed to delinquent peers. In addition, Rosario et al. (2003) found that high levels of support from peers amplified antisocial responding in male and female Black and Hispanic sixth graders who were victimized.

Consistent with the social interactional model, evidence from the Oregon Youth Study (OYS), a longitudinal study of fourth-grade White boys, indicated that inept parental disciplining and poor parental monitoring were related to the early onset of boys' antisocial conduct (Patterson, Capaldi, & Bank, 1991; Patterson & Yoerger, 1997). OYS data indicated a bidirectional relation between steadily increasing antisocial conduct and increased hesitancy in parents to exert control. Patterson et al. found that early antisocial behavior paves the way for affiliation with deviant peers in school and elsewhere. Dishion, Andrews, and Crosby (1995) found that antisocial boys' interactions with friends were often of low quality, somewhat less durable, and fraught with coercion and bossiness. Dishion, Patterson, and Griesler (1994) also found that even the most difficult children have at least one reciprocating friend based on common-ground activities, such as rule breaking, and that conversations within such friendships were more deviant than were those of comparison boys.

The SL and social interaction research programs allow investigators to get close to the actual transactions that take place in the lives of children in order to identify the behavioral and psychological processes that lead children to violence and other forms of antisocial conduct. The SL and social interaction research programs underline the role of mechanisms of learning and cognition that have been well established in the field of psychology in elucidating the processes by which children, in their *immediate* social environments, learn to engage in violent behavior.

Social Information Processing Models

Social information processing (SIP) models underline the role children's cognitions play in the development of aggressive behavior. In this section, I focus on the SIP-related research of Kenneth Dodge and his colleagues. The model represents an extension of historically important basic research in cognitive psychology (Miller, Galanter, & Pribram, 1961; Neisser, 1967) into consequential new domains. The SIP model advanced by Dodge, Pettit, McClaskey, and Brown (1986) posits a sequence of cognitive activities in which individuals engage in social situations. First, the individual encodes social cues and then interprets those cues. Next, the individual draws from a repertoire of behavioral responses stored in long-term memory (LTM) and then evaluates the likely consequences of the accessed responses. Finally, the individual selects and enacts a response. Aggressive children process information differently from their nonaggressive peers. Aggressive children manifest problems encoding relevant social cues; they show biases in the direction of interpreting others' intentions as reflecting hostility when the intentions are unclear; compared with peers, they have stored in LTM fewer competent, prosocial responses and more aggressive responses; aggressive children are more disposed to retrieve aggressive responses from LTM; and they are more likely to evaluate favorably anticipated consequences of aggressive actions (Dodge et al., 1986).

Dodge et al. (1986) compared the social cognitions of highly aggressive, socially rejected second through fourth graders and nonaggressive "average" peers. In laboratory tasks, the aggressive children were not as competent as the control children in SIP, notably in the number of antisocial responses they generated and their propensity to enact aggressive responses. In the classroom, the aggressive children were more antisocial and disruptive and were more ignored by classmates, although this is not surprising given that teachers helped select the children. The competency of the children in a staged peer-group entry task was judged by adult observers and two peer confederates. Success at the entry task was related to SIP variables, including self-monitoring and number of prosocial solutions generated to questions. Responses in a live peer-group provocation situation were also related to SIP variables, including endorsing aggressive responses and making hostile attributions.

Dodge, Lochman, Harnish, Bates, and Pettit (1997) assessed the SIP capabilities in reactively and proactively aggressive children and nonaggressive peers entering the third grade. Reactively aggressive children were at higher risk for having experienced harsh physical punishment; consistent with this finding, the reactively aggressive children showed more problems encoding social cues. Proactively aggressive children were more likely to anticipate positive consequences for aggressive responses. Dodge et al. (1997) suggested that cognitive factors such as general intelligence could account for the observed differences in SIP. IQ-related differences between aggressive and nonaggressive children have been widely observed (e.g., Hirschi & Hindelang, 1977; Huesmann, Eron, & Yarmel, 1987; Loeber et al., 1998; Schonfeld, Shaffer, O'Connor, & Portnoy, 1988).

Although the above studies indicate that aggressive children think differently from other children, none of the studies demonstrated that deviant SIP plays a causal role in the development of aggressive behavior. Other evidence implicates SIP in the development of aggressive behavior. In a six-month longitudinal study, Weiss, Dodge, Bates, and Pettit (1992) found that Time-1 SIP partly mediated the link between early harsh parental discipline and Time-2, kindergarten aggression, controlling for Time-1 aggression and temperament. In a test of the specificity of the model, Weiss et al. found that SIP did not mediate the link between early harm and Time-2 internalizing. A follow-up of the sample into third and fourth grades suggests that SIP partly mediates the relation of early abuse to later teacher-reported aggression (Dodge, Pettit, Bates, & Valente, 1995).

Like the SL theories of Bandura, Akers, and Patterson, the SIP model of Dodge and his colleagues outlines processes thought to pave the way for the development of aggressive conduct in and out of school. Clues from the studies by Weiss et al. (1992) and Dodge et al. (1995) suggest that harsh parental discipline, a variable well connected to antisocial outcomes as early as kindergarten, helps shape the biases in SIP that partly contribute to aggressive responding.

A Final Word About Models of School Violence

No one model provides a "complete" explanation of violence in school and elsewhere. The models complement each other and the more atheoretical, "risk factor" approaches to antisocial conduct in youth (Farrington, 1998). One of the leading longitudinal risk factor studies, the Pittsburgh Youth Study (Loeber et al., 1998), identified multiple developmental pathways into aggressive behaviors, as well as sets of child (e.g., behavioral impulsivity, hyperactivity, intelligence, negative emotionality, early onset, lack of guilt, reading difficulties), family (e.g., poor supervision and communication, physical punishment, parental discord), contextual (e.g., welfare dependency, broken home, bad neighborhood), and peer factors (e.g., exposure to deviant peers) that are associated with increased risk of antisocial conduct. Many of these factors have been identified in other studies and have been largely replicated in a longitudinal study conducted in England (Farrington, 1998). It is expected that what is learned from research associated with theoretical, and atheoretical, approaches to youth violence would inform prevention programs.

Preventive Interventions

This section examines public health and school-associated interventions that have been aimed at reducing violence and that have at least 200 participants (in the interest of conserving space, details of each preventive treatment are found in Table 9.6). Few interventions, however, are aimed at violence alone. The interventions are aimed at preventing violence and a variety of other types of antisocial conduct. The section is organized by the ages of the children to whom the interventions apply. The section examines interventions carried out before school entrance and during the elementary school years, the periods when behavioral difficulties frequently emerge (cf. Tremblay, Pagani-Kurtz, Mâsse, Vitaro, & Pihl, 1995) yet are most manageable. The extent of teacher-reported violence in the early grades is highly stable over time (Broidy et al., 2003), making early prevention critically important. The section also addresses the idea of early warning systems that apply to all grade levels but are thought to be most applicable in high school.

Prevention Before Entrance Into School

I briefly note that interventions that occur before the child enters school can affect the likelihood of the child's engaging in antisocial conduct later.

Table 9.6   Summary of Intervention Programs

Authors	Ages/Grades Implemented	Key Components of the Index Intervention
Olds et al. (1998)	Birth to age 2; poor White families in upstate New York	Nurse made home visits to mothers. Emphasized competent care, health behaviors, and mothers' personal growth (e.g., job preparation). Emphasized the ecology of the home and attachment à la Bowlby (by implication Hirschi) and parent self-efficacy à la Bandura.
Schweinhart et al. (1986a)	Ypsilanti, Michigan, preschool children; 65% were Black	Child-centered curriculum emphasized active learning à la Piaget and social competence training.
Webster-Stratton (1998)	Washington State Head Start children; 63% were White	Trained parents à la Patterson to better supervise children, effectively set limits, and improve the children's social skills and prosocial behaviors. Taught parents to use less harsh discipline.
CPRG (1999a and 1999b)	Diverse 1st graders in 4 impoverished areas in the U.S.	Two components: (a) Component that targeted most at-risk children included tutoring, social cognitive skills training, training of parents to be more effective; and (b) in universal component, teachers followed curriculum for all children; focus on "understanding and communicating emotions," friendship skills, self-control, and social problem solving.
Tremblay et al. (1995)	Disadvantaged, White, French-speaking (Montreal), kindergarten boys	Two-year "bimodal" program consisting of (a) home-based component à la Patterson aimed at helping parents effectively reinforce prosocial behaviors and reduce antisocial behaviors; and (b) a school-based component involving at-risk and normal peers aimed at strengthening prosocial behaviors, social cognitive problem solving, and self-control in the context of conflict situations.
Dolan et al. (1993)	Baltimore 1st graders; 64% were Black	Application of the Good Behavior Game (GBG), which involves the creation of teams comprising aggressive and normal children who compete as groups for contingently awarded reinforcements by enacting prosocial behavior. The GBG increasingly became part of the school day.
Grossman et al. (1997)	Mostly White Seattle area 2nd and 3rd graders	*Second Step* program consisted of 30 lessons in which teachers teach empathy, impulse control, social cognitive problem solving, and anger management; role playing and teacher modeling of social skills.
Mayer et al. (1983)	Vandalism-plagued elementary and middle schools in Los Angeles	Teachers were specially trained; then they delivered behavioral treatment (e.g., contingently praising children for specific accomplishments).

(Continued)

Table 9.6 (Continued)

Authors	Ages/Grades Implemented	Key Components of the Index Intervention
Olweus (1991)	Norwegian children in Grades 5–8	Teachers were trained to apply key antibullying principles including firm limit-setting, placing sanctions on rule breakers, careful monitoring of children in class and in the playground, initiating serious discussions with bullies and victims. Teachers were also instructed on showing warmth and avoiding corporal punishment.
Flay et al. (2004)	Disadvantaged, Black Chicago 5th graders	Social Development Curriculum (SDC) included 21 culturally sensitive lessons focused on cognitive-behavioral skills pertaining to anger management, social problem solving, and resisting peer pressure. The School/Community Intervention (SCI) included the SDC and a parent program aimed at improving parenting skills. Attention to community ecology.
Reid et al. (1999)	White Oregon 1st and 5th graders from lower- and middle-class homes and living in areas with above-average delinquency rates	Lift Prevention Program. Teacher component involved 20 1-hour lessons devoted to social-skills training (e.g., identifying feelings, cooperating), social problem solving (with the help of the GBG), and daily reinforcement of prosocial behavior during free play. Parent component involved instructing parents in managing their children without coercive practices à la Patterson. Parent-teacher component included a special phone line to facilitate communication.
Flannery et al. (2003)	Grades K–5 in 8 southern Arizona school districts having high rates of delinquency; half the students were Hispanic and 13%, Native American	PeaceBuilders program. Included reinforcement of prosocial behaviors, "story and live models for positive behavior," rehearsal of solutions to aversive incidents, response cost as a consequence for negative behaviors, teachers sending home notes of praise, specific prompts to promote the generalization of prosocial behavior to other contexts. Engagement of family members.
Hawkins et al. (1999)	18 Seattle schools "serving high-crime" areas, Grades 1–6; schools were 40–50% White	In-school component consisted of strengthening classroom management, which includes clear instructions, reinforcement for students who comply with teachers' requests; interactive teaching, which includes modeling appropriate behavior, checking for understanding, and remediation; cooperative learning in which heterogeneous learners depend on each other to earn reinforcers. The parent component included training in managing the child à la Patterson and helping the child succeed in school.

Olds et al. (1998; also see Olds, Kitzman, Cole, & Robinson, 1997) in a 15-year follow-up of a field experiment found that children who were assigned in infancy to the index treatment, compared with controls, had a lower incidence of arrests, disruptive behavior in school, and school suspensions.

Research on preschool programs suggests that such programs have a role to play in later violence prevention. The long-term follow-up into adolescence of children who participated in the High/Scope Perry Preschool Project field experiment (Parks, 2000; Schweinhart, Weikart, & Larner, 1986a and 1986b) found that exposure to the program was related to a lower incidence of fighting and other types of antisocial conduct, fewer arrests, less drug dealing, better attitudes toward school, and higher levels of academic achievement. Webster-Stratton (1998) found that both immediately after an intervention involving preschoolers' mothers and 1 year posttreatment (when the children were in kindergarten), the mothers displayed less harsh discipline and were less critical of their children. Compared with controls, experimental children exhibited fewer home-related conduct problems immediately after the program and 1 year later. The differences in school-related conduct problems were less clear. Although the study was not concerned with violence, Lazar and Darlington (1982) demonstrated that high-quality "early education interventions" can pave the way for significantly greater academic achievement and lower levels of grade retention and special education placement, risk factors for school violence and other aggressive behaviors.

Prevention During the Elementary School Years

A number of interventions have been aimed at benefiting elementary school children. The Fast Track Program (Conduct Problems Prevention Research Group [CPPRG], 1999a and b) is unique because it is a large randomized preventive trial that includes multimodal targeted and universal program components. The component targeted for at-risk children showed evidence of reducing disruptive and aggressive behavior, improving the children's grades, and improving parenting skills. The universal component showed evidence of improving the classroom climate and reducing in-class disruption and aggression. Dolan et al. (1993), in an experimental study, found that a first-grade, behaviorally oriented, classroom-based intervention led to a decline in aggressive behavior. Among the more aggressive first-grade boys, the effects of exposure to the intervention in first and second grades were evident in sixth grade (Kellam, Rebok, Ialongo, & Mayer, 1994). Grossman et al. (1997) found that the *Second Step* curriculum program for second and third graders led to reductions, 6 months later, in physically aggressive behavior as assessed by blind observers (although differences on parent- and teacher-reported behaviors were nonsignificant).

Tremblay et al. (1995) found long-term effects for a 2-year, preventive treatment begun in kindergarten. With boys randomly assigned to the index treatment and attentional and no-treatment control conditions, the treated boys were (a) through age 12 more likely to be in age-appropriate regular classes, (b) through age 13 less likely to disrupt classes, and (c) through age 15, the last year data were collected, less delinquent.

Mayer, Butterworth, Nafpaktitis, and Sulzer-Azaroff (1983) found that children attending elementary and middle schools randomly assigned to a behavioral treatment showed a greater drop since baseline in disruptive and nontask behavior and vandalism over the 3 years of the study. Olweus (1991, 1994, 1997, 1999), using a quasi-experimental design involving Norwegian children in Grades 5 to 8, found that a bullying prevention program was associated with decrements in bullying and victimization in and out of school, fighting, and vandalism, as well as an increase in satisfaction with recess, an important marker of program success. Olweus's antibullying principles have been successfully implemented elsewhere (Smith, 1997).

Reid and his colleagues (Reid, Eddy, Fetrow, & Stoolmiller, 1999; Stoolmiller, Eddy, & Reid, 2000) found first and fifth graders attending schools randomly assigned to a school-and-home, behaviorally oriented prevention program, compared with children attending control schools, showed a greater pre-to-postintervention decline in physical aggression in the playground; however, among first graders, the decline was greatest in children with the highest levels of preintervention aggression. The program was also associated with a greater decline from preintervention levels in harsh verbal behavior mothers directed at children, among mothers who were above the preintervention mean but not among other mothers. Flay, Graumlich, Segawa, Burns, and Holliday (2004) found that, compared with boys attending control schools, fifth-grade boys attending schools randomly assigned to a combined school-and-parent intervention, when in Grades 6, 7, and 8, showed greater deceleration in the trajectory of violent behavior, provoking behavior, school delinquency, and substance use. Effects for girls were nonsignificant.

Flannery and his colleagues (Flannery et al., 2003; Embry, Flannery, Vazsonyi, Powell, & Atha, 1996) found that, compared with children attending control schools, children attending elementary schools randomly assigned to a universal, school-based violence prevention program after 1 year showed higher levels of social competence and prosocial behavior. Children in Grades 3 through 5 showed a greater decrement in aggressive behavior. These changes were largely maintained into the 2nd year of the evaluation. The intervention children in Grades 3 through 5 who manifested the highest baseline levels of aggression showed the greatest decrements. Hawkins, Catalano, Kosterman, Abbott, and Hill (1999) conducted a long-term follow-up of the students in Grades 1 to 5 whose schools were assigned, in a quasi-experiment, to a multimodal prevention intervention. By age 18, individuals who were assigned to the full intervention, compared with controls, showed higher levels of commitment and attachment to school, higher achievement, less school misconduct, and less violence.

Although beyond the scope of this chapter, there is some evidence that violence prevention programs aimed at disadvantaged middle and high school students (Farrell & Meyer, 1997; Hausman, Pierce, & Briggs, 1996) show a degree of success, but not consistently (Harrington, Giles, Hoyle, Feeney, & Yungbluth, 2001; Orpinas, Kelder, Frankowski, Murray, Zhang, & McAlister, 2000). An ambitious multisite, multicomponent middle school violence-prevention effort (Ikeda et al., 2004) is in progress, but evaluation data were not available as of the writing of this chapter. Researchers recognize that beginning with middle school, preexisting patterns of antisocial conduct escalate in seriousness. A need for interventions in middle school, however, suggests that earlier efforts aimed at preventing violence have not succeeded.

Early Warning Systems

Preventing the type of violence that has erupted in schools such as Columbine High School in Littleton, Colorado, is a great concern. McGee and DeBernardo (1999) described what is involved in developing profiles of individuals who could potentially launch lethal attacks in schools. The profiles are expected to lead to early detection and prevention. A profile would include precipitating incidents such as a humiliating experience as well as demographic and dispositional factors. Problems in predicting school violence, however, are manifold. Because the base rate for attacks such as shootings is extremely low, a large number of false positives would be identified (Mulvey & Cauffman, 2001). If, in response to the base rate problem, officials widen the definition of the target behavior to include fighting and bullying, the target behaviors become more heterogeneous and common, changing the meaning of the profile.

There are two other complications in profiling. First, shooters in recent high-profile incidents manifested internalizing problems and experienced rejection by peers, conditions that are less visible to teachers and staff (Reinke & Herman, 2002). Second, students with a diagnosed mental illness are not especially likely to engage in school violence; in general, violence is at best weakly associated with mental illness (Burns, Dean, & Jacob-Timm, 2001).

Borum, Fein, Vossekuil, and Berglund (1999) noted that the Secret Service, one of whose functions is to protect U.S. and foreign officials, has moved away from profiling potential attackers (obtaining "descriptive, demographic, or psychological profiles") and concerns itself more with assessing individuals who pose a threat. The approach is actuarial and consistent with a large body of psychological research supporting the view that actuarial prediction is more accurate than clinical prediction. A characteristic of the approach is that it is fact-based and dependent on objectively ascertained information (e.g., recent preparatory behavior, the occurrence of a major SLE, disciplinary events). Borum et al. suggested that such an approach could be applied to preventing school violence. Consistent with the actuarial approach, Tobin and Sugai (1999) found that the frequency of official disciplinary referrals for school violence in the sixth grade predicted referrals for violence in the eighth.

The actuarial approach also has limitations. First, disciplinary violations occur for heterogeneous reasons and become too unfocused to precisely predict future violence (Morrison & Skiba, 2001). Second, violence and other types of antisocial conduct that go undetected by school officials cannot be factored into the model (Tobin & Sugai, 1999). Third, relying on peers to report (e.g., through a tip line) on threats and violence (Band & Harpold, 1999) that go undetected by school officials can be problematic because such reporting can only take place in schools where students feel genuinely safe and confident that officials are vigilant (Mulvey & Cauffman, 2001). Such a description does not fit many schools where students have safety concerns. Fourth, the actuarial approach has not been subjected to the kinds of reliability, validity, and utility research that would promote confidence (Burns et al., 2001). It is unlikely that in the near future school officials can establish a distance early warning (DEW) line that will prevent the worst cases of school violence.

Given that early warning systems are problematic, it is important to note that there is evidence that secondary schools have an effect on school violence and a host of related problems. Rutter, Maughan, Mortimore, Ouston, and Smith (1979)—in what was, in effect, a natural quasi-experiment involving 12 London secondary schools—found that school quality, adjusting for student characteristics at intake, affects the rates of fighting, rule breaking, and disruptive behavior, along with outcomes such as achievement and job finding. The characteristics of the most effective secondary schools included good administrative leadership and support for teachers; an ethos that fosters civility and achievement; effective classroom management practices that include spotting disruptive behavior early and taking firm appropriate action; positive feedback from teachers; and high expectations.

Final Comments

Methodological Concerns

Grossman et al. (1997) advanced two reasons for the view that teacher reports of aggressive behavior, a commonly employed dependent variable, militate against detecting the effects of violence prevention programs. First, aggressive behavior is less common in the classroom than in other parts of the school, such as the playground. Second, the expectations of teachers assigned to experimental treatments may lead teachers to judge child behavior overly stringently, making it more difficult to demonstrate the efficacy of treatments. The possibility exists, however, that when the teacher is both intervention agent and rater (e.g., Dolan et al., 1993), bias could apply in the opposite direction. The deployment of blind observers (e.g., Grossman et al., 1997; Reid et al., 1999) in and out of the classroom would be most useful in evaluating the effects of antiviolence interventions.

Given the constraints of research conducted in schools, the modal research design has been to randomly assign a small number of units, either schools or classes, to treatment and control conditions (e.g., Flannery et al., 2003; Flay et al., 2004; Grossman et al., 1997; Mayer et al., 1983; Reid et al., 1999). In other words, the school or class, not the individual child, is the unit being randomized. It should be borne in mind that such designs, although true experiments, limit statistical power. Power is influenced by the number of units being randomized. If the within-unit intraclass correlation (ICC) is high, that is, the students within each unit being randomized (e.g., a school or a class) are very similar to each other, power is reduced. If the ICC is close to zero, power is increased to close to what it would be if the student were the unit being randomized. The constraint on power works against antiviolence interventions demonstrating effects. An example of this phenomenon comes from the CPPRG (1999b). There was little dependency in observers' and sociometric ratings of children's aggressive behavior, and intervention effects were statistically significant; however, when teachers' ratings, which showed in-class dependency (ICC = .15), were used, intervention effects were nonsignificant.

What the Research Tells Us About Prevention

To intervene early is to intervene strategically. The antecedents of violent and aggressive behavior are evident in first grade (e.g., Kellam et al., 1998) and earlier (Webster-Stratton, 1998). Aggressiveness in later grades becomes increasingly dangerous. An important idea attached to interventions in the early grades (and in preschool and even earlier) is that of changing the course of developmental trajectories bearing on violence.

Elements of the earlier described theoretical models are reflected in the interventions. Some interventions reflect the theoretical notion that SIP bears on social skills and social problem solving that provide alternatives to aggressive solutions (CPPRG, 1999a, 1999b; Flay et al., 2004; Tremblay et al., 1995). A number of interventions reflect control theory ideas regarding attachment to school (Flay et al., 2004; Flannery et al., 2003; Hawkins et al., 1999), culture (Flay et al., 2004), and home (Olds et al., 1998; Webster-Stratton, 1998) as important to preventing aggression. Several interventions embody behavioral (Dolan et al., 1993; Flannery et al., 2003; Mayer et al., 1983; Reid et al., 1999; Tremblay et al., 1995; Webster-Stratton, 1998) and cognitive behavioral (Flannery et al., 2003; Flay et al., 2004) principles of social learning. A number of interventions have taken preventive remedial action to reduce the risk of school failure (e.g., CPPRG, 1999a, 1999b; Hawkins et al., 1999; Schweinhart et al., 1986a), a major stressor that, according to strain theory, increases the likelihood of antisocial conduct. Successful schools identified by Rutter et al. (1979) were effective in promoting achievement and curbing misconduct.

Although behaviorally oriented interventions have shown promise, one problem associated with implementing individualized behavioral programs is that many teachers prefer not to commit themselves to such programs because the programs often require a great deal of record keeping and well-honed management skills; moreover, the availability of "natural" reinforcers in classrooms is limited (Dolan et al., 1993). Reliance on extrinsic motivators could, for some children, undermine intrinsic motivation. Group-level behavioral interventions such as the Good Behavior Game (GBG) reduce some of the burden on teachers and make prosocial classroom interactions more enjoyable (Embry, 2002).

Flay et al. (2004) suggested that comprehensive interventions that address multiple risk behaviors and that involve both school and families are more likely to succeed than more narrowly focused programs. Several programs that have been successful in reducing aggressive conduct include both school and parent components (e.g., CPPRG, 1999a; Flay et al., 2004; Hawkins et al., 1999; Olweus, 1991; Reid et al., 1999; Tremblay et al., 1995). An advantage to such programs is that they allow the school to develop an ally at home who will reinforce the antiaggression lessons taught in school.

Tremblay et al. (1995) recommended that after successful early interventions have been implemented, it is useful to provide later "booster sessions" to help blunt the potential for growth in antisocial behavior that peaks in midadolescence. Perhaps more important, the implementation of a successful prevention program in the early grades should be followed with the reimplementation of the program in later grades, with adjustments for the changing developmental levels of the children. Interventions such as the GBG have worked with children in the early grades and can be adjusted to work with older children (Embry, 2002). Other adjustments to help improve the efficacy of antiviolence programs include the deployment of both universally applied program components and program components specially targeted at the children at highest risk (e.g., CPPRG, 1999a), which is important given evidence that a subgroup of children, beginning at school entry, manifests chronically high levels of physical violence (Broidy et al., 2003).

References

Agnew, R. (1992). Foundation for a general strain theory of crime and delinquency. *Criminology, 30,* 47–87.

Agnew, R., Brezina, T., Wright, J. P., & Cullen, F. T. (2002). Strain, personality traits, and delinquency: Extending general strain theory. *Criminology, 40,* 43–72.

Agnew, R., & White, H. R. (1992). An empirical test of general strain theory. *Criminology, 30,* 475–499.

Akers, R. L. (2000). *Criminological theories: Introduction, evaluation, and application* (3rd ed.). Los Angeles: Roxbury.

Akers, R. L., Krohn, M. D., Lanza-Kaduce, L., & Radosevich, M. (1979). Social learning and deviant behavior: A specific test of a general theory. *American Sociological Review, 44,* 635–655.

Anderson, C. A., & Bushman, B. J. (2001). Effects of violent video games on aggressive behavior, aggressive cognition, aggressive affect, physiological arousal, and prosocial behavior: A meta-analytic review of the scientific literature. *Psychological Science, 12,* 353–359.

Anderson, M., Kaufman, J., Simon, T. R., Barrios, L., Paulozzi, L., Ryan, G., et al. (2001). School-associated violent deaths in the United States, 1994–1999. *Journal of the American Medical Association, 286,* 2695–2702.

Appendix C: Assaulted and / or battered employee policy. Guidelines for workplace violence for a healthcare and social service workers. US Department of Labor occupational safety and health administration, OSHA 3148, 1996, pp. 25–26.

Arcus, D. (2002). School shooting fatalities and school corporal punishment: A look at the states. *Aggressive Behavior, 28,* 173–183.

Astor, R. A., Benbenishty, R., Zeira, A., & Vinokur, A. (2002). School climate, observed risky behaviors, and victimization as predictors of high school students' fear and judgments of school violence as a problem. *Health Education and Behavior, 29,* 716–736.

Band, S. R., & Harpold, J. A. (1999). School violence. *FBI Law Enforcement Bulletin, 68,* 9–16.

Bandura, A. (1977). *Social learning theory.* Englewood Cliffs, NJ: Prentice Hall.

Bandura, A. (1983). Psychological mechanisms of aggression. In R. G. Geen & E. I. Donnerstein (Eds.), *Aggression: Theoretical and empirical reviews.* New York: Academic.

Benbenishty, R., Astor, R. A., Zeira, A., & Vinokur, A. (2002). Perceptions of violence and fear of school attendance among junior high school students in Israel. *Social Work Research, 26,* 71–87.

Bezilla, R. (1993). *America's youth in the 1990s.* Princeton, NJ: Gallup International Institute.

Bloch, A. M. (1978). Combat neurosis in inner-city schools. *American Journal of Psychiatry, 135,* 1189–1192.

Bonny, A. E., Britto, M. T., Klostermann, B. K., Hornung, R. W., & Slap, G. B. (2000). School disconnectedness: Identifying adolescents at risk. *Pediatrics, 106,* 1017–1021.

Borowsky, I. W., Ireland, M., & Resnick, M. D. (2002). Violence risk and protective factors among youth held back in school. *Ambulatory Pediatrics, 2,* 475–484.

Borum, R., Fein, R., Vossekuil, B., & Berglund, J. (1999). Threat assessment: Defining an approach for evaluating risk of targeted violence. *Behavioral Sciences and the Law, 17,* 323–337.

Bowen, N. K., & Bowen, G. L. (1999). Effects of crime and violence in neighborhoods and schools on the school behavior and performance of adolescents. *Journal of Adolescent Research, 14,* 319–342.

Boxer, P., Edwards-Leeper, L., Goldstein, S. E., Musher-Eizenman, D., & Dubow, E. F. (2003). Exposure to "low-level" aggression in school: Associations with aggressive behavior, future expectations, and perceived safety. *Violence and Victims, 18,* 691–704.

Brener, N. D., Kann, L., McManus, T., Kinchen, S. A., Sundberg, E. C., & Ross, J. G. (2002). Reliability of the 1999 youth risk behavior survey questionnaire. *Journal of Adolescent Health, 31,* 336–342.

Brezina, T. (1996). Adapting to strain: An examination of delinquent coping responses. *Criminology, 34,* 39–60.

Broidy, L. M., Nagin, D. S., Tremblay, R. E., Bates, J. E., Brame, B., Dodge, K. A., et al. (2003). Developmental trajectories of childhood disruptive behaviors and adolescent delinquency: A six-site, cross-national study. *Developmental Psychology, 39,* 222–245.

Bronfenbrenner, U. (1979). *The ecology of human development experiments by nature and design.* Cambridge, MA: Harvard University Press.

Bronfenbrenner, U. (2005). *Making human beings human: Bioecological perspectives on human development.* Thousand Oaks, CA: Sage.

Bronfenbrenner, U., & Ceci, S. (1994). Nature-nurture reconceptualized: A bio-ecological model. *Psychological Review, 101,* 568–586.

Bureau of Labor Statistics. (2004a). *1992–2001 Census of fatal occupational injuries (CFOI)* [Revised data]. Washington, DC: U.S. Department of Labor, Bureau of Labor Statistics. www.bls.gov/iif/oshwc/cfoi/cftb0166.pdf

Bureau of Labor Statistics. (2004b). *Civilian labor force (seasonally adjusted)* (LNS11000000). Washington, DC: U.S. Department of Labor, Bureau of Labor Statistics. http://data.bls.gov/cgi-bin/surveymost

Burns, M. K., Dean, V. J., & Jacob-Timm, S. (2001). Assessment of violence potential among school children: Beyond profiling. *Psychology in the Schools, 38,* 239–247.

Bushman, B. J., & Huesmann, L. R. (2001). Effects of televised violence on aggression. In D. G. Singer & J. L. Singer (Eds.), *Handbook of children and the media* (pp. 223–254). Thousand Oaks, CA: Sage.

Campbell, C., & Schwarz, D. F. (1996). Prevalence and impact of exposure to interpersonal violence among suburban and urban middle school students. *Pediatrics, 98,* 396–402.

Centers for Disease Control and Prevention. (2003). Source of firearms used by students in school-associated violent deaths: United States 1992–1999. *Morbidity and Mortality Weekly Report, 52,* 169–172.

Centers for Disease Control and Prevention. (2004). Violence-related behaviors among high school students: United States 1991–2003. *Morbidity and Mortality Weekly Report, 53,* 651–655.

Chang, J. J., Chen, J. J., & Brownson, R. C. (2003). The role of repeat victimization in adolescent delinquent behaviors and recidivism. *Journal of Adolescent Health, 32,* 272–280.

Cleary, S. D. (2000). Adolescent victimization and associated suicidal and violent behaviors. *Adolescence, 35,* 671–682.

Coggeshall, M. B., & Kingery, P. M. (2001). Cross-survey analysis of school violence and disorder. *Psychology in the Schools, 38,* 107–116.

Conduct Problems Prevention Research Group. (1999a). Initial impact of the fast track prevention trial for conduct problems: 1. The high-risk sample. *Journal of Consulting and Clinical Psychology, 67,* 631–647.

Conduct Problems Prevention Research Group. (1999b). Initial impact of the fast track prevention trial for conduct problems: 2. Classroom effects. *Journal of Consulting and Clinical Psychology, 67,* 648–657.

Cornell, D. G., & Loper, A. B. (1998). Assessment of violence and other high-risk behaviors with a school survey. *School Psychology Review, 27,* 317–330.

Cretacci, M. A. (2003). Religion and social control: An application of a modified social bond on violence. *Criminal Justice Review, 28,* 254–277.

DeVoe, J. F., Peter, K., Kaufman, P., Ruddy, S. A., Miller, A. K., Planty, M., et al. (2003). *Indicators of school crime and safety: 2003* (NCES 2004-004/NCJ 201257). Washington, DC: U.S. Departments of Education and Justice. http://nces.ed.gov or www.ojp.usdoj.gov/bjs/

Dillon, S. (1994, July 7). Report finds more violence in the schools: Board says principals covered up incidents. *New York Times,* pp. B1, B7.

Dishion, T. J., Andrews, D. W., & Crosby, L. (1995). Antisocial boys and their friends in early adolescence: Relationship characteristics, quality, and interactional process. *Child Development, 66,* 139–151.

Dishion, T. J., Patterson, G. R., & Griesler, P. C. (1994). Peer adaptations in the development of antisocial behavior: A confluence model. In L. R. Huesmann (Ed.), *Aggressive behavior: Current perspectives* (pp. 61–95). New York: Plenum.

Dodge, K. A., Lochman, J. E., Harnish, J. D., Bates, J. E., & Pettit, G. S. (1997). Reactive and proactive aggression in school children and psychiatrically impaired chronically assaultive youth. *Journal of Abnormal Psychology, 106,* 37–51.

Dodge, K. A., Pettit, G. S., Bates, J. E., & Valente, E. (1995). Social information-processing patterns partially mediate the effect of early physical abuse on later conduct problems. *Journal of Abnormal Psychology, 104,* 632–643.

Dodge, K. A., Pettit, G. S., McClaskey, C. L., & Brown, C. L. (1986). Social competence in children. *Monographs of the Society for Research in Child Development, 51*(2, Serial no. 213).

Dolan, L. J., Kellam, S. G., Brown, C. H., Werthamer-Larsson, L., Rebok, G. W., Mayer, L. W., et al. (1993). The short-term impact of two classroom-based preventive interventions on aggressive and shy behaviors and poor achievement. *Journal of Applied Developmental Psychology, 14,* 317–345.

Durkheim, E. (1979). *Suicide: Study in sociology* (J. A. Spaulding & G. Simpson, Trans.). New York: Free Press. (Original work published in 1897)

Embry, D. D. (2002). The Good Behavior Game: A best practice candidate as a universal behavioral vaccine. *Clinical Child and Family Psychology Review, 5,* 273–296.

Embry, D. D., Flannery, D. J., Vazsonyi, A. T., Powell, K. E., & Atha, H. (1996). PeaceBuilders: A theoretically driven, school-based model for early violence prevention. *American Journal of Preventive Medicine, 12*(Suppl. 5), 91–100.

Evans, G. W. (2004). The environment of childhood poverty. *American Psychologist, 59,* 77–92.

Farrell, A. D., & Meyer, A. L. (1997). The effectiveness of a school-based curriculum for reducing violence among urban sixth-grade students. *American Journal of Public Health, 87,* 979–984.

Farrington, D. P. (1998). Predictors, causes and correlates of male youth violence. In M. Tonry & M. Moore (Eds.), *Youth violence* (Crime and Justice, Vol. 24). Chicago: University of Chicago Press.

Felson, R. B., Liska, A. E., South, S. J., & McNulty, T. L. (1994). The subculture of violence and delinquency: Individual vs. school context effects. *Social Forces, 73,* 155–173.

Flannery, D. J., Vazsonyi, A. T., Liau, A. K., Guo, S., Powell, K. E., Atha, H., et al. (2003). Initial behavior outcomes for the PeaceBuilders universal school-based violence prevention program. *Developmental Psychology, 39,* 292–308.

Flay, B. R., Graumlich, S., Segawa, E., Burns, J. L., & Holliday, M. Y. (2004). Effects of 2 prevention programs on high-risk behaviors among African American youth: A randomized trial. *Archives of Pediatrics and Adolescent Medicine, 158,* 377–384.

Furlong, M., & Morrison, G. (2000). The school in school violence: Definitions and facts. *Journal of Emotional and Behavioral Disorders, 8,* 71–82.

Glueck, S., & Glueck, E. (1950). *Unraveling juvenile delinquency.* New York: Commonwealth Fund.

Gottfredson, G. D., & Gottfredson, D. C. (1985). *Victimization in schools.* New York: Plenum.

Gottfredson, M. R., & Hirschi, T. (1990). *A general theory of crime.* Stanford, CA: Stanford University Press.

Grossman, D. C., Neckerman, H. J., Koepsell, T. D., Liu, P. Y., Asher, K. N., Beland, K., et al. (1997). Effectiveness of a violence prevention curriculum among children in elementary school: A randomized controlled trial. *Journal of the American Medical Association, 277,* 1605–1611.

Guerra, N. G., Huesmann, L. R., & Spindler, A. (2003). Community violence exposure, social cognition, and aggression among urban elementary school children. *Child Development, 74,* 1561–1576.

Harrington, N. G., Giles, S. M., Hoyle, R. H., Feeney, G. J., & Yungbluth, S. C. (2001). Evaluation of the All Stars character education and problem behavior prevention program: Effects on mediator and outcome variables for middle school students. *Health Education and Behavior, 29,* 533–546.

Hashemi, L., & Webster, B. S. (1998). Non-fatal workplace violence workers' compensation claims (1993–1996). *Journal of Occupational and Environmental Medicine, 40,* 561–567.

Hausman, A., Pierce, G., & Briggs, L. (1996). Evaluation of comprehensive violence prevention education: Effects on student behavior. *Journal of Adolescent Health, 19,* 104–110.

Hawkins, J. D., Catalano, R. F., Kosterman, R., Abbott, R., & Hill, K. G. (1999). Preventing adolescent health-risk behaviors by strengthening protection during childhood. *Archives of Pediatrics and Adolescent Medicine, 153,* 226–234.

Hirschi, T. (1969). *Causes of delinquency.* Berkeley: University of California Press.

Hirschi, T., & Hindelang, M. J. (1977). Intelligence and delinquency: A revisionist review. *American Sociological Review, 42,* 571–587.

Hoffmann, J. P., & Cerbone, F. G. (1999). Stressful life events and delinquency escalation in early adolescence. *Criminology, 37,* 343–373.

Huesmann, L. R., Eron, L. D., & Yarmel, P. W. (1987). Intellectual functioning and aggression. *Journal of Personality and Social Psychology, 52,* 232–240.

Ikeda, R., Farrell, A. D., Horne, A. M., Rabiner, D., Tolan, P. H., & Reid, J. (Eds.). (2004). Prevention of youth violence: The multisite violence prevention project. *American Journal of Preventive Medicine, 26*(Suppl. 1), 1–82.

Islam, S. S., Edla, S. R., Mujuru, P., Doyle, E. J., & Ducatman, A. M. (2003). Risk factors for physical assault: State-managed workers' compensation experience. *American Journal of Preventive Medicine, 25,* 31–37.

Johnston, L. D., O'Malley, P. M., & Bachman, J. G. (2001). *Monitoring the future: National survey results on drug use, 1975–2000* (Secondary school students, Vol. 1) (NIH Publication No. 01-4924). Bethesda, MD: National Institute on Drug Abuse.

Kachur, S. P., Stennies, G. M., Powell, K. E., Modzeleski, W., Stephen, R., Murphy, R., et al. (1996). School-associated violent deaths in the United States, 1992 to 1994. *Journal of the American Medical Association, 275,* 1729–1733.

Kandel, D. B. (1978). Homophily, selection, and socialization in adolescent friendships. *American Journal of Sociology, 84,* 427–436.

Kellam, S. G., Ling, X., Merisca, R., Brown, C. H., & Ialongo, N. S. (1998). The effect of the level of aggression in the first grade classroom on the course and malleability of aggressive behavior into middle school. *Development and Psychopathology, 10,* 165–185.

Kellam, S. G., Rebok, G. W., Ialongo, N. S., & Mayer, L. S. (1994). The course and malleability of aggressive behavior from early first grade into middle school: Results of a developmental epidemiology-based preventive trial. *Journal of Child Psychology and Psychiatry and Allied Disciplines, 35,* 259–281.

Kerres Malecki, C., & Demaray, M. K. (2003). Carrying a weapon to school and perceptions of social support in an urban middle school. *Journal of Emotional and Behavioral Disorders, 11,* 169–178.

Kingery, P. M., & Coggeshall, M. B. (2001). Surveillance of school violence, injury, and disciplinary actions. *Psychology in the Schools, 38,* 117–126.

LaMar, W. J., Gerberich, S. G., Lohman, W. H., & Zaidman, B. (1998). Work-related physical assault. *Journal of Occupational and Environmental Medicine, 40,* 317–324.

Lansford, J. E., Deater-Deckard, K., Dodge, K. A., Bates, J. E., & Pettit, G. S. (2004). Ethnic differences in the link between physical discipline and later adolescent externalizing behaviors. *Journal of Child Psychology and Psychiatry and Allied Disciplines, 45,* 801–812.

Lazar, I., & Darlington, R. (1982). Lasting effects of early education: A report from the consortium for longitudinal studies. *Monographs of the Society for Research in Child Development, 47*(2/3, Serial No. 195).

Lewin, K. (1935). *A dynamic theory of personality.* New York: McGraw-Hill.

Loeber, R., Farrington, D. P., Stouthamer-Loeber, M., Moffitt, T. E., & Caspi, A. (1998). The development of male offending: Key findings from the first decade of the Pittsburgh Youth Study. *Studies on Crime and Crime Prevention, 7,* 141–171.

Mayer, G. R., Butterworth, T., Nafpaktitis, M., & Sulzer-Azaroff, B. (1983). Preventing school vandalism and improving discipline: A three-year study. *Journal of Applied Behavior Analysis, 16,* 355–369.

Mayer, M. J., & Leone, P. E. (1999). A structural analysis of school violence and disruption: Implications for creating safer schools. *Education and Treatment of Children, 22,* 333–356.

McGee, J. P., & DeBernardo, C. R. (1999). The classroom avenger: A behavioral profile of school-based shootings. *Forensic Examiner, 8,* 16–18.

Merton, R. K. (1938). Social structure and anomie. *American Sociological Review, 3,* 672–682.

Metropolitan Life Insurance Company. (1999). *The Metropolitan Life survey of the American teacher, 1999: Violence in America's public schools—five years later.* New York: Lou Harris.

Miller, G. A., Galanter, E., & Pribram, K. H. (1961). *Plans and the structure of behavior.* New York: Holt, Rinehart & Winston.

Minden, J., Henry, D. B., Tolan, P. H., & Gorman-Smith, D. (2000). Urban boys' social networks and school violence. *Professional School Counseling, 4,* 95–104.

Moffitt, T. E. (1990). Juvenile delinquency and attention deficit disorder: Boys' developmental trajectories from age 3 to age 15. *Child Development, 61,* 893–910.

Morrison, G. M., & Skiba, R. (2001). Predicting violence from school misbehavior: Promises and perils. *Psychology in the Schools, 38,* 173–184.

Mulvey, E. P., & Cauffman, E. (2001). The inherent limits of predicting school violence. *American Psychologist, 56,* 797–802.

Nansel, T. R., Craig, W., Overpeck, M. D., Saluja, G., & Ruan, W. J. (2004). Cross-national consistency in the relationship between bullying behaviors and psychosocial adjustment. *Archives of Pediatric and Adolescent Medicine, 158,* 730–736.

Nansel, T. R., Overpeck, M. D., Haynie, D. L., Ruan, W. J., & Scheidt, P. (2003). Relationships between bullying and violence among U.S. youth. *Archives of Pediatric and Adolescent Medicine, 157,* 348–353.

Nansel, T. R., Overpeck, M., Pilla, R. S., Ruan, W. J., Simons-Morton, B., & Scheidt, P. (2001). Bullying behaviors among U.S. youth: Prevalence and association with psychosocial adjustment. *Journal of the American Medical Association, 285,* 2094–2100.

National Center for Educational Statistics. (2000). *Indicators of school crime and safety: 2000.* Washington, DC: Author. http://nces.ed.gov/pubsearch/pubsinfo .asp?pubid'2001017

National Center for Education Statistics. (2004). *Digest of education statistics tables and figures: 1996.* Washington, DC: Author. http://nces.ed.gov/programs/digest/ d96/D96T004.asp

National Educational Goals Panel. (2000). *Building a nation of learners.* Washington, DC: Author. www.negp.gov/page3.htm

Natvig, G. K., Albrektsen, G., & Qvarnstrøm, U. (2001). School-related stress experience as a risk factor for bullying behavior. *Journal of Youth and Adolescence, 30,* 561–575.

Neisser, U. (1967). *Cognitive psychology.* New York: Appleton-Century-Crofts.

O'Keefe, M. (1997). Adolescents' exposure to community and school violence: Prevalence and behavioral correlates. *Journal of Adolescent Health, 20,* 368–376.

Olds, D., Henderson, C. R., Jr., Cole, R., Eckenrode, J., Kitzman, H., Luckey, D., et al. (1998). Long-term effects of nurse home visitation on children's criminal and antisocial behavior: 15-year followup of a randomized controlled trial. *Journal of the American Medical Association, 280,* 1238–1244.

Olds, D., Kitzman, H., Cole, R., & Robinson, J. (1997). Theoretical foundations of a program of home visitation for pregnant women and parents of young children. *Journal of Community Psychology, 25,* 9–25.

Olweus, D. (1991). Bully/victim problems among schoolchildren: Basic facts and effects of a school-based intervention. In D. Pepler & K. Rubin (Eds.), *The development and treatment of childhood aggression* (pp. 411–448). Hillsdale, NJ: Erlbaum.

Olweus, D. (1994). Annotation: Bullying at school: Basic facts and effects of a school-based intervention program. *Journal of Child Psychology and Psychiatry and Allied Disciplines, 35,* 1171–1190.

Olweus, D. (1997). Bully/victim problems in school: Knowledge base and an effective intervention program. *Irish Journal of Psychology, 18,* 170–190.

Olweus, D. (1999). The nature of school bullying: A cross-national perspective. In P. K. Smith, J. Junger-Taqs, D. Olweus, R. Catalano, & P. Slee (Eds.), *The nature of school bullying: A cross-national perspective* (pp. 7–27). New York: Plenum.

O'Malley, P. M., Johnston, L. D., Bachman, J. G., & Schulenberg, J. (2000). A comparison of confidential versus anonymous survey procedures: Effects on reporting of drug use and related attitudes and beliefs in a national study of students. *Journal of Drug Issues, 30,* 35–54.

Orpinas, P. K., Basen-Engquist, K., Grunbaum, J. A., & Parcel, G. S. (1995). The co-morbidity of violence-related behaviors with health-risk behaviors in a population of high school students. *Journal of Adolescent Health, 16,* 216–225.

Orpinas, P., Kelder, S., Frankowski, R., Murray, N., Zhang, Q., & McAlister, A. (2000). Outcome evaluation of a multi-component violence-prevention program for middle schools: The Students for Peace project. *Health Education Research, 15,* 45–58.

Orpinas, P. K., Murray, N., & Kelder, S. (1999). Parental influences on students' behaviors and weapon carrying. *Health Education and Behavior, 26,* 774–787.

Paik, H., & Comstock, G. (1994). The effects of television violence on antisocial behavior: A meta-analysis. *Communication Research, 21,* 516–546.

Parks, G. (2000). The High/Scope Perry Preschool Project. *Juvenile Justice Bulletin.* Washington, DC: U.S. Department of Justice, Office of Justice Programs. www .ncjrs.org/html/ojjdp/2000_10_1/contents.html

Paternoster, R., & Mazerolle, P. (1994). General strain theory and delinquency: A replication and extension. *Journal of Research in Crime and Delinquency, 31,* 235–263.

Patterson, G. (1982). *Coercive family process.* Eugene, OR: Castalia.

Patterson, G. R. (1992). *Antisocial boys: A social interactional approach.* Eugene, OR: Castalia.

Patterson, G. R. (1995). Coercion as a basis for early age of onset for arrest. In J. McCord (Ed.), *Coercion and punishment in long-term perspectives* (pp. 81–105). New York: Cambridge University Press.

Patterson, G. R., Capaldi, D., & Bank, L. (1991). An early starter model for predicting delinquency. In D. J. Pepler & K. H. Rubin (Eds.), *Development and treatment of childhood aggression* (pp. 139–168). Hillsdale, NJ: Lawrence Erlbaum.

Patterson, G. R., & Yoerger, K. (1997). A developmental model for late-onset delinquency. In D. W. Osgood (Ed.), *Nebraska symposium on motivation* (Motivation and Delinquency, Vol. 44, pp. 119–177). Lincoln: University of Nebraska Press.

Peek-Asa, C., Howard, J., Vargas, L., & Kraus, J. F. (1997). Incidence of non-fatal workplace assault injuries determined from employer's reports in California. *Journal of Occupational and Environmental Medicine, 39,* 44–50.

Pettit, G. S., Clawson, M. A., Dodge, K. A., & Bates, J. E. (1996). Stability and change in peer-rejected status: The role of child behavior, parenting, and family ecology. *Merrill-Palmer Quarterly, 42,* 267–294.

Pine, D. S., Shaffer, D., Schonfeld, I. S., & Davies, M. (1997). Minor physical anomalies: Modifiers of environmental risks for psychiatric impairment? *Journal of the American Academy of Child and Adolescent Psychiatry, 36,* 395–403.

Raine, A. (1993). *The psychopathology of crime: Criminal behavior as a clinical disorder.* San Diego, CA: Academic.

Raine, A. (2002). Biosocial studies of antisocial and violent behavior in children and adults: A review. *Journal of Abnormal Child Psychology, 30,* 311–326.

Reid, J. B., Eddy, J. M., Fetrow, R. A., & Stoolmiller, M. (1999). Description and immediate impacts of a preventive intervention for conduct problems. *American Journal of Community Psychology, 27,* 483–517.

Reinke, W. M., & Herman, K. C. (2002). A research agenda for school violence prevention. *American Psychologist, 57,* 796–797.

Resnick, M. D., Bearman, P. S., Blum, R. W., Bauman, K. E., Harris, K. M., Jones, J., et al. (1997). Protecting adolescents from harm: Findings from the National

Longitudinal Study on Adolescent Health. *Journal of the American Medical Association, 278,* 823–832.

Robinson, W. S. (1950). Ecological correlations and the behavior of individuals. *American Sociological Review, 15,* 351–357.

Rosario, M., Salzinger, S., Feldman, R. S., & Ng-Mak, D. S. (2003). Community violence exposure and delinquent behaviors among youth: The moderating role of coping. *Journal of Community Psychology, 31,* 489–512.

Rosenblatt, J. A., & Furlong, M. J. (1997). Assessing the reliability and validity of student self-reports of campus violence. *Journal of Youth and Adolescence, 26,* 187–202.

Rutter, M. (1980). *Changing youth in a changing society: Patterns of adolescent development and disorder.* Cambridge, MA: Harvard University Press.

Rutter, M., Maughan, B., Mortimore, P., Ouston, J., & Smith, A. (1979). *Fifteen thousand hours: Secondary schools and their effects on children.* Cambridge, MA: Harvard University Press.

Sampson, R. J., & Groves, W. B. (1989). Community structure and crime: Testing social-disorganization theory. *American Journal of Sociology, 94,* 774–802.

Sampson, R., & Laub, J. (1993). *Crime in the making: Pathways and turning points through life.* Cambridge, MA: Harvard University Press.

Schonfeld, I. S. (1992). Assessing stress in teachers: Depressive symptoms scales and neutral self-reports of the work environment. In J. C. Quick, L. R. Murphy, & J. J. Hurrell Jr. (Eds.), *Work and well-being: Assessments and instruments for occupational mental health* (pp. 270–285). Washington, DC: American Psychological Association.

Schonfeld, I. S. (2001). Stress in 1st-year women teachers: The context of social support and coping. *Genetic, Social, and General Psychology Monographs, 127,* 133–168.

Schonfeld, I. S., Shaffer, D., O'Connor, P., & Portnoy, S. (1988). Conduct disorder and cognitive functioning: Testing three causal hypotheses. *Child Development, 19,* 993–1007.

Schreck, C. J., & Fisher, B. S. (2004). Specifying the influence of family and peers on violent victimization: Extending routine activities and lifestyles theories. *Journal of Interpersonal Violence, 19,* 1021–1041.

Schweinhart, L. J., Weikart, D. P., & Larner, M. B. (1986a). Consequences of three preschool curriculum models through age 15. *Early Childhood Research Quarterly, 1,* 15–45.

Schweinhart, L. J., Weikart, D. P., & Larner, M. B. (1986b). Child-initiated activities in early childhood programs may help prevent delinquency. *Early Childhood Research Quarterly, 1,* 303–312.

Sieving, R. E., Beurhing, T., Resnick, M. D., Bearinger, L. H., Shew, M., Ireland, M., et al. (2001). Development of adolescent self-report measures from the National Longitudinal Study of Adolescent Health. *Journal of Adolescent Health, 28,* 73–81.

Smith, P. K. (1997). Bullying in schools: The UK experience and the Sheffield anti-bullying project. *Irish Journal of Psychology, 18,* 191–201.

Stoolmiller, M., Eddy, J. M., & Reid, J. B. (2000). Detecting and describing preventive intervention effects in a universal school-based randomized trial targeting delinquent and violent behavior. *Journal of Consulting and Clinical Psychology, 68,* 296–306.

Stouthamer-Loeber, M., Loeber, R., Wei, E., Farrington, D. P., & Wikström, P.-O. H. (2002). Risk and promotive effects in the explanation of persistent serious delinquency in boys. *Journal of Consulting and Clinical Psychology, 70,* 111–123.

Straus, M. A. (1991). Discipline and deviance: Physical punishment of children and violence and other crime in adulthood. *Social Problems, 38,* 133–154.

Tobin, T. J., & Sugai, G. M. (1999). Using sixth-grade school records to predict school violence, chronic discipline problems, and high school outcomes. *Journal of Emotional and Behavioral Disorders, 7,* 40–53.

Tremblay, R. E., Pagani-Kurtz, L., Mâsse, L. C., Vitaro, F., & Pihl, R. O. (1995). A bimodal preventive intervention for disruptive kindergarten boys: Its impact through mid-adolescence. *Journal of Consulting and Clinical Psychology, 63,* 560–568.

Valois, R. F., & McKeown, R. E. (1998). Frequency and correlates of fighting and carrying weapons among public school adolescents. *American Journal of Health Behavior, 22,* 8–17.

Valois, R. F., Vincent, M. L., McKeown, R. E., Garrison, C. Z., & Kirby, S. D. (1993). Adolescent risk behaviors and the potential for violence: A look at what's coming to campus. *Journal of American College Health, 41,* 141–147.

Webster-Stratton, C. (1998). Preventing conduct problems in Head Start children: Strengthening parenting competencies. *Journal of Consulting and Clinical Psychology, 66,* 715–730.

Weiss, B., Dodge, K. A., Bates, J. E., & Pettit, G. S. (1992). Some consequences of early harsh discipline: Child aggression and a maladaptive social information processing style. *Child Development, 63,* 1321–1335.

Wiesner, M., & Windle, M. (2004). Assessing covariates of adolescent delinquency trajectories: A latent growth mixture modeling approach. *Journal of Youth and Adolescence, 33,* 431–442.

Williams, L. E., Winfree, L. T., & Clinton, L. (1989). Trouble in the schoolhouse: New views on victimization, fear of crime, and teacher perceptions of the workplace. *Violence and Victims, 4,* 27–44.

Wilson, W. J. (1987). *The truly disadvantaged.* Chicago: University of Chicago Press.

Wright, B. R. E., Caspi, A., Moffitt, T. E., & Silva, P. A. (2001). The effects of social ties on crime vary by criminal propensity: A life-course model of interdependence. *Criminology, 39,* 321–351.

10 Workplace Violence in the Police

Stephen B. Perrott
E. Kevin Kelloway

In many ways, police officer is the archetypal occupation for discussions of workplace violence. In contrast to occupations for which violence is a rare and unanticipated occurrence, violence is an expected part of the police officer's role. Police are regularly exposed to many of the occupational risk factors for workplace violence (e.g., LeBlanc & Kelloway, 2002). Moreover, in a very real sense, police officers are the individuals tasked with handling or dealing with violent individuals and situations. In this chapter, we review the experience of workplace violence by police officers. We review both predictors and outcomes of workplace violence experienced by police officers and begin with a consideration of the prevalence of workplace violence among police occupations.

Prevalence of Workplace Violence

In the United States between 1993 and 2002, 636 police officers were murdered and 574, 990 were victims of assault. In 2002 alone, on average, an officer was killed every 66 hours and was the victim of an assault every 9 minutes (Federal Bureau of Investigation [FBI], 2002). Repeated analyses show that American police experience violent crime at much higher rates than any other occupational group. Between 1993 and 1999, for example, the rate of violent victimization was 261 for every 1,000 police officers, about twice the rate for taxicab drivers, the next most victimized group (U.S. Department of Justice, 2001). Earlier research in the state of California covering the period between 1979 and 1981 provided similar findings, with the homicide rate for police officers pegged at 20.8 per 100,000, the highest of all occupational groups and 10 times greater than the average for men

(Kraus, 1987). Furthermore, these statistics reflect only officer victimization and do not include the much broader exposure to violent criminal acts perpetrated on the public that police officers witness. Hostility and violence are such integral parts of the American police officer's day-to-day activities that the work is often likened to being at war or characterized as civilian combat (Paton & Violanti, 1996; Violanti & Paton, 1999).

The situation in industrialized English-speaking countries outside of the United States is less well understood due to a surprising absence of data. In Canada, for example, Statistics Canada does not disaggregate assaults on police from a hodgepodge "other assaults" category. From what can be determined, it appears that police in other countries cope with similar, albeit much less severe, circumstances. For example, the homicide rate for police officers in Canada does not appear to be elevated against the general population (see Parsons, 2004); however, Canadian police officers do face extremely high levels of citizen assault, at least insofar as can be gauged from the experience in British Columbia. Boyd (1995) culled statistics from Workers Compensation Board claims in that province and determined that between 1982 and 1991, police officers submitted over 250 claims for every 1,000 workers, a rate just surpassing that of health care workers. The claims for these two groups more than doubled those of all other groups combined. Furthermore, the rate of serious violence incidents perpetrated against the police, such as stabbings and shootings, surpassed those against health care workers at the rate of more than tenfold (in this category, the experience of taxi drivers more closely approximated that of the police). Nonetheless, as Boyd points out, this single snapshot of workplace violence leaves many questions unanswered about the Canadian experience.

Even fewer data are available from Europe. As Parsons (2004) points out in her review, European researchers have undertaken a more micro- and systems-oriented analysis, focusing on such things as situational dynamics, officer characteristics, and offender characteristics and generally neglecting an investigation of base rates. One interesting finding regarding officer gender indicates that female officers suffer assaults proportionate to their representation in police forces. This discovery contradicts assertions that female officers are less likely to face assault because of enhanced interpersonal skills or because males are reticent to assault female officers. On the other hand, this finding, albeit qualified by limited data, might be interpreted as evidence that female officers are more closely approaching occupational parity with their male counterparts.

Limited research also has addressed the experiences of police officers in developing nations and in nations with high levels of civil strife, such as South Africa (Kopel & Freidman, 1997) and Northern Ireland (Hamilton, 1995). Although rates of violent victimization are, not surprisingly, much higher than in most Western nations, sharp differences in societal structure and the nature of policing led to a decision to exclude these countries within the current review.

Danger, Violence, and
the Police Stress Hypothesis

Although widespread scholarly attention to violence in the workplace only emerged in the last two decades, researchers have been interested in the effects of violence experienced by police officers from the beginning of academic study of this group. In Skolnick's (1966) landmark treatise, *Justice Without Trial*, typically seen as the starting point for the police literature, he discusses how the experience of facing a hostile and violent public socializes the police officer's "working personality" and social identity. The two most fundamental features of police culture, according to Skolnick, are danger and authority. The police transform those who threaten and assault them into a collective composite, the *symbolic assailant*. The other seminal contribution to the early literature was Niederhoffer's (1967) *Behind the Shield*, in which cynicism as a coping mechanism for dealing with hostile and violent experiences was first clearly explicated. Others soon expanded on these largely anecdotal analyses with more systematic and empirical approaches to understand the link between workplace violence and psychological outcomes in the police. By the mid-1970s, the study of police stress, typically linked to the experience of danger and violence, had developed into a substantial body of literature that continued to grow rapidly into the late 1980s (see Farmer, 1990, for a review).

Despite a growing body of empirical evidence, the decade of police stress research was guided as much by folklore as evidence. By the mid-1980s, obvious limitations with the danger-stress link and, for that matter, the entire police stress hypothesis were being documented. It became increasingly clear that levels of danger faced by the police and the magnitude of the resulting stress responses were exaggerated by officers, researchers, and the public. For example, Somodevilla (1978) claimed that "it is an accepted fact that a police officer is under stress and pressure unequaled by any other profession" (p. 21) but did not offer any empirical evidence to support this contention.

Although Somodevilla's view remains an accepted tenet of police mythology, reviews sharply contradict the police stress hypothesis (Malloy & Mays, 1984; Terry, 1981). First, as Walker and Katz (2005) note, other occupations, including mining and construction work, have always had higher workplace death rates as compared with police work. In their review of Justice Department statistics, these researchers also note how policing has become significantly safer insofar as felonious death rates in the United States have fallen from nearly 30 to less than 10 per 100,000 from 1976 to 1998. Nonetheless, the police do stand out from other dangerous occupations, as the danger faced is typically directed out of hostility.

The police danger-stress hypothesis is further brought into question by the faulty assumption that danger and violence are inevitably stressful for the typical officer. Kroes, Margolis, and Hurrell (1974) first challenged this premise by demonstrating that the police find a negative public image, administrative policies, nonsupport from the courts, and problems with equipment more distressing than violent experiences. On the contrary, facing danger and violence is often highly meaningful for police officers and may actually increase levels of job satisfaction (Jermier, Gaines, & McIntosh, 1989). Kroes et al. (1974) argue that second-level stressors involving police-community conflict are coped with relatively well, provided that care is taken to protect the professional image of officers.

The experience of violence as role congruent with the police mandate is likely the single most important variable mediating potentially deleterious outcomes. That the police are expected to deal with violent people is most explicitly acknowledged by their possession of sidearms, batons, and pepper spray. Although police officers typically see themselves as crime-fighting warriors, a major part of their occupational identity is that of a helping professional (Yarmey, 1990; see also Perrott & Taylor, 1995b). Insofar as violent experiences can be simultaneously appraised as congruent with both crime-fighting and helping roles, the construction of the meaning of a violent encounter is likely to be quite different in police officers from that of other helping professionals.

In addition to role congruity, the meaning of violent episodes is strongly moderated by the degree of social support received from fellow officers. The police are known more than any other occupational group for legendary levels of solidarity (or in-group identification) and for their inclination to alienate non–police officers in an us-versus-them dichotomy (Shernock, 1988). These dual processes are likely flip sides of the same coin. Although police solidarity is typically viewed as an alienating, ethnocentric phenomenon, Perrott and Taylor (1994) have provided evidence that solidarity may contribute to officer well-being and provide benefits to the public.

A recent well-designed study conducted with 527 New Zealand police officers supports this view with the finding that peer support moderated the severity of posttraumatic stress disorder (PTSD) symptoms (Stephens & Long, 1999). Perrott and Kelloway (2003) drew similar conclusions with their sample of urban officers who were relatively unaffected by citizen-initiated hostility and violence, provided they perceived that peers provided a supportive, nonhostile work environment. Thus, the degree to which violent activities are viewed as role congruent and the extent to which an officer perceives support from the public, supervisors, and especially peers are probably more important in determining likely stress responses from a violent encounter than is the nature or severity of the stressor.

Contextual variables, especially role congruity and peer solidarity, make the police unique in the consideration of workplace violence. Most of the current literature deals with hostility directed from others within the same setting, whether this is supervisor bullying, sexual harassment from a peer, or overt acts of violence from a disgruntled employee. For most occupational groups, the experience of violence in the workplace is not part of what is to be expected and typically is directed from others within the workplace. For another family of occupations, most notably public school teachers and health workers, facing violent acts is not explicitly part of the job mandate but can nonetheless be anticipated as an episodic, albeit not role-congruent, experience. The police belong to an even smaller group of occupational groups, including correctional officers and military personnel, for whom coping with and using violence is an explicit job requirement.

The experience of police stress, including that stemming from violent and hostile encounters, can be viewed across two separate dimensions. The first juxtaposes reactions to highly stressful but relatively infrequent critical events, often of a violent nature, to the cumulative effects of less remarkable but highly frequent "hassles" (Hart, Wearing, & Headey, 1993). The second dimension considers stress reactions that emerge from context variables (e.g., problems with equipment, frustration with the court system, and critical examination from the general public, especially minority groups; Jefferson, 1988; Kroes et al., 1974) and those that emerge from content variables (the day-to-day challenges confronted in the workplace including acts of violence experienced directly or vicariously). These dimensions are alternatively referred to as organizational and operational stressors (e.g., Biggam, Power, MacDonald, Carcary, & Moodie, 1997). Unfortunately, these two sources of stressors are often not clearly separated in the literature, and those studies linking outcomes to violent acts have provided weak or ambiguous findings partly because of the aforementioned limitations in using low-frequency violent episodes (Hart et al., 1993).

Although rates of violent victimization are often not high enough to provide sufficient power when incorporated in multivariate analyses, the police are nonetheless still disproportionately affected by violent acts usually arising from unpredictable and ambiguous circumstances. In a recent qualitative analysis of 35 UK police officers reporting to a counseling service, Dick (2000) found that acute operational stressors, usually in the form of citizen-initiated violence, were as often the source of referral as were intra-occupational context stressors. Additionally, a number of her referrals for context stressors were based in conflict with peers or supervisors, a source of hostility usually not considered in the police research but almost always incorporated in the emerging workplace violence literature.

Furthermore, the tendency to include only explicitly physically violent acts excludes lower-level but more chronic negative events and the perception, albeit an arguably distorted one, that the general public presents the police with a continuously hostile and potentially violent workplace (see Perrott & Taylor, 1994, 1995a). Furthermore, the one area in which the police accurately perceive significant levels of public hostility is that directed from minority communities (see Wortley, Macmillan, & Hagan, 1997, for an extended discussion of this issue). In particular, young Black man, a group composed of individuals most readily placed in the symbolic assailant category, appear to hold a special antipathy toward the police (Jefferson, 1988).

Although the perception of a hostile environment was considered relevant to early contributors, it has generally not been incorporated in subsequent empirical studies incorporating more easily measured discrete acts of citizen-initiated violence. Furthermore, little attention is focused on the special strain caused by negative interactions with and complaints from minority communities, criticism that is almost always amplified by liberal activists and academics. Political proclivities within the academy have led to a heavy research focus in which the police are unilaterally condemned for racism without sufficient attention to sociopolitical context, the mandate of the police in maintaining the societal status quo, or the interactive nature of conflict escalation in incidents involving minority group members (see Wortley et al., 1997, for an exemplar of a sophisticated yet heavily skewed analysis).

It is beyond the scope of this chapter to review theories about the genesis of police-minority community tensions or to apportion responsibility. Rather, we simply propose that it is necessary to include these tensions as a significant factor in any discussion of workplace violence in the police. Indeed, police-minority tension is the single greatest challenge facing the police institution in industrialized nations.

Intraoccupational Hostility

There is little research dealing with the experience and effect of hostility and violence within police organizations. One exception, often cited by line officers, is the lack of support and empathy provided by police supervisors and administrators for the reality of work on the street (Van Maanen, 1984). Another exception is the experience of female and minority officers who traditionally have been viewed as police outsiders (Balkin, 1988; Cashmore, 2001; Martin, 1994). Nonacceptance is likely to have a particularly negative effect in an occupation so dependent on solidarity and camaraderie.

There is some evidence that female officers bring a gentling factor into potentially violent situations and are more troubled by exposure to human tragedy and danger than are their male colleagues (see Norvell, Hills, & Murrin, 1993). In general, however, female officers report the same stressors and respond in ways similar to male officers (Bartol, Bergen, Volckens, & Knoras, 1992; Grennan, 1987). A notable exception is that female officers must also face hostility and nonacceptance from male officers. In an early study on this topic, Wexler and Logan (1983) found that 80% of their sample of 25 female officers reported being exposed to negative attitudes of male officers. They cited rumors and open comments about sexual behavior, sexual orientation, and their inability to perform the police role as frequent stressors. Other less vocal male officers did not demonstrate their hostility with overt acts but rather by simply ignoring female officers. Nonacceptance by men and the belief that promotion through the ranks is unlikely contribute to the high attrition rate of women in policing (Poole & Pogrebin, 1988).

The relationship between minority and majority officers, in many regards, reflects racial tensions at a societal level. One of the largest problems with relations between White and minority officers is the mirror image perception that those of the other race are provided preferential treatment by police administration, a phenomenon that seems unaffected by any appeal to objective reality. This reciprocal perception, referred to by Toch (2002) as the Roshamon phenomenon, currently seems irreconcilable. A similar perception, referred to as the across-perceiver discrepancy, extends to police-community relations more generally (Perrott & Taylor, 1994). In this phenomenon, the police report general acceptance of African Canadian citizens but perceive Blacks as distancing themselves from the police. Perrott (1999) reported that African Canadian police applicants held the same mirror image perception of the police, a reality that not only undermines minority recruitment efforts but also attempts to improve police-minority relations more generally.

Minority officers face the additional challenge of facing hostility from their own racial community. They are often viewed as traitors by a significant number of Black citizens, promoting significant feelings of dissonance for many of these officers (Cashmore, 1991; Holdaway, 1991; Perrott, 1999). Having their legitimacy questioned by the Black community and also not being fully accepted by White peers places minority officers in the position of being doubly marginalized (Campbell, 1980).

There are some indications that the situation of female and minority officers has improved in recent years due to their increasing numbers. In larger American cities especially, the proportion of African American officers has grown significantly, though it is clear that this has not presented a panacea for healing the rift between the police and minority communities. A sample of minority officers recently interviewed by Cashmore (2001) offered a mixture of views on this topic, suggesting that minority officers in the UK view their status within the institution with considerable uncertainty and ambivalence.

Women are also providing mixed evaluations about their status within the institution. Furthermore, on outcome variables that should be reflective of systemic bias against women, findings are also mixed. Although some studies provide expected results (e.g., Parker & Griffen, 2002), others show no gender differences (e.g., Dantzger & Kubin, 1998), and still others have resulted in counterintuitive findings. For example, Norvell and her colleagues (1993) found female highway patrol officers to be less stressed and higher in job satisfaction than their male counterparts.

Future research about the amount of workplace hostility faced by women in policing and their reaction to it will need to employ increasingly nuanced techniques to capture more subtle effects. For example, Krimmel and Gormley (2003) found that higher levels of job satisfaction for female officers depended on whether their department employed a critical mass (> 15%) of women, whereas Parker and Griffen (2002) found that gender harassment was related to overperformance demands and psychological distress. Of particular interest in the Parker and Griffen study was the finding that although the locker room banter characteristic of the police culture was innocuous to male officers, it was harmful to women.

Vicarious Violence

The effects of vicariously experienced violence, especially that formed from criminal malice, provide a significant and unique form of operational stressor, as demonstrated with mean scores and factor loadings in a study of 601 British officers (Brown, Fielding, & Grover, 1999). Police officers almost universally report that situations in which children are victims of violence are the most profoundly disturbing of those with which they must deal (Toch, 2002). Outside of medical personnel, the police confront death more commonly than any other group, presenting them with a frequent reminder of their own mortality (Henry, 1995). The callous disregard for humanity reflected by violent acts presents an additional dimension with which police officers must cope (Carlier, 1999; Figley, 1999).

Although recognized only recently, PTSD is experienced at exceptionally high levels in the police. In an early investigation, Martin, McKean, and Veltkamp (1986) found that 26% of officers in their convenience sample met the DSM-III criteria for PTSD. Female officers reported more PTSD symptoms than male officers experiencing similar traumas but were also more willing to reach out to others for support. Strikingly, shooting someone placed officers at greater risk than did being shot; and, in general, other forms of vicariously experienced violence were more likely than being personally victimized to result in clinical levels of distress.

Harvey-Lintz and Tidwell (1997) examined the consequences of being a police officer assigned to South Central Los Angeles during the riots associated with the Rodney King trial. Nineteen months after the civil unrest, they found that 17% of their sample of 141 officers met the criteria for PTSD (15% of male and 28% of female respondents). Although only 7 respondents were injured during the disturbances, 77 (54%) had personal knowledge of other officers or citizens being injured. The recovery period during which they worked was otherwise noteworthy due to the extreme antipathy directed toward the LAPD. Those respondents reporting PTSD symptomatology used about twice as many avoidance coping strategies as did those who were symptom free.

Exposure to events typically outside the range of human experience is often within the normal range of experience for police officers. It seems possible that police officers are relatively well inoculated against the impact of violent acts such that they are less likely than most to develop PTSD. Their chronic exposure to violence and victimization may necessitate utilizing a variety of avoidance-coping strategies that protect them from developing full-blown PTSD symptoms or other clearly diagnosable anxiety disorders. It may also reduce the likelihood that officers are sufficiently open to recognize bona fide psychological symptoms when they are present. Harvey-Lintz and

Tidwell (1997) hypothesize that this factor was in play with the officers they surveyed from South Central Los Angeles and that the real rate of PTSD in their sample was significantly higher than the 17% reported.

Individual and Family Outcomes

Outside of anecdotal reports, there is little literature directly addressing the consequences of violence. There is, however, an extensive literature attributing negative outcomes to workplace stress. As indicated above, police stress results from both organizational and content stressors, the latter category including hostility and violence. Directly attributing sequelae to workplace violence is further complicated by the failure to disentangle the extent to which negative outcomes are the result of stress as opposed to the product of socialization factors resulting from exposure to police culture. Nonetheless, even if police culture plays a larger role than typically accounted for, it is clear that danger, violence, and hostility play a significant role in the formation of police culture.

Police officers rely heavily on avoidance-coping strategies like displacement, none so destructive as the excessive use of alcohol (Beehr, Johnson, & Nieva, 1995; Violanti, Marshall, & Howe, 1985). In an Australian study examining police lifestyle choices, Richmond, Wodak, Kehoe, and Heather (1998) found that 48% of male and 40% of female officers drank excessively (the corresponding community percentages were 10.5 and 7). These researchers also found a plethora of other health-compromising behaviors, including higher than normative levels of smoking and lack of exercise, with one half of the sample reporting being overweight. These risk factors not only compromise general health but also raise concerns about the ability to function optimally while on duty.

Terry (1981) undertook a critical analysis of the legitimacy of the stress-related maladies reported by police researchers. He found that although many of the claims had merit, most were exaggerated or compromised by methodological problems. For example, although the police do experience a relatively high number of physiological and somatic complaints, the frequency is eclipsed by a variety of other occupational groups. The most serious stress-related consequence is the often cited epidemic level of suicide in the police, although this literature is also suspect due to methodological deficiencies (Loo, 1999).

Given this attention to individual stress-related outcomes, it is not surprising that researchers have turned their attention to effects on the police officer's family. The most dramatic effects, clearly, are in cases in which officers lose their lives while on duty (Violanti, 1999a). It is commonly assumed that the police suffer from exceptionally high levels of divorce; Terry's (1981) review, however, suggests that this assumption is not supported by empirical evidence and that police divorce rates have been exaggerated by flawed data and popular folklore; but even if divorce rates are not elevated relative to the general population, there is little doubt that the stress police officers encounter at work negatively impacts family life. Maynard and Maynard (1982) found that spouses of police officers frequently reported incompatibility between family life and job demands, departmental insensitivity about family needs, and their spouse's exclusive and excessive socialization with other officers as significant sources of stress. The tendency for officers to bring the residuals of work-related problems home yet remain secretive also places increased strain on marital relations. Because officers suppress affect associated with negative events at work, this unresolved distress is transferred home, remains unacknowledged, and manifests in ways that bring conflict and frustration to the relationship (Roberts & Levenson, 2001).

The Police Culture and Avoidance Coping

Police officers have consistently been found to be avoidance copers, with cynicism being the most widely used strategy. Niederhoffer (1967) first outlined how cynicism acts as a coping mechanism and how police culture encourages the use of this style. As outlined above, the abuse of alcohol is also another form of avoidance coping (Beehr et al., 1995). The assessment of more general coping styles has also demonstrated a strong inclination toward avoidance or emotion-focused strategies (Dick, 2000; Perrott, Corey, & Kelloway, 2004; Reiser & Geiger, 1984) that are, on balance, viewed as less optimal than approach- or problem-focused strategies, especially when relied on by men (Moos, 1993).

Avoidance coping likely results from (a) the limited mandate of police officers as first responders and (b) certain aspects of the police subculture (Lennings, 1997). Some contributors have not recognized avoidance coping because of the action-oriented activities of the police; however, there is a sharp distinction between being action oriented and being a problem solver. Police officers have traditionally provided first aid in crisis situations and, although often superficially successful, quickly come to learn about the intractable nature of the problems with which they deal. This band-aid approach to facing challenges encourages short-term solutions that not only affect society as a whole but also promote a more generic coping style in officers.

Police culture also contributes to avoidance coping in a variety of ways. Although providing police officers with essential social support, the culture also supports an "us-versus-them" alienated worldview, exaggerates the perception of violence on the job, and underestimates the actual level of public support. The "John Wayne" culture (Herbert, 1998) also discourages the expression of distress and acts as a mechanism of emotional suppression. The tendency to become trapped in a singular police role further restricts the range of coping options when the officer is off duty (Violanti, 1999b). Thus, although police culture and solidarity provide a useful buffer against hostility, they ultimately serve to prevent officers from fully working through their experiences and engaging in the "uncovering" process thought to be especially critical following traumatic events.

Conclusions

Despite folklore and an abundance of scholarly literature, both the prevalence and effect of workplace violence in the police remain poorly understood because of methodological weaknesses and conceptual confounds. First, there remains a dearth of basic epidemiological data, and what is available is ambiguous due to a failure to clearly separate violence and hostility from the larger study of police stress. Far too much of the literature is based on anecdotal reports and/or samples of limited size. The use of small samples has likely artificially reduced the magnitude of findings about the negative impact from infrequent but severe traumatic events.

There also is little consistency in how violence and hostility are operationally defined, so much so that many events that might be considered workplace violence are placed under the umbrella of organizational rather than operational stressors. Most specifically, although intraoccupational hostility and an environment characterized by low-level but chronic hostility are typically considered significant in the emerging workplace violence literature, these sources of stress are not included in traditional conceptualizations of the danger and violence faced by the police.

Researchers have constantly emphasized that the police are considerably more stressed by organizational events and climate than by operational stressors, the category that incorporates danger and violence. This has been an important emphasis not only because it properly refutes certain basic premises proposed by early researchers but also because a grossly exaggerated perception of the role of danger and violence in the day-to-day work lives of officers stubbornly clings to the mythology of police work. Concomitant with this focus has been an increased understanding that coping with violence is often role-congruent and meaningful for the police.

Although this focus has been necessary in challenging unfounded myths, it has nonetheless shifted the police research pendulum too far in the other direction. The recognition that organizational stressors trump danger and violence in deleterious effects overall does not lead to the conclusion that the violence and danger faced by police officers are innocuous forces. Furthermore, although the risk to the physical safety of police officers has been exaggerated, the data we do have indicate that police officers are at a grossly disproportionate risk for injury relative to the general workforce. The fact that this risk is usually borne out of malice rather than the result of workplace accidents adds a significant psychological dimension when considering the meaning that is placed on injury incidents.

Policy Implications

Boyd (1995) outlines five areas of consideration for dealing with workplace violence, and we draw from his framework in our consideration of policy initiatives involving the police.

Arguments About Rules

Much workplace violence can be traced to the interpretation of rules within the workplace and between workers and their occupational clientele. This is especially the case in care-providing occupations requiring controlling contact and the need to maintain institutional rules (Castillo & Jenkins, 1994). For example, public school teachers and nurses, two occupational groups that face disproportionately high levels of client aggression, must ensure that a plethora of rules are adhered to if they hope to deliver the services with which they are mandated. For the police, rule maintenance is not so central to their ability to meet job requirements, as *it is* their central mandate.

In order to reduce violent episodes, the police need to continually reevaluate just which rules (i.e., laws) are actually necessary to enforce and, if enforced differentially, determine the contextual variables that need be considered in decision making. This consideration falls within the domain of police discretion and involves making judgments that open the police to criticism, whether the judgment involves positive or negative discrimination. For example, although it would typically be considered poor judgment to effect arrests for possession during a rally to legalize marijuana, the failure to make arrests also carries significant implications. Similarly, uniform enforcement of the law across communities may lead to conflict and charges the police lack cultural sensitivity, whereas differential treatment may lead to accusations that the police do not care about certain segments of society. Either choice can lead to allegations of racial or other discrimination.

The police already routinely reevaluate how best to match policy to law, such as is the case with pursuit policy governing high-speed chases. There are no simple solutions here other than the need to remain flexible and to constantly reassess shifting societal standards. One step the police can take is to make sure that rules violations represent a breech of societal standards and not personal affronts to individual officers, such as was exemplified by the Rodney King incident. This shift in attitudes will not result simply from new training initiatives but will also require that certain aspects of police culture be challenged.

Environmental Design

Police forces have been vigilant in recent years to enhance the environmental design of the workplace to enhance safety. For example, where the purchase of bulletproof vests was once the responsibility of individual officers, they are now typically issued by the employer and mandated by safety codes. Similarly, technological advances, such as the development of the Taser gun, have made it possible for the police to utilize equipment that is both more effective and less dangerous to officer and offender.

Perhaps the current greatest challenge in this area involves the more organic changes to environment that must be adopted as conflicts with citizens evolve. In terms of large-scale demonstrations, much has been learned in the era of antiglobalization protests since the Seattle protests. Police response in these types of episodes need not only be concerned with appropriate equipment and environmentally designed strategies to effectively extract crowd "escalators" but also incorporate greater knowledge about psychological and social psychological dynamics to help determine when a show of force or a softer approach is more likely to deescalate tension. Although public safety units are becoming better versed in these dynamics, additional attention should be directed toward the rank-and-file officer acting in more day-to-day conflict situations, such as when traffic stops signal the potential for the escalation of hostility into violence.

The Institution as a Source of Violence

Boyd provides an example of how long-term care facilities provide a recipe for conflict between health care workers and their clientele. It is not possible to draw direct analogies to police work other than to point to the symbolic importance of the police as maintainers of the societal status quo. This is especially problematic when the police interact with minority group members or others who see themselves as disenfranchised by society.

Steps here need to extend well beyond police administrators to policymakers and the public realm. There must be even greater outreach efforts and education of the public to promote knowledge of the police role and reduce the perception of the police as enemy. To date there has been little useful debate about public expectations for the police; rather, most commentators take polarized positions either as police defenders or as critics. There also needs to be a clearer recognition that individual officers will continue to bear the brunt of criticism for conflict that is more appropriately attributed to forces within a society characterized by inequities. The two most significant initiatives to address the gap between the police and the public, especially minority communities, have been community-based policing and the focused recruitment of minority group members to serve in the police service (see Perrott, 1999). To date, the extent that these initiatives have been successful in attenuating police-community conflict remains a topic of heated debate.

Finally, steps have been taken in recent years by police administrators and unions to recognize the deleterious effects of violence and the need of individual officers to be professionally supported following victimization. Although the macho policing culture has traditionally not been receptive to the notion of psychological vulnerability, this began to change in the 1980s with growing recognition of PTSD with police officers as victims (Reiser & Geiger, 1984). Through employee assistance programs, Western police forces now typically provide counseling services, including critical incident stress debriefings, and police officers are often required to attend mandatory counseling sessions as part of the emerging major incident protocols (see, for example, Amaranto, Steinberg, Castellano, & Mitchell, 2003).

Staffing

In the past 30 years, the police have moved from being a poorly educated blue-collar occupational group to a highly educated and sophisticated group achieving at least semiprofessional status. Police salaries have dramatically increased to meet this change in status, presenting an ongoing budgetary challenge for maintaining sufficient numbers to ensure public safety and officer safety. The police have responded by ensuring that civilians replace highly paid officers in positions that do necessitate a police presence. Community groups, business owners, and the police themselves have typically viewed this redeployment as inadequate. Disgruntled business owners have been, albeit grudgingly, at the forefront of promoting the exponential growth in the private policing industry (a term that the police see as a misnomer for the activities of underqualified security guards).

Staffing deficiencies need to be addressed in a coherent and thoughtful manner as they represent a direct threat to the physical safety of both officers and citizens. Having fewer officers on the front line also presents a less direct threat insofar as the remaining officers are increasingly being forced to return to a "fire-brigade" policing style to the detriment of the more proactive and inclusive community-based policing approach. Unfortunately, most public debate has been politically driven, with considerable rhetoric employed by both politicians and police unions. Consequently, the drive for greater numbers of police officers is often based in rather crude calculations to the detriment of considering a more strategic and empirically supported allocation of resources. In this regard, the police find themselves facing a challenge similar to military forces that are currently being required to deliver more with less.

Education and In-Service Training

Relative to comparable occupational groups such as health care workers, the police have the opportunity to receive reasonable levels of ongoing in-service training (Boyd, 1995). Much of this training focuses on tactical techniques for self-defense, video simulations of crisis situations, use of emerging technologies, and crowd control. There also is some attention given to interpersonal techniques, such as those used during mediation, hostage negotiation, and conflict resolution.

Not surprisingly, less attention is given to providing police officers with exposure to the social sciences. Although most Western officers join police forces holding or having partially completed a baccalaureate degree, this is not an entry requirement, nor is there particular consistency in the course exposure of those who do have university training. Furthermore, because there is a tendency for undergraduates to attend university before attaining much real-world experience, the opportunity to be exposed to aspects of disciplines like sociology, psychology, and political science in a continuing education context would provide serving officers with a new framework for viewing academic offerings and allow them the chance to integrate the material with their front-line experiences. Such exposure would allow officers to stand back from the grittier realities of their everyday experiences and allow them a more macrolevel perspective through which to interpret the hostility and aggression they face. This may not only prove beneficial to individual officers but might also result in their adopting modifications to approach that reduce the probability that certain problematic interactions emerge in the first place.

The concept of the symbolic assailant remains highly relevant to the work of frontline police officers nearly 40 years after Skolnick first outlined the notion. Policing is a difficult and dangerous occupation, and officers need to recognize genuine assailants. Sensing signs of danger, including recognizing characteristics of individuals likely to present a threat, is an understandable and necessary strategy for coping with an ambiguous and unpredictable work environment. Too often police critics and the general public fail to appreciate the magnitude of this challenge. At the same time, however, a significant proportion of violent and hostile incidents occur or escalate because of the tendency to overgeneralize those individuals who should be included in the dangerous category, a problem unnecessarily amplified by certain aspects of police culture. The challenge for training programs is to work toward stemming these overgeneralizations and ensure that the police accurately identify those who pose an actual threat.

References

Amaranto, E., Steinberg, J., Castellano, C., & Mitchell, R. (2003). Police stress interventions. *Brief Treatment and Crisis Intervention, 3,* 47–53.

Balkin, J. (1988). Why policemen don't like policewomen. *Journal of Police Science and Administration, 16,* 29–38.

Bartol, C. R., Bergen, G. T., Volckens, J. S., & Knoras, K. M. (1992). Women in small-town policing: Job performance and stress. *Criminal Justice and Behavior, 19,* 240–259.

Beehr, T. A., Johnson, L. B., & Nieva, R. (1995). Occupational stress: Coping of police and their spouses. *Journal of Organizational Behavior, 16,* 3–25.

Biggam, F. H., Power, K. G., MacDonald, R. R., Carcary, W. B., & Moodie, E. (1997). Self-perceived occupational stress and distress in a Scottish police force. *Work & Stress, 2,* 118–133.

Boyd, N. (1995). Violence in the workplace in British Columbia: A preliminary investigation. *Canadian Journal of Criminology, 37,* 491–519.

Brown, J., Fielding, J., & Grover, J. (1999). Distinguishing traumatic, vicarious, and routine operational stressor exposure and attendant adverse consequences in a sample of police officers. *Work & Stress, 14,* 312–325.

Campbell, V. (1980). Double marginality of Black policemen: A reassessment. *Criminology, 17,* 477–484.

Carlier, I. V. E. (1999). Finding meaning in police traumas. In J. M. Violanti & D. Paton (Eds.), *Police trauma: Psychological aftermath of civilian combat* (pp. 227–240). Springfield, IL: Charles C Thomas.

Cashmore, E. (1991). Black Cops Inc. In E. Cashmore & E. McLaughlin (Eds.), *Out of order? Policing Black people* (pp. 87–108). New York: Routledge.

Cashmore, E. (2001). The experiences of ethnic minority police officers in Britain: Underrecruitment and racial profiling in a performance culture. *Ethnic and Racial Studies, 24,* 642–659.

Castillo, D. N., & Jenkins, E. L. (1994). Industries and occupations at high risk for work-related homicide. *Journal of Occupational Medicine, 36,* 125–132.

Dantzger, M. L., & Kubin, B. (1998). Job satisfaction: The gender perspective among police officers. *American Journal of Criminal Justice, 23,* 19–31.

Dick, P. (2000). The social construction of the meaning of acute stressors: A qualitative study of the personal accounts of police officers using a stress counseling service. *Work & Stress, 14,* 226–244.

Farmer, R. E. (1990). Clinical and managerial implications of stress research in the police. *Journal of Police Science and Administration, 17,* 205–218.

Federal Bureau of Investigation. (2002). *Uniform crime reports: Law enforcement officers killed and assaulted.* Washington, DC: Department of Justice.

Figley, C. R. (1999). Police compassion fatigue (PCF): Theory, research, assessment, treatment, and prevention. In J. M. Violanti & D. Paton (Eds.), *Police trauma: Psychological aftermath of civilian combat* (pp. 37–53). Springfield, IL: Charles C Thomas.

Grennan, S. A. (1987). Findings on the role of officer gender in violent encounters with citizens. *Journal of Police Science and Administration, 15,* 78–85.

Hamilton, A. (1995). Policing Northern Ireland: Current issues. *Studies in Conflict and Terrorism, 18,* 233–242.

Hart, P. M., Wearing, A. J., & Headey, B. (1993). Assessing police work experiences: Development of the Police Daily Hassles and Uplifts Scale. *Journal of Criminal Justice, 21,* 553–572.

Harvey-Lintz, T., & Tidwell, R. (1997). Effects of the 1992 Los Angeles civil unrest: Post traumatic stress disorder symptomatology among law enforcement officers. *Social Science Journal, 34,* 171–183.

Henry, V. E. (1995). The police officer as survivor: Death confrontations and the police subculture. *Behavioral Sciences and the Law, 13,* 93–112.

Herbert, S. (1998). Police subculture revisited. *Criminology, 36,* 343–369.

Holdaway, S. (1991). Race relations and police recruitment. *British Journal of Criminology, 31,* 365–382.

Jefferson, T. (1988). Race, crime, and policing: Empirical, theoretical and methodological issues. *International Journal of the Sociology of Law, 16,* 521–539.

Jermier, J. M., Gaines, J., & McIntosh, N. J. (1989). Reactions to physically dangerous work: A conceptual and empirical analysis. *Journal of Organizational Behaviour, 10*, 15–33.

Kopel, H., & Freidman, M. (1997). Posttraumatic symptoms in South African police exposed to violence. *Journal of Traumatic Stress, 10*, 307–317.

Kraus, J. F. (1987). Homicide while at work: Persons, industries, and occupations at high risk. *American Journal of Public Health, 77*, 1285–1289.

Krimmel, J. T., & Gormley, P. E. (2003). Tokenism and job satisfaction for police-women. *American Journal of Criminal Justice, 28*, 73–88.

Kroes, W. H., Margolis, B. L., & Hurrell, J. J. (1974). Job stress in policemen. *Journal of Police Science and Administration, 2*, 145–155.

LeBlanc, M. M., & Kelloway, E. K. (2002). Predictors and outcomes of workplace violence and aggression. *Journal of Applied Psychology, 87*, 444–453.

Lennings, C. J. (1997). Police and occupationally related violence: A review. *Policing: An International Journal of Police Management and Strategies, 20*, 555–566.

Loo, R. (1999). Police suicide: The ultimate stress reaction. In J. M. Violanti & D. Paton (Eds.), *Police trauma: Psychological aftermath of civilian combat* (pp. 241–254). Springfield, IL: Charles C Thomas.

Malloy, T. E., & Mays, G. L. (1984). The police stress hypothesis: An empirical evaluation. *Criminal Justice and Behavior, 11*, 197–224.

Martin, C. A., McKean, H. E., & Veltkamp, L. J. (1986). Post-traumatic stress disorder in police and working with victims: A pilot study. *Journal of Police Science and Administration, 14*, 98–101.

Martin, S. E. (1994). "Outsider within" the station house: The impact of race and gender on black women policing. *Social Problems, 41*, 383–400.

Maynard, P. E., & Maynard, N. E. (1982). Stress in police families: Some policy implications. *Journal of Police Science and Administration, 10*, 302–314.

Moos, R. (1993). *Coping Responses Inventory Manual*. Lutz, FL: Psychological Assessment Resources.

Niederhoffer, A. (1967). *Behind the shield: The police in contemporary society*. Garden City, NY: Doubleday.

Norvell, N. K., Hills, H. A., & Murrin, M. R. (1993). Understanding stress in female and male law enforcement officers. *Psychology of Women Quarterly, 17*, 289–301.

Parker, S. K., & Griffen, M. A. (2002). What is so bad about a little name-calling? Negative consequences of gender harassment for overperformance demands and distress. *Journal of Occupational Health Psychology, 7*, 195–210.

Parsons, J. R. L. (2004). *Occupational health and safety issues of police officers in Canada, the United States and Europe*. SafetyNet, Newfoundland Centre for Applied Health Research, Memorial University of Newfoundland. St. John's: Newfoundland. Retrieved October 11, 2004, from www.safetynet.mun.ca/about1.htm

Paton, D., & Violanti, J. M. (1996). *Traumatic stress in critical occupations: Recognition, consequences and treatment*. Springfield, IL: Charles C Thomas.

Perrott, S. B. (1999). Visible minority applicant concerns and assessment of occupational role in the era of community-based policing. *Journal of Community and Applied Social Psychology, 9*, 339–353.

Perrott, S. B., Corey, S. A., & Kelloway, E. K. (2004, June). *Coping with violence and hostility: Evidence from police officers, schoolteachers, and registered nurses.* Poster session presented at the Canadian Psychological Association Convention, St. John's, Newfoundland.

Perrott, S. B., & Kelloway, E. K. (2003, May). *Consider the source: Outcomes of workplace aggression among police officers.* Poster session presented at the 11th European Congress on Work and Organizational Psychology, Lisbon, Portugal.

Perrott, S. B., & Taylor, D. M. (1994). Ethnocentrism and authoritarianism in the police: Challenging stereotypes and reconceptualizing ingroup identification. *Journal of Applied Social Psychology, 24,* 1640–1664.

Perrott, S. B., & Taylor, D. M. (1995a). Attitudinal differences between police constables and their supervisors: Potential influences of personality, work environment, and occupational role. *Criminal Justice and Behavior, 22,* 326–339.

Perrott, S. B., & Taylor, D. M. (1995b). Crime fighting, law enforcement, and service provider role orientations in a sample of community-based police officers. *American Journal of Police, 14,* 173–195.

Poole, E. D., & Pogrebin, M. R. (1988). Factors affecting the decision to remain in policing: A study of women officers. *Journal of Police Science and Administration, 161,* 49–55.

Reiser, M., & Geiger, S. P. (1984). Police officer as victim. *Professional Psychology: Research and Practice, 15,* 315–323.

Richmond, R. L., Wodak, A., Kehoe, L., & Heather, N. (1998). How healthy are the police? A survey of life-style factors. *Addiction, 93,* 1729–1737.

Roberts, N. A., & Levenson, R. W. (2001). The remains of the workday: Impact of job stress and exhaustion on marital interaction in police couples. *Journal of Marriage and the Family, 63,* 1052–1067.

Shernock, S. K. (1988). An empirical examination of the relationship between police solidarity and community orientation. *Journal of Police Science and Administration, 16,* 182–194.

Skolnick, J. H. (1966). *Justice without trial.* New York: Wiley.

Somodevilla, S. A. (1978). The psychologist's role in the police department. *The Police Chief, 45,* 21–23.

Stephens, C., & Long, N. (1999). Posttraumatic stress disorder in the New Zealand police: The moderating role of social support following traumatic stress. *Anxiety, Stress, and Coping, 12,* 247–264.

Terry, W. C. (1981). Police stress: The empirical evidence. *Journal of Police Science and Administration, 9,* 61–75.

Toch, H. (2002). *Stress in policing.* Washington, DC: American Psychological Association.

U.S. Department of Justice. (2001). Violence in the workplace, 1993–99. *Bureau of Justice Statistics: Special Report.* Washington, DC: Author.

Van Maanen, J. (1984). Making rank: Becoming an American police sergeant. *Urban Life, 13,* 155–176.

Violanti, J. M. (1999a). Death on duty: Police survivor trauma. In J. M. Violanti & D. Paton (Eds.), *Police trauma: Psychological aftermath of civilian combat* (pp. 139–158). Springfield, IL: Charles C Thomas.

Violanti, J. M. (1999b). Trauma in police work: A psychosocial model. In J. M. Violanti & D. Paton (Eds.), *Police trauma: Psychological aftermath of civilian combat* (pp. 88–96). Springfield, IL: Charles C Thomas.

Violanti, J. M., Marshall, J. R., & Howe, B. (1985). Stress, coping, and alcohol use: The police connection. *Journal of Police Science and Administration, 13,* 106–110.

Violanti, J. M., & Paton, D. (Eds.). (1999). *Police trauma: Psychological aftermath of civilian combat.* Springfield, IL: Charles C Thomas.

Walker, S., & Katz, C. M. (2005). *The police in America: An introduction* (5th ed.). Toronto: McGraw-Hill.

Wexler, J. G., & Logan, D. D. (1983). Sources of stress among women police officers. *Journal of Police Science and Administration, 11,* 46–53.

Wortley, S., Macmillan, R., & Hagan, J. (1997). Just des(s)erts? The racial polarization of perceptions of criminal injustice. *Law and Society Review, 31,* 637–676.

Yarmey, A. D. (1990). *Understanding police and police work.* New York: New York University Press.

11

Crossing the Line

Violence on the Picket Line

Lori Francis
James E. Cameron
E. Kevin Kelloway

I n late May 1992, the management of Royal Oak Mines Inc. locked out its workers at the Giant Gold Mine in the Canadian Northwest Territories. The lockout came one day before approximately 240 members of the Canadian Association of Smelter and Allied Workers (CASAW) were set to go on strike ("Giant Mine: Timeline," 2003). The lockout followed a tense and frustrating round of bargaining, during which the union executive and Royal Oak management reached a tentative agreement that was ultimately rejected by the union membership ("Trouble Began at Bargaining Table," 2003). The union hoped to gain a contract without major concessions. Royal Oak Mines wanted concessions, including pay cuts, and contentious issues such as downsizing were on the table.

Within days, the picket line at the Giant Mine operation became the site of violence. Then CEO of Royal Oak Mines, Peggy Witte, opted to keep the plant in operation during the labor dispute. Newly hired replacement workers and strikebreaking union members were escorted across the picket line by security and ultimately transported into the mine by helicopter ("Giant Mine: Timeline," 2003). Strikers were enraged about continued production. Several

Authors' Note: This work was supported by grants from the Nova Scotia Health Research Foundation and the Social Sciences and Humanities Research Council of Canada to the first and third authors.

acts of violence followed; the mine itself and the homes of individuals crossing the picket lines were vandalized. Striking union members snuck into the mine and left insulting graffiti for the replacement workers. Police were forced to intervene in riots on the picket line between Royal Oak's security provider, Pinkerton's Security, and strikers. Additionally, a number of explosions set by strikers occurred at the mine. Throughout the summer, Royal Oak was reportedly warned by police and the security provider that safety was an issue at the mine.

The violence reached a climax in the fourth month of the strike. On September 18, 1992, nine miners were killed in an underground explosion while riding a mine car ("Giant Mine: Timeline," 2003). Six of the dead were union members who crossed the picket line and three were replacement workers. Thirteen months later, union member Roger Warren confessed that he had set the explosives with the intention of doing property damage to the mine. He was convicted on nine counts of second-degree murder in January 1995 and is now serving a life prison sentence ("Giant Mine: Timeline," 2003).

The Giant Mine strike lasted for 17 months. Union members returned to work in December 1993 following a decision by the Canada Labour Relations Board against Royal Oak Mines ordering an end to the lockout; however, the dispute did not end with the return to work. In 1997, the Workers' Compensation Board of the North West Territories launched a lawsuit against a number of stakeholders in the Giant Mine lockout on behalf of the families of the nine miners who were killed in 1992 ("WCB Details Defendants," 2003). Among the accused were the former CEO Peggy Witte, Royal Oaks Mines, Inc., Pinkerton's Security, the union, and a number of high-profile strikers, including Roger Warren. The Workers' Compensation Board claimed that negligence on the part of a number of parties set the stage for the deadly violence that occurred during the labor dispute. For instance, the Compensation Board criticized the security procedures that permitted strikers to sneak into the mine at will; the management of Royal Oak who maintained plant operations during a violent strike, fired a number of striking employees during the dispute, and wanted to cut security throughout the strike; and the regional chief inspector of mines, who did not shut the mine down despite the property damage it sustained.

In December 2004, the Supreme Court of the Northwest Territories awarded over $10.7 million in damages to the widows and family members of the nine miners killed in the blast (*Fullowka et al. v. Royal Oak Ventures et al.*, 2004). A further $600,000 was awarded to James O'Neill, a miner who developed posttraumatic stress disorder after witnessing the immediate aftermath of the blast. In allocating fault among the various defendants, Justice A. M. Lutz concluded that Royal Oak, the union, and Roger Warren share substantial and approximately equal portions of blame for the fatal blast (*Fullowka et al. v. Royal Oak Ventures et al.*).

The labor dispute at Giant Mine is illustrative of the nature and ramifications of picket line violence. From this case, it is evident that the escalation of violence during a labor dispute can lead to such immediate outcomes as property damage, injury, and even death. It also illustrates the potential for longer term implications for those involved, such as criminal and civil lawsuits launched against a number of stakeholders, including strikers, the union, and company management.

Certainly, the Giant Mine dispute is not the only well-publicized case of picket lines turning violent. Consider the 3-year labor dispute between Overnite Transportation Company, which had been the trucking subsidiary of Union Pacific Corporation, and the International Brotherhood of Teamsters. This strike was precipitated by the union's claim that Overnite's management engaged in unfair labor practices, including unlawful discharge and harassment, against Teamsters' members who constituted a small portion of Overnite's workforce ("Teamsters Notebook," 1999). During this nationwide strike, while Overnite maintained operations, there were numerous incidents, including vandalism, cut brake lines on trucks, and more than 50 shootings (Schulz, 2000; "Teamster Promise," 2003). Following this strike, as part of a settlement with the National Labor Relations Board in the United States, the Teamsters were required to post a notice on their Web site and at their locals promising that union members will not engage in acts of violence such as threatening death or the use of a weapon, disabling vehicles, or assaulting nonstriking workers at Overnite (International Brotherhood of Teamsters [IBT], n.d.).

In this chapter, we examine the issue of picket line violence. In particular we consider the prevalence of violent episodes during labor disputes, introduce theoretical frameworks that help explain why strikes and lockouts can turn violent, and identify factors that predict violence on the picket line. Following our empirical and theoretical review of picket line violence, we highlight a number of future research needs on this issue and identify implications for practice, policy, and intervention.

Nature and Prevalence of Violence on the Picket Line

Thieblot, Haggard, and Northrup (1999) provide a recent discussion on the characteristics and incidence of picket line violence in the United States. They define picket line violence as the "non-privileged physical interference with the person or property of another, or the threat, express or implied of such interference" (Thieblot & Haggard, 1983, p. 14). Note that this definition includes such physical acts as assault, sabotage, blocking access to a work site, and vandalism. Furthermore, it incorporates acts of aggression that are more psychological in nature, including threats and intimidation. Thieblot et al. note that this definition excludes privileged acts, such as union members refusing to work during a legal strike, although such refusal may contribute to economic or competitive losses for the company. Thieblot et al.'s inclusion of a range of activities in their definition of picket line violence is in keeping with conceptions of workplace violence in general. For instance, Robinson and Bennett (1995) include both minor and serious events in their typology of deviant workplace behavior, and Schat and

Kelloway (2005) incorporate both physical and psychological aspects of workplace aggression in their definition of that construct.

In characterizing picket line violence, Thieblot et al. (1999) point out that labor disputes tend to involve two large categories of violent acts: confrontational and purposeful. *Confrontational violence* is that which breaks out at the spur of the moment during a conflict. For instance, following a trade of verbal insults, a group of picketers may throw rocks at line crossers. Similar to Anderson and Bushman's (2002) description of *hostile aggression*, confrontational violence is event-driven, reactive, spontaneous, and driven by anger. In the collective context of the picket line, confrontational violence is relatively common, and its origin or instigator usually remains unknown. Such is not necessarily the case with the broader label, *hostile aggression*.

Thieblot et al. (1999) describe *purposeful violence* as planned and deliberate. Parallel to Anderson and Bushman's (2002) conception of *instrumental aggression*, purposeful violence is enacted to help achieve a goal. For instance, in the Giant Mine dispute, the use of explosives by strikers in an attempt to deter replacement workers from continuing employment at the mine is illustrative of purposeful violence. With respect to group settings like a picket line, an investigation might reveal the perpetrator of an act of purposeful violence.

The incidence of picket line violence must be considered in concert with the prevalence of unionization in general. In the United States, 13.2% of the workforce belonged to a labor union in 2002, with union membership rising to over 20% in states such as New York, Alaska, Hawaii, and Michigan (U.S. Department of Labor [USDL], n.d.). Unionization rates are higher in other countries. In 2002, union density among employees in the UK was 29% (National Statistics Online, n.d.) and 30.3% in Canada (Akyeampong, 2003). In terms of Canadian public servants, more than 70% were unionized in 2002.

Picket lines are usually set up as a form of labor protest when there is a breakdown of labor-management relations (Bluen, 1994). As such, picket lines arise during strikes and lockouts. In a strike situation, the union executive makes a decision, with endorsement of the majority of union members, to walk off the job. In the case of lockouts, the company's management prevents employees from working. In 2001, 379 strikes lasting more than 10 days occurred in Canada, resulting in 223,800 individuals off the job and 2,231,100 missed workdays (International Labour Office, [ILO], n.d.). Comparable statistics for strikes that occurred in the United States include only those events involving more than 1,000 employees, resulting in a lower number of reported strikes. Nonetheless, during 2001, 29 strikes in the United States involved more than 1,000 employees, resulting in 99,100 workers off the job and 1,151,300 missed workdays.

Violence on the picket line has a long history. For instance, Baker (2002) details incidents of violence between police and union members during the 1928 Australian maritime strike. Other research examines the historical prevalence of collective violence in the European labor movements in the 19th and early 20th centuries (Snyder & Kelly, 1976; Snyder & Tilly, 1972).

Additionally, detailed reviews of violent strikes in the United States are readily available (Taft & Ross, 1969; Thieblot et al., 1999). Some of the frequently referenced strikes include the Detroit News strike of 1995, the UK coal strike of 1984–1985, and the Pullman strike of 1894.

Using data gathered by the National Institute for Labor Relations Research in the United States, Thieblot et al. (1999) estimated that the annual average number of incidents of union and strike-related violence in the United States was 432 for the period from 1975 to 1995. They provide a context for this value by pointing out that although there has been a decrease in the union movement in general, and strike activity specifically, there has actually been an increase in the amount of violence on a per strike basis. In the time frame they examined, the number of strikes declined by about two thirds, but the number of violent incidents related to labor disputes decreased by only one third. These authors conclude that violence is a continuing and potentially increasing element on picket lines.

To extend Thieblot et al.'s analysis, we examined the available statistics for union- and strike-related violence in the years following 1995. Complete data were available for 1966 through 2002 (National Institute for Labor Relations Research [NILRR], personal communication, January 22, 2004). The number of violent events fluctuated from a low of 31 in 2001 to a high of 184 in 1997. The annual average number of violence incidents for this 7-year period was 127.86. This average incidence of violence is lower than for the period from 1976 to 1995. The reasons for this difference are difficult to ascertain and range from potential changes in the reporting and recording of violent events to a possible decline in the prevalence of strike activity in general to an actual decrease in the true incidence of strike-related violence in more recent years.

In keeping with Robinson and Bennett's (1995) typology of deviant workplace behavior, the picket line violence recorded in the NILRR database and analyzed by Thieblot et al. (1999) ranged from relatively minor incidents involving such aggressive acts as name-calling, shouting, and pushing to serious incidents involving weapons such as guns and explosives, which result in serious injury and death. In the approximately 20-year period considered by Thieblot et al. (1999), approximately 10% (1,021 events) of the recorded incidents involved guns. These incidents ranged from incidents when individuals produced and threatened to use a firearm to those when actual shots were fired. Another 5% (427 events) of the reported cases involved explosives, including firecrackers, firebombs, and bombs. In total, the NILRR database reported 248 incidents of picket line violence resulting in death. In almost 60% (143) of those cases, the victims were third parties who had no direct involvement with the strike. Another 20% of the victims were strikers, company officials, or line crossers. The remaining cases involved a mixed group of victims, including union officials and business agents.

A second dimension of workplace aggression and violence identified in Robinson and Bennett's (1995) typology is interpersonal versus organizational.

Interpersonal violence is that directed at other people and includes such acts as verbal abuse and sexual harassment. Alternatively, organizational violence is intended bring harm to the company and includes such acts as stealing from the organization and sabotaging equipment. Thieblot et al.'s (1999) analysis of picket line violence can also be considered along this dimension. Confrontational incidents on the picket line account for 24% of the violence episodes in the NILRR database. Confrontational incidents are somewhat difficult to classify as exclusively organizational or interpersonal, as these events can fall under either classification. For instance, throwing rocks at a company vehicle as it crosses the line is organizational, whereas throwing objects at individuals crossing the line is interpersonal. Another 30% of strike-related violence is clearly organizational, directed at the struck company and its suppliers. Incidents in this category include vandalizing company buildings and equipment.

Interpersonal attacks are the most frequent type of strike-related violence, accounting for 43% of the incidents in the NILRR database (Thieblot et al., 1999). In particular, picket line crossers are noted targets for such acts of violence as vandalism of their vehicles and homes. Stennett-Brewer's (1997) study of picket line crossers showed that exposure to violence is high in this population. Fully 100% of the individuals surveyed reported they had been the subject of verbal assaults by picketers while crossing the line; more than 40% experienced damage to their vehicle; more than 20% had received phone threats against them or their family members; and approximately 11% experienced gunshots directed at their vehicle or property.

Unique Qualities of Picket Line Violence

A number of qualities of strikes, and picket lines in particular, make them unique settings in which to examine work-related violence. First, the collective nature of strikes provides a special context for research on work-related violence. Numerous other studies of workplace violence focus on cases in which individuals with varying relationships to the organization (e.g., client, employee, member of the general public) commit an aggressive or violent act (e.g., Barling, 1996; Braverman, 1999; LeBlanc & Barling, 2005; Rogers & Kelloway, 1997; Schat & Kelloway, 2000). In contrast, strikes provide researchers with the opportunity to examine cases of aggression and violence when individuals perform a violent act as members of shared social groups. In collective situations, the predictors and appropriate theoretical models of violence likely differ from those involving an isolated perpetrator. As such, the study of picket line violence may expand our conceptions of work-related violence. Further, to the extent that both confrontational and purposeful violence characterize picket lines, strikes provide a unique setting in which to examine and compare the precursors and outcomes of both of these categorizations of violence.

Compared with other types of workplace aggression and violence, situations arising on the picket line involve a number of distinctive predictors. For example, the hiring of replacement workers and strikebreakers by management to maintain operations during a strike is associated with increased incidents of picket line violence (Grant & Wallace, 1991; Thieblot et al., 1999). Furthermore, the length of the strike and complexity of the outstanding labor issues appear to predict violence (Snyder & Kelly, 1976). Generally, strikes that are longer and characterized by a large number of outstanding issues tend to be more violent. To the extent that picket lines are characterized by unique precursors to violent acts, they allow researchers a unique environment in which to study violence and its causes.

Picket lines also provide a unique setting for the study of workplace violence in the diversity of acts and targets that characterize strike-related incidents. With respect to aggressive and violent acts, studies of strikes show that in a single strike, incidents of aggression and violence can range from name-calling and verbal threats to acts of assault, sabotage, and murder (Thieblot et al., 1999). Furthermore, strike-related violence has multiple foci. On picket lines, aggression and violence can be directed toward the company, other organizations that carry out business with the targeted company, and various groups of individuals, most notably replacement workers, strikebreakers, and managers who are crossing the picket line (Thieblot et al., 1999). We also note that members of the public are potential victims of picket line violence if they have to cross a picket line or are in the vicinity of a demonstration that erupts in violence. Although most of the existing research studies cases when picketers enact violence against other groups or objects, we also note that the strikers themselves are sometimes the object of picket line violence. They may be the targets of aggression and violence by individuals who are crossing the picket line or by security forces and police who are tasked with maintaining order during strikes (Baker, 2002; Grant & Wallace, 1991; Thieblot et al., 1999). As such, the varying nature of strike-related violence provides a unique opportunity to study a wide range of multiply directed violent and aggressive acts.

Perhaps most interesting, picket line violence is a unique form of workplace violence because some scholars suggest that strike-related violence is viewed as legitimate. General opinion is that a degree of aggression and violence are part and parcel of picketing (Thieblot et al., 1999). Thieblot et al. conclude that the interpretation and implementation of existing laws in the United States are ineffective in restraining labor violence. In fact, some have charged that federal laws and the National Labor Relations Board actually condone strike-related violence (Bovard, 1994; Brinker, 1985; Kendrick, 1998; Thieblot et al., 1999). Courts are hesitant to apply antiracketeering laws in cases of picket line violence following the 1973 case of the United States v. Enmons, in which the Supreme Court concluded that union violence is exempt from federal anti-extortion laws if such violence is aimed at furthering legitimate union objectives (e.g., job protection or better wages) (Brinker, 1985; Kendrick, 1998; Thieblot et al., 1999). Furthermore, some suggest that the 1947 Taft-Hartley revision to the National Labor Relations Act, which outlaws union violence and coercion, is in fact tolerant of such acts, as it provides inadequate remedies to address union violence. In implementing the act, the National Labor Relations Board has condoned union violence to the extent that violence occurring during a strike is not defined as an unfair labor practice unless it becomes excessive (Thieblot et al., 1999). Under Section 303 of the National Labor Relations Act, employers can seek redress against unions if they suffer injury only when the union engages in unfair labor practice. Furthermore, acts of violence on the picket line are rarely considered just cause for employers to dismiss striking employees. Thieblot et al. (1999) attribute this to the tendency to view picket line violence as a byproduct of emotions on the picket line and therefore not a just cause for dismissal. Nonetheless, there are some avenues of recourse in cases of picket line violence. For instance, criminal actions under both federal and state laws and civil actions under the Racketeer Influenced and Corrupt Organizations (RICO) Act are possible forms of redress (Thieblot et al., 1999).

To the extent that aggression and violence on picket lines are considered by the public and legal system as expected or legitimate, picket line violence is separate from other forms of workplace violence. For instance, some acts of violence such as threats, sabotage, and assaults, which are generally viewed as reprehensible in work settings, may be viewed as legitimate and acceptable when they occur on the picket line.

Theoretical Models of Picket Line Violence

Prior researchers have presented a number of theoretical propositions about strike-related violence. Some assess picket line violence using models of group relations (e.g., Diener, 1980; Tajfel, 1978; Tajfel & Turner, 1979) to account for acts of violence on the picket line, whereas others examine characteristics of particular industries and the personalities of union members to explain picket line violence (e.g., Kerr & Siegel, 1954). In this section, we both summarize and extend the existing theoretical models of picket line violence, drawing on the deindividuation (Diener, 1980; Festinger, Pepitone, & Newcomb, 1952; Zimbardo, 1969) and social identity models (Tajfel, 1978; Tajfel & Turner, 1979) of group behavior from social psychology; and we consider the characteristics of labor unions and union members (Brinker, 1985; Kerr & Siegel, 1954; Thieblot et al., 1999). Furthermore, we introduce a novel theoretical perspective that has not been identified by previous researchers in this area, namely picket line violence as a behavioral outcome of strike-related stressors (Barling & Milligan, 1987; Bluen & Barling, 1988; Francis & Kelloway, 2005).

The Deindividuation Model

The concept of *deindividuation* (Diener, 1980; Festinger et al., 1952; Zimbardo, 1969) involves a number of psychological and situational elements associated with being in groups, including reduced accountability for one's actions, anonymity, arousal, and reduced self-awareness. Notwithstanding various and often imprecise definitions of deindividuation (for a recent review, see Postmes & Spears, 1998), the essential theme—that the group somehow engenders a loss of self that in turn renders individuals prone to antisocial and/or aggressive behavior—is one that runs from the earliest explanations of crowd behavior (Le Bon, 1895/1960). The deindividuated member of the group is, according to this view, someone whose rationality is compromised and whose behavior is consequently chaotic (Zimbardo, 1969), antinormative, and potentially violent.

Given that the deindividuation model has assumed a place in the social psychological canon (Postmes & Spears, 1998), it is not surprising that accounts of violence on the picket line also rely on the concept of deindividuation (e.g., Baron, 1986); however, it has been recently challenged from both sociological (e.g., McPhail, 1991) and psychological (e.g., Reicher, 2001; Reicher, Spears, & Postmes, 1995) perspectives. Postmes and Spears's (1998) meta-analysis of 60 relevant experimental investigations indicated, for example, that deindividuation effects were more variable and less robust than is generally assumed. Even more problematic for the deindividuation model was the absence of evidence that supposedly deindividuating conditions led to "deregulated" behavior; instead, the manipulations tended to elicit behavior that was *consistent* with situational norms. In other words (Postmes & Spears, 1998), "the factors that social psychologists have identified as playing a crucial role in the formation of collective behavior appeared to lead to a specific form of social regulation rather than its breakdown" (p. 253). Understanding the nature of this regulation requires attention to an aspect of collective violence that the deindividuation model generally neglects: that it often takes place (as it does on the picket line) in contexts where there is more than one group and where violent behavior thus can be understood as an *intergroup* phenomenon.

The Social Identity Model

According to social identity theory (Tajfel, 1978; Tajfel & Turner, 1979), intergroup behavior is fundamentally different from interpersonal behavior because it reflects a collective aspect of the self: social identity (which reflects shared group memberships) as opposed to personal identity (which reflects one's unique characteristics). Group behavior is thought to result from a shift in self-concept from personal to social identity (Turner, Hogg, Oakes, Reicher, & Wetherell, 1987), which is more likely to happen when (a) individuals identify relatively strongly with an in-group, and (b) this group membership—as distinct from some other category—is perceptually prominent in a particular context (Turner et al., 1987). The social identity theory explanation of group violence differs from the deindividuation model in the important sense that collective behavior is viewed as guided by the norms of the group, rather than as the chaotic product of a "loss" of self (e.g., Reicher, 2001; Reicher et al., 1995). From this perspective, understanding picket line violence requires an appreciation of how strikers identify with their group and how the salience of an intergroup distinction (e.g., between strikers and replacement workers or between strikers and management), combined with consensual prescriptions for group action, make aggressive responses available and even desirable. It is necessary, then, to maintain a distinction between *general* norms for appropriate conduct, which deindividuation theory emphasizes, and those that prescribe acceptable behavior in a particular intergroup context (Postmes & Spears, 1998).

In terms of social identity theory, strike-related behaviors can be considered forms of *collective action,* which Wright, Taylor, and Moghaddam (1990) defined as behavior that arises "any time that [the individual] is acting as a representative of the group and [that] is directed at improving the conditions of the entire group" (p. 995). There is substantial evidence that group identification predicts collective action intentions, including protest in industrial contexts (Haslam, 2001; Kelly & Kelly, 1994; Veenstra & Haslam, 2000); however, although Tajfel and Turner (1979) predicted that direct forms of collective action would be preferred when group members perceived their situation as illegitimate and unstable, the precise precursors of particular behavioral options are not well understood (Taylor & Moghaddam, 1987). Nevertheless, there is some agreement that group members opt for aggressive and potentially illegal forms of collective action as a last resort, after less risky strategies have been exhausted and proven ineffective (e.g., Kawakami & Dion, 1995; Wright, 2001). There are also a handful of experimental indications that extreme varieties of protest arise in situations when high levels of illegitimacy and unfairness are perceived (Lalonde & Cameron, 1994; Wright et al., 1990).

A number of psychological consequences of social categorization (i.e., an us-versus-them distinction) and social identification can contribute to the sharpening of intergroup perceptions and behavior, particularly during a protracted strike or lockout. These include in-group-favoring social comparisons, heightened stereotyping of both in-group and out-group members, an atmosphere of competition and mutual mistrust (e.g., Hoyle, Pinkley, & Insko, 1989), and enhanced in-group cohesion (e.g., Dion, 1979), particularly among highly identified members (Branscombe, Ellemers, Spears, & Doosje, 1999). Certainly, union solidarity increases during a strike (Stagner & Eflal, 1982). As group positions become more polarized, norms can shift in such a way that behavior that would normally be seen as inappropriate becomes desirable in the intergroup context. As Grant and Wallace (1991) note with respect to striker-enacted picket line violence, "tactics that seem unthinkable in the early days of a conflict may seem the only logical course of action in later days" (p. 1119). In recent testimony in the Giant Mine civil trial, Roger Warren, who was recognized as a strong union loyalist and is now serving a life sentence for second degree murder, was quoted as saying, "In a normal time I would have known that amount of explosives would have killed people. I never did anything so crazy in my . . . life" (e.g., "Lawyers Focus," 2004).

Such shifts in perception can be gradual or immediate, as during a situated confrontation. Thus, even in cases when violence erupts in a seemingly surprising and unpredictable fashion, the "confrontational" violence (Thieblot et al., 1999) that is often explained with reference to deindividuation can be understood as a function of the dynamics of intergroup relations. Analyses of crowd behavior by Reicher and colleagues (see Drury & Reicher, 2000; Reicher, 2001) suggest, for example, that previously moderate group members who nevertheless believe in the legitimacy of their collective position can be radicalized by their perceived mistreatment by out-group members (e.g., police). This leads to an aggravation of conflict, as individuals on both sides respond in kind.

A potentially useful theoretical basis for further study on the precursors of aggressive and violent acts on the picket line may be Klandermans's (e.g., 1984, 1986, 1993, 1997) model of participation in protest. Klandermans's framework, which incorporates collective identification, also includes a cost-benefit analysis as a factor influencing one's willingness to engage in various forms of social protest. Although Klandermans's model focuses on participation in protest rather than on specific protest behaviors such as the use of violence, it is possible that shifting perceptions of the costs and benefits associated with acts of aggression and violence as a strike wears on prompt people to act in a violent manner to further the position of their group. Such an approach is limited, in that it assumes that acts of violence and aggression during strikes are the result of a rational, strategic process, which may or may not be the case with acts of purposeful aggression and is unlikely the case in confrontational violence, which occurs in the heat of the moment. We offer this theory, however, as a potential starting point for future studies in this area and caution that its value in addressing questions of picket line violence is subject to empirical investigation.

Industry Characteristics and Union Member Personality: The Kerr-Siegel Hypotheses

Following a study of strike propensity in 11 countries from the 1920s through the 1940s, Kerr and Siegel (1954) developed a theory regarding the predictors of the propensity to strike, which they further linked to labor-related violence. They noted that certain industries have a higher propensity to strike than others. In particular, mining and longshore industries had the highest, trade and agriculture unions the lowest, and the lumber and textile industries intermediate propensity to strike. They presented two hypotheses to account for these interindustry differences.

Kerr and Siegel (1954) proposed that workers in industries that (a) provide little opportunity for occupational or social mobility, (b) involve isolation, and (c) offer little communication with management would form a strong sense of group. Their strong group identity would contribute to their viewing management as an out-group. Kerr and Siegel (1954) suggested that strikes would be perceived by such workers as a viable way to deal with tensions caused by management.

Further, Kerr and Siegel's (1954) theory addressed the characteristics of the job itself. They proposed that jobs that were physically demanding, involved difficult working conditions, and required little formal training would attract tough and combative individuals who were naturally prone to striking and violence.

There are interindustry differences in both the number of strikes and incidence of violence. To some extent, these differences are in keeping with patterns noted by Kerr and Siegel (1954). For example, coal mining had the highest incidence of violence per employee in the period from 1975 to 1995, whereas government and public trust unions had the lowest (Thieblot et al., 1999). In general, skilled trade and service industries tend to display less violence during strikes than does the mining industry (Brinker, 1985). In explaining the large number of violence charges against the Teamsters, some have suggested that trucking appeals to tough individuals with a high propensity to strike (Brinker, 1985). Further, it is possible that striking members of Teamsters model aggressive behavior that they have witnessed in other members and leaders of their union in previous labor disputes. Other studies, however, contradict Kerr and Siegel's (1954) classification. Examining the history of labor violence in Italy, Snyder and Kelly (1976) found that those industries considered most militant under Kerr and Siegel's classification (e.g., mining) had lower incidence of violence than some of those considered less militant (e.g., agriculture).

Other scholars have criticized Kerr and Siegel (1954) on theoretical grounds. For instance, Hyman (1972) noted that Kerr and Siegel's model does not account for international differences in an industry's propensity to strike. Edwards (1977) critiqued the model on the basis that they linked strike rates to dissatisfaction with management but did not offer an explanation of why such dissatisfaction arises. He asserted that an isolated group of workers simply having a strong sense of group identity would not necessarily result in more dissatisfaction, increased conflict, and accordingly more frequent strikes. Others (e.g., Nelson & Grams, 1978; Poole, 1981) have suggested that inter-industry differences in the propensity to strike are related to the extent to which workers view problems in structural rather than personal terms.

Stress and Picket Line Violence

A more individualistic account of picket line violence would see violence as emerging as a reaction to threat and frustration (Fox & Spector, 1999; Spector, 1997). Certainly there is both conceptual (e.g., Bluen & Barling,

1987, 1988; Francis & Kelloway, 2005) and empirical (Barling & Milligan, 1987) evidence for the suggestion that strikes are stressful events for participants, nonparticipant employees who may continue to work during a strike (e.g., Lusa, Häkkänen, Luukkonen, & Viikari-Juntera, 2002), and third parties who might be affected by the action (see, for example, Day, Stinson, & Catano, 2002).

Empirically, most researchers have focused on the experience of strike participants. Symptoms of strain, such as job withdrawal and exhaustion (Milburn, Schuler, & Watman, 1983); increased psychological distress, decreased perceptions of health, and decreased general functioning (MacBride, Lancee, & Freeman, 1981); and decreased marital functioning, psychological distress, and psychosomatic complaints (Barling & Milligan, 1987) have all been associated with participation in a strike. Moreover, these negative outcomes may persist for as long as 6 months following the resolution of the strike (Barling & Milligan, 1987).

Francis and Kelloway (2005) identify several of the stressors associated with strike participation, including both intra- and interrole conflicts, increased financial strain (Bluen, 1994), and an increased sense of job insecurity. Collective bargaining is, in itself, a stressful experience (Bluen & Jubiler-Lurie, 1990), and these stressors may be exacerbated in a strike. Like other forms of protest (see, for example, Francis, Teed, Kelloway, & Catano, 2004; Kelloway, Francis, & Catano, 2004), strikes are fundamentally an expression of perceived injustice, and there is now mounting evidence that injustice is also a stressor (see, for example, Elovainio, Kivimaki, & Helkama, 2001; Francis & Barling, 2005; Francis & Kelloway, 2005; Tepper, 2001). In this sense, a strike may be an acute stressor (Pratt & Barling, 1988) and appropriately viewed as a major life event (Dohrenwend & Dohrenwend, 1974) requiring considerable adaptation on the part of the individual.

Although there are, at present, few data linking industrial relations stressors directly with strike-related violence, there are several lines of evidence suggesting the existence of such a link. First, studies have illustrated that aggression is a reaction to frustration (e.g., Fox & Spector, 1999; Spector, 1978, 1997). Frustrating events are those that interfere with or prevent goal achievement (Spector, 1997). Workplace stressors such as role ambiguity and role conflict are noted frustrators (Keenan & Newton, 1984) and potentially relevant industrial relations stressors (Francis & Kelloway, 2005). As such, individuals experiencing heightened exposure to stressors during a labor dispute may react aggressively. Further, models of the frustration-aggression relationship suggest that frustrated individuals may be more likely to react aggressively when they perceive they have little situational control and do not fear they will be punished for their actions (Fox & Spector, 1999). Certainly the picket line setting may enhance both of these factors. In cases of persisting strikes when bargaining talks have stalled, individual stakeholders may feel they have little control over the outcome of the dispute and react with acts of aggression and violence. Further, in the case of confrontational violence, when it is often difficult to identify the perpetrators, individuals with little fear of reprimand may respond to their frustration with aggression.

Perceived injustice is an acknowledged workplace stressor that has also been linked to aggression. For example, Skarlicki and Folger (1997) found that perceptions of distributive, procedural, and interactional injustice accounted for a large proportion of variance in organizational retaliatory behavior. Greenberg and Barling (1999) demonstrated that perceived procedural injustice and organizational use of surveillance and monitoring technology predict aggression directed toward supervisors but not toward coworkers or subordinates. Certainly, perceived injustice is at the core of many labor disputes. Members of the union likely feel that company management, by failing to meet the bargaining demands, is treating them unfairly. Similarly, those in management may perceive the union's position as unfair. Overall, organizational injustice is identified as one of the most promising avenues in the study of workplace aggression (e.g., Jawahar, 2002). Combined with the core role of perceived injustice in labor disputes, these findings suggest that individual perceptions of injustice may be experienced as stressors and lead to more aggression and violence on the picket line.

Predictors of Picket Line Violence

There are a number of predictors of picket line violence, ranging from characteristics of the strike and management reactions to the strike to sociopolitical forces (Grant & Wallace, 1991). Some researchers have considered political and socioeconomic factors as potential predictors of strike violence. For instance, Grant and Wallace (1991) reported greater incidence of picket line violence during strikes that occurred when a centrist, as opposed to right-leaning government, is in power, suggesting that strikes may be more violent when there is less fear of union repression by political powers. Alternatively, models of strike violence reported by Snyder and Tilly (1972) suggest a curvilinear relationship between incidences of picket line violence and the political ideology of ruling governments. Specifically, labor-related violence will be low under left-leaning governments that permit collective action and support civil liberties, as well as under oppressive regimes that outlaw collective action.

Others have examined the impact of forthcoming government elections on strike violence. Snyder and Tilly (1972) reported that collective violence in France increased during election years, whereas Grant and Wallace (1991) indicated that picket line violence in Canada decreased during election years. The divergent results may be explained by the differing study contexts. The unions in the Canadian sample were largely recognized bodies who would prefer not to tarnish labor's reputation in an election year. Alternatively, the strikes under consideration in the French sample involved less recognized unions aiming to gain power.

Some researchers have advanced the argument that picket line violence is more likely during strikes occurring during a downturn in the economy (e.g., Ashenfelter & Johnson, 1969); however, empirical evidence does not support this claim (Grant & Wallace, 1991; Snyder & Tilly, 1972). For example, strikes that occurred in times of high unemployment or when rises in the cost of living outpaced wage increases were not characterized by more violence than those that occurred during better economic times (Grant & Wallace, 1991).

Industry has been identified as a potential predictor of picket line violence (Kerr & Siegel, 1954; Thieblot et al., 1999), but as described in the previous section, mixed results make it difficult to establish which industries and unions are more likely to encounter violence during strikes (Brinker, 1985; Kerr & Siegel, 1954; Snyder & Kelly, 1976; Thieblot & Haggard, 1983; Thieblot et al., 1999). The skill level of the striking employees has also been examined as a predictor of union violence. It appears that unions composed mostly of skilled workers are the least prone to picket line violence, and those with predominantly unskilled strikers are the most likely to erupt in violence (Grant & Wallace, 1991). Interestingly, unlike other combinations of skills levels, strikes involving unskilled, semiskilled, and skilled workers were not less violent than those involving only unskilled workers, suggesting that there may be problems maintaining order during strikes with a mixed group of picketers (Grant & Wallace, 1991).

Researchers have also examined the predictive role of the issues at play in the dispute. Snyder and Kelly (1976) reported that although the exact nature of outstanding issues, such as wages, working conditions, or union recognition, did not predict picket line violence, strikes that were characterized by multiple issues, termed by the researchers as complex, were more prone to violence than single-issue disputes. Others have argued that the nature of the underlying issues does affect strikes. In particular, strikes that are launched over ideological differences such as work conditions or union recognition may be more susceptible to violence than those over material issues such as wages because such conflicts are potentially less conducive to compromise (Taft & Ross, 1969); however, an archival study of a large number of strikes illustrated that when controlling for other predictors such as the skill composition of the strikers, strike issues, including working conditions and union recognition, did not predict picket line violence (Grant & Wallace, 1991).

The duration of strikes is also a predictor of picket line violence, with violence being more likely to emerge during longer disputes (Grant & Wallace, 1991; Snyder & Kelly, 1976). There are at least three plausible explanations for this finding (Snyder & Kelly, 1976). First, increased incidence of violence during longer strikes may be purely probabilistic. More days spent on the picket line provide a greater opportunity for events that precipitate violence to occur. Second, longer strikes may reflect more complex outstanding issues, a recognized predictor of picket line violence. Third, longer strikes may contribute to increased anger and desperation among the strikers, prompting them to engage in increased violent behavior. We suggest that this third explanation fits well with the stress-related account of picket line violence presented earlier. Longer term exposure to stressors during a lengthy strike can increase behavioral manifestations of stress, including acts of violence and aggression. Furthermore, longer strikes may result in increased group identification and thus relate to violence in the manner outlined in our earlier discussion of social identity theory.

Grant and Wallace (1991) examined the legal status of a strike as a predictor of violence. They found that one category of illegal strikes, those that started in the postconciliation waiting period (a mandated waiting period in their Canadian sample), were more violent than their legal counterparts. The relationships among other categories of illegal strikes (e.g., precertification, during an existing contract) and picket line violence were in the predicted direction but did not reach significance.

Researchers have also considered the impact of the size of a strike on picket line violence. Evidence suggests that strikes involving a larger number of picketers are more violent (Snyder & Kelly, 1976). Other researchers have examined strike size in terms of the proportion of eligible workers adhering to the strike (participation rate). It appears that the relationship between participation rate and strike-related violence may be curvilinear, such that violence is highest when the portion of the workforce striking is intermediate and lowest when participation is either very low or very high (Grant & Wallace, 1991). Grant and Wallace suggest that intermediate participation rates increase the number of union members attempting to cross the picket line, amplifying the potential for violence. During strikes in which the participation rate is very low, a small group of strikers may be less likely to confront the larger number of union members crossing the picket line (cf. resource mobilization theory, Jenkins, 1983; Klandermans, 1984). In cases of high participation, there are fewer union members attempting to cross the picket line.

The factor that has been most often and consistently reported as a predictor of picket line violence is continued organizational operations—via the use of nonstriking employees, replacement workers, or managers—on the part of the targeted organization (Grant & Wallace, 1991; Thieblot et al., 1999). Maintenance of operations during a strike may contribute to violence via a number of routes. First of all, continued operations means increased traffic across the picket line as replacement workers, nonstriking employees, and managers attempt to report for work (Grant & Wallace, 1991). Certainly, a large portion of reported incidents of picket line violence are attributable to confrontational violence on the picket line (Thieblot et al., 1999). Furthermore, strikers who feel threatened by maintained operations may engage in purposeful violence to deter individuals from crossing the picket line.

Continued company operations also tend to increase police and security presence on the picket line, as these forces are called on by management to provide escorts across the line (Grant & Wallace, 1991). These security agents may aggress against strikers who are trying to slow progress through the line. Furthermore, the mere presence of police and security guards may aggravate strikers and result in violence.

Continued operations during a strike may also exacerbate other predictors of picket line violence and therefore indirectly lead to violence and aggression. For instance, maintained operations may increase the job insecurity of strikers. Job insecurity is a noted stressor (e.g., Barling & Kelloway, 1996) that may increase strain and accordingly contribute to violence. Additionally, maintained operations may place less pressure on management to reach a settlement and may therefore increase the duration of a strike.

Major Empirical Studies

There is very little empirical research on picket line violence, and the studies that are available tend to fall into two main categories. Some researchers have taken the case study approach, using illustrative examples of strikes to reach determinations about the predictors, characteristics, and outcomes of picket line violence (e.g., Baker, 2002; Taft & Ross, 1969). Other researchers study picket line violence via quantitative analysis of archival data (e.g., Grant & Wallace, 1991; Snyder & Kelly, 1976; Snyder & Tilly, 1972). One other major empirical work used a combination of these two approaches (Thieblot et al., 1999).

Case Studies

Taft and Ross's (1969) qualitative discussion of several widely publicized, violent strikes from the 1870s to the mid-20th century is a widely cited reference on American labor violence. The authors noted that most incidents of picket line violence arise when strikers attempt to hinder continued company operations by stopping replacement workers and strikebreakers who try to cross the picket line. They theorize that strikes launched over issues of union recognition are the most likely to erupt in violence because employers who are aware of strikers' resentment regarding the lack of organized representation may heighten defensive strike measures. Defensive acts such as hiring security guards to police the picket line and provide escorts to line crossers increase the potential for confrontations between strikers, line crossers, and security forces. Taft and Ross (1969) firmly conclude that strike-related violence leads to negative outcomes for unions. Further, they assert that in the quarter century leading up to their publication, picket line violence was on the decline, a trend they attribute to legislation requiring employers to recognize unions.

Although it is widely cited, Taft and Ross's (1969) analysis is limited in a number of ways. First of all, their discussion includes only a small number of well-publicized, violent strikes. The lack of consideration given to nonviolent disputes precludes a consideration of the differences between strikes that turn violent and those that do not (Grant & Wallace, 1991). Taft and Ross's (1969) claims regarding union recognition as a predictor of picket line violence have been refuted by quantitative analyses of large numbers of strikes (Grant & Wallace, 1991; Snyder & Kelly, 1976). Additionally, their claim that strike-related violence is declining is contrary to the conclusions reached by other scholars (e.g., Brinker, 1985; Thieblot et al., 1999). Furthermore, even the most recent strikes in Taft and Ross's (1969) analysis occurred more than 40 years ago, and a study considering more recent strikes would provide a better illustration of the current nature of picket line violence.

Baker (2002) examined the role the police play in labor-related violence. Via a case study of the 1928 maritime strike that saw the death of a union stevedore in Port Melbourne, Australia, Baker (2002) concluded that police presence in labor disputes places both strikers and police officers in a precarious situation. For instance, when police escort individuals across the picket line, both the officers and the strikers can easily become victims of violence. Baker (2002) noted that the volatility of such situations may stem from the historical fact that police are not usually a neutral party in labor disputes and are often willing to operate in a forceful manner at the request of employers. Strikers receive the brunt of police aggression during a strike, and most often the strikers are victims of such violence rather than vice versa. This analysis is interesting in that it presents a less frequently discussed aspect of picket line violence, the case in which the striker is the victim. Baker (2002) concludes that both police forces and unions must appreciate the value of avoiding violence during strikes as both sides aim to gain public support.

Quantitative Studies

Researchers have also used archival data on strikes to examine the factors pertaining to industrial violence. Snyder and Kelly's (1976) examination of industrial violence in Italy provides an illustrative example of this approach. Using a database compiled by the Italian government pertaining to all of the work stoppages in that country from 1878 to 1903, the researchers were able to identify whether or not the stoppages were violent, the issues at stake in each strike, situational aspects of strikes (e.g., size, duration), and characteristics of the resolution. They found that strikes involving a large number of participants and of longer duration are more likely to erupt in violence. They also found industry differences in picket line violence, but these were not in line with the pattern predicted by Kerr and Siegel (1954). For instance, contrary to the predictions of Kerr and Siegel, Snyder and Kelly reported that agricultural strikes were more violent than those in the mining or textile industries.

Snyder and Kelly (1976) also examined the relationship among the issues that prompted the strike and the prevalence of violence during the dispute. In particular, they considered three dimensions. First, they noted whether the strike was an offensive effort, in which workers were asking for increased benefits, or defensive, in which strikers walked off the job to protest a decrease in workers' welfare. Second, they investigated the impact of two broad types of outstanding issues, namely wages and working conditions versus union-related matters such as recognition. Finally, they considered the complexity of the issues at the root of the strike. Strikes characterized by a great number of issues were considered more complex. Interestingly, only complexity predicted picket line violence. Snyder and Kelly suggested that multiple outstanding issues, likely perceived by management as demands, may decrease the company's perceived legitimacy of the strike and accordingly intensify the conflict. The failure of type of outstanding issues to predict violence was surprising to the extent that other scholars had, on the basis of qualitative studies, asserted that ideological issues such as union recognition are less open to compromise than material matters (Taft & Ross, 1969); however, Snyder and Kelly noted that such an assertion had not previously been empirically analyzed.

With respect to the outcomes associated with picket line violence, controlling for other characteristics of the dispute (e.g., nature of issues, size, and type of industry), Snyder and Kelly (1976) concluded that peaceful strikes result in better outcomes for the union. Strikes that are characterized by violence tended to result in concessions on the part of the union, with violence between groups of workers (e.g., strikers versus those crossing the picket line) having a larger negative impact than violence directed at security forces or the struck company. Nonetheless, Snyder and Kelly noted that violence on the picket line does not necessarily result in negative outcomes for the union as has been suggested by other researchers (e.g., Taft & Ross, 1969).

Grant and Wallace (1991) also examined the predictors of strike violence using archival data collected by a government organization. In this case, the strikes in question happened between 1958 and 1967 in Ontario, Canada. Their analysis included several classes of predictors, including political and economic factors, strike and picket line characteristics, skill level of workers, and strategies used by employers during the strike. In some ways, this study confirms the conclusions reached by Snyder and Kelly (1976). For instance, larger strikes that were of longer duration were more likely to be violent. Again in keeping with previous findings (Snyder & Kelly, 1976), the nature of the outstanding issues did not predict picket line violence. Extending the work of Snyder and Kelly, Grant and Wallace (1991) reported a relationship between maintained company operations during a strike and picket line violence. Violence was more likely to emerge in strikes when the targeted company maintained production. Additionally, the skill level of strikers was an important predictor of violence. For the most part, the lower the skill level of the strikers, the more violence on the picket line. The exception was the case of strikes including a wide range of skill levels among the picketers. Such strikes were no less violent than those involving only unskilled labor. This study also adds to the literature on picket line violence showing that strikes that occurred illegally during a mandated waiting period were more likely to be violent.

Thieblot and Haggard (1983) used a combination of qualitative and quantitative approaches in their analyses on picket line violence. Their original work was revised and published as Thieblot et al. (1999). In both cases,

Thieblot and colleagues combined the presentation of descriptive statistics on the incidence of strike-related violence using data collected by the National Institute for Labor Relations Research with illustrative case discussions of violent strikes in various industries such as mining and construction.

In both versions (Thieblot & Haggard, 1983; Thieblot et al., 1999), the researchers concluded that picket line violence is a substantial aspect of strikes and an increasing concern. They also noted that picket line violence is becoming a less effective tactic for unions trying to seek a resolution to the strike, as companies are more effective at maintaining production during disputes via the use of specialized security forces and therefore less economically pressured to reach a deal with unions. Throughout their analysis, Thieblot and colleagues noted several trends in picket line violence, particularly regarding the industry involved, and the purpose and targets of violence. With respect to industrial sectors, their conclusions about the industries and unions more likely to experience strike-related violence were largely in keeping with the classifications offered by Kerr and Siegel (1954), with the mining industry reporting the largest number of labor-related violent events per employee.

Thieblot et al. (1999) noted that strike-related violence can arise either from spontaneous confrontations on the picket line or deliberate attempts to influence the strike. Strikers may engage in planned acts of violence for a number of reasons, including to get attention, advance bargaining, and generate fear among those who may cross the picket line. As we discussed earlier in the section on the nature and prevalence of picket line violence, an increasing proportion of violence appears to be directed toward individuals as opposed to the struck company. Company attempts to maintain operations during a strike appear to increase the likelihood of picket line encounters and the motivation of strikers to use deliberate violence to invoke fear.

Thieblot and colleagues (Thieblot & Haggard, 1983; Thieblot et al., 1999) added uniquely to the literature on strike violence with their consideration of the legal response to incidents of violence on the picket line. They conclude that the application of existing law in the United States does not restrain labor violence because the courts and regulatory bodies tend not to seek charges in cases in which violence enacted by union members is considered to be aimed at seeking legitimate goals such as a collective agreement. Their negative evaluation of the American legal response has received some criticism. Craft (2001) argued that Thieblot et al. (1999) do not give enough credence to the group processes that contribute to confrontations on the picket line and suggested that what they present as leniency on the part of the National Labor Relations Board reflects the tendency of the board to take into account the context that surrounds violent episodes on the picket line before pursuing restrictive action.

There are other potential weaknesses with Thieblot et al.'s approach. Their quantitative descriptions are based on information collected by the National Institute for Labor Relations Research. The database was generated by gathering clippings from newspaper reports of strikes across the United States. Thus only those strikes that were covered by the popular press in the

United States were included. The incidents recorded in the database are predominantly American, and it seems that only violent strikes are included. As such, it is difficult to engage in a comparative analysis of violent and nonviolent disputes and to consider potential international differences in picket line violence. They have also been critiqued for undervaluing the role of some potential causative factors of strike violence. For instance, they downplay the role of personality and the frustration that strikers feel in response to management intransigence during the strike (Craft, 2001).

Key Measurement Issues

The core measurement concern in studying strike-related violence is that it is quite difficult to obtain reliable data on strike behavior in general and picket line violence in particular. The existing studies have relied on after-the-fact case studies of well-known violent strikes (e.g., Baker, 2002; Taft & Ross, 1969), data sources reliant on the popular press (e.g., Thieblot & Haggard, 1983; Thieblot et al., 1999), or arguably outdated government databases (Grant & Wallace, 1991; Snyder & Kelly, 1976). Each of these approaches comes with a unique set of concerns.

Case studies of violent strikes do not permit a direct comparison of the different predictors, characteristics, and outcomes of violent and nonviolent strikes. Using data documented from media sources is problematic in that only those events dramatic enough to make the news are subject to analysis. Such an approach may overestimate the prevalence of major acts of violence and underplay the incidence of aggressive, but more commonplace, occurrences such as name-calling and swearing during strikes. Moreover, media portrayals of labor unions tend to be unfavorable (Beharrell & Philo, 1977; Puette, 1992). Such a bias may result in an overestimate of incidents involving violence in which the strikers are the perpetrators and an underestimate of cases when other parties (e.g., replacement workers, police forces, managers, or members of the public) instigate acts of violence. With respect to historical analyses, reaching conclusions about the predictors and outcomes of picket line violence using data gathered as long ago as the late 19th century may not provide an accurate depiction of the current reality during strikes. Changes in the past century regarding the extent to which labor unions are organized, accepted, and protected by regulatory bodies such as labor relations boards mean that the practice of industrial relations today is very different that it was even 25 years ago.

Future Research Needs

The largest outstanding research need in the area of industrial relations violence is a systematic examination of the predictors, prevalence, nature, and outcomes of picket line violence in recent strikes. We were unable to locate any existing studies of the emergence, nature, and outcomes of violence in the context of an ongoing strike. Although we acknowledge the difficulties surrounding data collection during a strike, we suggest that there are ways to circumvent them. For instance, researchers could carry out interviews or diary studies asking strikers and line crossers to reflect on their experiences and thus gain insight into picket line violence in today's industrial relations climate. Further, we suggest surveys of individuals who have recently been on strike would permit researchers to test some of the theoretical accounts of picket line violence. Questions regarding group processes and exposure to stressors would elucidate our understanding of why violence so frequently emerges on picket lines.

The current body of research emphasizes violent events enacted by strikers against other constituents (e.g., Taft & Ross, 1969; Thieblot et al., 1999); however, strikers can also be victims of violent acts. Given this, future research should more directly examine violence on the part of picket line crossers and security forces and compare the motivations and outcomes of picket line violence when it is used as a tactic by different stakeholder groups during a strike.

We urge scholars studying workplace violence to pay increased attention to strike-related violence in general. The prevalence of picket line violence, along with its unique predictors and purposes, makes it a viable focus for research on a wide range of violent acts. In fact, we suggest that collective violence be explicitly recognized in categorizations of workplace violence. Currently, there are four identified classes of workplace violence (e.g., LeBlanc & Barling, 2005). In Type I, a member of the public with no legitimate relationship to the organization commits a violent, usually criminal, act (e.g., a robbery). In Type II, a member of the public who has a legitimate service relationship with the organization (e.g., client, patient) commits an act of violence. In Type III, the perpetrator is a current or former employee of the organization. Type IV involves cases of domestic violence that spill over to the workplace. To an extent, incidents of picket line violence are illustrative of Type III violence in that the perpetrators are most often employees of the struck company representing either union or management; however, we suggest that the existing classes of violence do not fully capture the collective nature and other unique aspects of strike-related violence, and an expansion of the mainstream research on workplace violence to better incorporate violence stemming from industrial relations is in order.

Personal, Organizational, and Social Costs of Picket Line Violence

Picket line violence carries a number of costs for the unions, companies, and individuals affected by it. In terms of personal costs, picket line violence can lead to injury and even death for individuals, including strikers, managers, replacement workers, police and security forces, and members of the public who may cross the picket line. Additionally, individuals who have been victims of strike-related violence may experience a number of negative outcomes, including emotional and physical symptoms of strain (Schat & Kelloway, 2000).

Although Thieblot et al. (1999) questioned the effectiveness of the current legal response to picket line violence, individual stakeholders can face criminal charges for violent acts committed on the picket line, just as Roger Warren did in the Giant Mine case. Furthermore, given that civil suits are a possibility following a violent strike (Thieblot et al., 1999), multiple stakeholders could face civil legal proceedings if they perpetrated a violent act during a strike or did not take adequate measures to prevent one.

The organizational costs of picket line violence are also substantial. From the union perspective, research suggests that violence during a strike decreases the likelihood of a successful resolution (Snyder & Kelly, 1976; Taft & Ross, 1969; Thieblot et al., 1999). Furthermore, picket line violence captures media attention. A negative portrayal in the media (Puette, 1992) may further damage labor's reputation in society and decrease public support for strikes. From a company perspective, violent strikes can result in substantial property damage and tarnish future union-management relations, perhaps irreparably so.

The societal costs of picket line violence are less tangible but no less real than individual and organizational losses. Violence during strikes may reduce community members' trust in labor organizations and damage the long-term viability of unions as protectors of workers' rights. Additionally, when members of the public see police and security forces acting in a violent manner during a strike, their respect for and trust in these groups may decline. From a social learning perceptive (Bandura, 1977), everyone bears the cost of picket line violence to the extent that the use of violence to advance one's position in a labor dispute may send a message that violent tactics are an accepted and viable means of conflict resolution. If so, those who witness or hear about acts of aggression and violence on the picket line may perpetrate future violence by modeling those actions as a form of conflict resolution in their own organizations. Furthermore, some have noted that aggression and violence on the picket line are expected aspects of labor disputes (e.g., Thieblot et al., 1999). To the extent that violence becomes legitimized, expected, and accepted, society loses some of its sensitivity to issues of violence and aggression—that is perhaps the biggest societal cost associated with picket line violence.

Implications for Practice, Policy, and Intervention

Picket line violence has numerous and broad implications. Union officials and managers who are involved in a pending or current labor dispute must recognize the problem of strike-related violence and take measures to minimize it. Advanced recognition and swift treatment of the problem may slow the progression of violence and ultimately lessen its impact. The social psychological literature on intergroup conflict suggests that the union and management may attempt to decrease violence by increasing perceptions of individual accountability. If people are reminded that, even in a collective situation, they are responsible for their own actions, they may be less prone to engage in acts of violence on the picket line. Union and management leaders can also emphasize that strikes bring increased public and media attention. Such a reminder of public scrutiny may decrease violence on the picket line (Postmes & Spears, 1998). Leading up to and during a strike, union members and managers should be encouraged to question their assumptions about the nature of strikes. If people expect a strike to be aggressive and violent, then violence may be a foregone conclusion. Changing expectations about the acceptability of violence on the picket line may, in fact, reduce violence. Furthermore, union and company leaders can communicate norm-based information to their constituents. If prescriptive examples of less dangerous ways to express grievances with the other party can be provided, violence may not be perceived as the only outlet for emotions.

All stakeholder groups must closely examine the impact of their own practices on picket line violence. Unions must consider the extent to which their strike rituals and procedures explicitly or implicitly justify aggression and violence during a strike and work to remove any perceived legitimation of such acts. Employers must also acknowledge that their reactions to strikes can contribute to violence. Employers must seriously examine company policies regarding continued production during a strike, given that maintained operations during a strike is the most consistent predictor of strike-related violence and is theoretically linked to both spontaneous, confrontational violence at the line and more deliberate acts of violence designed to induce fear. Although maintained operations during a strike are viewed favorably by employers on a purely economic basis, management officials must seriously weigh this benefit against the very real costs. Continued production jeopardizes the physical and psychological (Francis & Kelloway, 2005) well-being of strikers, replacement workers, strikebreakers, and managers. Keeping production up and running during a strike angers the union, potentially slows negotiations, and can irreversibly damage future labor-management relations. Furthermore, the company may be vulnerable to legal action if a violent attack that is deemed preventable results in injury or death. In light of these costs, employers might be well advised to forego the short-term economic benefit of continued production in return for less acrimonious and violent strikes, reduced liability, and an improved industrial relations climate.

Police and security forces also need to examine their practices and policies when called on to maintain order in labor disputes. They should consider the impact of using violence against strikers on their public image.

Furthermore, they must be willing to take a strong stand in interactions with the company on matters of safety during hostile strikes. As evidenced by Pinkerton's Security being named a defendant in the Giant Mine case, if security and police forces are aware of safety hazards and do not take action to address them, they can face legal ramifications.

_____ **Epilogue**

Picket line violence is a very real concern in industrial relations practice but remains a largely understudied form of workplace violence. Researchers should take action to explore the predictors, characteristics, and outcomes of picket line violence. In doing so, they may gain an increased understanding of workplace violence in general and increased insight into the nature of collective violence in particular. Researchers and practitioners alike must search for strategies to change existing assumptions about the normative nature of aggression and violence on the picket line and provide union leaders and employers with tools to avoid strike-related violence whenever possible and better manage it when it does occur.

_____ **References**

Akyeampong, E. B. (2003, July). Fact sheet on unionization. *Perspectives on labor and income* (47, no. 7, pp. 2–25). Ottawa, ON: Statistics Canada.

Anderson, C. A., & Bushman, B. J. (2002). Human aggression. *Annual Review of Psychology, 53,* 27–51.

Ashenfelter, O., & Johnson, G. (1969). Bargaining theory, trade unions, and industrial strike activity. *American Economic Review, 59,* 35–49.

Baker, D. (2002). "You dirty bastards, are you fair dinkum?" Police and union confrontation on the wharf. *New Zealand Journal of Industrial Relations, 27,* 33–47.

Bandura, A. (1977). *Social learning theory.* Englewood Cliffs, NJ: Prentice Hall.

Barling, J. (1996). The prediction, experience, and consequences of workplace violence. In G. R. VandenBos & E. Q. Butlatao (Eds.), *Violence on the job* (pp. 29–49). Washington, DC: American Psychological Association.

Barling J., & Kelloway, E. K. (1996). Job insecurity and health: The moderating role of workplace control. *Stress Medicine, 12,* 253–260.

Barling, J., & Milligan, J. (1987). Some psychological consequences of striking: A six month, longitudinal study. *Journal of Occupational Behavior, 8,* 127–138.

Baron, R. A. (1986). *Behavior in organizations: Understanding and managing the human side of work* (2nd ed.). Boston: Allyn & Bacon.

Beharrell, P., & Philo, G. (Eds.). (1977). *Trade unions and the media.* London: Macmillan.

Bluen, S. D. (1994). The psychology of strikes. In C. L. Cooper & I. T. Robertson (Eds.), *International review of industrial and organizational psychology* (Vol. 9, pp. 113–135). London: John Wiley.

Bluen, S. D., & Barling, J. (1987). Stress and the industrial relations process: Development of the Industrial Relations Event Scale. *South African Journal of Psychology, 17,* 150–159.

Bluen, S. D., & Barling, J. (1988). Psychological stressors associated with industrial relations. In C. L. Cooper & R. Payne (Eds.), *Causes, coping and consequences of stress at work.* London: John Wiley.

Bluen, S. D., & Jubiler-Lurie, V. G. (1990). Some consequences of labor-management negotiations: Laboratory and field studies. *Journal of Organizational Behavior, 11,* 105–118.

Bovard, J. (1994, June 2). Union goons' best friend. *Wall Street Journal,* p. A4.

Branscombe, N. R., Ellemers, N., Spears, R., & Doosje, B. (1999). The context and content of social identity threat. In N. Ellemers, R. Spears, & B. Doosje (Eds.), *Social identity: Context, commitment, content* (pp. 35–58). Oxford, UK: Blackwell.

Braverman, M. (1999). *Preventing workplace violence: A guide for employers and practitioners.* Thousand Oaks, CA: Sage.

Brinker, P. A. (1985). Violence by U.S. labor unions. *Journal of Labor Research, 6,* 417–427.

Craft, J. A. (2001). Union violence: A review and critical discussion. *Journal of Labor Research, 22,* 679–688.

Day, A. L., Stinson, V., & Catano, V. M. (2002, April). *Strike threats: Predictors of strain outcomes in affected third parties.* Paper presented at the annual meeting of the Society for Industrial and Organizational Psychology, Toronto.

Diener, E. (1980). Deindividuation: The absence of self-awareness and self-regulation in group members. In P. B. Paulus (Ed.), *Psychology of group influence* (pp. 209–242). Hillsdale, NJ: Lawrence Erlbaum.

Dion, K. L. (1979). Intergroup conflict and intragroup cohesiveness. In W. G. Austin & S. Worchel (Eds.), *The social psychology of intergroup relations* (pp. 211–224). Monterey, CA: Brooks-Cole.

Dohrenwend, B. S., & Dohrenwend, B. P. (Eds.). (1974). *Stressful life events.* New York: John Wiley.

Drury, J., & Reicher, S. (2000). Collective action and psychological change: The emergence of new social identities. *British Journal of Social Psychology, 39,* 579–604.

Edwards, P. K. (1977). A critique of the Kerr-Siegel hypothesis of strikes and the isolated mass: A study of the falsification of sociological knowledge. *Sociological Review, 25,* 551–570.

Elovainio, M., Kivimaki, M., & Helkama, K. (2001). Organizational justice evaluations, job control, and occupational strain. *Journal of Applied Psychology, 86,* 418–424.

Festinger, L., Pepitone, A., & Newcomb, T. (1952). Some consequences of de-individuation in a group. *Journal of Abnormal and Social Psychology, 47,* 522–552.

Fox, S., & Spector, P. E. (1999). A model of work frustration-aggression. *Journal of Organizational Behavior, 20,* 915–931.

Francis, L., & Barling, J. (2005). Organizational injustice and psychological strain. *Canadian Journal of Behavioral Science, 37,* 250–261.

Francis, L., & Kelloway, E. K. (2005). Industrial relations. In J. Barling, M. Frone, & E. K. Kelloway (Eds.), *Handbook of work stress* (pp. 325–352). Thousand Oaks, CA: Sage.

Francis, L., Teed, M., Kelloway, E. K., & Catano, V. M. (2004, June). Solidarity and injustice as predictors of activism. In E. K. Kelloway (Chair.), *Predicting protest*. Symposium presented at the meeting of the Canadian Psychological Association, St. John's, NL.

Fullowka et al. v. Royal Oak Ventures et al. (2004, December 16). Docket CV 05408, 2004 NWTSC 66. Retrieved January 3, 2005, from www.justice .gov.nt.ca/pdf/CourtLibrary/Giantmine.pdf

Giant mine: Timeline. (2003). Canadian Broadcasting Corporation. Retrieved Oct. 29, 2003, from http://north.cbc.ca/north/archive/gianttrial/archives.htm

Grant, D. S., II, & Wallace, M. (1991). Why do strikes turn violent? *American Journal of Sociology, 96*, 1117–1150.

Greenberg, L., & Barling, J. (1999). Predicting employee aggression against co-workers, subordinates and supervisors: The roles of person behaviors and perceived workplace factors. *Journal of Organizational Behavior, 20*, 897–913.

Haslam, S. A. (2001). *Psychology in organizations: The social identity approach.* London: Sage.

Hoyle, R. H., Pinkley, R. L., & Insko, C. A. (1989). Perceptions of behavior: Evidence of differing expectations for interpersonal and intergroup interactions. *Personality and Social Psychology Bulletin, 15*, 365–376.

Hyman, R. (1972). *Strikes.* Glasgow: Fontana/Collins.

International Brotherhood of Teamsters. (n.d.). *Notice to Employees and Members: Posted pursuant to a settlement stipulation approached by a regional director of the National Labor Relations Board.* Retrieved March 16, 2003, from www.teamster .org/overnite/pdfs/overnitecb.pdf

International Labour Office. (n.d.). *Yearbook of labor statistics*. In Statistics Canada (2003). *Strikes and lockouts, workers involved and workdays not worked.* Retrieved July 25, 2003, from www.statcan.ca/english/Pgdb/labor30a.htm

Jawahar, I. M. (2002). A model of organizational justice and workplace aggression. *Journal of Management, 28*, 811–834.

Jenkins, J. C. (1983). Resource mobilization theory and the study of social movements. *Annual Review of Sociology, 9*, 527–553.

Kawakami, K., & Dion, K. L. (1995). Social identity and affect as determinants of collective action: Toward an integration of relative deprivation and social identity theories. *Theory & Psychology, 5*, 551–577.

Keenan, A., & Newton, T. A. (1984). Frustration in organizations: Relationships to role stress, climate, and psychological strain. *Journal of Occupational Psychology, 57*, 57–65.

Kelloway, E. K., Francis, L., & Catano, V. M. (2004, June). Third party support for strike action. In E. K. Kelloway (Chair.), *Predicting protest*. Symposium presented at the meeting of the Canadian Psychological Association, St. John's, NL.

Kelly, C., & Kelly, J. E. (1994). Who gets involved in collective action? Social psychological determinants of individual participation in trade unions. *Human Relations, 47*, 63–88.

Kendrick, D. (1998, Sept. 9). *Freedom from union violence* (Cato Institute for Public Policy Research Policy Analysis No. 316). Document retrieved October 18, 2004, from www.cato.org/pubs/pas/pa-316es.html

Kerr, C., & Siegel, A. (1954). The interindustry propensity to strike: An international comparison. In A. Kornhauser, R. Dubin, & A. Ross (Eds.), *Industrial conflict* (pp. 189–212). New York: McGraw-Hill.

Klandermans, B. (1984). Mobilization and participation in trade union action: An expectancy-value approach. *Journal of Occupational Psychology, 57,* 107–120.

Klandermans, B. (1986). Perceived costs and benefits of participation in union action. *Personnel Psychology, 39,* 379–397.

Klandermans, B. (1993). A theoretical framework for comparisons of social movement participation. *Sociological Forum, 8,* 383–402.

Klandermans, B. (1997). *The social psychology of protest.* Oxford, UK: Blackwell.

Lalonde, R. N., & Cameron, J. E. (1994). Behavioral responses to discrimination: A focus on action. In M. P. Zanna & J. M. Olson (Eds.), *The psychology of prejudice: The Ontario Symposium* (Vol. 7, pp. 257–288). Hillsdale, NJ: Lawrence Erlbaum.

Lawyers focus on Warren's changing testimony. (2004, April 22). Canadian Broadcasting Corporation. Retrieved July 6, 2004, from http://north.cbc.ca/north/archive/gianttrial/news.html

LeBlanc, M. M., & Barling, J. (2005). Understanding the many faces of workplace violence. In S. Fox & P. E. Spector (Eds.), *Counterproductive workplace behavior: An integration of both actor and recipient perspective on causes and consequences* (pp. 41–63). Washington, DC: American Psychological Association.

Le Bon, G. (1960). *The crowd: A study of the popular mind.* New York: Viking. (Original work published 1895)

Lusa, S., Häkkänen, M., Luukkonen, R., & Viikari-Juntura, E. (2002). Perceived physical work capacity, stress, sleep disturbance and occupational accidents among firefighters working during a strike. *Work & Stress, 16,* 264–274.

MacBride, A., Lancee, W., & Freeman, S. J. J. (1981). The psychosocial impact of a labor dispute. *Journal of Occupational Psychology, 54,* 125–133.

McPhail, C. (1991). *The myth of the madding crowd.* New York: Aldine de Gruyter.

Milburn, T. W., Schuler, R. S., & Watman, K. H. (1983). Organizational crisis: Part II. Strategies and responses. *Human Relations, 36,* 1161–1180.

National Statistics Online. (n.d.). *Union membership: Broadly flat in 2002 compared with 2001.* Retrieved July 28, 2003, from www.statistics.gov.uk/CCI/nugget.asp

Nelson, J. I., & Grams, R. (1978). Union militancy and occupational communities. *Industrial Relations, 17,* 342–346.

Poole, M. (1981). *Theories of trade unionism.* London: Routledge.

Postmes, T., & Spears, R. (1998). Deindividuation and antinormative behavior: A meta-analysis. *Psychological Bulletin, 123,* 238–259.

Pratt, L. I., & Barling, J. (1988). Differentiating between daily events, acute and chronic stressors: A framework and its implications. In J. J. Hurrell Jr., L. R. Murphy, S. L. Sauter, & C. L. Cooper (Eds.), *Occupational stress: Issues and development in research* (pp. 41–53). London: Taylor & Francis.

Puette, W. J. (1992). *Through jaundiced eyes: How the media view organized labor.* Ithaca, NY: ILR Press.

Reicher, S. (2001). The psychology of crowd dynamics. In R. Brown & S. L. Gaertner (Eds.), *Blackwell handbook of social psychology: Intergroup processes* (Vol. 3, pp. 182–208). Oxford, UK: Blackwell.

Reicher, S., Spears, R., & Postmes, T. (1995). A social identity model of deindividuation phenomena. In W. Stroebe & M. Hewstone (Eds.), *European review of social psychology* (Vol. 6, pp. 161–198). Chichester, UK: John Wiley.

Robinson, S. L., & Bennett, R. J. (1995). A typology of deviant workplace behaviors: A multidimensional scaling study. *Academy of Management Journal, 38,* 555–572.

Rogers, K., & Kelloway, E. K. (1997). Violence at work: Personal and organizational outcomes. *Journal of Occupational Health Psychology, 2,* 63–71.

Schat, A. C. H., & Kelloway, E. K. (2000). The effects of perceived control on the outcomes of workplace aggression and violence. *Journal of Occupational Health Psychology, 4,* 386–402.

Schat, A. C. H., & Kelloway, E. K. (2004). Workplace aggression. In J. Barling, E. K. Kelloway, & M. Frone (Eds.), *Handbook of work stress* (pp. 189–218). Thousand Oaks, CA: Sage.

Schulz, J. D. (2000, January 17). Violence rises at Overnite. *Traffic World,* pp. 25–26.

Skarlicki, D. P., & Folger, R. (1997). Retaliation in the workplace: The roles of distributive, procedural and interactional justice. *Journal of Applied Psychology, 82,* 434–443.

Snyder, D., & Kelly, W. R. (1976). Industrial violence in Italy, 1878–1903. *American Journal of Sociology, 82,* 131–163.

Snyder, D., & Tilly, C. (1972). Hardship and collective violence in France, 1830–1960. *American Sociological Review, 37,* 520–532.

Spector, P. E. (1978). Organizational frustration: A model and review of the literature. *Personnel Psychology, 31,* 815–829.

Spector, P. E. (1997). The role of frustration in antisocial behavior at work. In R. A. Giacalone & J. Greenberg (Eds.), *Antisocial behavior in organizations* (pp. 1–17). Thousand Oaks, CA: Sage.

Stagner, R., & Eflal, B. (1982). Internal union dynamics during a strike: A quasi-experimental study. *Journal of Applied Psychology, 67,* 37–44.

Stennett-Brewer, L. (1997). *Trauma in the workplace: The book about chronic work trauma.* Mount Zion, IL: Nepenthe.

Taft, P., & Ross, P. (1969). American labor violence: Its causes, character, and outcome. In H. D. Graham & T. R. Gurr (Eds.), *Violence in America: Historical and comparative perspectives* (pp. 281–396). New York: Frederick A. Praeger.

Tajfel, H. (1978). *Differentiation between social groups.* London: Academic.

Tajfel, H., & Turner, J. C. (1979). An integrative theory of intergroup conflict. In W. G. Austin & S. Worchel (Eds.), *The social psychology of intergroup relations* (pp. 33–47). Monterey, CA: Brooks-Cole.

Taylor, D. M., & Moghaddam, F. M. (1987). *Theories of intergroup relations: International social psychological perspectives.* New York: Praeger.

Teamster promise. (2003, Sept. 30). *Wall Street Journal,* p. A20.

Teamsters notebook: Strike at overnite. (1999, November). Socialist Action. Retrieved August 22, 2005, from www.socialistaction.org/news/199911/teamsters.html

Tepper, B. J. (2001). Health consequences of organizational injustice: Tests of main and interactive effects. *Organizational Behavior and Human Decision Processes, 86,* 197–215.

Thieblot, A. J., & Haggard, T. R. (1983). *Union violence: The record and the response by the courts, legislatures, and the NLRB.* Philadelphia: Industrial Research Unit, Wharton School, University of Pennsylvania.

Thieblot, A. J., Haggard, T. R., & Northrup, H. R. (1999). *Union violence: The record and the response by the courts, legislatures, and the NLRB* (Rev. ed.). Fairfax, VA: George Mason University, John M. Olin Institute of Employment Practice and Policy.

Trouble began at bargaining table, Giant trial hears. (2003, Oct. 8). Canadian Broadcasting Corporation. Retrieved Oct. 29, 2003, from http://north.cbc.ca/north/archive/gianttrial/news.html

Turner, J. C., Hogg, M. A., Oakes, P. J., Reicher, S. D., & Wetherell, M. S. (1987). *Rediscovering the social group: A self-categorization theory.* Oxford, UK: Blackwell.

U.S. Department of Labor, Bureau of Labor Statistics. (n.d.). *The union difference: Union membership by state.* Retrieved August 22, 2005, from www.aflcio.org/joinaunion/why/uniondifference/uniondiff16.cfm

United States v. Enmons, 410 US 396, 406, n. 16 (1973).

Veenstra, K., & Haslam, S. A. (2000). Willingness to participate in industrial protest: Exploring social identification in context. *British Journal of Social Psychology, 39,* 153–172.

WCB details defendants. (2003, Oct. 1). Canadian Broadcasting Corporation. Retrieved Oct. 29, 2003, from http://north.cbc.ca/north/archive/gianttrial/news.html

Wright, S. C. (2001). Strategic collective action: Social psychology and social change. In R. Brown & S. L. Gaertner (Eds.), *Blackwell handbook of social psychology: Intergroup processes* (pp. 409–430). Malden, MA, and Oxford, UK: Blackwell.

Wright, S. C., Taylor, D. M., & Moghaddam, F. M. (1990). Responding to membership in a disadvantaged group: From acceptance to collective action. *Journal of Personality and Social Psychology, 58,* 994–1003.

Zimbardo, P. G. (1969). The human choice: Individuation, reason, and order vs. deindividuation, impulse, and chaos. In W. J. Arnold & D. Levine (Eds.), *Nebraska symposium on motivation* (pp. 237–307). Lincoln: University of Nebraska Press.

12 Public-Initiated Violence

Manon Mireille LeBlanc
Kathryne E. Dupré
Julian Barling

December 10, 2003, Florida, United States:

> Zhi Hui Dong, 20, was just finishing his first day of work at the
> China Star restaurant when two masked men entered through the back
> door. After robbing the restaurant, they forced the young employee
> to lie on the ground and then they shot him in the head. Zhi died at
> the hospital. ("Employee Shot," 2003; "Man Shot," 2003; "Police Nab
> Suspect," 2004)

The majority of workplace homicides in the United States are perpetrated by members of the public during the commission of a robbery or similar crime (see, e.g., Bureau of Labor Statistics, 1998). Individuals employed
in the retail (e.g., convenience stores), services (e.g., restaurants), security
(protective agencies), and transportation (e.g., taxi) industries are at highest
risk (e.g., Casteel & Peek-Asa, 2000; Castillo & Jenkins, 1994; Peek-Asa,
Runyan, & Zwerling, 2001). Research suggests that there are several
job-related tasks that place employees at increased risk for robbery-related
violence, often referred to as *Type I violence*: contact with the public, working alone or in small numbers, working in the late evening or early morning,
guarding something of value, handling money, and working in high-crime
areas (Canadian Centre for Occupational Health and Safety [CCOHS],
1999; Castillo & Jenkins, 1994; Davis, 1987; Kraus, 1987). In Type I
violence, the perpetrator does not have a legitimate relationship with the
targeted workplace or its employees. In other words, the assailant and victim

are strangers (see Merchant & Lundell, 2001; University of Iowa Injury Prevention Research Center [UIIPRC], 2001).

Although robbery is the primary risk factor for occupational homicide, it is not the primary risk factor for nonfatal assaults (Amandus et al., 1996). Providing service, care, advice, or education can put employees at increased risk for assault (e.g., CCOHS, 1999; see also LeBlanc & Kelloway, 2002), especially if clients, customers, inmates, or patients are experiencing frustration, insecurity, or stress (see Lamberg, 1996; National Institute for Occupational Safety and Health [NIOSH], 2002; Painter, 1987). Workers who have the authority to deny the public a service or request may also be at increased risk for violence (Hearnden, 1988; LeBlanc & Kelloway, 2002; NIOSH, 2002). Working alone or interacting with unstable (e.g., psychiatric patients) or volatile (e.g., criminals) populations, as well as interacting with individuals who are under the influence of drugs or alcohol, may increase employee risk (CCOHS, 1999; LeBlanc & Kelloway, 2002; NIOSH, 2002). Contrary to Type I violence, the perpetrator in *Type II violence* has a legitimate relationship with the victim and commits an act of violence while being served by the organization (e.g., a nurse is assaulted by a patient). Industries reporting high rates of nonfatal assaults include health care, education, social services, and law enforcement (Casteel & Peek-Asa, 2000; NIOSH, 2002; Occupational Safety and Health Administration [OSHA], 2004).

The focus of this chapter is on both Type I (robbery-related) and Type II (non-robbery-related) violence. We begin by discussing prevention strategies for robbery-related violence, and we focus our discussion on predicting and preventing violence in the taxi and retail industries. We discuss the taxi industry because taxi drivers in the United States have the highest risk of workplace homicide of any occupation (see Sygnatur & Toscano, 2000) and the retail industry because the majority of research on Type I violence is focused on convenience stores (Casteel & Peek-Asa, 2000). Following this, we explore Type II violence. We discuss prevention strategies for the health care and social service industries. We focus on health care and social services because these two industries face a significant risk of job-related assault (OSHA, 2004). We conclude our chapter with suggestions for future research within the realm of Type I and Type II workplace violence.

Type I Violence

Because most workplace homicides occur during the commission of a robbery, actions aimed at preventing robberies will likely reduce the number of workplace homicides (see Amandus, Hunter, James, & Hendricks, 1995). To understand why some targets (e.g., convenience stores) are robbed more frequently than others, it is useful to consider the decision-making processes of criminals. Rational choice theory portrays criminals as active decision makers, taking into account risks and benefits when choosing a particular target (see Desroches, 1995; Gill, 2000). This is not to suggest that all offenders are completely and equally rational (Gabor & Normandeau, 1989) or that they assess targets in similar ways (Gill, 2000). Offenders will have varying levels of knowledge about risks, be willing to assume more or less risk, and be satisfied with different monetary gains.

Because studies confirm that criminals do behave, at least to a limited extent, in a rational way (e.g., Gill, 2000), robbery reduction strategies focus on increasing the risks, reducing the rewards, and increasing the effort associated with robbery (Desroches, 1995; Hendricks, Landsittel, Amandus, Malcan, & Bell, 1999; OSHA, 1998). Three principles—increasing visibility, reducing rewards, and target hardening—underlie most robbery reduction strategies (Mayhew, 2000b; see also Mayhew, 2000a; OSHA, 1998). Increasing visibility by using security cameras, for example, may deter would-be robbers by increasing their perceptions of risk. Reward reduction strategies make committing a robbery less lucrative (e.g., less money is kept in the cash register). Target hardening approaches involve engineering design or redesign of the workplace to make committing a robbery more difficult (e.g., using a protective screen to shield store clerks from customers). These robbery reduction strategies should be considered and, to the extent deemed appropriate, utilized when trying to reduce workplace robberies. Because risk factors for robbery will differ among workplaces, no single strategy is appropriate for all organizations (OSHA, 1998). Hence, prevention strategies must be customized to work sites (Mayhew, 2000b). Prevention strategies should also be routinely evaluated to determine their level of effectiveness, and they should be upgraded when necessary (Mayhew, 2000b).

Employees in high-risk industries should be provided with training to anticipate and respond to robberies and violence. Although employee training may not necessarily prevent robberies, it may reduce the likelihood that employees will be injured or killed during a robbery. To date, there is no research examining the effectiveness of employee training.

Robbery and Violence in the Taxi Industry

"No job is worth risking your life for. There were lots of times when I was scared out of my mind and I really had to keep my wits about me or who knows what could have happened?"

After working for 13 years as a taxi driver in Calgary, Alberta, where five taxi drivers were assaulted in as many weeks, Paul Murray, 37, quit working as a taxi driver and took a job with a trucking company. (Bourette & Hanes, 2000)

Paul Murray had good reason to be afraid. Driving a taxi is dangerous work. Between 1992 and 1998, 510 taxi drivers and chauffeurs in the United States were murdered on the job (U.S. Department of Labor, 1999). Taxi drivers and chauffeurs are also among the occupations with the highest rates of nonfatal victimization (OSHA, 2000). Although precise statistics on homicide and assault rates of taxi drivers who work outside of the United States are hard to obtain, research suggests that taxi drivers around the globe experience workplace violence (International Labour Organization [ILO], 1998; see also Mayhew, 2000c). For example, Haines (1997) conducted a survey of taxi drivers in Victoria, Australia. One third of the 3,634 respondents reported being assaulted, and 14% reported being robbed over the course of their careers. In a Canadian study, 36% of taxi drivers who were questioned reported being robbed at least once during their careers (Stenning, 1996). The following prevention strategies may reduce the risk for robbery and violence in the taxi industry:

Increasing Visibility

Surveillance techniques used in the taxi industry include global positioning systems (GPS), external emergency lights, and in-car video cameras. GPS allows dispatchers and police to accurately locate a taxi driver in distress (OSHA, 2000). External emergency lights are located on the roofs of taxis; hence, perpetrators should be unaware when they are flashing. Of course, they are ineffective if there are no people around to see them flashing (Mayhew, 2000a). Another strategy is in-car surveillance cameras. Cameras allow identification of perpetrators (Appleby, 2000; Mayhew, 2000a) and may act as a deterrent for robbery and violence (Jackman & Smith, 2001). Surveillance cameras, mandatory in Perth since December 1997, resulted in a 60% decrease in assaults within a year after their introduction (cf. Mayhew, 2000a). Cameras debuted in the United States in 1999 and are currently being used in several American cities (Jackman & Smith, 2001). Crimes against taxi drivers have been reduced by more than 50% since the implementation of a bylaw in Toronto requiring taxi owners to install either security cameras or GPS in their cars (Calleja, 2002).

Reducing Rewards

Cash handling practices such as carrying minimal amounts of money and making frequent cash deposits may deter would-be robbers because money is the most frequent motive for robberies (Gill, 2000). Cashless taxi payment systems, which would require passengers to pay cabdrivers with credit cards or vouchers, would also likely deter would-be robbers (Appleby, 2000; Mayhew, 2000a). To date, there is no research examining the effectiveness of cash-handling practices for reducing robberies and robbery-related violence in the taxi industry.

Target Hardening

Protective screens have been found to reduce the number of assaults experienced by taxi drivers. Stone and Stevens (1999) examined taxi driver assaults in Baltimore prior to and following a 1996 citywide shield mandate. In 1991, when 5% of cabs had shields, there were 203 assaults; by 1995, when 50% of taxis were shielded, there were 131 assaults. In 1996, following the mandate, taxi drivers experienced 25 assaults, a decrease of 56% from 1995, and 88% from 1991. The authors also reported a 17-to-1 benefit-to-cost ratio of estimated savings from reduced injuries versus the cost of citywide shield installations. Despite Stone and Stevens's (1999) findings, opinions on screens remain mixed (Appleby, 2000; Mayhew, 2000a). Many taxi drivers and customers do not like them because they can restrict air circulation, leave little leg room, and limit communication between drivers and passengers (see Appleby, 2000; Mayhew, 2000a). There are also taxi drivers who argue that shields will do little to protect them if assailants are intent on robbing and hurting them; perpetrators can simply find a way to lure them out of the car (Fallding, 2001). To date, screens are mandatory in several American and Australian cities (Mayhew, 2000a; Stone & Stevens, 1999), but they are not currently being used in any Canadian cities (Marlowe, 2001).

Driver Training

Driver training may also potentially prevent robberies and reduce the incidence of assaults. Drivers need to be knowledgeable about current policies and procedures (e.g., mandatory safety equipment). They also need to learn how to use safety equipment such as surveillance cameras and external emergency lights. Taxi drivers should also receive training on how to prevent robberies. For example, they need to be aware that they may be able to avoid random attacks by keeping their car doors locked when waiting in a queue. Drivers also need information on how to react during a robbery to lessen the likelihood of injury (e.g., drivers should never resist or fight back; Mayhew, 2000a).

Research suggests that some taxi drivers refuse to pick up certain passengers because they fear for their safety (see Dao, 2003; Haines, 1997). Although to some extent this is understandable, given the level of violence in this field of work, this practice has resulted in unfair discrimination against certain groups. A review of 1999 dispatch records from one Washington taxi company showed that an individual calling for taxi service from a northwest Washington address was 14 times more likely to receive service than an individual calling from an address in the city's southeast district, a low-income, mainly Black neighborhood. Northwest Washington is the city's most wealthy section and is predominately White (see Dao, 2003). In 2001, police officers gave out 94 citations in 3 days to taxi drivers because they picked up White undercover officers posing as customers but not Black undercover officers (see Dao, 2003). This is not just an issue in the United States: A recent study of taxi drivers in Victoria, Australia, found that most drivers have refused rides to some passengers because they feared for their safety (Haines, 1997). It has been argued that training may help alleviate discriminatory practices among taxi drivers (see "Taxi Discrimination," 1999). Making the taxi industry safer in general would also presumably reduce such practices by reducing the level of fear in drivers and making violence in this industry less of an issue.

Robbery and Violence in the Retail Industry

February 12, 2004, Massachusetts, United States:

A 26-year-old store clerk who was working alone at a 7-Eleven store was stabbed during an early morning robbery. The young man, married only 2 months, died in the hospital. There were apparently no witnesses. ("Lynn Store Clerk," 2004)

Employees in the retail industry face an above-average risk for workplace homicide. In the early 1990s, for example, the average risk of workplace homicide for all occupations was 0.7 per 100,000 employees, whereas the risk for homicide in the retail industry was 1.6 per 100,000 employees (OSHA, 1998). Not all occupations in the retail sector have the same risk of homicide, however. From 1990 to 1992, convenience stores (including grocery stores) had a rate of 3.8 per 100,000 workers, and jewelry and liquor stores had a rate of 4.7 and 7.5, respectively (see OSHA, 1998). Because the majority of research studies in the retail industry have used convenience stores as samples, our discussion of prevention strategies is predominately focused on convenience stores.

Increasing Visibility

Robbers appear to be deterred by the presence of witnesses (see Purpura, 1993). Research suggests, for instance, that commercial robberies occur more often in the late evening or early morning hours when there are few if any customers (e.g., D'Alessio & Stolzenberg, 1990). Of course, the risk of late-night robbery may vary depending on other factors, including whether or not the organization is located in close vicinity to other businesses that are open late (OSHA, 1998). Robbery rates are also higher during the winter months, presumably because there are more dark hours during the day in winter compared with summer (Van Koppen & Jansen, 1999). In their study of 30 randomly sampled convenience stores in Leon County, Florida, D'Alessio and Stolzenberg (1990) found that more than 50% of the robberies they studied occurred between November and February. Hence, strategies that increase the visibility of would-be robbers may reduce crime by increasing perceptions of risk (Mayhew, 2000b).

To increase visibility, retail establishments should keep their windows clear of signs (e.g., advertisements) to allow passersby to see inside (Purpura,

1993). Good interior and exterior lighting, as well as a cash register location that can be seen from the outside (e.g., in the center of the store), may also reduce criminal behavior (Mayhew, 2000b). Hendricks et al. (1999) found that poor visual access to the inside of stores and cash registers located along the wall rather than in the center of stores were strongly associated with increased risk of robbery.

Closed circuit televisions (CCTV) and video cameras may also deter criminal behavior by increasing would-be robbers' perceptions of risk (OSHA, 1998). Of course, for maximum deterrence, retail establishments should display signs informing customers and would-be criminals that surveillance equipment is in use (OSHA, 1998). A recent study of imprisoned robbers found that the presence of cameras had deterred some criminal activity (Gill, 2000). Ironically, the presence of cameras can also affect the amount of violence used during robberies. For example, in certain instances, perpetrators have destroyed surveillance cameras by firing shots at them (Gill, 2000).

Store clerks should make eye contact with customers and greet them as they enter the store (e.g., Desroches, 1995; Gabor & Normandeau, 1989). This behavior may be effective in deterring crime by making would-be robbers feel conspicuous (Desroches, 1995; Gabor & Normandeau, 1989). OSHA (1998) suggests that employing two clerks during evening shifts may also reduce the incidence of robberies; however, employing multiple clerks as a method of deterring robberies is controversial (see Amandus et al., 1996) and is not recommended by either the National Association of Convenience Stores (NACS) or NIOSH (see Richman, 1998). Critics of OSHA's (1998) two-clerk condition argue that there is limited empirical evidence supporting the validity of the two-clerk provision, hiring two clerks is expensive, and employing more than one clerk potentially increases the number of workers exposed to robbery-related violence (see Casteel & Peek-Asa, 2000). Although there is some support that stores employing two clerks during late-night shifts experience fewer robberies (e.g., Calder & Bauer, 1992), more research is required before a decision can be made about whether this is an effective strategy for reducing robberies (Casteel & Peek-Asa, 2000). Commercial establishments should have practices in place to ensure the safety of employees who work alone (e.g., routinely check on individuals who work alone; Mayhew, 2000b).

Reducing Rewards

Retail stores should establish cash-handling practices. Keeping a minimal amount of cash on hand and using drop safes may reduce the rewards associated with robbery (see Desroches, 1995; Gill, 2000; OSHA, 1998). Hendricks et al. (1999) examined 400 convenience stores that were robbed and 1,201 that were not. The stores were located in three metropolitan areas of Virginia. Cash-handling policy exhibited the strongest association with robberies: Stores that were categorized as having good cash-handling policies were at a significantly reduced risk for robbery. Stores were coded as having either good, fair, or poor cash-handling policies. To receive a *good* rating, stores had to post a sign informing patrons of their cash limit policy, the amount of the cash limit, and the hours of the cash limit. As well, they had to use a drop safe, have a sign posted informing customers that a drop safe is used, and have the drop safe situated in a location visible to the public. Bank deposits should be made at irregular times so that would-be robbers are unable to predict employee behavior (Desroches, 1995).

Target Hardening

Given that many robbers suggest that an important consideration in choosing a target is their subsequent escape (Gill, 2000), making it difficult for criminals to flee from the scene of the crime may deter robbery (Desroches, 1995). Potential strategies to make retail stores less attractive targets include blocking off lane ways and using speed bumps in parking lots (Desroches, 1995). Revolving doors and longer rather than shorter distances between the cash register and the exit may also help to deter crime (Gill, 2000).

In addition to preventing robberies, some target hardening strategies may also reduce the likelihood that employees will be hurt during the commission of a robbery. Commercial establishments can install high and wide counters with raised floors on the employee side to prevent robbers from jumping over counters to assault employees (Desroches, 1995; Mayhew, 2000b). Personnel can also be shielded by bullet-resistant barriers (Desroches, 1995; Mayhew, 2000b). A recent study conducted by Hendricks et al. (1999) found that the presence of bullet-resistant shielding is associated with reduced risk for robbery. Locking doors that lead behind counters or to cash registers may also make it more difficult for criminals to physically attack employees (Desroches, 1995).

Employee Training

Employees should be taught how to act in the event of a robbery. Having instructions on how to behave may give employees a sense of control of the situation and lessen the possibility that they will be injured. Employee training should stress cooperation with robbers because there is ample evidence that employees who cooperate with robbers sustain fewer injuries (e.g., Faulkner, Landsittel, & Hendricks, 2001). Employees who refuse to cooperate with robbers can also endanger the lives of customers. One example of this will suffice to explain the importance of cooperation with robbers: On April 17, 1998, a robber entered Caisse Populaire de Saint-Simon-Apotre, a credit union in Ahuntsic, Quebec, and demanded money from a teller. The teller refused. The credit union's policy is to *not* hand over money during a robbery. All the tellers are protected by bullet-resistant glass. Paradoxically, the effectiveness of protections for employees may have unintended negative consequences. The robber threatened to shoot a customer if he did not get the money. The teller did nothing, and the robber shot 35-year-old Claude Mailhot in the spine, paralyzing him for life. He is currently suing the credit union (Brownstein, 2002; Fitterman, 2003).

Workers should also be told not to make any sudden moves during a robbery, to keep their hands in plain sight at all times, and to inform the robbers of what they are doing when they are doing it (see Tyler, 1999). Staff should also be told to activate the silent alarm only when it is safe to do so (see Tyler, 1999). Employees should also be aware that it is not constructive to confront shoplifters. On February 17, 2004, an 18-year-old CVS Pharmacy store clerk was stabbed to death and another employee was injured when they confronted a shoplifter ("CVS Clerk Killed," 2004).

Robbery-related violence is responsible for the majority of workplace homicides. Taxi drivers and retail workers are among those occupations at highest risk for Type I violence (see Casteel & Peek-Asa, 2000; Castillo & Jenkins, 1994; ILO, 1998; OSHA, 1998; Sygnatur & Toscano, 2000). Methods of preventing and responding to violence include increasing risk, reducing rewards, and increasing the effort associated with robbery (Desroches, 1995; Hendricks et al., 1999; OSHA, 1998). Employee training may also be useful for preventing robbery-related violence. More research is needed to assess the effectiveness of these strategies.

Type II Violence

Service providers (health care workers, teachers, social service workers, prison guards, and police officers) are among the most common victims of nonfatal workplace violence (UIIPRC, 2001). In the United States in the year 2000, 48% of all nonfatal assaults occurred in the health care and social service industries (see OSHA, 2004). Although the average rate of nonfatal assaults in the private sector was 2 per 10,000 full-time workers, nursing and personal care facility workers had a rate of 25, and social service workers had a rate of 15 (see OSHA, 2004); however, the actual number of incidents is likely much higher because of underreporting (UIIPRC, 2001).

There are generally three approaches to preventing or dealing with Type II violence (e.g., Merchant & Lundell, 2001; Peek-Asa et al., 2001). The first is environmental and involves looking at physical risk factors related to building layout or design (e.g., the organization should be well lit). The second approach is organizational or administrative and involves the development of policies and practices specific to workplace violence. The third, behavioral or interpersonal, involves training employees to anticipate and respond to violence.

Violence in the Health Care Industry

January 10, 2001, Quebec, Canada:

A 6-ft., 2-in., 225-lb. psychiatric patient repeatedly punched and kicked male nurse Daniel Begin, 41, in the emergency room at the Louis-Hippolyte Lafontaine Psychiatric Hospital. Mr. Begin died 3 weeks later of internal bleeding; because Mr. Begin had a preexisting medical condition, chronic pancreatitis, experts were unable to conclude definitely that the assault was the direct cause of his death. ("Discharge Ruling," 2003; Parkes, 2003c)

The vast majority of aggressive acts directed against health care workers are perpetrated by patients and, to a lesser extent, visitors (e.g., NIOSH, 2002). Although violent incidents can occur anywhere in hospitals, they are more likely to occur in psychiatric wards, emergency departments, waiting rooms, and geriatric units (NIOSH, 2002). There are several factors that increase employee risk. For example, health care workers may be at risk when they attempt to set limits on behavior (e.g., tobacco use; NIOSH, 2002), particularly if the employee's actions are perceived as being unfair or unreasonable (see, e.g., Boyd, 1995). Violence can also occur when patients are involuntarily admitted into the hospital (NIOSH, 2002). Long waits for service may result in frustration and increase the propensity of patients and visitors to become aggressive (e.g., Hoag-Apel, 1998; Levin, Hewitt, & Misner, 1998).

Environmental Strategies

In a recent study, focus groups of nurses argued that the physical work environment is critical to preventing violence (Levin et al., 1998). Security devices that may reduce employee risk include metal detectors, surveillance cameras, and bullet-resistant glass surrounding reception areas and nursing stations (NIOSH, 2002; OSHA, 2004). Other suggestions include effective lighting both inside and outside hospitals and curved mirrors at hallway intersections (OSHA, 2004). The presence of security personnel may also be effective at preventing assaults (e.g., Levin et al., 1998). Card-controlled entrances and security checks for identification could be used to limit public access to restricted areas (Levin et al., 1998; NIOSH, 2002; OSHA, 2004).

Hospitals should provide patients and their families with comfortable waiting rooms designed to minimize stress (e.g., soothing colors on walls, toys for children to play with, reading materials; NIOSH, 2002). Waiting areas and patient-care rooms should also be designed with safety in mind: Furniture should be lightweight, have few sharp edges, and be laid out to ensure that staff can not be trapped in rooms (OSHA, 2004). Rooms and waiting areas should also be sparsely decorated with accessories (e.g., few pictures on the walls or vases on the tables) to limit the number of possible weapons that can be used against staff (see OSHA, 2004). Patient-care rooms should have two exits and be equipped with phones and panic buttons (OSHA, 2004).

Organizational or Administrative Strategies

Hospitals should have policies and practices in place to prevent aggression. A written policy should outline what constitutes unacceptable behavior in the workplace (Scalora, Washington, Casady, & Newell, 2003), and patients, visitors, and employees should be aware of the document. Policies that encourage reporting of violence are also necessary, and management should stress to employees the importance of reporting acts of aggression. A point worth emphasizing is that accurate information on the incidence of violence is essential to assess employee risk, to implement appropriate prevention strategies, and to evaluate the effectiveness of intervention strategies.

Management should also take all reports of aggression seriously, and they should ensure that employees are aware of their commitment to safety. Levin et al. (1998) found that nurses in their study were consistent in dismissing any benefits that reporting violence to management might have on preventing future incidents of aggression. Employees who report being victimized should be treated with respect by their superiors. It is not uncommon for nurses and health care workers to express concerns about reporting incidents of violence because they fear their employers will assume that they provoked the incident (see Boyd, 1995; Elliot, 1997; Scalora et al., 2003). Hospitals also need to have detailed plans for dealing with violent attacks when they occur (Health Services Advisory Committee [HSAC], 1987).

Hospitals should also develop procedures to ensure that information about aggressive patients and visitors is shared between employees and departments so that employees can take necessary precautions to avoid being victimized (HSAC, 1987). One possibility is for the charts of high-risk patients to be flagged (Levin et al., 1998); another possibility is for a notice board to be posted on wards with ratings for patients' potential for violence (Parkes, 2003b). Although access to patient information must be balanced with patients' rights for confidentiality, when staff members are not informed of patients' or visitors' propensity for violence, the consequences can be devastating. On July 1, 2003, a female employee working at the Douglas Psychiatric Hospital (Quebec, Canada) was sexually assaulted by a male patient with a history of sexual violence. The doctor and head nurse on the ward were aware of his history, but they did not inform the female staff member who was assigned to watch him. The female employee was alone with the patient when the attack occurred (Parkes, 2003a).

When health care employees work inside their patients' homes, access to protections that are afforded to employees who work within traditional organizational settings is delayed or limited at best (Barling, Rogers, & Kelloway, 2001). Hence, organizations need to have policies and procedures in place that are targeted at home health care providers. For example, home care workers could be required to keep a designated colleague informed of their whereabouts throughout their work shift (OSHA, 2004). Health care workers should also be accompanied to a patient's home by a coworker or a police escort if their personal safety may be threatened (HSAC, 1987; OSHA, 2004). In a similar vein, employees should be prohibited from working alone in emergency areas or walk-in clinics, especially during late-night and early-morning shifts (Elliott, 1997; NIOSH, 2002; OSHA, 2004). Policies and practices should also be in place to restrict public (e.g., patients, visitors) movement in hospitals (NIOSH, 2002).

Behavioral or Interpersonal Strategies

Employees should be required to attend training sessions on preventing and responding to violent incidents. In addition to providing staff with necessary knowledge and skills, training may give employees the confidence to deal with potentially dangerous situations (HSAC, 1987; Levin et al., 1998). Schat and Kelloway (2000) found that hospital workers who received training targeting workplace violence reported higher levels of perceived control compared with workers who did not receive training. In their study, perceptions of control were positively correlated with employee emotional well-being and negatively associated with employee fear of future violence.

Staff should be taught customer service skills, how to resolve conflicts, how to recognize escalating agitation, and how to manage and respond to aggressive behavior (DelBel, 2003; NIOSH, 2002; OSHA, 2004). Because violence is related to patient wait times (see Hoag-Apel, 1998; Hunter & Love, 1996; NIOSH, 2002), staff should provide patients and their families with sufficient information when there are long delays for service (e.g., explain how long the delay will be and why there is a long delay; see HSAC, 1987). Answering patients' and visitors' questions during stressful medical procedures and times of crises may also reduce the risk for aggression. Employees who have direct patient contact (e.g., security guards, nurses, orderlies) should also be trained on how and when to physically restrain patients (HSAC, 1987). Follow-up training is necessary if employees are to maintain the skills and confidence that they have acquired (Levin et al., 1998; Maggio, 1996).

Violence in the Social Services Industry

Summer 1999, Ottawa, Canada:

A 24-year-old social worker employed at a social services group home was hit on the head with a fire extinguisher by a resident. (McCoy, 1999)

Social service employees are at high risk for violence from their clients, many of whom may be experiencing stressful life circumstances and feelings of frustration or despair. A 1999 survey of Ontario social workers found that 71% of respondents had experienced physical assaults, verbal abuse, or threats at work (McCoy, 1999). Newhill (1996) conducted a random survey of members of the National Association of Social Workers from Pennsylvania and California and found that 57% of respondents experienced one or more types of client violence, including threats, property damage, and physical attacks, over the course of their careers.

Abusive behavior may be directed at social workers and other social service employees for a number of reasons, one being the role that these employees play in the lives of their clients. Social service workers must be caring and controlling (Newhill, 1996). For example, when clients are ineligible for resources, they may have to assume the role of service denier (Newhill, 1995). When denied service or resources, some clients may become frustrated and hostile. Social service workers may also have regular contact with involuntary clients who must unwillingly reveal personal information about themselves and their families (Shields & Kiser, 2003). When clients face situations that are highly unpleasant (e.g., child abuse allegations), their interactions with social service workers can be particularly tense and unpredictable (Shields & Kiser, 2003).

The strategies that have been recommended to prevent violence against social service workers are identical to those that have been recommended to reduce violence directed at health care workers (e.g., OSHA, 2004). Environmental strategies—for example, design of the workplace (e.g., interview rooms with two exists and lightweight furniture) and security systems (e.g., emergency buttons, security personnel)—are required to ensure the safety of social service workers. Policies and practices aimed at preventing and responding to violent incidents should also be put into place (Rey, 1996). Home visits and outreach work can be extremely risky (Newhill, 1995), and policies should be developed that allow social service workers to request the accompaniment of coworkers or law enforcement personnel when the risk for violence is high (e.g., when the client lives in a dangerous neighborhood; when the client has a drug or alcohol addiction). Social service workers should also receive ongoing on-the-job training appropriate to the client population served and settings (e.g., Newhill, 1995; Weisman & Lamberti, 2002). They need to develop skills to identify potentially dangerous clients and de-escalate violent interactions, as well as be aware of existing organizational policies and practices.

Clients, customers, patients, and inmates are responsible for the vast majority of nonfatal assaults. Health care workers and social service employees are among the occupations at highest risk for Type II violence (OSHA, 2004). Preventing and responding to this type of violence requires environmental, administrative, and interpersonal strategies. To date, only nine studies have evaluated organizational or behavioral interventions aimed at preventing or responding to Type II violence, and they are all based in the health care industry (Runyan, Zakocs, & Zwerling, 2000). To our knowledge, there are no studies that have examined the effectiveness of environmental approaches to preventing Type II violence.

Directions for Future Research

In this section, we discuss directions for future research specific to Type I and Type II violence.

Type I Violence

Previous research suggests that prevention strategies are effective at reducing robberies in the retail industry (see Casteel & Peek-Asa, 2000, for a review); however, because this research has limitations, there are many unanswered questions that need to be addressed. The study population in the majority of these studies is convenience stores (see Amandus et al., 1996). Hence, it is impossible to conclude whether strategies that are effective in preventing convenience store robberies will also be effective in other business settings (e.g., jewelry stores). Future research should examine prevention strategies across a variety of different retail settings.

Another limitation of existing studies is that they examine the effectiveness of programs comprising multiple intervention components (Casteel & Peek-Asa, 2000). As a result, it is not possible to determine the value of specific strategies. It would be important for future researchers to evaluate single-component programs. To date, the majority of studies that have examined single-component programs have shown reductions in robbery frequency (see Casteel & Peek-Asa, 2000); however, many have not controlled for other prevention strategies that may have been employed at the same time or may have been added at a later point in time (see Casteel & Peek-Asa, 2000). Future research needs to address these concerns.

Currently there is no consensus on whether employing two clerks is an effective strategy for reducing robberies. As previously mentioned, OSHA (2004) recommends that late-night retail establishments employ two clerks, whereas NIOSH and the NACS disagree with OSHA's recommendation (see Richman, 1998). It would be important for controlled studies to be conducted to determine whether employing two clerks is an effective strategy for preventing robberies.

Although employee training targeting workplace violence is widely recommended as a method for preventing robberies and employee injuries (e.g., Desroches, 1995; Gabor & Normandeau, 1989; Mayhew, 2000a), few studies have evaluated the effectiveness of this form of intervention (Runyan et al., 2000). When staff training has been studied, it has been imbedded in a multiple-component program (see Casteel & Peek-Asa, 2000). Hence, information on the effectiveness of training targeting workplace violence is limited. Future research should evaluate employee training in a single component program. It would be important to know whether training on how to behave during a robbery situation reduces worker injuries and increases employee confidence to deal with dangerous situations.

Schat and Kelloway (2000) found that health care workers who receive training targeting workplace violence have higher perceptions of control compared with health care employees who are not provided with training. Future research could examine whether providing training to employees who work in the retail industry will lower fear and increase perceptions of control during a robbery situation. Because many retail employees are teenagers (Janicak, 1999), researchers should investigate whether young employees would benefit from the same type of training as more mature employees.

Experts suggest that retail employees who make eye contact with and greet customers may reduce the risk for robbery by making would-be robbers feel conspicuous (e.g., Desroches, 1995; Gabor & Normandeau, 1989). To our knowledge, this suggestion has not been examined empirically. It has also been proposed that retail organizations should implement practices to ensure the safety of employees who work alone (e.g., routinely check on employees; Mayhew, 2000b). Future research needs to determine what organizational policies and practices will be the most effective at preventing injuries to employees who work alone.

Although research has shown that cash-handling practices can reduce the risk for robbery in retail settings (e.g., Hendricks et al., 1999), we are unaware of any studies that have examined whether cash-handling practices (e.g., cashless system) are effective at preventing robberies in the taxi industry. In addition to determining whether cash-handling practices deter would-be robbers from targeting taxi drivers, future research should examine whether training programs can reduce injuries to taxi drivers. Stenning (1996) conducted a qualitative study of 150 Canadian taxi drivers. In his study, taxi drivers who at some point in their careers received training in safety and risk awareness did not report fewer victimizations compared with drivers who did not receive training. Researchers need to investigate whether driver training targeting workplace violence is effective at reducing injuries.

Type II Violence

Although environmental strategies are widely recommended for decreasing violence directed at health care and social service workers (e.g., OSHA, 2004), they have been neglected in intervention studies aimed at reducing Type II violence. Hence, future research should examine whether environmental strategies (e.g., lighting, surveillance cameras, metal detectors) are effective at reducing Type II violence.

Research on the effectiveness of policies and practices to reduce Type II violence is also limited (Runyan et al., 2000). It would be important to know if restricting public access in hospitals and social service agencies can reduce employee injuries. Another question worth investigating is whether postings declaring zero tolerance for violence deter aggressive behavior from the public. Researchers also need to determine what are the most effective policies and practices for ensuring the safety of employees who work inside their clients' homes.

The few studies that have focused on preventing Type II violence have been conducted in health care settings (Runyan et al., 2000), limiting the generalizability of the results. The majority of these studies have evaluated training programs aimed at teaching hospital employees how to handle aggressive patients (Runyan et al., 2000); however, these studies have used methodologically weak designs and their results are inconclusive (Runyan et al., 2000). Future research should investigate intervention programs in a variety of work settings (e.g., social services settings, educational settings). As well, intervention programs should be examined using methodologically sound research designs. Questions worth investigating include the following: Do training programs aimed at teaching employees customer service and conflict resolution skills reduce injuries to workers? How effective are programs that train employees how to recognize and respond to aggressive behavior? Do employees who are trained on proper restraining techniques sustain fewer injuries?

Conclusion

Members of the public are responsible for the vast majority of workplace homicides (Sygnatur & Toscano, 2000) and assaults (Peek-Asa & Howard, 1999; Peek-Asa, Schaffer, Kraus, & Howard, 1998). Although numerous strategies have been recommended to prevent and reduce workplace violence (e.g., Merchant & Lundell, 2001), studies evaluating these strategies, when available, have been plagued with shortcomings, including weak research designs and limited samples. We urge researchers to continue to investigate methods of reducing Types I and II violence given their devastating consequences for victims and their organizations.

References

Amandus, H. E., Hunter, R. D., James, E., & Hendricks, S. (1995). Reevaluation of the effectiveness of environmental designs to reduce robbery risk in Florida convenience stores. *Journal of Occupational and Environmental Medicine, 37,* 711–717.

Amandus, H. E., Zahm, D., Friedmann, R., Ruback, R. B., Block, C., Weiss, J., et al. (1996). Employee injuries and convenience store robberies in selected metropolitan areas. *Journal of Occupational and Environmental Medicine, 38,* 714–720.

Appleby, T. (2000, January 4). *How to make the job safer for cabbies.* Retrieved March 1, 2004, from http://taxi-world.home.att.net/toronto02.htm

Barling, J., Rogers, A. G., & Kelloway, E. K. (2001). Behind closed doors: In-home workers' experience of sexual harassment and workplace violence. *Journal of Occupational Health Psychology, 6,* 255–269.

Bourette, S., & Hanes, A. (2000, January 5). *Drivers concerned about job safety: Assaults, slayings from Halifax to Calgary frightening cab operators*. Retrieved March 1, 2004, from http://taxi-world.home.att.net/toronto02.htm

Boyd, N. (1995, October). Violence in the workplace in British Columbia: A preliminary investigation. *Canadian Journal of Criminology*, 491–519.

Brownstein, B. (2002, July 18). Caisses ignore protest at their peril. (Montreal) *Gazette*, p. A6.

Bureau of Labor Statistics. (1998). *National census of fatal occupational injuries 1997* (USDL 98-336). Washington, DC: Author.

Calder, J. D., & Bauer, J. R. (1992). Convenience store robberies: Security measures and store robbery incidents. *Journal of Criminal Justice, 20*, 553–566.

Calleja, F. (2002). *Cab hold-ups on Web*. Retrieved March 1, 2004, from http://taxi-world.home.att.net/safety.htm

Canadian Centre for Occupational Health and Safety. (1999). *Violence in the workplace*. Retrieved March 1, 2004, from http://www.ccohs.ca/oshanswers/psychosocial/violence.html

Casteel, C., & Peek-Asa, C. (2000). Effectiveness of Crime Prevention Through Environmental Design (CPTED) in reducing robberies. *American Journal of Preventive Medicine, 18*, 99–115.

Castillo, D. N., & Jenkins, E. L. (1994). Industries and occupations at high risk for work-related homicide. *Journal of Occupational Medicine, 36*, 125–132.

CVS clerk killed trying to stop shoplifter. (2004, February 17). Retrieved February 24, 2004, from http://www.thebostonchannel.com/news/2851551/detail.html

D'Alessio, S., & Stolzenberg, L. (1990). A crime of convenience: The environment and convenience store robbery. *Environment and Behavior, 22*, 255–271.

Dao, J. (2003, October 8). Report cites persistent bias among cabbies in Washington. *New York Times*, p. A24.

Davis, H. (1987). Workplace homicides of Texas males. *American Journal of Public Health, 77*, 1290–1293.

DelBel, J. C. (2003). De-escalating workplace aggression. *Nursing Management, 34*, 30–34.

Desroches, F. J. (1995). *Force and fear: Robbery in Canada*. Scarborough, Ontario: Nelson Canada.

Discharge ruling in ER death warrants appeal. (2003, October 29). (Montreal) *Gazette*, p. A30.

Elliott, P. P. (1997, December). Violence in health care: What nurse managers need to know. *Nursing Management*, 38–41.

Employee shot in head during restaurant robbery. (2003, December 11). *WFTV News*. Retrieved on February 15, 2004, from http://www.wftv.com/news/2697967/detail.html

Fallding, H. (2001). *Government launches action plan for cab safety: Mandatory shields an option in preventing abuse of drivers*. Retrieved March 1, 2004, from http://taxi-world.home.att.net/winnipeg01.htm

Faulkner, K. A., Landsittel, D. P., & Hendricks, S. A. (2001). Robbery characteristics and employee injuries in convenience stores. *American Journal of Industrial Medicine, 40*, 703–709.

Fitterman, L. (2003, April 3). Bank robber sentenced to life for shooting bystander: No remorse, no explanation why he wounded credit union customer, leaving him paralyzed. (Montreal) *Gazette*, p. A9.

Gabor, T., & Normandeau, A. (1989). Preventing armed robbery through opportu-
    nity reduction: A critical analysis. *Journal of Security Administration, 12*, 3–18.

Gill, M. (2000). *Commercial robbery.* London: Blackstone.

Haines, F. (1997). *Taxi driver survey—Victoria: Understanding Victorian taxi dri-
    vers' experiences of victimization and their preferred preventative measures*
    (Report for the Victorian Taxi Driver Safety Committee). Criminology
    Department, University of Melbourne.

Health Services Advisory Committee. (1987). *Violence to staff in the health services.*
    London: HMSO.

Hearnden, K. (1988). *Violence at work* (Industrial Safety Data File). London: United
    Trade Press.

Hendricks, S. A., Landsittel, D. P., Amandus, H. E., Malcan, J., & Bell, J. (1999). A
    matched case-control study of convenience store robbery risk factors. *Journal of
    Occupational and Environmental Medicine, 41*, 995–1004.

Hoag-Apel, C. M. (1998, July). Violence in the emergency department. *Nursing
    Management,* 60–61.

Hunter, M. E., & Love, C. C. (1996). Total quality management and the reduction
    of inpatient violence and costs in a forensic psychiatric hospital. *Psychiatric
    Services, 47*, 751–754.

International Labour Organization. (1998). *Violence on the job: A global problem.*
    Retrieved August 31, 2000, from http://www.ilo.org/public/english/bureau/inf/
    pr/1998/30.htm

Jackman, T., & Smith, L. (2001). *Taxi camera develops its first lead for police:
    Armed robbery in Mount Vernon caught in digital clarity.* Retrieved March 1,
    2004, from http://taxi-world.home.att.net/wp_22aug01.htm

Janicak, C. A. (1999). An analysis of occupational homicides involving workers 19
    years old and younger. *Journal of Occupational and Environmental Medicine,
    41*, 1140–1145.

Kraus, J. F. (1987). Homicide while at work: Persons, industries, and occupations at
    high risk. *American Journal of Public Health, 77*, 1285–1289.

Lamberg, L. (1996). Don't ignore patients' threats, psychiatrists told. *JAMA, 275*,
    1715–1716.

LeBlanc, M. M., & Kelloway, E. K. (2002). Predictors and outcomes of workplace
    violence and aggression. *Journal of Applied Psychology, 87*, 444–453.

Levin, P. F., Hewitt, J., & Misner, T. S. (1998). Insights of nurses about assault
    in hospital-based emergency departments. *Image: The Journal of Nursing Scholar-
    ship, 30*, 249–254.

Lynn store clerk stabbed to death. (2004, February 12). Retrieved February 24,
    2004, from www.officer.com/news/IBS/wcvb/news-2005857.html

Maggio, M. J. (1996). Keeping the workplace safe: A challenge for managers. *Federal
    Probation, 60*, 67–71.

Man shot during robbery dies from injuries. (2003, December 12). *WFTV
    News.* Retrieved February 15, 2004, from http://www.wftv.com/news/2700717/
    detail.html

Marlowe, T. (2001). *Mandatory shields the answer? Several cities in the U.S. claim
    they work.* Retrieved March 1, 2004, from http://taxi-world.home.att.net/
    winnipeg01.htm

Mayhew, C. (2000a). Preventing assaults on taxi drivers in Australia. *Trends and
    Issues in Crime and Criminal Justice, 179*, 1–6.

Mayhew, C. (2000b). *Violence in the workplace—preventing armed robbery: A practical handbook* (Research and Public Policy Series, No. 33). Canberra, ACT: Australian Institute of Criminology.

Mayhew, C. (2000c). Violent assaults on taxi drivers: Incidence patterns and risk factors. *Trends and Issues in Crime and Criminal Justice, 178,* 1–6.

McCoy, H. J. (1999, November 13). Social workers face increased violence: Survey. *Ottawa Citizen,* p. A12.

Merchant, J. A., & Lundell, J. A. (2001). Workplace Violence Intervention Research Workshop, April 5–7, 2000, Washington, DC: Background, rationale, and summary. *American Journal of Preventive Medicine, 20,* 135–140.

National Institute for Occupational Safety and Health. (2002). *Violence: Occupational hazards in hospitals* (DHHS Publication No. 2002-101). Retrieved March 5, 2004, from http://www.cdc.gov/niosh/2002-101.html#intro

Newhill, C. E. (1995). Client violence toward social workers: A practice and policy concern for the 1990s. *Social Work, 40,* 631–636.

Newhill, C. E. (1996, October). Prevalence and risk factors for client violence toward social workers. *Families in Society: Journal of Contemporary Human Services,* 488–495.

Occupational Safety and Health Administration. (1998). *Recommendations for workplace violence prevention programs in late-night retail establishments.* Retrieved March 5, 2004, from http://www.osha-slc.gov/Publications/osha3153.pdf#search='Occupational%20Safety%20and%20Health%20Administration.%20(1998).%20Recommendations%20for%20workplace%20violence%20prevention%20programs%20in%20latenight%20retail%20establishments'

Occupational Safety and Health Administration. (2000). *Risk factors and protective measures for taxi and livery drivers.* Retrieved March 1, 2004, from http://www.osha.gov/OSHAFacts/taxi-livery-drivers.pdf

Occupational Safety and Health Administration. (2004). *Guidelines for preventing workplace violence for health care and social service workers.* Retrieved March 5, 2004, from www.osha.gov/Publications/osha3148.pdf

Painter, K. (1987). "It's part of the job": Violence at work. *Employee Relations, 9,* 30–40.

Parkes, D. (2003a, October 29). Outrage at the Douglas: Patient attacks. Female employee victim of hospital's neglect of policies, union boss says. (Montreal) *Gazette,* p. A1.

Parkes, D. (2003b, November 3). Douglas Hospital officials move to improve safety: Meeting this week with clinic workers to discuss need for guard, other measures. (Montreal) *Gazette,* p. A6.

Parkes, D. (2003c, December 27). Inquiry demanded into nurse's slaying: Death caused by beating: Coroner. Grieving girlfriend is outraged after psychiatric patient who pleaded guilty to assault is granted a discharge. (Montreal) *Gazette,* p. A7.

Peek-Asa, C., & Howard, J. (1999). Workplace-violence investigations by the California division of occupational safety and health, 1993–1996. *Journal of Occupational and Environmental Medicine, 41,* 647–653.

Peek-Asa, C., Runyan, C. W., & Zwerling, C. (2001). The role of surveillance and evaluation research in the reduction of violence against workers. *American Journal of Preventive Medicine, 20,* 141–148.

Peek-Asa, C., Schaffer, K., Kraus, J., & Howard, J. (1998). Surveillance of nonfatal workplace assault injuries using police and employers' reports. *Journal of Occupational and Environmental Medicine, 40,* 707–713.

Police nab suspect in restaurant robbery, murder. (2004, January 12). *WESH News.* Retrieved February 15, 2004, from http://www.wesh.com/news/2758356/detail.html

Purpura, P. P. (1993). *Retail security and shrinkage protection.* Stoneham, MA: Butterworth-Heinemann.

Rey, L. D. (1996, January). What social workers need to know about client violence. *Families in Society: Journal of Contemporary Human Services, 33*–39.

Richman, T. (1998). What does science say about crime prevention? *Security Management, 42,* 109–110.

Runyan, C. W., Zakocs, R. C., & Zwerling, C. (2000). Administrative and behavioral interventions for workplace violence prevention. *American Journal of Preventive Medicine, 18,* 116–127.

Scalora, M. J., Washington, D., Casady, T., & Newell, S. P. (2003). Nonfatal workplace violence risk factors: Data from a police contact sample. *Journal of Interpersonal Violence, 18,* 310–327.

Schat, A. C. H., & Kelloway, E. K. (2000). Effects of perceived control on the outcomes of workplace aggression and violence. *Journal of Occupational Health Psychology, 5,* 386–402.

Shields, G., & Kiser, J. (2003). Violence and aggression directed toward human service workers: An exploratory study. *Families in Society: Journal of Contemporary Human Services, 84,* 13–20.

Stenning, P. (1996). *Fare game, fare cop: Victimization of, and policing by, taxi drivers in three Canadian cities.* Retrieved March 1, 2004, from http://taxi-world.home.att.net/safety.htm

Stone, J. R., & Stevens, D. C. (1999). *The effectiveness of taxi partitions: The Baltimore case.* Retrieved March 1, 2004, from http://taxi-library.home.att.net/stone99.pdf

Sygnatur, E. F., & Toscano, G. A. (2000, Spring). Work-related homicides: The facts. *Compensation and Working Conditions,* 3–8.

Taxi discrimination. (1999, November 12). *New York Times,* p. A32.

Tyler, K. (1999). Targets behind the counter. *HR Magazine, 44,* 106–111.

University of Iowa Injury Prevention Research Center. (2001). *Workplace violence: A report to the nation.* Retrieved May 31, 2002, from http://www.public-health.uiowa.edu/iprc/NATION.PDF

U.S. Department of Labor, Bureau of Labor Statistics. (1999). *National census of fatal occupational injuries, 1998* (New Bulletin USDL-99-208). Washington, DC: Author.

Van Koppen, P. J., & Jansen, R. W. J. (1999). The time to rob: Variations in time of number of commercial robberies. *Journal of Research in Crime and Delinquency, 36,* 7–29.

Weisman, R. L., & Lamberti, J. S. (2002). Violence prevention and safety training for case management services. *Community Mental Health Journal, 38,* 339–348.

13

The Battlefield as Workplace

Violence in Warfighting

LCol Kelly M. J. Farley
Victor M. Catano

Fear is the natural state of the soldier.

(Regan, 1995, p. 247)

The very nature of warfare is based on violence, and combat zones remain the most dangerous and violent places on earth. Unlike workers in traditional workplaces, soldiers are trained to inflict violence on the enemy and minimize the danger to themselves and their peers. Soldiers in war are therefore doubly at risk; in addition to being victims of violence, there is a psychological cost for killing other human beings. In fact, these risks are generally acknowledged as the central tenet of the military ethos known as *unlimited liability*. This shared understanding that soldiers can be ordered into harm's way under conditions that could lead to the loss of their lives "lies at the heart of the military professional's understanding of duty" (Canadian Forces, 2003, p. 26).

Although this central theme of the military ethos is as old as warfare itself, the 20th century saw a revolution in weapons and soldier systems designed to increase the potential for enemy casualties and minimize the loss of friendly forces. In particular, the high-cost strategies such as close-quarter, direct-fire attrition warfare as seen in the American Civil War have been replaced by more targeted practices, such as effects-based operations that strike at the enemy's ability to make war rather than confront him on the

Table 13.1   United States Military Casualties

War/Conflict	Number Serving	Total Deaths (% Number Deaths)	Battle Deaths (% Total Deaths)	Other Deaths (% Total Deaths)	Wounds Not Mortal (% Serving)
Civil War (Union Forces only) 1861–1865	2,213,363	364,511 (16.4)	140,414 (38.5)	224,097 (61.5)	281,881 (12.7)
World War 1 1917–1918	4,734,991	116,516 (2.5)	53,402 (45.8)	63,114 (54.2)	204,002 (4.3)
World War 2 1941–1946	16,112,566	405,399 (2.5)	291,557 (71.9)	113,842 (28.1)	671,846 (4.1)
Korean War 1950–1953	5,720,000	36,574 (0.7)	33,374 (91.1)	2,833 (8.7)	103,284 (1.8)
Vietnam Conflict 1964–1973	8,744,000	58,209 (0.6)	47,424 (81.5)	10,785 (18.5)	153,303 (1.7)
Persian Gulf War 1990–1991	2,225,000	382 (0.1)	147 (38.5)	235 (61.5)	467 (0.2)
Op Iraqi Freedom* 2003–	Unknown	1,871	1,452 (77.6)	419 (23.4)	14,265

SOURCE: U.S. DoD Web site: http://web1.whs.osd.mil/mmid/mmidhome.htm

NOTE: * Indicates data current as of August 27, 2005.

battlefield. These practices are not totally risk free, as friendly forces and combat soldiers will also continue to engage the enemy with "bullets and bayonets," so militaries continue to invest in improving battlefield survivability.

In this chapter, we will examine changes to the experience of violence on the battlefield, including advances in technology, doctrine, training, and the treatment of medical and psychological casualties. We will also examine the psychological cost of killing and the role of unit climate in moderating the effects of combat stress, as well as the impact of warfighting on civilians.

Survivability on the Battlefield

The industrial revolution provided the backdrop for changes in warfighting, improving the specificity and lethality of individual engagements but at the same time enhancing the overall survivability of soldiers in war. In fact, the *rates* of battle casualties have declined drastically since the major conflicts of the 19th and 20th centuries. Improvements in soldier protection and medical treatment on the battlefield can account for the greatest portion of this change. American data are illustrative of this trend.

As can be seen in Table 13.1, over 16% of Union Army soldiers died during the American Civil War. Although 40% of this number were killed in action or died from their wounds, the majority (60%) died from non-battlefield causes, such as disease, starvation, and accidents.

By WW1 some 50 years later, advances in medical treatment and soldier protection helped reduce the overall number of deaths dramatically. Compared with the Civil War death rate of 16%, the American forces' losses of less than 3% of all soldiers in WW1 is much lower, although the number of deaths by other causes (54%) compared with those killed in action (46%) remained high.

Although overall the proportion of deaths for WW2 (2.5%) was about the same as that for WW1, the numbers of soldiers dying from noncombat causes began to fall. About 28% of those who died in WW2 were noncombat deaths compared with 54% for WW1 and 61% for the Civil War.

During the Korean War, the sophistication of emergency medical treatment, including surgical suites close to the front and the introduction of helicopters for casualty evacuation, dramatically reduced deaths due to combat and noncombat sources alike. Less than 1% of American soldiers died during the war, and of these most were killed in action (91%).

The trend in reduction of killed-in-action casualties continued for the American military in Vietnam (0.6%) and Gulf Wars (0.1%); however, the downward trend of deaths due to other causes reversed itself during the same period. In fact, deaths due to other causes were almost twice (235) those for combat deaths (147) during the Gulf War (1990–1991; at the time of writing, deaths due to other causes accounted for 23.4% of all U.S. military deaths so far in the war in Iraq, March 2003–present). Unlike non-battle casualties in 19th- and early-20th-century wars in which disease, starvation, and exposure were the main causes, modern nonbattle casualties are more likely due to friendly-fire incidents. The terms *friendly fire* and *fratricide* are used interchangeably in the military literature.

This is not to say the accidental killing of friendly forces is a new phenomenon. Shrader (1992) reported evidence of the problem as early as the wars between Greek and Roman armies. More famously, Stonewall Jackson was mortally wounded by friendly fire at Chancellorsville during the Civil War (Regan, 1995). Although there are no authoritative figures for friendly fire in earlier conflicts, data from more recent wars indicate the problem is on the rise (Ayers, 1993; Shrader, 1992), and estimates of fratricide deaths in the first Gulf War are as high as 50% of all casualties (Hackworth, 1992).

The recent conflicts in Afghanistan and Iraq are similarly replete with examples of friendly-fire casualties. For example, four Canadian soldiers were killed and eight others wounded when a coalition fighter jet mistakenly attacked the soldiers in Afghanistan in 2002. (During their 6 months in Afghanistan, the Canadians suffered no losses from enemy action.) In this particular case, a disciplinary hearing found that the pilot "disregarded a direct order from the controlling agency, exercised a lack of basic flight discipline over [his] aircraft, and blatantly ignored the applicable rules of engagement and special instructions" (U.S. Air Force, 2004). Although the findings of the hearing focused on the negligence of the pilot alone, a Board of Inquiry (Canadian Forces, 2002a) investigation indicated other factors such as stress, leadership failures, and confusion in communications might have contributed to the tragedy.

In his examination of friendly-fire incidents during the Vietnam and the Gulf Wars, Ayers (1993) found that most were due to the combination of battle stress, environmental factors (e.g., smoke, noise, confusion), technological failures, and negligence. Similarly, in his comprehensive review of friendly-fire incidents since medieval times, Regan (1995) categorized the causes of friendly-fire incidents into two main themes: the use of technology beyond the capability of soldiers to use it effectively and "simple human error" exacerbated by stress, fear, anger, and drug use. Many cases of friendly fire appear to combine both of these themes.

For example, the use of chlorine gas by the British forces against the Germans in WW1 resulted in a recorded 2,361 friendly casualties when the wind shifted and blew the poison gas back over the British positions (Regan, 1995). Both the technology of dispensing chlorine gas and the decision-making process to assess the direction and speed of the wind were faulty. To be effective against the Germans, who by then were outfitted with personal respirators, the British staff calculated that they needed 40 minutes of sustained poison gas on the German location to overwhelm the respirator filtration systems. The problem was that there was not enough chlorine gas in the British Army to produce such a prolonged effect; and, moreover, after the gas was released, there was no telling where it might drift. Compounding these difficulties was the insistence by the British commanding general—and resulting pressure on others—to use the weapon as soon as possible. Incredibly, General Sir Douglas Haig actually gave the order to release the gas after satisfying himself about the wind direction by watching the cigarette smoke of his aide curl toward the German lines.

Although the technical improvement of weapon systems continues to be a main research and development activity for many militaries, the stress of combat and its effects has received the most attention in the psychological literature.

Combat Stress

Combat stress is stress that a soldier experiences while engaged in combat or in a combat-related mission. Internal and external stressors lead to combat stress. These stressors may be generated by enemy actions or from the soldier's own unit leaders and mission demands. In small-scale engagements of the type encountered in combating terrorist activities, stress may result from rules of engagement that differ from those for traditional combat, the proximity of the combatants to one another, or the severity of the fighting.

Table 13.2   Examples of Combat Stressors

Physical Stressors	Mental Stressors
Environmental	**Cognitive**
Heat, Cold, Wetness	Information: Too Much, Too Little
Vibration, Noise, Blast	Sensory Overload Versus Deprivation
Hypoxia (Insufficient Oxygen),	Ambiguity, Uncertainty, Isolation
Fumes, Poison, Chemicals	Time Pressure Versus Waiting
Directed-Energy Weapons/Devices	Unpredictability
Ionizing Radiation	Rules of Engagement,
Infectious Agents	Difficult Judgment
Physical Work	Organizational Dynamics
Bright Lights, Darkness, Haze,	Hard Choice Versus No Choice
and Obscurations	Recognition of Impaired
Difficult or Arduous Terrain	Functioning
Physiological	**Emotional**
Sleep Debt	Fear- and Anxiety-Producing Threats
Dehydration	(of Death, Injury, Failure, Loss)
Malnutrition, Poor Hygiene	Grief-Producing Losses (Bereavement)
Muscular and Aerobic Fatigue	Resentment, Anger- and Rage-Producing
Impaired Immune System	Frustration, Threat, Loss, and Guilt
Overuse or Underuse of	Boredom-Producing Inactivity
Muscles, Organ Systems	Conflicting Motives (Worries About
Illnesses or Injury	Home, Divided Loyalties)
	Spiritual Confrontation or Temptation
	Causing Loss of Faith
	Interpersonal Feelings

SOURCE: U.S. Army (1994) pp. 8–51

Combat stress may have several different origins. Table 13.2 presents common combat stressors grouped into four domains: environmental, physiological, cognitive, and emotional (U.S. Department of the Army [U.S. Army], 1994). One of the strongest stressors is the soldier's fear of dying (Thomas & O'Hara, 2000).

Combat stress (also known as *operational stress*) has been studied in several military operational environments (e.g., Adler, Litz, & Bartone, 2003; Farley, 2002; Griffith, 1997; Lamerson & Kelloway, 1996), and its long-term effects for psychological health are well known (e.g., Dekel, Solomon, Ginzburg, & Neria, 2003; Green, Grace, & Lindy, 1990; Solomon & Mikulincer, 1990). These include committing criminal or other acts of misconduct, including mutilation of enemy soldiers, looting, alcohol abuse, riding sick call, desertion, and killing noncombatants. *Battle fatigue*, which is characterized by hyper alertness, fear, impaired performance of duty, and apathy is another well-known consequence of combat stress.

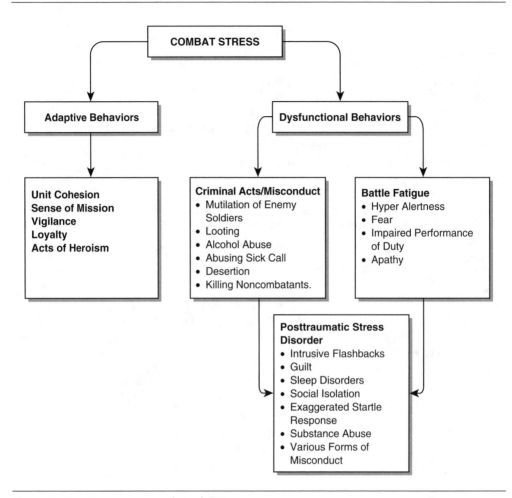

Figure 13.1   Consequences of Combat Stress

In the longer term, combat stress can lead to posttraumatic stress disorder (PTSD), which produces intrusive flashbacks, guilt, sleep disorders, social isolation, exaggerated startle responses, substance abuse, and/or various forms of misconduct. The fourth edition of the *Diagnostic and Statistical Manual of Mental Disorders* (*DSM-IV*) estimates the prevalence of PTSD in the U.S. general population at about 8%. The rate of PTSD among combat veterans appears to be considerably higher than in the general population. Nathan, Gorman, and Salkind (1999) suggested that the rate of PTSD among American war veterans was as high as 30%, and a Canadian Forces study estimated that 20% of members returning from overseas missions suffer from the disorder (Canadian Forces, 2002b). A recent study of 6,201 U.S. Army or Marine troops who had served in either Afghanistan or Iraq reported that 11% and 17%, respectively, exhibited PTSD symptoms; furthermore, less than 40% of those afflicted with PTSD sought help (*Combat Stress: The War Within*, 2004).

On the other hand, combat can also produce adaptive behaviors. Unit cohesion, a sense of mission, vigilance, loyalty, and acts of heroism are positive behaviors that may defend against combat stress (Thomas & O'Hara, 2000). Figure 13.1 summarizes these possible outcomes of combat stress. Dekel, Solomon, Ginzburg, and Neria (2003) examined the exposure to battlefield stress in terms of both wartime performance and long-term adjustment. Almost 25 years following the war, they reviewed the history of three groups of Israeli veterans of the 1973 Yom Kippur War. The first group had suffered combat stress reactions during the war, and the second group had been decorated for bravery and heroism. A control group was randomly selected from the war veterans who had not been treated for combat stress reactions or decorated for heroism. The decorated heroes reported having experienced higher levels of battlefield stressors than either the combat stress victims or the controls. They reported experiencing more combat, exposure to death and injury, and more exposure to their own army's failures. They and those affected by combat stress had experienced the same level of life-threatening situations. Yet, the decorated heroes had significantly lower rates of PTSD than the combat stress casualties. At the time of the war, about 37% of those in the combat stress group were treated for PTSD compared with 7.5% of the decorated heroes. At the time of the study, 13.4% of the combat stress group were still experiencing PTSD compared with 2.2% of the decorated heroes, whose PTSD rates were on a par with those in the control group. The decorated heroes also had better general psychological health than the combat stress casualties and adjusted substantially better after the war. Dekel et al. speculated that the reason for these differences might have been the beneficial effect of the decorations on the heroes' mental health in later life. The decorated veterans had the highest level of perceived self-esteem among the three groups (Ginzburg, Solomon, Dekel, & Neria, 2003). The U.S. Army recognizes the role that courage or bravery plays in promoting effective unit performance; the development of fortitude through training programs is seen as one way of reducing combat stress as well as enhancing maximum effectiveness and survival in battle (Ozkaptan, 1994).

Dekel et al. (2003) also found that officers in the Israeli Defence Forces had lower rates of PTSD and general psychiatric symptomatology than those in noncommissioned ranks. They attributed this difference to the officers' greater robustness and personal resources, as well as to their special training and the responsibility they assume for their troops. Sharkansky et al. (2000) made a similar point in discussing the lowered rates of PTSD among U.S. Army veterans of the Gulf War. Although the officers had exposure to more combat than the other ranks, they also used more approach-based coping strategies. Apparently, the officers were more prepared to deal with combat stressors than were noncommissioned personnel. Sharkansky et al. attributed this difference in coping to the officers' better training, greater personal resources, and/or greater control in combat situations, which allowed them to make use of coping strategies that were unavailable to the noncommissioned ranks. Personal resources and social support are two categories of variables that moderate the effects of stress (Lazarus & Folkmann, 1984). *Personal resources* include personality characteristics as well as beliefs and attitudes about killing and war; *social support* includes such variables as group cohesion, loyalty to the unit, and unit morale (Milgram, Orenstein, & Zafrir, 1989). Milgram et al. related this latter group of variables to effective combat performance by Israeli veterans during operations in Lebanon during the 1980s. Solomon and Mikulincer (1990) examined Israeli veterans from the same war who had been treated for combat-related stress and, subsequently, PTSD. They concluded that lack of social support was a major contributing factor to PTSD.

Social support and group cohesion are similar, overlapping constructs. For example, *cohesion* is often defined in terms of communication, teamwork, and collective action (Griffith & Vaitkus, 1999; Siebold, 1999), and *social support* involves giving tangible support in the form of material assistance or information, advice, and guidance (Curtona, 1990). *Cohesion* includes both attraction to the group and an emotional component indicated by the degree of trusting, caring, and liking, or interpersonal support (Griffith & Vaitkus, 1999; Siebold, 1999), which are similar to social support characteristics of social companionship—emphasizing the individual in the context of the group (Flannery, 1990)—and of interpersonal connectedness (Sarason, Sarason, & Pierce, 1990). According to Griffith and Vaitkus (1999), cohesion and social support function similarly in facilitating the productivity of the group member and successful interaction of the group as a whole.

Leadership as Social Support

Optimally effective leaders in small army units capitalize on general processes of social influence (Bartone & Kirkland, 1991). These leaders model behavior that demonstrates competence in soldier skills, caring for the welfare of unit members, respect for subordinates as worthy and competent members of the unit, commitment to the importance of group goals and activities, and open sharing of information. Thus, leadership becomes an important social support mechanism; however, the views of leaders and their subordinates on the impact and performance of the leader often vary greatly. Studies carried out in the U.S. Army (Gabriel, 1985), in the Swedish Army (Korpi, 1965), and in the Canadian Forces (Eyres, 1998) reached similar conclusions. Officers tend to overestimate unit morale and the favorable impressions of their subordinates about them. There is a feeling among subordinates that officers do not really "care" for them. On the other hand, officers believe that they are doing a good job in forming bonds with their unit. These and other studies suggest that soldiers do not hold their leaders in particularly high regard, whereas officers believe they have a positive impact on their unit morale. These discordant views may have a negative effect on operational performance and lead to a greater incidence of combat stress reactions.

The officers' overestimation of their subordinates' morale and confidence in them may result from a lack of knowledge about, or experience with, unit climate issues (Yates, 1990). In the context of confidence research (e.g., Lichtenstein & Fischhoff, 1977), officer overconfidence might indicate poor calibration. Overconfident individuals may have insufficient experience in a specific situation to know how little they actually know (Yates, 1990). Lichtenstein, Fischhoff, and Phillips (1982) suggested that people could be trained to become better calibrated by receiving outcome feedback. Until recently, there were few if any sound psychometric instruments that could provide reliable information about a military unit's climate. The Canadian Forces has now developed a unit climate survey that allows collection of data from subordinates in situ with rapid feedback of the survey results to field commanders (Farley, 2002; Farley & Veitch, 2004a; Murphy & Farley, 1998, 2000).

Clearly, high morale and cohesion together with strong confidence in leaders represent strong social support mechanisms that buffer the effects of stress on strain. It follows that it should be possible to measure the effects of these variables on the experience of stress for soldiers on deployed operations. What has been missing so far in the military environment is a comprehensive model of the relations among morale, cohesion, and confidence in leadership in the context of a stress, coping, and strain framework. Such a model, however, must be seen in the larger context of the occupational stress. Indeed, stress in military operations can be viewed as a special case of occupational stress.

Farley (2002) adapted the model developed by Griffith (Griffith, 1997; Griffith & Vaitkus, 1999) to focus on the moderating effects of confidence in leadership on the relationship between stress and strain. Specifically, he extended the notion of social support to include soldiers' confidence in leadership, which was expected to buffer the effects of stressors on strain. As well, the model included individual coping styles, rank (officer vs. soldier), and time (early in tour vs. late in tour). Unlike Griffith's research, data to test the model shown in Figure 13.2 were collected from soldiers and officers actually serving in a theater of operations.

Canadian Forces played a major peacekeeping role in postwar Bosnia and participated in combat actions in Afghanistan following the events of 9/11. These settings allowed a rare comparison of the model between the two types of operational environments, peacekeeping and combat. Farley and Veitch (2004b) found that although the soldiers in both peacekeeping and combat environments identified similar stressors, other unit climate factors such as social and task cohesion operated differently. Specifically, social cohesion both mediated and moderated the relationship between stress and strain for soldiers in the peacekeeping environment, but there were no similar effects for a similar group of soldiers in the combat setting. That is, increases in cohesion in the peacekeeping units led to decreases in strain, but cohesion did not have a similar effect for units engaged in combat. In fact, social cohesion scores were much lower in the combat sample compared with those in the peacekeeping sample. On the other hand, stress, strain, and task cohesion scores were significantly higher in the combat environment.

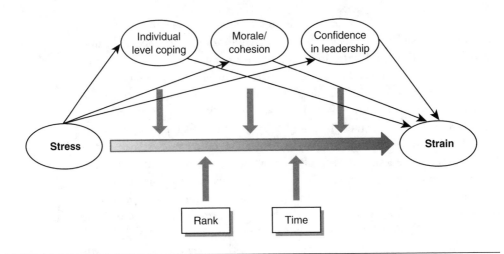

Figure 13.2   Proposed Model of the Relations Between Stress, Coping, Confidence in
Leadership, Morale/Cohesion, and Strain

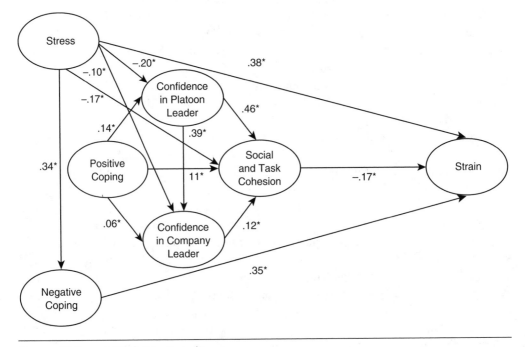

Figures 13.3a and 13.3b (Continued)

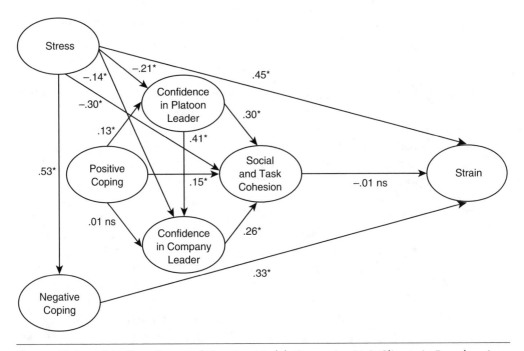

Figures 13.3a and 13.3b. Structural Equation Models Comparing Unit Climate in Peacekeeping and Warfighting

NOTE: Values represent standardized regression coefficients.

	GFI	AGFI	RMSR
13.3(a) Bosnia (N = 1,897)	.91	.90	.05
13.3(b) Afghanistan (N = 876)	.89	.87	.06

This strict focus on task cohesion at the expense of social cohesion appeared to put soldiers at greater risk of experiencing increased strain. Structural equation modeling and hierarchical regression showed that confidence in leadership at the platoon and company level and positive coping strategies (such as problem solving and seeking social support) generated the interaction between social cohesion and stress in the peacekeeping sample. The result was that social cohesion rather than task cohesion played the major role buffering the relation between stress and strain. Figures 13.3a and 13.3b present the final structural equation models, respectively, for data collected from Canadian soldiers in Bosnia (peacekeeping environment) and Afghanistan (combat environment), along with the fit indices for the models.

In summary, there is limited research comparing stress experiences in peacekeeping and combat environments, but the available evidence suggests that unit climate plays an important role in moderating the relation between stress and strain. In particular, a strict focus on task cohesion at the expense of social cohesion appears to put soldiers at greater psychological risk. Confidence in leadership and positive coping skills also play key roles in stress reduction. In addition to identifying moderators of combat stress, recent research has used unit climate information to estimate the potential for stress casualties under various combat conditions.

Predicting Combat Stress Casualties

In terms of deployment in war, any army wants to know the likelihood of casualties. Can the number of combat-related stress outcomes be estimated? Recently, U.S. Army researchers (Stokes, Belenky, Bradford, & Elliott, 2003) have developed a stress casualty forecasting method that takes into account local conditions such as physical stress (e.g., cumulative days in-theater, physical load, dehydration, sleep loss), mental stress (e.g., anticipated level of danger to own troops, seeing harm and suffering among locals, cultural friction), unit readiness (e.g., unit cohesion, leadership, soldier quality), and wounded in action (WIA—numbers of wounded per day or per contact).

According to the authors, this method of forecasting stress casualties has been validated in recent U.S. operations. Values assigned to each variable are products of unit climate data or based on unit-level observations. As examples, a highly trained larger unit with high morale and cohesion, taking significant casualties, produced a ratio of WIA to stress casualties of approximately 10 to 1. For an untrained or demoralized unit with major known problems, taking significant casualties, the formula produced a ratio of 2 to 1. The following equations are used to calculate the ratio of wounded to stress casualties:

$$OI = (0.000015 \times \text{Troop Population})$$
$$\text{WIA Impact} = (\text{WIA Admissions}/20) \times ([PS + MS] / UR)$$

where OI = operational impact stress; WIA = wounded in action; PS = physical stress; MS = mental stress; and UR = unit readiness.

One limitation of this method is that it produces an estimate as a ratio of WIA to stress casualties only. It is well known that stress casualties can occur in the absence of WIA when conditions are particularly difficult (e.g., Rwanda).

Thomas and O'Hara (2000), in their survey of Russian reports on PTSD following the war in Chechnya, reported that the environment was one that was prone to increase PTSD:

Chechnya was clearly a war infested with a special psychological flavor for Russian combatants because of the special circumstances of the conflict (fighting their own citizens under the toughest of circumstances, that is, combat in cities using a poorly trained and informed force vulnerable to intimidation, persuasion, deception, and provocation). The emotional environment was high risk. (p. 52)

It is not surprising then that up to 1996, over 35,000 Russian military who had served in Chechnya and their families had received some form of psychological counseling (Kucher, 1997). Ruzduev (1996) predicted that in future wars, Russia would expect that a minimum of 20% of its troops would return home with some type of postwar psychological syndrome.

One conclusion that can be drawn from these studies is that combat-related stress outcomes will be high. In modern wars in which casualties are relatively low, the number of combat stress–related incidents and more severe PTSD will likely outnumber physical casualties. One change that has occurred on battlefields is the recognition that combat-related stress outcomes are legitimate war injuries and must be treated as such close to the battlefront.

The Treatment of Stress Casualties in Combat

Morale, cohesion, physical exhaustion, training, living conditions, and traumatic events such as seeing one's friends wounded or killed in combat are all variables found to contribute to combat stress (Stokes et al., 2003). Far from a new phenomenon, combat stress reaction has been identified as a distinct psychological dysfunction since the American Civil War (Hammond, 1883). During that war, William Hammond, the surgeon general of the Union Army, identified a mental condition he called "nostalgia" that made soldiers incapable of performing their duties, even in the absence of any physical injury. The Union Army reported 5,213 cases of nostalgia in the first year of the war alone. Hammond observed that treatment near the front where soldiers remained close to their peers and units seemed to produce better results than when soldiers were removed to hospitals in the rear. Treatment consisted of rest, food, and regular but nonstressful work such as caring for horses and preparing supplies.

The evolution of the identification and treatment of nostalgia through to the present day combat stress reaction is as complex as the evolution of psychology itself. Variously known as "shell shock," "traumatic war neurosis," "combat exhaustion," and "combat fatigue," the etiology of the disorder and subsequent long-term effects, such as posttraumatic stress disorder, have been hotly debated by mental health specialists of all theoretical stripes (e.g., Beveridge, 1997; Bourne, 1970). Current procedures for dealing with combat stress are based on a three-stage model that emphasizes prevention in the first stage by controlling and, when possible, reducing the stressors identified in Table 13.2. The second stage attempts to minimize acute disability by training leaders, chaplains, and medical personnel to identify troops exhibiting signs of combat stress, particularly acts of misconduct, and to take action to control the relevant stressors and to obtain treatment with the goal of reintegrating the affected soldier into the unit as quickly as possible. The third stage attempts to minimize the possibility of PTSD by having an active prevention program and conducting tour debriefings for units and the members' families (U.S. Army, 1994). Interestingly, however, the treatment principles first outlined by Hammond in the 1860s look very similar to the military mental heath doctrine embraced by Western armies today. In particular, the principle known as *proximity,* the treatment of combat stress reaction casualties close to the front, remains a fundamental tenet of modern military mental health services.

The intent of treating soldiers close to the combat zone is to reduce the stigma attached to PTSD by treating it as just another combat-related injury and to return troops to their posts as quickly as possible. Nearly all soldiers treated for PTSD at the front return to duty. Rather than wait for those suffering from PTSD to go to a clinic for help, the U.S. Army commanders now have the obligation to order troops to go to "rest centers" if they become unable to do their jobs. The U.S. Navy has now developed education programs on combat stress and encourages sufferers to seek help at its facilities in war zones ("U.S. Tries Combat Stress Program," 2004).

In addition to proximity, the *Textbook of Military Medicine* (U.S. Army, 1993) includes three other principles as doctrinal guideposts for treatment of stress casualties in combat. These are *immediacy*—the intervention should begin immediately on recognition; *expectancy*—treatment personnel should develop the expectancy that the soldier will recover and return to duty rapidly; and *simplicity*—the use of straightforward interventions are encouraged rather than longer term therapeutic strategies. As an *aide-mémoir* for military personnel, these principles are referred to as the PIES treatment (proximity, immediacy, expectancy, and simplicity).

Thomas and O'Hara (2000) report that the Russian military used much the same approach to treat PTSD among Russian soldiers who had fought in Chechnya. They reported that Russian psychologists based PTSD treatment on six principles:

1. The PTSD victims must realize they need help and must trust the psychologist completely if the process is to succeed.

2. Assistance must be offered immediately, even during pauses in combat.

3. The assistance must be offered in the proximity of the battlefield.

4. The structure of the daily activity of the soldier and composition of the unit must be preserved.

5. Information/education must be oriented toward recognition of the high value of the missions completed.

6. The amount of time spent on treatment of an individual must be limited.

If the brief treatment in the combat zone is not effective and more extensive treatment is required, the PTSD victim is sent to division medical facility for up to 2 weeks.

The deployment of mental health professionals to combat zones is a relatively new activity but is now widespread across most Western militaries, in addition to Russia. The deployment of specialized combat stress control (CSC) units in the U.S. Army is one example. These units are usually colocated with field hospitals and can provide mental health assessment and support to units at or near the front lines. Although the numbers vary according to need, there are about 10 CSC units of 25 mental health personnel each in the U.S. Army at any given time. Prevention of combat stress is a main thrust of the CSC unit's work, and much activity is focused on consultation with commanders with respect to monitoring and improving conditions of unit climate described earlier. In addition to these climate issues, however, stress reactions in the field and long-term psychological dysfunction often occur as a result of killing other human beings.

Treatment of PTSD does not end with the combat assignment, as the effects of PTSD may be long lasting. In the United States, the Department of Veterans Affairs medical centers run an extensive network of programs that deal with PTSD. These programs include outpatient clinics that provide assessment, evaluation, and therapy on a one-on-one or group basis; day hospital PTSD programs that provide social, recreational, and vocational counseling, in addition to therapy; and inpatient PTSD programs that provide 24-hour care for up to 90 days for the most severe cases of PTSD (National Center for PTSD, 2004).

The Psychological Cost of Killing

To this point in the chapter, we have considered the soldier as victim of violence on the battlefield. The soldier, however, is also a perpetrator of violence, and as Grossman (1996) concluded in his examination of killing in battle, the psychological cost for soldiers can be devastating.

According to Grossman (1996), at the root of the psychological dysfunction is the natural hesitancy of humans to kill other humans. Support for this thesis can be found in both the biological and psychological literature. For example, most mammals appear to have an aversion to killing members of their own species (Eibel-Eibesfeldt & Mosbacher, 1979; Fossey, 1983; Goodall, 1986; Lorenz, 1963). Of course, intraspecies killing does occur on occasion among mammals, but this general aversion to killing other members represents a general threshold beyond which many will not cross. For many soldiers who have been trained to kill, the decision is sometimes too difficult to make, even in the face of grave danger to themselves.

In his seminal work on soldiers' reactions to combat in WW2, S. L. A. Marshall (1966) found that only about 15% of American riflemen in combat had fired at the enemy. According to Marshall, the fear of killing, rather than the fear of being killed, was the most common cause of battle failure in the individual. In response to Marshall's research, the U.S. Army instituted a number of fundamental reforms to training aimed at increasing the rate at which soldiers would fire at the enemy. These reforms included desensitizing the soldier to the act of killing by changing the language used in training (for example, "enemy soldiers" became "targets," and "killing" became "engaging" or "servicing the target") and the introduction of automatic weapons for individual soldiers, which enabled "massing fire" on locations where "targets" might be hiding.

Respondent and operant conditioning were also used to increase firing rates. Targets in the shape, size, and color of enemy soldiers (conditioned stimulus) were presented to soldiers on the firing range and immediate, accurate firing (conditioned response) resulted in positive reinforcement in the form of shooting proficiency badges and praise from instructors and peers. These reforms seemed to have worked because by the end of the Vietnam War, estimates of firing on the enemy had increased to about 90% to 95% in combat (Grossman, 1996).

Although the aversion threshold to killing other human beings seems to have been overcome by a focus on training, such methods did little to counter the psychological reaction to killing. For example, soldiers in Vietnam who killed, or believed that they had, were found to have much higher rates of PTSD compared with other soldiers who participated in combat (MacNair, 2000). Indeed, according to the *Textbook of Military Medicine*, "Casualties that the soldier inflicted himself on enemy soldiers were usually described as the most stressful events" (U.S. Army, 1993, p. 298).

One variable that seems to influence the resistance to killing and severity of the stress reaction is the distance at which the killing occurs (Grossman, 1996). Both the resistance to killing and resulting stress reaction increase as the distance decreases between the soldier and enemy. It appears easier to kill with high-altitude bombing and artillery than with bullets and bayonets.

Given recent and ongoing relatively close-quarter combat environments, the prognosis for psychological dysfunction among soldiers appears grim. In fact, close contact with the enemy and exposure to terrorist attacks is one factor cited in a recent finding that one in six American veterans of the Iraq war (2003–2004) shows signs of PTSD or other related disorders (Hoge et al., 2004). Equally troubling is the finding that more than half of the soldiers who met the criteria for a psychiatric disorder reported that they had not sought help out of concern that their careers would suffer.

Although the costs of killing are becoming obvious for the individual soldier, the wider community and society at large also pay a price. Grossman (1996) points out that the price to be paid is felt in terms of violence and suicide among returning combat veterans and a general desensitization of society to violence as a result of media coverage of combat, movies that glamorize violence, and—particularly disturbing—the proliferation of killing-oriented video games aimed at children and teenagers.

In summary, militaries have developed training and socialization techniques to reduce the natural inhibition to kill, but the immediate and long-term psychological reactions to killing remain pernicious problems that continue to threaten the individual soldier and the society to which he returns.

_____ Battlefield Violence: Impact on Civilians

In most cases, workplace violence is restricted to the work site and to those employees who happen to be in the line of fire. In almost all cases, the victims were employed at the work site. Very rarely does the violence spread over to other locations or involve people who are not related to the work site. The battlefield as a work site is an exception. The battlefield is not nicely contained in isolated areas. Modern wars have involved bombing and destruction of cities and neighborhoods. Many of us watched the live news reports of sophisticated bombardments on Baghdad and other Iraqi cities and marveled at those aerial pyrotechnics. These attacks not only do violence to enemy soldiers but also civilians who find themselves in harm's way. So far we have discussed what soldiers experience in warfighting and their exposure to traumatic events and combat stress. It seems fitting that we should also discuss what is known about the effects of traumatic war-related events on civilians. Most of the existing research in this area is descriptive.

Civilians who are not involved in a war also experience many of the same war-related stressors encountered by soldiers. They suffer various deprivations due to shortages of food and water; they are displaced from their homes; their lives are threatened; and they see family members killed or maimed. Civilians are also jailed and tortured or abused both physically and sexually; they are forced to watch family members or friends executed. All of these experiences constitute stressors, described in Table 13.2, that will produce negative outcomes. Studies of civilian war refugees in Rwanda and Burundi (de Jong, Scholte, Koeter, & Hart, 2000) and in Bosnia (Mollica et al., 1999) found high levels of PTSD, as well as depression and other psychiatric problems, among the refugees. Similarly, large levels of PTSD were found in nonrefugee civilians who had been exposed to war or other forms of mass violence such as terrorist attacks (de Jong et al., 2000).

Exposure to severe stress may have long-lasting effects. Landau and Litwin (2000) found that 46% of 124 holocaust survivors living in Israel were still exhibiting symptoms of PTSD. This rate was about seven times higher for men and three times higher for women when compared with rates for other Israelis of similar ages. Civilians exposed to traumatic events in war also have higher mortality rates. Civilians in Beirut who had experienced at least five traumatic events were two to three times more likely to die than other civilians (Sibai, Fletcher, & Armenian, 2001).

Most of the research on civilian war-related stress has involved studies of adults. The few studies conducted with samples of children suggest that they are more resilient in coping with war-related stress. Studies of Israeli children who had been exposed to Scud missile attacks during the Gulf War showed few if any signs of PTSD except for sensitivity to loud noises (Klingman, 1995). Children living in refugee camps, however, were more like adults in exhibiting higher rates of PTSD and other disorders (Paardekooper, de Jong, & Herman, 1999).

The PTSD treatment of civilians differs from that of soldiers in combat. In cases of noncombat-related PTSD, treatment begins only after the survivor has been removed from the crisis situation. The first step in treating PTSD in civilians is to attempt to resolve the crisis that precipitated the PTSD, if at all possible. Treatment of PTSD in civilians generally involves (a) educating the survivor and family about the nature of PTSD, (b) having the survivor reexperience the traumatic event through imagery while in a safe controlled environment, (c) having the survivor reexamine feelings associated with the traumatic event, and (d) teaching the survivor how to cope with posttraumatic memories. There are several recognized therapeutic approaches used in dealing with PTSD. The most preferred is cognitive-behavioral therapy, which involves working with cognitions to change emotions, thoughts, and behaviors. Pharmacotherapy, or drug therapy, is used to reduce extreme cases of anxiety and depression. Group therapy and brief psychodynamic psychotherapy have also been used to teach victims how to confront and deal with PTSD. Most of these therapies are better suited for use with adults than children. These therapies, however, have been used with civilians who did not experience PTSD in combat-related events but rather through domestic or other forms of violence.

Future Trends and Implications for Psychology

This chapter has followed the dramatic changes in warfighting and, in particular, violence on the battlefield over the past 150 years. The attrition warfare strategies of the American Civil War and WW1 have given way to maneuver warfare in which modern militaries have managed to maximize the lethality of their weapon systems and reduce their own casualty rate from enemy fire. Paradoxically, it appears that technology, stress, and fatigue have often conspired to create an environment in which soldiers stand a better chance of being killed by their own forces than the enemy. And the psychological costs of warfighting, of course, remain high, with consequences far beyond the individual soldier and the battlefield.

What of the future then? How will the wars of today shape the warfighting of tomorrow, and how will violence on the battlefield manifest itself? Effects-based operations and the three-block war are trends that provide a glimpse into the battlefields of the future.

Effects-Based Operations

Effects-based operations are strategies that do not necessarily depend on physical force for attaining a desired outcome or effect on the enemy

(Canadian Forces, 2004). The intent of effects-based operations is to attack an opponent's will and capacity to wage war. The desired result is to render the enemy either physically or morally incapable of pursuing an objective. The consequences of this strategy would be an overall reduction in violence and, ideally, the surrender of the enemy before fighting actually begins. In addition to weapons such as "smart" bombs designed to strike with precision a military target and minimize collateral damage, effects-based operations include "hearts and minds" methods, such as psychological operations, civil-military cooperation, and the use of special forces.

According to the *U.S. Doctrine for Joint Psychological Operations* (U.S. Department of Defense [DoD], 2003), "Psychological operations are planned to convey selected information and indicators to foreign audiences to influence emotions, motives, objective reasoning and ultimately the behavior of foreign governments, groups and individuals" (p. ix). At the tactical level, common psychological operations practices include dropping leaflets from aircraft on enemy positions with messages encouraging them to surrender or loudspeaker messages encouraging locals to identify unwanted insurgents in their location. For example, during the 78-day air campaign over Serbia in 1999, U.S. psychological operations forces dropped 104.5 million leaflets of 40 different types. They also produced television programming in Serbian and Albanian languages that was transmitted from a specially equipped aircraft. During the first Gulf War in 1991, thousands of Iraqi prisoners surrendered waving psychological operations leaflets promising fair treatment by the coalition forces. Psychological operations outcomes are difficult to measure, but the use of such methods has likely saved thousands of friendly, enemy, and civilian lives.

Like psychological operations, civil-military cooperation operations are designed to influence behavior, but the focus is on civilian populations in the theater of operations. Examples of civil-military operations are reconstruction of damaged infrastructure such as schools, police stations, community water wells, and roads. Canadian civil-military operations in Afghanistan have been credited with stimulating a positive shift in the attitudes of several small village communities, improving the lives of civilians, and making them safer areas in which troops can operate (Department of National Defence [DND], 2004).

Special forces have long been used to create changes in the affiliation of local military and paramilitary groups (e.g., U.S. Army, 1989). For example, the U.S. Army was very successful in obtaining the loyalty of the Montagnards during the Vietnam War. According to the U.S. Department of the Army (1989),

> The Montagnards and other minority groups were prime targets for Communist propaganda, partly because of their dissatisfaction with the Vietnamese government, and it was important to prevent the Viet-Cong from recruiting them and taking complete control of their large and strategic land holdings. (p. 21)

Although the U.S. eventually lost the war, the conversion of the Montagnards to U.S. loyalties was an effective use of special forces in this context as it reduced the overall threat to U.S. forces in the region and became a model for the use of special forces in the future. Indeed, the extensive use of coalition special forces in Afghanistan and Iraq today is built on many of the same principles developed in the jungles and mountains of Vietnam. The extent to which they have succeeded in reducing the threat to coalition forces in the region has yet to be determined.

The use of effects-based operations methods such as psychological operations, civil-military cooperation, and special forces will become increasingly important, as modern conflicts in built-up areas will require soldiers to change strategy and tactics quickly, even from city block to city block.

The Three-Block War

The trend toward fighting in built-up areas in places like Iraq will force Western militaries to exploit and perhaps reconsider effects-based operations strategies to defeat small but determined groups that use the maze of city streets and the civilian population for protection. The problem of engaging enemy forces in built-up areas has been referred to as the *three-block war* (Canadian Forces, 2004). The idea is that on one city block, soldiers might be engaged in high-intensity warfare against a well-trained and well-equipped enemy. On another, they might face light, irregular forces fighting a guerrilla-style or insurgency campaign. In yet another area, soldiers might be engaged in peacekeeping and distributing humanitarian aid. The scenario is three city blocks with three very different types of military activity—hence, the three-block war. Exacerbating the problem of defeating an enemy in this scenario is the requirement to transition from one type of activity to another, which "could be measured in minutes" (Canadian Forces, 2004, p. 4). In reality, of course, clear boundaries from one area to another will be blurred as fighting continues, and the situation in one area alone could cycle through all these options (and perhaps back again) in the same day. Of all warfare scenarios, fighting in built-up areas and in scenarios like the three-block war is the most difficult and dangerous for soldiers.

Rules of engagement for such scenarios are notoriously complex and add to the long list of stressors soldiers must confront. On one hand, if soldiers know that they will face serious consequences for violating rules of engagement that result in the death of civilians, they might be overly cautious and put themselves at risk of being killed by enemy forces masquerading as civilians. On the other hand, the mistaken killing of civilians and destruction of property will undoubtedly cause a wave of anger in the civilian community that might align the sympathies of the population with the enemy. It is in the three-block war that the physical and psychological risk to the soldier will be the greatest.

The full exploitation and novel uses of effects-based operations like psychological operations, civil-military cooperation, and special forces—and the development of new strategies—will be necessary to mitigate the potential physical and psychological violence of the three-block war of the future.

Implications for Practice

In addition to the physical and psychological threats outlined earlier in this chapter, future trends like the three-block war represent unique and complex environments that are not easy to predict and therefore pose problems for military and mental health professionals alike.

Military professionals have responded to these scenarios by changing both the way soldiers operate and the technologies they use. For example, small, semiautonomous groups of soldiers laden with sophisticated communications and other command-and-control systems can be more effective in built-up areas for surveillance and fighting than larger, more traditionally sized groups in which command and control can be more difficult. This trend toward smaller operational groupings of soldiers in turn poses problems in the psychological framework of unit climate.

In particular, the isolation of individuals and small groups puts social cohesion at risk. Recall that unit climate research showed that strict focus on task cohesion to the exclusion of social cohesion put soldiers at a greater risk for psychological strain (Farley & Veitch, 2004b). Psychologists who work in military settings will need to continue to research the implications of the evolution of combat on soldiers and develop effective preparation, adaptation, and recovery programs and services as needed.

Psychological Preparation

Many Western militaries already include a variety of predeployment training sessions on psychological topics, including stress management, identification of combat stress in fellow soldiers and themselves, and psychological first aid. In the Canadian military, for example, trained mental health professionals deliver these sessions based on current information in the literature and "lessons learned data" from previous deployments. The result is a blend of theory and practical advice designed for an audience of soldiers.

For example, the importance of social cohesion in unit climate theory has led to practical changes in how individual replacements are integrated into the unit. These include the forming and fixing of sections, platoons, and companies as early as possible after the warning order for deployment is issued; and if the use of replacements cannot be avoided, every effort should be made to include them in the social, as well as work, activities of the group.

For the Canadian Forces, unit climate data is collected before, during, and postdeployment, and the results are fed back to commanding officers at each stage. In line with future warfighting trends, unit climate data will need to be refined to identify morale, cohesion, and leadership issues in smaller, more autonomous work groups.

Psychological Adaptation

The primary role of mental health professionals in deployed settings is to advise the commander on issues related to the human dimension of operational readiness. They also must identify soldiers who are experiencing adaptation or stress-related problems and provide short-term counseling as required, using the principles of proximity, immediacy, expectancy, and simplicity (PIES). Mental health professionals rely on unit climate data as well as interviews and participant observation to accomplish their tasks. The key issue for the deployed mental health professional is access to soldiers in the field. As access to soldiers in new environments such as the three-block war will necessarily become more limited, mental health professionals will need to consider novel ways of interacting with soldiers under challenging conditions.

The employment of peer counselors is one way mental health professionals can maintain a connection with soldiers, even under severe conditions. The selection and training of peer counselors must take place before the deployment and be adequate to ensure peer counselors can identify stress casualties and report on unit climate issues to the deployed mental health professional. Recently, American and Canadian militaries have used peer counselors on a trial basis in operations in Iraq and Afghanistan, respectively, with positive results. The challenge for deployed mental health workers in the future will be to coordinate and supervise peer counselors in more isolated conditions.

Recovery

Earlier we described the long-term effects of combat exposure. These include mental health problems such as PTSD and a host of related family and societal effects. Typically, militaries follow up with soldiers after they return from duty and provide psychological and medical care as appropriate. The challenge for the future will be the identification of soldiers and units that are at higher risk for potential problems.

Given the physical and psychological hazards of the three-block war scenario, those participating in these environments might benefit from decompression periods prior to being sent back home. For example, one Canadian unit was sent to Guam for a week of rest and monitoring after a particularly difficult experience in Afghanistan. This period allowed mental health professionals time to evaluate soldiers and units and to provide information sessions on family reintegration issues and other topics.

Considering the changing face of combat, the use of decompression periods for returning soldiers may become the norm rather than the exception.

Summary

The military occupation is unique in that its "employees" are made aware from Day 1 that they may be called on to make the ultimate sacrifice for their country in taking up arms against an enemy of the state. Soldiering is not just a risky occupation in which death may occur on the job through accident; it is a job in which the ability to commit violence and to be subject to it are part of the everyday job description. Although soldiers may have nonviolent jobs in the military, every soldier must be prepared for combat, though fewer soldiers are called on to fight in modern wars.

The continued evolution of modern warfare with its emphasis on increased technology and weapons of mass destruction has ironically led to a reduction in deaths and physical injuries of the soldiers who engage in warfighting. Modern warfighting, however, has offset combat death and injury with increased psychological scars on the soldiers who participate in the fighting and on the civilians who experience the carnage and destruction of war.

Now combat stress rather than cowardice is recognized as a legitimate mental health problem that may have severe consequences after the traumatic event has occurred. Recent wars in Vietnam, the Persian Gulf, and Iraq have seen increases in combat stress and its treatment at the front lines, like any other battle injury. Combat stress is not unique to North American soldiers; Russians fighting in Chechnya and Israelis in the Middle East have exhibited the same etiology and outcomes.

Plain and simple, exposure to the violence of war, whether on a large battlefield or in a three-block area of a city, may have severe and long-lasting negative consequences for a significant portion of the men and women who are asked to engage in battle and for the civilian adults and children who are exposed to the consequences of that fighting. Posttraumatic stress disorder, the most severe outcome of combat stress, may have repercussions long after the soldier has returned to civilian life. The soldier's war with PTSD continues for a long time after the actual fighting has stopped and takes place far from the battlefield where the violence occurred. Violence on the battlefield has an impact not only on the workers (soldiers) in that environment but also on their families, friends, and society at large, as well as on the practice of health professionals.

References

Adler, A. B., Litz, B. T., & Bartone, P. T. (2003). The nature of peacekeeping stressors. In T. W. Britt & A. B. Adler (Eds.), *Psychology of the peacekeeper: Lessons from the field* (pp. 149–167). Westport, CT: Praeger/Greenwood.

Ayers, W. (1993). *Fratricide: Can it be stopped?* Unpublished master's thesis, Marine Corps University and Staff College, Decatur, GA.

Bartone, P. T., & Kirkland, F. R. (1991). Optimal leadership in small army units. In R. Gal & A. D. Mangelsdorff (Eds.), *Handbook of military psychology* (pp. 393–409). New York: Wiley.

Beveridge, A. (1997). On the origins of post-traumatic stress disorder. In D. Black, M. Newman, J. Harris-Hendriks, & G. Mezey (Eds.), *Psychological trauma: A developmental approach* (pp. 3–9). London: Gaskell.

Bourne, P. (1970). *Men, stress and Vietnam.* Boston: Little, Brown.

Canadian Forces. (2002a). *Board of inquiry final report Tarnak Farm 2002.* Retrieved from www.vcds.forces.gc.ca/boi/finalv2/fr-19_e.asp

Canadian Forces. (2002b). *Special report: Systemic treatment of CF members with post-traumatic stress disorder* (Ombudsman Report). Ottawa: Department of National Defence, Ombudsman.

Canadian Forces. (2003). *Duty with honour: The profession of arms in Canada.* Kingston, ON: Department of National Defence, Canadian Forces Leadership Institute.

Canadian Forces. (2004). *Purpose defined: The force employment concept for the Army.* Ottawa: Department of National Defence, Chief of Land Staff.

Combat stress: The war within. (2004, July 1). Retrieved September 1, 2004, from www.CNN.com

Curtona, C. E. (1990). Stress and social support: In search of optimal matching. *Journal of Social and Clinical Psychology, 9,* 3–14.

de Jong, J., Scholte, W., Koeter, M., & Hart, A. (2000). The prevalence of mental health problems in Rwandan and Burundese refugee camps. *Acta Psychiatrica Scandinavica, 102,* 171–177.

Dekel, R., Solomon, Z., Ginzburg, K., & Neria, Y. (2003). Combat exposure, wartime performance, and long-term adjustment among combatants. *Military Psychology, 15,* 117–131.

Department of National Defence. (2004). *Canadian CIMIC completes renovation of Chahar Asiab police station.* Retrieved September 7, 2004, from www.forces.gc.ca/site/Feature_Story/2004/ju104/16_f_e.asp

Eibel-Eibesfeldt, I., & Mosbacher, E. (1979). *The biology of peace and war: Men, animals, and aggression.* New York: Viking Press.

Eyres, S. A. T. (1998). *Measures to assess perceptions of leadership and military justice in the Canadian Army: Results from the 1997 personnel survey* (Sponsor Research Report 98-5). Ottawa Department of National Defence, Directorate for Human Resource Research and Evaluation.

Farley, K. M. J. (2002). *A model of unit climate and stress for Canadian soldiers on operations.* Unpublished doctoral dissertation, Carleton University, Ottawa, Ontario, Canada.

Farley, K. M. J., & Veitch, J. A. (2004a). Measuring morale, cohesion and confidence in leadership: What are the implications for leaders? *Canadian Journal of Police and Security Services, 1*(4), 353–364.

Farley, K. M. J., & Veitch, J. A. (2004b, June). *A model of unit climate and stress for Canadian soldiers on peace support and warfighting operations.* A paper presented at the Annual Convention of the Canadian Psychological Association, St. John's, Newfoundland, Canada.

Flannery, R. B. (1990). Social support and psychological trauma: A methodological review. *Journal of Traumatic Stress, 3,* 593–611.

Fossey, D. (1983). *Gorillas in the mist.* Boston: Houghton Mifflin.

Gabriel, R. A. (1985). *Military incompetence: Why the American military doesn't win.* New York: Hill & Wang.

Ginzburg, K., Solomon, Z., Dekel, R., & Neria, Y. (2003). Battlefield functioning and chronic PTSD: Associations with perceived self-efficacy and causal attribution. *Personality and Individual Differences, 34,* 463–476.

Goodall, J. (1986). *The chimpanzees of Gombe: Patterns of behavior.* Boston: Harvard University Press.

Green, B. L., Grace, M. C., & Lindy, J. D. (1990). Buffalo Creek survivors in the second decade: Comparison with unexposed and nonlitigant groups. *Journal of Applied Social Psychology, 20,* 1033–1050.

Griffith, J. (1997). Test of a model incorporating stress, strain, and disintegration in the cohesion-performance relation. *Journal of Applied Social Psychology, 27,* 1489–1526.

Griffith, J., & Vaitkus, M. (1999). Relating cohesion to stress, strain, disintegration, and performance: An organizing framework. *Military Psychology, 11,* 27–55.

Grossman, D. (1996). *On killing: The psychological cost of learning to kill in war and society.* Boston: Back Bay.

Hackworth, D. H. (1992). Friendly fire casualties. *Marine Corps Gazette, 92,* 46–48.

Hammond, W. A. (1883). *A treatise on insanity in its medical relations.* New York: Appleton.

Hoge, C. W., Castro, C. A., Messer, S. C., McGurk, D., Cotting, D. I., & Koffman, R. L. (2004). Combat duty in Iraq and Afghanistan, mental health problems, and barriers to care. *New England Journal of Medicine, 351,* 13–22.

Klingman, A. (1995). Israeli children's responses to the stress of the Gulf War. *School Psychology International, 16,* 303–313.

Korpi, W. (1965). A note on the ability of military leaders to assess opinions in their units. *Acta Sociologica, 8,* 293–303.

Kucher, A. (1997). Life after military service. *Independent Military Review, 43,* 8.

Lamerson, C. D., & Kelloway, E. K. (1996). Towards a model of peacekeeping stress: Traumatic and contextual influences. *Canadian Psychology, 37,* 195–204.

Landau, R., & Litwin, H. (2000). The effects of extreme early stress in very old age. *Journal of Traumatic Stress, 13,* 473–487.

Lazarus, R. S., & Folkmann, S. (1984). *Stress, appraisal and coping.* New York: Springer.

Lichtenstein, S., & Fischhoff, B. (1977). Do those who know more also know more about how much they know? *Organizational Behavior and Human Performance, 20,* 159–183.

Lichtenstein, S., Fischhoff, B., & Phillips, L. D. (1982). Calibration of probabilities: The state of the art to 1980. In D. Kahneman, P. Slovic, & A. Tversky (Eds.), *Judgment under certainty: Heuristics and biases.* Cambridge, UK: Cambridge University Press.

Lorenz, K. (1963). *On agression.* New York: Bantam.

MacNair, R. (2000, August). *Perpetration-induced traumatic stress: Severity and patterns.* A paper presented at the Annual Convention of the American Psychological Association, Washington, DC.

Marshall, S. L. A. (1966). *Men against fire.* New York: Morrow.

Milgram, N. A., Orenstein, R., & Zafrir, E. (1989). Stressors, personal resources and social supports in military performance during wartime. *Military Psychology, 1,* 185–199.

Mollica, R., McInnes, K., Sarajlic, N., Lavelle, J., Sarajlic, I., & Massagli, M. (1999). Disability associated with psychiatric comorbidity and health status in Bosnian refugees living in Croatia. *Journal of the American Medical Association, 282,* 433–439.

Murphy, P., & Farley, K. M. J. (1998). *The postdeployment status of CF personnel: Preliminary findings* (Research Note 98-1). Ottawa: Department of National Defence, Personnel Research Team.

Murphy, P., & Farley, K. M. J. (2000). Morale, cohesion and confidence in leadership: Unit climate dimensions for Canadian soldiers on operations. In C. McCann & R. Pigeau (Eds.), *The human in command: Exploring the modern military experience* (pp. 311–331). New York: Kluwer/Plenum.

Nathan, P. E., Gorman, J. M., & Salkind, N. J. (1999). *Treating mental disorders: A guide to what works.* New York: Oxford University Press.

National Center for PTSD. (2004). *Specialized PTSD treatment programs in the U.S. Department of Veterans Affairs.* Retrieved October 4, 2004, from www .ncptsd.org/facts/veterans/fs_treatment_programs.html

Ozkaptan, H. (1994). Determinants of courage. In R. F. Holz & J. F. Hiller (Eds.), *Determinants of effective unit performance: Research on measuring and managing unit training readiness* (pp. 233–253). Alexandria, VA: U.S. Army Research Institute for the Behavioral and Social Sciences.

Paardekooper, B., de Jong, J., & Herman, J. (1999). The psychological impact of war and the refugee situation on South Sudanese children in refugee camps in Northern Uganda: An exploratory study. *Journal of Child Psychology and Psychiatry, 40,* 529–536.

Regan, G. (1995). *Backfire: A history of friendly fire from ancient warfare to the present day.* London: Robson.

Ruzduev, V. (1996). Saved scorched souls. *Orienteer, 7,* 43–45.

Sarason, I. G., Sarason, B. R., & Pierce, G. R. (1990). Social support: The search for the theory. *Journal of Social and Clinical Psychology, 9,* 133–147.

Sharkansky, E. J., King, D. W., King, L. A., Wolfe, J., Erickson, D. J., & Stokes, L. R. (2000). Coping with Gulf War combat stress: Mediating and moderating effects. *Journal of Abnormal Psychology, 109,* 188–197.

Shrader, C. R. (1992, Autumn). Friendly fire: The inevitable price. *Parameters,* 29–43.

Sibai, A., Fletcher, A., & Armenian, H. (2001). Variations in the impact of long-term wartime stressors on mortality among the middle aged and older population in Beirut, Lebanon, 1983–1993. *American Journal of Epidemiology, 154,* 128–137.

Siebold, G. L. (1999). The evolution of the measurement of cohesion. *Military Psychology, 11*(1), 5–26.

Solomon, Z., & Mikulincer, M. (1990). Life events and combat-related posttraumatic stress disorder: The intervening role of locus of control and social support. *Military Psychology, 2,* 241–256.

Stokes, J. W., Belenky, G., Bradford, A., & Elliott, C. W. (2003, April–June). Stress casualty forecasting. *U.S. Army Medical Department Journal,* 9–14.

Thomas, T. L., & O'Hara, C. P. (2000, January–March). Combat stress in Chechnya: "The equal opportunity disorder." *Army Medical Department Journal,* PB 8-00-1/2/3, 46–53.

U.S. Air Force. (2004, July 6). *U.S. Air Force verdict.* Retrieved September 7, 2004, from www.cbc.ca/news/background/friendlyfire/verdict.html

U.S. Department of Defense. (2003). *Doctrine for joint psychological operations 3-53*. Washington, DC: Department of Defense, Joint Chiefs of Staff.

U.S. Department of the Army. (1989). *U.S. Army Special Forces: 1961–1971*. Washington, DC: Author.

U.S. Department of the Army. (1993). *Textbook of military medicine: War psychiatry*. Washington, DC: Office of the Surgeon General, Department of the Army.

U.S. Department of the Army. (1994). *FM 8-51: Combat stress control in a theatre of operations—tactics, techniques and procedures* (Booklet 1). Washington, DC: Author. Retrieved September 7, 2004, from www.vnh.org/FM851/Booklet1.html

U.S. tries combat stress program. (2004, April 27). *Philadelphia Inquirer*. Retrieved September 7, 2004, from www.duckdaotsu.org/ptsd_combat_program.html

Yates, J. F. (1990). *Judgment and decision making*. Englewood Cliffs, NJ: Prentice Hall.

14

Violence in Peacekeeping

Michelle Inness
Julian Barling

In the past 15 years, the violence caused by civilian warfare around the world has reached unprecedented proportions and has included severe humanitarian crises such as genocide, massacres, rape, and community destruction. Today at least 30 million people live in conflict zones, often in horrendous conditions. By the end of 2003, there were 23 major ongoing armed conflicts throughout the world, and all but 3 of these conflicts were fought by civilians (Bailes, 2003). Unlike interstate warfare in which the militaries of combating nations defend their countries in an organized way, wars fought among civilians tend to be more volatile and are not constrained by traditional rules of engagement. Quelling this "unstructured" civilian violence requires that outside, third-party forces intervene, and the task of doing so now frequently falls to peacekeepers.

In this chapter, we look at peacekeeping as a job that often takes place in violent, volatile environments where the methods and strategies used are most likely to be successful during times of peace. We will examine the impact of violence on peacekeepers and peacekeeping operations, present a conceptual framework with which to examine peacekeeping stressors such as violence.

Recent Shifts in the Nature of Peacekeeping

Peacekeeping originally emerged from the political conditions of the Cold War. At a time when fears of nuclear proliferation ran high, peacekeeping operations developed for the purpose of allaying conflict between nations and averting the potential for nuclear war. In this sociopolitical environment, conflicts that erupted were handled by the militaries of the combating nations and were well organized and controlled, and ceasefires were achievable through a process of negotiation. Traditional peacekeeping missions, referred to as "classic" or "Chapter VI" missions, were originally designed for this type of situation, in which an agreed-upon ceasefire had already been established between previously conflicting parties, and the parties were sovereign nations that gave their consent for the presence of peacekeepers. The primary purpose of peacekeepers in this milieu was to maintain a ceasefire while the combatants sought a more permanent resolution to their political disputes. Typically, under these circumstances, there existed a relatively low level of violence or aggression between groups at the time when the peacekeepers' presence was required (Langholtz, 1998; Moskos, 1975). This contrasted with other peace missions such as peacemaking, which was characterized by a more active enforcement of peaceful relations and negotiations between parties. Since the end of the Cold War, the distinction between peacekeeping and peacemaking has blurred. According to a more recent definition, the duties involved in peacekeeping include both the prevention of conflict and the making of peace (Boutros-Ghali, 1992).

Many expected the end of the Cold War to usher in an era of international peace and harmony. Contrary to expectations, however, when the international political tensions that characterized the Cold War began to subside, repressed intranational conflict based on historic long-standing ethnic and religious differences soon erupted (e.g., Rwanda, East Timor). Although fears of nuclear war waned at the end of the Cold War, the demand for a peacekeeping presence increased to address emerging intrastate conflicts around the world; however, this new warfare environment proved to differ in a number of respects from that for which peacekeeping was originally established. In the international conflicts common during the Cold War, militaries of the conflicting nations were on the front lines, governments were intimately involved in these disputes, and rules of engagement constrained soldiers' behavior. When conflicts occur primarily *within* nations, it is usually civilians who are on the front lines, often with minimal if any accountability to anyone except their leaders and compatriots, who are often extremist forces with strong political agendas. The increase of such conflicts and resulting humanitarian crises is reflected in an illustrative statistic: In the early 1900s, approximately 80% of casualties of war were military personnel. By the end of the 20th century, approximately 80% of casualties were civilians (Garfield & Neugut, 1997).

Although the rules governing the behavior of peacekeepers have not changed since the end of the Cold War, the characteristics of the contexts in which peacekeepers must intervene have changed dramatically. Civilian-fought warfare tends to be more complex than military battles and frequently involves more challenging mandates compared with those of classic peacekeeping operations. Peacekeepers' tasks often include humanitarian assistance, promoting national reconciliation, and the reconstruction of "failed states" in which the government is no longer functioning, the police and judiciary have collapsed, and populations have been uprooted, such as in Rwanda and Somalia (Boutros-Ghali, 1995). In this context, the risk for civilian violence is heightened.

Intrastate civilian combat often challenges the appropriateness of the principles of classic peacekeeping. These principles include (a) the necessity for impartiality among peacekeepers toward combatants, (b) the restraint from the use of force except in self-defense, (c) the consent of all parties for the presence of the peacekeepers, and (d) carrying a minimum of weapons (Langholtz, 1998). Peacekeepers are still required to restrain themselves from the use of aggression, even when confronting aggression from others, and to function as an impartial third party; however, they must uphold these behaviors in contexts in which ceasefires are not in place; in which their presence is not always supported by the local parties; and in which the contexts are much more volatile and often include ongoing civilian combat, violence, terrorism, and genocide (Orsillo, Roemer, Litz, Ehlich, & Friedman, 1998). Although the level of violence peacekeepers may confront can be akin to warfighting, peacekeepers are generally outnumbered by civilian combatants and are often without a comparable arsenal of weapons (Dirkzwager, Bramsen, & van der Ploeg, 2003). To make matters even more complex, peacekeepers are often given more challenging and diverse objectives compared with those of classic peacekeeping operations, including intervening in violent clashes and providing humanitarian assistance (Boutros-Ghali, 1995).

Peacekeeping is considered to be an integral part of a continuum of activities in the process of establishing peaceful relations among societies. The UN General Assembly has stated that peacekeeping operations "constitute a considerable part of the efforts of the United Nations to maintain international peace and security and to enhance the effectiveness of the United Nations" (UN Department of Public Information, 1996, p. 99). However, given the recent changes in international combat, the question arises as to whether peacekeepers are adequately poised to attain their objectives and protect their well-being while deployed to theaters in which there is no peace to keep.

Contemporary peacekeepers are a potentially valuable group to examine to advance research and understanding of workplace violence. Peacekeepers often find themselves in the business of managing violent situations while dealing with a great deal of ambiguity regarding their role, how to attain their objectives, and what to expect from the local populace. Further, because peacekeeping often occurs in environments characterized by violence and social disorganization, peacekeeping operations offer a fruitful opportunity for the testing of boundary conditions of models of stress and workplace violence.

_____ The Frequency of Violence in Peacekeeping

Peacekeepers often operate in volatile environments where they may frequently be the target of violence (including lethal violence), may be witness to injury of other soldiers or civilians by someone else's actions, may cause the death of another person as a result of their own actions, and may have to deal with the aftermath of violence, including handling bodies (MacDonald, Chamberlain, Long, & Mirfin, 1999; Weisæth, 2003).

Researchers who have examined peacekeepers' experiences have offered some insights regarding the exposure of peacekeepers to violent events. Although soldiers deployed to peacekeeping missions are less likely than soldiers in combat to have confronted violence, exposure to violence is not uncommon for peacekeepers. In one study (Lamerson, 1995) of 428 infantry combat engineers engaged in peacekeeping, 68% reported coming under direct fire, approximately half of the sample witnessed a colleague and/or a civilian being killed or wounded, 27% reported handling injured people, and 19% reported handling bodies. In a second sample (Lamerson, 1995), similar results were obtained with 72% receiving fire, 55% seeing a colleague wounded or killed, 47% seeing civilians killed or wounded, 28% handling the wounded, and 28% involved in body handling. In a sample of U.S. peacekeepers who had returned from a mission in Somalia, approximately half reported having experienced direct violence, including having rocks thrown at their unit (51%), shots fired on them (36%), and hostile rejection of help by locals (32%; Bolton, Glenn, Orsillo, Roemer, & Litz, 2003). It is important to note that these findings emerged from samples of peacekeepers who worked in some of the most volatile and violent environments; however, studies such as these provide valuable information about the extent to which violence may be a part of peacekeepers' work experience and the kinds of violence they may confront.

Costs of Violence to Peacekeepers: Empirical Findings

Violence can affect peacekeepers in at least two significant ways. It can affect directly the well-being of the peacekeepers, and it can affect the ability of peacekeepers to perform their duties, with the latter having potential implications for the well-being of the populations the peacekeepers serve. Recent changes in peacekeepers' roles have created a need to better understand the nature of the stressors experienced on peacekeeping deployments and the implications of these experiences for individual well-being and organizational effectiveness (Lamerson & Kelloway, 1996). Much research has focused on the effects of violence in peacekeeping on peacekeepers' well-being, including psychiatric morbidity (Litz, King, King, Orsillo, & Friedman, 1997), posttraumatic stress disorder (PTSD; Bartone, Adler, & Vaitkus, 1998), deleterious behaviors such as alcohol and drug abuse (McFall, Mackay, & Donovan, 1992), and combat-related casualties (Blood, Zhang, & Walker, 2002). Indeed, most empirical studies on peacekeepers to date have focused on well-being outcomes. As such, a review of the effect of violence on these outcomes provides an overview of much of what has been empirically tested on violence in peacekeeping.

Psychological Outcomes

It has been suggested that one unique aspect of violence in peacekeeping operations is that unlike traditional combat, violence may be unanticipated and unpredictable for soldiers on peacekeeping missions and that this may render peacekeepers more vulnerable to the harmful psychological effects of violence (Bartone et al., 1998). Research on peacekeepers suggests that exposure to violence, both direct and vicarious, and experiencing hostile opposition to their presence by local populations may be associated with reactions of fear and helplessness (Litz, King, et al., 1997).

The frequency of exposure to combat-type events has been found to be related to psychiatric symptoms (Ward, 1997). In a sample of U.S. peacekeepers who had returned from deployment in Somalia, one of the most violent and dangerous of UN peacekeeping missions, peacekeepers' exposure to warlike conditions was the strongest predictor of symptomatology. Other negative interpersonal experiences such as hostile reactions on the part of the locals and frustrations with the locals also had a significant impact on subsequent symptomatology (Orsillo et al., 1998). In a sample of Australian veterans of Somalia 15 months after returning home, at least one fifth of peacekeepers had significant psychiatric morbidity, almost twice as much as their nondeployed counterparts and higher rates than reported in previous studies of UN soldiers deployed where the theaters were less volatile and violent (Ward, 1997). In a study comparing Australian peacekeepers who were deployed to Somalia with a nondeployed control group, the deployed group experienced significantly higher levels of psychopathology, although there was a tendency for those symptoms to lessen over a 12-month period (Litz, King, et al., 1997).

The most commonly reported forms of distress included depression, psychoticism, hostility, and paranoid ideation. Problems related to depression are also fairly common in peacekeeping, particularly when the theater is violent or volatile, as this may lead to feelings of demoralization or concerns that the mission was not successful or important (Orsillo et al., 1998). Problems with anger management are not uncommon following exposure to combat-like conditions, given the degree of threat the individual faces and the concomitant sensitivity to possible external threats. For peacekeepers, this may be exacerbated by various frustrations associated with peacekeeping operations, such as being rejected by the local population and overly restrictive rules of engagement.

Posttraumatic Stress Disorder

PTSD is a recognized consequence of experiencing stressful life events. PTSD is characterized by persistent intrusive memories about the traumatic event, persistent avoidance of stimuli associated with the trauma, and persistent symptoms of increased arousal (American Psychiatric Association, 1994). Because it has become widely recognized that peacekeepers may be at risk for developing PTSD, it deserves special focus.

A wealth of research suggests that soldiers who are exposed to war zone stressors (Fairbank, Schlenger, Caddell, & Woods, 1993; Kulka et al., 1990) or involved in operations in which violence is occurring also have a heightened susceptibility for developing PTSD (Litz, King, et al., 1997). The intensity of traumatic events, as well as the extent to which the individual is exposed to traumatic events, have been found to be related to PTSD symptom severity (Bartone et al., 1998; Donovan, Padin-Rivera, Dowd, & Blake, 1996; Hotopf, David, Ismail, Unwin, & Wessely, 2003; Lauterbach & Vrana, 2001).

A large-scale study of U.S. military personnel deployed to Somalia reported that 8% of peacekeepers met the diagnostic criteria for PTSD, a rate comparable to soldiers in Operation Desert Storm. In another study, a difference in the rates of PTSD was found between peacekeepers and nondeployed soldiers following a tour in Somalia (MacDonald et al., 1999). The greatest predictors of PTSD included the stresses of being in a warlike environment characterized by violence and human suffering and confronting various frustrating events associated with peacekeeping duty in general, such as restrictive rules of engagement (Litz, Orsillo, Frieman, Ehlich, & Batres, 1997). Other research suggests that the impact of witnessing violent traumatic events on the development of PTSD is cumulative over time, such that prior exposure to such events increases the likelihood that traumatic events that occur during deployment will result in PTSD symptoms (Bolton, Litz, Britt, Adler, & Roemer, 2001), a finding that has implications for soldiers who are deployed to multiple peacekeeping assignments (Mehlum & Weisæth, 2002).

Alcohol and Drug Abuse

The stressors of peacekeeping have been found to be related to both alcohol and drug abuse, although individual difference factors have been found to moderate each relationship. Specifically, among peacekeepers, drug abuse has been found to be associated with the use of avoidance as a coping strategy and the desire for emotional numbing; alcohol abuse has been found to be associated with overarousal and the inability to calm down or to sleep (McFall et al., 1992). In a study of Vietnam veterans, approximately 60% to 80% of veterans who sought treatment for PTSD were abusing drugs or alcohol, demonstrating the use of these substances to self-medicate.

Casualties

Peacekeeping operations can vary widely in terms of the number of casualties incurred. For instance, British troops in Operation Resolute 2 in Bosnia suffered no wounded or killed-in-action casualties, whereas in Somalia's "Blackhawk Down" incident, 18 soldiers died and another 75 were wounded in a 24-hour period. In Somalia a few months earlier, another 24 soldiers died and 58 were wounded in an ambush of troops on a UN mission. The UN maintains records of fatalities that have occurred on their missions. Records up until March 2001 suggest that 1,681 fatalities have occurred on almost 70 different peacekeeping missions and that military personnel made up 85.4% of these casualties (Blood et al., 2002). A startling statistic illustrates the relative volatility of post–Cold War peacekeeping: From 1948 to 1990 (42 years), 844 peacekeepers died in action; between 1991 and 2000 (9 years), 814 peacekeepers died in action (UN Department of Peacekeeping Operations, 2005).

Costs of Violence to the Organization

There is no single governing organization to which peacekeepers belong. Although peacekeepers are immediately accountable to their own national militaries, they are ultimately responsible for upholding the values and principles of peacekeeping as established by the UN. As such, when violence affects peacekeepers' performance, it has ramifications for their militaries and for the UN; however, not many of these ramifications have been addressed in current research on peacekeeping. As such, many of the possible costs to the UN and to peacekeepers' units and militaries remain speculative.

Performance

There is a paucity of research examining the effects of violence on peacekeepers' performance; however, research has suggested that the stress of confronting violent situations may make people more prone to errors in judgment and decision making (Janis & Mann, 1977). Research from the literature on workplace violence may offer some insights regarding the effect of violence on work performance. For instance, in a study by Barling, Rogers, and Kelloway (2001), experiencing workplace aggression and sexual harassment was found to negatively affect work performance and other outcomes, although the effects were indirect and mediated by negative emotions.

Resource Costs

What have been traditionally thought of as combat casualties—casualties resulting from bodily injury and death—are now becoming costly to peacekeeping operations as well. Although the resources dedicated to these casualties in the context of traditional combat far outweigh those of peacekeeping operations, the shift in peacekeeping from primarily monitoring ceasefires to the more recent need to intervene in combat-like situations has made the provision of resources to deal with these casualties a necessity. Although researchers do not mention a dollar amount, it has been suggested that casualties are highly resource-intensive in terms of supplies and personnel (Blood et al., 2002).

Conceptualizing the Peacekeeping Experience Through the Lens of Acute and Chronic Stressors

A *stressor* has been defined in the literature as any event external to the individual that the individual perceives as demanding or, frustrating, or that in some way exceeds personal resources (Lazarus & Folkman, 1991). One of the most commonly evoked formulations of stressors in the literature distinguishes between acute and chronic stressors (Wheaton, 1999). Although no single study can fully encapsulate the entire experience of peacekeeping stress, this formulation may aid in the development of a rich yet parsimonious picture of these experiences. *Acute* stressors refer to stressful events that are infrequent, take place within a relatively discrete period of time, and are intense (Meichenbaum, 1994; Pratt & Barling, 1988; Wheaton, 1997). In the context of peacekeeping, acute stressors most often involve experiences with violence, including being the target of violence, a witness to acts of violence, and the perpetrator of violence, as well as nonhuman sources of danger such as land mines.

Chronic stressors refer to stressors that have a relatively consistent presence and are typically lower in intensity. Chronic stressors are not associated with a particular event, per se, but rather are often part of one's typical day-to-day experiences in a given role, such as within one's work role. Unlike acute stressors in which the event and its resolution occur fairly quickly, resolving chronic stressors may be postponed until the source of the stress is removed (Pearlin, 1989; Wheaton, 1997). Examples of chronic peacekeeping stressors include working with an unclear mandate or role expectations, working in an unpredictable environment, dealing with an unsupportive local population, either excessive or insufficient role demands, unclear rules of engagement, separation from family, feeling ill-prepared for or uninterested in peacekeeping duties, and experiencing conflict between the tasks and one's personal morals and values.

A few points should be made about acute and chronic stressors in the peacekeeping context. First, both acute and chronic stressors are an integral part of the post–Cold War peacekeeping experience (Lamerson & Kelloway, 1996). Historically, an inherent aspect of peacekeeping operations has always been the threat of confronting acute stressors, such as witnessing violence and torture, being the target of violence, body-handling, and witnessing intense suffering (MacDonald et al., 1999). Although acute stressors such as these may be increasingly common in post–Cold War peacekeeping, chronic stressors are also playing a new and important role in the experiences of peacekeepers. Chronic stressors are increasingly likely as the nature of the environmental demands, task directives given by the UN, personal feelings about the mission and tasks, and the tools the peacekeepers have to do their job may be incompatible with one another (Lamerson & Kelloway, 1996).

Second, although peacekeeping stressors overlap with stressors typical of combat operations, they are not necessarily identical. Similarities between peacekeeping and combat exist with respect to both the daily hassles and the combat-related events experienced in both types of missions (Adler, Litz, & Bartone, 2003). Many of these common sources of chronic stress involve the experience of ambiguity or uncertainty and the experience of conflicting work role demands. For instance, working in an unsupportive environment creates ambiguity about the problems and issues one might face on the job; working with an unclear mandate creates ambiguity about one's role; and rules of engagement that seem unclear or insensitive to the social context may create ambiguity about whether one's work is useful and morally justified. Conflicting work role demands may emerge if task directives are not sensitive to the external environment or if the individual peacekeeper does not prefer the tasks he or she has been given. Peacekeepers may also have an expectation that local populations will be grateful for their presence, which may not always be the case. In recognition of the unique combination of chronic and contextual stressors such as violence that are common to peacekeeping operations, researchers have coined the terms *peacekeeping stress* and *UN soldier's stress syndrome* (Weisæth, 2003).

Third, research suggests that the simultaneous experience of violence and chronic stressors has multiplicative effects. Exposure to violence or other acute stressors may not only exacerbate the effects of chronic stressors (Michel, Larsson, & Lundin, 2000) or heighten individual reactions to stressful or traumatic events on subsequent missions (Adler et al., 2003) but may also attenuate the positive or beneficial aspects of peacekeeping, such as seeing one's self as a humanitarian (Litz, Orsillo, et al., 1997). This vulnerability hypothesis will be discussed in greater detail in the following section.

A Specific Model Examining Violence in the Work Lives of Peacekeepers

The formulation of stressors as acute and chronic events facilitates the empirical examination of violence and other stressors in peacekeeping. Consistent with this perspective, Lamerson and Kelloway (1996) developed a model of peacekeeping stress. Their model conceptualizes peacekeeping as exposure to traumatic stressors such as violence in the context of chronic stressors such as role stressors. According to their model, exposure to violence along with the experience of chronic stressors may have implications for a number of outcomes related to peacekeeper well-being as well as various organizational outcomes. They suggest that peacekeepers who experience chronic stressors may be particularly vulnerable to the effects of traumatic stressors such as violence. Conversely, it is also possible that peacekeepers who experience violence either directly or as a witness may be less able to cope with chronic stressors such as role stressors (Lamerson & Kelloway, 1996); however, they acknowledge that not all peacekeepers who experience a combination of violence and chronic stressors will suffer deleterious outcomes. They propose that the extent to which these stressful experiences affect their performance and well-being depends on the individual's subjective appraisal of these events, a finding that has also been suggested by research on traumatization (Udwin, Boyle, Yule, Bolton, & O'Ryan, 2000).

According to their classification of stressful peacekeeping experiences, peacekeeping stressors can be categorized as either combat stressors, which include potentially traumatic events, or chronic stressors, which include all stressors that are chronic to the work role of peacekeeping, such as unclear mandates or overly restrictive rules of engagement, harsh working conditions, and interpersonal frustrations with the local population. Classifying experiences in this way draws on research in the stress literature that classifies stressors as being either acute or chronic. This formulation is a parsimonious way of conceptualizing peacekeeping experiences with violence and role stressors and facilitates the empirical examination of these stressors.

Although most peacekeeping missions have met with success, one common feature of missions that has not achieved their objectives is the presence of both acute and chronic stressors. For instance, on Operation Restore Hope in Somalia (ORH), peacekeepers were deployed primarily for humanitarian and policing duties but found themselves confronted with hostility and violence directed toward them by locals, as well as extreme violence between well-armed clans. Against this hostile and violent background, peacekeepers also confronted a number of chronic stressors, such as being constrained from the use of force to defend themselves or to interject when violence was occurring and being frustrated by the hostile rejection of their help by locals, leaving them feeling demoralized (Litz, 1996).

It is often in contexts such as these that some of the most high-profile scandals involving criminal acts by peacekeepers have emerged. In the case of the missions in Somalia, for instance, a number of peacekeepers engaged in severe abuses toward local populations. Although the individuals involved were ultimately and individually responsible for these abuses, it speaks to the need to recognize how intense acute and chronic stress may contribute to these abusive violations.

Moderators

Little is known about the factors that buffer peacekeepers from the negative outcomes associated with experiences of violence in peacekeeping or the factors that place peacekeepers at greater risk, particularly when violence occurs against a backdrop of chronic stressors (Bolton, Glenn, Orsillo, Roemer, & Litz, 2003). From of the research that has been done on this important question, findings suggest that social support in the forms of leadership and group cohesion, active coping, and individual differences is associated with psychological adjustment (e.g., Fairbank, Hansen, & Fitterling, 1991; Green, Grace, Lindy, Gleser, & Leonard, 1990). Given that the availability of many of these resources—including social support, group cohesion, and leadership—can be controlled from within the military, understanding the impact of these resources on peacekeeper well-being is particularly valuable.

Social Support

Social support is considered to be a key factor influencing individuals' reactions to stress, whether acute or chronic. Two main models delineating the effect of social support have been suggested in the literature. The *main effects model* suggests that social support offers benefits to individuals regardless of whether or not they are experiencing stress. The *buffering model* suggests that social support mainly provides benefits to individuals under stress. Given that many psychological problems such as PTSD result from stress, to the extent that social support buffers the individual from stress, it should help to minimize the risk for PTSD (Dirkzwager et al., 2003) and perhaps other negative psychological outcomes as well. In a longitudinal study, Dirkzwager, Bramsen, and van der Ploeg (2001) found that seeking social support was negatively related to PTSD symptomatology among military veterans, even after controlling for the presence of symptomatology at an earlier time.

Some studies have shown that people who engage in open discussion about a traumatic experience with others tend to suffer lower levels of psychological distress (Lepore, Silver, Wortman, & Wayment, 1996). Self-disclosure is particularly likely to be beneficial if the confidant's reactions are supportive and understanding (Bolton et al., 2003). Bolton et al. (2003) examined the relationship between confidants' reactions to self-disclosure and PTSD severity of peacekeepers who returned from a mission to Somalia. Results of this study suggest that self-disclosure and the confidants' supportiveness were related to lower levels of psychological strain. Further, these effects were independent of the degree of exposure to violent or combat-like situations during the mission.

Group Cohesion

One of the most important sources of social support peacekeepers may receive comes from within their work unit (Orsillo et al., 1998). Cohesion serves two main functions, both of which would be critical for effectiveness and well-being: cohesion helps to (a) establish standards of behavior and (b) support and sustain individuals during times of stress (Griffith, 1997).

Military leaders, policymakers, and social scientists have considered cohesion to be critical to combat effectiveness and performance. In a study of United States Army soldiers from 112 different companies, Griffith (1997) found that cohesion had a moderating effect on the relationship between stress and strain and between strain and performance and that task cohesion was particularly related to group performance. Group cohesion may also have an impact on outcomes related to peacekeepers' well-being. One study suggests that group cohesion was found to be one of the most powerful buffers against the harmful effects of experiencing stressful events during a peacekeeping mission (Orsillo et al., 1998).

Leadership

There is accumulating evidence to suggest that the quality of leadership can affect employee performance, including in the military context (Dvir, Eden, Avolio, & Shamir, 2002). Research suggests that leaders can make their followers feel more efficacious, that is, believe in their own capabilities to perform their job and tasks (Bandura, 1997). According to Chen and Bliese (2002), leadership influences followers' efficacy perceptions by providing followers with social support and by enhancing role clarity. These beliefs affect an individual's persistence in attaining his or her goals and, in turn, affect job performance (Stajkovic & Luthans, 1998) and buffer the negative effects of work stressors on well-being (Jex & Bliese, 1999). In addition, social support may also increase the likelihood that the individual employee will feel a sense of autonomy and empowerment, which can be self-motivating (Kark, Shamir, & Chen, 2003).

Coping Strategies

Coping refers to the cognitive and behavioral efforts used to manage stress (Lazarus, 1993). Coping has two main functions: to deal directly with the problem that is causing the stress (problem-focused coping) and to regulate one's own emotions about the problem (emotion-focused coping). Research that has examined coping strategies among combat veterans suggests that the coping strategies employed by the soldiers had different effects on psychological outcomes. In a study on the impact of coping strategy on the development of PTSD, soldiers who used a problem-focused coping strategy were less likely to develop PTSD, supporting a buffering hypothesis, whereas those who employed and emotion-coping strategy were more likely to develop PTSD (Fairbank et al., 1991; Sharkansky et al., 2000). Compelling support for the differential effects of using problem- and emotion-focused coping on the development of PTSD is offered by longitudinal research examining the use of different coping strategies at Time 1 and subsequent rates of PTSD. This research supports the differential effects of problem- and emotion-focused coping and suggests that problem-focused coping can offer benefits over time and emotion-focused coping can have deleterious effects over time (Dirkzwager et al., 2003; Farley & Veitch, 2003).

Occupational Identity

There is variability between soldiers with respect to the extent to which they identify with being a "warrior." Some research suggests that soldiers who adhere strongly to the warrior identity tend to find active combat more rewarding than peacekeeping and are less likely to have a positive attitude toward peacekeeping (Franke, 1997). Further, they may lack a sense of personal meaning in performing humanitarian work and may feel that this is not an appropriate role for them personally (Britt, 1998). It has been suggested that those soldiers who identify themselves as warriors have a greater tendency to treat hostile local populations as enemies and to generalize the behavior of individual members of the local population to all members of the population. By contrast, soldiers who identified themselves as "humanitarians" were more likely to eschew the use of force and seek political and cultural explanations for hostile behavior on the part of the local population (Miller & Moskos, 1995).

Personal Characteristics

Researchers have examined some of the risk factors for developing PTSD and found that two factors were significantly associated with subsequent traumatization following a violent peacekeeping mission: certain personality traits, including neuroticism (as this may tend to encourage negative interactions with others; Bramsen, Dirkzwager, & van der Ploeg, 2000; Lauterbach & Vrana, 2001), and various demographic characteristics (being relatively younger, unmarried, lower rank, and having relatively less education; Bolton et al., 2001).

Methodological and Ethical Issues

Conducting research on violence in peacekeeping poses a few practical challenges and evokes ethical considerations. At the time of the deployment of peacekeeping troops to a mission, it is not always clear whether the mission will involve violent encounters. Peacekeeping theaters change notoriously quickly, and what may begin as a purely humanitarian mission may deteriorate into a complete breakdown in social order. As such, it is not always possible to have data collection strategies in place prior to a violent event. The time needed to organize data collection may preclude early assessments of outcomes to the peacekeepers' well-being and performance. Even if data collection strategies are in place, careful considerations must be made as to the ethical appropriateness of collecting research data on a group of people who have recently witnessed or have been victims of violence. Each peacekeeper's psychological response to these events may be unique, peacekeepers may only be prepared to discuss these events after they have returned to the safety and normalcy of their own lives and have had time to readjust to post-deployment life.

Second, it has been suggested (Castro, 2003) that because research on peacekeepers has emerged only recently, researchers may not yet be completely familiar with the uniqueness of this group and of their experiences. Therefore, it may be desirable for preliminary data collection to include interview data, which would allow for the spontaneous emergence of relevant issues that may not otherwise be acknowledged by the researcher. Castro (2003) also suggests that because researchers are often focused on the development of theory and respondents tend to be more concerned with identifying practical solutions to existing problems, research conducted on peacekeeping can and should be directed toward accomplishing both of these goals.

Third, causal comparisons need to be made between peacekeeping and nonpeacekeeping experiences. This requires that nondeployed control groups be examined for comparison with deployed and nondeployed peacekeepers. In addition, obtaining good predeployment data would allow for predeployment-postdeployment comparisons.

Policy and Prevention

The shift in the nature of peacekeeping from the monitoring of ceasefires to the broad spectrum of activities that characterizes current peacekeeping operations has motivated serious discussion on the development of peacekeeping policies that are suitable to a variety of missions, including those missions characterized by ongoing violence. The Panel on United Nations Peace Operations convened in 2000 to review UN activities related to peace and security. This panel consisted of people who had been involved in various aspects of peace support operations, and their task was to examine shortcomings of the existing system, identify lessons that have been learned, and make recommendations for change. The panel successfully elucidated questions and concerns that needed addressing and provided directions for future policy. At this early stage, the testing and implementation of these policies are still in their infancy.

Nevertheless, many of the main concerns of the panel have focused on examining the principles of peacekeeping in a volatile or violent environment (e.g., Spieker, 2000). The panel recommends that some of the principles of classic peacekeeping be reexamined. First, the panel recognizes that the principle of maintaining impartiality and the use of nonviolence is wholly unsuited to conditions of ongoing conflict. In some cases, impartiality may actually hinder peacekeepers from achieving their objectives when those objectives include quelling violence. For instance, witnessing the slaughter of innocent, unarmed civilians and being prevented from intervening contributed to the mass slaughter of people in Bosnia-Herzegovina. Although the panel is now recommending that peacekeepers be able to exercise force, their mandates have to specifically dictate exactly how much, under what circumstances, and the means with which they are able to do so.

Second, it has been suggested that the principle of attaining the consent of all parties to intervene is inappropriate during conflict, when the UN is unlikely to get that consent from combating parties who are achieving their agendas. Although the UN is not yet prepared to interfere when their presence is not desired, they are seeking alternative means of obtaining consent; however, they have not yet established the criteria to determine which institutions should be called upon to make these judgments.

Third, clear mission mandates and objectives must be in place. The tasks peacekeepers are asked to perform must be realistically achievable in the time they're given. The rules of engagement must be clear and outline specifically when a peacekeeper can actively defend him- or herself and others and the means with which they are able to do so. To this end, the panel recommends that resources should be spent prior to a mission on fact-finding and, assessment and analysis of the situation, including information regarding how dangerous the situation is and how volatile it may become. The UN has been accused of assuming a best-case scenario prior to many peacekeeping deployments and therefore being ill prepared for less than ideal circumstances.

Fourth, one feature of peacekeeping is that on any given mission, troops may be sent on repeated periods of deployment with alternating periods of time spent at home. Although some theories have contended that having breaks between exposure to trauma may be refreshing or help build a resilience to future trauma, research on the relationship between exposure to trauma and PTSD suggests that repeated exposures to traumatic events at different points in time may be just as detrimental as ongoing trauma (Neria, Bromet, Sievers, Lavelle, & Fochtmann, 2002). Given this, the effects of experiencing multiple incidents of trauma over time may be cumulative, calling into question the existing norm of multiple deployments in which peacekeepers may be exposed to traumatic events on a repeated basis.

Fifth, the UN needs to be involved in conflict prevention at the earliest stages of a potential problem. This requires that member nations provide political and financial support to such missions; however, this has not always proven to be a simple task for the UN.

Intervention

At present, there is no clear consensus regarding appropriate or effective psychiatric interventions (Shigemura & Nomura, 2002). Given research findings that suggest that interpersonal processes such as social support

(Dirkzwager et al., 2003), group cohesion (Orsillo et al., 1998), and leadership (Chen & Bliese, 2002) may buffer the negative effects of experiencing violence in peacekeeping operations, efforts by the military to cultivate supportive social relationships may reduce the likelihood of deleterious psychological outcomes.

For a considerable time, conventional wisdom has suggested that following exposure to extremely traumatizing events, the optimal treatment strategy was to offer and sometimes mandate single sessions of *crisis intervention stress debriefing* (CISD). Recent research now strongly challenges that conventional wisdom. A recent meta-analysis by Van Emmerik, Kamphuis, Hulsbosch, and Emmelkamp (2002) suggests that, at best, single-session CISD may have no positive effects and in some cases may worsen the trauma. The potential for this well-intended intervention to cause harm may be so great as to require immediate and serious rethinking of a long held and pervasive belief about interventions for peacekeepers and other groups exposed to acute stressors.

One intervention that has met with success is that of *stress inoculation training* (SIT). Given that strain results from the individual's negative subjective appraisal of an event, SIT focuses on changing the individual's appraisal process through a series of steps. The individual is first asked to reconceptualize an event in a realistic manner. The second step involves the acquisition and rehearsal of coping skills to deal with the potentially stressful events. In the final step, these new coping skills are tested during the presentation of successively greater stressors (Thompson & Pasto, 2003).

Future Research Needs

The deleterious impact of violence on peacekeepers' well-being has been consistently established in multiple studies; however, little is known about the effects of violence on other outcomes, including peacekeeper performance and turnover, and how these ultimately affect organizational outcomes such as the success of peacekeeping operations. Outcomes such as performance and success are highly contextual and determined by the unique goals of each mission. As such, operationalization of these variables across contexts may be a challenge to researchers. One strategy may be to examine success and performance by asking peacekeepers about their perceptions of their own and their unit's success and performance. Understanding the strategies and methods that meet with success in intrastate peacekeeping is highly important given that peacekeepers' effectiveness has direct implications for the well-being of those whom they serve.

Another fruitful area for research for which peacekeepers may be an appropriate group for study is that of working in conditions of uncertainty. The violent and volatile environments in which peacekeepers often work, the unpredictability of these unstable environments, the presence of sometimes unclear objectives and strategies for conducting operations in nonpeaceful environments, and the potential for hostilities and lack of support by local populations may constitute a recipe for an intense experience of uncertainty in one's work. This may provide researchers with an opportunity to uncover some of the processes by which workers in ambiguous conditions make sense of their work and communicate this meaning to others.

Summary

Changes in peacekeeping since the end of the Cold War have led to a shift in the conditions in which peacekeepers must work. Peacekeeping was originally created to monitor relatively peaceful theaters, and the principles on which peacekeeping was founded are best suited to more stable environments. Now more than ever before, peacekeepers are required to confront theaters of violence and civil unrest. It has been suggested that these principles are wholly unsuited to unstable environments, and policymakers have recently called for the reexamination and refurbishing of these principles. Indeed, the notion that traditional peacekeeping is unsuited to violent environments is supported by grim data on how the well-being of peacekeepers has suffered as a result of these inconsistencies. Finding new methods for peacekeepers to achieve their objectives in contemporary, often violent, peacekeeping missions is of paramount importance. Doing so can help protect the well-being of peacekeepers, enhance the success of peacekeeping operations, and ultimately result in better outcomes for the populations the peacekeepers serve.

References

Adler, A. B., Litz, B. T., & Bartone, P. T. (2003). The psychology of the peacekeeper: Lessons from the field. *Psychological dimensions to war and peace* (pp. 149–167). Westport, CT: Praeger.

American Psychiatric Association. (1994). *Diagnostic and statistical manual of mental disorders* (4th ed.). Washington, DC: Author.

Bailes, A. J. K. (2003). Trends and challenges in international security. *SIPRI yearbook 2003: Armaments, disarmament and international security.* Oxford, UK: Oxford University Press.

Bandura, A. (1997). *Self-efficacy: The exercise of control.* New York: W. H. Freeman.

Barling, J., Rogers, A. G., & Kelloway, E. K. (2001). Behind closed doors: In-home workers' experience of sexual harassment and workplace violence. *Journal of Occupational Health Psychology, 6,* 255–269.

Bartone, P. T., Adler, A. B., & Vaitkus, M. A. (1998). Dimensions in psychological stress in peacekeeping operations. *Military Medicine, 163,* 587–593.

Blood, C. G., Zhang, J., & Walker, G. J. (2002). Implications for modeling casualty sustainment during peacekeeping operations. *Military Medicine, 167,* 868–872.

Bolton, E. E., Glenn, D. M., Orsillo, S., Roemer, L., & Litz, B. T. (2003). The relationship between self-disclosure and symptoms of posttraumatic stress disorder in peacekeepers deployed to Somalia. *Journal of Traumatic Stress, 16,* 203–210.

Bolton, E. E., Litz, B. T., Britt, T. W., Adler, A., & Roemer, L. (2001). Reports of prior exposure to potentially traumatic events and PTSD in troops poised for deployment. *Journal of Traumatic Stress, 14,* 249–256.

Boutros-Ghali, B. (1992). *An agenda for peace.* New York: United Nation.

Boutros-Ghali, B. (1995, January 3). *Supplement to an agenda for peace* (Position paper of the secretary-general on the occasion of the fiftieth anniversary of the United Nations). New York: United Nations.

Bramsen, I., Dirkzwager, A. J. E., van der Ploeg, H. M. (2000). Predeployment personality traits and exposure to trauma as predictors of posttraumatic stress symptoms: A prospective study of former peacekeepers. *American Journal of Psychiatry, 157,* 1115–1119.

Britt, T. W. (1998). Psychological ambiguities in peacekeeping. In H. J. Langholtz (Ed.), *The psychology of peacekeeping* (pp. 111–128). Westport, CT: Praeger.

Castro, C. A. (2003). Considerations when conducting psychological research during peacekeeping missions: The scientist and the commander. In T. W. Brit & A. Adler (Eds.), *The psychology of the peacekeeper: Lessons from the field* (Psychological dimensions to war and peace, pp. 11–27). Westport, CT: Praeger.

Chen, G., & Bliese, P. D. (2002). The role of different levels of leadership in predicting self- and collective efficacy: Evidence for discontinuity. *Journal of Applied Psychology, 87,* 549–556.

Dirkzwager, A. J. E., Bramsen, I., & van der Ploeg, H. M. (2001). The longitudinal course of posttraumatic stress disorder symptoms among aging military veterans. *Journal of Nervous and Mental Disease, 189,* 846–853.

Dirkzwager, A. J. E., Bramsen, I., van der Ploeg, H. M. (2003). Social support, coping, life events, and posttraumatic stress symptoms among former peacekeepers: A prospective study. *Personality and Individual Differences, 34,* 1545–1559.

Donovan, B. S., Padin-Rivera, E., Dowd, T., & Blake, D. D. (1996). Childhood factors and war zone stress in chronic PTSD. *Journal of Traumatic Stress, 9,* 361–368.

Dvir, T., Eden, D., Avolio, B. J., & Shamir, B. (2002). Impact of transformational leadership on follower development and performance: A field experiment. *Academy of Management Journal, 45,* 735–744.

Fairbank, J. A., Hansen, D. J., & Fitterling, J. M. (1991). Patterns of appraisal and coping across different stressor conditions among former prisoners of war with and without posttraumatic stress disorder. *Journal of Consulting and Clinical Psychology, 59,* 274–281.

Fairbank, J. A., Schlenger, W. E., Caddell, J. M., & Woods, M. G. (1993). Posttraumatic stress disorder. In P. B. Sutker & H. E. Adams (Eds.), *Comprehensive handbook of psychopathology* (2nd ed., pp. 145–165). New York: Plenum.

Farley, K. M. J., & Veitch, J. A. (2003). Measuring morale, cohesion and confidence in leadership: What are the implications for leaders? *Military leadership, 1,* 353–364.

Franke, V. (1997). Warriors for peace: The next generation of military leaders. *Armed Forces and Society, 24,* 33–59.

Garfield, R. M., & Neugut, A. I. (1997). The human consequences of war. In B. S. Levy & V. W. Sidel (Eds.), *War and public health* (pp. 27–38). New York: Oxford University Press.

Green, B. L., Grace, M. C., Lindy, J. D., Gleser, G. C., & Leonard, A. (1990). Risk factors for PTSD and other diagnoses in a general sample of Vietnam veterans. *American Journal of Psychiatry, 147,* 729–733.

Griffith, J. (1997). Test of a model incorporating stress, strain, and disintegration in the cohesion-performance relation. *Journal of Applied Social Psychology, 27,* 1489–1526.

Hotopf, M., David, A. H. L., Ismail, K., Unwin, C., & Wessely, S. (2003). The health effects of peacekeeping (Bosnia, 1992–1996): A cross-sectional study—comparison with nondeployed military personnel. *Military Medicine, 168,* 408–413.

Janis, I. L., & Mann, L. (1977). Emergency decision making: A theoretical analysis of responses to disaster warnings. *Journal of Human Stress, 3,* 35–48.

Jex, S. M., & Bliese, P. D. (1999). Efficacy beliefs as a moderator of the impact of work-related stressors: A multilevel study. *Journal of Applied Psychology, 84,* 349–361.

Kark, R., Shamir, B., & Chen, G. (2003). The two faces of transformational leadership: Empowerment and dependency. *Journal of Applied Psychology, 88,* 246–255.

Kulka, R. A., Schlenger, W. E., Fairbank, J. A., Hough, R. L., Jordan, B. K., Marmar, C. R., et al. (1990). *Trauma and the Vietnam War generation: Report of findings from the National Vietnam Veterans Readjustment Study* (Brunner/Mazel Psychosocial Stress Series, No. 18). Philadelphia: Brunner/Mazel.

Lamerson, C. D. (1995). *Peacekeeping stress: Testing a model of organizational and personal outcomes.* Unpublished doctoral dissertation.

Lamerson, C. D., & Kelloway, E. K. (1996). Towards a model of peacekeeping stress: Traumatic and contextual influences. *Canadian Psychology, 37,* 195–204.

Langholtz, H. J. (1998). *The psychology of peacekeeping.* Westport, CT: Praeger.

Lauterbach, D., & Vrana, S. (2001). The relationship among personality variables, exposure to traumatic events, and severity of posttraumatic stress symptoms. *Journal of Traumatic Stress, 14,* 29–45.

Lazarus, R. S. (1993). Coping theory and research: Past, present, and future. *Psychosomatic Medicine, 55,* 234–247.

Lazarus, R. S., & Folkman, S. (1991). The concept of coping. In A. Monat & R. S. Lazarus (Eds.), *Stress and coping: An anthology* (3rd ed., pp. 189–206). New York: Columbia University Press.

Lepore, S. J., Silver, R. C., Wortman, C. B., & Wayment, H. A. (1996). Social constraints, intrusive thoughts, and depressive symptoms among bereaved mothers. *Journal of Personality and Social Psychology, 70,* 271–282.

Litz, B. T. (1996). The psychological demands of peacekeeping for military personnel. *NCP Clinical Quarterly, 6,* 1–8.

Litz, B. T., King, L. A., King, D. W., Orsillo, S. M., & Friedman, M. J. (1997). Warriors as peacekeepers: Features of the Somalia experience and PTSD. *Journal of Consulting and Clinical Psychology, 65,* 1001–1010.

Litz, B. T., Orsillo, S. M., Friedman, M., Ehlich, P., & Batres, A. (1997). Posttraumatic stress disorder associated with peacekeeping duty in Somalia for U.S. military personnel. *American Journal of Psychiatry, 54,* 178–184.

MacDonald, C., Chamberlain, K., Long, N., & Mirfin, K. (1999). Stress and mental health status associated with peacekeeping duty for New Zealand defence force personnel. *Stress Medicine, 15,* 235–241.

McFall, M. E., Mackay, P. W., & Donovan, D. M. (1992). Combat-related posttraumatic stress disorder and severity of substance abuse in Vietnam veterans. *Journal of Studies on Alcohol, 53,* 357–363.

Mehlum, L., & Weisæth, L. (2002). Predictors of post-traumatic stress reactions in Norwegian U.N. peacekeepers one year after service. *Journal of Traumatic Stress, 15,* 17–26.

Meichenbaum, D. (1994). *A clinical handbook/practical therapist manual for assessing and treating adults with post-traumatic stress disorder (PTSD).* Waterloo, ON, Canada: Institute Press.

Michel, P., Larsson, G., & Lundin, T. (2000). Systematic assessment of mental health following various types of posttrauma support. *Military Psychology, 12,* 121–135.

Miller, L. L., & Moskos, C. (1995). Humanitarians or warriors? Race, gender, and combat status in Operation Restore Hope. *Armed Forces and Society, 21,* 615.

Moskos, C. C. (1975). The American combat soldier in Vietnam. *Journal of Social Issues, 31,* 25–37.

Neria, Y., Bromet, E. J., Sievers, S., Lavelle, J., & Fochtmann, L. J. (2002). Trauma exposure and posttraumatic stress disorder in psychosis: Findings from a first-admission cohort. *Journal of Consulting and Clinical Psychology, 70,* 246–251.

Orsillo, S. M., Roemer, L., Litz, B. T., Ehlich, P., & Friedman, M. J. (1998). Psychiatric symptomatology associated with contemporary peacekeeping: An examination of post-mission functioning among peacekeepers in Somalia. *Journal of Traumatic Stress, 11,* 611–625.

Pearlin, L. I. (1989). The sociological study of stress. *Journal of Health and Social Behavior, 30,* 241–256.

Pratt, L. I., & Barling, J. (1988). Differentiating between daily events, acute and chronic stressors. In J. R. Hurrell, L. R. Murphy, S. L. Sauter, & C. L. Cooper (Eds.), *Occupational stress: Issues and development in research* (pp. 42–50). London: Taylor Francis.

Schumm, W. R., & Bell, D. B. (2000). Soldiers at risk for individual readiness or morale problems during a six-month peacekeeping deployment to the Sinai. *Psychological Reports, 87,* 623–633.

Sharkansky, E. J., King, D. W., King, L., Wolfe, J., Erickson, D. J., & Stokes, L. R. (2000). Coping with Gulf War combat stress: Mediating and moderating effects. *Journal of Abnormal Psychology, 109,* 188–197.

Shigemura, J., & Nomura, S. (2002). Mental health issues of peacekeeping workers. *Psychiatry and Clinical Neurosciences, 56,* 483–491.

Spieker, H. (2000). The international criminal court and non-international armed conflicts. *Leiden Journal of International Law, 13,* 395–425.

Stajkovic, A. D., & Luthans, F. (1998). Social cognitive theory and self-efficacy: Going beyond traditional motivational and behavioral approaches. *Organizational Dynamics, 26,* 62–74.

Thompson, M. M., & Pasto, L. (2003). Psychological interventions in peace support operations: Current practices and future challenges. In T. W. Britt & A. B. Adler (Eds.), *The psychology of the peacekeeper: Lessons from the field.* Westport, CT: Praeger.

Udwin, O., Boyle, S., Yule, W., Bolton, D., & O'Ryan, D. (2000). Risk factors for long-term psychological effects of a disaster experienced in adolescence: Predictors of post traumatic stress disorder. *Journal of Child Psychology and Psychiatry and Allied Disciplines, 41,* 969–979.

UN Department of Peacekeeping Operations. (2005). Retrieved from www.un .org/Depts/dpko/fatalities/

UN Department of Public Information. (1996). *Blue helmets: A review of United Nations peace-keeping.* New York: Author.

Van Emmerik, A. A. P., Kamphuis, J. H., Hulsbosch, A. M., & Emmelkamp, P. M. G. (2002). Single-session debriefing after psychological trauma: A meta analysis. *Lancet, 360,* 766–771.

Ward, W. (1997). Psychiatric morbidity in Australian veterans of the United Nations peacekeeping force in Somalia. *Australian and New Zealand Journal of Psychiatry, 31,* 184–193.

Weisæth, L. (2003). Psychological dimensions to war and peace. In T. W. Britt & A. B. Adler (Eds.), *The psychology of the peacekeeper: Lessons from the field* (pp. 207–222). Westport, CT: Praeger.

Wheaton, B. (1997). The nature of chronic stress. In B. H. Gottlieb (Ed.), *Coping with chronic stress* (Plenum Series on Stress and Coping, pp. 43–73). New York: Plenum.

Wheaton, B. (1999). The nature of stressors. In A. V. Horwitz & T. L. Scheid (Eds.), *A handbook for the study of mental health: Social contexts, theories, and systems* (pp. 176–197). New York: Cambridge University Press.

15 Community Sources of Workplace Violence

Joerg Dietz
Harjinder Gill

W orkplace violence, extreme acts of aggression against employees while they are fulfilling their organizational duties, is a complex phenomenon with multiple antecedents. The vast majority of research on workplace violence has examined its individual and organizational antecedents, such as aggressive personalities (Douglas & Martinko, 2001) and mistreatment by managers and coworkers or excessive stress (e.g., Neuman & Baron, 1998). This individual and organization-internal approach to workplace violence, however, may not fully capture its complexity (cf. Howard & Voss, 1996).

Heeding Bennett and Robinson's (2003) call for more research on organization-external antecedents of workplace violence, this chapter presents a model of the community-based sources of violence in the workplace. In the remainder of this introduction, we describe the motivation for and importance of studying these sources, followed with a brief review of empirical research. We then discuss a theoretical model that links community variables, such as poverty and family disruption, to workplace violence.

The scientific interest in the communal antecedents of workplace violence has been very sparse (for an exception, see Dietz, Robinson, Folger, Baron, & Schulz, 2003). The first author became curious about these antecedents after colleagues reported that practitioners repeatedly raised the possibility that workplace violence constituted spillover from society at large into the workplace (see also Beugre, 1998; Laabs, 1999). The spillover perspective may be more than a self-serving rationalization by managers who would like to attribute workplace violence to factors beyond their responsibility (Dietz et al., 2003). It might echo the understanding of violence as a phenomenon that has many causes (e.g., Berkowitz, 1993) and is learned in different contexts (e.g., Guerra, Eron, Huesmann, Tolan, & Van Acker, 1997).

Authors' Note: The Social Sciences and Humanities Research Council of Canada supported this research with a grant (#410-2002-0637) to the first author.

A relation between variables in the communities in which organizations reside and violence in organizations would not surprise macro theorists (e.g., DiMaggio & Powell, 1983; Meyer & Rowan, 1977; Scott, 1992, 1995), who for many years have emphasized the impact of external environments on organizations. Because an organization is embedded in the social and cultural frameworks of its environment and therefore, at least partially, reflects features of it (Scott, 1992), Davis and Powell (1992) suggested that researchers should include an organization's environment in their studies of organizational behavior. On the basis of Scott's argument that the informal, normative aspects of an organization can have their roots in its environment, it is plausible that communal factors may transcend organizational boundaries and, hence, affect workplace violence.

Understanding the relation between communal factors and workplace violence is important for several reasons. First, given the severe implications of workplace violence for the involved individuals and organizations, any added knowledge about its antecedents is critical. For example, at the United States Postal Service (USPS), the extremely low number (statistically speaking) of 48 murdered postal workers killed by coworkers or others in a time span ranging from 1986 to 1999 in a workforce of over 900,000 employees led to an organizational image of the USPS as a violent place to work. Workplace violence also increases employee fears about becoming victims of workplace violence (e.g., U.S. Postal Service Commission on a Safe and Secure Workplace, 2000), decreases customer satisfaction (e.g., Walkup, 1999), and can have expensive legal ramifications (Dolan, 2000). Second, a theoretical model that allows the comparison of workplace violence with violence in the community is critical for establishing the utility of studying workplace violence as a unique phenomenon. If the antecedents for workplace and community violence were the same, one might question why (a) scientists only rarely conduct joint studies of workplace and communal violence and (b) at least some governments (e.g., the United States of America) have invested significant resources in understanding and combating workplace violence when extensive programs against communal violence already exist. Third, a model of communal factors of workplace violence is needed for understanding not only workplace violence in which employees are the instigators but also workplace violence in which employees are the victims. Despite the fact that the vast majority of workplace violence (e.g., homicides) is committed by organizational outsiders, theoretical models typically ignore outsider-instigated workplace violence (Howard & Voss, 1996). Finally, if workplace violence can, even partially, be traced back to communal factors, then organizational (and federal or communal) interventions against it should be restructured to address these factors.

Empirical Research

Despite acknowledgment that community factors may play a role in the prevalence of workplace violence, little empirical work has examined this important issue. For instance, health scientists have noted that violence in health care facilities is in part due to the characteristics of the community in which these facilities are located (Boyd, 1995; Hobbs & Keane, 1996; Holness, Somerville, Kosny, Gadeski, Mastandrea, & Sinclair, 2004); yet these researchers have not provided any empirical evidence to support this argument. Below, we review the few empirical studies on violence in organizations and schools. The reviewed studies were all conducted in the United States.

Violence in Organizations

Dietz et al. (2003), in a longitudinal study of 250 plants of a nationally operating public service organization, found that the 1992–1994 violent crime rates for the communities (cities and towns) where plants resided predicted the occurrence of assaults and credible threats of physical aggression by plant employees in a 14-month period in 1995 and 1996. Community violent crime rates, in fact, were a better predictor of these employee-instigated violent acts than were organization-internal climates of procedural justice (organizational members' shared perceptions of how they are treated in the workplace by other organizational members). Other community variables that indicated levels of poverty and family disruption, as well as the existence of subcultures of violence, did not predict workplace aggression.

In addition, a few studies have examined the antecedents of workplace homicides. Workplace homicides are willful or nonnegligent killings of employees in the line of duty by employees, former employees, or others (e.g., robbers) (Bureau of Labor Statistics, 2000). Dietz and Nolan (2001), in a state level study of 50 U.S. states, found that in states where in 1995 the killings of employees on the job were particularly prevalent, other homicides also occurred more frequently. Furthermore, workplace and other homicide rates shared several antecedents such as poverty rates, divorce rates, robbery rates, and cultures of violence. Loomis, Wolf, Runyan, Marshall, and Butts (2001) examined 105 workplaces in North Carolina where killings of employees occurred between 1994 and 1998 and compared them with similar workplaces where such killings did not occur. These researchers reported that the risk of homicide was modestly higher in counties with a higher population and higher rates of crime.

Violence in Schools

Gottfredson and Gottfredson (1985), in a seminal study, examined the relations between community characteristics and overall disruption, teacher victimization, and student victimization in a national sample of 642 public high schools. They found that teacher victimization and overall disruption was greater in schools that were located in urban communities characterized by poverty and social disorganization (communities with a high proportion of families headed by females, high rates of divorce or separation, high unemployment, and a high proportion of families on welfare). These schools were also more likely to be located in high population areas and away from business districts.

Consistent with Gottfredson and Gottfredson (1985), Hellman and Beaton (1986), in a study of the 120 public schools in Boston, found that community characteristics were related to suspension rates in middle and high schools. These suspensions typically result from violent or otherwise extremely deviant student behavior. These researchers observed that as community crime rates decreased, so did suspension rates. In addition, suspension rates were lower in communities characterized by a large number of traditional working class families. In these communities, for example, the proportion of nonfamily households is lower, few community members participate in the labor force (indicating a greater proportion of stay-at-home parents), and the percentage of the population who are children and the percentage of blue-collar workers are greater. Finally, suspension rates were also lower in districts with better housing conditions and a lower population density.

Mansfield, Alexander, and Farris (1991), in the 1990–1991 National Center for Education Statistics study of a national sample of 1,350 public school teachers, reported that differences across communities were related to teacher reports of school disorder. Teachers reported being threatened with physical violence more often in schools with a greater number of poor students (as indicated by the percentage of free or subsidized lunches) and in schools located in cities (as compared with rural communities). Felson, Liska, South, and McNulty (1994), in a sample of 2,213 male students from 67 randomly selected public high schools, similarly reported a greater prevalence of interpersonal violence and delinquency in schools with a greater proportion of low SES students. Welsh, Greene, and Jenkins (1999), in a study of 11 middle schools in the Philadelphia School District, also reported a link between communal poverty and student misconduct.

Summary of Empirical Research

Two observations about empirical research on community factors and workplace violence stand out. First, few studies have been conducted. Second, although the findings are not always consistent, several communal factors appear to be related to violence in organizations and schools. Most notably, communal violent crime rates tend to be related to violence in organizations and schools, and poverty tends to be related to school violence.

Theoretical Model of Community Sources of Workplace Violence

Overview

The proposed model of the community sources of workplace violence that is presented in Figure 15.1 has two levels of theory. Communal variables are

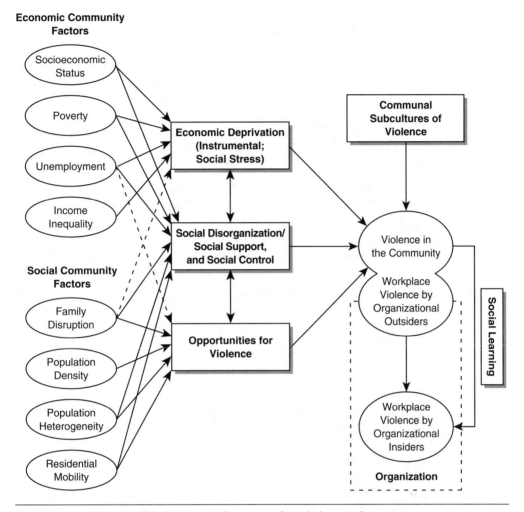

Figure 15.1　Basic Model of Communal Sources of Workplace Violence

conceptualized at the community level. *Community* has been defined as a geographic location determined by its members and local area organizations such as law enforcement, educators, and faith community (Bowen, Gwiasda, & Brown, 2004). Community violence research operationalizes communities typically on the basis of federal, city, town, or county categorizations. Communal variables affect workplace violence, which is conceptualized at the organizational level. As social entities, organizations are goal-directed, deliberately structured activity systems with identifiable boundaries (Bedeian, 1980). These boundaries demarcate the organization from the community.

Workplace violence refers to violence against employees while they fulfill their organizational duties. It can be instigated by organizational outsiders or insiders. Our model distinguishes outsider-instigated and insider-instigated workplace violence as they are expected to (a) have different antecedents and (b) be related such that outsider-instigated workplace violence predicts insider-instigated workplace violence (cf. LeBlanc & Kelloway, 2002). As an organizational level phenomenon, workplace violence is expected to differ systematically across organizations. The proposed model does not intend to predict which individuals are more likely to engage in workplace violence but rather (a) in which communities workplace violence rates are likely to be higher and (b) which organizations are likely to have higher rates of workplace violence.

Below we focus on fundamental theoretical processes that we argue drive communal violence and, indirectly or directly, also workplace violence. For the sake of simplicity, our approach is limited to the impact of community factors on workplace violence, although we acknowledge that an open systems perspective suggests reciprocal relationships between communities and the organizations that reside in them (see, for example, Catalano, Novaco, and McConnell's 1997 research that relates the fear of job losses to violence outside organizations). We open with a discussion of social learning processes that explain links between communal violence and workplace violence. Next, we briefly review cultural, economic, social, and opportunity-based explanations of violence.[1] We conclude with a discussion of additional explanations for effects of communal factors on workplace violence.

Social Learning

Dietz et al. (2003) proposed and found empirical support for a social learning perspective (e.g., Bandura, 1983) on the effects of communal violence on workplace violence (see also O'Leary-Kelly, Griffin, & Glew, 1996, for a social learning model of workplace aggression). Social learning theory suggests that aggressive behaviors are learned from others through several related processes such as imitating models of violence, reacting to situational cues, reacting to aversive treatment, and desensitization.

Members of organizations located in violent communities are more likely to be exposed to people who engage in violent behaviors. From these aggressive models, organizational members learn violent behavior through imitation and experience (e.g., Berkowitz, 1993; Robinson & O'Leary-Kelly, 1998). As a side effect, observing violent models heightens emotional arousal, which in turn can enhance aggressive tendencies (Berkowitz, 1993). Although family models of violence are particularly powerful, members of organizations in violent communities may learn violent behavior not only from their own family but also from customers and coworkers. Violent behavior may also be acquired through symbolic modeling (Wood, Wong, & Chachere, 1991). *Symbolic modeling* refers to the influence of reports of violence in media (e.g., newspaper and television) on violent behavior.

Furthermore, social learning theory suggests that people react to situational cues for violent behavior. *Aggression-cueing stimuli* include paired experiences and response consequences (Bandura, 1973). In *paired experiences,* a previously neutral stimulus, when repeatedly associated with aggressive action, begins itself to trigger aggression. For example, employees of organizations in violent communities may more frequently encounter abusive and aggressive customers. As a result, these employees may start to become aggressive as soon as customers enter the organization. *Response consequences* refer to the rewards or punishments associated with violent behavior. Social learning theory proposes that individuals learn not only violent behavior but also the circumstances in which this behavior is rewarded or punished. For example, a salesperson who observes that aggressive customers receive better service than do nonaggressive customers might be motivated to engage in aggressive behavior to receive better service as well.

Members of organizations in violent communities are also more likely to become victims of aversive treatment as a result of aggression. According to Bandura (1973), aversive treatment is the most reliable means of provoking aggression. In particular, the experience of physical aggression is commonly associated with violent responses. An example of an employee reacting to aversive treatment would be a store clerk who had been held at gunpoint by a robber subsequently lashing out against fellow employees and other customers.

Finally, the social learning effects of violent communities may also include the desensitization associated with watching aggressive models (O'Leary-Kelly et al., 1996). As Baron and Richardson (1994) stated, "Individuals exposed to aggressive actions on the part of others frequently may experience sharp reductions in the strength of their restraints against engaging in such behavior. After all, they may reason, if others aggress with impunity, it is all right for them to do likewise" (p. 104). Research has shown that the repeated exposure to aggression can make people more indifferent toward it (e.g., Rule & Ferguson, 1986; Thomas, Horton, Lippincott, & Drabman, 1977).

In summary, it is plausible that social learning processes might foster the diffusion of violence from communities into organizations. Moreover, these processes are likely to occur in violent communities more often. We view community violence as the most proximal communal antecedent to workplace violence and argue that social learning is a key process in explaining how violence spills over from communities into organizations. As Scott (1992, p. 20) noted, "Employees come to the organization with heavy cultural and social baggage obtained from interactions in other social contexts." We propose that employees develop violent "baggage" in violent communities.

Cultural Theories of Violence

In the model depicted in Figure 15.1, community violence is proposed to affect workplace violence by both organizational outsiders and insiders. Furthermore, the model proposes community violence is a mediating variable for the more distal influences of several other community factors on workplace violence. One such factor is a communal subculture of violence.

The fundamental assumption of theories about subcultures of violence is that individuals are socialized into deviant entities. As a result of the socialization process, group members share values, attitudes, and beliefs that promote or tolerate violent behaviors. Although several theories of subcultures of delinquency have been proposed (e.g., Cohen, 1955; Miller, 1958), we briefly review Wolfgang and Ferracuti's (1967) thesis of the subculture of violence and Nisbett and Cohen's (1996) theory about cultures of honor because of their focus on violence.

Wolfgang and Ferracuti (1967) proposed that violence among young poor men from minority groups could be explained by a set of values around machismo. In these groups, members value physical arguments as a means of showing courage and defending status. Furthermore, group members value toughness and excitement and show disregard for the value of human life. Nisbett and Cohen (1996) argued that certain regions in the United States (parts of the South and the West) historically had predominantly herding-based economies. Because herders are economically vulnerable to theft, they are particularly protective of their possessions and tend to rely on violence as a means of retaliation. This behavior led to development of cultures of honor, which continue to be influential in these regions.

Our model proposes an indirect effect of communal subcultures of violence on employee-instigated workplace violence. Essentially, within their organization, employees are assumed to adhere to organizational cultural norms and rules first (and to other cultural norms, including communal ones, second). Most organizations have very strict norms and rules against violence (among other things, most organizations do not allow weapons in the workplace), and violations of these rules and norms are typically associated with dismissal from the organization.

Theories of Economic Deprivation

A second group of theories that explain community violence are theories of economic deprivation. These theories assert that communal violence is more likely in communities with fewer economic resources. Economic deprivation is expected to lead to violence primarily through two mechanisms: First, economic deprivation is associated with a lack of resources for obtaining valued outcomes, and violence may provide an alternative means for getting these outcomes (the instrumental hypothesis). Second, economic deprivation is associated with greater stress and frustration, and violence may provide a cathartic release for these emotions (the social stress hypothesis). Economic deprivation, which can be conceptualized as absolute deprivation (operationalized as, for example, poverty and unemployment) or relative deprivation (operationalized as income inequality), has been consistently linked to violent crime (e.g., Boggs, 1965; Chiricos, 1987; Hsieh & Pugh, 1993; Miethe & Meyer, 1994).

Instrumental Hypothesis

The *instrumental hypothesis* is based on the assumption that members of poor communities value the same outcomes as do members of more affluent communities. Members of poor communities, however, are blocked from opportunities for achieving these outcomes (cf. Merton, 1957). They lack the financial resources, educational attainment, or access to legal recourse that members of more affluent communities have. Members of poorer communities then may resort to violence in order to obtain these desired outcomes.

Social Stress Hypothesis

The *social stress hypothesis* of economic deprivation can be viewed as a restatement of the frustration-aggression hypothesis at the macrolevel. Members of communities with fewer economic resources, or material disadvantage, experience a greater number of stressor events. The increased stress stems not only from a higher number of daily hassles but also from the humiliation that is associated with poverty (Kramer, 2000). The resulting strain may exceed their ability to cope and result in diffused hostility and violent aggression (Linsky, Bachman, & Straus, 1995).

Economic Deprivation and Workplace Violence

Economic deprivation has several implications for workplace violence: First, economic deprivation is likely a driver of outsider-instigated workplace violence that results from robberies and botched thefts. Second, economic deprivation is unlikely to be a direct antecedent of insider-instigated workplace violence because such violence is associated with job losses, reduced opportunities for reemployment, and, hence, enhanced economic deprivation (Catalano et al., 1997).

Theories of Social Disorganization, Social Support, and Social Control

Whereas theories of subcultures of violence and economic deprivation focus on mechanisms that provoke violent behavior, theories of social disorganization (Shaw & McKay, 1942), social support (Kramer, 2000), and social control (e.g., Hirschi, 1969) explain mechanisms that inhibit communal violence. This latter set of theories essentially proposes that violence is relatively rare in communities that are socially organized and where processes of social support and control are in place. Our review focuses on social disorganization theory as the potentially most comprehensive formulation of this approach to community violence.

Social disorganization theory posits that community level differences in violence may be explained by community level differences in the degree of social organization, characterized by solidarity, cohesion, and integration among community members. Socially organized communities have well-developed and connected local friendship networks, a high degree of involvement and participation in local organizations and institutions, and the ability to exercise social control over their members (cf. Akers, 2000) and provide social support for them. *Social control* refers to the sanctions and controls used in an effort to curb violent behavior, and *social support* refers to the provisions made to encourage the use of behaviors other than violence (Kramer, 2000). Both social control and support are exercised by significant others, friends, neighbors, and community networks (cf. Hirschi, 1969).

Numerous economic and social factors have been related to social disorganization (e.g., Sampson & Groves, 1989). Communities characterized by low socioeconomic status (SES), poverty, and high unemployment have fewer resources to invest in community organizations and, therefore, community members are less involved in these local institutions. This lack of involvement reduces opportunities to form close social networks necessary to maintain effective social control and support.

Population heterogeneity (the level of diversity in a community) decreases the social glue in a community. That is, in demographically diverse communities, the degree of solidarity, cohesion, and integration is lower. Consequently, there are fewer interactions among community members, resulting in fragmented and weakened social networks and a reduced ability to provide social support and exercise social control. Like population heterogeneity, high residential mobility (the extent to which people change dwellings) has a negative effect on social organization within communities. The consistent change of neighbors prevents the formation of strong local friendship networks.

Finally, in communities with a high degree of *family disruption* (a high percentage of single-parent families), the levels of social support and social control are also reduced. First, family disruption reduces a community's collective resources (e.g., fewer adults) for social support and control. Second, family disruption often leads to greater need for parents to work outside the home, thereby reducing the amount of supervision for youth and guardianship of community property. Third, family disruption typically curtails the economic resources available to invest in local area institutions.

Taken together, a lack of social organization through reduced social support and social control is associated with higher rates of community violence. Our model, however, does not propose a direct effect of communal social disorganization on workplace violence. Organizations as social entities exercise social control over and provide social support for their members independent of the surrounding community. Organizations' contractual relationships with their members and their smaller size are expected to make them more efficient in their exercise of control and the provision of support than are communities.

Opportunity Theories

The previously reviewed theories speak to the motivations (incentives or inhibitions) for or against engaging in violent behavior. Community members, even if they are motivated to engage in violent behavior, can only do so, however, if the opportunities for this behavior are available. *Opportunity theories* identify community characteristics that enhance or reduce the likelihood of opportunities for violence. In doing so, these theories (e.g., Bennett & Wright, 1984; Cohen, Kluegel, & Land, 1981; McIntosh, 1971, 1975) draw on characteristics that attract offenders (situational selection theories) and/or increase victimization (routine activity theories) (Birkbeck & LaFree, 1993).

Situational Selection Theories

McIntosh (1971, 1975) argued that a number of community factors (population density, family disruption, residential mobility, and unemployment) were associated with enhanced opportunities for offenders. As population density increases, offenders have more potential victims. Family disruption provides more opportunities for violence because it is associated with less guardianship of people and community property as fewer adults reside in the community and the remaining parents are more likely to work outside the home. Residential mobility sets up more opportunities for violence because of its association with weakened social ties. Weakened ties, in turn, mean greater anonymity and less likelihood that strangers (as offenders or victims) will be recognized.

Victimization Theories

Routine activities theory (Cohen & Felson, 1979; Cohen et al., 1981) is an opportunity theory that focuses on victimization (i.e., activity patterns under which community members are more likely to become victims of violence). The basic thesis of the routine activities approach is that differences in individuals' daily routines may explain differences in victimization. Weaker guardianship, greater attractiveness of targets (e.g., desirability of persons or property), and greater exposure are key factors that promote victimization (Cohen & Felson, 1979). Family disruption, population heterogeneity, and residential mobility can be associated with daily routines that enhance the likelihood of victimization.

Opportunity Theories and Workplace Violence

For understanding how opportunity theories explain workplace violence, it is interesting to note that these theories have provided contradictory propositions about the role of unemployment. On the one hand, it has been argued that higher unemployment rates mean that more community members have more time to get into troublesome situations that lead to violence (Crutchfield, 1989). On the other hand, according to the routine activities approach, greater unemployment should be negatively related to violence because fewer community members are in the public as employees (less exposure) and more community members are around their homes (greater guardianship). Furthermore, if population density is associated with a higher percentage of service organizations and customer contact employees, opportunity theories may predict in which communities workplace violence constitutes a relatively higher proportion of overall violence. It is noteworthy that there is variance across organizations in the provision of opportunities for violence (i.e., some organizations, because they store and possess money and valued goods, are more attractive to offenders than are other organizations). This variance, however, does not stem from community factors but from organizational factors, on which we will briefly touch below.

Additional Explanations for Effects of Communal Factors on Workplace Violence

Our model proposes that with the exception of community violence, communal factors affect workplace violence only indirectly. We view this model as outlining the basic and predominant processes for the communal sources of workplace violence. We acknowledge, however, that communal sources may affect workplace violence also through three other processes, which are graphically represented in Figure 15.2: (a) If the permeability of organizational boundaries is high, communal factors may directly affect workplace violence; (b) if the attractiveness of organizations for violence (e.g., because they possess valued goods and money) is particularly high, they are more likely to have high rates of outsider-instigated workplace violence; and (c) communal factors may affect organizational constructs other than workplace violence, such as organizational cultures, which in turn may affect workplace violence. These processes, on which we elaborate below, complement those outlined in the basic model.

Permeability of Organizational Boundaries

As mentioned earlier, organizations are demarcated from communities through their boundaries. The permeability of these boundaries for community influences varies by organization: Schools, for example, can be expected to have more permeable boundaries with their communities than do manufacturing plants. As boundary permeability increases, boundaries lose their buffering function against outside influences. Then organizational phenomena, including workplace violence, become more susceptible to these influences.

It is important to acknowledge that students of organizational design (e.g., Sherman & Schultz, 1998) have observed the rise of the open-boundary organization. The design of open-boundary organizations is particularly popular

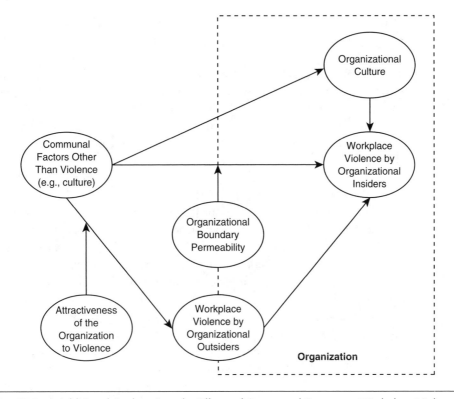

Figure 15.2   Additional Explanations for Effects of Communal Factors on Workplace Violence

in the growing service sector. Although open boundaries are viewed as having many advantages for organizations (e.g., increased customer involvement and loyalty), it is logical that open boundaries also increase the vulnerability of organizations to negative communal factors such as poverty and family disruption. We speculate that the inconsistent effects of communal factors on workplace violence can partially be explained by boundary permeability. For example, the fact that poverty is consistently linked to school violence, but rarely if at all linked to violence in work organizations, may have to do with the higher permeability of school boundaries.

Attractiveness of Organizations to Violence

As indicated above, an application of opportunity theories to organizations implies that some organizations are more attractive to violent offenders than are others. In particular, organizations that store and possess money and valued goods are likely to be the targets of robberies and thefts. Other factors, such as the relatively low protection of organizational property (for example, in mom-and-pop stores), also make organizations attractive targets for violent offenders. Therefore, the impact of communal factors on outsider-instigated workplace violence varies as a function of the attractiveness of organizations to violent offenders.

Boundary Permeability and Attractiveness to Violence as Explanations for Cross-Level Effects

As mentioned earlier, community factors are community level constructs, whereas workplace violence is an organizational level construct. As an organizational level construct, workplace violence can vary across organizations, although they are located within the same community. In other words, our model suggests cross-level effects of community factors on workplace violence. The question arises: How can this be the case, as all organizations within the same community are subject to the same community influences (cf. Klein, Dansereau, & Hall, 1994)?

The answer to this question lies in our arguments on boundary permeability and attractiveness to violence. These arguments can be recast as *interaction hypotheses:* (a) The permeability of organizational boundaries moderates the effects of communal factors on workplace violence such that these effects grow stronger as organizational boundaries become more permeable; and (b) the attractiveness of organizations to violence moderates the effects of communal factors on outsider-instigated workplace violence such that these effects become stronger as organizations become more attractive targets for violent offenders. In other words, depending on their boundary permeability and attractiveness to violent offenders, organizations vary in their receptiveness to community influences. These moderation hypotheses account for differences in the rates of workplace violence between organizations within the same community. It also explains the cross-level effects of community factors. If there were no moderators of the relationship between community factors and workplace violence, workplace violence rates across organizations within a community would be equally affected by community factors and, hence, could be conceptualized at the same level as community factors (the community level).

Effects of Communal Factors on Organizational Cultures

Earlier we mentioned that organizational macro theorists have for many years argued that organizations are affected by their environments, including the communities in which they are embedded. Scott (1992), for example, noted that the "social structure of the organization will reflect important features borrowed from or impressed on it by the environment" (p. 21) and that both formal and informal elements of the organization can have their roots in the environment. Thus, although communal factors, with the exception of community violence, may not directly affect workplace violence, they likely affect other organizational constructs such as organizational cultures. Organizational cultures, in turn, affect workplace violence (cf. O'Leary-Kelly et al., 1996).

Cohen and Nisbett (1997) theorized about the link between regional norms that legitimized violence in certain conditions and organizational norms for violence. According to their arguments, organizations (a) are affected by communal norms for violence, (b) perpetuate norms of violence congruent with the cultures in their surrounding communities, and (c) provide public representations of norms that establish guidelines for acceptable behavior. In a fascinating U.S. study, Cohen and Nisbett found that when organizations received letters from job applicants who had allegedly killed someone, organizations in geographical areas with aggression-tolerating cultures of honor reacted more positively to these letters than did organizations that were not located in these areas. In their examination of the effect of community and organizational variables on workplace violence, Dietz et al. (2003) found that two communal variables, unemployment rates and regional cultures of honor, were negatively related to organizational procedural justice climates and that median household income was positively related to organizational procedural justice climates. Procedural justice climate, in turn, had a weak positive zero-order effect on rates of workplace assaults and credible threats of such assaults. These studies do not provide evidence of a direct relation between communal factors and workplace violence, but they do imply the possibility of an indirect link that is mediated by other organizational constructs.

Conclusion

A model is presented that links community factors to workplace violence. Among these community factors, only community violence is proposed to directly affect insider-instigated workplace violence. Other economic and social community factors, such as poverty and family disruption, may affect insider-instigated workplace violence through community violence. Our model, however, allows for direct effects of these other community factors on workplace violence under two conditions: if organizations (a) have highly permeable boundaries and (b) are particularly attractive to violent offenders.

At the beginning of the chapter, we argued that a model of the communal antecedents of workplace violence is important for four reasons. First, workplace violence has enormous costs for the involved individuals and organizations. For their earlier reviewed study of 250 plants of a nationwide operating U.S. organization, Dietz et al. (2003) estimated that whether these plants were located in more or less violent communities was associated with an annual $1,100,000 difference in costs for workplace violence. Second, our model suggests a more fine-grained distinction between workplace violence and community violence. In our model, community factors have the same effects on community violence and outsider-instigated workplace violence, but insider-instigated violence is differently affected by community factors. Hence, a distinction between insider-instigated workplace violence and community violence is conceptually justified. Third, heeding Howard and Voss's (1996) call, our model explains outsider-instigated and insider-instigated workplace violence, thereby covering the full range of the violence that affects employees. Finally, our model points out that interventions against workplace violence can not be limited to organization-internal factors but must include community factors as well. To conclude, we hope that the proposed model inspires research on a largely neglected but important topic: the impact of community factors on workplace violence.

Note

1. For the sake of clear presentation, these explanations are presented under separate headings. Note that this does not imply that these explanations are conceptually independent. The contrary is the case, as these explanations are related to each other and partially overlap.

References

Akers, R. L. (2000). *Criminological theories: Introduction, evaluation, and application* (3rd ed.). Los Angeles: Roxbury.

Bandura, A. (1973). *Aggression: A social learning analysis.* Englewood Cliffs, NJ: Prentice Hall.

Bandura, A. (1983). Psychological mechanisms of aggression. In R. G. Geen & E. I. Donnerstein (Eds.), *Aggression: Theoretical and empirical reviews* (Vol. 1, pp. 1–40). New York: Academic.

Baron, R. A., & Richardson, D. R. (1994). *Human aggression.* New York: Plenum.

Bedeian, A. G. (1980). *Organizations, theory and analysis.* Hinsdale, IL: Dryden.

Bennett, R. J., & Robinson, S. L. (2003). The past, present, and future of workplace deviance research. In J. Greenberg (Ed.), *Organizational behavior: The state of the science* (2nd ed., pp. 247–281). Mahwah, NJ: Lawrence Erlbaum.

Bennett, T., & Wright, R. (1984). Constraints on burglary: The offender's perspective. In R. Clarke & T. Hope (Eds.), *Coping with burglary* (pp. 181–200). Boston: Kluwer-Nijhoff.

Berkowitz, L. (1993). *Aggression: Its causes, consequences, and control.* Philadelphia: Temple University Press.

Beugre, C. D. (1998). Understanding organizational insider-perpetrated workplace aggression: An integrative model. In P. A. Bamberger & W. J. Sonnenstuhl (Eds.), *Research in the sociology of organizations: Deviance in and of organizations* (Vol. 15, pp. 163–196). Greenwich, CT: JAI.

Birkbeck, C., & LaFree, G. (1993). The situational analysis of crime and deviance. *Annual Review of Sociology, 19,* 113–137.

Boggs, S. L. (1965). Urban crime patterns. *American Sociological Review, 30,* 899–908.

Bowen, L. K., Gwiasda, V., & Brown, M. M. (2004). Engaging community residents to prevent violence. *Journal of Interpersonal Violence, 19,* 356–367.

Boyd, N. (1995). Violence in the workplace in British Columbia: A preliminary investigation. *Canadian Journal of Criminology, 37,* 491–519.

Bureau of Labor Statistics. (2000). *National census of fatal occupational injuries, 1999.* Washington, DC: Author.

Catalano, R., Novaco, R., & McConnell, W. (1997). A model of the net effect of job loss on violence. *Journal of Personality and Social Psychology, 72,* 1440–1447.

Chiricos, T. G. (1987). Rates of crime and unemployment: An analysis of aggregate research evidence. *Social Problems, 34,* 187–212.

Cohen, A. (1955). *Delinquent boys.* New York: Free Press.

Cohen, D., & Nisbett, R. E. (1997). Field experiments examining the culture of honor: The role of institutions in perpetuating norms about violence. *Personality and Social Psychology Bulletin, 23,* 1188–1199.

Cohen, L. E., & Felson, M. (1979). Social change and crime rate trends: A routine activity approach. *American Sociological Review, 44,* 588–608.

Cohen, L. W., Kluegel, J. R., & Land, K. C. (1981). Social inequality and predatory criminal victimization: An exposition and test of a formal theory. *American Sociological Review, 46,* 505–524.

Crutchfield, R. D. (1989). Labor stratification and violent crime. *Social Forces, 68,* 489–512.

Davis, G. F., & Powell, W. W. (1992). Organization-environment relations. In M. D. Dunnette & L. M. Hough (Eds.), *Handbook of industrial and organizational psychology* (Vol. 3, pp. 315–375). Palo Alto, CA: CPP.

Dietz, J., & Nolan, N. (2001, August). *Workplace homicides: A state-level study.* Paper presented at the 2001 Academy of Management Conference, Washington, DC.

Dietz, J., Robinson, S. L., Folger, R., Baron, R. A., & Schulz, M. (2003). The impact of community violence and an organization's procedural justice climate on workplace aggression. *Academy of Management Journal, 49,* 317–326.

DiMaggio, P. J., & Powell, W. W. (1983). The iron cage revisited: Institutional isomorphism and collective rationality in organizational fields. *American Sociological Review, 48,* 147–160.

Dolan, J. B.. (2000). Workplace violence: The universe of legal issues. *Defense Counsel Journal, 67,* 332–341.

Douglas, S. C., & Martinko, M. J. (2001). Exploring the role of individual differences in the prediction of workplace aggression. *Journal of Applied Psychology, 86,* 547–559.

Felson, R. B., Liska, A. E., South, S. J., & McNulty, T. L. (1994). The subculture of violence and delinquency: Individual vs. school context effects. *Social Forces, 73,* 155–173.

Gottfredson, G. D., & Gottfredson, D. C. (1985). *Victimization in schools.* New York: Plenum.

Guerra, N. G., Eron, L. D., Huesmann, L. R., Tolan, P., & Van Acker, R. (1997). A cognitive-ecological approach to the prevention and mitigation of violence and aggression in inner-city youth. In D. P. Fry & K. Björkqvist (Eds.), *Cultural variation in conflict resolution: Alternative to violence* (pp. 199–213). Mahwah, NJ: Lawrence Erlbaum.

Hellman, D. A., & Beaton, S. (1986). The pattern of violence in urban public schools: The influence of school and community. *Journal of Research in Crime and Delinquency, 23,* 102–127.

Hirschi, T. (1969). *Causes of delinquency.* Berkeley: University of California Press.

Hobbs, F. D. R., & Keane, U. M. (1996). Aggression against doctors: A review. *Journal of the Royal Society of Medicine, 89,* 69–72.

Holness, L. D., Somerville, S., Kosny, A., Gadeski, J., Mastandrea, J. J., & Sinclair, G. M. (2004). Workplace health and safety concerns in service organizations in the inner city. *Journal of Urban Health, 81,* 489–497.

Howard, J. L., & Voss, R. B. (1996). "Organization-motivated aggression: A research framework": Comment. *Academy of Management Review, 21,* 920–922.

Hsieh, C. C., & Pugh, M. D. (1993). Poverty, income inequality, and violent crime: A meta-analysis of recent aggregate data studies. *Criminal Justice Review, 18,* 182–202.

Klein, K. J., Dansereau, F., & Hall, R. J. (1994). Levels issues in theory development, data collection, and analysis. *Academy of Management Review, 19,* 195–229.

Kramer, R. C. (2000). Poverty, inequality, and youth violence. *Annals of the American Academy of Political and Social Science, 567,* 123–129.

Laabs, J. (1999). Columbine tragedy sparks HR debate over workplace violence. *Workforce, 78,* 20–21.

LeBlanc, M. M., & Kelloway, E. K. (2002). Predictors and outcomes of workplace violence and aggression. *Journal of Applied Psychology, 87,* 444–453.

Linsky, A. S., Bachman, R., & Straus, M. A. (1995). *Stress, culture and aggression.* London: Yale University Press.

Loomis, D., Wolf, S. H., Runyan, C. W., Marshall, S. W., & Butts, J. D. (2001). Homicide on the job: Workplace and community determinants. *American Journal of Epidemiology, 154,* 410–417.

Mansfield, W., Alexander, D., & Farris, E. (1991). *Teacher survey on safe, disciplined, and drug-free schools.* Washington, DC: National Center for Education Statistics.

McIntosh, M. (1971). Changes in the organization of thieving. In S. Cohen (Ed.), *Images of deviance* (pp. 98–133). London: Penguin.

McIntosh, M. (1975). *The organization of crime.* London: Macmillan.

Merton, R. K. (1957). *Social theory and social structure* (Rev. ed.). New York: Free Press.

Meyer, J. W., & Rowan, B. (1977). Institutionalized organizations: Formal structure as myth and ceremony. *American Journal of Sociology, 83,* 340–363.

Miethe, T. D., & Meyer, R. F. (1994). *Crime and its social context: Toward an integrated theory of offenders, victims, and situations.* Albany: State University of New York Press.

Miller, W. B. (1958). Lower class culture as a generating milieu of gang delinquency. *Journal of Social Issues, 14,* 5–19.

Neuman, J. H., & Baron, R. A. (1998). Workplace violence and workplace aggression: Evidence concerning specific forms, potential causes, and preferred targets. *Journal of Management, 24,* 392–419.

Nisbett, R. E., & Cohen, D. (1996). *Culture of honor: The psychology of violence in the South.* New York: Westview.

O'Leary-Kelly, A. M., Griffin, R. W., & Glew, D. J. (1996). Organization-motivated aggression: A research framework. *Academy of Management Review, 21,* 225–253.

Robinson, S. L., & O'Leary-Kelly, A. M. (1998). Monkey see, monkey do: The influence of work groups on the antisocial behavior of employees. *Academy of Management Journal, 41,* 658–672.

Rule, B. G., & Ferguson, T. J. (1986). The effects of media violence on attitudes, emotions, and cognitions. *Journal of Social Issues, 42,* 29–50.

Sampson, R., & Groves, W. (1989). Community structure and crime: Testing social-disorganization theory. *American Journal of Sociology, 94,* 774–802.

Scott, W. R. (1992). *Organizations: Rational, natural, and open systems* (3rd ed.). Englewood Cliffs, NJ: Prentice Hall.

Scott, W. R. (1995). *Institutions and organizations.* Thousand Oaks, CA: Sage.

Shaw, C. R., & McKay, H. D. (1942). *Juvenile delinquency and urban areas.* Chicago: University of Chicago Press.

Sherman, H., & Schultz, R. (1998). *Open boundaries: Creating business innovation through complexity.* Reading, MA: Perseus Books.

Thomas, M. H., Horton, R. W., Lippincott, E. C., & Drabman, R. S. (1977). Desensitization to portrayals of real-life aggression as a function of exposure to television violence. *Journal of Personality and Social Psychology, 35,* 450–458.

U.S. Postal Service Commission on a Safe and Secure Workplace. (2000, August). *Report of the United States Postal Service Commission on a Safe and Secure Workplace.* New York: National Center on Addiction and Substance Abuse at Columbia University.

Walkup, C. (1999, September 13). Customer satisfaction: Security. *Nation's Restaurant News,* pp. 102–104.

Welsh, W. N., Greene, J. R., & Jenkins, P. H. (1999). School disorder: The influence of individual, institutional, and community factors. *Criminology, 37,* 73–115.

Wolfgang, M. E., & Ferracuti, F. (1967). *The subculture of violence: Towards an integrated theory in criminology.* London: Tavistock.

Wood, W., Wong, F. Y., & Chachere, G. J. (1991). Effects of media violence on viewers' aggression in unconstrained social interaction. *Psychological Bulletin, 109,* 371–383.

16 The Consequences of Partner Violence on Employment and the Workplace

Jennifer E. Swanberg
TK Logan
Caroline Macke

The phenomenon of partner violence is a pervasive social problem that plagues many people. According to data from the National Violence Against Women Survey (NVAWS), lifetime prevalence rates of partner violence have been estimated at 25% for women and 8% for men (Tjaden & Thoennes, 2000). The study further indicated that 1.5% of women and 0.9% of men have experienced partner violence in the past year (Tjaden & Thoennes, 2000). These figures suggest that approximately 1.5 million women and 834,732 men are subjected to partner violence annually in the United States alone (Tjaden & Thoennes, 2000). Though already alarming, these numbers may be underestimates of partner violence because victims may underreport partner violence on surveys and/or because data sources may lack information identifying victim-perpetrator relationships (Bachman & Salzman, 1995; Straus & Gelles, 1990).

Data further indicate that partner violence is not just a domestic issue; rather, it has workplace implications. According to the National Crime Victimization Survey, between 1992 and 1996, an average of 18,000 people were assaulted by an intimate partner at work each year (Warchol, 1998). The Bureau of Justice Statistics reports that among the 1 to 2 million employees victimized at work, intimates are identified as the perpetrator in approximately 1% to 3% of all workplace violence incidents (Duhart, 2001). Moreover, women are five times more likely than men to be attacked at work by a current or former intimate partner (Bachman, 1994). More specifically, 2.2% to 5% of female victimizations and 0.2% to 1% of male victimizations on the job are perpetrated by a current or former intimate partner (Bachman, 1994).

Furthermore, despite recent increased attention to employee-motivated aggression in the workplace, analysis of the National Crime Victimization Survey data shows that employees are nearly as likely to be assaulted by a partner at work as by a coworker, and female employees killed in the workplace are more likely to be killed by a partner than by a coworker (Warchol, 1998).

The organizational costs associated with partner violence when it spills over into the workplace, further referred to as workplace partner violence (WPV), are significant. The Bureau of National Affairs (BNA; 1990) estimates that employers spend $3 to $5 billion yearly on consequences related to WPV, including lost productivity, employee turnover, and health care costs. Further, partner violence interferes with victims' ability to maintain consistent employment and results in an approximate loss of $18 million in earnings each year for victims of partner violence (Greenfeld, Rand, Craven, Klaus, Perkins, & Ringel, 1998).

Although the Occupational Safety and Health Administration (OSHA) includes "violence by personal relations" as a form of workplace violence and provides voluntary measures for addressing WPV, there has been limited attention to partner violence as a workplace violence issue. Few organizations have taken an active stance against partner violence or have developed formal policies to address this problem when it traverses the workplace (Johnson & Indvik, 1999). Furthermore, as Bell, Moe, and Schweinle (2002) assert, the management field has neglected to focus on the intersection of partner violence and the workplace. In a review of literature using the ABI/Inform database,[1] Bell et al. found that between 1990 and 2000, 551 articles pertaining to *workplace violence* and 269 pertaining to *domestic violence* were published in management journals. Yet, when the two terms were combined, the search resulted in only 23 articles published in six management journals.

The purpose of this chapter is to illuminate the relationship between partner violence and workplaces by reviewing what is known about the consequences of partner violence on employment from an individual perspective and an organizational perspective. Specifically, the chapter reviews research and related literature pertaining to the following: (a) definitions and consequences of partner violence; (b) job interference tactics used by perpetrators; (c) victimized employee level consequences of WPV; (d) organizational level consequences of WPV; (e) employer responses to WPV; and (f) the issues surrounding workplace disclosure of partner violence. Implications for future research and practice are discussed.

Definitions and Consequences

Working definitions of partner violence vary from study to study. For our purpose, we have adopted the definition used by the Centers for Disease Prevention and Control (cf. Saltzman, Fanslow, McMahon, & Shelley, 1999):

Intimate partner violence is actual or threatened physical or sexual violence or psychological and emotional abuse directed toward a spouse, ex-spouse, current or former boyfriend or girlfriend, or current or former dating partner. Intimate partners may be heterosexual or of the same sex. Typical terms used to describe intimate partner violence include *domestic abuse, spouse abuse, partner violence,* and *battering,* among others. The term *partner violence* is used in this chapter because it refers to violence specifically between intimate partners rather than other terms that may go beyond the intimate relationship to include violence in the family. Because the terms *intimate partner violence* and *partner violence* are often used interchangeably, we opted to use the latter to simplify the writing and reading of the chapter.

Interference Tactics: Actions That Negatively Affect Employment

Exerting control over victims' employment or job opportunities is a form of victimization used by batterers to intimidate their partners (MacMillan & Gartner, 1999). Studies have estimated that 36% to 75% of employed partner violence victims were bothered by their abusive partners while at work (Shepard & Pence, 1988; Swanberg, Macke, & Logan, 2005; Taylor & Smith Barusch, 2004). The strategies used by abusers are varied, yet somewhat universal. A review of the research literature implies that job interference tactics can be grouped into two primary categories: work disruption and work-related stalking.

Work Disruption

Work disruption consists primarily of actions that prevent the victim from reaching the workplace either on time or at all; as such, these actions predominantly take place in the home or off the workplace premises. A review of the few studies that focus on this topic reported a variety of techniques (Brandwein, 2000; Moe & Bell, 2004; Raphael, 1995, 1996; Swanberg & Logan, 2005). Results from a national 12-site, welfare-to-work evaluation study indicated that participants' abusers disrupted employment efforts by depriving victims of sleep, refusing to care for children while participants went to work, hiding or destroying clothing or books, inflicting physical injury on participants prior to work, turning off the alarm clock, cutting off participants' hair to prevent victims from going to work, or creating an embarrassing or threatening situation at participants' work (Raphael, 1995, 1996).

Qualitative studies reported similar findings. In a qualitative study of 34 employed or recently employed women, participants identified tampering with the car or failing to show up with the car as examples of tactics used by their partner or former partner to interfere with work (Swanberg & Logan,

2005). A qualitative study of 24 ethnically diverse battered women receiving public assistance in two regionally disparate states reported such work-disruptive tactics as hiding clothes, not showing up to care for young children, or beating respondent women prior to work, thereby preventing them from reporting to their jobs (Brandwein, 2000). In another qualitative study using semistructured interviews, 19 study participants who were all residents of domestic violence shelters reported that the physical ramifications of the abuse (bruises, cuts, ripped clothing) were the primary way abusers sabotaged employment (Moe & Bell, 2004). In summary, the primary work disruption tactics used by perpetrators to interfere with victims' job performance include (a) direct physical abuse to prevent victim from going to work and (b) indirect interference by not providing child care, sabotaging transportation, destroying work clothing, and threatening to cause harm.

Work-Related Stalking

Workplaces are common arenas for perpetrators to stalk victims because the work location often remains unchanged even when the residence has changed, and perpetrators may know the work schedule of their partner or former partner (Chenier, 1998; Libbus, Sable, Huneke, & Anger, 1999). *Stalking* is generally defined as the unwelcome and repeated harassing or threatening behavior directed at one individual (Tjaden & Thoennes, 1997; Westrum & Fremouw, 1998). Examples of stalking behavior include following a person, appearing outside or showing up at a person's home or place of business, leaving written messages or objects, or vandalizing a person's property. Analysis of the NVAWS reveals that 81% of women who were stalked by an intimate also reported physical assault by that same partner, and 31% also reported sexual assault by that partner (National Institute of Justice and Centers for Disease Control [NIJ/CDC], 1998). Lifetime prevalence rates suggest that between 5% and 8% of women and between 1% and 2% of men will be stalked at some time in their lives (Tjaden & Thoennes, 1998, 2000), whereas data suggest that between 0.5% and 1% of women and between 0.2% and 0.4% of men suffer at the hands of a stalker each year (Tjaden & Thoennes, 1998, 2000).

The literature suggests that work-related stalking behavior parallels general stalking behavior. Specifically, the types of behaviors exhibited by a batterer at or near a victim's workplace can be grouped into two dimensions of work-related stalking: on-the-job surveillance and on-the-job harassment. On-the-job surveillance behaviors identified in the literature include perpetrator looking into the window of the workplace, perpetrator waiting for the victim at the end of the workday, or perpetrator waiting for victim along commuting route (Raphael, 1996; Swanberg & Logan, 2005). On-the-job harassment incidents were identified as events in which the perpetrator physically appeared on the workplace premises or when the perpetrator made telephone calls to victims, their coworkers, or supervisors.

In the literature reviewed, the prevalence of *on-the-job surveillance* ranged from 35% to 52% (Raphael, 1996; Swanberg et al., 2005; Swanberg & Logan, 2005; Tolman & Rosen, 2001). For instance, among employed women who filed domestic violence orders (DVOs) within the previous 12 months, 35% reported that they had been observed or closely watched by their abusive partner within the last year (Swanberg et al., 2005). Raphael's (1996) previously described study of a dozen welfare-to-work programs identified on-the-job surveillance as a primary interference tactic used by batterers. Similar patterns emerged in Swanberg and Logan's (2005) qualitative study of 34 employed or recently employed victims of partner violence. Designed to examine the effects of partner violence on women's employment using semi-structured interviews and focus groups, their study found that about half the women in the sample reported specifically being stalked at work. Finally, an employer-based survey of 46 Canadian corporations brought a slightly different perspective to the study of on-the-job surveillance (Schell, 2003). The cross-section study of 46 firms—randomly selected from 1,782 corporations listed in a Canada-based human resource directory to participate in a survey—focused on the prevalence of work-related stalking and sexual harassment among employees. The study reported that 8 of the 46 firms reported stalking incidents in their organizations. In total, 19 stalking incidents were reported to human resource professionals over the 5-year span of the study. A spouse or boyfriend perpetrated 32% of reported stalking cases.

The prevalence of *on-the-job harassment* ranged from 8% to 75% (for example, see Brush, 2000, 2002; Friedman & Couper, 1987; Stanley, 1992; Swanberg et al., 2005; Taylor & Smith Barusch, 2004; Tolman & Rosen, 2001). On-the-job harassment tactics included appearing at work, disallowing employed victims to complete work functions (Brush, 2002; Friedman & Couper, 1987; Swanberg et al., 2005; Swanberg & Logan, 2005; Taylor & Smith Barusch, 2004), or making frequent telephone calls to victims, coworkers, or supervisors (Brush, 2000; Friedman & Couper, 1987; Swanberg & Logan, 2005). One study conducted by the Victim Services Unit in New York surveyed 50 employed or recently employed intimate partner victims to better understand how violent partners interfere with women's work (Friedman & Couper, 1987). Seventy-five percent of respondents reported that their abusive partner harassed them on the job either in person or on the phone over the previous 12 months. Comparable findings were reported by Stanley's (1992) study of 118 women victimized by their partners and receiving services from a domestic violence intervention service agency in Tulsa, Oklahoma. Among the sample of employed or recently employed respondents, 70% were telephoned excessively while at work. Swanberg et al. (2005), in their previously mentioned study, reported that in the previous 12 months, 40% of respondents were harassed in person, 34% had been threatened at work, and 24% bothered coworkers while at work. Similar results emerged from an in-depth, descriptive study of long-term welfare recipients (Browne, Salomon, & Bassuk, 1999).

Other research investigations indicated that on-the-job harassment occurred less frequently. Using the first wave of the Women's Employment Study, a three-wave study of welfare recipients in an urban Michigan county, Tolman and Rosen (2001) examined the prevalence of partner violence and its association with health, mental health, and economic well-being. Among the 753 female participants, 23% reported they had been harassed at work or school at some time in their lives and 7% in the previous 12 months. Slightly more conservative statistics were reported in Lloyd's (1997) study of a random household survey that examined the effects of partner violence on the labor force participation of 824 women living in a low-income neighborhood. Among the 802 female respondents who were or had been in an adult relationship with a man in the past, 8.7% of the sample reported on-the-job harassment by phone and 7.8% reported on-the-job harassment in person during their lifetimes. Thus, as evidenced by the reviewed literature, partner violence traverses the workplace in a variety of ways posing challenges to employees and employers.

The consequences of partner violence in general and work interference specifically have major ramifications for the victimized employee (individual level consequences) and the workplace where the victim is employed (organizational level consequences). The following two sections review these consequences. As will be discussed, individual level consequences can lead to some of the identified organizational level consequences.

Victimized Employee Level Consequences of Workplace Partner Violence

Information gleaned from the limited number of small studies suggests that at least 66% of employed victims of partner violence report problems in the workplace as a result of the abuse (Friedman & Couper, 1987; Stanley, 1992; Swanberg & Logan, 2005; Tolman & Rosen, 2001). For instance, Swanberg et al. (2005) report that in a study of women with a DVO against an intimate partner, 71% of women were unable to concentrate at work because of recent partner victimization, and 63% were unable to perform on the job to the best of their ability. Similarly, Stanley (1992) found that 96% of employed victims of partner violence reported that their jobs were affected by victimization, and Friedman and Couper (1987) reported 66% of their sample were late to work because of the abuse.

Yet the research pertaining to the relationship between partner violence and employment, including victims' employment patterns, is complex. Studies focusing on the effect of partner violence on victims' employment can be grouped into two general categories: (a) empirical studies of the relationship between experiencing partner violence and employment patterns and (b) empirical studies identifying and documenting the extent to which abusers' actions interfere with victims' ability to work and perform on the job (see Tolman & Raphael, 2000, for review).

Workplace Partner Violence and Employment Patterns

The studies focusing on the relationship between partner violence and employment patterns are inconclusive as to the exact effects of partner violence on victims' employability. It is difficult to determine at this time the effect that partner violence has on short-term and long-term job stability, employability, and earnings (Riger & Staggs, 2004; Tolman & Raphael, 2000). In their comprehensive literature review of research on welfare and domestic violence, Tolman and Raphael (2000) report that some victims of partner violence struggle to obtain employment, others manage to secure a job but fail to maintain it, and still others cannot obtain employment at all. Thus, the authors conclude that partner violence does interfere with employment but does not necessarily prevent it. That is, cumulative findings suggest that partner violence does not affect employment status; rather it affects the victim's ability to sustain consistent employment for long periods of time.

Two cross-sectional studies (Lloyd, 1997; Lloyd & Taluc, 1999) report no evidence to suggest that victims of partner violence are employed at different rates than their nonvictim counterparts. Analyses using data collected on the effects of male violence on women's labor force participation indicated that women who experienced partner violence were as likely to be employed as women who had not experienced such victimization; however, findings from both studies indicate that victims of partner violence were more likely to have been unemployed in the past and that partner violence may depress socioeconomic status and occupational attainment over time (Lloyd, 1997; Lloyd & Taluc, 1999).

Another set of studies further illuminates the complexity of the long-term relationship between partner violence and women's employment. Data from the second and third wave of a longitudinal study of an ethnically diverse group of extremely poor women were analyzed to determine the relationship between partner violence and work over time (Browne & Bassuk, 1997; Browne et al., 1999). Controlling for demographic, psychosocial, and health factors, the study found that "women who were victimized by male intimate partners during the previous year had only one third the odds of maintaining employment for at least 30 hours per week for 6 months or more during the subsequent year as compared with women without victimization experiences" (p. 417). The effect was even greater for women working 40 hours or more per week. Specifically, women working full-time who had been victimized (within the past year) were only about 20% as likely to work full-time for 6 months or more the following year, compared with nonvictimized women. As such, these studies suggest that partner violence may negatively affect employment intensity (hours worked per week) rather than employment status.

Workplace Partner Violence and Employee Outcome Consequences

Although it is difficult to draw persuasive and strong conclusions about the long-term consequences of partner violence on women's employment because of the limited studies conducted to date, studies that identify and document the extent to which abusers' actions interfere with victims' ability to work and perform on the job appear to allow for some tentative conclusions. Overall, the research seems to be in agreement that compared with nonvictims, victims of partner violence are more likely to report lower productivity, higher absenteeism rates, more frequent tardiness, and higher job turnover rates and job losses (Raphael, 1996; Shepard & Pence, 1988; Tolman & Rosen, 2001). Furthermore, the literature is conclusive that partner violence has a profound impact on health, mental health, and substance use (for reviews see Campbell, 2002; Logan, Walker, Cole, & Leukefeld, 2002; Logan, Walker, Jordan, & Campbell, 2004; Logan, Walker, Jordan, & Leukefeld, 2005).

The following section reviews the research literature pertaining to the following four negative job-related consequences of partner violence: reduced productivity, increased absenteeism, increased tardiness, and job loss, as well as negative health-related consequences.

Productivity

Using the ability to concentrate on the job as a proxy measure for productivity, several cross-sectional studies report that partner violence victims' productivity was compromised by their victimization (Brush, 2000, 2002; Raphael, 1996; Stanley, 1992; Swanberg et al., 2005; Swanberg & Logan, 2005). The lack of concentration may result from before-work circumstances, on-the-job harassment, phone harassment, stalking, or depression resulting from the abuse (Friedman, Brown Tucker, Neville, & Imperial, 1996; Raphael, 1996; Stanley, 1992). As an example, Stanley's (1992) study of 82 battered employed women who were enrolled in domestic violence related treatment services reported that 70% of participants were too distracted by the violence to perform well at work. Swanberg et al. (2005) found that 71% of employed or recently employed women reported they were unable to concentrate at work because of the abuse at home. Sixty-three percent of women in this same study were unable to perform on the job to the best of their ability during the previous year. Data also suggest that partner violence victims' inability to concentrate is strongly associated with their fear of the perpetrator (Raphael, 1996; Swanberg & Logan, 2005).

The relationship between cognitive distraction and interrole conflict has been established in the literature (Barling, Zacharatos, & Hepburn, 1999; MacEwen & Barling, 1991). When pressures within the work or family domain interfere with the fulfillment of role responsibilities in another domain, employees may become distracted or suffer cognitive difficulties. In essence, WPV is an extreme form of interrole conflict. Further, research has also demonstrated a relationship between sexual harassment, cognitive distraction, and impaired academic performance (Barling et al., 1996). Students who have experienced sexual harassment suffered from cognitive distraction, which resulted in lower academic performance (Barling et al., 1996). Because very little research has explored the intersection between partner violence and employment outcomes, looking to the related literature, including the sexual harassment literature, may provide some valuable insight into the possible consequences of partner violence on work performance.

Absenteeism

Partner violence victims also have significant absenteeism rates (Brush, 2002; Johnson, 1995; Sable, Libbus, Huneke, & Anger, 1999; Shepard & Pence, 1988; Swanberg et al., 2005). Research found that between 23% and 85% of employed partner violence victims reported being absent from work due to the abuse, with between 4% and 6% reporting that this happened frequently (Allard, Albelda, Collen, & Cosenza, 1997; Friedman & Couper, 1987; Raphael, 1996; Shepard & Pence, 1988; Stanley, 1992; Taylor & Smith Barusch, 2004; Tolman & Rosen, 2001). Friedman and Couper (1987) found that 54% of their employed and victimized sample of 50 women had missed an average of 3 days of work per month because of injuries, shame, depression, or attending appointments with lawyers or law enforcement for issues directly related to the partner violence. Taylor and Smith Barusch (2004) reported that 36% of women receiving public assistance had to stay home from work because of domestic violence. Nearly 6% of women in Tolman and Rosen's (2001) study missed work as a direct result of the victimization.

In response to this absenteeism, Shepard and Pence (1988) found that 44% of their sample of 71 battered women had been reprimanded by their employer. Reasons partner violence victims failed to report to work included reports of being prohibited or prevented from going to work, fearing for children's safety, fatigue related to abuse, and fearing for their own safety (Lloyd, 1997; Raphael, 1996; Raphael & Tolman, 1997; Shepard & Pence, 1988; Stanley, 1992). Between 12% and 75% of employed partner violence victims reported being prohibited from attending work in this way in their lifetime (Friedman & Couper, 1987; Lloyd, 1997; Raphael, 1996). Furthermore, data from one quantitative study of an ethnically diverse female sample of 734 women receiving public welfare found that abused women in their sample were more likely than those never victimized to have a current or former partner who would not want them to go to work or school (Allard et al., 1997). Specifically, partner violence victims were 15 times more likely to be involved with a partner who would not want the victim to be involved in professional activities compared with women who did not have an abusive partner. In addition, women reported having to leave work early (Brush, 2002; Swanberg & Logan, 2005). The culmination of similar findings led Raphael and Tolman (1997) to conclude that victims with partners who do not want them to work are more likely to report late or miss work.

Tardiness

Employed partner violence victims also experience higher rates of tardiness (Friedman & Couper, 1987; Raphael, 1996; Shepard & Pence, 1988). Studies suggest that 50% to 65% of partner violence victims reported being late for work or leaving work early due to the partner violence (Friedman & Couper, 1987; Raphael, 1996; Shepard & Pence, 1988; Swanberg & Logan, 2005). Further, Raphael (1996) found that 13% of the victims who reported being late to work also reported that this type of tardiness occurred frequently. Friedman and Couper (1987) reported that 20% of their sample was late for work because their partners tried to prevent them from going to work by engaging in a variety of prework tactics. Similarly, Swanberg and Logan (2005) found that nearly two thirds of participants frequently reported to work late because of batterers' prework tactics. Reported reasons for tardiness in all three studies included the abuser turning off an alarm clock or the victim being too exhausted after violent or aggressive incidents the night before, needing extra time to cover bruises, waiting for painkillers to take effect, or the batterer physically restraining the woman from leaving for work, hiding her car keys, and refusing at the last minute to assist with child care.

Job Loss and Turnover Rates

Cross-sectional studies indicate that 5% to 27% of victims reported a job loss as a direct result of the partner violence (Riger, Raja, & Camacho, 2002; Romero, Chavkin, Wise, & Smith, 2003; Sable et al., 1999; Shepard & Pence, 1988; Stanley, 1992; Swanberg & Logan, 2005). In addition, partner violence victims experience higher turnover rates than nonvictims (Romero et al., 2003). Romero et al.'s longitudinal study of 504 low-income mothers found that women with victimization histories were more than twice as likely to lose a job because of health-related issues as nonvictimized women. Shepard and Pence (1988) reported that 24% of their sample of 71 employed victimized women lost a job in the last year as a direct result of the abuse. Similarly, one third of participants in another study reported that the abuse had caused them to lose a job (Stanley, 1992). Swanberg and Logan (2005) reported that 91% of respondents had resigned or had lost a job in the last year as a direct result of victimization.

Women's reasons for quitting their jobs included shame associated with the victimization situation, fear for their own and their children's safety, embarrassment associated with abusers' continued on-the-job harassment, unreliability of child care, and abuser forcing them to resign (Moe & Bell, 2004; Shepard & Pence, 1988). Moe and Bell also found that battered women quit jobs because they feared for their lives and as a consequence needed to seek safety.

Health and Mental Health Consequences

Extensive research pertaining to partner violence indicates that partner violence has deleterious effects on victims' physical and mental health (see Campbell, 2002; Campbell et al., 2002; Logan et al., 2002; Logan et al., 2004; Logan et al., 2005; Plitcha, 1996, for review). Health consequences of victimization can be broken down into three main categories: acute health problems (e.g., bruises, broken bones); chronic health problems, which may be directly associated with the violence or may have been existing and are exacerbated by the violence; and stress-related health problems (e.g., pain, unexplained symptoms, sleep difficulties). Partner violence is more than twice as likely to cause injury as stranger violence (Bachman & Salzman, 1995). Moreover, 41% of violent attacks by intimates that cause injury require medical attention, compared with 20% of stranger attacks involving injury (Bachman & Salzman, 1995). In addition, partner violence is associated with mental health problems such as posttraumatic stress disorder, anxiety, and depression, as well as higher rates of substance use and abuse (Campbell, 2002; Campbell et al., 2002; Logan et al., 2002; Logan et al., 2004; Logan et al., 2005). These more indirect results of partner violence may affect work performance in a number of ways, including productivity, absenteeism (due to sick days or doctor or mental health visits), and job loss due to poor performance.

Summary

Although research on individual level consequences of WPV is scarce, available studies suggest that perpetrator interference tactics affect victimized employees in a variety of deleterious ways. The personal ramifications of WPV include lowered productivity, increased absenteeism and tardiness, and heightened job loss and turnover rates. The ramifications associated with WPV are particularly disconcerting as they result in a compromised employability of the victim. Specifically, although victims may not be employed at lower rates as compared with nonvictims, they are less likely to maintain consistent employment.

Organizational Level Consequences
of Workplace Partner Violence

Until recently, partner violence has been a social problem that has virtually been ignored by workplaces (Duffy, Scott, & O'Leary-Kelly, 2005; Johnson & Indvik, 1999). Within the past decade, some organizations have become more aware of partner violence as a social problem and its associated economic and social costs and consequences to workplaces. As a result, some firms have taken action to combat this social issue at the workplace level. Data suggest that 10,000 to 60,000 partner violence incidents are perpetrated within the workplace each year (Bachman, 1994; Warchol, 1998). As illustrated in the previously reviewed literature, the impact that WPV has on employee victims is evident; however, the negative consequences of WPV may also transfer over to secondary victims (see Bell et al., 2002, for review; Brownell, 1996; Duffy et al., 2005; Kinney, 1995; Zachary, 2000). Secondary victims are individuals who are not the primary target of the aggressive or violent episode but rather are accidentally injured or harmed by it. In the workplace, this might include coworkers or supervisors of the primary target or customers or other individuals who happen to be in the work area at the time of the WPV episode. Secondary victims may also be traumatized or harmed by witnessing or physically affected by the incident and, as such, may suffer similar negative effects including physical and psychological health problems (Bell et al., 2002; Brownell, 1996; Duffy et al., 2005; Kinney, 1995). In turn, these health effects may result in similar consequences as experienced by the primary victims: reduced productivity, increased tardiness, and increased turnover or job loss.

The organizational consequences associated with partner violence have the possibility of costing employers enormous sums of money (BNA, 1990). In contrast, when the social issue is addressed as a workplace issue, the social and economic costs can be significantly reduced (Friedman et al., 1996; Pereira, 1995; Petty & Kosch, 2001). Identifying and quantifying these costs is a first step in persuading organizational leaders that partner violence has significant consequences for workplaces and that action is needed to eradicate its radiating effects (Duffy et al., 2005). The following section reviews the limited literature on the four types of organizational costs associated with partner violence: production, medical, administrative, and liability costs.

Organizational Costs

Production Costs

As was noted earlier, primary and secondary victims of partner violence frequently display lowered productivity within the organization (see Bell et al., 2002, for review; Brownell, 1996; Duffy et al., 2005; East, 1999; Johnson,

1995; Kinney, 1995; Raphael, 1996; Zachary, 2000). Over half of partner violence victims miss 3 or more workdays per month (Zachary, 2000). Lowered productivity may result from partner violence victims' use of work time to secure resources or make phone calls prohibited at home (Wilson, 1997). Such lowered productivity at the individual level (e.g., through difficulties in concentrating) results in an overall lowered productivity of the company, involving a lowered quality and/or quantity of organizational output (Brownell, 1996; Chenier, 1998; Johnson & Indvik, 1999; Zachary, 2000).

Medical Costs

The second prominent cost increase experienced by organizations due to partner violence occurs in the area of medical expenses. As mentioned above, partner violence has been associated with health and mental health problems that may increase health-related costs. In other words, the consequences of partner violence on primary victims may lead to higher employee benefit costs, increased health insurance premiums, and increased sick leave expenditures (Bell et al., 2002; Brownell, 1996; Chenier, 1998; Family Violence Prevention Fund [FVPF], 1999; Greenfeld et al., 1998; Johnson & Indvik, 1999; Moe & Bell, 2004; Reynolds, 1997; Wisner, Gilmer, Saltzman, & Zink, 1999; Zachary, 2000). As an example, Wisner et al. (1999) found that $1,775 more was spent on each partner violence victim annually compared with that spent on a random sample of health plan enrollees. One hundred and twenty-six women were randomly identified by using diagnostic codes indicative of partner violence. All women were referred to mental health services for partner violence–related treatment from 1992 to 1994 and were continuously enrolled in the health plan for 2 years. A random selection of 1,007 nonvictimized women from the same health plan was used as a comparison group to determine if there was variation in health expenditure costs. Computerized analyses of health plan records suggest that partner violence victims had more general ambulatory clinic and mental health clinic visits than the other women. In particular, mental health costs were 800% higher among identified victims (Wisner et al., 1999). It is important to note that strained economic circumstances are associated with stress, health problems, and mental health symptoms and likely to decrease access to health and mental health services (Pamuk, Makuc, Heck, Reuben, & Lochner, 1998; Scott Collins et al., 1999). Thus, if health records were not inclusive of lower-income women, the health cost differential between victims of partner violence and other women may be higher than noted in the above-described study.

Administrative and Liability Costs

Increased absenteeism, tardiness, and turnover of primary and secondary victims result in increased administrative costs for the organization (Bell et al., 2002; Brownell, 1996; Chenier, 1998; Johnson & Indvik, 1999; Reynolds,

1997; Zachary, 2000). These administrative costs include leave or transfer costs, separation costs, and replacement costs (hiring and training costs; Bell et al., 2002).

Legal liability is also an important consideration for organizations battling with partner violence. Employers are obligated to protect employees at work from "recognized hazards that are causing or are likely to cause death or serious harm . . . to employees" as is stipulated by OSHA's General Duty Clause (Chenier, 1998; Johnson & Indvik, 1999; Petty & Kosch, 2001). According to Petty and Kosch (2001), "Employers are obligated to do everything reasonably necessary to protect the life, safety, and health of employees." This suggests that an employer, once informed of a potential partner violence–related risk situation, may be held liable if reasonable steps were not taken to protect the safety of the employees. If the organization was aware of an impending danger yet didn't take steps to prevent it, OSHA may fine the organization between $25,000 and $70,000 for serious health hazard (Petty & Kosch, 2001).

In contrast, when employees see their organizations investing in them and going out of their way to help them, perceptions of organizational support increase (Eisenberger & Huntington, 1986), as does affective commitment (Meyer & Allen, 1991, 1997). As such, organizations that consider partner violence as a workplace issue may cultivate secondary benefits. Implementing policies aimed to thwart aggressive acts and cultivating cultures of zero tolerance of any aggressive or violent acts may promote employee loyalty and commitment to the company.

Additional costs borne by employers as a result of partner violence include increased security costs, increased workers' compensation costs, increased legal costs, lost business, damaged reputation, and damaged property (Bell et al., 2002; Chenier, 1998; Johnson & Indvik, 1999).

Summary

Workplace partner violence places a heavy financial burden on employers in the form of increased production, medical, administrative, and liability costs. These costs, incurred by both primary and secondary victims of WPV, add up to an estimated $3 to $5 billion annually (BNA, 1990). Addressing WPV at the organizational level would subsequently benefit not only the victims but also the organization's bottom line.

Employer Responses to Workplace Partner Violence

The previous cost assessments associated with partner violence expose the possible fiscal liability that organizations are likely to incur if and when intimate partner violence is disregarded as a workplace concern. The following section reviews the current knowledge about employers' responses to partner violence.

Employer Attitudes and Actions

Given the potential expenses incurred by organizations due to partner violence (BNA, 1990), executives have slowly begun to view partner violence as an issue worthy of attention in the workplace. As noted in the information compiled by the FVPF (1999; see Table 16.1), it is apparent from several studies pertaining to employer views of partner violence that there is an awareness of the problem but not a general consensus on the negative consequences associated with this social ill when it spills over into the workplace.

Although over half of business executives recognize that partner violence is a workplace issue and that there are significant expenses associated with partner violence, research suggests that few organizations have taken an active stance against partner violence or have developed formal policies for dealing with it (Johnson & Indvik, 1999); however, as illustrated in the popular press, businesses are slowly beginning to take the issue seriously. A *Wall Street Journal* article published in 1995 suggested that a concern to "keep talent, reduce absenteeism, and avoid liability" is moving organizations to take action against partner violence (Pereira, 1995, p. B1). For instance, corporations, including Liz Claiborne, Polaroid Corporation, and CoreStates Financial Corporation, have developed a set of companywide personnel and management policies and support services specifically tailored to victims of partner violence (Friedman et al., 1996). As a result, they have set an

Table 16.1   Corporate Attitudes Pertaining to Partner Violence

- 57% of senior corporate executives believe partner violence is a major social problem
- 33% of senior corporate executives believe partner violence has a negative impact on their companies' bottom lines
- 40% of senior corporate executives reported that they were personally aware of employees and other individuals affected by partner violence
- 66% of senior corporate executives believed that their organization's financial performance would benefit from addressing partner violence within their organizations
- 47% of senior corporate executives believed that partner violence has a negative impact on their organizations' productivity
- 44% of senior corporate executives believed that partner violence increases the health care costs of the organization
- 94% of security directors from 248 companies across 27 states ranked partner violence as "high" on the scale of security problems
- 78% of human resource professionals polled by *Personnel Journal* said domestic violence is a workplace issue

SOURCE: Family Violence Prevention Fund [FVPF] (1999)

example for other businesses to follow (Friedman et al., 1996; Pereira, 1995; Petty & Kosch, 2001).

Although information in the popular press and in a few studies reports that some firms are working to reduce the risk of WPV by creating prevention and protection programs, empirical evidence suggests that employers sometimes respond to partner violence incidents perpetrated on the job by terminating the primary victim (Browne et al., 1999; Moe & Bell, 2004; Shepard & Pence, 1988; Stanley, 1992; Swanberg & Logan, 2005). For instance, Swanberg and Logan reported that a participant was terminated because her partner did not comply with her supervisor's request to stay off the workplace premises. Other research participants in the same study were asked to leave because of excessive absences, poor work performance, or a general concern that her abusive partner placed coworkers at risk for harm. Shepard and Pence (1988) found that many research participants lost their jobs because of excessive absences, tardiness, and poor productivity. Further, although participants did not report termination as the reason for job loss, Browne et al. (1999) report that only one third of women in their study were able to maintain their jobs for 6 months or more the year following a partner violence incident.

Job termination by employers for behaviors related to victimization may exacerbate the economic abuse from which victims often already suffer and lead women to turn to public programs for financial assistance (Tolman & Raphael, 2000). Substantial research has documented the importance of financial independence in overcoming violent relationships (Campbell, Rose, Kub, & Nedd, 1998; Gelles, 1976; Lloyd, 1997; Moe & Bell, 2004; Shepard & Pence, 1988; Strube & Barbour, 1984); thus, terminating partner violence victims may be especially detrimental from the victim's perspective. Additionally, such actions have economic ramifications for businesses. Termination of employees is associated with heightened administrative costs (see Bell et al., 2002, for review; Brownell, 1996; Chenier, 1998; Johnson & Indvik, 1999; Reynolds, 1997), including separation and replacement costs (hiring and training costs; Bell et al., 2002). As such, terminating partner violence victims may not be in the best interest of the organization either.

Workplace Supports

Research within the interdisciplinary field of work and family demonstrates that a growing number of organizations have implemented policies and practices to help employees balance their work and family responsibilities (Galinsky & Bond, 1998); however, research also suggests that unless organizations create a workplace culture that promotes the use of the policies and practices, programs will have little impact on employees' well-being and organizational outcomes (see Allen, Herst, Bruck, & Sutton, 2000, for a review; Bond, Galinsky, & Swanberg, 1998). Accordingly, workplace supports are generally categorized into two groups: informal and formal. Examples of informal workplace supports include supervisor or coworker offering informal emotional support or supervisor allowing for occasional flexibility with starting and quitting times. Examples of formal workplace supports include employee assistance programs (EAPs), flexible schedule arrangements, or the opportunity for telecommuting.

Though research within the work and family field has reported positive employee outcomes with the adoption of formal and informal "family-friendly" workplace practices, few organizations have recognized WPV as a work-family matter, as well as a workplace violence matter. Thus, limited research has investigated the relationship between WPV, workplace supports, and employee outcomes. The limited literature that does address the topic suggests that organizations have other options besides terminating victims of partner violence. As one example, employers have the option of providing formal and/or informal support as a strategy to assist employees.

Three studies were identified that specifically examined whether organizations provided any type of workplace support to WPV victims. Swanberg and Logan (2005), Swanberg et al. (2005), and Swanberg and Macke (in press) conducted investigations on the consequences of partner violence on employment and the role of workplace supports. The first study (Swanberg & Logan, 2005) asked participants if they received any type of support at work to assist with the partner violence and if so whether it helped them maintain their job. About half the participants received either formal or informal supports. Informal supports included supervisors and coworkers providing a listening ear, screening phone calls, or allowing an employee to leave early on occasion. Formal supports included management allowing an employee to modify his or her starting and quitting times as a strategy to enhance victim's security, referring an employee to an EAP, or referring employees to the organization's formal workplace violence policy specific to partner violence.

In the second study (Swanberg et al., 2005), among the 331 women who told someone at work about the abuse, the majority received either informal or formal supports from coworkers or supervisors. Examples of informal supports included a "listening ear" (90%), assistance from coworkers during break times (62%), screening intrusive telephone calls from the abusive partner (46.5%), assistance with creating a security plan should partner threaten to come to the workplace (44%), and general information about where to go for help with violence at home (32%). Examples of formal supports offered by workplaces included supervisor approved schedule flexibility to attend to personal matters (73%), workload flexibility (49.5%), and referrals to counseling (15%).

In the third study (Swanberg & Macke, in press), a workplace violence study ($N = 868$) conducted within a medium size municipality, 34 employees reported experiencing partner violence within the last year. Among these employees, 15 received some type of formal or informal workplace support. As in the first study, the types of informal supports included supervisor or coworker providing a listening ear, screening phone calls, or allowing an employee to leave early on occasion. Formal supports included supervisor allowing an employee to adjust starting and quitting times, referring an employee to an EAP, or referring employees to the organization's formal WPV policy and resource list. Among the 15 employees who received some type of workplace support, all employees were completely satisfied with the support they received, and they reported that it helped them to stay employed and to stay focused at work.

In contrast, another study reported less positive findings. Stanley's (1992) study indicated that only 20% of the research participants had been offered any assistance by their employer. The quality of the assistance, as reported by research participants, was either value-laden or simplistic in nature, as evidenced by such comments to the victims as, "Why don't you just leave him?" The limited research available suggests that receiving both informal and formal workplace supports is valued and consequently promotes loyalty among employed victims. Yet given the extremely small sample size and study limitations, conclusions must be drawn with caution.

Nonetheless, drawing on organizational research within the employee assistance field, Brownell (1996) recommends that employers maximize workplace safety and therefore workplace productivity by instituting a range of formal employer policies specific to partner violence. Brownell offers a broader definition of workplace supports. She categorizes possible formal workplace supports as prevention, protection, or intervention services. Examples of such services are provided in Table 16.2.

Prevention-focused formal supports such as security personnel are often already in place within medium and larger firms to assume the responsibility of handling workplace violence incidents; however, security personnel may need to be trained on how to manage WPV, or new personnel may need to be hired to provide prevention and intervention supports (Brownell, 1996). Protection-focused formal supports such as flexible work arrangements, screening phone calls, or providing leave with job security are workplace policies designed to keep employees safe and to keep them employed, whether it be at an alternate job site or an alternate work schedule. The third type of formal workplace support includes programs such as EAPs. EAPs in particular can be especially effective in assisting employees who are experiencing partner violence (Chenier, 1998). EAPs can benefit employees and also result in an economic saving for the employer by increasing productivity, decreasing absenteeism, and strengthening morale (Chenier, 1998). The U.S. Department of Labor concluded that every dollar invested in EAPs resulted in savings of $5 to $16 (Chenier, 1998).

Though several companies, such as Polaroid, Liz Claiborne, and Marshall's (Brownell, 1996), have pioneered the provision of such formal workplace supports to their employees, there is no research indicating the outcomes of such supports. Although it is speculated that such supports may enhance victims' ability to maintain employment, empirical evidence is lacking. This clearly constitutes an area for further research.

Table 16.2   Formal Employer Supports

Prevention	Protection	Intervention
Partner violence education programs for supervisors: helping supervisors recognize warning signs and enhancing familiarity with community partner violence resources	Leave time without penalty so employee can keep court appointments or go to safe shelters	Employee assistance programs (EAPs) staffed with partner violence professionals
	Flexible work hours	Counseling services through EAPs
Partner violence education programs for employees encouraging disclosure	Workplace transfers	Resource referrals to outside partner violence services
	Alter work schedule to confuse perpetrator	
Partner violence education for security personnel	Relocation of victim's work station	Assistance with safety planning
	Temporarily altering job responsibilities or adjusting expectations	Emergency funds for crisis situations
	Observation of protection or restraining orders	
	Provision of legal assistance	
	Provision of a cell phone	
	Phone call screenings	
	Silent alarms at victim's work station	
	Providing photo of perpetrator to security personnel to spot intruder	
	Security camera	
	Security escort to vehicle	
	Priority parking near building	
	Enhanced parking lot lighting	

SOURCES: Brownell (1996); Johnson and Indvik (1999); Kinney (1995); Moe and Bell (2004); Reynolds (1997)

Victimized Employee Responses to Partner Violence: Disclosure—To Tell or Not to Tell _____

Although workplaces may have formal and informal support systems available to employees to assist with WPV, employees may be uninformed about them. Thus, the first step in receiving employer support requires victims of partner violence to tell someone at work about the victimization. Workplace attitudes or organizational culture can influence whether employees choose to disclose such sensitive information. The stigma associated with partner violence often inhibits victims from disclosing to family members or friends; the limited research to date suggests that the stigma may also prevent victims from disclosing their situation at work (Lemon, 2001; Swanberg & Logan, 2005; Swanberg & Macke, in press). For instance, fear of job loss is one of the primary reasons reported by employed victims of partner violence for remaining silent (Lemon, 2001; Swanberg et al., 2005; Swanberg & Logan, 2005).

Swanberg and Logan (2005) found that employed victims of partner violence had significant concerns about the reactions and subsequent actions taken by employer representatives if they disclosed their experience of victimization. In this study, 46% of respondents reported informing supervisors or managers, whereas 43% informed a coworker about their victimization situation. Safety concerns, needing time off, or wanting to explain workplace absences were reasons that influenced employees to tell someone at work. In contrast, 54% of the sample opted *not* to tell someone at work because of fear of job loss, sense of shame about their situation, and perceived ability to handle situation independently. Respondents' reasons for disclosing victimization pertained to either safety reasons or because victims assumed people "figured out what was going on." Although findings from Swanberg and Logan's (2005) study suggested that victims who disclosed to someone at work and consequently received supports from their employer experienced positive outcomes such as increased concentration on the job, the relationship between the utilization of workplace supports and respondents' job retention was inconclusive. Comparable findings were reported in Swanberg and Macke's (in press) study of employed victims of partner violence. As noted previously, 15 of the 34 employees who reported experiencing partner violence in the past year reported telling someone at work about the abuse for the same reasons as noted above. Employees who remained silent about the issue did so because they wanted to save their reputations, felt it was a personal matter, or feared for their safety if they told someone at work.

Although fear of job loss is a main theme that emerged from these two studies (Swanberg & Logan, 2005; Swanberg & Macke, in press), Lemon (2001) suggests other reasons why victims may be reluctant to come forward about their abuse-related situation. Victims may fear that the batterer may seek retribution for disclosing sensitive information to someone at work, or victims may want to protect their partner or former partner from harm or punishment that could occur if the violence is reported. Further, victims of partner violence might be embarrassed to disclose because of the stigma associated with partner violence or because of concerns that the employer may not be responsive to the abuse-related problems. The limited available research pertaining to disclosure implies that victims' decisions to disclose or not disclose in the workplace may be dependent on the extent to which the partner violence affects their work performance, the prevailing organizational attitudes about partner violence, and the subsequent availability of workplace supports.

Research Implications

Although research has revealed the complex nature of the link between partner violence and employment, extant literature continues to be plagued by limitations and caveats. These shortcomings and future research directions are discussed below.

One of the primary limitations of the studies reviewed is that most are cross-sectional in nature and do not take into account temporal factors such as the relationship between violent outbursts and poor work performance (Browne et al., 1999). The one longitudinal study conducted to date (Browne et al., 1999) demonstrated a relationship between severe partner violence and job instability. Additional longitudinal studies are needed to further build on this finding.

Another limitation of partner violence and employment studies is that many of the studies conducted to date have been focused on partner violence as a barrier to employment. As a result, they have relied on samples of women seeking employment or employed in lower-wage jobs, and thus employment outcome variables focus on job attainment and job tenure. Although this is an important social issue that needs to be addressed, the line of inquiry pertaining to partner violence and employment needs to be more reflective of the social problem. Partner violence cuts across all economic levels. Accordingly, research is needed to determine the relationship between partner violence and other employment and economic factors that may be strongly related to partner violence. For instance, what are the long-term economic effects of job instability resulting from partner violence? Or for women who are able to maintain stable employment despite experiencing partner violence, what effects do the consequences associated with the abuse have on performance reviews and promotional opportunities?

From the perspective of the workplace, further research is needed in three areas: First, the reviewed research demonstrates that partner violence has a significant impact on the workplace; however, there is limited information on the employee prevalence of partner violence and its effects on employment and job performance. Additionally, there is limited data on the prevalence and effects of partner violence spilling over into the workplace. Thus further research is needed to understand the scope and effects of this social problem as it pertains to the workplace.

Second, although OSHA has set out guiding regulations pertaining to workplace violence and the handling of partner violence when it spills over into the workplace, very little research has been conducted on employers' knowledge of the consequences that partner violence may have on the workplace, attitudes and perceptions about partner violence, and actions taken once partner violence incidents become apparent within the workplace. Furthermore, no information could be found about the prevalence of employers that implement partner violence management and staff education or training programs. Additionally, the reviewed literature implies that the stigma associated with partner violence sometimes prevents victims from seeking assistance at the workplace. If employees felt more comfortable coming forward about their domestic situations and coworkers and managers understood how to manage the information, then the workplace might become a safer place to seek assistance. Thus, further research is needed to understand partner violence from a workplace perspective, specifically focusing on employers' knowledge and attitudes about partner violence and the actions taken when it spills over into the workplace.

Third, assuming other longitudinal data confirm Browne et al.'s (1999) findings that partner violence does not prevent employment but rather affects job stability, further investigation into the strategies that employers could utilize to help victims of partner violence maintain employment for longer periods of time is warranted. For instance, research within the interdisciplinary field of work-family suggests that workplace supports (e.g., supervisor support, flexible work schedules, alternate work hours) are associated with reduced job turnover, reduced tardiness, and increased job satisfaction (see Allen et al., 2000, for review; Bond et al., 1998). As such, considering the relevant reviewed findings (Swanberg et al., 2005; Swanberg & Logan, 2005; Swanberg & Macke, in press) and borrowing from research within the work-family field, it seems plausible that workplace supports may also have positive work outcomes for victims of partner violence. Thus, an intervention study focusing on the relationship between workplace supports and job outcomes among victims of partner violence is another important area of inquiry.

From the perspective of the employed victim, longitudinal research focusing on the complex nuances associated with partner violence and employment is long overdue for three primary reasons: First, authors concur with Browne et al. (1999) that future research is needed that follows partner violence victims over time, specifically documenting temporal relationships between violent episodes and employment factors. A more precise assessment between batterers' violent behaviors and employment behaviors will allow for more effective clinical interventions with victims and batterers, and it will allow for appropriate workplace interventions aimed to prevent and protect people in the workplace. Second, longitudinal research should include a focus on victims of partner violence who manage to stay employed for longer periods of time as such research will help determine what individual and workplace factors might contribute to stable employment. Third, a richer and more comprehensive understanding of the effects of partner violence on employment could be gathered if research samples included victims across economic brackets, occupational levels, and all age-groups.

Practical Implications

Within the workplace, there are several steps employers can take depending on the organization's size, commitment to the issue, and resources. In general, workplace partner violence policies should focus on prevention, in the first instance, but also protection and assistance (Friedman et al., 1996; Hoffman & Baron, 2001; Petty & Kosch, 2001). Possible steps organizations may take include the following:

• *Develop a workplace violence policy that specifically addresses workplace partner violence.*[2] Petty and Kosch (2001) recommend that workplace violence policies include two key components: (a) a zero-tolerance policy for any type of violent behavior and (b) a procedure for confidential reporting of violence-related matters. This policy can be expanded to include workplace partner violence by explicitly identifying partner violence–related behaviors that are prohibited at the workplace and on its property and the specific procedures that will be taken if such actions are discovered. The workplace partner violence policy should be written in a way that encourages victims to come forward and emphasizes that by doing so they will receive the necessary protection and referrals to appropriate services to assist with the situation. As well, the policy should create a set of clear and simple steps that should be taken by managers, supervisors, security personnel, and coworkers if partner violence incidents come into the workplace. It is recommended that all employees should be made aware of workplace partner violence policies and procedures and that the information should be distributed and displayed in anonymous locations.

• *Develop and implement partner violence education and workplace partner violence prevention programs.* Given the shame and stigma associated with partner violence, it is important to demystify the disgrace associated with the social problem in order to encourage employees to come forward and thereby reduce or eliminate the risk of partner violence spilling over into the workplace. Employer strategies might include requiring all employees to attend general information sessions on partner violence that provide information about community resources, distributing information materials about partner violence and where to seek help, and posting materials in public and private places. Further, some recommend (Friedman et al., 1996) that partner violence education be incorporated into all training seminars, including office safety and employee health or employee benefits training, as a way to destigmatize the issue.

• *Mandatory training for managers and supervisors.* Numerous publications on workplace violence strongly recommend that employers require managers and supervisors to participate in workplace violence–prevention training programs (Hoffman & Baron, 2001; Lemon, 2001; Petty & Kosch, 2001). As such, the workplace violence–prevention programs should include a component dealing with workplace partner violence. Recommended topics include recognizing partner violence–related symptoms among employees, employee confidentiality, organizational procedures for handling partner violence incidents, OSHA's general duty-to-warn clause, EAPs, community resources available to help employees, and workplace policies and practices that are available to accommodate victims' needs (leaves of absences, flexible work hours, Family Medical Leave Act).

• *Tailor HR policies and programs to accommodate the needs of partner violence victims.* Specific HR policies can be created to protect partner violence victims (Friedman et al., 1996; Petty & Kosch, 2001). Such policies might include paid time off, extended leave of absence, workplace relocation policies, flexible work hours that may allow victims to apply for court orders or seek new housing arrangements, or escort services to and from employees' cars.

Social Service Agency Applications

Research findings suggest that because partner abuse is not limited to the home, it seems to be an issue that social service workers may need to integrate (if they have not already) into their counseling interventions with employed victims of partner violence. There are several steps that partner violence counselors and advocates may take to help victims continue working despite the abuse. Examples of possible interventions include the following:

• *Develop and implement work-related safety plans.* Counselors and advocates generally consider home-related safety plans; however, research suggests that it is critical that safety plans be extended into the workplace (Petty & Kosch, 2001). Safety plans need to be created for various work-related situations, including periods when victims go to and return from work and situations when a batterer shows up or calls at work or harasses coworkers or supervisors.

• *Consider disclosing abuse-related situations to someone at work.* Given the research evidence, it may be beneficial if counselors could help victims determine if they need to tell someone at work about their abusive situation, despite their probable reluctance to do so (Lemon, 2001; Swanberg & Logan, 2005). Two studies indicate that when victims asked for help from coworkers or supervisors, positive outcomes resulted. Thus, it may be important for counselors and advocates to assist employed victims in carefully considering the advantages and disadvantages of disclosing this information to an employer or work colleagues.

- *Expand counselor role to include job coaching.* A third approach that counselors could take with the victim's permission is to act as an intermediary between the victim and the employer (Lemon, 2001). That is, a counselor or victim's advocate could speak to the employee's supervisor, educating him or her about partner violence and the employee's situation and possibly collaboratively creating a plan to keep the employee and workplace safe while also allowing the employee to continue working.

Conclusion

As the stigma associated with partner violence fades away, more women and men are sharing their experiences of victimization with friends, family, and health professionals. Partner violence has a significant effect on employed victims' day-to-day work lives; yet the long-term employment consequences remain unclear. Further research is needed to address the social, psychological, and economic costs of workplace partner violence; however, even given the limited information, increasing employees', supervisors', and managers' knowledge about the consequences of partner violence spilling over into the workplace would seem to be advantageous for employees and employers alike. Moreover, expanding social services to include topics related to workplace safety planning could assist victims of partner violence in keeping their jobs and organizations in keeping their valuable employees.

Notes

1. ABI/INFORM is a database that contains content from over 1,000 journals that provide information about business trends, management techniques, corporate strategies, and industry-specific topics.

2. For the purpose of this chapter, we specifically address workplace partner violence policies that could be included within broader workplace violence policies.

References

Allard, M. A., Albelda, R., Collen, M. E., & Cosenza, C. (1997). *In harm's way? Domestic violence, AFDC receipt, and welfare reform in Massachusetts.* Boston: University of Massachusetts, McCormack Institute and Center for Survey Research.

Allen, T. D., Herst, D. E. L., Bruck, C. S., & Sutton, M. (2000). Consequences associated with work-to-family conflict: A review and agenda for future research. *Journal of Occupational Health Psychology, 5*(2), 278–308.

Bachman, R. (1994). *Violence and theft in the workplace.* Washington, DC: U.S. Department of Justice.

Bachman, R., & Salzman, L. E. (1995, August). *Violence against women: Estimates from the redesigned survey* (Special Report). Washington, DC: U.S. Department of Justice, Bureau of Justice Statistics.

Barling, J., Dekker, I., Loughlin, C. A., Kelloway, E. K., Fullagar, C., & Johnson, D. (1996). Prediction and replication of the organizational and personal consequences of workplace sexual harassment. *Journal of Managerial Psychology, 11*(5), 4–15.

Barling, J., Zacharatos, A., & Hepburn, G. (1999). Parents' job insecurity affects children's academic performance through cognitive difficulties. *Journal of Applied Psychology, 84*(3), 437–444.

Bell, M., Moe, A., & Schweinle, W. (2002). Partner violence and work: Not just a "domestic issue." *Academy of Management Best Paper Proceedings,* 1–27.

Bond, J. T., Galinsky, E., & Swanberg, J. (1998). *The 1997 national study of the changing workforce.* New York: Families and Work Institute.

Brandwein, R. A. (2000). Toward real welfare reform: The voices of battered women. *AFFILIA: Journal of Women and Social Work, 15*(2), 224.

Browne, A., & Bassuk, S. S. (1997). Intimate violence in the lives of homeless and poor housed women: Prevalence and patterns in an ethnically diverse sample. *Journal of Orthopsychiatry, 67,* 261–278.

Browne, A., Salomon, A., & Bassuk, S. S. (1999). The impact of recent partner violence on poor women's capacity to maintain work. *Violence Against Women, 5*(4), 393.

Brownell, P. (1996). Domestic violence in the workplace: An emergent issue. *Crisis Intervention, 3,* 129–141.

Brush, L. (2000). Battering, traumatic stress, and welfare-to-work transition. *Violence Against Women, 6*(10), 1039–1065.

Brush, L. (2002). Work-related abuse: A replication, new items and persistent questions. *Violence and Victims, 17*(6), 743–757.

Bureau of National Affairs. (1990). *Violence and stress: The work/family connection* (Special Rep. No. 32). Washington, DC: Author.

Campbell, J. (2002). Health consequences of intimate partner violence. *Lancet, 359*(9314), 1331–1337.

Campbell, J., Jones, A., Dienemann, J., Kub, J., Schollenberger, J., O'Campo, P., et al. (2002). Intimate partner violence and physical health consequences. *Archives of Internal Medicine, 162*(10), 1157–1164.

Campbell, J., Rose, L., Kub, J., & Nedd, D. (1998). Voices of strength and resistance: A contextual and longitudinal analysis of women's responses to battering. *Journal of Interpersonal Violence, 743*(1), 743–762.

Chenier, E. (1998). The workplace: A battleground for violence. *Public Personnel Management, 27*(3), 557–568.

Duffy, M., Scott, K., & O'Leary-Kelly, A. (2005). The radiating effects of intimate partner violence on occupational stress and well-being. *Research in Occupational Stress and Well-Being, 4,* 30–57.

Duhart, D. T. (2001). Violence in the workplace, 1993–1999 (Special Report). Washington, DC: U.S. Department of Justice.

East, J. F. (1999). Hidden barriers to success for women in welfare reform. *Families in Society: The Journal of Contemporary Human Services, 80*(3), 295–305.

Eisenberger, R., & Huntington, R. (1986). Perceived organizational support. *Journal of Applied Psychology, 71*(3), 500–507.

Family Violence Prevention Fund. (1999). *Workplace impact: Fact sheet.* San Francisco: Author.

Friedman, L. N., Brown Tucker, S., Neville, P. R., & Imperial, M. (1996). The impact of domestic violence on the workplace. In G. R. VandenBos & E. Q. Bulatao (Eds.), *Violence on the job: Identifying risks and developing solutions* (pp. 153–161). Washington, DC: American Psychological Association.

Friedman, L. N., & Couper, S. (1987). *The cost of domestic violence: A preliminary investigation of the financial costs of domestic violence.* New York: Victim Services.

Galinsky, E., & Bond, J. T. (1998). *The 1998 Business Work-Life Study: A sourcebook.* New York: Families and Work Institute.

Gelles, R. J. (1976). Abused wives: Why do they stay? *Journal of Marriage and the Family, 38,* 659–668.

Greenfeld, L. A., Rand, M. R., Craven, D., Klaus, P. A., Perkins, C. A., & Ringel, C. (1998). Violence by intimates: Analysis of data on crimes by current or former spouses, boyfriends, and girlfriends. Washington, DC: U.S. Department of Justice.

Hoffman, S., & Baron, S. A. (2001). Stalkers, stalking, and violence in the workplace setting. In J. A. Davis (Ed.), *Stalking crimes and victim protection.* Washington, DC: CRC Press.

Johnson, H. (1995). The truth about white-collar domestic violence. *Working Woman, 20*(3), 55.

Johnson, P. R., & Indvik, J. (1999). The organizational benefits of assisting domestically abused employees. *Public Personnel Management, 28*(3), 365–374.

Kinney, J. A. (1995). When domestic violence strikes the workplace. *HRMagazine, 40*(8), 74.

Lemon, N. (Ed.). (2001.) *Domestic violence law: A comprehensive overview of cases and sources.* Eagan, MN: West Group.

Libbus, M. K., Sable, M., Huneke, D., & Anger, K. (1999). Domestic violence and implications for welfare-to-work: A qualitative investigation. *Employee Assistance Quarterly, 14*(4), 1–15.

Lloyd, S. (1997). The effects of domestic violence on women's employment. *Law & Policy, 19*(2), 139–167.

Lloyd, S., & Taluc, N. (1999). The effects of male violence on female employment. *Violence Against Women, 5*(4), 370–392.

Logan, T., Walker, R., Cole, J., & Leukefeld, C. (2002). Victimization and substance use among women: Contributing factors, interventions, and implications. *Review of General Psychology, 6*(4), 325–397.

Logan, T., Walker, R., Jordan, C., & Campbell, J. (2004). An integrative review of separation and victimization among women: Consequences and implications. *Violence, Trauma, & Abuse, 5*(2), 143–193.

Logan, T., Walker, R., Jordan, C., & Leukefeld, C. (2005). *Adult interpersonal victimization, mental health and substance abuse among women: Contributing factors, treatment and implications.* Washington, DC: American Psychological Association.

MacEwen, K., & Barling, J. (1991). Effects of maternal employment experiences on children's behavior via mood, cognitive difficulties, and parenting behavior. *Journal of Marriage and the Family, 53,* 635–644.

MacMillan, R., & Gartner, R. (1999, November). When she brings home the bacon: Labor-force participation and the risk of spousal violence against women. *Journal of Marriage and the Family, 61,* 947–958.

Meyer, J. P., & Allen, N. J. (1991). A three-component conceptualization of organizational commitment. *Human Resource Management Review, 1,* 161–189.

Meyer, J. P., & Allen, N. J. (1997). *Commitment in the workplace: Theory, research, and application.* Thousand Oaks, CA: Sage.

Moe, A. M., & Bell, M. P. (2004). Abject economics: The effects of battering and violence on women's work and employability. *Violence Against Women, 10*(1), 29–55.

National Institute of Justice and Centers for Disease Control. (1998, April). *Research in brief. Stalking in America: Findings from the National Violence Against Women Survey.* Washington, DC: Author.

Pamuk, E., Makuc, D., Heck, K., Reuben, C., & Lochner, K. (1998). *Socioeconomic status and health chartbook: Health, United States.* Hyattsville, MD: National Center for Health Statistics.

Pereira, J. (1995, March 2). Employers confront domestic abuse. *Wall Street Journal,* p. B1.

Petty, R. A., & Kosch, L. M. (2001). Workplace violence and unwanted pursuit: From an employer's perspective. In J. A. Davis (Ed.), *Stalking crimes and victim protection.* Washington, DC: CRC Press.

Plitcha, S. B. (1996). Violence and abuse: Implications for women's health. In M. M. Falik & K. S. Collins (Eds.), *Women's health: The commonwealth fund survey* (pp. 237–270). Baltimore: Johns Hopkins University Press.

Raphael, J. (1995). *Domestic violence: Telling the untold welfare-to-work story.* Chicago: Taylor Institute.

Raphael, J. (1996). *Prisoners of abuse: Domestic violence and welfare receipt.* Chicago: Taylor Institute.

Raphael, J., & Tolman, R. M. (1997). *Trapped by poverty, trapped by abuse: New evidence documenting the relationship between domestic violence and welfare.* Chicago: Project for Research on Welfare, Work, and Domestic Violence of Taylor Institute and University of Michigan Research Development Center on Poverty, Risk, and Mental Health.

Reynolds, L. (1997). Fighting domestic violence in the workplace. *HRFocus, 74*(11), 8.

Riger, S., & Staggs, S. (2004). Welfare reform, domestic violence, and employment. *Violence Against Women, 10*(9), 961–990.

Riger, S., Raja, S., & Camacho, J. (2002). The radiating impact of intimate partner violence. *Journal of Interpersonal Violence, 17(2), 184–205.*

Romero, D., Chavkin, W., Wise, P., & Smith, L. (2003). Low-income mothers' experience with poor health, hardship, work, and violence. *Violence Against Women, 10*(9), 1231–1244.

Sable, M., Libbus, K., Huneke, D., & Anger, K. (1999). Domestic violence among AFDC recipients: Implications for welfare-to-work programs. *AFFILIA, 14*(2), 199–216.

Saltzman, L. E., Fanslow, J. L., McMahon, P. M., & Shelley, G. A. (1999). *Intimate partner violence surveillance: Uniform definitions and recommended data elements.* Atlanta: National Center for Injury Prevention and Control.

Schell, B. (2003). The prevalence of sexual harassment, stalking, and false victimization syndrome cases and related human resource management policies in a cross-section of Canadian Companies from January 1995 through January 2000. *Journal of Family Violence, 18*(6), 351–360.

Scott Collins, K., Schoen, C., Joseph, S., Duchon, L., Simantov, E., & Yellowitz, M. (1999). *Health concerns across a woman's lifespan: The commonwealth fund 1998 survey of women's health.* New York: Commonwealth Fund.

Shepard, M., & Pence, E. (1988). The effect of battering on the employment status of women. *AFFILIA, Journal of Women and Social Work, 3*(2), 55–61.

Stanley, C. (1992). *Workplace efficiency: The effect of family violence on work performance.* Tulsa, OK: Domestic Violence Intervention Services.

Straus, M., & Gelles, R. J. (1990). *Physical violence in American families: Risk factors and adaptations to violence in 8,145 families.* New Brunswick, NJ: Transaction.

Strube, M. J., & Barbour, L. S. (1984). Factors related to the decision to leave an abusive relationship. *Journal of Marriage and the Family, 46*(4), 837–844.

Swanberg, J., & Logan, TK (2005, January). The effects of intimate partner violence on women's labor force attachment: Experiences of women living in rural and urban Kentucky. *Journal of Occupational Health Psychology, 10*(1), 3–17.

Swanberg, J., & Macke, C. (in press). The intersection between intimate partner violence and the workplace: Consequences, disclosure rates and employer supports. *AFFILIA: Journal of Women and Social Work.*

Swanberg, J., Macke, C., & Logan, TK. (2005). *Intimate partner violence, women and work: A descriptive look at work interference tactics, coping with violence on the job, and informal workplace support.* Manuscript submitted for publication, University of Kentucky.

Taylor, M. J., & Smith Barusch, A. (2004). Personal, family, and multiple barriers of long-term welfare recipients. *Social Work, 49*(2), 175–183.

Tjaden, P., & Thoennes, N. (1997). *Stalking in America: Findings from the National Violence Against Women Survey.* Denver, CO: Center for Policy Research.

Tjaden, P., & Thoennes, N. (1998). *Prevalence, incidence, and consequences of violence against women: Findings from the National Violence Against Women Survey.* Washington, DC: U.S. Department of Justice, Office of Justice Programs.

Tjaden, P., & Thoennes, N. (2000). *Extent, nature, and consequences of intimate partner violence.* Washington, DC: U.S. Department of Justice, National Institute of Justice.

Tolman, R. M., & Raphael, J. (2000). A review of research on welfare and domestic violence. *Journal of Social Issues, 56*(4), 655–682.

Tolman, R. M., & Rosen, D. (2001). Domestic violence in the lives of women receiving welfare: Mental health, substance dependence, and economic well-being. *Violence Against Women, 7*(2), 141–158.

Warchol, G. (1998). *Workplace violence, 1992–1996.* Washington, DC: U.S. Department of Justice, Office of Justice Programs.

Westrum, D., & Fremouw, W. J. (1998). Stalking behavior: A literature review and suggested functional analytic assessment technology. *Aggression and Violence Behavior, 3*, 255.

Wilson, K. L. (1997). *When violence begins at home: A comprehensive guide to understanding and ending domestic abuse.* Salt Lake City, UT: Publishers Press.

Wisner, C. L., Gilmer, T. P., Saltzman, L. E., & Zink, T. M. (1999). Intimate partner violence against women: Do victims cost health plans more? *Journal of Family Practice, 48*(6), 439–443.

Zachary, M.-K. (2000). Labor law for supervisors: Domestic violence as a workplace issue. *Supervision, 61*(4), 23–26.

17

Sexual Harassment in the Workplace

A Look Back and a Look Ahead

Collette Arens Bates
Lynn Bowes-Sperry
Anne M. O'Leary-Kelly

Targets of sexual harassment (SH) such as Kathy Durkin, who was training to be a police officer at the Chicago Police Academy (Thompson, 2003), understand clearly that SH is a form of workplace aggression. Durkin experienced many instances of gender harassment and unwanted sexual attention from both her instructor and her classmates. For example, while in a car with two classmates during driving school, one classmate exposed himself to her. She also was subjected to other forms of workplace aggression such as her instructor frequently berating her during firearms training, yelling obscenities, and even kicking her leg on one occasion. Although many people think of SH as a distinct behavior because it is sex-related, it is, in fact, one form of workplace aggression (O'Leary-Kelly, Paetzold, & Griffin, 2000).

Baron and Neuman (1996) define *workplace aggression* as "efforts by individuals to harm others with whom they work or the organizations in which they are employed" (p. 161). Previous theoretical (Bowes-Sperry, Tata, & Luthar, 2003; O'Leary-Kelly et al., 2000) and empirical (Barling, Rogers, & Kelloway, 2001; Baron, Neuman, & Geddes, 1999; Lucero, Middleton, Finch, & Valentine, 2003; Robinson & Bennett, 1995; Scalora, Washington, Casady, & Newell, 2003) research indicates that SH is a form of workplace aggression. Furthermore, SH is often accompanied by other forms of general workplace abuse such as disrespectful behavior, exclusion, and physical aggression (Rospenda, Richman, Wislar, & Flaherty, 2000). Barling et al. (2001) capture the connection between SH and workplace aggression well when they state, "sexual harassment may constitute an especially insidious form of workplace violence from the victim's perspective, because it appears to be socially or organizationally sanctioned" (p. 259).

This chapter will review the prevalence of SH in the workplace, major theoretical models of SH, and major empirical studies investigating SH. In addition, we will review the connection between theoretical and empirical research to point the way for future SH research.

Prevalence of Sexual Harassment

One commonly cited study estimates that 44% of working women and 19% of working men experience some form of unwanted sexual attention while at work (U.S. Merit Systems Protection Board [USMSPB], 1995). According to Welsh (2000), of the complaints filed with the Canadian Human Rights Commission during the period from 1978 through 1993, 74% dealt with unwanted sexual attention, 46% dealt with gender harassment, 25% involved relational advances, and 10% involved quid pro quo situations.[1] Welsh's (2000) results are consistent with research that finds the occurrence of different types of SH to be highly correlated (Fitzgerald, Gelfand, & Drasgow, 1995; Gelfand, Fitzgerald, & Drasgow, 1995). The research of Fitzgerald, Swan, and Magley (1997) indicates that *gender harassment* (i.e., behaviors that express hostile and insulting views toward women but are not aimed at achieving sexual cooperation) was experienced more frequently than *unwanted sexual attention* (unwanted behaviors that are aimed at achieving sexual cooperation but are not tied to job-related outcomes), which in turn was experienced more frequently than *sexual coercion* (unwanted behaviors that are aimed at achieving sexual cooperation and are tied to job-related outcomes).

During the decade from 1992 through 2002, the number of SH charges received by the Equal Employment Opportunity Commission (EEOC) and Fair Employment Practice Agencies (FEPAs) in the United States increased by almost 37% (from 10,532 in 1992 to 14,396 in 2002). The monetary benefits (excluding those obtained through litigation) associated with these charges increased by over 200% during the same time period (from $16.3 million[2] to $50.3 million). Whereas women filed the majority of SH complaints at both the beginning and end of the decade, the percentage of complaints filed during this time period by men increased approximately 64% (from 9.1% in 1992 to 14.9% in 2002).

It also is interesting to analyze the trend in resolution of charges filed with the EEOC. Resolutions can take the form of settlements, withdrawal with benefits, administrative closures, findings of reasonable cause, and findings of no reasonable cause. In both 1992 and 2002, administrative closure (whereby a charge is closed for administrative reasons such as failure to locate the charging party or the charging party requesting to withdraw a charge without having resolved the issue) was a primary method of resolution. Specifically, it was the number one method of resolution in 1992 and number two method of resolution in 2002. Although administrative closures represented a large portion of resolutions in both time periods, fewer charges were resolved via this method in 2002 (25.1% of all charges) than in 1992 (40.2% of all charges). The fact that a larger percentage of charging parties are sticking with their cases may mean that they have more faith in the system than those who filed charges a decade before them.

This faith in the system may be misplaced, however, because the primary method of resolution for charges of SH filed with the EEOC in 2002 was a determination of "no reasonable cause" (i.e., that no evidence of SH existed, thus the EEOC had decided not to pursue the case but will allow the charging party to bring private court action). Specifically, 47.1% of SH charges filed with the EEOC in 2002 were resolved by a finding of no reasonable cause compared with 32.8% in 1992. This represents an increase of 44% over the decade (however, it is important to note that findings of no reasonable cause ranked as the number two method of resolution even in 1992).

One potential reason for this substantial increase in findings of no reasonable cause is that as individuals become more familiar with the existence of SH laws, they are more likely to feel that their rights have been violated and to file charges; however, all behavior of a sexual nature is not considered *illegal* SH, so although a person bringing a charge may consider the behavior harassing, the behavior may not fit the legal definition of SH. Another potential explanation is that given the substantial increase in charges of SH filed during the past decade, the EEOC may be understaffed and thus not conducting thorough investigations. Therefore, charges of illegal SH may go undetected by the EEOC.

Perhaps most interesting, the occurrence of methods of resolution that are most favorable to individuals charging SH (i.e., findings of reasonable cause, settlements, and withdrawals with benefits) have changed very little during the decade from 1992 through 2002. These three categories represented 26.9% and 27.8% of total resolutions in 1992 and 2002 respectively. Now we look at what has been done to advance the theory that explains SH.

Major Theoretical Models of Sexual Harassment

Several recent reviews have looked at the domain of SH (e.g., Lengnick-Hall, 1995; Sbraga & O'Donohue, 2000; Welsh, 1999). Although these reviews and discussions can be helpful in furthering our understanding of the causes and consequences of SH, it is often difficult for those interested in the topic to get a comprehensive perspective of SH and be able to understand how, if at all, these varying perspectives fit together. In order to better present our discussion in this section, we have developed a framework for reviewing the SH literature (see Figure 17.1). In this framework, SH occurs as an actor communicates to a target something the target finds sexually harassing or

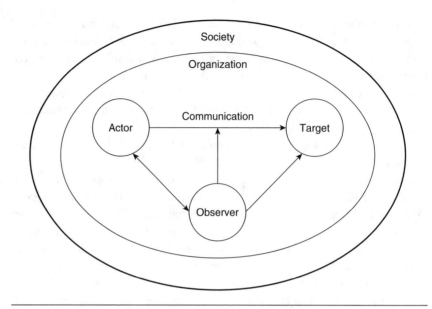

Figure 17.1   An Organizing Framework for SH Research

inappropriate. This occurs within the boundaries of the organization but is influenced by the larger society. This act is often communicated to and/or observed by others, such as coworkers, within the organization. It should be noted that this is not a model of SH, per se, but simply a useful way of organizing our discussion regarding theoretical perspectives on SH. Theory related to each component of the model (society, organization, actor, communication process, target, and observer) will be discussed next. Empirical research studies related to each component will be discussed in the next major section.

Societal Level Explanations of Sexual Harassment

At the most macro level, society can contribute to sexually harassing behavior. Events that occur in society have an impact on our behavior from the moment of our births and throughout our lives. What contributions does society make in influencing SH?

Within the SH literature, power differences between men and women are seen as the most evident cause of SH at the societal level. Perhaps one of the best known examples of this approach is the *sociocultural model* (Tangri, Burt, & Johnson, 1982). According to this model, SH is seen as a reflection of the power and status differential in our society. SH is a result of a patriarchal society in which men are known for their dominance and aggressive behaviors, whereas women are seen as passive, meek, and mild. From this perspective, our culture values and teaches these respective roles to boys and girls from the time they are very young. It is a culture based on male dominance, in which men control the decision-making process. SH, according to the sociocultural model, serves the function of maintaining this dominance by "intimidating, discouraging, or precipitating [in the] removal of women from work" (Tangri et al., 1982, p. 40), because the workplace is considered a man's domain.

Another societal level view of SH as a power demonstration is the general *feminist perspective.* The basis of this approach is much the same as the sociocultural model. One group is able to exert influence and control over other groups through cultural influences, behavioral expectations, and societal and political decisions (Dougherty, 2001). Men are seen in this approach as well as having a higher status and, therefore, more power (Cleveland & Kerst, 1993). SH, then, is seen as a means of maintaining the status quo. That is, SH is a means of oppression (Vaux, 1993) to prevent women from rising up and changing the social structure and cultural values.

A third approach to explaining SH at the societal level involves *moral exclusion* (Vaux, 1993), that is, processes to maintain or change the social order within our moral community. Individuals within our society acquire knowledge of what is right and wrong from the society at large. Those who are in power or hold the most power generally have the most influence on these values and morals. Using in-group/out-group reasoning, Vaux (1993) suggests people in the in-group (the people in power) are able to justify their negative or harmful behaviors by focusing on the greater humanity. Thus, SH is justified by denying that any harm may have been done or, at least, diminishing the harm done. In-group members may also justify sexually harassing behaviors by blaming the victim or somehow showing that society is better off with out-group members out of the workplace.

Organizational Explanations of Sexual Harassment

Because SH is defined as occurring within the workplace, it is necessary to look at what factors within the organization influence this behavior. One of the most obvious places to look is the structure of the organization. Within an organization's structure, relevant factors might include the hierarchy of the organization, the segregation or integration of men and women within the various workgroups, and possibly the culture or climate of the organization. Current theoretical approaches at the organizational level have ranged from the general (looking at the organizational structure as a whole) to the specific (looking at one piece within this structure that might be a contributing factor to SH). Many of these explanations also view SH as a manifestation of power and/or have ties back to societal level explanations.

Organizational Structures as a Cause of SH

Tangri et al. (1982) present the *organizational model,* which suggests that SH results from the opportunity structures created by the organizational climate, established hierarchy, and authority relations. It acknowledges that men are more likely to be the harassers, suggesting this is due to men having a higher position, thus having more power over women. An organization's climate can further contribute to the possibility of SH through sex-integrated work groups and organizational norms, as well as a relaxed or informal policy toward SH.

The *power differential perspective* (Cleveland & Kerst, 1993; Gutek & Morasch, 1982), which has direct ties to the feminist perspective, views SH as a function of differences in workplace power between men and women. Power includes not only formal power such as differences in authority structures (men as supervisors, women as subordinates) but also informal power such as differences in the relative influence in the workplace. Informal power can come from a variety of sources. Gutek and Morasch (1982) point out, for example, that although a male and female who work at the same job may *formally* have the same power, the larger physical size of the male may give him more *informal* power. In keeping with the feminist tradition, simply being a man in an environment that values the accomplishments of men is also a source of informal power (Gutek & Morasch, 1982).

Integrated Workplaces Contributing to SH

The *sex role spillover model* (Gutek & Morasch, 1982) suggests that the carryover of gender-based behavioral expectations into the workplace is the basis of SH. This spillover occurs because the societal level expectations for how one should behave generally cross over to become part of the expectations for how one should behave on the job. Such spill-over is most likely to occur when there is a skewed sex ratio within a job category or when jobs have come to be associated with the female gender. A skewed sex ratio occurs when there is a greater number of one gender in the work role than the other. When the skew is such that being female is made salient (e.g., one woman among many men), gender-based expectations may spill over to the workplace, and SH is more likely to occur (Gutek & Morasch, 1982). In traditionally female occupations, in which women are the majority, Gutek and Morasch (1982) suggest spillover of gender-based expectations also is likely to occur, which increases the likelihood of SH. Sexually harassing behavior is often not likely to be identified as harassment in these traditionally female occupations because it is often happening to everyone within the work role.

Another theoretical perspective, the *contact hypothesis*, states that in work settings where men and women come into greater contact with one another, men will initiate and women will report more sexualized behaviors (Gutek, Cohen, & Konrad, 1990). Prior research and theorizing by Gutek and her colleagues (e.g., Gutek, Morasch, & Cohen, 1983) showed that integrated work settings are more sexualized than nonintegrated ones. This non-work-related sexual behavior then can be translated or interpreted by some recipients as SH.

Organizational Culture as Cause of SH

A final theory of SH at the organizational level, *organizational tolerance for sexual harassment* (OTSH; Hulin, Fitzgerald, & Drasgow, 1996), suggests that SH is supported by, or at least tolerated through, the norms and values of the workplace. An organization's culture exists as a means for employees to make sense of their workplace surroundings, including the rules and practices of organizations (Keyton, Ferguson, & Rhodes, 2001), thus guiding employees' behaviors. How an organization responds to claims of SH will send a message to all those within the organization in terms of the tolerance or intolerance of such behaviors within the organization (Hulin et al., 1996). Whatever message the organization sends to some employees regarding SH will be sent to *all* employees within the organization, thus having consequences not only for current harassers and targets but also for future ones.

Initiators of Sexual Harassment: The Actor

Understanding that harassment occurs within the larger context of society and the organization, the sexually harassing act itself involves an *actor* (the harasser) and a *target* (the receiver of the harassment). The primary issue regarding the SH actor that has received theoretical attention in the literature to date is the question of *why* actors engage in SH. Researchers have provided several theoretical explanations, including (a) SH as a natural act, (b) SH as a misperception, (c) SH as an individual predisposition, (d) SH as a case of unethical decision making, (e) SH being driven by low accountability, and (f) SH as an aggressive work behavior. We briefly describe each of these theoretical explanations.

SH as a "Natural" Act

The underlying assumption of the natural or biological model (Tangri et al., 1982) is that SH results from the natural attraction between two people. It is argued in this model that SH actually does not occur, as there is an absence of intention to harass, and SH is actually the natural expression of a man's strong sex drive. The natural or biological model acknowledges that men are often the aggressors but argues this is due to a natural (biological) difference between the two sexes. Tangri et al. (1982) identify three basic assumptions of this model: (a) Men have a stronger sex drive, leading them to aggress sexually against women but without any intent to discriminate; (b) there is a mutual, natural attraction between men and women with both participating and enjoying sexually related behaviors; and (c) true SH can only be attributed to a minority of "sick" men.

SH as Misperceptions

The first stream of research that focused on the actor was the work developed by Antonia Abbey and her colleagues. Although this research did not deal directly with SH, it addressed the ways that social interactions might be interpreted differently by men and women, making it highly relevant to an understanding of harassment. In the aggregate, this research suggests that men are more prone to interpreting social encounters in sexual terms than are women. For example, men tend to interpret a female actor's behavior as promiscuous and seductive, whereas women interpret the same conduct as friendly (Abbey, 1982; Saal, Johnson, & Weber, 1989). These patterns appear to hold constant, regardless of issues such as the organizational power level of the female in the scenario or the severity of harassing conduct the female endured (Johnson, Stockdale, & Saal, 1991).

This research is relevant to SH because it implies, somewhat akin to the natural or biological model (Tangri et al., 1982), that SH may be driven by natural sexual desires but that male actors misperceive a woman's level of interest in receiving sexual attention, thereby leading to such harassment. The theoretical explanation behind this research is that men and women are socialized differently, thereby leading to these different perceptions in social encounters. In many ways, then, this is a dyadic version of the societal level explanations that were discussed earlier. Other researchers have explicitly linked the "misperceptions" explanation for SH to the sex role spillover theory. Essentially, this theoretical explanation suggests that a woman who acts in a friendly manner may be targeted for harassment by actors who bring gender-based expectations into the workplace and therefore interpret friendliness as sexual interest (Saal et al., 1989).

SH as an Individual Predisposition

The work of Pryor and his colleagues suggests that some men are predisposed to SH because of individual differences in personality, attitudes, and perceptions. This perspective suggests that men are exposed to different socialization messages than are women, which encourages some to develop adversarial sexual beliefs and attitudes (Pryor, 1987; Pryor & Giedd, 1995; Pryor, LaVite, & Stoller, 1993). These negative perceptions and attitudes are termed the *likelihood to sexually harass* (LSH) and include an inability to take the perspective of another, rape proclivity, authoritarian personality trait, and negative feelings about sex (Pryor, 1987). These LSH beliefs and attitudes, then, serve as a filter for interpretation in social encounters, leading such men to a predisposition to behave in sexually dominant and exploitive ways (Pryor & Stoller, 1994). Although the theoretical explanation here seems to emphasize individual difference explanations, there is recognition that situational conditions (e.g., role models, sexualization of the workplace, amount of contact between the sexes at work) also can influence the behavioral expression of these negative beliefs (Gutek, 1985; Pryor, 1987; Pryor et al., 1993).

SH as Unethical Decision Making

A quite different approach frames SH motives from a decision-making perspective. Here, an ethical decision-making model is used as a context for exploring the motives of a harasser (Bowes-Sperry & Powell, 1996, 1999; O'Leary-Kelly & Bowes-Sperry, 2001). Generally, it is suggested that harassers who do not regard their situation as involving a moral imperative (i.e., do not regard the situation as *morally intense;* Jones, 1991) are unlikely to engage ethics schemata and behave ethically. Research in this area suggests there are numerous reasons why an actor may not see a moral imperative in SH situations and that many of these reasons stem from the social context in which the harassing act occurs. For example, when actors do not believe that their actions harm the target (which is common because targets often are reluctant to respond negatively), when there is little agreement on what constitutes SH in a social environment, and when there is diffuse responsibility for preventing or responding to SH, then the social environment does not encourage moral intensity perceptions and SH becomes more likely.

SH as Motivated by Lack of Accountability

Another perspective that focuses on the social environment as a stimulus for SH is based in accountability theory (Frink & Klimoski, 1998; Schlenker, 1982; Tetlock, 1985). *Accountability* is the "perceived need to justify or defend a decision or action to some audience(s) which has potential reward and sanction power, and where such rewards and sanctions are perceived as contingent on accountability conditions" (Frink & Klimoski, 1998, p. 9). From this perspective, SH occurs when actors perceive that such behavior will not be negatively sanctioned in the social environment (that there are no behavioral prescriptions against the behavior). Research (O'Leary-Kelly, Tiedt, & Bowes-Sperry, 2004) suggests that accountability often is limited regarding SH because of ambiguity in role expectations (due to the necessarily subjective nature of SH definitions), reactance to threats to the identity of some actors that occur when behavioral prescriptions around SH are enacted in a work environment, competing behavioral prescriptions within the social environment, and diffusion of accountability that occurs when SH becomes a group phenomenon (common in many hostile environment cases).

SH as Aggressive Behavior

Perhaps the most comprehensive model outlining actor motives is that provided by O'Leary-Kelly et al. (2000). This perspective differs from the others described here in that it shifts the focus from how the social environment or individual predispositions facilitate SH to a focus on what it is that harassers are trying to achieve with their actions. SH is depicted as a form of aggressive behavior that allows the actor to achieve some valued personal goal.

Although the model recognizes both emotional and instrumental goals as motivators for SH, it emphasizes instrumental goals. One such goal is a *retributive justice goal* (i.e., a desire to punish another person for a perceived injustice). For example, a male employee who believes that a female coworker is behaving inconsistently with sex role expectations (a likely occurrence when women enter male-dominated work environments) may use SH to restore a desired social hierarchy. As with other aggressive behaviors, the harassment may at times be directed at the cause of the perceived injustice and at other times it may be directed toward someone who is perceived as similar to the offender. Interestingly, this suggests that some SH may reflect anger toward one party (e.g., a female boss) being displaced to another (e.g., a female subordinate). This model also suggests self-presentational goals as important to SH, suggesting that harassing actions may represent attempts by the actor to either create a valued social identity or protect a valued social identity.

Communicating Sexually Harassing Behavior

As shown in Figure 17.1, communication is a key link in terms of understanding SH. In order for a sexually harassing act to occur, the actor must *communicate* something to the target. Looking at research on communication, there are several relevant theoretical questions that could be addressed, including what form of communication a harasser might choose and whether there are some forms that might have a greater impact on the victim than others. Tying in to explanations from the organizational level, are there any organizational barriers or enhancers that might play a role in the communication process? Noise can also play an important role in disrupting the communication process, but what are the forms noise can take in terms of an event being perceived as sexually harassing? Little theoretical work, however, has focused on SH as communication between an actor and a target. Theory has been offered in terms of misperceptions, which can be thought of as a form of noise to disrupt the communication process. This is discussed below.

Noise in the Communication Process

The misperception theory suggests that the communication process for men and women is very different, and this accounts for a difference in attributions of sexual behavior between men and women (Stockdale, 1993). As stated earlier (see "SH as Misperceptions" in "The Actor" section), research has shown that men and women do not interpret behaviors the same way, especially friendly behaviors (e.g., Abbey, 1987; Johnson et al., 1991). Men tend to interpret more behaviors as sexual than do women, which contributes to a sexualized work environment (Gutek et al., 1983). Gutek et al. (1983) further suggest that much of the communication, particularly sexual communication, within the work setting is ambiguous. It is this ambiguity that contributes to the misperception of the intent of the behavior (Lee & Guerrero, 2001).

Stockdale (1993) suggests that this misperception can either be a moderating or mediating variable in the causal chain of SH. Misperception as a moderating variable suggests that, as part of one's attitudes and belief structure, misperceiving behaviors can vary throughout the population. In terms of misperception being a mediating factor, Stockdale (1993) suggests that misperceptions may occur within the communication process itself. This may be attributed to noise in the encoding and/or decoding stages of the communication process that affects whether or not a behavior is interpreted as sexually harassing.

Although not explicitly stated in misperception theory, it should be noted that not all communication is verbal. Nonverbal communication can also contribute to or be a cause of SH. Murphy, Driscoll, and Kelly (1999) identified a number of nonverbal behaviors related to dominance (power) and sexual interest, including staring, body posturing, eye contact, smiles, and head tilts. Furthermore, Lee and Guerrero (2001) identified touch as a form of nonverbal communication related to SH. Touch can be interpreted in a number of ways, from benign to friendly to sexual to harassing. For example, a face touch is perceived differently than an arm around the waist or a touch on the arm or knee (Lee & Guerrero, 2001). As with verbal forms, nonverbal forms of communication are also often perceived differently by men and women (Murphy et al., 1999).

_____ Receivers of Sexual Harassment: The Targets

Potentially, a variety of issues related to the target (see Figure 17.1) might provide an understanding of the SH phenomenon. These include the following: (a) When will a target interpret an action as SH? (b) How do targets react to such harassment? and (c) How does SH affect targets? The first issue will be discussed in the following section, which describes research on observers. Theoretical perspectives on the latter two issues are discussed here.

How Do Targets React to SH?

Although there has been relatively steady research on this issue, most research has been quite atheoretical. Much of the existing research tends to emphasize either specific variables that influence responses to SH (e.g., Baker, Terpstra, & Larantz, 1990 found that the severity of harassment incidents influenced the assertiveness of response) or atheoretical categorization of SH responses (e.g., Terpstra & Baker, 1989). This work has been helpful in creating knowledge about the domain of responses likely to be chosen by targets (i.e., *how* targets react) but has not provided theoretical models that explain *why* targets choose the reactions they do. There have, however, been a few attempts to add theory to this general research question.

Social Exchange Theory and Target Reactions

Social exchange theory suggests that social relationships will be regarded positively when there is an equitable exchange of resources. From this perspective, SH occurs when the target believes that the personal costs of sexual behavior are greater than the benefits (Jones & Remland, 1992). This perspective allows researchers to explain why and when targets will respond negatively to harassing acts (i.e., when they involve an inequitable exchange from the perspective of the target). For example, targets are likely to react more negatively when conduct is more severe (because this raises the costs for the target in the social exchange) or when they are receiving no rewards in exchange for tolerating the situation.

Personal Control Theory and Target Reactions

Thacker (1992) suggested that target reactions might be understood using two theories of personal control: reactance theory (Brehm, 1966, 1972) and learned helplessness (Seligman, 1974). According to *reactance theory,* people whose behavioral freedom is threatened will be intent on restoring a sense of control (Brehm, 1966; Thacker, 1992). SH targets, then, are expected to either act directly to restore control (e.g., complaining about the harassment, threatening to complain) or to make cognitive adjustments that provide an illusion of control (e.g., adjusting their perceptions of how offensive the behavior actually was). According to the second theoretical perspective, *learned helplessness,* individuals who are exposed to frequent negative conduct might develop the belief that they cannot restore control and will simply come to passively accept the negative circumstances (Seligman, 1974; Thacker, 1992). Thacker argues that learned helplessness is most likely to occur when organizational cultures tolerate SH or when the harasser has power over the target.

Target Reactions as Whistle-Blowing

Perry, Kulik, and Schmidtke (1997) depicted target reactions as a form of whistle-blowing. *Whistle-blowing* is the "disclosure by organization members . . . of illegal, immoral, or illegitimate practices under the control of their employers, to persons or organizations that may be able to effect action" (Near & Miceli, 1985, p. 4). This theoretical perspective suggests that factors such as the power of the whistle-blower and the receptiveness of the organizational environment may influence his or her decision to take this often risky action (Perry et al., 1997). Applying this to SH situations, it predicts that targets who react assertively to harassment by blowing the whistle (reporting it), do so because they can—that is, they do so when they have the personal or position power to take this action or when the organization has provided a safe environment (Perry et al., 1997). Adams-Roy and Barling

(1998) extended this by further suggesting that personal factors such as being assertive and having high self-esteem, as well as organizational factors, can influence the target's decision to take action.

More Comprehensive Models of Targets' Reactions

To date, perhaps the most comprehensive research to address target responses is research by Knapp, Faley, Ekeberg, and Dubois (1997). First, these authors provide more theoretical framing to the question of *how* targets might react. Here, they suggest that two dimensions can be used to categorize target responses: the focus of response (self-focused, initiator-focused) and the mode of response (self-response, supported response). These dimensions provide a clear conceptual basis for clustering of target responses. Second, the authors used theoretical perspectives such as whistle-blowing theory, stress/coping theory, and expectancy theory to explain how and why targets will choose among these varying responses. For example, they predict that the most extreme target reactions (e.g., self-focused and self-response; initiator-focused and supported response) will occur when targets experience great levels of distress from the harassment (e.g., because it is severe, because it is pervasive). This framework provides the most focused answer to date on the question of how and why targets react the way that they do.

A second comprehensive model is presented by O'Leary-Kelly et al. (2000), who regarded SH as a special case of aggressive work behavior. By incorporating the actor's goals and motives into the model, these authors examined both emotional and behavioral responses by targets, describing the attributional processes that determine the nature of these responses. Specifically, and based on attribution theory (Pyszcznski & Greenberg, 1981; Wong & Weiner, 1981), target responses were predicted to depend on factors such as perceived intentionality of the conduct, knowledge of the negative consequences of the conduct, and perceived alternatives to the conduct (Forgas, O'Connor, & Morris, 1983; Tedeschi & Felson, 1994). This model also suggests that target responses can be understood through greater consideration of target goals. Using theories that explain aggression as a framework (e.g., Tedeschi & Felson, 1994), it is suggested that targets are motivated by multiple, sometimes competing goals such as ending the conduct, maintaining status and reputation in the social environment, and retribution.

How Does SH Affect Targets?

Although there is research that outlines the types of consequences experienced by targets of SH (e.g., Gutek & Koss, 1993; Schneider, Swan, & Fitzgerald, 1997; Thacker & Gohmann, 1996), initial research provided little theoretical grounding. More recently, multiple researchers have used work stress theory to explain the effects of SH on targets. Specifically, SH is depicted as a specific type of work stressor that can negatively influence attitudinal and behavioral outcomes experienced by targets (Munson, Hulin, & Drasgow, 2000; Munson, Miner, & Hulin, 2001; Schneider et al., 1997). These outcomes include job withdrawal, health-related problems, turnover, absenteeism, and decrements in psychological well-being. From the stress-based perspective, even relatively mild sexually harassing conduct can, over time and over multiple experiences, lead to negative outcomes for victims.

Observers of Sexual Harassment

As with other areas discussed to this point, there are multiple research questions related to observers that have been addressed to date. These include examinations of (a) the factors that lead observers to label conduct as SH, (b) the consequences that witnessing SH has for the observer, and (c) the behavioral responses observers might take. The theoretical frameworks used for research in each of these areas will be described here. It should be noted that our focus is on *direct* observers of SH, not on more removed observers such as jurors or organizational decision makers.

Observers and the Labeling of Conduct as SH

There has been a significant amount of research addressing the factors leading individuals to label an act as SH. Although most of this research was not driven by any specific theoretical perspective, it has resulted in an impressive accumulation of findings (e.g., that gender predicts labeling, that personal experiences with SH predict labeling, that target attractiveness predicts labeling; Baker, Terpstra, & Cutler, 1989; Hartnett, Robinson, & Singh, 1989; Terpstra & Baker, 1986). Cohen and Gutek (1985) added some structural clarity when they found that such predictive factors cluster into four groups: (a) factors related to the interpersonal relationship between target and actor, (b) personal aspects of the situation, (c) factors related to the conduct itself, and (d) factors related to the likelihood of future conduct. Beyond this attempt at classification, there have been a few efforts (described next) to bring theoretical frameworks to bear on this question, although none have consistently been applied.

Konrad and Gutek (1986) examined three perspectives that might explain differences in individuals' perceptions of SH: (a) sex differences in definitions, (b) differential experiences by men and women, and (c) gender role spillover. The first two explanations are based on the socialized differences between men and women that were discussed previously (see "Societal Level Explanations" section). The final explanation uses sex role spillover theory by suggesting that gender-based segregation of jobs leads to integration of job roles and gender roles such that some gender-based expectations may develop into job-based expectations (Konrad & Gutek, 1986). For example, individuals who work in female-dominated jobs may be less likely to view sex-based behaviors as harassment because expectations regarding women behaving as sex objects (a gender-based role expectation) may become part of job-related expectations.

A second effort to bring theory to this area of research was led by Pryor and his colleagues (e.g., Pryor, 1985; Pryor & Day, 1988), who used attribution theory to explain laypeople's (e.g., observers') labeling of harassment. Specifically, they suggested that attributional factors (Kelley, 1973) such as the consistency of the actor's behavior toward the target, the actor's treatment toward other targets, and the treatment the target receives by other actors are critical to observers' interpretations. Other subsequent work has continued this focus on attributional sensemaking (e.g., Thomann & Wiener, 1987; Williams, Brown, Lees-Haley, & Price, 1995).

A third effort to bring theory to this area involved role theory (Dougherty, Turban, Olson, Dwyer, & LaPreze, 1996). Here the authors recognized the impact that differential role expectations might have on observers' perceptions. Specifically, they argued that differing contextual factors (e.g., nature of relationship between actor and target, job status of harasser, physical setting) prompt differing role expectations, which result in differential evaluations of the nature of the witnessed behavior.

Finally, researchers have proposed theory on ethical decision making as a viable framework for understanding observers' interpretations of conduct (Bowes-Sperry & Powell, 1996, 1999; Pierce, Broberg, McClure, & Aguinis, 2002). This framework suggests that observers' reactions may be predicted by "ethics" issues such as the moral intensity of the conduct and the ethics ideologies of observers.

Effects of SH on Observers

Interestingly, little research has examined the effects of SH on observers. Given that researchers and practitioners long have recognized that SH can be enacted through work *environments* (i.e., our society recognizes hostile environment harassment, which often involves not just the actor and target but also others in the work setting), it seems odd that the effects of SH on observers have been overlooked in research to date. Fortunately, recent research by Glomb et al. (1997) offered an important step in resolving this oversight. These authors used stress theory to argue that SH, like other forms of job stress, can have broad effects in the work environment. They further proposed that work environment stimuli can be either discretionary (directed at individuals differentially) or ambient (diffused to all individuals in the environment). They then argued that SH is a stimulus that can be experienced as ambient and/or as discretionary, suggesting that its negative stress-related effects (e.g., lower job satisfaction, greater psychological distress) can be experienced by observers as well as targets.

Observers' Behavioral Responses

A final question related to observers is how they will respond when they witness harassing conduct. A very recent effort (Bowes-Sperry & O'Leary-Kelly, 2005) to answer this question applies theoretical models on bystander intervention from the social psychology literature. Specifically, this research uses the Latané and Darley (1970) framework for bystander intervention, which suggests that observers decide about whether they will intervene based on answers to questions such as the following: Does this situation require action? Is it my personal responsibility to act, and what type of intervention should I undertake? Latané and Darley (1970) argued that bystanders will intervene when they have affirmative answers to these questions. Linking this to SH, Bowes-Sperry and O'Leary-Kelly (2005) identified aspects of SH situations that may encourage and discourage affirmative answers, thereby influencing the likelihood of observer intervention. Further, they made predictions about the type of interventions that observers might choose based on these situational factors. These types of interventions ranged from those that are immediate and high involvement (e.g., the observer tells the harasser to stop the SH while the harassing incident is occurring) to those that are delayed and low involvement (e.g., the observer provides private advice to the target about how to prevent future SH).

Major Empirical Studies Investigating Sexual Harassment

In the previous section, we described a great many theoretical explanations of SH. Next, we look at where the empirical work has occurred. Is the criticism—that the link between empirical studies and theory is lacking—fair? Or have researchers begun to answer the call? We now discuss major empirical work and, as shown in Table 17.1, match this work with the theoretical models.

Societal Level Explanations of Sexual Harassment

Societal level theories have focused on power differences between men and women, offering three theories: the sociocultural model, feminist perspective, and moral exclusion. Unfortunately, there has been little work in directly testing any of these theories within the organizational literature. We suspect this lack of empirical evidence is due to the relative difficulty in conducting societal level research; that is, focusing on societal level factors

Table 17.1

	Theoretical Models	*Empirical Research in Organizational Literature*
Society	Power differences • Sociocultural model • Feminist perspective • Moral exclusion	
Organization	Organizational structures • Organizational model • Power differential perspective • Sex role spillover model • Contact hypothesis • OTSH	 ✓ ✓ ✓
Actor	Motives for SH • Natural or biological model • Misperception • Individual predisposition • Ethical decision-making theories • Accountability theory • Workplace aggression theory	 ✓ ✓
Communication	Noise • Misperception theory	
Target	Target reactions • Social exchange theory • Personal control theory • Whistle-blowing • Comprehensive models	✓
	Effects on target • Work stress theory	✓
Observer	Labeling of SH • Individual differences • Attribution theory • Decision making	✓
	Effects on observer • Work stress theory (ambient SH)	
	Behavioral responses of observer • Bystander intervention	

within organizational research would be difficult to set up, and many organizational level factors could interfere with findings. Therefore, research done at the societal level is generally completed in other disciplines such as sociology.

The idea that society plays a role in SH, however, has raised some interesting ideas that do have a broad, macrolevel feel. For example, how is SH defined (e.g., legally, subjectively), and how is it conceptualized in research generally? Empirical research has conceptualized SH from subjective, objective, and legal perspectives. In his research, York (1989) employed the subjective perspective, in which SH is conceptualized as unwelcome behavior of a sexual nature that *an individual perceives to be offensive.* He found that both equal employment opportunity officers and naive individuals agree on a set of elements that constitute SH. Fitzgerald and colleagues (1995) examined SH from an objective perspective finding that it is a *stable behavioral construct* consisting of gender harassment, unwanted sexual attention, and sexual coercion. In their research examining the outcomes of court cases, Terpstra and his colleagues (Terpstra & Baker, 1988, 1992; Terpstra & Cook, 1985) focused on the legal perspective. In the United States, SH is considered a form of sex discrimination under Title VII of the Civil Rights Act of 1964. *Illegal sexual harassment* can take the form of either *quid pro quo harassment,* in which employees' job-related outcomes are tied to their compliance with requests for sexual favors, or *hostile environment harassment,* in which employees experience intimidating or offensive working conditions that interfere with their job performance (EEOC, 1980). In her analysis of SH complaints filed with the Canadian Human Rights Commission, Welsh (2000) found two categories of SH, poisoned environment and quid pro quo, both of which are illegal forms of harassment in the United States.

Organizational Factors Associated With Sexual Harassment

Theoretical approaches to organizational influences on SH have focused primarily on the structure of the organization and have ranged from the general to looking at specific pieces of the structure. As stated earlier, the organization's structure seems to be at least an influencing factor in sexually harassing behavior. Several theoretical viewpoints were discussed, including how the organization in general is structured, whether or not integrated workplaces may be a factor, and how an organization's culture might play a role. Empirical research has focused primarily on specific areas within the organization's structure, specifically looking at the contributions an integrated workplace and culture have on SH. Studies related to the sex-role spillover model, contact hypothesis, and OTSH will be discussed next.

Integrated Workplaces Contributing to SH

Gutek and colleagues have offered two separate but related models regarding the role of integrated workplaces on SH. The *sex role spillover model* (Gutek & Morasch, 1982) suggests that expectations for how men and women behave carry over into the workplace and thus contribute to SH.

Tests of this model have met with mixed results. Early studies found support in that women in traditionally male-dominated jobs are more likely to experience SH than those in traditionally female or gender-neutral jobs (Gutek & Cohen, 1987; Gutek & Morasch, 1982). More recent work looking at the gender ratio effect has not been as successful (Ragins & Scandura, 1995). Further work has been done to refine this model with tests indicating that factors such as age (Padavic & Orcutt, 1997) and the ambiguity of the behaviors (Sheffey & Tindale, 1992) can affect perceptions of SH.

The contact hypothesis (Gutek et al., 1990) has also found mixed support. Recall that this theory suggests that contact between men and women within the workplace will result in more SH. In their initial proposal of this theory, Gutek et al. (1990) found only limited support. Although contact can account for some of the findings of SH, it cannot account for all. Specifically, although people in their study who had more contact with members of the opposite sex were more likely to report more SH, women were more likely to report more SH regardless of contact. Ragins and Scandura (1995), on the other hand, found no support for the contact hypothesis. In their study, type of occupation (blue-collar vs. white-collar) rather than amount of contact with the opposite gender accounted for more reports of SH by women.

Organizational Culture as a Cause of SH

The effects of organizational tolerance of SH have received much attention, and results indicate that it is more likely to occur in organizations with cultures that are not concerned with preventing and dealing with SH (e.g., Fitzgerald, Drasgow, Hulin, Gelfand, & Magley, 1997). Alternatively, in organizations in which employees perceive sanctions against SH, lower rates of SH occur (Dekker & Barling, 1998). Further work indicates that the implementation practices have the greatest effect on reports of SH as well as job consequences (Williams, Fitzgerald, & Drasgow, 1999). Using structural equation modeling, Glomb, Munson, Hulin, Bergman, and Drasgow (1999) found that over time, an organization's climate is both an antecedent and an outcome of SH, thus indicating a vicious cycle occurring if organizations do not take the initiative in sending a message of intolerance regarding SH from the beginning.

_____ Initiators of Sexual Harassment: The Actor

Many theoretical perspectives were offered earlier in this chapter regarding an actor's motive(s) for SH. Although one would expect this to be a primary area for empirical research in the SH literature, more has been offered from the theoretical side than has actually been tested. Of the six theoretical areas discussed, much of the work has focused on misperceptions and individual predispositions, with a little offered that is related to workplace aggression theory.

SH as Misperceptions

Research regarding the different perceptions of social-sexual behaviors between men and women has a substantial history with little variance in the results. As described earlier, men tend to view more female behaviors as sexual than do women, thus often leading women to interpret men's responses to these behaviors as harassing. A recent meta-analysis regarding gender differences in perceptions of SH, however, has helped further this area by looking at the size of the differences in perceptions. Rotundo, Nguyen, and Sackett (2001) found that although gender differences do exist in terms of defining SH behaviors (women define a broader range of behaviors as SH than do men), the size of the difference or gap between men and women is not as large as previously thought (overall standardized mean difference of 0.30). The authors did find evidence for moderators to the perception differences–SH link, which suggests that the explanation for SH is far more complex than simply saying it is a case of misperception.

SH as an Individual Predisposition

Just as gender has played a significant role in perceptions of SH, it is also a primary determinant of sexually harassing behavior. Men engage in more sexually harassing behavior than do women (e.g., USMSPB, 1995), which may be due to the fact that they perceive fewer incidents to be sexually harassing than do women. Although men are more likely than women to harass, most men do not engage in sexually harassing behavior. Therefore, research has attempted to determine the characteristics associated with those who choose to engage in sexually harassing behaviors.

As described earlier, Pryor (1987) provided the first thorough examination of initiators of SH. He developed an instrument, the Likelihood to Sexually Harass (LSH) Scale, to assess proclivities for quid pro quo SH in men. High LSH men are more likely to approve of sexual violence, adhere to traditional gender roles, indicate a higher likelihood to rape, and have sexually permissive attitudes (e.g., Malamuth, Sockloskie, Koss, & Tanaka, 1991; Murphy, Coleman, & Haynes, 1986; Perry, Kulik, & Schmidtke, 1998; Pryor & Stoller, 1994; Osland, Fitch, & Willis, 1996). Furthermore, research indicates that high LSH men are more likely than low LSH men to send pornographic material to women (Dall'Ara & Maass, 1999), ask more sexist questions during an interview (Rudman & Borgida, 1995), rate a female's performance negatively (Driscoll, Kelly, & Henderson, 1998), and spend less time with a woman in a subordinate position (Murphy et al., 1999). These results are consistent with the findings of Begany and Milburn (2002) that hostile sexism (subjectively negative views toward women; Greenwood & Isbell, 2002) mediates the relationship between authoritarianism and men's self-reported proclivity to sexually harass.

SH as Aggressive Behavior

In keeping with the overall theme of this chapter, SH has been categorized as a form of workplace aggression. Although the common perception is that SH is typically initiated by those with hierarchical power toward those without such power, research indicates that 75% of targets reported that their harassers were coworkers (USMSPB, 1995). More recent research on initiators of SH focuses on a dynamic perspective of emergent perpetrator behavior (Lucero et al., 2003). An escalation perspective is consistent with research on general workplace violence finding that an employee history of prior violence is a risk factor for subsequent workplace violence (Greenberg & Barling, 1999). This research has empirically identified four types of sexual harassers: *Persistent harassers,* who initiate multiple incidents of SH directed at multiple targets, seem to be motivated by ego gratification. *Malicious harassers,* who also initiate multiple incidents of SH directed at multiple targets, seem to be motivated by competition and aggression. Perhaps such initiators are concerned with threats to the male social identity, which Dall' Ara and Maass (1999) found to be positively related to the likelihood to sexually harass. *Exploitive harassers,* who direct their behavior at multiple targets but do not necessarily target a given individual repeatedly, seem to be motivated by situations that allow their behavior to escape scrutiny or punishment. This is consistent with research by Dekker and Barling (1998), who found that men reported engaging in less sexually harassing behavior when they believed that they would be punished for it. Such men may also exhibit low self-monitoring, which has been linked to increased SH (Dall'Ara & Maass, 1999). Finally, *vulnerable harassers,* who initiate repeated incidents of SH toward a single target, appear to be motivated by the potential for a positive relationship with the target. Perhaps persistent and malicious harassers are most indicative of Perry et al.'s (1998) finding that men scoring high on the LSH Scale do not change their long-term attitudes regarding SH after attending SH awareness training.

_____ Communicating Sexually Harassing Behavior

The communication process, as shown in Figure 17.1, is an important link in understanding SH. Just as there is little theory, there is also a lack of empirical research within the organizational literature regarding the role of the communication process in SH. Borrowed from the communication literature, misperception theory (Stockdale, 1993) was offered as the lone theory, suggesting that misperceptions occurring within the communication process (possibly attributable to noise in the encoding or decoding stages) may be a factor. As is stated throughout this chapter, misperceptions are often a given explanation when SH occurs. Perhaps, however, looking at how misperceptions mediate the communication process might further our understanding of how these differing perceptions of sexual and sexually harassing behaviors influence our judgments of what is considered SH.

Receivers of Sexual Harassment: The Targets

In an attempt to understand the SH phenomenon, researchers have often approached the subject by looking at the target of the harassing behavior. As we stated earlier in the chapter, much of this research, although largely atheoretical, has helped in our understanding of why someone may be chosen as a target, how they are likely to react, and what sort of outcomes would be expected. A review of the research focusing on the target is presented below.

Target Responses to SH

Women of color (Bergman & Drasgow, 2003), unmarried women (USM-SPB, 1995), and women who are working as "temps" (Rogers & Henson, 1997) are among those with higher rates of SH. Regardless of who the targets of harassment are, research indicates that most do not take assertive action to stop the harassment. For example, targets of SH are especially reluctant to report it either internally to management or externally to a governmental office such as the EEOC (Gruber & Bjorn, 1982; Gutek, 1985; Knapp et al., 1997; Loy & Stewart, 1984). One study of federal employees found that only 6% of individuals who were sexually harassed took formal action (USMSPB, 1995). Individuals who decided not to report their harassment experiences explained that they feared retaliation or job loss (e.g., Cochran, Frazier, & Olson, 1997) or felt embarrassed by the situation (Gutek, 1985). It appears that their fears are realistic because women who file complaints are more likely than those who do not to experience adverse outcomes such as job loss (Welsh & Gruber, 1999) and to perceive the reporting process as unjust (Adams-Roy & Barling, 1998).

The most common response of targets is to ignore the behavior or avoid the harasser (Gutek & Koss, 1993; Knapp et al., 1997) in the hope that it will stop; however, this tactic is typically unsuccessful. One study (Adams-Roy & Barling, 1998) did find that women who were more assertive were more likely to confront the harasser; however, targets who do take more assertive actions tend to be older and have higher levels of self-esteem (Roth & Fedor, 1993), hold beliefs that SH is a vehicle men use to control women (Gruber & Smith, 1995), and reject traditional gender role stereotypes (Fitzgerald et al., 1988).

Effects of SH on Targets

Not surprisingly, outcomes for targets of SH are consistent with those for targets of workplace violence and aggression. As is suggested by theory from the work stress literature, negative psychological (e.g., anxiety and depression), somatic (e.g., migraines and sleep disturbances), and job-related (e.g., job satisfaction and turnover intentions) outcomes have been found to plague both targets of workplace violence or aggression, in general (e.g., Barling et al., 2001; LeBlanc & Kelloway, 2002; Schat & Kelloway, 2003), and SH more specifically (e.g., Barling et al., 2001; Fitzgerald et al., 1997; Gutek & Koss, 1993; Parker & Griffin, 2002; Schneider et al., 1997). In fact, some argue that SH meets the diagnostic criteria for posttraumatic stress disorder (PTSD; Avina & O'Donohue, 2002; Dansky & Kilpatrick, 1997). Simply witness workplace violence or SH has been associated with (perceived) lower levels of empowerment and teamwork (Bennett & Lehman, 1999).

Schat and Kelloway (2003) found that both instrumental support (i.e., direct help or support provided by coworkers and/or managers) and informational support (i.e., indirect help provided through mechanisms such as training programs) reduced the negative psychological health consequences emanating from workplace violence and aggression. Similarly, research indicates that targets of harassment who receive support from their supervisor experience fewer negative outcomes than those lacking such support (Murry, Sivasubramaniam, & Jacques, 2001).

Observers of Sexual Harassment

As shown in Figure 17.1, many factors play a role and are affected by harassing behavior in the workplace, observers being no exception. In looking to the environment to make sense of behaviors, targets and actors of SH will look to coworkers, the observers, for help in interpreting behaviors. Observing and reacting to SH will not only affect target and actor behaviors but also will have an effect on the observer in terms of consequences and further actions. Earlier we discussed theories related to three issues of the observer: (a) the labeling of SH by the observer, (b) effects of SH on the observer, and (c) behavioral responses of the observer. Empirical research has been done regarding the first two issues and will be discussed below.

Observers and the Labeling of Conduct as SH

Much of what we know about the labeling of SH comes from observers, that is, people watching (but not directly experiencing) a behavior. Perceptions play a significant role in how behavior is labeled. Harassing behaviors are often not perceived or labeled as such, even when they meet objective criteria of SH (Schneider et al., 1997). For example, individuals in Lee's (2001) research referred to behaviors that were clearly harassing as "sexism," "really unpleasant," "not very nice," and "quite unnecessary" rather than as SH. According to Fitzgerald et al. (1997), whether or not an individual interprets behavior as SH depends not only on personal factors (e.g., attitudes and previous experiences) but also on objective aspects of the behavior (e.g., duration, frequency) and contextual factors (e.g., the organization's response to reported harassment). This perspective combines both the subjective and objective perspectives described above and as such provides a more detailed description of SH perceptions.

The most conclusive finding from research examining individuals' perceptions of SH is that women perceive more behaviors as sexually harassing than do men but that both men and women are likely to perceive egregious behaviors as harassing (e.g., Collins & Blodgett, 1981; Gutek, Nakamura, Gahart, Handschumacher, & Russell, 1980; Gutek et al., 1983; Powell, 1986). Prior SH experiences and sexual abuse (e.g., child molestation), however, do not influence individuals' perceptions of SH (Stockdale, O'Connor, Gutek, & Geer, 2002). In other words, such individuals are typically not more likely than others to interpret behaviors as SH.

Situational Factors That Influence Perceptions of SH

Situational factors that influence individuals' identification of sexually harassing behaviors include status of the initiator, both in absolute terms and relative to the target, the initiator's intentions, evidence of coercion, the target's reaction, and job consequences for the target (e.g., Collins & Blodgett, 1981; York, 1989). Based on his research and the research of others (e.g., Reilly, Carpenter, Dull, & Barlett, 1982), Pryor (1985) concluded that "the general unexpectedness or inappropriateness of a behavior for an actor's role and status contributes to the labeling of a behavior as sexual harassment" (p. 274). This was his explanation for the finding that behaviors initiated by supervisors or married individuals are more likely to be perceived as sexually harassing.

Effects of SH on Observers

As stated earlier, little research has looked at the effects of SH on observers. In presenting their notion of ambient SH, Glomb et al. (1997) found that simply being exposed to SH can have negative effects. Specifically, they found that observers of SH suffer from lower job satisfaction and psychological distress, which can have a detrimental effect on an observer's health. Ultimately, this can lead to job withdrawal. More recent work has extended this work to show that ambient SH affects both male and female observers (Richman-Hirsch & Glomb, 2002).

Conclusions

We face one final task in this chapter: to share our general thoughts about the current state of knowledge regarding workplace SH. Fortunately, Table 17.1

provides a valuable framework to facilitate this task. As described earlier, this table summarizes the major theoretical models that have been developed around workplace SH, and it also identifies those theoretical approaches that have received the most empirical attention in organizational research. By juxtaposing the two columns in this table, we can identify those topic areas in which the strongest research contributions might be made.

Beginning with general topics, it is probably not surprising that theories that focus on the "Organization" concept in Figure 17.1 have received the most empirical attention in the organizations literature. Most of the theoretical models that posit organizational explanations for sexual harassment have received at least some investigation. Although there is certainly room for greater exploration of organizational contributions to SH, research to date provides clear evidence that organizational factors do play a role in SH. The findings around organizational influences continue to accumulate, suggesting that this is a lively area of research in which additional contributions will be made.

Less well investigated are the other concepts depicted in Figure 17.1. It is perhaps not surprising that the "Society"-based explanations have been given little attention in organizational research. As mentioned earlier, tests of these models are likely to be society level and therefore beyond the scope of interest and expertise of most organizational researchers. Societal factors, then, present the context for other investigations of workplace SH but are unlikely to be the focus of research by organizational scholars. Therefore, we would identify this as an area in which there is little empirical work and in which we would expect little empirical work within the organizational sciences in the future.

Research (both theoretical and empirical) on SH as a communication process also has received little attention in the organizations literature; however, contrary to our statement above regarding research on society-based explanations, we believe that research on SH as a form of communication presents an important opportunity for future research. Perhaps because organizational researchers have paid little attention to SH actors, they also have focused little on the choices these individuals make about *how* to enact sexual harassment. If SH is a motivated behavior, then actors must decide when and how they will act, and these decisions involve the communication process (i.e., how to encode the message, how to transmit the message). Therefore, we believe that the integration of theoretical perspectives from the communications literature could be very valuable to further explaining why SH actors act in the ways that they do (e.g., when they will choose verbal vs. nonverbal communication methods, whether they will deliberately introduce noise into the communication process).

Building on this, we also note the lack of empirical research on SH actors that is evident from a review of Table 17.1. By far, the majority of studies in this area address SH as occurring because of actor misperceptions or due to negative personality patterns. What is clearly missing here is research that looks at SH as a motivated behavior by actors. We know little about why or when actors will consciously choose to engage in sexually harassing behavior. Certainly, it is challenging to do research on the "perpetrator" of any negative work behaviors; however, researchers who study general workplace aggression have tackled this challenge in a way that SH researchers have not. Therefore, we put in a strong call for future research that focuses on SH actors: What motivates their harassing behavior? What goals are they pursuing when they harass? What cognitions are involved in their decision making? Fortunately, there is actor-based theoretical work (see Table 17.1) that can guide these empirical investigations, with models of ethical decision making and accountability being noteworthy.

Table 17.1 also reveals a mismatch between theoretical advances and empirical verifications about targets of SH. In recent years, there have been numerous models that predict how and when targets will react to SH, but few studies have followed to test these predictions. Again, this strikes us as an area in which significant empirical contributions may be made. As discussed in our review of theory, there certainly are a range of theoretical frameworks that can be invoked to develop such studies (e.g., learned helplessness, reactance theory, whistle-blowing, taxonomies of response behaviors, attribution theory, goal theory). Given the strong theoretical development in this area, it is somewhat surprising that more empirical work has not occurred. In contrast to our discussion of actors above, it is easier to locate and study individuals who identify themselves as victims of SH as opposed to perpetrators of SH. Therefore, the challenges of doing research on targets (vs. actors) are less daunting.

Finally, we are very excited about the potential for future research on SH observers. Hostile environment SH is a phenomenon that takes place within the workplace social system, suggesting that there often are observers of SH. Few empirical studies have explored the attitudes and experiences of observers, yet there are several good models to guide such work. Fortuitously, research on observers would appear to be the "easiest" type of SH research to pursue, given that observers are less directly involved and therefore less likely to be directly threatened by a recounting of their experiences.

To this point, our discussion of the state of the SH literature has focused on the model (Figure 17.1) and table (Table 17.1) that we developed throughout our literature review. Before closing, and because of the general topic of this volume, we also want to share some thoughts about the state of the literature if SH is conceptualized as a type of workplace aggression. We believe that thinking of SH as aggression offers some interesting insights into research contributions that might be made in future research.

Our thoughts in this regard develop from the general belief that popular conceptualizations of SH and of workplace aggression tend to be quite distinct. We argue that the general conceptualization of workplace aggression is such that aggression is something that is *activated* (or triggered) by organizations. That is, many of our theories and studies examine organizational policies and actions that drive employees to aggressive behavior (e.g., that workplace aggression occurs when employees perceive that they have been treated unfairly). Certainly, there is a recognition in the literature that some employees overreact to organizational actions (e.g., the employee who perceives injustice where none exists), yet still there is a notion that organizational actions trigger the negative behavior. On the other hand, we would argue that the general conceptualization of SH is that harassment is something that is *permitted* by organizations. That is, we tend to view harassment as something that exists in society generally (developed through the societal forces described in earlier sections), and an organization can either tolerate it or not.

We share these armchair theories here because we think it is interesting to consider how SH research might proceed differently if the conceptualization of workplace aggression were to be applied to SH. That is, what if SH were to be conceptualized as something that organizations *trigger*? What research topics would be front and center in our theories? What research questions would take on the most urgency?

From our perspective, this alternative conceptualization would shift the focus from organizational norms and culture (e.g., such as is evident in the organizational tolerance for sexual harassment research) to management actions. In the workplace aggression literature, there is some recent research that explores aggression norms and climates, but the primary focus has been on the actions that organizational managers take and how these prompt injustice perceptions and negative responses. Adopting this perspective for SH, perhaps some SH is triggered because of an actor's negative experiences at work. For example, a person who feels unfairly treated may enact SH (instead of some other form of workplace aggression) in order to release frustration or anger, in order to retaliate, or in order to restore equity. Thus, the motivating force behind SH is not simply the expression of views learned through societal level socialization (e.g., that it is appropriate for men to dominate women), but it also involves actions that an employer has taken against an employee that are negatively experienced. Then, the research issues that become central are ones such as the following: Which managerial actions against an actor are associated with SH responses by the actor? When will perceived injustice trigger SH (vs. some other form of workplace aggression)? Are some actor goals (e.g., retaliation vs. equity restoration) more likely to be pursued through SH? Are certain actors more likely to choose SH, as opposed to some other form of negative behavior? These types of questions have rarely been posed in research on sexual harassment but provide interesting avenues for future research.

In this chapter, it was our intent to present a review of the sexual harassment literature and to provide some clarity about the current state of the literature. It is not, in our minds, an exaggeration to say that there are *many* more good theories than good empirical studies in SH research to date. We strongly encourage SH researchers to focus their attention on theory testing. Certainly, that is one of the lessons that we personally have taken away from the experience of conducting this review.

Notes

1. These numbers do not add to 100% because several forms of sexual harassment were often experienced in conjunction with another.

2. The original figure provided by the EEOC was $12.7 million, but that was expressed in 1992 dollars. In order to make relevant comparisons, we expressed the 1992 figure in 2002 dollars by adjusting for inflation.

References

Abbey, A. (1982). Sex differences in attributions for friendly behavior: Do males misperceive females' friendliness? *Journal of Personality and Social Psychology, 42*(5), 830–838.

Abbey, A. (1987). Misperceptions of friendly behavior as sexual interest: A survey of naturally occurring incidents. *Psychology of Women Quarterly, 11*, 173–194.

Adams-Roy, J., & Barling, J. (1998). Predicting the decision to confront or report sexual harassment. *Journal of Organizational Behavior, 19*, 329–336.

Avina, C., & O'Donohue, W. (2002). Sexual harassment and PTSD: Is sexual harassment diagnosable trauma? *Journal of Traumatic Stress, 15*, 69–75.

Baker, D. D., Terpstra, D. E., & Cutler, B. D. (1989). Perceptions of sexual harassment: A re-examination of gender differences. *Journal of Psychology, 124*(4), 409–416.

Baker, D. D., Terpstra, D. E., & Larantz, K. (1990). The influence of individual characteristics and severity of harassing behavior on reactions to sexual harassment. *Sex Roles, 22*(5/6), 305–325.

Barling, J., Rogers, A. G., & Kelloway, E. K. (2001). Behind closed doors: In-home workers' experience of sexual harassment and workplace violence. *Journal of Occupational Health Psychology, 6*, 255–269.

Baron, R. A., & Neuman, J. H. (1996). Workplace violence and workplace aggression: Evidence of their relative frequency and potential causes. *Aggressive Behavior, 22*, 161–173.

Baron, R. A., Neuman, J. H., & Geddes, D. (1999). Social and personal determinants of workplace aggression: Evidence for the impact of perceived injustice and the Type A behavior pattern. *Aggressive Behavior, 25*, 281–296.

Begany, J. J., & Milburn, M. A. (2002). Psychological predictors of sexual harassment: Authoritarianism, hostile sexism, and rape myths. *Psychology of Men and Masculinity, 3*, 119–126.

Bennett, J. B., & Lehman, W. E. K. (1999). The relationship between problem coworkers and quality work practices: A case study of exposure to sexual harassment, substance abuse, violence, and job stress. *Work & Stress, 13*, 299–311.

Bergman, M. E., & Drasgow, F. (2003). Race as a moderator in a model of sexual harassment: An empirical test. *Journal of Occupational Health Psychology, 8*, 131–145.

Bowes-Sperry, L., & O'Leary-Kelly, A. M. (2005). To act or not to act: The dilemma faced by observers of sexual harassment. *Academy of Management Review, 30*, 288–306.

Bowes-Sperry, L., & Powell, G. N. (1996). Sexual harassment as a moral issue: An ethical decision-making perspective. In M. S. Stockdale (Ed.), *Sexual harassment in the workplace* (Vol. 5, pp. 105–124). Thousand Oaks, CA: Sage.

Bowes-Sperry, L., & Powell, G. N. (1999). Observers' reactions to social-sexual behavior at work: An ethical decision-making perspective. *Journal of Management, 25,* 779–802.

Bowes-Sperry, L., Tata, J., & Luthar, H. K. (2003). Comparing sexual harassment to other forms of workplace aggression. In A. Sagie, S. Stashevsky, & M. Koslowky (Eds.), *Misbehaviour and dysfunctional attitudes in organizations* (pp. 33–56). New York: Palgrave Macmillan.

Brehm, J. W. (1966). *A theory of psychological reactance.* New York: Academic.

Brehm, J. W. (1972). *Responses to loss of freedom: A theory of psychological reactance.* Morristown, NJ: General Learning.

Cleveland, J. N., & Kerst, M. E. (1993). Sexual harassment and perceptions of power: An under-articulated relationship. *Journal of Vocational Behavior, 42,* 49–67.

Cochran, C. C., Frazier, P. A., & Olson, A. M. (1997). Predictors of responses to unwanted sexual harassment. *Psychology of Women Quarterly, 21,* 207–226.

Cohen, A. G., & Gutek, B. A. (1985). Dimensions of perceptions of social-sexual behavior in a work setting. *Sex Roles, 13*(5/6), 317–327.

Collins, E. G. C., & Blodgett, T. B. (1981, March-April). Some see it . . . some won't. *Harvard Business Review,* 77–95.

Dall'Ara, E., & Maass, A. (1999). Studying sexual harassment in the laboratory: Are egalitarian women at higher risk? *Sex Roles, 41,* 681–704.

Dansky, B. S., & Kilpatrick, D. G. (1997). Effects of sexual harassment. In W. O'Donohue (Ed.), *Sexual harassment: Theory, research, and treatment* (pp. 152–174). Needham Heights, MA: Allyn & Bacon.

Dekker, I., & Barling, J. (1998). Personal and organizational predictors of workplace sexual harassment of women by men. *Journal of Occupational Health Psychology, 3,* 7–18.

Dougherty, D. S. (2001). Sexual harassment as [dys]functional process: A feminist standpoint analysis. *Journal of Applied Communication Research, 29*(4), 372–402.

Dougherty, T. W., Turban, D. B., Olson, D. E., Dwyer, P. D., & LaPreze, M. W. (1996). Factors affecting perceptions of workplace sexual harassment. *Journal of Organizational Behavior, 17,* 489–501.

Driscoll, D. M., Kelly, J. R., & Henderson, W. L. (1998). Can perceivers identify likelihood to sexually harass? *Sex Roles, 38*(7/8), 557–588.

Equal Employment Opportunity Commission. (1980). Guidelines on discrimination on the basis of sex. *Federal Register, 45*(219) 29 CFR, part 1604.

Fitzgerald, L. F., Drasgow, F., Hulin, C. L., Gelfand, M. J., & Magley, V. J. (1997). Antecedents and consequences of sexual harassment in organizations: A test of an integrated model. *Journal of Applied Psychology, 82,* 578–589.

Fitzgerald, L. F., Gelfand, M. J., & Drasgow, F. (1995). Measuring sexual harassment: Theoretical and psychometric advances. *Basic and Applied Social Psychology, 17,* 425–445.

Fitzgerald, L. F., Schullman, S. L., Bailey, N., Richards, M., Swecker, J., Gold, Y., et al. (1988). The incidence and dimensions of sexual harassment in academia and the workplace. *Journal of Vocational Behavior, 32*(2), 152–175.

Fitzgerald, L. F., Swan, S., & Magley, V. J. (1997). But was it really sexual harassment? Legal, behavioral, and psychological definitions of the workplace victimization of women. In W. O'Donohue (Ed.), *Sexual harassment: Theory, research, and treatment* (pp. 5–28). Boston: Allyn & Bacon.

Forgas, J. P., O'Connor, K. V., & Morris, S. L. (1983). Smile and punishment: The effects of facial expression on responsibility attribution by groups and individuals. *Personality and Social Psychology Bulletin, 9,* 587–596.

Frink, D. D., & Klimoski, R. J. (1998). Toward a theory of accountability in organizations and human resources management. In G. R. Ferris (Ed.), *Research in personnel and human resources management* (pp. 1–51). Stamford, CT: JAI.

Gelfand, M. J., Fitzgerald, L. F., & Drasgow, F. (1995). The structure of sexual harassment: A confirmatory analysis across cultures and settings. *Journal of Vocational Behavior, 47,* 164–177.

Glomb, T. M., Munson, L. J., Hulin, C. L., Bergman, M. E., & Drasgow, F. (1999). Structural equation models of sexual harassment: Longitudinal explorations and cross-sectional generalizations. *Journal of Applied Psychology, 84,* 14–28.

Glomb, T. M., Richman, W. L., Hulin, C. L., Drasgow, F., Schneider, K. T., & Fitzgerald, L. F. (1997). Ambient sexual harassment: An integrated model of antecedents and consequences. *Organizational Behavior and Human Decision Processes, 71*(3), 309–328.

Greenberg, L., & Barling, J. (1999). Predicting employee aggression against supervisors, coworkers, and subordinates. *Journal of Organizational Behavior, 20,* 897–913.

Greenwood, D., & Isbell, L. M. (2002). Ambivalent sexism and the dumb blonde: Men's and women's reactions to sexist jokes. *Psychology of Women Quarterly, 26,* 341–351.

Gruber, J. E., & Bjorn, L. (1982). Blue-collar blues: The sexual harassment of women autoworkers. *Work and Occupations, 9,* 271–298.

Gruber, J. E., & Smith, M. (1995). Women's responses to sexual harassment: A multivariate analysis. *Basic and Applied Social Psychology, 17,* 543–562.

Gutek, B. (1985). *Sex and the workplace.* San Francisco: Jossey-Bass.

Gutek, B. A., & Cohen, A. G. (1987). Sex ratios, sex role spillover, and sex at work: A comparison of men's and women's experiences. *Human Relations, 40,* 97–115.

Gutek, B. A., Cohen, A. G., & Konrad, A. M. (1990). Predicting social-sexual behavior at work: A contact hypothesis. *Academy of Management Journal, 33*(3), 560–577.

Gutek, B. A., & Koss, M. P. (1993). Changed women and changed organizations: Consequences of and coping with sexual harassment. *Journal of Vocational Behavior, 42,* 28–48.

Gutek, B. A., & Morasch, B. (1982). Sex-ratios, sex-role spillover, and sexual harassment of women at work. *Journal of Social Issues, 38*(4), 55–74.

Gutek, B. A., Morasch, B., & Cohen, A. G. (1983). Interpreting social-sexual behavior in a work setting. *Journal of Vocational Behavior, 22,* 30–48.

Gutek, B. A., Nakamura, C. Y., Gahart, M., Handschumacher, I., & Russell, D. (1980). Sexuality and the workplace. *Basic and Applied Psychology, 1,* 255–265.

Hartnett, J. J., Robinson, D., & Singh, B. (1989). Perceptions of males and females toward sexual harassment and acquiescence. *Journal of Social Behavior and Personality, 4*(3), 291–298.

Hulin, C. L., Fitzgerald, L. F., & Drasgow, F. (1996). Organizational influences on sexual harassment. In M. S. Stockdale (Ed.), *Sexual harassment in the workplace* (Vol. 5, pp. 127–150). Thousand Oaks, CA: Sage.

Johnson, C. B., Stockdale, M. S., & Saal, F. E. (1991). Persistence of men's misperceptions of friendly cues across a variety of interpersonal encounters. *Psychology of Women Quarterly, 15,* 463–475.

Jones, T. M. (1991). Ethical decision making by individuals in organizations: An issue-contingent model. *Academy of Management Review, 16,* 366–395.

Jones, T. S., & Remland, M. S. (1992). Source of variability in perceptions of and responses to sexual harassment. *Sex Roles, 27*(3/4), 121–142.

Kelley, H. H. (1973). The process of causal attribution. *American Psychologist, 27,* 107–128.

Keyton, J., Ferguson, P., & Rhodes, S. C. (2001). Cultural indicators of sexual harassment. *Southern Communication Journal, 67*(1), 33–50.

Knapp, D. E., Faley, R. H., Ekeberg, W. C., & Dubois, C. L. Z. (1997). Determinants of target responses to sexual harassment: A conceptual framework. *Academy of Management Review, 22,* 687–729.

Konrad, A. M., & Gutek, B. A. (1986). Impact of work experiences on attitudes toward sexual harassment. *Administrative Science Quarterly, 31,* 422–438.

Latané, B., & Darley, J. M. (1970). *The unresponsive bystander: Why doesn't he help?* New York: Appleton-Century-Crofts.

LeBlanc, M. M., & Kelloway, E. K. (2002). Predictors and outcomes of workplace violence and aggression. *Journal of Applied Psychology, 87,* 444–453.

Lee, D. (2001). "He didn't sexually harass me, as in harassed me for sex . . . he was just horrible": Women's definitions of unwanted male sexual conduct at work. *Women's Studies International Forum, 24,* 25–38.

Lee, J. W., & Guerrero, L. K. (2001). Types of touch in cross-sex relationships between coworkers: Perceptions of relational and emotional messages, inappropriateness, and sexual harassment. *Journal of Applied Communication Research, 29*(3), 197–220.

Lengnick-Hall, M. L. (1995). Sexual harassment research: A methodological critique. *Personnel Psychology, 48,* 841–864.

Loy, P. H., & Stewart, L. P. (1984). The extent and effects of sexual harassment of working women. *Sociological Focus, 17*(1), 31–43.

Lucero, M. A., Middleton, K., Finch, W., & Valentine, S. (2003). An empirical investigation of sexual harassers: Toward a perpetrator typology. *Human Relations, 56,* 1461–1483.

Malamuth, H. S., Sockloskie, R., Koss, M., & Tanaka, J. (1991). The characteristics of aggressors against women: Testing a model using a national sample of college students. *Journal of Consulting and Clinical Psychology, 59,* 670–681.

Munson, L. J., Hulin, C., & Drasgow, F. (2000). Longitudinal analysis of dispositional influences and sexual harassment: Effects on job and psychology outcomes. *Personnel Psychology, 53,* 21–46.

Munson, L. J., Miner, A. G., & Hulin, C. (2001). Labeling sexual harassment in the military: An extension and replication. *Journal of Applied Psychology, 86*(2), 293–303.

Murphy, W. D., Coleman, E. M., & Haynes, M. R. (1986). Factors related to coercive sexual behavior in a non-clinical sample of males. *Violence and Victims, 4,* 255–278.

Murphy, W. D., Driscoll, D. M., & Kelly, J. R. (1999). Differences in the nonverbal behavior of men who vary in the likelihood to sexually harass. *Social Behavior and Personality, 14,* 113–129.

Murry, W. D., Sivasubramaniam, N., & Jacques, P. H. (2001). Supervisory support, social exchange relationships, and sexual harassment consequences: A test of competing models. *Leadership Quarterly, 12,* 1–29.

Near, J. P., & Miceli, M. P. (1985). Organizational dissidence: The case of whistle-blowing. *Journal of Business Ethics, 4,* 1–16.

O'Leary-Kelly, A. M., & Bowes-Sperry, L. (2001). Sexual harassment as unethical behavior: The role of moral intensity. *Human Resource Management Review, 11,* 73–92.

O'Leary-Kelly, A. M., Paetzold, R. L., & Griffin, R. W. (2000). Sexual harassment as aggressive behavior: An actor-based perspective. *Academy of Management Review, 25,* 372–388.

O'Leary-Kelly, A. M., Tiedt, P., & Bowes-Sperry, L. (2004). Answering accountability questions in sexual harassment: Insights regarding harassers, targets, and observers. *Human Resource Management Review, 14,* 85–106.

Osland, J. A., Fitch, M., & Willis, E. E. (1996). Likelihood to rape in college males. *Sex Roles, 35,* 171–183.

Padavic, I., & Orcutt, J. D. (1997). Perceptions of sexual harassment in the Florida legal system: A comparison of dominance and spillover explanations. *Gender & Society, 11*(5), 682–698.

Parker, S. K., & Griffin, M. A. (2002). What is so bad about a little name-calling? Negative consequences of gender harassment for overperformance demands and distress. *Journal of Occupational Health Psychology, 7*(3), 195–210.

Perry, E. L., Kulik, C. T., & Schmidtke, J. M. (1997). Blowing the whistle: Determinants of responses to sexual harassment. *Basic and Applied Social Psychology, 19*(4), 457–482.

Perry, E. L., Kulik, C. T., & Schmidtke, J. M. (1998). Individual differences in the effectiveness of sexual harassment awareness training. *Journal of Applied Social Psychology, 28,* 698–723.

Pierce, C. A., Broberg, B. J., McClure, J. R., & Aguinis, H. (2002). Responding to sexual harassment complaints: Effects of a dissolved workplace romance on decision-making standards. *Organizational Behavior and Human Decision Processes, 95,* 66–82.

Powell, G. N. (1986). Effects of sex role identity and sex on definitions of sexual harassment. *Sex Roles, 14,* 9–19.

Pryor, J. B. (1985). The lay person's understanding of sexual harassment. *Sex Roles, 17*(5/6), 273–286.

Pryor, J. B. (1987). Sexual harassment proclivities in men. *Sex Roles, 17,* 269–290.

Pryor, J. B., & Day, J. D. (1988). Interpretations of sexual harassment: An attributional analysis. *Sex Roles, 18*(7/8), 405–417.

Pryor, J. B., & Giedd, J. L. (1995). A social psychological model for predicting sexual harassment. *Journal of Social Issues, 51*(1), 69–86.

Pryor, J. B., LaVite, C. M., & Stoller, L. M. (1993). A social psychological analysis of sexual harassment: The person/situation interaction. *Journal of Vocational Behavior, 42,* 68–83.

Pryor, J. B., & Stoller, L. M. (1994). Sexual cognition processes in men high in the likelihood to sexually harass. *Personality and Social Psychology Bulletin, 20,* 163–169.

Pyszcznski, T. A., & Greenberg, J. (1981). Role of disconfirmed expectancies in the instigation of attributional processing. *Journal of Personality and Social Psychology, 40,* 31–38.

Ragins, B. R., & Scandura, T. A. (1995). Antecedents and work-related correlates of reported sexual harassment: An empirical investigation of competing hypotheses. *Sex Roles, 32*(7/8), 429–455.

Reilly, T., Carpenter, S., Dull, V., & Barlett, K. (1982). The factorial survey technique: An approach to defining sexual harassment on campus. *Journal of Social Issues, 38,* 99–110.

Richman-Hirsch, W. L., & Glomb, T. M. (2002). Are men affected by the sexual harassment of women? Effects of ambient sexual harassment on men. In J. M. Brett & F. Drasgow (Eds.), *Psychology of work: Theoretically based empirical research* (pp. 121–140). Mahwah, NJ: Lawrence Erlbaum.

Robinson, S. L., & Bennett, R. J. (1995). A typology of deviant workplace behaviors: A multidimensional scaling study. *Academy of Management Journal, 38,* 555–572.

Rogers, J. K., & Henson, K. D. (1997). "Hey, why don't you wear a shorter skirt?" Structural vulnerability and the organization of sexual harassment in temporary clerical employment. *Gender and Society, 11,* 215–237.

Rospenda, K. M., Richman, J. A., Wislar, J. S., & Flaherty, J. A. (2000). Chronicity of sexual harassment and generalized work-place abuse: Effects on drinking outcomes. *Addiction, 95,* 1805–1820.

Roth, J., & Fedor, D. B. (1993, August). *In the eye of the beholder: Naming, blaming, and claiming in the sexual harassment process.* Paper presented at the Annual Meeting of the Academy of Management, Atlanta, GA.

Rotundo, M., Nguyen, D. H., & Sackett, P. R. (2001). A meta-analytic review of gender differences in perceptions of sexual harassment. *Journal of Applied Psychology, 86*(5), 914–922.

Rudman, L. A., & Borgida, E. (1995). The afterglow of construct accessibility: The behavior consequences of priming men to view women as sex objects. *Journal of Experimental Social Psychology, 31,* 493–517.

Saal, F. E., Johnson, C. B., & Weber, N. (1989). Friendly or sexy? It may depend on whom you ask. *Psychology of Women Quarterly, 13,* 263–276.

Sbraga, TP., & O'Donohue, W. (2000). Sexual harassment. *Annual Review of Sex Research, 11,* 258–285.

Scalora, M. J., Washington, D. O., Casady, T., & Newell, S. P. (2003). Nonfatal workplace violence risk factors: Data from a police contact sample. *Journal of Interpersonal Violence, 18,* 310–327.

Schat, A. C. H., & Kelloway, E. K. (2003). Reducing the adverse consequences of workplace aggression and violence: The buffering effects of organizational support. *Journal of Occupational Health Psychology, 8,* 110–122.

Schlenker, B. R. (1982). Translating actions into attitudes: An identity-analytic approach to the explanation of social conduct. In L. Berkowitz (Ed.), *Advances in experimental social psychology* (Vol. 15, pp. 193–247). San Diego, CA: Academic.

Schneider, K. T., Swan, S., & Fitzgerald, L. F. (1997). Job-related and psychological effects of sexual harassment in the workplace: Empirical evidence from two organizations. *Journal of Applied Psychology, 82,* 401–415.

Seligman, M. E. P. (1974). Depression and learned helplessness. In R. J. Friedman & M. J. Katz (Eds.), *The psychology of depression: Contemporary theory and research* (pp. 83–113). Washington, DC: Winston-Wiley.

Sheffey, S., & Tindale, R. S. (1992). Perceptions of sexual harassment in the workplace. *Journal of Applied Social Psychology, 22*(19), 1502–1520.

Stockdale, M. S. (1993). The role of sexual misperceptions of women's friendliness in an emerging theory of sexual harassment. *Journal of Vocational Behavior, 42,* 84–101.

Stockdale, M. S., O'Connor, M., Gutek, B. A., & Geer, T. (2002). The relationship between prior sexual abuse and reactions to sexual harassment: Literature review and empirical study. *Psychology, Public Policy, and Law, 8,* 64–95.

Tangri, S. S., Burt, M. R., & Johnson, L. B. (1982). Sexual harassment at work: Three explanatory models. *Journal of Social Issues, 38*(4), 33–54.

Tedeschi, J. T., & Felson, R. B. (1994). *Violence, aggression, and coercive actions.* Washington, DC: American Psychological Association.

Terpstra, D. E., & Baker, D. D. (1986). Psychological and demographic correlates of perception of sexual harassment. *Genetic, Social, and General Psychology Monographs, 112*(4), 459–478.

Terpstra, D. E., & Baker, D. D. (1988). Outcomes of sexual harassment charges. *Academy of Management Journal, 31*(1), 185–194.

Terpstra, D. E., & Baker, D. D. (1989). The identification and classification of reactions to sexual harassment. *Journal of Organizational Behavior, 10,* 1–14.

Terpstra, D. E., & Baker, D. D. (1992). Outcomes of federal court decisions on sexual harassment. *Academy of Management Journal, 35*(1), 181–190.

Terpstra, D. E., & Cook, S. E. (1985). Complainant characteristics and reported behaviors and consequences associated with formal sexual harassment charges. *Personnel Psychology, 38,* 559–574.

Tetlock, P. E. (1985). Accountability: A social check on the fundamental attribution error. *Social Psychology Quarterly, 48,* 227–236.

Thacker, R. A. (1992). A descriptive study of behavioral responses of sexual harassment targets: Implications for control theory. *Employee Responsibilities and Rights Journal, 5*(2), 155–171.

Thacker, R. A., & Gohmann, S. F. (1996). Emotional and psychological consequences of sexual harassment: A descriptive study. *Journal of Psychology, 130*(4), 429–446.

Thomann, D. A., & Wiener, R. L. (1987). Physical and psychological causality as determinants of culpability in sexual harassment cases. *Sex Roles, 17*(9/10), 573–591.

Thompson, T. D. (2003). Employee's "atrocious" behavior didn't give rise to liability for city of Chicago. *Illinois Employment Law Letter, 14.*

U.S. Merit Systems Protection Board. (1995). *Sexual harassment in the federal workplace: Trends, progress and continuing challenges.* Washington, DC: U.S. Government Printing Office.

Vaux, A. (1993). Paradigmatic assumptions in sexual harassment research: Being guided without being misled. *Journal of Vocational Behavior, 42,* 116–135.

Welsh, S. (1999). Gender and sexual harassment. *Annual Review of Sociology, 25,* 169–190.

Welsh, S. (2000). The multidimensional nature of sexual harassment: An empirical analysis of women's sexual harassment complaints. *Violence Against Women, 6*(2), 118–141.

Welsh, S., & Gruber, J. E. (1999). Not taking it anymore: Women who report or file complaints of sexual harassment. *Canadian Review of Sociology and Anthropology, 36,* 559–583.

Williams, C. W., Brown, R. S., Lees-Haley, P. R., & Price, J. R. (1995). An attributional (causal dimensional) analysis of perceptions of sexual harassment. *Journal of Applied Social Psychology, 25*(13), 1169–1183.

Williams, J. H., Fitzgerald, L. F., & Drasgow, F. (1999). The effects of organizational practices on sexual harassment and individual outcomes in the military. *Military Psychology, 11*(3), 303–328.

Wong, P. T. P., & Weiner, B. (1981). When people ask "why" questions and the heuristics of attributional search. *Journal of Personality and Social Psychology, 40,* 650–663.

York, K. M. (1989). Defining sexual harassment in the workplace: A policy-capturing approach. *Academy of Management Journal, 32,* 830–850.

18

Young Workers

Sean Tucker
Catherine Loughlin

A lthough incidents of bullying in schools have received increased public attention in recent years, young people's exposure to aggression and violence in other contexts has been neglected. Previous work has identified young workers as an at-risk population for exposure to workplace violence and aggression (e.g., Chappell & Di Martino, 2000); however, to our knowledge, this chapter is the first to offer a comprehensive review of the literature related to this issue. We will review research from a range of academic disciplines, including developmental psychology, organizational behavior, the medical sciences, and criminology. In this chapter, we begin by framing the topic (e.g., Who are young workers? What are the patterns of workplace aggression and violence among youth?). Thereafter, we consider the major theoretical models of relevance. We will then review the specific predictors (e.g., gender), mediators (e.g., anger), moderators (e.g., social support), individual outcomes (e.g., well-being), and organizational outcomes (e.g., turnover intentions) of exposure to work-related aggression or violence. Next, we will address key measurement issues and outline future research needs (e.g., What are the long-term outcomes of adolescent exposure to aggression in the workplace?). Finally, we consider the implications for policy and intervention.

Authors' Note: This chapter was supported by a grant from the Social Sciences and Humanities Research Council of Canada to Dr. Catherine Loughlin.

Definitions

Aggression and Violence

Researchers have found it useful to distinguish between the terms *aggression* and *violence* in the literature. Both constructs lie within the realm of personal aggression (e.g., see Robinson & Bennett, 1995); however, aggression is more common than violence and typically precedes it (Barling, 1996; LeBlanc & Kelloway, 2002). *Aggression* includes hostile verbal behavior (e.g., swearing or yelling) and nonverbal behavior (e.g., ostracizing or stalking). Aggressive behaviors may take many forms, including harassment and *bullying* (i.e., the long-term, systematic harassment of a person by one or more persons). *Violence* describes more serious acts of aggression (Anderson & Bushman, 2002), a range of behaviors including physical assaults and threats directed toward persons, including forms of direct physical harm such as homicide, kicking, pushing, and sexual harassment during which physical coercion is used.

Barling, Rogers, and Kelloway (2001) proposed that sexual harassment and workplace violence are conceptually similar and that they may co-occur. In this chapter, we discuss workplace aggression and violence, including sexual harassment, that is both enacted and experienced by young workers, including acts that are perpetrated by their managers or supervisors, members of the public (customers and robbers), and coworkers. Our investigation is limited to person-to-person violence and aggression; hence, we exclude from this review studies that examine harm that is self-inflicted (suicide) and those primarily concerned with physical damage to employer or employee property (see Robinson & Bennett, 1995).

Work and Workplace

Throughout this chapter *work* will refer to a diverse range of employment arrangements in the formal and informal sectors in which labor is voluntarily exchanged for pay. We use a relatively broad definition of *workplace*, which accounts for incidents that occur while on duty, either on or away from the work site. We include in this discussion young workers employed in the military. It is generally accepted that soldiers are inherently different from other workers and that their work experiences may involve exposure to extreme violence; however, we would point out that all early work experiences are relevant to civilian employers because a large proportion of young soldiers eventually acquire civilian jobs, whereas others maintain a dual role as reservist and employee. In fact, military recruiters often publicize the potential benefits of military service to civilian employers. An additional reason for focusing on young soldiers is that previous research suggests that exposure to violent cultures is associated with higher levels of enacted aggression or violence, both inside and outside the workplace (e.g., Douglas & Martinko, 2001).

Young Workers

The term *young workers* typically refers to workers between the ages of 15 and 24; however, "arbitrary age boundaries for the category 'youth' does not provide an adequate basis for either public policy or research" (Barling & Kelloway, 1999, p. 259). Thus, in this chapter we will also consider studies in which the majority of participants are identified as youth (see Table 18.1 for a list of articles included) or in which those studied have jobs typically occupied by young workers. We do not focus on studies that include child laborers, that is, workers below the age of 15, because international labor law prohibits employment below this age. This is not to suggest that children are not exposed to significant levels of aggression and/or violence in the workplace; however, their experiences may be different from young people above 15 years of age, who are, in many jurisdictions, afforded at least minimum employment protections (see International Labour Organization [ILO], 2004, for a review on child labor).

It should be noted that neither young workers nor their employment experiences are homogeneous. Although these workers share some things in common with their age cohort, their work varies based on job characteristics, employment and educational status, and individual differences. We are interested in young workers who attend school on a full- or part-time basis and work during the evening or weekends, young workers employed full-time during the summer months, and those who have left school and have full-time jobs. Given the wide differences in work status, work intensity (hours per week), and human development, young workers have unique needs and experiences in the workplace. A review of the workplace violence and aggression literature shows that very few studies use samples of young people, and those studies that are relevant are typically cross-sectional and retrospective.

National labor force participation rates show that the vast majority of young people are employed. For example, 67% of Canadian youth (aged 15 to 24) participated in the workforce in 2002 (Statistics Canada, 2005), a rate roughly equivalent to the overall labor force participation rate in the United States and the UK (Duffield, 2002; Bureau of Labor Statistics, 2005). These figures do not capture youth employment in the informal sector (e.g., babysitting, newspaper carriers). Almost half of employed young people work in the retail and service sector in the United States (Zakocs, Runyan, Schulman, Dunn, & Evensen, 1998), which suggests that many young workers have jobs that involve direct interaction with the public. It is important to note that "gendering" of certain occupations, including those in the retail environment, occurs relatively soon after workers enter the labor force (e.g., Kouvonen & Kivivuori, 2001).

Table 18.1   Workplace Violence and Aggression Studies Involving Young Workers

Author	Occupational Group	N	Mean Age (SD)		Age Range
Zakocs et al. (1998)	various	117	16.6		14–17
Vaez et al. (2004)	various	863	na		20–34
Ostvik & Rudmin (2001)	soldiers	696	20		19–27
Mayhew & Quinlan (2002)	fast food restaurant	304	na		na
Kouvonen & Kivivuori (2001)	various	4,347	na		15–16
Keashly et al. (1994)	various	59	19 mode		18–40
Keashly et al. (1997)	student residence assistants	79	21.1		na
Hughes & Tadic (1998)	retail workers	60	≤ 19	20%	
			20–29	62%	
			≥ 30	18%	
Gottfredson (1985)	various				
Grandey et al. (2002)	various	36	18	43%	18–35
Glomb & Liao (2003)	health care	149	23.6 (7.5)		17–40
Frone (2000)	various	319	17.7 (1.0)		16–19
Folgero & Fjeldstad (1995)	various	10	First-year university students		na
Fitzgerald et al. (2003)	various	230	22.0 (3.0)		na
Fineran (2002)	various	381	16.3		14–19
Dupre et al. (in press)	various	131	17.0 (1.2)		na
Bachman et al. (2003)	various	>300,000	~16		~13–19
Bachman et al. (1993)	various	>70,000	18 mode		na
Bey & Zecchinelli (1974)	soldiers	43	na		19–24
Bellair et al. (2003)	various	14,738	na		11–20

Unions may offer workers greater protection from workplace violence. In Canada, Britain, and the United States, however, union density among young workers is significantly lower compared with rates among older workers. For example, only 13.5% of Canadian workers age 15 to 24 are unionized, compared with 30.3% of all other workers (Statistics Canada, 2002). In the United Sates, these rates are 5% and 15.9%, respectively (Bryson, Gomez, Gunderson, & Meltz, 2001). Commentators have noted that young workers, particularly those in the retail sector, are less likely to have access to mechanisms common to most collective agreements that can increase employees' voice (Mayhew & Quinlan, 2002), ensure necessary job training on how to handle abusive situations (DeLaurier, 2001), and provide access to a formal grievance process when work abuse occurs (Moskowitz, 2000).

Prevalence of Aggression and Violence Among Young Workers

On a societal level, national statistics reveal that young people are disproportionately involved in more violent crimes than adults. For instance, in 2002, Canadians aged 15 to 24 years represented 13% of the population; however, they accounted for 31% of individuals charged with violent crimes, including homicide, assault, and sexual assault (Wallace, 2003). Higher rates of criminal victimization are also found among youth. According to the U.S. National Crime Victimization Survey, Americans aged 12 to 24 years were only 22% of the population, but they account for 35% of murder victims and 49% of victims of serious violent crimes, including rape, robbery, and aggravated assault (Perkins, 1997). In terms of workplace violence, the U.S. Bureau of Labor Statistics notes that workers aged 15 to 24 years represented 18% of victims in reported cases of nonfatal work-related assaults and violent acts by person(s) in 2001 (U.S. Department of Justice, 2002). Even young workers aged 15 to 18 experience levels of extreme workplace violence (e.g., assaults and violent acts) similar to working adults (National Institute for Occupational Safety and Health [NIOSH], 2003).

In terms of employment sectors, youth working in the service industry (e.g., restaurant, hospitality, and retail) consistently report high rates of exposure to customer aggression, ranging from low-level verbal and emotional abuse (e.g., Keashly, Hunter, & Harvey, 1997) to sexually harassing behaviors (e.g., Hughes & Tadic, 1998). A study of young Australian fast-food workers found that 48% of employees reported being verbally abused, almost 8% were threatened, and 1% were assaulted during the previous 12 months of employment. In nearly all cases, the perpetrator was identified as someone other than a coworker (Mayhew & Quinlan, 2002). A survey of London Underground Limited (UK) employees found that workers aged 18 to 24 and 25 to 30 experienced the highest per capita rates of assaults during a 2.5-year period compared with all other age cohorts (unpublished report cited in Chappell & Di Martino, 2000). Finally, although Janicak (1999) reported that adult retail workers were more likely to be victims of homicide than young retail workers, NIOSH (2003) recently reported that between 1992 and 2000, 63% of workplace fatalities involving U.S. retail workers under the age of 18 were due to assaults and other violent acts. In addition, Janicak (1999) noted that U.S. workers 19 years of age and younger employed in retail trades experience a 2.5 times greater risk of violent death than youth employed in other industries. Not surprisingly, the largest group of young workers affected by violence is combat soldiers. Kneisler and White (n.d.) have compiled data based on U.S. Central Command press releases on fatalities attributed to hostile fire in Iraq between March 2003 and January 2004. They note that 38% (140/365) of victims were aged 23 years or younger (the youngest soldiers killed being 18 years), although the relative proportion of combat soldiers in this age-group is not reported.

Based on international surveys, we know that young workers are at higher risk than adult workers of being targets of certain forms of aggression and violence and that gender interacts with these experiences as well. Results from the British Crime Survey (BCS) consistently show that young workers are at risk of being victimized by work aggression and violence initiated by members of the public (Budd, 1999). A survey of employees in European Union (EU) countries also found that 5% of young workers reported sexual harassment compared with 2% of all EU workers (Chappell & Di Martino, 2000). A recent survey examining mobbing in German workplaces (defined as frequent harassment, torment, or discrimination by colleagues and/or superiors over a relatively long period) found that significantly more workers under the age of 25 reported this experience in the previous year compared with all other age-groups (Meschkutat, Stackelbeck, & Langenhoff, 2002). A survey of adolescent workers in the United States noted that one third reported being sexually harassed at work over a 1-year period and that young females were more likely than young males to report being victimized (Fineran, 2002).

Concerning other gender differences, males aged 16 to 24 were more likely to report being assaulted at work (including assaults against personal property) than both women and men above 44 years of age (Budd, 1999), and women aged 16 to 24 were more likely to say that they were threatened at work than other age-groups. Meschkutat, Stackelbeck, and Langenhoff (2002) noted that young female workers faced a greater risk of being mobbed than their male counterparts. The 1996 U.S. National Violence Against Women Survey (Tjaden & Thoennes, 2001) indicated that coworker violence (including rape, physical assault, stalking, and threats) is extremely rare. These results are likely understated because workers 15 to 17 years were not surveyed.

In summary, in regard to prevalence rates, the evidence suggests that young people as a whole (whether employed or not) are exposed to more aggression and violence than adults. The sector in which young workers are employed and the type of aggression or violence under discussion also affect the prevalence rates. Certain groups of young workers are more likely to encounter aggression and/or violence in the workplace (e.g., young female workers are at higher risk of being victims of sexual harassment or mobbing). In general, the patterns and frequency of exposure will vary widely based on occupation and other factors that we will discuss shortly. In the next section, we will discuss major empirical studies and the most dominant theoretical model used to explain work aggression and violence enacted and experienced by young workers.

Theoretical Models
and Major Empirical Studies

Explanatory theoretical models of aggression or violence in the workplace consider situational, individual, or interactional models between environmental and individual factors and aggressive behavior (see Griffin, O'Leary-Kelly, & Collins, 1998). In general, these frameworks are not specific to age of either perpetrators or victims of work abuse. The dominant available theory offering insight into young-worker victimization and the expression of work violence and aggression is social learning theory. According to social learning theory (Bandura, 1973), people learn vicariously through observing the behaviors of others (e.g., peers, parents, teachers, coworkers) regarding appropriate responses to perceived interpersonal unfairness or injustice.

Employment, family, and school serve as socializing agents for young people (e.g., Chermack & Walton, 1999; Frone, 1999; Loughlin & Barling, 2001). Young people who witness parents, coworkers, or supervisors responding aggressively to work-related mistreatment could be more likely to adopt similar coping strategies when faced with these situations. A study of young Norwegian Army soldiers found that senior soldiers may model some behaviors (those associated with hazing) to young recruits (Ostvik & Rudmin, 2001). Similarly, Kenway, Fitzclarence, and Hasluck (2000) propose that male-to-male coworker violence in the skilled manual trades is learned and passed from one generation to the next.

As previously mentioned, there are a small number of studies of young workers and workplace aggression. In this section, we discuss four studies (two that examined workplace aggression and two that explored work aggression including violence).

Aggression

A study by Keashly, Trott, and MacLean (1994) of 59 undergraduate students (modal age 19 years) examined the impact of nonsexual, nonphysical, abusive work behavior on job satisfaction and intention to quit. They found that 14% of young workers reported at least 10 abusive interpersonal events (from a list of 28 events) over the previous 12 months and that nearly an equal proportion reported exiting a job due to interpersonal abuse. Supervisors and managers accounted for almost 60% of cases of abusive behavior, followed by coworkers (38%) and subordinates (5%). Approximately equal proportions o   ther the perpetrator or target of aggressio   a hostile event was to talk to others about   avior (55.9%), and avoid the person (44.1   those cited by young female retail worker   assed (Hughes & Tadic, 1998). The least   rceived ability to improve a situation was   ing.

In a later study, Keashly and colleagues (1997) examined the effect of hostile interpersonal interaction by dormitory residents and other guests toward 76 student (mean age = 21 years) residence assistants (RAs) in terms of emotional abuse, role stressors (e.g., role conflict), and other variables, including stress, job satisfaction, job commitment, and intention to leave. Because RAs are responsible for counseling and disciplining students living in college residences, the risk of experiencing abuse is relatively high, and thus it is not surprising that the proportion of the sample that reported 10 or more abusive events in the previous 6 months was markedly greater than in the previous study (48% versus 14%). Finally, RAs with longer tenure cited more and a greater frequency of abusive events, which led to higher job-related tension.

Aggression and Violence

Two cross-sectional studies by Ostvik and Rudmin (2001) examined the social and cognitive elements of bullying (i.e., harassment over time) and hazing (i.e., harassment associated with initiation rituals) among Norwegian Army conscripts (mean age = 20 years). Overall, 12% of recruits reported being bullied, and 22% indicated being hazed in the military. The first study of 696 soldiers found that witnesses more often than victims cited internal characteristics (e.g., personality) as the cause of bullying (23% vs. 11%), whereas victims more often than witnesses reported external characteristics (e.g., appearance and body type) as the cause (25% vs. 18%). Previous exposure to hazing predicted the likelihood that these soldiers would haze others in the future, which supports social learning theory. Hazing was more often directed toward soldiers who were strangers, whereas bullying occurred when perpetrators and victims were familiar with one another and frequency of interaction was high. Also, the youngest soldiers, those 18 years of age, were at highest risk of being victimized.

Their second study focused on the attitudes of 77 officers and 88 soldiers toward bullying. Soldiers were more likely than officers to blame a victim for bullying and report that it was more difficult to prevent peer-on-peer abuse. In cases when soldiers and officers blamed the victim for bullying, soldiers condoned the act whereas officers were more likely to intervene. In terms of effective interventions, soldiers were more likely to agree that to transfer the target of bullying, not the perpetrator, to another unit was appropriate.

Dupre, Inness, Connelly, Barling, and Hoption (in press) controlled for trait anger in a cross-sectional study of 131 part-time Canadian workers (mean age = 17.1 years) and found that the prevalence of enacted aggression was similar to that in studies of adult employees; however, rates of physical violence directed toward supervisors were lower than in studies of adult employees. They found that when financial reasons for working were high and interpersonal injustice and abusive supervision were also high, aggression was higher. The authors suggest that teenagers who work for financial reasons have fewer options because they perceive the consequences of exiting as high. This study also reported that with high interpersonal injustice, work aggression was found to be higher when personal fulfillment was low. The authors propose that young workers who work primarily for personal fulfillment may exit before supervision becomes abusive, whereas workers who do not expect personal fulfillment may believe that they have less to lose and be more likely to demonstrate aggressive behaviors toward supervisors to restore a sense of justice.

In summary, there are few empirical studies on the topic of work aggression and young workers. Although some of the findings are interesting (e.g., that ignoring abusive behavior is perceived as ineffective), these studies tend to deal with small samples and collect data of a self-report and often retrospective nature. Given that studies on workplace aggression have only emerged in the literature in the last decade, the characteristics of these studies are not surprising and simply reflect the stage of development of the literature. The same issue will arise in the next section where, in some places, we will use studies of adults to extrapolate the individual and situational predictors of work aggression and violence experienced and enacted by young workers, as well as probable interactions between predictors.

Predictors of Work Aggression and Violence Related to Young Workers

Individual Predictors

Although few studies have considered young workers in particular, reviews of the literature among adult workers have identified several important individual differences that predict enacted work aggression and violence (see Douglas & Martinko, 2001; Hershcovis et al., in press). We will discuss the role of age and gender in particular in predicting patterns of workplace violence and aggression.

Previous research shows that, in general, enacted aggression is negatively related to age (see Douglas & Martinko, 2001). This is not surprising given that longitudinal studies find that youth between the ages 12 and 17 demonstrate the highest levels of aggression and violence in society as well; by the age of 20, the probability of violent behavior decreases (see Thornberry & Krohn, 2003). In keeping with these findings, Baron, Neuman, and Geddes (1999) found that workers aged 19 to 24 years reported demonstrating aggressive behaviors more often than workers over the age of 34 years. Glomb and Liao's (2003) study of health care workers revealed that younger workers were more likely to enact a range of aggressive behaviors (e.g., swearing, yelling, and damaging property). Interestingly, in contrast to the findings, a recent meta-analysis of 40 studies of full-time employees found that age was *not* a significant predictor of enacted aggression and violence (Hershcovis et al., in press). As mentioned in the previous section, Dupre et al. (in press) found that rates of nonphysical and physical aggression directed toward supervisors were similar to levels reported by adult workers. The reason for these recent counterintuitive findings is not readily apparent but certainly suggests the need for further research on age and enacted workplace aggression and violence.

In terms of victimization, there is some evidence that age also interacts with the type of aggression and violence experienced. For example, a study of adolescent part-time workers found that younger workers were more likely to report experiencing incidents of abusive supervision than older teenage workers (Dupre et al., in press). In a study of Swedish workers aged 20 to 34, Vaez, Ekberg, and Laflamme (2004) found that women and men aged 20 to 24 experienced significantly more threats and violence compared with older age-groups. Ostvik and Rudmin (2001) found that the youngest soldiers were more likely to be targets of bullying and hazing. In contrast, Fineran (2002) reported that young male and female victims of workplace sexual harassment (aged 14 to 19 years) were older than those who reported no sexual harassment.

Gender is another important predictor and research on adolescent development indicates that young males exhibit more severe aggression and violence than do young females (see Thornberry & Krohn, 2003). A study of young fast-food restaurant workers (Mayhew & Quinlan, 2000) found that young female workers more often reported being verbally abused by customers compared with the frequency of such incidents reported by their male counterparts (59.9% vs. 35.2%), but young males were more likely than were young females to cite being threatened with violence (12.3% vs. 5.8%). It is possible that young males engage in more aggressive behavior when provoked by a customer or coworker because they are socialized differently regarding how to respond appropriately to interpersonal conflict (Frone, 2000). Another study of young workers aged 14 to 19 years found that females were more likely to report being the target of sexual harassment than males (Fineran, 2002). This being said, situational constraints can be powerful, and evidence suggests that gender interacts with situational predictors of aggression and violence. For example, a study of young Norwegian Army soldiers found that gender did not predict the frequency of bullying or hazing in this environment (Ostvik & Rudmin, 2001).

Situational Predictors

Various environmental factors predict workplace violence and aggression involving adults (Hershcovis et al., in press). In this section, we discuss the role of youth aggression climate, work opportunities, employment characteristics (e.g., work intensity, interpersonal injustice, work status, handling cash, working alone, working evening hours), and occupational cultures and norms in predicting work aggression and violence experienced and enacted by youth.

Studies of middle school students show that community violence predicts levels of student aggression reported in schools (e.g., Menacker, Weldon, & Hurwitz, 1990). Although long suspected by researchers (e.g., VandenBos & Bulatao, 1996), a longitudinal study by Dietz, Robinson, Folger, Baron, and Schulz (2003) was the first to show an empirical link between community violence climate (e.g., murders, robberies, aggravated assaults) and incidents of serious workplace violence (e.g., physical assaults, threats, harm to employee property). Evidence from the British Crime Survey suggests that youth violence has a significant spillover effect to organizations. Although British youth between the ages of 16 and 24 years are about 12% of the population (National Statistics, 1999), a large sample of employees who reported being assaulted by a member of the public cited that the perpetrator was a young person in 35% of incidents (Budd, 2001). In addition, victims of threatening behavior (including threats and damaging property) at work alleged that the offender(s) was between the age of 16 and 24 in 41% of incidents (Budd, 2001). Glomb and Liao (2003) found that young health care workers who were targets of aggression in their work group were also more likely to engage in aggression, controlling for individual differences (e.g., negative affectivity) and other relevant variables (e.g., organizational injustice). Previous authors have also argued that the initiation of aggression and violent behavior is the result of previous exposure to violent subcultures (Douglas & Martinko, 2001). Nonetheless, evidence suggests that young workers who have previously been victimized in the home, school, or work domain are not necessarily at greater risk of being victimized on the job (Ostvik & Rudmin, 2001).

Research findings conflict concerning the extent to which employment opportunity may be linked to enacted work and nonwork youth violence. Bellair, Roscigno, and McNulty (2003) measured rates of serious violence (e.g., fighting, being shot or stabbed) among middle-aged adolescents in relation to local labor market conditions. Their results indicated that youth residing in areas characterized by "low-wage service sector employment" reported higher violence than in areas where higher-quality opportunities existed (i.e., professional or primary resource sector), controlling for prior violence, socioeconomic variables (i.e., family attachment, school achievement, school attachment, peer delinquency, unemployment, family income) and microindicators (e.g., age, ethnicity, gender, access to guns, drug use). Using longitudinal data, Gottfredson (1985) reached the opposite conclusion; that is, she found that being employed had no effect on levels of interpersonal aggression across settings and that individual differences were most likely the cause. Again, more research is needed to reconcile these results and to determine the extent to which there are links between employment opportunity and quality and enacted aggression.

Researchers have also examined links between work intensity and self-reports of delinquent behavior, including violence and aggression in both work and nonworkplace settings. Bachman and Schulenberg (1993) found that high school seniors working more than 30 hours per week reported twice as much aggressive behavior as those working 15 hours per week, controlling for racial background and educational success. Kouvonen and Kivivuori's (2001) study of 4,347 Finnish adolescents aged 15 and 16 years found that those who worked 10 or more hours per week were significantly more likely to report beating someone up compared with reports of nonworkers, controlling for several relevant variables (e.g., gender, peer criminality, parental control). This study also reported no significant relationship between students who worked less than 10 hours and nonworkers on physical abuse. A more recent study by Bachman, Safron, Sy, and Schulenberg (2003) of working and nonworking high school students replicated earlier findings. The authors argue that young people who work longer hours may be most disposed to engaging in interpersonal aggression.

Studies of adult workers show a link between higher interpersonal injustice (the degree to which one perceives being treated with a lack of respect, dignity, sensitivity, and courtesy by those responsible for executing procedures) and increased levels of aggression directed toward supervisors (see Inness, Barling, & Turner, 2005). Dupre et al. (in press) found that teenage workers who reported experiencing abusive supervision were more likely to reciprocate aggression toward their supervisors. The consequences of higher interpersonal injustice may be particularly salient to young people employed in the food service industry where Schlosser (2002) notes that the majority of robberies, many of which involve violence, are perpetrated by current or former employees. He argues that workplace injustice motivates some young ex-fast-food workers to engage in violent criminal behavior toward their former employers to retaliate for poor interpersonal treatment.

Employment status (full-time vs. part-time) may also predict exposure to work aggression and violence. A high proportion of young people work nonstandard (i.e., part-time, temporary, or contract) jobs, and the majority of these jobs involve direct interactions with the public. A study of younger Swedish workers found that experience of threat and violence was more frequent among part-time workers (Vaez et al., 2004). Mayhew and Quinlan (2000) tentatively concluded that contingent workers may be exposed to more occupational violence than permanent workers but emphasized that "industry-specific risks [remain] the prime determinant" (p. 197). Unfortunately, their study did not report comparative data on enacted aggression among nonstandard workers. Further, the lines between part-time and full-time work can be blurry, particularly in the retail sector.

In terms of employment characteristics, a relatively small segment of young workers routinely confront aggression and violence because it is inherent in their work. Professional athletes who play contact sports (e.g., rugby, North American football, ice hockey, and boxing) voluntarily consent to levels of violence and aggression that are significantly higher compared with levels of violence faced by those in other occupations (Young, 1991). Younger police officers, nightclub bouncers, and door attendants also experience higher rates of physical violence due to the nature of their work. Finally, younger aged military soldiers, deployed on combat missions or in peacekeeping or police-like roles, are exposed to more violence than older soldiers due to their lower military rank.

Other employment characteristics, such as handling cash, working alone, and working evening hours, also increase the risk of exposure to violence, especially in retail outlets at risk for robbery (NIOSH, 2003). Janicak (1999) notes that a disproportionately high percentage (57%) of fatalities involving workers aged 19 and under occurred between 7:00 P.M. and 3:00 A.M. LeBlanc and Kelloway (2002) compared high-risk job characteristics and found that denying the public a service or interacting with frustrated individuals, situations that young, frontline service sector workers commonly encounter, were less likely to lead to incidents of aggression and physical violence than were other high-risk job characteristics such as handling guns and exercising security functions. Leidner (1993) acknowledges that policies adopted by fast-food corporations, such as training workers to follow scripted verbal responses when faced with difficult interpersonal situations, provide workers with tools to defuse customer hostility. Nonetheless, when service delivery systems fail to meet heightened expectations of prompt service, customers may direct aggression toward frontline workers, who are easy targets for abuse.

Strong customer service cultures, which promote the slogan "the customer is always right," have also been cited as a factor in certain kinds of harassment and abuse of young service sector workers. Studies have found that the "sexualized culture" of some restaurants, bars, and retail settings coupled with service norms indirectly contribute to sexual harassment (Folgero & Fjeldstad, 1995; Hughes & Tadic, 1998). Albeit using a small randomly drawn sample size ($N = 10$), an exploratory study using female Norwegian college students, who reported having at least 2 years frontline work experience, found that all cited at least one incident of being verbally or physically harassed by a customer (Folgero & Fjeldstad, 1995). Hughes and Tadic's (1998) study of young women employed in a variety of retail service settings found that two thirds had been sexually harassed by customers. The authors argue that strong customer service norms may explain why only 5% of workers told the client-harasser to stop. Other evidence suggests that negative public perceptions of the status of fast-food restaurant workers, the majority of whom are young workers, lead to more verbal abuse and intimidation of these workers by customers (Leidner, 1993).

Arguably the most insidious norms related to work aggression and violence are "rites of passage," which are found in some predominately male occupational groups (Kenway et al., 2000). Although not commonplace, newcomers to professional sports teams, military units, and skilled manual crafts are at particular risk. Kenway et al. (2000) studied cases of young male Australian manual trades apprentices who were victims of severe hazing and bullying. The issue of hazing is particularly relevant to military organizations.

Ostvik and Rudmin's (2001) study of Norwegian recruits concluded that hazing is a norm that is common to military cultures and that more senior soldiers may model this behavior when training recruits. Senior troops in a former elite unit of the Canadian Forces would sometimes deliberately ostracize young male recruits and/or compel them participate in extreme forms of initiation (e.g., intentional electrocution; Winslow, 1999).

Mediators and Moderators

Whereas *mediators* more accurately specify causal chains between predictors and outcomes, *moderators* change the strength of relationships between variables. That is, the strength of a relationship between two variables is determined by a third variable. Because the literature on young workers and workplace aggression is in the formative stage, few mediators and moderators have been explored.

In terms of mediators, *trait anger,* the tendency to view situations as frustrating or annoying and to respond to these situations with strong negative emotions, has been identified as a partial mediator between negative affectivity and aggression and violence (Anderson & Bushman, 2002; Douglas & Martinko, 2001). Hershcovis et al. (in press) found trait anger to be significantly positively correlated with enacted aggression toward coworkers but not toward supervisors. Two studies found that outward-projected anger and work aggression were significantly correlated in samples of younger workers (Dupre et al., in press; Glomb & Liao, 2003). It is important to note that researchers have distinguished between situational anger (i.e., demonstrating strong negative emotions to events) and trait anger. There may be a relatively strong relationship between state and trait anger and enacted aggression in the workplace. For example, Douglas and Martinko (2001) found evidence that "high-trait-anger individuals are more likely to both perceive a wider range of situations as anger provoking and engage in acts of workplace aggression than are low-trait-anger individuals" (p. 549).

The relationship between predictors and work aggression and violence is moderated by personal, situational, and social factors. Several moderating variables in this area were mentioned in our review of major empirical studies and will not be repeated here (e.g., Dupre et al., in press, found that when financial reasons for working were high and interpersonal injustice and abusive supervision were also high, aggression was higher). Experienced and enacted workplace aggression can also be moderated by age, gender, and other personal variables, as discussed in the predictors section. For example, studies show that females experience more sexual harassment compared with young males (Fineran, 2002). The latter group, however, may be exposed to more workplace assaults (Budd, 1999). We will now briefly review moderators not covered in previous sections of this review.

Personal Variables

Douglas and Martinko (2001) found a significant relationship between low self-control and workplace aggression. Further, self-control moderated the relationship between trait anger and aggression in this study. Qualitative evidence suggests that workers in fast-food settings with high self-monitoring personalities (i.e., those who are able to read customers' moods and respond in appropriate ways) were able to maintain control and minimize hostile interactions (Leidner, 1993).

Social Variables

Social support has also been identified as an important moderator of work aggression and violence in studies of adult workers (e.g., Schat & Kelloway, 2003). A study of young workers found that lower supervisor support was associated with higher levels of situational anger directed toward supervisors (Fitzgerald, Haythornthwaite, Suchday, & Ewart, 2003). In this study, coworker support moderated the relationship between job control and anger directed at peers, an important predictor of coworker-targeted aggression (Hershcovis et al., in press). Specifically, anger with coworkers was highest when job control and coworker support was relatively low; however, anger directed toward coworkers was reduced under conditions of low job control and moderate to high levels of coworker support. Social support also appears to have beneficial effects in military settings. Ostvik and Rudmin (2001) reported that social isolation was significantly related to being bullied. Low support in military units engaged in combat was cited as a factor contributing to violent outbursts by U.S. soldiers under the age of 24 deployed to Vietnam (Bey & Zecchinelli, 1974; Grossman, 1995). Studies show that social support, both during and after violent combat missions, can reduce the magnitude of posttraumatic stress disorder (PTSD) among soldiers (see Grossman, 1995). These finding may also have implications for young workers who experience traumatic workplace events such as violent robberies.

In some cases, however, it is possible that high social cohesion may interact with violent cultures to produce less positive outcomes. For example, Ostvik and Rudmin (2001) found that familiarity and a social network were necessary for bullying to occur in a military unit. A study of younger aged health care workers reported that being a target of aggression in a work group was associated with victims engaging in aggression (Glomb & Liao, 2003).

Situational Variables

Different workplace characteristics have been shown to affect the experience of workplace aggression. Perceived job control plays an important role in moderating the effects of enacted and experienced aggression and violence in a range of occupations. Interviews with young female workers revealed that perceived control during retail sales interactions was perceived as important to prevent unwanted sexual behavior from customers (Hughes & Tadic, 1998). Young female retail workers who consciously play a role while at work alleviated the objective experience of sexual harassment (Folgero & Fjeldstad, 1995; Hughes & Tadic, 1998). Qualitative data suggest that fast-food workers who perceived their job as having more prestige may be less likely to view customer behaviors as personally aggressive (Leidner, 1993). Chermack and Walton (1999) found that young males may aggress less often (and in some cases, less severely) in work relationships than in other relationships. A sample of college-aged males reported using less severe violence (e.g., beating up or threatening someone with a knife or gun) toward coworkers, bosses, police officers, and romantic partners compared with other relationships (friends, people in bars, and strangers). Rates of moderate level violence directed toward bosses and police officers were lowest compared with all other relationships. Moreover, coworkers were identified as the target of moderate violence at a rate equal to other relationships with the exception of friends, who were the most frequent targets of moderate violence. Chermack and Walton concluded that "specific relationship types or situational characteristics appear to influence the expression of aggression" among young males (1999, p. 264).

Outcomes

Until this point, we have discussed the predictors, mediators, and moderators of work-related aggression. Now, we turn to both the individual (psychological and psychosomatic) and organizational outcomes of experienced aggression and violence.

Psychological Outcomes

Strain is the most common result of exposure to work violence or aggression and refers to outcomes (e.g., anxiety, tension) resulting from *stress*, the individual response to perceived *stressors* (e.g., harassment, verbal abuse). Sources show that young females generally report higher levels of strain to work stressors than do males. For instance, the British Crime Survey found that 16- to 24-year-old females were more likely than their male peers to report being "very or fairly worried" about work-related threats (22% vs. 14%, respectively) and assaults (19% vs. 11%, respectively) initiated by the public (Budd, 2001). A study of part-time employed high school students reported that females were more upset and threatened by work-related sexual harassment than were males (Fineran, 2002). In this study, females were most threatened when workplace sexual harassment was perpetrated by "others" (i.e., members of the public), whereas males were most threatened when sexually harassed by a supervisor.

Self-reports of the effects of customer-initiated harassment among a small sample of young female retail workers found that anger, worry, and fear were the most common emotional responses to these situations (Hughes & Tadic, 1998). Nine percent of these workers also reported illness as a perceived result of sexual harassment (Hughes & Tadic, 1998). Interestingly, in this study, a greater proportion of victims of work-related sexual harassment reported that customer harassment had no effect on their job performance compared with personal outcomes (41% vs. 3%). Although it is possible that these young workers underestimated the impact of this form of aggression on their work performance, it is also probable that the strain associated with hostile events is personally borne by the young worker or moderated by other factors in the environment (e.g., social support). Perhaps not surprisingly, Grandey, Tam, and Brauburger (2002) found that young workers faked emotions more often when the source of anger was a customer compared with anger that was instigated by a coworker (55% vs. 13%).

Psychosomatic Outcomes

Frone (2000) found that interpersonal conflict (which includes aggressive verbal behavior) with coworkers was associated with higher depression and somatic symptoms and lower self-esteem among a sample of teenage workers. Lubbers, Loughlin, and Zweig (2005) found that the relationship between interpersonal conflict early in a work term and job performance and psychological and physical health several months later was mediated by both job self-efficacy and work-related affect in young workers. For example, participants with low self-efficacy who experienced high interpersonal conflict (including aggressive verbal behavior) were more likely to experience lowered somatic and psychological health.

One of the most serious outcomes of exposure to work violence, in terms of both severity and long-term adverse health effects, is PTSD, which is caused by witnessing or being the target of an extreme traumatic stressor. According to the U.S. National Center for PTSD, individuals diagnosed with PTSD "relive the experience through nightmares and flashbacks, have difficulty sleeping, and feel detached or estranged" (www.ncptsd.org). Numerous health-related problems (e.g., headaches and gastrointestinal problems) and negative effects on relationships have been found (National Center for Post-traumatic Stress Disorder [NCPTSD], n.d.). Findings from empirical studies show that between 8% and 50% of young soldiers (mean age 26 to 29 years) involved in intense military combat did experience PTSD (e.g., Grossman, 1995; Litz, Orsillo, Friedman, Ehlich, & Batres, 1997; Stretch et al., 1996). Estimates of PTSD among U.S. veterans of the Vietnam War (also known as the "teenaged war" because the average age of soldiers was 19 years) range between 18% and 54% (Grossman, 1995). There is some evidence that PTSD may increase levels of aggression among former combat soldiers (Begic & Jokic-Begic, 2001). Given the large numbers of young soldiers currently involved in frontline combat, policing, and peace-keeping roles and the lack of effective treatments, the potential scope of this problem is large and likely to pose a challenge for years to come. Victims of robberies and other extreme violence in civilian workplaces are also at risk of experiencing PTSD, though no studies have examined PTSD in the context of workplace violence among young workers.

Organizational Outcomes

Organizations experience direct and indirect effects when their younger employees enact or are victimized by workplace aggression. Frone (2000) found that higher interpersonal conflict with supervisors (including forms of aggressive behaviors) was associated with lower job satisfaction, lower organizational commitment, and higher turnover intentions. Keashly et al. (1994) reported that job satisfaction and satisfaction with coworkers and supervisors decreased as the number, impact, and frequency of abusive events increased for student residence assistants. An investigation of the job-related outcomes for female service workers of customer-initiated sexual harassment found that a majority (59%) indicated that such incidents had an effect on their jobs (Hughes & Tadic, 1998). Self-reported consequences ranged from avoiding or ignoring male customers (20%) to being less friendly to customers (16%), losing interest in work (6%), and having lower job performance (6%). Given that a majority of young workers occupy frontline customer service jobs and that job satisfaction and job performance are positively related in customer service roles, lower job satisfaction may indirectly decrease customer satisfaction and organizational performance.

Increased turnover and absenteeism also occur when young workers are exposed to work violence and aggression. A retrospective study found that 4% of young female retail workers responded to customer harassment by quitting or transferring (Hughes & Tadic, 1998). A sample of undergraduate students revealed that almost 14% reported that they had left an employer because of work-related abuse (Keashly et al., 1994), and 3% indicated that they were absent or used a sick day when victimized by low-level aggression or violence. Keashly et al. (1997) reported that high-impact abusive events experienced by university students who were residence assistants were associated with higher job-related tension and intentions to quit.

Finally, in some cases, young workers' perceptions of unjust treatment can have even more direct and serious implications for employers. One outcome of exposure to work injustice and abusive supervision is increased aggression toward supervisors and managers (Dupre et al., in press). Schlosser (2002) provides examples of robberies that involved extreme violence and points out that, "according to industry studies, about two thirds of the robberies at fast food restaurants involve current or former employees" (p. 84). There are signs that high-profile cases of violent crime have negatively affected recent campaigns to recruit food service workers (Elan, 2001).

_____ Key Measurement and Methodological Issues

What is considered aggressive behavior will no doubt vary based on age and group norms (e.g., in teenage vs. adult subcultures). The degree to which young workers identify their own personal experiences at work as "aggressive" or "violent," as defined by researchers, is an important measurement issue. Keashly et al. (1997) noted that the labeling of abusive behaviors by victims is influenced by the relationship between the perpetrator and victim and organizational norms. Interestingly, however, young people employed in a variety of service settings (e.g., restaurant, retail, and hospitality) view behaviors that policymakers and researchers define as aggressive (e.g., verbal abuse and low-level sexual harassment) as "normal" or "just part of the job" (see Hughes & Tadic, 1998, p. 217; Mayhew & Quinlan, 2002, p. 272). One explanation may be that certain nonphysical abusive behaviors are socially permissible in some groups (Keashly et al., 1994). Nonetheless, perceptual differences between middle-aged and adolescent workers regarding behaviors that constitute unwelcome conduct can complicate reporting (Moskowitz, 2000; Ostvik & Rudmin, 2001). To overcome this challenge, researchers should avoid asking young workers direct questions about their experience with a particular construct (e.g., Have you been sexually harassed at work in the past 12 months?). Instead they should inquire about specific behaviors associated with a construct (e.g., Has a customer unnecessarily touched you in the past 12 months?).

Reliance on official reports of aggressive or violent incidents is also problematic. For example, Hughes and Tadic (1998) found that only 18% of young female retail workers reported incidences of work-related sexual harassment to management or security personnel. The limitations associated with using self-reports of incidents of workplace violence and aggression, especially in retrospective studies, are documented in the adult literature. Given that individual perception is influenced by different individual and situational factors and that official reports often understate prevalence, there is a compelling need for using a combination of measures to accurately record these variables.

Finally, young workers present a unique set of challenges to researchers due to differences in their work-school status (Loughlin & Barling, 2001), their work roles, and the forms of work aggression and violence they experience and enact. For these reasons, direct comparisons with samples of adult workers are difficult. Another challenge in the current research is that studies of young workers aged 19 to 24 rely heavily on university undergraduate students whose expectations of work may differ from those of young nonstudent workers (Grandey et al., 2002). Researchers also need to identify, and control for, individual factors that may cause selection into certain jobs (Fitzgerald et al., 2003).

Implications for Practice, Policy, and Intervention

Several authors have made proposals for ways to improve young people's experience of work with regard to workplace aggression. Janicak (1999) and DeLaurier (2001) note that there is considerable room to improve young worker education, training, and policies related to prevention of violence during interactions with hostile customers and during robberies. Zakocs et al. (1998) surveyed teenagers employed in restaurants, grocery stores, and other retail organizations (e.g., gas stations, convenience, clothing stores) about forms of workplace safety training. Table 18.2 shows the percentage of these workers who agreed to statements relevant to workplace violence and aggression. These results suggest that work aggression and violence prevention training is relatively infrequent across industries. Workers classified as employed in "other retail" were significantly more likely to be taught how to respond to an angry customer or a robbery. This may be due to the fact that the frequency of interaction with the public and other job characteristics (e.g., handling cash) were not controlled for in this study. In each case, a much smaller proportion reported being trained to deal with sexual assault than a robbery or angry customer.

Young workers also cite incongruent employer policies related to customer service and handling customer abuse as contributing to sexual harassment and aggression (Hughes & Tadic, 1998; Leidner, 1993; Zakocs et al., 1998). Hughes and Tadic found that reporting incidents of customer sexual harassment was perceived to have a negative impact on individual performance evaluations and thus to overall compensation and other rewards. Because of this, some workers may be willing to put customer satisfaction ahead of their own comfort and safety. Findings from both qualitative and quantitative studies show that sexual harassment, in particular, is a significant workplace concern to young female workers employed in the service

Table 18.2   Number of Working Teens Who Responded "Yes" to Questions About Specific Training to Prevent Work Violence and Aggression

	Total (%)	Food Service (n = 50)	Grocery Store (n = 24)	Other Retail (n = 43)
Trained to deal with angry customer (n = 116)	53	20	12	30
Trained to deal with robbery (n = 117)	38	13	8	23
Trained to deal with sexual assault (n = 116)	21	11	5	8

SOURCE: Zakocs et al. (1998)

sector. Folgero and Fjeldstad (1995) propose that "public recognition and condemnation of sexual harassment at the service workplace" (p. 311) is critical to changing the apparent social acceptability of even low levels of harassment toward young working females.

Members of the public may also engage in aggressive behavior toward certain young workers because they perceive these jobs as having a low status (Leidner, 1993). One approach would be for industry associations and government to develop public awareness campaigns that educate customers, coworkers, and supervisors about forms of inappropriate conduct. Given the low rates of unionization of young workers and the relative powerlessness they have compared with working adults, it is important that regulatory bodies enforce existing laws and offer protection to young people who report work-related abuse (Dale, Tobin, & Wilson, 1998).

Finally, in terms of the most serious outcomes, longitudinal studies of soldiers who have been exposed to high-intensity combat show a relatively high prevalence of PTSD. Available treatments such as psychological debriefing "produce only partial symptom relief" (Deahl et al., 2000, p. 78). At present, research is examining the degree to which selection, training, and early intervention can mitigate the severity of PTSD (Deahl et al., 2000); however, severe forms of experienced and enacted aggression are likely to make an indelible mark on most individuals that they will carry into future work and nonwork contexts. The extent to which individual intervention can mitigate the effects from these experiences is limited.

Future Research Needs

Research examining the work experiences of young people in general is underrepresented in the management literature. Several issues affecting young workers warrant greater empirical attention, and few are as important from a developmental and human capital perspective as early career exposure to workplace aggression, including sexual harassment. What are the long-term health and developmental effects of work-related aggression or violence experienced by young people? Based on social learning theory, workers who engage in aggressive and violent behavior early in their careers may continue and escalate these behaviors at later stages. Given the potential for serious personal and organizational outcomes, longitudinal studies are needed to determine the consequences of adolescent victimization and instigation of aggression and violence in the workplace (Dupre et al., in press; Fineran, 2002; Frone, 2000; Kouvonen & Kivivuori, 2001) and to measure the effectiveness of early intervention in both cases.

Research findings conflict on whether the quantity of hours worked by adolescents is a cause or consequence of enacted aggression in work and nonwork settings (see Bachman et al., 2003; Frone, 1999). Bachman et al. (2003) suggest that third variables (e.g., poor educational success and adjustment) may be responsible for significant association between work intensity and general levels of aggression. Were studies to show that aggression and work hours covary, additional research would be needed to identify the specific work-related mechanisms that underlie this association among young workers and, more important, in what settings (e.g., school, home, workplace) young workers more frequently engage in aggressive or violent behaviors (Kouvonen & Kivivuori, 2001).

It also remains unclear whether age cohorts performing comparable employment tasks are exposed to similar forms and frequency of aggression and violence, controlling for variables such as individual propensity toward aggression, relevant job characteristics (e.g., interaction with the public and work hours), age-based perceptions, and work status. Comparative studies related to the situational (e.g., workplace justice) and individual causes (e.g., gender) of workplace aggression and violence affecting young people and adults are also required to better understand patterns of work aggression and violence.

The prevalence of aggression and violence in many societies is highest among young people, and evidence shows that members of organizations are not immune to violent crime in society (Dietz et al., 2003). Research needs to measure the impact of youth aggression climate on young workers and the organizations that either employ them or have large numbers of young people as their clientele.

A final avenue for future research relates to work that is either morally or physically tainted. Although an unconventional area for research by North American standards, young people can be employed in a variety of ways and in a wide range of capacities (as pointed out with the example of young soldiers), and their experiences of aggression and violence will vary accordingly. In several countries (e.g., Germany, Australia, Holland), there is a growing public recognition of adult sex work as legitimate employment. Empirical studies find that approximately 50% of street and brothel workers, the majority of whom are young females, report being victimized by severe client-initiated violence (e.g., Church, Henderson, Barnard, & Hart, 2001). The individual consequences of exposure to extreme physical violence are particularly salient; one multinational study found that 70% of prostitutes met the criteria for a diagnosis of PTSD (Farley, Baral, Kiremire, & Sezgin, 1998).

Epilogue

This chapter considers young workers' experiences and enactment of workplace aggression and violence. On the basis of this review, there is evidence to suggest that certain groups of young workers are at greater risk of being victimized by certain forms of work aggression or violence (e.g., young females' experience with sexual harassment). Some factors that may account for differences between adult and young workers' experiences with work aggression or violence include public attitudes toward service sector workers, age-based norms concerning aggression and violence, job characteristics (e.g., handling cash), and insufficient coping mechanisms to deal with aggression, particularly from the public. Given the potential for serious developmental consequences due to early exposures to workplace aggression and violence and the number of young people currently exposed to such threats (e.g., young soldiers), there is a pressing need for more research in this area for the benefit of both young workers and society as a whole.

References

Anderson, C. A., & Bushman, B. J. (2002). Human aggression. *Annual Review of Psychology, 53,* 27–51.

Bachman, J. G., Safron, D. J., Sy, S., & Schulenberg, J. E. (2003). Wishing to work: New perspectives on how adolescents' part-time work intensity is linked to educational disengagement, substance use, and other problem behaviours. *International Journal of Behavioral Development, 27,* 301–315.

Bachman, J. G., & Schulenberg, J. (1993). How part-time work intensity relates to drug use, problem behavior, time use, and satisfaction among high school seniors: Are these consequences or merely correlates? *Developmental Psychology, 29,* 220–235.

Bandura, A. (1973). *Aggression: A social learning analysis.* Englewood Cliffs, NJ: Prentice Hall.

Barling, J. (1996). The prediction, experience, and consequences of workplace violence. In G. R. VandenBos & E. Q. Bulatao (Eds.), *Violence on the job: Identifying risks and developing solutions* (pp. 29–49). Washington, DC: American Psychological Association.

Barling, J., & Kelloway, E. K. (1999). *Young workers: Varieties of experience.* Washington, DC: American Psychological Association.

Barling, J., Rogers, G. A., & Kelloway, E. K. (2001). Behind closed doors: In-home workers' experience of sexual harassment and workplace violence. *Journal of Occupational Health Psychology, 6,* 255–269.

Baron, R. A., Neuman, J. H., & Geddes, D. (1999). Social and personal determinants of workplace aggression: Evidence for the impact of perceived injustice and the type A behavior pattern. *Aggressive Behavior, 25,* 281–296.

Begic, D., & Jokic-Begic, N. (2001). Aggressive behavior in combat veterans with post-traumatic stress disorder. *Military Medicine, 166,* 671–676.

Bellair, P. E., Roscigno, V. J., & McNulty, T. L. (2003). Linking local labor market opportunity to violent adolescent delinquency. *Journal of Research in Crime and Delinquency, 40,* 6–33.

Bey, D. R., & Zecchinelli, V. A. (1974). G.I.s against themselves: Factors resulting in explosive violence in Vietnam. *Psychiatry, 37*(3), 221–228.

Bryson, A., Gomez, R., Gunderson, M., & Meltz, N. (2001). *Youth-adult differences in the demand for unionisation: Are American, British, and Canadian workers all that different?* London: Centre for Economic Performance, London School of Economics and Political Science.

Budd, T. (1999). *Violence at work: Findings from the British Crime Survey.* London: Home Office, Research, Development and Statistics Directorate.

Budd, T. (2001). *Violence at work: New findings from the 2000 British Crime Survey*. London: Health and Safety Executive; British Home Office. Retrieved January 2004 from www.homeoffice.gov.uk/rds/pdfs/occ-violence.pdf

Bureau of Labor Statistics, U.S. Department of Labor. (2005). *Employment and unemployment among youth: Summer 2005*. Retrieved August 2005 from www.bls.gov/news.release/youth.nr0.htm

Chappell, D., & Di Martino, V. (2000). *Violence at work* (2nd ed.). Geneva: International Labour Office.

Chermack, S. T., & Walton, M. A. (1999). The relationship between family aggression history and expressed aggression among college males. *Aggressive Behavior, 25*, 255–267.

Church, S., Henderson, M., Barnard, M., & Hart, G. (2001, March). Violence by clients towards female prostitutes in different work settings: Questionnaire survey. *British Medical Journal, 322*, 524–525.

Dale, R., Tobin, W., & Wilson, B. (1998). Ganged up on, victimized and alone: Young people and workplace violence. In J. Bessant & S. Cook (Eds.), *Against the odds: Young people and work*. Hobart: Australian Clearinghouse for Youth Studies.

Deahl, M., Srinivasan, M., Jones, N., Thomas, J., Neblett, C., & Jolly, A. (2000). Preventing psychological trauma in soldiers: The role of operational stress training and psychological debriefing. *British Journal of Medical Psychology, 73*, 77–85.

DeLaurier, G. (2001, September/October). Dying to serve you: Violence in the retail workplace. *Dollars and Sense*, 27–29.

Dietz, J., Robinson, S. L., Folger, R., Baron, R. A., & Schulz, M. (2003). The impact of community violence and an organization's procedural justice climate on workplace aggression. *Academy of Management Journal, 46*(3), 317–326.

Douglas, S. C., & Martinko, M. J. (2001). Exploring the role of individual differences in the prediction of workplace aggression. *Journal of Applied Psychology, 86*(4), 547–559.

Duffield, M. (2002). *Trends in female employment 2002*. Economy and Labour Market Division, UK Department for Work and Pensions. Retrieved January 2004 from www.statistics.gov.uk/articles/labour_market_trends/Trends_in_female_employment_nov2002.pdf

Dupre, K., Inness, M., Connelly, C., Barling, J., & Hoption, C. (in press). Adolescent antagonism: Predicting workplace aggression among part-time teenage employees. *Journal of Applied Psychology*.

Elan, E. (2001). A career in foodservice—cons: Poor image. *Nation's Restaurant News, 21*, 98–99.

Farley, M., Baral, I., Kiremire, M., & Sezgin, U. (1998). Prostitution in five countries: Violence and post-traumatic stress disorder. *Feminism & Psychology, 8*(4), 405–426.

Fineran, S. (2002). Adolescents at work: Gender issues and sexual harassment. *Violence Against Women, 8*, 953–967.

Fitzgerald, S. T., Haythornthwaite, J. A., Suchday, S., & Ewart, C. K. (2003). Anger in young black and white workers: Effects of job control, dissatisfaction, and support. *Journal of Behavioral Medicine, 26*(4), 283–296.

Folgero, I., & Fjeldstad, I. (1995). On duty–off guard: Cultural norms and sexual harassment in service organizations. *Organization Studies, 16*(1), 299–313.

Frone, M. R. (1999). Developmental consequences of youth employment. In J. Barling & E. K. Kelloway (Eds.), *Young workers: Varieties of experiences* (pp. 89–128). Washington, DC: American Psychological Association.

Frone, M. R. (2000). Interpersonal conflict at work and psychological outcomes: Testing a model among young workers. *Journal of Occupational Health Psychology, 5,* 246–255.

Glomb T. M., & Liao, H. (2003). Interpersonal aggression in work groups: Social influence, reciprocal, and individual effects. *Academy of Management, 46,* 486–496.

Gottfredson, D. C. (1985). Youth employment, crime, and schooling: A longitudinal study of a national sample. *Developmental Psychology 21,* 419–432.

Grandey, A. A., Tam, A. P., & Brauburger, A. L. (2002). Affective states and traits in the workplace: Diary and survey data from young workers. *Motivation and Emotion, 26,* 31–55.

Griffin, R. W., O'Leary-Kelly, A., & Collins, J. M. (Eds.). (1998). *Dysfunctional behavior in organizations: Violent and deviant behavior.* Stamford, CT: JAI.

Grossman, D. (1995). *On killing: The psychological cost of learning to kill in war and society.* Boston: Little, Brown.

Hershcovis, S. M., Turner, N., Barling, J., Arnold, K. A., Dupré, K. E., Inness, M., et al. (in press). Predictors of workplace aggression: A meta-analysis. *Journal of Applied Psychology.*

Hughes, K. D., & Tadic, V. (1998). "Something to deal with": Customer sexual harassment and women's retail service work in Canada. *Gender, Work, and Organization, 5*(4), 207–219.

Inness, M., Barling, J., & Turner, N. (2005). Situational specificity, individual differences, and workplace aggression. *Journal of Applied Psychology, 90,* 731–739.

International Labour Organization. (2004). *Child labour: A textbook for university students.* Geneva: ILO.

Janicak, C. A. (1999). An analysis of occupational homicides involving workers 19 years old and younger. *Journal of Occupational and Environmental Medicine, 41*(12), 1140–1145.

Keashly, L., Hunter, S., & Harvey, S. (1997). Abusive interaction and role state stressors: Relative impact on student residence assistant stress and work attitudes. *Work & Stress, 11*(2), 175–185.

Keashly, L., Trott, V., & MacLean, L. M. (1994). Abusive behavior in the workplace: A preliminary investigation. *Violence and Victims, 9*(4), 341–357.

Kenway, J., Fitzclarence, L., & Hasluck, L. (2000). Toxic shock: Understanding violence against young males in the workplace. *Journal of Men's Studies, 8*(2), 131–152.

Kneisler, P., & White, M. (n.d.). *Iraq coalition casualty count.* Retrieved February 3, 2004, from http://icasualties.org/oif/

Kouvonen, A., & Kivivuori, J. (2001). Part-time jobs, delinquency and victimization among Finnish adolescents. *Journal of Scandinavian Studies in Criminology and Crime Prevention, 2,* 191–212.

LeBlanc, M. M., & Kelloway, K. E. (2002). Predictors and outcomes of workplace violence and aggression. *Journal of Applied Psychology, 87*(3), 444–453.

Leidner, R. (1993). *Fast food, fast talk: Service work and the routinization of everyday life.* Berkeley: University of California Press.

Litz, B. T., Orsillo, S. M., Friedman, M., Ehlich, P., & Batres, A. (1997). Posttraumatic stress disorder associated with peacekeeping duty in Somalia for U.S. military personnel. *American Journal of Psychiatry, 154,* 178–184.

Loughlin, C. A., & Barling, J. (2001). Young workers' work values, attitudes, and behaviors. *Journal of Occupational and Organizational Psychology, 74,* 543–558.

Lubbers, R., Loughlin, C., & Zweig, D. (2005). Common pathways to health and performance: Job-self-efficacy and affect among young workers. *Journal of Vocational Behavior, 67,* 199–214.

Mayhew, C., & Quinlan, M. (2000). The relationship between precarious employment and patterns of occupational violence: Survey evidence from thirteen occupations. In K. Isaksson, C. Hogstedt, C. Eriksson, & T. Theorell (Eds.), *Health effects of the new labour market* (pp. 183–205). New York: Kluwer Academic/Plenum.

Mayhew, C., & Quinlan, M. (2002). Fordism in the fast food industry: Pervasive management control and occupational health and safety for young temporary workers. *Sociology of Health and Illness, 24*(3), 261–284.

Menacker, J., Weldon, W., & Hurwitz, E. (1990). Community influences of school crime and violence. *Urban Education, 25,* 68–80.

Meschkutat, B., Stackelbeck, M., & Langenhoff, G. (2002). *Mobbing report.* German Federal Ministry for Labour and Social Affairs (*Eine Repräsentativstudie für die Bundesrepublik Deutschland*). Berlin: Dortmund Institute for Social Research.

Moskowitz, S. (2000). Adolescent workers and sexual harassment. *Labor Law Journal, 51,* 78–85.

National Center for Post-traumatic Stress Disorder. (n.d.). Retrieved January 15, 2004, from www.ncptsd.org/

National Institute for Occupational Safety and Health. (2003). *Preventing deaths, injuries, and illnesses of young workers* (Publication No. 2003-128). Cincinnati, OH: NIOSH Publications Dissemination.

National Statistics. (1999). *Population trends.* Government Statistical Service. Retrieved August 25, 2005, from www.statistics.gov.uk/downloads/theme_population/PT97book.pdf

Ostvik, K., & Rudmin, F. (2001). Bullying and hazing among Norwegian Army soldiers: Two studies of prevalence, context, and cognition. *Military Psychology, 13*(1), 17–39.

Perkins, C. A. (1997). *Special report: Age patterns of victims of serious violent crime.* Bureau of Justice Statistics. Retrieved December 30, 2003, from www.ojp.usdoj.gov/bjs/pub/pdf/apvsvc.pdf

Robinson, S. L., & Bennett, R. J. (1995). A typology of deviant workplace behaviors: A multi-dimensional scaling study. *Academy of Management Journal, 38,* 555–572.

Schat, A. C. H., & Kelloway, E. K. (2003). Reducing the adverse consequences of workplace aggression and violence: The buffering effects of organizational support. *Journal of Occupational Health Psychology, 8,* 110–122.

Schlosser, E. (2002). *Fast food nation: The dark side of the all-American meal.* Boston: Houghton Mifflin.

Statistics Canada. (2002). Fact sheet on unionization. *Perspectives on Labour and Income, 3,* 8.

Statistics Canada. (2005). *Labour force and participation rates by sex and age group.* Retrieved August 2005 from www40.statcan.ca/l01/cst01/labor05.htm

Stretch, R. H., Marlowe, D. H., Wright, K. M., Bliese, P. D., Knudson, K. H., & Hoover C. H. (1996). Post-traumatic stress disorder symptoms among Gulf War veterans. *Military Medicine, 161,* 407–410.

Thornberry, T. P., & Krohn, M. D. (2003). *Taking stock of delinquency: An overview of findings from contemporary longitudinal studies.* New York: Kluwer Academic/Plenum.

Tjaden, P. G., & Thoennes, N. (2001). Coworkers, violence and gender: Findings from the National Violence Against Women Survey. *American Journal of Preventive Medicine, 20*(2), 85–89.

U.S. Department of Justice, Bureau of Justice Statistics. (2002). *National Crime Victimization Survey.* Retrieved December 15, 2003, from http://www .bls.gov/iif/oshwc/osh/case/ostb1215.txt

Vaez, M., Ekberg, K., & Laflamme, L. (2004). Abusive events at work among young working adults: Magnitude of the problem and its effect on self-rated health. *Relations Industrielles/Industrial Relations, 59,* 569–583.

VandenBos, G. R., & Bulatao, E. Q. (Eds.). (1996). *Violence on the job: Identifying risks and developing solutions.* Washington, DC: American Psychological Association.

Wallace, M. (2003). Crime statistics in Canada. *Juristat: Canadian Centre for Justice Statistics, 23*(5).

Winslow, D. (1999). Rites of passage and group bonding in the Canadian Airborne. *Armed Forces and Society, 25*(3), 429–457.

Young, K. (1991). Violence in the workplace of professional sport from victimological and cultural studies perspectives. *International Review for the Sociology of Sport, 26*(1), 3–13.

Zakocs, R. C., Runyan, C. W., Schulman, M. D., Dunn, K. A., & Evensen, C. T. (1998). Improving safety for teens working in the retail trade sector: Opportunities and obstacles. *American Journal of Industrial Medicine, 34,* 342–350.

19

A Case of Cyberdeviancy

Cyberaggression in the Workplace

Terrance Weatherbee
E. Kevin Kelloway

The Orwell law of the future: any new technology that can be tried will be. Like Adam Smith's invisible hand (leading capitalist economies toward ever-increasing wealth), Orwell's Law is an empirical fact of life.

(Gelernter, D., n.d.)

O ver the last decade, the increasing incidents of aggressive acts perpetrated against coworkers in the workplace have become a growing concern for practitioners and researchers alike. Major research perspectives being brought to bear on these activities include the conceptualization of workplace aggression and violence as deviant behaviors (Robinson & Bennett, 1995), antisocial behaviors (Giacalone & Greenberg, 1997), uncivil behaviors (Anderson & Pearson, 1999), bullying and mobbing (Keashley & Jagatic, 2002; Vandekerckhove & Commers, 2003), counterproductive work behaviors (Gruys & Sackett, 2003; Sackett & DeVore, 2001), actions resulting from experienced frustration (Fox & Spector, 1999; Spector, 1997), and revenge or retaliatory behaviors (Skarlicki & Folger, 1997; Sommers, Schell, & Vodanovich, 2002).

Despite the broad interest and the wide theoretical approaches spurred on by the more dramatic of these violent phenomena in our workplaces (Jockin, Arvey, & McGue, 2001), there is as yet no consensus to our understanding.

Our attention to this topic has left us with a complex multiplicity of definitions, concepts, constructs, and terms and a wide range of potential antecedents, processes, outcomes, or consequences of these behaviors (Bennett & Robinson, 2003). The wider body of research on aggression and violence in the workplace remains largely fragmented, existing across multiple and often independently conceived efforts. As a consequence, our understanding of this behavioral domain still remains very much in a nascent stage, and the empirical substantiation to move us forward is only now becoming sufficient (Glomb, 2002).

To further complicate this expansive theoretical diversity, it is becoming increasingly apparent, as demonstrated by the growing body of anecdotal evidence, that a newer and increasingly prevalent form of aggression in the workplace now involves the use of information and communication technologies (ICTs). In our increasingly computer-enabled workplaces, individuals are using the capabilities of ICTs to engage in a wide range of behaviors that may be conceived of as aggressive, hostile, antisocial, uncivil, or even criminal.

On almost a daily basis, it is possible to peruse the popular press or media and practitioner publications and observe examples of these phenomena. These activities range across a spectrum of behaviors from relatively benign and harmless to blatantly illegal and dangerous, from employees simply idling away company time by using corporate ICTs for personal rather than work purposes to playing at office politics through selective e-mailing, to the commission of fraud, or even to the outright destruction or sabotage of an organization's data or information. Located at the more benign end of this range of behaviors is so-called cyberslacking or cyberloafing (Mirchandani & Motwani, 2003) in which employees spend work time surfing the Internet, chatting through some form of instant messaging, or just playing games. Although perhaps innocent enough, this type of behavior in the aggregate is estimated to cost billions of dollars in lost organizational productivity (Barlow, Bean, & Hott, 2003) through consumption of employees' work hours or firm resources, such as processing time, network bandwidth, and storage or other computing resources. Internet abuse is a growing trend in the workplace (Churchman, 2003), and related productivity losses have now become a major organizational concern. Some employees have even been terminated from their employment as a result of the time spent in chat rooms and personal e-mailing (Levitt, 2003). In response, many firms are beginning to monitor their employees' use of organizational ICTs in order to reduce these losses, or employee monitoring (Wheelwright, 2003; Zall, 2001) is put in place to avoid the potential liability associated with the actions of employees when engaged in nonorganizationally sanctioned behaviors (Fertell, 2002; Freeman, 2004; Rothman & Taffae, 2003).

Unfortunately, the domain of ICT misuse includes many more harmful behaviors, from both an interpersonal and an organizational perspective. For example, software piracy—the illegal copying, downloading, and use of software programs by employees—is another growing area of concern for organizations (Makris, 2004; Sundararajan, 2004). Many employees actively use freely available peer-to-peer (P2P), or PC-to-PC, networking software to engage in trade of digital music, digital video, software, or pornographic material on company time using company resources (AssetMetrix, 2003; Lang, 2003; Freeman, 2004; Donaldson, 2001). Organizational members are also using the technological capability of ICTs to perpetrate deliberate harms. Through the use of software programs such as *spyware* (Stafford & Urbaczewski, 2004)—a program specifically designed to surreptitiously monitor and record keyboard or computer activity—to engage in *cybertapping,* which is the computer equivalent of wiretapping, for the purposes of discovering passwords needed to access restricted or confidential corporate databases (Gentile, n.d.) or to track what another computer user was doing with the intent of using this information against her or him. Once this information and subsequent access to either corporate confidential or employees' personal data has been acquired, this information may then be used for personal gain (Schroeder, 2002), for fraud (Trembly, 2004), or for the commission of other crimes, like identity theft (Fertell, 2003).

Some employees have hacked into their supervisors' computers in order to go through their e-mail or to find any other information that may be used against them for purposes of office politics, revenge, or retaliation. There are cases of employees having done this in order to expose their superiors' sexual proclivities to other corporate executives in attempts to discredit them or ruin their reputation at work (Bruce, 2004). This was easily achieved through investigating the *cookies* (small text files left behind on the users' computers). These files are often placed on users' hard drives when they visit pornographic, gambling, or other Web sites (Johnston, 2004). In other cases, the reverse can occur. Rather than discovering where a computer user has been through cookie tracking or through e-mail inspection, there is a new trend that has been coined cyberextortion (Reed, 2004; Salkever, 2000). *Cyberextortion* is the threat of having pornographic or other damaging contents placed on your work computer system by the extortionist or even uploaded to an entire organization's Web site (Jurgensen, 2004). It may also consist of the threat of having your personal information broadcast electronically to other coworkers or to the public through the Internet. Research also shows this as a rapidly growing form of misuse (Stahl, 2004; Swartz, 2004), and this type of information—the personal details about other organizational employees or customers—has even been used for the more insidious purpose of cyberstalking (Brandt, 2003; "Cyber Stalking," 2004; Rosenwald & Allen, 2004).

Surveys of corporate information systems' security reveal that over 50% of firm respondents report some form of unauthorized access to corporate information or databases (Davis & Braun, 2004), with the majority of unauthorized access committed by employees (Casselman, 2002; Mearian, 2002) during working hours (Reddy Randazzo, Keeney, Kowalski, Cappelli, & Moore, 2004). Disgruntled employees have gained access to corporate payroll and financial details and subsequently e-mailed the information to the entire firm's employee complement (McBride, 2004). The misuse of, or damage potential to, corporate electronic information and databases is so prevalent that it has created a market opportunity for new forms of liability, or *cyberinsurance* (Aarsteinsen, 2002), within the insurance industry.

In addition to the risk to corporate information, this type of employee activity may also increase corporate liability by contributing to a hostile work environment. In one case, numerous government employees were found to have collected and distributed significant masses of pornographic material using government servers, e-mail systems, and PCs over an extended period. Several hundred employees were involved, having either received, traded, or sent this material through e-mail, and many of the employees were subsequently fired or censured for their actions ("Yukon's Computer Porn Scandal," 2004). The electronic duplication and distribution of pornographic material as well as sexually explicit jokes in e-mail systems is becoming so widespread that an electronic form of sexual harassment, *e-harassment*, has been coined in the courts to describe this phenomenon and its impact on other employees in the workplace (Towns & Johnson, 2003).

Despite the amazing prevalence of ICT misuse, research into this new domain has significantly lagged the reporting of the practice (Bennett & Robinson, 2003). As the workplace incorporates the ubiquitous PC into almost all aspects of our daily work, their ultimate use—for production avoidance through personal use, to engage in office politics, or as tools to facilitate or enable acts of aggression directed at coworkers, management, customers, or others—should have been neither surprising nor unexpected. A comprehensive electronic and manual search, however, of several major management, behavioral, and technical journals (*Journal of Applied Psychology, Personnel Psychology, MIS Quarterly, Information Systems Research, Journal of Management Information Systems, Organizational Behavior,* and the *Academy of Management Journal*) reveals a significant and distinct paucity of attention to the use of ICTs for intentional negative workplace behaviors.

Within the information systems literatures, most recent effort has been focused on three broad areas: research concerning the development and deployment of information systems, studies concerning the impacts of ICTs on organizational structure and processes, and research on how these systems are subsequently managed within the organizational context (Orlikowski & Barley, 2001). Not unexpectedly, both theoretical and empirical work within the information systems discipline(s) has largely treated technology as the primary subject, with focus on the technical elements (Sproull & Kiesler, 1994), usually highly divorced and somewhat abstracted from the context and practices of actual use (Orlikowski & Iacono, 2001). This is achieved at the expense of attention to the equally important user or the psychological elements (Lyytinen & Yoo, 2002) behind use.

Similarly, within the management and behavioral sciences, there is also a lacuna concerning the use of information technology as a tool for the facilitation of negative behaviors or the prosecution of aggression (Bennett & Robinson, 2003). As mentioned previously, this state of affairs continues to exist, even as we observe a marked increase in the misuse of computers or ICTs within organizations (Allan & Salter, 1997). Several reasons may be advanced to explain the scarcity of research into this phenomenon.

First, the extremely rapid rates of adoption and the widespread organizational use of ICTs have in many ways outstripped our ability to effectively research and understand their impacts at multiple levels of analysis (Sussman & Sproull, 1999; Turnage, 1990). The time needed to observe the new technology in practice and to develop research questions concerning its use, the time required for the subsequent conceptualization and necessary theory development, and finally the time needed for investigation and testing often exceed the more compressed time frame in which the design and deployment of newer generations of ICTs within organizations take place.

Second, our understanding of the nature of the synergism of the complex product that is the user, the ICT, and the organizational process is, understandably, still in an emergent state, given that technology changes often outpace our research capability. In addition to the challenge of empirically based understanding against this backdrop of rapidity of change, the study of the emergent phenomenon that is the *human-computer-work fusion* remains largely in a disciplinarily isolated state. Our limited understanding of the various elements of this fusion or composite is mostly "research stream–dependent" (Orlikowski & Barley, 2001) or singular discipline–dependent. Many conceptual gaps and conceptual overlaps exist within and across the different discipline-based approaches used in the study of information systems in organizations (Weatherbee, 2004). This has left us with either an overly narrow or an overly restrictive basis for gaining more theoretical insight into ICTs and their use in the workplace.

Finally, research into negative workplace behaviors has tended to concentrate on the more dramatic of behaviors or on those with the more serious and adverse outcomes (Glomb & Liao, 2003), including hostility, violence, or aggression. Therefore, the less serious but perhaps more prevalent forms of aggression (Rogers & Kelloway, 1997), normally those short of physical violence, seriously suffer from a lack of focused scholarly attention (Neumann & Baron, 1997). This is the case for the more recent forms of workplace violence or aggression with or through the misuse of ICTs.

Based on content analysis of ICT use and misuse in the practitioner and popular media, it is apparent that when ICTs are used for acts that involve negative behaviors, hostility, or aggression, the potential for severity in degree of adverse impact at the individual, group, organizational, and public levels (Kiesler, Siegel, & McGuire, 1984) is much greater than for other more conventional forms. Therefore, from both theoretical and practical standpoints, it is critical for our research effort to focus on this form of behavior. Study and understanding of the unique nature of this form of aggressive workplace behavior may only be achieved from a multidisciplinary perspective, a call that in the past has too often been ignored by people investigating technological impacts (Kiesler et al., 1984).

In order to identify areas of research potential, this work draws from the technical, behavioral, organizational, and practitioner literatures for the study of ICT-based misuse, focusing on ICT aggression within the broader domain construct of deviant workplace behavior. In the first section, we briefly review the scope of ICT use and impact in organizational settings. In the next section, we draw a representative selection of events from the practitioner and popular media to demonstrate the potential for ICT misuse and for conceptual development and dimensionalization. Further, we discuss demonstrative examples when ICTs have been used for the commission of aggressive or hostile acts. These behaviors are then mapped on Robinson and Bennett's (1995) deviant workplace behavior typology, and the overarching conceptualization of *cyberdeviancy* is defined. The unique dimensionality of ICT-based aggressive workplace behavior is then discussed in relation to this typology as well as the general body of aggression research. We then shift focus to the more specific construct of *cyberaggression,* defined as the commission of aggressive or hostile workplace behaviors committed either through or with ICTs. Finally, a process model is proposed that situates the cyberaggression construct within a larger nomological network of antecedents and outcomes. The concluding section then offers a number of research questions that we believe are needed to carry the study of both cyberdeviancy and cyberaggression forward.

ICTs in Organizations

Technology, like aggression, has been subject to a great variety of definitions, largely dependent on the context in which the term is used. Technology itself is multidimensional in nature, and definitions have been based on invention, innovation and scientific knowledge, material artifacts, transformation and physical processing, or a body of knowledge (Zyglidopoulos, 1999). Conceptually, when technology and users are married into systems, the human-computer-work construct contains both explicit and tacit elements (Nonaka, 1994; von Krogh, 2002) and may be mechanical-, human-, or knowledge-centered (Roberts & Grabowski, 1996).

Historically, the term *information systems,* synonymous with ICT, was first coined in the literature almost 50 years ago (Clark, 1993). At that time, the term was intended to be uniquely descriptive of a class of automated business tools used by managers (Haigh, 2001) that combined mechanical, data, and computers together electronically as a system for the management of work-relevant information (Leavitt & Whisler, 1958). The modern definition of information systems does not stray too far from this earlier view. The organizational focus concerning the use of these systems, however, has been expanded. An information system, or ICT, within an organizational setting may now more properly be considered as a computer-based "systematic arrangement for providing a defined group of people with information for purposeful action" (Ulrich, 2001, p. 61).

The information element in the system is generated not only by computers but also by other networked electronic sources like personal data assistants, cell phones, text messaging systems, and other mobile devices. Their introduction is radically altering organizational communication processes (Roberts & Grabowski, 1996; Straub & Watson, 2001), and the original envisioning of information systems as solely a management tool can now be extended into a broader domain that includes any user(s) within any technologically enabled work environment. With the introduction and use of the Internet and Internet-based communications technologies for networking (Brynjolfsson, 1993; Feraud, 2000), linkages between people, machinery, and computers lay at the core of most modern work processes.

The interconnectivity of these systems, their ubiquity and mobility (March, Hevner, & Ram, 2000), and their capability of reaching across organizational boundaries into the interorganizational or public spheres (Lyytinen & Yoo, 2002) implies that the potential domain of ICT misuse, cyberdeviancy, or cyberaggression is much broader than those of conventional constructs. The limitations of organizational communication in a non-ICT environment are removed as boundaries are electronically breached or dissolved. This difference is the result of three capabilities enabled by the technological characteristics of most ICTs: the ease of use of these systems, the multipath connectivity when they are networked, and the consequent potential for mass reach (Sproull, 1994).

First, access and use of these systems pervades all organizational levels, from the most junior to the most senior employee. These systems are no longer the sole domain of technical mandarins. The increasing user-friendliness of these systems allows a broader range of task accomplishment by professional, managerial, administrative, and line personnel, and their organizational ubiquity provides ready access for almost all organizational employees.

Second, the multipath connectivity of these systems yields the potential for any employee located anywhere in the organization to transact with any other person, whether inside or outside the organization (Flynn & Khan, 2003). This capability effectively removes any perceived or practical boundaries between organizational personnel. It also opens the organization to vertical, lateral, and external communications and influence from a wide range of stakeholders, including employees, other partnered or connected firms, customers, and the public at large.

Finally, the potential for mass reach grants any one individual the ability to transact with a multiplicity of others (Sproull, 1994), both within the organization and simultaneously with the public at large. This allows any individual with access to organizational ICTs the capability of mass broadcast communications, essentially granting them a type of public forum in which to communicate.

The complex nature of the technology, the unique nature of the human-work-computer fusion, and the rapid pace of their introduction within organizations has resulted in both anticipated and unanticipated impacts (Orlikowski,

2000; Roberts & Grabowski, 1996). Although the functional characteristics of ICTs serve to drive initial changes in organizational work processes (Sankar, 1988), the use of ICTs also results in increasing reliance on them for task accomplishment by employees (Hitt & Brynjolfsson, 1997), engendering even further change. These changes may be classed into categories of the first or second order (Sproull & Kiesler, 1994): *First-order effects* are those expected impacts normally founded on concepts of technology-as-tool, usually designed to increase organizational efficiency or enhance firm productivity. These effects are normatively associated with the planned implementation trajectories as foreseen and desired by the organization.

The *second-order effects* are those changes or impacts that are usually unintended by-products of first-order implementation. These are normally unforeseen and are primarily social in nature. These unanticipated effects may be generated as a result of the changes to organizational work processes or changes to communication and social networks within organizations, or as a function of the emergent nature of the resulting human-computer-work fusions that are created. From this perspective, the nonorganizationally sanctioned use, or misuse, of ICTs may be considered a second-order effect.

Second-Order Effects in Practice

E-mail has rapidly assumed prominence in organizational communications (Markus, 1994a, 1994b; Survey, 2003), and its use is truly pervasive (Kuzmits, Sussman, Adams, & Raho, 2002). It has become the current organizational communications medium of choice (Negroponte, 1995), and it is expected to remain so for the immediate future (Straub & Watson, 2001). The prevalent use of e-mail in organizations, its presence at the individual, group, organizational, and public levels—combined with the wealth of practitioner evidence of its misuse—permits this form of ICT-based behavior to be used as an exemplar to explore the scope and scale of ICT-based misuse in organizational settings.

Once predominantly an internal communicative medium, the advent of networks and the Internet has resulted in an environment in which e-mail is now widely used for both internal and external organizational communications. A recent IDC survey estimates that organizational e-mail use will continue to grow exponentially in the near future and form the backbone of business communications (Howard-Martin, n.d.). Paralleling the growth in the use of e-mail are the incidents of its misuse. The latest American Management Association (2003) survey of companies in the United States found that the misuse of e-mail by employees is on the rise. These findings are similar to those of firms in the United Kingdom where the number of incidents of e-mail abuse—including rude e-mail or the distribution of pornographic material—is growing ("Firms Face Up," 2003). On a global basis, many major corporations are experiencing both e-mail misuse and abusive use (Trombly & Holohan, 2000).

So complex and frequent is the misuse of e-mail that these electronic communications are increasingly being subpoenaed as evidence for legal proceedings, and organizations are increasingly concerned with issues of liability (Feldman, 2003; White & Pearson, 2001). This may be considered an indirect measure of the seriousness, level, and extent of these behaviors in the workplace. Legal systems are now managing greater numbers of cases involving a broad range of behaviors using organizational ICTs, including sexual harassment (Towns & Johnson, 2003), racial discrimination, age discrimination, securities fraud, and stock manipulation (Cohen, 1997; Varchaver & Bonamici, 2003; Verespej, 1998).

Misuse of ICTs also includes their use as a tool to commit fraud, for intentionally unauthorized access to either systems or the information within them, for hacking and sabotage, for eavesdropping or masquerading, for the deliberate denial of access, the introduction and spread of viruses, and the distribution of offensive pornography (Allan & Salter, 1997). Damage from cyber attack and liability for misuse or abuse of ICTs by employees has become such a frequent phenomenon that there is now a burgeoning business for third-party insurance coverage within the market (Foster, 2003).

Within the workplace, the use of e-mail for engaging in sexually suggestive behaviors—including flirtation (Whitty, 2003), the transmission of sexually graphic images, or sexual jokes—is fairly common (Middelton, 2001). Misuse of this type has been considered a form of workplace harassment, which actually contributes to a hostile work environment for others (Solomon, 1999). Organizational reactions in some instances have been quite strong. They have included the firing of employees for violating corporate e-mail policies themselves, or employees have been fired for sexual harassment when they were found to have collected, stored, and distributed (using organizational systems) pornographic or violent graphics and images (American Management Association, 2003). Xerox terminated 40 employees in 1999 when their network system was affected by the downloading and distribution of pornographic material. Dow Chemical terminated employees for distribution of sexually explicit jokes using their corporate e-mail. Similarly, Chevron Corporation was found culpable in permitting a hostile work environment to develop through employee use of sexual e-mail and had to settle a multimillion dollar sexual harassment lawsuit based on e-mail evidence ("Employee Misuse," 2004). An employee of the Carlyle Group e-mailed a friend declaring his intent to turn his corporate-provided residence into a venue for sexual exploitation. The e-mail was subsequently forwarded to several other parties and eventually was released publicly onto the Internet. The employee was subsequently returned to the host country and his employment terminated by his employer (Sorkin, 2001). Incidents of this form of sexual bragging being released into the public Internet are growing (Doward & Reilly, 2003; Walker, 2001).

Employees may also use the more public forum of corporate bulletin boards or the Internet, as well as internal e-mail systems, to express negative, derogatory, or defamatory comments about supervisors, coworkers (Rosman, 2002), or the organization (Abelson, 2001) or to release information to the public about internal corporate practices. E-mail misuse is not limited to line or operational employees (Morris, 2003). An e-mail from the CEO of Cerner Corporation to organizational managers that contained negative comments on the performance and commitment level of employees was subsequently released to the public in a Yahoo bulletin board (www.yahoo.com) where it would be accessible by corporate investors. Market and investor reaction was relatively swift, and the stock price declined by almost 30% in a matter of a few days ("Be Careful," 2001). Many of these acts are increasingly the grounds for censure or dismissal of the offending individual, regardless of position within the organization (Doward & Reilly, 2003).

In addition to organizational members misusing e-mail during the normal course of work activities, dismissed or terminated employees may take the opportunity to send negative good-bye e-mails. These e-mails often contain derogatory comments about supervisors, coworkers, or the organization itself (Rosman, 2002). One employee used the e-mail address directory of Intel Corporation to e-mail critical comments concerning the corporate practices of the firm to employees. Six e-mails were sent over several months to as many as 35,000 employees (Post & Brown, 2003).

Organizations themselves may misuse or abuse e-mail. E-mail has been used inappropriately to notify individuals that they are being laid off or fired (Goodnough, 2002). Misuse is not limited to business settings, and examples can be found across all forms of organizational settings. E-mail containing racist epithets has been sent to groups of ethnic minority students within a university setting (Flaherty, 1998), and e-mail incidents of sexual harassment occur within educational institutions and universities (MacGregor, 2000) and within the public sector, or government, as well (Muhl, 2003).

In addition to hostile expression or communications (Hamin, 2000), ICTs may be used to spread viruses or other programs designed to damage personal or organizational ICT systems (Sophos, 2004). The intentional and unintentional release of viruses, with e-mail a major vector for their spread, is increasing in frequency and caused an estimated $55 billion worth of damage to American businesses in 2003 alone (Tan, 2003). One of the most spectacular and damaging incidents of this type of behavior is the case of Timothy Lloyd, an employee who believed he had been treated unfairly. This apparently served as his motivation to leave a time-delayed, software logic bomb within the company's information systems. The damage to the organizational computing systems included the destruction of corporate software, data, and proprietary software control systems. The direct cost was estimated in the millions of dollars, with the indirect cost including loss of business and the subsequent layoff of 80 employees. It took the firm an estimated 5 years to recover from the damage done (Gaudin, 2000). Similar incidents have occurred at UBS PaineWebber (Lemos, 2002), and other firms are concerned enough to ensure that they provide major training initiatives, such as Merrill Lynch's institution of mandatory training for all employees (Dobbs, 2002).

Other uses and misuses of e-mail include use for furtherance of personal agendas in organizational settings (Kuzmits et al., 2002) and facilitation of petty tyranny (Romm & Pliskin, 1997, 1999). It may be used in an abusive fashion by managers and supervisors through a desire to avoid social interaction with employees or others (Markus, 1994a), for the delivery of bad news (Markus, 1994b), for the commission of hostile and aggressive interactions (Alonzo & Aiken, 2002; O'Sullivan & Flanagan, 2003), or as a tool to enact hostility by subgroups within the organization itself (Romm & Pliskin, 1997).

Hostile or aggressive acts occurring through e-mail may be either intentional or unintentional. The potential for unintentional hostile communications may arise from either the perception of the communication by the target (Carlson & Zmud, 1999), as individuals construct their own meanings through a process of contextualization and incorporation of the communicative message into their own knowledge base and experience, or from the very features and characteristics of e-mail itself (Sproull, 1994). Flaming is a common form of intentional behavior in ICTs, which may be considered aggressive in nature.

Although *flaming* has been defined variously by a number of researchers, it may generally be considered as the intentional use of insulting, uncivil, obscene, or profane language designed to inflict harm on the communicative target, whether an individual, group, or organization (Aiken & Waller, 2000; Alonzo & Aiken, 2002; Reinig, Briggs, & Nunamker, 1998; Sproull & Kiesler, 1994). Flaming behaviors may be enacted through a variety of text-based ICTs, including e-mail (Siegel, Dubrovsky, Kiesler, & McGuire, 1986), group support systems (Alonzo & Aiken, 2002), distance learning environments (Valacich, Nunamker, & Vogel, 1994), or publicly on the Internet (Kayany, 1998).

The examples presented demonstrate that ICTs are being misused within organizational settings in various ways. Misuse may occur between coworkers with employees engaging in discriminatory, racial, hostile, abusive, or sexually motivated behaviors. It may be used between those in authority and subordinates in similar fashions. Targets of these behaviors include both persons and the organization itself. Adverse impacts occur both internally and externally. As more organizations experience these behaviors or become cognizant of the organizational and legal implications, they can be expected to respond in a number of ways. They may respond either through termination of employees engaged in these behaviors, through remedial training programs to prevent future occurrences, or through redress sought in the courts. In order to determine the optimum methods for the prevention or reduction in frequency of these behaviors, however, or to mitigate the impacts of adverse outcomes, it is first necessary to identify and more fully understand the relationship between antecedents and mediating or moderating factors in organizational settings.

Cyberdeviancy and Cyberaggression

Aggression is known to be a complex and multifaceted behavioral phenomenon (Neumann & Baron, 1997), and this complexity is reflected in the treatment of aggression and workplace violence within and across different literatures (Bennett & Robinson, 2003; Gruys & Sackett, 2003; Robinson & Bennett, 1995; Schat & Kelloway, 2005; Spector, 1997). Because culture, language, and context permeate our various understandings of these definitions and constructs, the derivation of a common and coherent definition remains challenging (Chappel & Di Martino, 2000). Although theoretically diverse to a certain extent, they conceptually overlap (Anderson & Pearson, 1999) with a greater or lesser focus on different elements of the phenomena of interest. These may include the targets of aggressive acts (Robinson & Bennett, 1995), antecedents and predictors of these actions, their process or episodic nature (Spector, 1997), and finally their consequences and outcomes (Schat & Kelloway, 2005).

ICTs are multidimensional technologies, and different users employ them in a multiplicity of ways (Orlikowski, 2000; Rice & Gattiker, 2001; Zack & McKenney, 1995). Potentially nonorganizationally sanctioned use—or misuse—of ICTs may then be situated using any number of dimensions, frameworks, or models, based on patterns of usage. Given the recent nature of these behaviors, however, and as these behaviors are still emergent phenomena, we are encouraged to take as broad an approach as possible, incorporating all forms of use (Glomb, 2002). The media and practitioner evidence suggests that cyberaggression may first be considered a unique form of the more general phenomenon of the misuse of ICTs within an organizational context. Consequently, the deviancy framework as conceived by Robinson and Bennett (1995) is a sufficiently inclusive framework in which to type misuse or cyberdeviant behaviors.

Robinson and Bennett (1995) define *organizational deviance* as "voluntary behavior that violates significant organizational norms and in so doing threatens the well-being of an organization, its members, or both" (p. 556). They type deviant work behaviors within a two-dimensional framework, with one dimension reflecting the level or degree of harm from minor to serious and the second reflecting the focus of the behaviors, which may range from dyadic to organizational. This dimensionality results in a quadratic space within which deviant behaviors may be situated. The typology includes *Political Deviance,* consisting of minor interpersonal behaviors; *Production Deviance,* consisting of minor forms of deviance at the organizational level that consume work time; *Property Deviance,* a more serious form of deviance at the organizational level where organizational properties may be sabotaged, damaged, or destroyed; and finally *Personal Aggression,* which is interpersonal behavior ranging in form from verbal abuse to more serious forms of aggression, including physical violence.

Within Robinson and Bennett's deviancy typology, ICTs may be considered as an object of aggression, as in Property Deviancy, with the target either organizational systems or personal systems or as a tool for facilitating Production Deviant behaviors, as in cyberloafing (Greenfield, 2000; Lim, 2002). It may be used as a tool to support Political Deviancy, such as attacking or blaming (Kuzmits et al., 2002), or acts of petty tyranny or supervisor abuse (Tepper, 2000; Zellars, Tepper, & Duffy, 2002). It may be used for other political purposes such as information disclosure and selective informing, as in a strike action or for management and administrative response to such actions (Kuzmits et al., 2002; Romm & Pliskin, 1997). Finally, ICTs themselves may be used as tools to enact Interpersonal Aggression (Bennett & Robinson, 2003), or they may be the proxy subjects of interpersonal aggressive acts.

As shown in Figure 19.1, there are some forms of misuse that may be enacted or facilitated through ICTs that do not neatly fall into the conceptual quadratic declarations of the deviancy framework, such as internal forms of whistle-blowing or interpersonal aggressive acts that are released into the public domain. This demonstrates the limitation of using the deviancy frame to type the *process nature of behaviors* using ICTs, as the dimensions of the typology do not yield the entirely clear and distinctive types needed for subsequent taxonomic development, empirical measurement, and analysis (Rich, 1992).

As the deviancy framework is essentially bound by the construct of organizational context, deviant behaviors are largely defined by the firm as a function of the target or the outcome reflecting the underlying axial dimensions. The interconnectivity of organizational information systems and the features of ICTs, however, permit misuse behaviors to be targeted directly or indirectly at individuals, groups, the organization as a whole, or even outside of the firm. The ability for mass reach and the capability for direct and indirect communications imply that targets and outcomes alone may no longer be sufficient to differentiate the observed forms of aggressive behaviors using ICTs. When moving outside of the organizational boundaries into the broader domain, the nature of the aggressive act is potentially qualitatively different. ICT misuse therefore may blend two or more of the statically defined quadratic spaces. Additionally, as deviant or counterproductive work behaviors may also be "undertaken as acts of aggression" (Jockin et al., 2001, p. 1267), the typology breaks down.

For example, an aggressive or hostile action using ICTs may be performed by one individual against another, a form of Interpersonal Aggression. If the act itself is channeled through the public domain, the mediation of the act while within the public domain may in turn result in additional harm-doing to the organization, a form of Property Deviance. This was the case for Cerna, where the release of the internal e-mail, probably designed to harm

Production Deviance	Property Deviance	
Cyber loafing/Slacking	Virus Introduction / Transmission	
Online Chatting	Data Diddling / Erasure	
Online Gaming	Downloading Pornography	
Internet Telephony	Downloading Copyrighted Material	
E-mail Joke Rings	Software Copying / Theft	
Personal E-mails	Hacking Systems	
Shopping	Security Breaches	Breaking Confidence
		Public Flaming

		Cyber Whistle-Blowing
E-Politics	Verbal Abuse – Flaming / Inappropriate Tone / Threats	
Selective Information Distribution	Harassment – Attachments (Jokes, Images)	
Self-Serving Information Distribution	Sexual Harassment – E-flirtation, Cyberstalking	
Blame Shifting	Hacking Users – Damage to Personal Systems	
	Identity Theft – Unauthorized Use of Accounts / Names	
Political Deviance	Personal Aggression	

Figure 19.1   Cyberdeviancy

SOURCE: Adapted from Robinson and Bennett, 1995.

the reputation of the originator, actually had an impact on the stock price and reputation of the firm overall. Hence, once beyond the organizational boundaries, consideration must now be given for the incorporation of the effects as mediated through other organizations, the public, or a specific subset of the public. This mediation process, and the blending of quadratic spaces, is not easily accounted for within the deviancy framework's static target/outcome-oriented conceptualization. This is viewed as particularly problematic, as most of the conceptualizations of organizational aggression and violence take a static perspective, either because they focus on one element—for example, the target—or because they do not account for the potential for ongoing or process behaviors—for example, where the outcome of aggression serves as an input (Robinson & Greenberg, 1999) or trigger for subsequent behaviors (Anderson & Bushman, 2002; Rogers & Kelloway, 1997; Schat & Kelloway, 2005).

The challenge involved in differentiating aggressive behaviors, acts, intents, and outcomes remains a complex endeavor. Although these issues have in a certain sense been resolved in several of the aggression models through limiting construct definitions to targets, victims, or proximal outcomes (Schat & Kelloway, 2005), we argue that within the cyberaggression context this approach is problematic. The unique dynamic and process nature of cyber-aggression should not be "defined" away.

The typification and separation of misuse behaviors into quadratic spaces may also introduce conceptual limitations when attempting to type misuse behaviors that either incorporate elements drawn from each or that evolve over time. For example the use of e-mail to forward humorous material may be initially considered a form of Production Deviancy. For this behavior, the time consumed may detract from the time needed for other organizationally productive activities. If the behavior is viewed from the perspective of the potential impact on other persons in the organization, this activity may also be considered as a contributory factor leading perceptually to a more dis-criminatory or hostile work environment on the behalf of others. We argue that whether the behavior is characterized as intentional or not is of less importance than the potential for perception of the material content and form—as in the case of sexually explicit text or graphics—by recipients. Although the harmful outcome may never have been intended, the outcome may still be justly typed as a form of interpersonal aggression. This reflects the complexity of both aggressive behaviors using ICTs and the potential for adverse second-order, social interaction effects.

ICTs are radically changing the patterns of communication and decision making (Roberts & Grabowski, 1996). Whereas technology affects these structures and practices within organizations (Daft & Lengel, 1986; Orlikowski & Barley, 2001), when ICTs are introduced, the social structures related to work practices also change due to both first- and second-order effects. The potential for the paradigmatic change sponsored by ICTs may be so pervasive and all encompassing that the impact on the nature of social relationships is assessed as greater than any other previous communicative technology (Sproull & Kiesler, 1986). Most organizational communications are now mediated by some form of technology (D'Ambra & Rice, 1994), and conceptually and practically "technology and communication are now intimately interrelated" (Cheseboro & Bonsall, 1989, p. 7).

ICTs have generally increased social connectivity within organizational settings by enabling greater levels of lateral and vertical communications (Jarvenpaa & Staples, 2001; Orlikowski & Barley, 2001) both within and between organizations. This capability has served to transform how and between whom communication in organizations occurs. Or, in other words, ICTs have changed the social context of organizational relationships. Therefore, when organizations deploy and employ ICTs, not only are they creating a first-order technological system, but they are also "building a social system" (Carpenter, 1983, p. 11) or defining a "new social arena" (Cheseboro & Bonsall, 1989) within which work takes place.

As "human behavior is context-dependent" (Cheseboro & Bonsall, 1989, p. 54), the frames of reference within these new arenas may blur the classic distinctions between what have been previously considered personal, organizational, and public communication contexts (Williams & Rice, 1983), yet another second-order effect. Organizationally, technology and social context may no longer be considered in isolation (Orlikowski, 2000), a unique property of the evolving human-computer-work fusion. Consequently, organizational communication enabled through technical systems—such as e-mail, voice mail, group support systems, cooperative work systems, conferencing and video systems, video telephone systems, instant messaging, and other horizon technologies—will continue to affect the social dimensions of work (Yates, Orlikowski, & Okamura, 1999) and generate new forms of individual and social behavior as they are used.

As organizational ICTs are densely used for the purposes of organizational communication, such as e-mail, we believe that the study of e-mail used in the commission of aggressive or hostile acts would serve as a foundational entry point into the study of aggression and ICTs in organizational settings. E-mail has been the subject of a tremendous amount of research that, however, is primarily oriented toward explicating the differences between the organizational use of e-mail as an alternative to face-to-face communications (Sussman & Siegal, 2003). The use of e-mail and the differences in communicative content and use from face-to-face communications has been investigated from a media richness perspective (Rice, 1992), from a naturalness perspective (Kock, 2002), using social presence theory (Rice, 1992), and using channel expansion theory (Carlson & Zmud, 1999). A more recent stream of literature using the lens of social interactionism attempts to more clearly conceptualize, define, and explain the new forms of behaviors that are being evidenced with the use of ICTs (Markus, 1994a, 1994b; O'Sullivan & Flanagan, 2003). Despite this attention and focus, the results of much of this research remain equivocal, and there is evidence to suggest that the use of e-mail in organizational settings cannot yet be fully explained by extant theory.

E-mail differs from other communication technologies as a function of the features and characteristics enabled by their design. These include its asynchronous nature, its speed, text content, multiple addressability, external recordability, and external processability (Sproull, 1994). The practitioner literature citing e-mail misuse indicates that ICTs may serve as simply another tool or method to facilitate aggressive acts or, second, that the features and characteristics of the ICTs may themselves be harbingers of new forms of aggressive behaviors. These newer forms may be uniquely ICT-based and permit augmentation of aggressive expression beyond conventional forms and in ways not possible without the use of ICTs themselves.

The use of ICTs may be conceptualized along two dimensions based on their technical characteristics and their use. At one end of the continuum, ICTs may be used for interpersonal dyadic communication, with a social or public audience located at the other extreme. In the second dimension, the "reach" capability of ICTs may be defined in comparison with other conventional communicative forms found in organizations, such as physical conversation. ICTs may then be seen to *facilitate* conventional, or conventionally defined, interpersonal communication, in that the content of an e-mail may simply be an electronic proxy for a conversation or a written memorandum.

The capability of ICTs to permit simultaneous communication when utilizing multiple addressability is considered a method to *amplify* interpersonal communication and behaviors. Extension includes social others beyond the intended dyadic target, such as when using the carbon-copy (CC) ability to keep others within a team or group informed.

Finally, ICTs may *augment* interpersonal communication capability when used as a communications medium. This may be achieved when large numbers of others are communicated with—such as every employee within an entire organization—or when moving beyond the organizational boundaries and into public or extraorganizational spheres. This type of reach is generally impossible to achieve without the use of ICTs and is a technologically dependent effect. The instantaneity of the communications achieved through the multiple addressability of ICTs implies that any individual use of ICTs may fall into one or more of these categorizations simultaneously.

Figure 19.2 represents a graphical portrayal of the capability of ICTs versus the potential domain of effect, based on the categorizations as discussed. It should be noted that this is an extremely general classification that is equally applicable whether the ICT is used for positive or organizationally sanctioned uses, for example, transferring information in the form of an attachment to an e-mail to a multiplicity of outside client organizations or, for more negative uses, the posting of confidential internal organizational memoranda to the Internet or the deliberate infection of organizational ICTs with a virus with the intent to destroy or damage these systems or the data that is on them. For the purposes of this discussion, this graphic portrayal is used to highlight the potentials inherent in the use of ICTs for cyberdeviant and cyberaggressive behaviors over more conventional forms.

As will be argued, especially for those forms of negative, hostile, or aggressive interactions that are socially dependent (Anderson & Pearson, 1999), cyberaggression contains a strong communicative dimension and therefore may be considered primarily a socially based phenomenon. As "human aggression is intrinsically a social affair" (Graumann, 1998, p. 41), this necessitates a careful consideration of the use of ICTs as communicative tools (Anderson & Pearson, 1999).

"Aggression itself is largely performed or enacted in words" (Graumann, 1998, p. 45), and *verbal aggression* is defined as "an exchange of messages between two people where at least one person in the dyad attacks the self-concept of the other person in order to hurt the person psychologically" (Infante & Wigley, 1986, p. 62). We extend this definition such that this form of aggressive behavior may be incorporated within the cyberaggression construct as aggression expressed in a communication between two or more people using ICTs, wherein at least one person in the communication aggresses against another in order to effect harm. Causes of verbal aggression that have been empirically identified include a reaction to experienced frustration (through social learning or the modeling of the behaviors of others), other

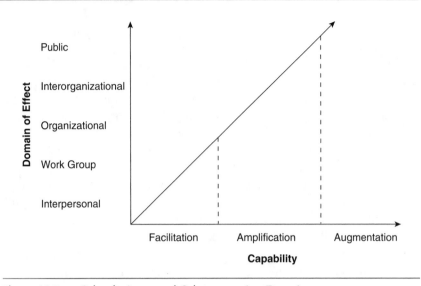

Figure 19.2   Cyberdeviancy and Cyberaggression Domains

psychopathological factors, or even argumentative skill deficiency (Infante & Wigley, 1986). Verbal forms of aggression, however, still remain as a significant gap in the broader domain of research concerning aggression and violence in the workplace (Graumann, 1998). This still may be considered a potentially critical failure as verbal aggression in social communications has the potential to result in greater psychological damage or harm (Infante & Wigley, 1986) than that of events or incidents of physical forms of aggression (Buss, 1971).

Within ICT-based communicative aggression, there are three types of actors involved: the initiator or perpetrator of the aggression, the recipient or victim(s), and vicarious victims or observers (Graumann, 1998). Social context influences ICT-based communicative acts through two major processes (Sproull & Kiesler, 1986). First, the user's (or users') perception of both dynamic and static cues contained within communications and, second, the cognitive interpretation and related affective states these perceptions generate (Sproull & Kiesler, 1986). Therefore all persons in this social triad may perceive different degrees of intentionality or harm in the actions taken by themselves or others. The socially reciprocal nature, therefore, again impels us to reflect a process basis for this phenomenon. The utility in using this approach is that it will permit the incorporation of antecedent, moderating, and mediating variables, as well as proximal and distal outcomes (Schat & Kelloway, 2005; Spector, 1997) and better capture the process nature of the phenomena.

Potential Antecedents

As cyberaggression is a relatively new and emergent phenomenon, the identification of potential predictors must be drawn from both the technical and behavioral literatures. Not surprisingly, within the technical literature, much of the research into the use of ICTs attempts to identify what factors influence individuals and groups to adopt and use ICTs. A major focus of effort in this area has been on the acceptance of technology as defined through the *technology acceptance model* or TAM (Davis, 1989). This model and its recent extensions have been used to predict the use and acceptance of technology in the workplace (Venkatesh, 2000). The level and types of use of new communication technologies have been found to be dependent on the utility (as perceived by the individual user), the ease of use in task accomplishment, and the social norms concerning the use of the technology in either group or work settings; however, the conceptualization for the TAM has been within a first-order context with little or no recognition of emergent second-order effects.

In their study of the introduction of a new phone technology in a large Fortune 500 firm, Manross and Rice (1986) observed that there is a distinct difference between the organizational and individual use of new technologies. As different individuals and groups within the same organization use technology differently, it is possible that actual use is more a function of emergent social context related to the technological features and characteristics (Zack & McKenney, 1995) than planned use. Consequently, the potential relationships that exist between variables that influence why and how employees adopt and use the technology and subsequent local emergent phenomena have not been well investigated.

The group support and cooperative work systems stream has also seen a major effort to identify the differences in behaviors between face-to-face and ICT-based communications and team or group level variables. Behavioral effects such as participation equalization, uninhibited behaviors, group norms, and conformity have been studied (Coovert & Thompson, 2001) in an effort to understand the interactive effects that occur among individuals, the technology, and their behaviors. Much of this work has attempted to explicate the observed behavioral differences through various media-based theories or through the study of the mediation of the communication process in relation to the features and characteristics of the ICTs in use. Much of this work remains equivocal and contradictory (Dennis & Kinney, 1998), though mediation effects observed include the acceleration of response expectancy, acceleration of work tasks, coordination of tasks over larger distances, a lack of immediacy in regulating feedback, the reduction of social status or positional cues, and a lack of social context information (Kiesler et al., 1984; Sproull, 1994).

The realization of the social impacts unique to computer-mediated communications are well recognized and have been widely studied, with the construct of social presence a mainstay within this line of research (Short, Williams, & Christie, 1976). Social presence reflects the level of perceived "personalness" of communications. ICT-based communications are a less rich communicative medium, as most of the nonverbal communication cues—those normally derived from face-to-face communication exchanges—are missing (Herbert & Vorauer, 2003). Consequently, ICTs mediate communications by restricting the range of communicative cues, and therefore it is argued that social presence may be reduced (Rice, 1984). This reduction may then contribute to deindividuation, disinhibition and deregulation effects (Hiltz, Turoff, & Johnson, 1989), or reduced inhibitions in communications (Siegel et al., 1986) or promote increased levels of impulsivity (Diener, Fraser, Beaman, & Kelem, 1976). Within the sociological study of criminals' impulsivity, an individual personality characteristic has been positively related to criminal and antisocial behaviors, with vandalism, rule breaking, and aggression as major correlates (Luengo, Carillo-de-la-Pena, Otero, & Romero, 1994). As ICTs are becoming a common and readily accessible feature of workplaces, they may contribute to impulsive decision-to-action cycles based on their availability and the immediate versus distal gratification involved in their use (Kuzmits et al., 2002).

Personal information that reflects or indicates an individual's status, such as a signature block incorporating an organizational hierarchical cue, has been shown to influence behaviors in the absence of other social information cues (Gueguen & Jacobs, 2002). In the absence of this information, particularly for communications when one of the communicants is unknown, such as in multiple addressing systems, Sproull and Kiesler (1986) found empirical support for reduced social context. They found increases in antisocial behavior within communications, such as flaming, negative comments, and a violation of what would be considered conventional communicative norms. Interestingly, greater experience with the use of the ICTs did not seem to attenuate the rate of misuse.

Flaming behaviors have also been related to the social context (Kayany, 1998), the perceived proximity or distance between communicants (Valacich et al., 1994), the effects of deindividuation or disinhibition associated with the use of ICTs (Hiltz et al., 1989), the perceived dehumanization of the message and the lack of politeness strategies influencing the construction of the message (Sussman & Sproull, 1999), the perception of violation of self-interests and hostility (Reinig et al., 1998), or the content or the subject of the communication itself (Garramone, Harris, & Anderson, 1986).

Less inhibited language choice with increased use of hostile tone, insulting language, or swearing (Kiesler et al., 1984) may result in aggressive exchanges that may then be further exacerbated by perceptions of the social isolation effects or depersonalization effects of ICTs (Markus, 1994b). The use of e-mail to deliver negative messages is subject to less positive distortion than that found in face-to-face exchanges (Sussman & Sproull, 1999). Consequently, civil communicative behavioral norms become more critical in an ICT-based communicative world, particularly because incivility and the violation of accepted communication behavioral norms may serve as precursors to escalation in ICTs (Sussman & Sproull, 1999) or different and more aggressive or hostile behaviors (Anderson & Pearson, 1999).

As the level and rate of use of such ICTs increases within organizational settings, so too do the opportunities for observation and modeling of behaviors of others. As we have shown, the reach of hostile or aggressively postured communications activities, both within and without an organization, increases this potential and may serve to provide a negatively contributory social environment. This in turn creates more opportunity for response, either from direct or indirect communications, thereby increasing the potential for escalatory aggression.

Social learning is one process in which individuals learn, adopt, and replicate normative social practices (Bandura, 1973). This enactment, based on observation and experiences in the workplace, results in the modeling of the behaviors of others. O'Leary-Kelly, Griffin, and Glew (1996) use social learning theory to explain acts of aggression within an organizational context. Similarly, Robinson and O'Leary-Kelly (1998) found empirical support to conclude that aggression may be the result of modeled behaviors, or in other words, it is a behavior that may be learned from coworkers.

This research identifies the importance of group work norms and practices and reinforces the importance of situational factors when these factors, activities, and behaviors that surround individuals in the workplace may serve to function as models or triggers to subsequent behaviors. This is a pattern similar to the more direct feedback spiral proposed by Anderson and Pearson (1999), explaining how acts of incivility classed as low-level or minor forms of workplace aggression may function as precursors to an escalation of aggressive behaviors among communicants so engaged. In addition to the interactive effects that may reduce social presence or adversely affect social context and normative behaviors, there are other contextual or organizational factors that contribute to aggressive behaviors. As ICTs are now a mainstay in most organizations, this implies that non-ICT-related predictors should also contribute to cyberaggressive behaviors: workload, work stress, fear, organizational climate and culture, or newer forms of stress such as technostress (Weatherbee, 2004).

As noted by Spector (1997), role ambiguity, role conflict, workload, and interpersonal conflicts may also function as stressors, which can then act as triggers. These "frustrators" may then lead to negative affective reactions ranging from minor irritation to serious negative affect, such as overt anger. Behavioral reaction may then be directed at the perceived source of these frustrations, with actions focused on the frustrators or displaced onto other targets such as coworkers or the organization.

Rapid technological change may contribute to experienced frustration at work (Neumann & Baron, 1997), and individuals may be expected to contribute to a greater degree than previously demanded within the organizations that have undergone downsizing or where new technology has been introduced. The resulting increases in workloads amplify experienced frustration. The resultant stress, generating increased feelings of resentment (Carll, 1999; Neumann & Baron, 1997), leads to negative affective reactions overall.

Research suggests that there are demographic variables that influence the use and misuse of ICTs. Evidence suggests that there is a gendered pattern to ICT communications (Alonzo & Aiken, 2002). Savicki and Kelley (2000) empirically differentiated communication patterns among single-gender and mixed-gender groups who were using ICTs. They found that gender influenced the normative style and content of communications with single-gender groups at the extremes of a continuum, with mixed gender groups between these two. Either individual males or all-male groups were more likely to engage in flaming behaviors, with females or all-female groups less likely to. Similarly, Herring (1996) also found that men and women use e-mail differently and that men are more likely than women to violate communicative norms, using e-mail in an abusive fashion.

Gruys and Sackett (2003) have shown that older workers or workers with greater levels of experience are less likely to engage in counterproductive behaviors. Alternatively, some studies show that there is little correlation between personality factors and deviant workplace behaviors like aggression. These studies suggest that interaction between personality variables and situational variables, as well as mediation effects, have a greater potential to provide more promising understanding of workplace deviance (Peterson, 2002; Sussman & Sproull, 1999).

Potential Outcomes

Outcomes of workplace aggression and violence still largely remain an under-researched area (Glomb, 2002) within the general violence, hostility, and aggression domains. Although research has primarily focused on primary effects, cyberaggression within the organizational context can have additional secondary or tertiary impacts that go far beyond the temporal immediacy of the primary act. These impacts roughly correlate with individual, group, or organizational levels as a function of the reach capabilities of the ICTs. *Primary effects* are those affecting the target or victim of the aggression. *Secondary effects* are those that affect coworkers or other observers or witnesses within the work group. *Tertiary impacts* are those in which the aggressive behaviors are enacted or evidenced beyond the work group and may span the organizational level or go beyond the organizational boundaries into the public sphere.

At the individual level where an "other" is the primary target, ICT-expressed aggression between a dyadic communication pair, such as in flaming, may result in anger or other negative affect (Alonzo & Aiken, 2002) and can negatively affect task perception and decision making (Martin, Hiesel, & Valencic, 2001). Receipt of a hostile or aggressive communication may also result in a mirrored response leading to an "incivility spiral" (Anderson & Pearson, 1999), as the initial hostile or aggressive message may serve as a trigger for a response escalating the level of hostility within each subsequent exchange.

Secondary impacts may fall on other coworkers who are observers or witnesses to the aggressive acts or who reside within the hostile environment itself. These vicarious impacts include fear and both psychological and physical ill effects similar to those experienced by the original target or victim (Rogers & Kelloway, 1997). Consequently, the resultant sociopsychological impact on secondary victims may be as potentially negative as those on the immediate target. In the case of Pettit & Martin, a legal firm that experienced a workplace homicide committed by an aggrieved client, the adverse psychological impact on the survivors was so great that the employees never recovered, the organization became dysfunctional, and the firm eventually dissolved (Carll, 1999).

In a group setting in which individuals share the communication, observers may be vicarious parties to the aggression, or multiple individuals in the group may be the target. Behaviors of this type within a group setting can lead to increased conflict among group members (Sia, Tan, & Wei, 2002). Similarly, at the organizational level, this behavior may affect not only the specific target but potentially all the organizational members who have access to the corporate ICT and who were observers (Rosman, 2002).

Tertiary impacts are hostile or aggressive ICT behaviors that may result in a number of other additional outcomes and have the potential to negatively affect individuals beyond dyadic relationships, including groups and organizations. It also has the potential to cross organizational boundaries, affecting other organizations or segments of the public (Kayany, 1998). Boundary violation may occur in two fashions: First, aggressive behaviors may be directed outward by an organizational employee or employees at targets such as other electronically linked organizations or customers (Alonzo & Aiken, 2002). Second, the behaviors may be directed at targets within the organization or the organization as a whole by employees of linked organizations, members of the public, or internal employees.

When subject to harassment or other aggressive behaviors, victims may react in a number of ways. They may choose to invoke authority for the purposes of stopping the behaviors, confront the aggressor, confront the aggressor and report the behaviors, or do nothing (Adams-Roy & Barling, 1998). The choice of which of these actions to take may be predicted by the relationship between perceived organizational justice and individual assertiveness attributes. Drawing from the extensive work on whistle-blowing over the last two decades (Dozier & Miceli, 1985; Miceli & Near, 1985, 1988; Miceli, Near, & Schwenk, 1991; Near, Dworkin, & Miceli, 1993; Near & Miceli, 1986, 1987), we see emerging evidence of what may be considered new and variant forms of reporting or whistle-blowing.

When employees perceive injustice within the organizational context, they may be motivated to take action to rectify the injustice through whistle-blowing (Gundlach & Douglas, 2003). Whistle-blowing may then be conceptualized as either an internal or external mechanism used in an attempt to influence others when needed to bring about changes to behaviors or circumstances that are perceived as illegitimate (Miceli et al., 1991). Motivated by fear, anger, or resentment (Gundlach & Douglas, 2003), employees may choose to cyber whistle-blow through ICTs in an attempt to halt the behaviors by invoking either formal or informal mechanisms (Somers & Casal, 1994). Victims' perceptions of injustice may motivate ICT reporting behaviors as a deterrent to behavior (Farrell & Peterson, 1982), to influence the behaviors of others (Miceli et al., 1991), or to resolve the situations they find themselves in (Gundlach & Douglas, 2003). As internal reporting to supervisors has been found to be more prevalent than external whistle-blowing behaviors (Somers & Casal, 1994), it is possible that victims in ICT-enabled environments may first choose to use ICTs, as they are often perceived as less formal communications (Kiesler et al., 1984). The ability of ICTs to have either specifically targeted small or broad audiences, to jump levels of hierarchy, or to bridge organizational boundaries may be permitting individuals to seek remedy or redress in new forms or in new ways. Reporting of hostility or aggression in the workplace is an area of research that has not been addressed sufficiently in general; and given the potential use of ICTs for these behaviors, this is an area of research that must be opened for exploration

Potential Interventions

Scholarly and practitioner recommendations for organizational interventions to reduce the risk of misuse or abuse of information systems have been a perennial topic of study and prescription. The interventions designed to reduce cyberdeviancy or cyberaggression may be classed into a threefold design: *technical interventions* wherein the characteristics of the underlying computational systems are designed to reduce or prevent misuse; *managerial interventions,* such as the propagation and enforcement of organizational policies of appropriate use that are designed to prevent or reduce the occurrence of these behaviors; and most recently, *social interventions,* such as the institution of appropriate norms of usage, which may be fostered in organizational settings.

Within the information systems literatures much of the work looks at deterrence, prevention, detection, and remedy solely from a technical perspective (Forcht, 1994). For example, the intentional or accidental forwarding or transmission of personal, confidential, or related information has become so prevalent that it has been recommended that this feature be removed from systems' capability (Jackson, Dawson, & Wilson, 2003). Alternative to their removal, information systems also have the potential to become self-monitoring. That is, the characteristics of computing systems and networks that permit their use in organizational settings may be used to automate the process of monitoring and scanning e-mails for key words or phrases to prevent users from sending objectionable, harassing, vulgar or insulting language, or pornographic and erotic materials (Solomon, 1999).

Boye and Jones (1997), however, argue that reliance on solely punitive and preventative security (e.g., technical interventions) will not be as effective as a more comprehensive approach. This suggests that factors that may be influenced by management or organizational members as a whole, such as organizational values, interpersonal and work group norms, preventative security, and disciplinary management of infractions together should do more to reduce unwanted or undesirable behaviors.

Corporations are now becoming aware that technical and managerial interventions are insufficient to prevent abuse of ICTs. Training in the appropriate use of ICTs has been identified as a critical requirement for the reduction of the potential for miscommunication in ICTs (Cornelius & Boos, 2003), and Klein, Clark, and Herskovitz (2003) recommend that training in writing and communication using ICTs may reduce nonunderstanding or misunderstanding of communications, which could subsequently reduce some of triggers of cyberaggression. Organizations are taking steps to make employees aware of these issues (Fusaro, 1998), and others such as Merrill Lynch are designing training programs on the appropriate use of corporate e-mail (Varchaver & Bonamici, 2003).

The creation of an amenable organizational environment (Bies, Tripp, & Kramer, 1997; Sommers et al., 2002) or culture of norms for appropriate use should also reduce cyberaggressive behaviors, as these may be influenced by social learning and modeling. To this end, Neumann and Baron (1997) recommend improved screening processes for prospective employees using in-depth background checks, reference reports, preemployment testing, and situational and stress interviews as potential managerial and human resource intervention mechanisms for prevention. By screening prospective employees in this fashion, the potential for individual factors contributing to cyberaggression may be reduced, which in turn would contribute to more positive behavioral norms and social context.

A Dynamic Model of Cyberdeviancy and Cyberaggression

Drawing widely from the technical, organizational, and behavioral literatures, we have identified a range of technological, individual, group, and organizational level variables that we propose contribute to these forms of workplace aggression in organizational settings. We view the unique nature of cyberaggression as a second-order effect arising out of the social nature of ICT use in the workplace and as a dynamic phenomenon that not only emerges from but influences the organizational settings in which it occurs. Cyberaggression in organizational settings is a behaviorally complex interplay of antecedents, moderating and mediating variables, and direct and indirect outcomes. These outcomes contain the potential to recycle and to subsequently influence the factors and variables that result in further aggressive behavior and so must be considered as both inputs and outputs. Therefore, we have chosen a process model (see Figure 19.3) as the most appropriate theoretical vehicle to commence the empirical investigation of the relationships between the potential factors and variables we have identified. Process models have been used within the broader work stress and workplace aggression domains to capture the dynamic relationships between variables at all levels, and their utility in capturing the temporal, reciprocal, or process nature of phenomena is well recognized (Schat & Kelloway, 2005).

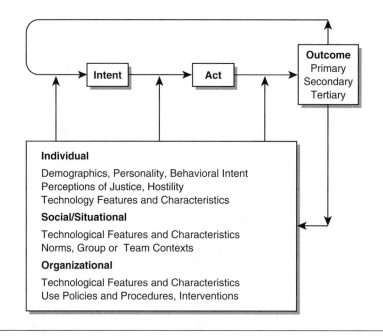

Figure 19.3   Process Model of Cyberaggression

This model portrays the proposed relationships between the events, factors, variables, and outcomes involved in cyberaggressive behaviors found in organizational settings. It is a multilevel model of ICT-based aggression and incorporates both technical and behavioral variables situated at the individual, group, organizational, and extraorganizational levels.

Future Research

It is critical that we move beyond typologies and static perspectives concerning the social effects of aggressive behaviors (Anderson & Pearson, 1999) and begin to take a more process or interactive view of these phenomena, as ICTs are so inextricably bound up with organizational communications, relationships, context, and behavior, all of which are reciprocal and socially constructed phenomena. As we have shown, the potential domain within which cyberaggressive behaviors exist is perhaps much larger than conventional constructs. We can no longer afford to view workplace aggression statically with separation of intent from act or outcomes. We must move forward and more fully investigate ICT use as an intervening or moderating variable (Sussman & Sproull, 1999) in a nomological network; for as the domain broadens, so too does the necessity for investigation into a broader set of variables of interest at all levels.

We need to determine if there are qualitative and empirically distinct differences in the nature of interpersonal aggression when ICTs are employed to simply facilitate conventional forms of aggression such as swearing—insulting or abusive verbal language in a dyadic context—versus those other forms when the ICTs are used to involve others. For example, upon what motivational basis are decisions made to involve coworkers and/or supervisors—potentially the entire organizational membership or even the public? Is this form of cyber whistle-blowing different from other forms of internal whistle-blowing? Is this behavior more or less prevalent in a formal or informal context? Is the invoking of intervention by authority empirically distinct from creating awareness through the desired involvement of coworkers? What contextual factors influence the decisions to report hostile or aggressive behaviors by others? What variables affect the manner in which this is done and to whom? Not only must individual and group processes be identified and differentiated, but we need to look at the relationships between and across groups as the technical reach capabilities are used. Is there a quantitative difference between individual dyadic communications and those in which one of the dyad escalates the behavior through the use of ICT features such as carbon copy or blind carbon copy? We believe that when these systems are used for hostile and aggressive purposes, empirically it is important to identify the potential differences in the intent behind informing others, whether aggressor- or victim-initiated. Is the invoking of authority for intervention different from informing for the purposes of awareness? Is informing for awareness a different process than invoking group loyalties or normative behaviors? What circumstances lead to this behavior: individual, contextual, or group? Group behaviors influence individual behaviors (Glomb & Liao, 2003), but how intensely and under what circumstances? For what types of groups? Virtual or distance or conventional and physically colocated?

Are there differences between cyberaggressive behaviors based on the motivation found in instrumental versus hostile aggressive acts (Bushman & Anderson, 2001)? Are there potential differences in antecedents and outcomes (Glomb, 2002)? Does impulsive aggressive behavior take a different form (Diener et al., 1976)? How does impulsive response contribute to escalation versus a more ruminative one?

ICTs have been used against organizational elements by groups within the organization. Is this a form of interpersonal aggression? Are the communicants on the other side of the ICT perceived as individuals or members of the group? As research into status and social hierarchy cues transmitted through ICTs remains equivocal (Weisband & Schneider, 1995) and technology furthers group interactive capability, the subject remains an area of interest and potentially fruitful research.

Beyond the immediate target(s) of aggression, we need to understand the impact of exposure to what may be considered vicarious ICT aggression (Rogers & Kelloway, 1997). There is growing evidence to suggest that these "minor" forms of workplace aggression, such as verbal abuse, may have a more severe impact than initially conceptualized (Chappel & Di Martino, 2000), and we need to understand the impacts of the essentially cumulative, longer term harm potential. Not only do we need to understand the impacts on the intended victim, the indirect victim, or vicarious victim; we also need to more fully understand the overall impact on the social dynamics and context within the organization where this behavior takes place.

We need to determine when and why hostile aggressive acts may serve as triggers for retaliatory behavior (Patten & Woods, 1978), revenge (Bies et al., 1997), or the perpetuation of a hostile environment through the initiation of a spiral pattern of escalation (Anderson & Pearson, 1999). As group aggressive behaviors positively influence individual aggressive behaviors (Glomb & Liao, 2003) through modeling and social learning (Bandura, 1973), we need to further investigate the group construct for this use of ICTs. Is there a difference between the spiral pattern of incivility and the chain effect when ICT carbon-copy/blind carbon-copy (CC/BCC) mechanisms are used (Kuzmits et al., 2002)? Physical verbal incivilities or other socially rude behaviors are mostly constrained by the physics of the work environment, by time and space. As ICTs remove or lessen these constraints, does this leave us with a new and distinct spiral or chain phenomenon?

Additionally, we need to investigate the potential for bundles or groups of negative behaviors committed through ICTs (Glomb, 2002; Glomb & Liao, 2003). Does engagement in forms of cyber-based verbal aggression lead to other more serious forms? Are individuals who engage in these behaviors also likely to engage in other forms of cyber or conventional aggression? Is the use of ICTs for aggression simply a function of ubiquity and ease of access, or is this form of aggression perceived as something distinct? As ICTs are married into almost all organizational work processes and as they provide ample opportunity for deviant use, we need to understand the temporal pattern of their use for aggression by both individuals and groups. Attempting to answer these questions should enable a more focused investigation of antecedents or predictors (Anderson & Pearson, 1999; Gruys & Sackett, 2003).

ICTs will become more prevalent, and as newer forms such as wearable or nomadic systems (Lyytinen & Yoo, 2002) are introduced, these systems will continue to affect and change the social nature of work processes in organizations. As research into newer forms of computer-mediated communication technologies such as instant messaging (IM), shared hypermedia workspaces, and Web communications logs (Weblogs) is just now commencing (Riva, 2002), this represents another rapidly burgeoning area for research.

There is evidence to suggest that the synchronicity of ICT communications is more critical for social development processes in groups than that of the available bandwidth needed for increased cue transmission (Irmer, Chang, & Bordia, 2000). This has implications, as one of the significant technological differences between e-mail systems and instant messaging is synchronicity, and IM use in organizational settings is on the rise (Rafaeli & Noy, 2002), an area where technological adoption provides a challenge for timely research.

These newer or different technologies will be increasingly found within the organizational context as horizon technology is adopted. They will also undoubtedly have first-order and second-order effects, and we must expect that they will be used for the commission of aggressive or hostile acts. Arguably, it will become even easier for an initiator to perpetrate these types of behaviors, as wireless, wearable, and nomadic technologies grant access 24 hours a day from one individual to another, from anywhere in the world to anywhere else. As the requirement for physical presence is lessened in the workplace and replaced by technological capability, the number of contingent and part-time workers employed by firms is growing. As the percentage of contingent and contract workers in the organizational workforce grows, it becomes critical to understand if remote workers (Kelloway, Barling, Kelley, Comtois, & Gatien, 2003) who are more socially isolated from their colleagues (Gephart, 2002) are more or less likely to engage in or be victims of these behaviors.

As organizations increase their use of global virtual teams as they globalize their operations, cultural differences will also become increasingly important. Rice, D'Ambra, and More (1998) have observed that there are differences in what are perceived as appropriate and inappropriate behaviors when using ICT across national cultures (Hofstede, 1980). ICTs have been found to mediate cultural variables due to reduced social cues, which variably affect cultural patterns, such as high- versus low-context cultures, or high versus low power distance cultures (Kersten, Koeszegi, & Vetschera, 2003). Are aggression antecedents and predictors different across cultures? What features of ICTs act to mediate or moderate particular forms of cyberaggressive acts? Are the impacts of social context different in cultures that form groups differently or that perceive the social dimensions of ICTs differently?

Cyberaggression also needs to be linked more fully with other organizational constructs such as whistle-blowing, exit, and voice (Harlos, 2001). Are more specific or unique forms of cyberaggression, such as departure or "good-bye" e-mails (Rosman, 2002), different from those that occur during normal work?

Do different perpetrators differentiate in victim selection? As ICTs enable both lateral and vertical communications directly to specified recipients, is victim selection upward different than downward or lateral? Is there a difference in the form of the behaviors themselves? Are targets in subordinate positions selected more than others? Are there intentional differences in the selection of targets? Are subordinates who target supervisors or superiors more likely to include others in the distribution of the communication? Does this behavior vary by the primary motivation for the action, for example, frustration versus justice perception or for perceived formal versus informal actions?

There is evidence to suggest that there are generational differences in the use of ICTs: Older workers rely more on social norms (Morris & Venkatesh, 2000). Are younger generations, who have either always had access to ICTs or had greater exposure to ICTs, more familiar with the social uses of these technologies? Will their experience with ICTs, including acceptance of the reduced social cues or social presence, make them more or less likely to use ICTs for hostility or aggression?

Many complaints of hostile behaviors such as sexual harassment suffer from the "deaf-ear" syndrome, if they are reported at all; and victims are hesitant to take action (Adams-Roy & Barling, 1998). As formal versus informal voice mechanisms appear to operate differently in different contexts based on supervisor and employee perceptions (Harlos, 2001), ICTs may represent a mechanism of reporting through informal or unofficial channels (Peirce, Smolinski, & Rosen, 1998). If policies, procedures, and guidelines are overly complex or not well understood, victims of workplace aggression or hostility may become frustrated and seek alternative methods of dealing with the situation (Peirce et al., 1998). ICTs' capability to reach others within the organization may be perceived as an informal and accessible route that victims may choose over others.

There is growing evidence to suggest that there are distinct and different perceptual and practical differences in how ICTs are used across genders (Fiore & Nelson, 2003; Fredrick, 1999; Gruber, 1999). Another area that mandates concerted study is the shifting gender balance in our workplaces and the increasing diversity of our workforce.

Finally, we are now observing that other technologies are also being used in new and innovative ways with both positive and negative implications for organizations and the public. In one incident, members of a police department were caught on a cell phone camera engaging in what has been described as racial harassment. A police car with a large stuffed gorilla tied to the grill was photographed outside a popular downtown bar whose cliental were mostly African Americans. A patron of the establishment perceiving this behavior as racist used a camera-enabled digital cell phone, and pictures were sent to local media as attachments to e-mail. The media subsequently broadcast the pictures on television, the Internet, and in print (Giegerich, 2003). In another case, a man was using a concealed cell phone camera for voyeuristic purposes by wandering the local malls taking illicit pictures of female mall and store patrons (Raphael, 2003). Camera-enabled cell phones are now being banned from organizational settings for just these reasons. As newer technologies appear and are adopted in society at large, they may serve as precursor indicators or represent potential trends or patterns of behaviors that may soon be expected to be found within organizational settings.

Research Challenges

Research into cyberdeviancy or cyberaggression will face two distinct challenges that may not necessarily be encountered in areas surrounding more conventional research topics: first, the challenges associated with data gathering, capture, and interpretation; and second, the unique ethical challenges associated with research involving aggression as a focus or with data concerning such acts or behaviors gathered from information systems themselves.

Regardless of the terminology employed, or how aggression and violence are operationalized, one óf the significant challenges for the study of cyberdeviancy or the more severe forms of cyberaggression remains the (potentially) low base rate phenomenon. For some of these types of acts, it is difficult to assess whether it is the low prevalence of the behavior itself or the lack of the reporting of the behavior that is the issue, despite some of the media evidence to the contrary. There is evidence to suggest that extremely violent behaviors loom large as a focus of media attention but that lesser forms of aggressive or hostile behaviors are more prevalent and underreported (Schat & Kelloway, 2005). Because they are socially proscribed behaviors, there may be a low prevalence rate in the general population; or, alternatively, many organizations may simply be reluctant to inform either shareholders or the public concerning incidents or events of this type, particularly those that involve organizational information systems, as reporting highlights the potential weaknesses in corporate systems (D'Amico, 2002). In any event, the often contradictory evidence concerning the rates of these behaviors still poses a challenge to solid empirically grounded research (Schat & Kelloway, 2005).

Methodologically, experimental methods may also be constrained. Exposure to violent or aggressive stimuli is not generally considered an acceptable practice from an ethical perspective (Bertilson, 1990). Because measuring an act of aggression when it occurs is rarely possible and because exposing experimental participants to acts of violence or aggression is unethical, research must generally rely on self-report data. This raises the pragmatic issue of socially desirable response and monomethod biases in empirical investigation. The base rate and prevalence challenge, as well as the potential ethical constraints of experimental design, imply that cross-sectional survey designs will likely form the bulk of study into cyberdeviancy and cyberaggression. This methodology raises these two constraints or empirical limitations: self-report data in aggression and violence studies are prone to social desirability bias (Saunders, 1991), and there is the potential of monomethod bias associated with single-source cross-sectional designs. Additionally, studies of this type (that is, nonlongitudinal) will also be limited to correlation-based analysis, and causality may not be inferred. Researchers will have to mitigate these effects through careful methodological and analytical strategies.

Finally, the interpretation of communicative cyberaggressive data itself may be problematic. For example, content analysis of communications using ICTs may only be accomplished in a post hoc fashion. The implication here is that the communication itself (the e-mail, listserv posting, etc.) may be analyzed completely outside of the context in which it was generated and used. In isolation of contextual norms of use and without cognizance of the social circumstances at the time of its generation and transmission, interpretation is potentially problematic. There is growing evidence to suggest that aggressive expression is contextually relational: hence the determination or classification of aggressive or hostile behaviors in ICT-based exchange must account for the relationship existing between perpetrator and victim (Aquino & Lamertz, 2004). For without acknowledgment of the context and relationship, it will be difficult to ensure that we are measuring cyber-aggression when ICTs are used with the intent to harm.

Conclusion

The actual use of ICTs in organizational settings for the commission of deviant acts and cyberaggressive behaviors is ample evidence that there is now an imperative to move beyond anecdotal reports (Peterson, 2002) and develop a body of research that investigates individual, interpersonal, contextual, and social interactions. Despite the fragmented nature of the general domain of aggression and violence at work, the practical pressures for understanding these growing phenomena no longer permit complacency in awaiting a greater research consensus.

The emergence of cyberaggression and our growing realization of the importance of the research agenda concerning workplace aggression in general make it critical that we also incorporate this emergent and burgeoning phenomenon, firmly situating the use of workplace ICTs to commit aggressive acts within the body of workplace aggression research. The space existing between the information systems, or management of information systems, literature and the organizational or psychological literatures means that the potential for new understanding will only be further restricted if a multidisciplinary approach is not taken. The psychological and behavioral constructs that facilitate our understanding of aggression and violence from a human perspective must now be married with our technological understanding concerning the unique features, characteristics, and potentials that exist within these systems.

The emergence and adoption rates of information systems continue to accelerate, paralleling the introduction of new generations of information technologies, greater levels of technology transfer, increased globalization of markets and firm presence, and greater levels of competition in the market (Yates & VanMaanen, 1996). The growing dependence on ICTs for most work processes (Roberts & Grabowski, 1996) dictates that they will remain a readily accessible means for the prosecution of aggressive acts. This potential can only be further compounded as ICTs continue to change how individuals, groups, and organizations communicate and achieve work (Gephart, 2002). It may also be argued that the workplace is on the cusp of a generational change (Kanter, 2001) wherein a younger generation, with a potentially significantly different perspective on the use of ICTs, will be entering the workplace. As the first truly wired generation, it may be assumed that the values and beliefs they hold concerning workplace ICTs will be different from those of their predecessors (Smola & Sutton, 2002) and that these may manifest as behavioral differences.

Without a firm theoretical grounding, it will be difficult to capture and understand the dynamic and changing nature of these complex and heavily contextualized behaviors, as they are in many ways dependent on the technological capability of ICTs and how these are perceived by the user; however, in identifying the importance of the emerging phenomenon of cyberdeviant behaviors and cyberaggression, we offer a forewarning, an extension of Gelernter's insight that opened this chapter, our Orwellian Corollary: Any technology that *can* be misused *will* be.

References

Aarsteinsen, B. (2002). New risks in the wired world. *Canadian Insurance, 107*(9), 10.

Abelson, R. (2001, April 29). By the water cooler in cyberspace, the talk turns ugly. *New York Times,* p. 11.

Adams-Roy, J., & Barling, J. (1998). Predicting the decision to confront or report sexual harassment. *Journal of Organizational Behavior, 19*(4), 329–336.

Aiken, M., & Waller, B. (2000). Flaming among first-time group support system users. *Information & Management, 37,* 95–100.

Allan, G. W., & Salter, S. (1997). Computer use and misuse. *Computer Audit Specialist Group Journal, 7*(1), 7–14.

Alonzo, M., & Aiken, M. (2002). Flaming in electronic communications. *Decision Support Systems, 36,* 205–213.

American Management Association. (2003). *E-mail survey finds e-mail abuse a firing offense.* Retrieved March 2, 2004, from www.econtentmag.com? Articles/Article Reader.asp

Anderson, C. A., & Bushman, B. J. (2002). Human aggression. *Annual Review of Psychology, 53,* 27–51.

Anderson, L. M., & Pearson, C. M. (1999). Tit for tat? The spiraling effects of incivility in the workplace. *Academy of Management Review, 24*(3), 452–471.

Aquino, K., & Lamertz, K. (2004). A relational model of workplace victimization: Social roles and patterns of victimization in dyadic relationships. *Journal of Applied Psychology, 89*(6), 1023–1034.

AssetMetrix. (2003, August 25). Employee misuse of computers said widespread. (Montreal) *Gazette,* p. B8.

Bandura, A. (1973). *Aggression: A social learning analysis.* Englewood Cliffs, NJ: Prentice Hall.

Barlow, J., Bean, L., & Hott, D. D. (2003). Employee "spy" software: Should you use it? *Journal of Corporate Accounting & Finance, 14*(4), 7.

Be careful how you crack the e-whip. (2001). *Business and Health, 19*(5), 16.

Bennett, R. J., & Robinson, S. L. (2003). The past, present and future of deviance research. In J. Greenburg (Ed.), *Organizational behavior: The state of the science* (2nd ed., pp. 247–282). Mahwah, NJ: Lawrence Erlbaum.

Bertilson, H. S. (1990). Can aggression be justified in order to study aggression? *American Behavioral Scientist, 33*(5), 594.

Bies, R. J., Tripp, T. M., & Kramer, R. M. (1997). At the breaking point: Cognitive and social dynamics of revenge in organizations. In R. A. Giacalone & J. Greenburg (Eds.), *Antisocial behavior in organizations* (pp. 18–36). Thousand Oaks, CA: Sage.

Boye, M. W., & Jones, J. W. (1997). Organizational culture and employee counterproductivity. In R. A. Giacalone & J. Greenburg (Eds.), *Antisocial behavior in organizations* (pp. 172–184). Thousand Oaks, CA: Sage.

Brandt, A. (2003). Growing threat: Stalking over the web. *PC World, 21*(8), 56.

Bruce, I. S. (2004). *Kissing their jobs goodbye?* Retrieved August 15, 2005, from www.sundayherald.com/46225

Brynjolfsson, E. (1993). The productivity paradox of information technology. *Communications of the ACM, 36*(12), 67–77.

Bushman, B. J., & Anderson, C. A. (2001). Is it time to pull the plug on the hostile versus instrumental aggression dichotomy? *Psychological Review, 108*(1), 273–279.

Buss, A. H. (1971). Aggression pays. In J. L. Singer (Ed.), *The control of aggression and violence: Cognitive and psychological factors* (pp. 7–18). New York: Academic.

Carll, E. K. (1999). *Violence in our lives: Impact on workplace, home, and community.* London: Allyn & Bacon.

Carlson, J. R., & Zmud, R. W. (1999). Channel expansion theory and the experiential nature of media richness perceptions. *Academy of Management Journal, 42*(2), 153–171.

Carpenter, T. (1983, September 6). Reach out and access. *Village Voice*, pp. 8–11.

Casselman, G. (2002, December 16). The enemy from within: Internal staff pose greatest threat to information security. *Calgary Herald*, p. C1.

Chappel, D., & Di Martino, V. (2000). *Violence at work* (2nd ed.). Geneva: International Labour Office.

Cheseboro, J. W., & Bonsall, D. G. (1989). *Computer-mediated communication: Human relationships in a computerized world.* Tuscaloosa: University of Alabama Press.

Churchman, P. (2003). Technology abusing the net: How to curb work surfers. *New Zealand Management*, 46–47.

Clark, J. (1993). Line manager, human resource specialist and technical change. *Employee Relations, 15*(3), 22.

Cohen, S. (1997). E-mail is no joke. *Training & Development, 51*(7), 37–46.

Coovert, M. D., & Thompson, L. F. (2001). *Computer supported cooperative work: Issues and implications for workers, organizations, and human resource management.* Thousand Oaks, CA: Sage Publications.

Cornelius, C., & Boos, M. (2003). Enhancing mutual understanding in synchronous computer-mediated communication by training: Trade-offs in judgmental tasks. *Communication Research, 30*(2), 147–177.

Cyber stalking: ID theft rise in Maine. (2004). *Crime Control Digest, 38*(42), 3.

Daft, R. L., & Lengel, R. H. (1986). Organizational information requirements, media richness and structural design. *Management Science, 32*(5), 554–570.

D'Ambra, J., & Rice, R. E. (1994). Multimethod approaches for the study of computer-mediated communication, equivocality, and media selection. *IEEE Transactions on Professional Communication, 37*(4), 231.

D'Amico, E. (2002). Cyber crime is on the rise, but let's keep it quiet. *Chemical Week, 164*(38), 25.

Davis, F. D. (1989). Perceived usefulness, perceived ease of use, and user acceptance of information technology. *MIS Quarterly, 13*(3), 319–340.

Davis, H. E., & Braun, R. L. (2004). Computer fraud: Analyzing perpetrators and methods. *CPA Journal, 74*(7), 56.

Dennis, A. R., & Kinney, S. T. (1998). Testing media richness theory in the new media: The effects of cues, feedback, and task equivocality. *Information Systems Research, 9*(3), 256–274.

Diener, E., Fraser, S., Beaman, A. L., & Kelem, R. T. (1976). Effects of deindividu-ating variables on stealing by Halloween trick-or-treaters. *Journal of Personality and Social Psychology, 33*(2), 178–183.

Dobbs, L. (2002). *Merrill's new focus: E-mail.* Retrieved March 31, 2004, from http://money.cnn.com/2002/10/02/commentary/dobbs

Donaldson, T. (2001). Ethics in cyberspace: Have we seen this movie before? *Business and Society Review, 106*(4), 273.

Doward, J., & Reilly, T. (2003, August 17). Dude, the threesome's off . . . That last e-mail cost me my job. (London) *Observer,* p. C2.

Dozier, J. B., & Miceli, M. P. (1985). Potential predictors of whistle-blowing: A prosocial behavior perspective. *The Academy of Management Review, 10*(4), 823–836.

Employee misuse and abuse of corporate computer assets creates HR nightmares. Retrieved March 2, 2004, from www.epolicyinstitute.com/training

Farrell, D., & Peterson, J. (1982). Patterns of political behavior in organizations. *Academy of Management Review, 7,* 403–412.

Feldman, J. E. (2003). *Essentials of electronic discovery: Finding and using cyber evi-dence.* Little Falls, NJ: Glasser LegalWorks.

Feraud, G. (2000). A century of information management. In D. A. Marchand, T. H. Davenport, & T. Dickson (Eds.), *Mastering information management* (pp. 27–31). London: Prentice Hall.

Fertell, D. (2002). Cyber-slacking kills productivity. *National Underwriter, 106*(38), 41.

Fertell, D. (2003). Identity and the insider threat. *USBanker, 113*(5), 58.

Fiore, R. N., & Nelson, H. L. (2003). *Recognition, responsibility, and rights: Feminist ethics and social theory.* Lanham, MD: Rowman & Littlefield.

Firms face up to Internet abuse. (2003, November 10). *BBC News.* Retrieved March 2, 2004, from http://news.bbc.co.uk/1/hi/business/3256753.stm

Flaherty, J. (1998, October 7). Racist e-mail is sent to 13 at Boston College. *New York Times,* p. B8.

Flynn, N., & Khan, R. (2003). *E-mail rules: A business guide to managing policies, security, and legal issues for e-mail and digital communication.* New York: AMACOM.

Forcht, K. A. (1994). *Computer security management.* Danvers, MA: Boyd and Fraser.

Foster, S. (2003). Virus victims weigh cyber-insurance options. *Computing Canada, 29*(19), 10.

Fox, S., & Spector, P. E. (1999). A model of work frustration-aggression. *Journal of Organizational Behavior, 20*(6), 915.

Fredrick, C. A. N. (1999). Feminist rhetoric in cyberspace: The ethos of feminist usenet newsgroups. *Information Society, 15*(3), 187–197.

Freeman, E. H. (2004). Corporate liability for illegal downloading of copyrighted music. *Information Systems Security, 13*(4), 6.

Fusaro, R. (1998). Training video tackles E-mail abuse. *Computerworld, 32*(29), 39.

Garramone, G., Harris, A., & Anderson, R. (1986). Uses of political bulletin boards. *Journal of Broadcasting and Electronic Media, 30*(3), 325–339.

Gaudin, S. (2000, June 27). The Omega Files. *Computerworld.*

Gelernter, D. (n.d.). *The second coming: A manifesto.* Retrieved February 17, 2004, from www.edge.org/3rd_culture/gelernter/gelernter_p1.html

Gentile, G. (n.d.). *Man cleared in keyboard-wiretapping case.* Retrieved December 2, 2004, from www.usatoday.com/tech/news/internetprivacy/2004/

Gephart, R. P. (2002). Introduction to the brave new workplace: Organizational behavior in the electronic age. *Journal of Organizational Behavior, 23*(4), 327–344.

Giacalone, R. A., & Greenberg, J. (1997). *Antisocial behavior in organizations.* Thousand Oaks, CA: Sage.

Giegerich, A. (2003). *Can you see me now? Gorilla case highlights cell phone vigilantiism.* Retrieved August 15, 2005, from www.portlandtribune.com/archview .cgi?id=21655

Glomb, T. M. (2002). Anger and aggression: Informing conceptual models with data from specific encounters. *Journal of Occupational Health Psychology, 7*(1), 20–36.

Glomb, T. M., & Liao, H. (2003). Interpersonal aggression in work groups: Social influence, reciprocal, and individual effects. *Academy of Management Journal, 46*(4), 486–496.

Goodnough, A. (2002, November 23). Klein lays off 70 employees in city schools. *New York Times,* p. 1.

Graumann, C. F. (1998). Verbal discrimination: A neglected chapter in the social psychology of aggression. *Journal for the Theory of Social Behaviour, 28*(1), 41–60.

Greenfield, D. (2000). *Web@work employer survey 2000: Cyberslacking: 5.* West Hartford, CT: Center for Internet Studies.

Gruber, S. (1999). Communication gone wired: Working toward a "practiced" cyberfeminism. *Information Society, 15*(3), 199–208.

Gruys, M. L., & Sackett, P. R. (2003). Investigating the dimensionality of counterproductive behavior. *International Journal of Selection and Assessment, 11*(1), 30–42.

Gueguen, N., & Jacobs, C. (2002). Solicitation by e-mail and the solicitor's status: A field study of social influence on the web. *CyberPsychology and Behaviour, 5*(4), 377–383.

Gundlach, M. J., & Douglas, S. C. (2003). The decision to blow the whistle: A social information processing framework. *Academy of Management Review, 28*(1), 107–123.

Haigh, T. (2001). Inventing information systems: The systems men and the computer, 1950–1968. *Business History Review, 75*(1), 15–61.

Hamin, Z. (2000). Insider cyber-threats: Problems and perspectives. *International Review of Law, Computers and Technology, 14*(1), 105–114.

Harlos, K. P. (2001). When organizational voice systems fail: More on the deaf-ear syndrome and frustration effects. *Journal of Applied Behavioral Science, 37*(3), 324.

Herbert, B. G., & Vorauer, J. D. (2003). Seeing through the screen: Is evaluative feedback communicated more effectively in face-to-face or computer-mediated exchanges? *Computers in Human Behavior, 19*(1), 25–38.

Herring, S. (1996). Linguistic and critical analysis of computer-mediated communication: Some ethical and scholarly considerations. *Information Society, 12,* 153–168.

Hiltz, S., Turoff, M., & Johnson, K. (1989). Experiments in group decision making: Disinhibition, deindividuation, and group process in pen name and real name computer conferences. *Decision Support Systems, 5*(2), 217–232.

Hitt, L., & Brynjolfsson, E. (1997). Information technology and internal firm organization: An exploratory analysis. *Journal of Management, 14*(2), 81–101.

Hofstede, G. H. (1980). *Culture's consequences: International differences in work-related values.* Beverly Hills, CA: Sage.

Howard-Martin, J. (n.d.). *Prevent e-mail misuse in your company.* Retrieved January 2004 from www.usatoday.com/money/jobcenter/workplace/employment-law/2002-12-18-e-mail_x.htm

Infante, D. A., & Wigley, C. J. (1986). Verbal aggressiveness: An interpersonal model and measure. *Communication Monographs, 53*(1), 61–69.

Irmer, B. E., Chang, A. M., & Bordia, P. (2000, August). *The development of social and task cohesion in computer-mediated and face-to-face task groups.* Paper presented at the Academy of Management Symposium, Toronto.

Jackson, T. W., Dawson, R., & Wilson, D. (2003). Understanding e-mail interaction increases organizational productivity. *Communications of the ACM, 46*(8), 80–85.

Jarvenpaa, S. L., & Staples, D. S. (2001). Exploring perceptions of organizational ownership of information and expertise. *Journal of Management Information Systems, 18*(4), 151–183.

Jockin, V., Arvey, R. D., & McGue, M. (2001). Perceived victimization moderates self-reports of workplace aggression. *Journal of Applied Psychology, 86*(6), 1262–1269.

Johnston, D. C. (2004, September 30). Court says ex-IRS employee deserves whistle-blower status. *New York Times,* p. C4.

Jurgenson, J. (2004). Hackers setting up racket for 21st century: Cyber extortion threatens web sites, (Montreal) *Gazette,* p. B1.

Kanter, R. M. (2001). *Evolve! Succeeding in the digital culture of tomorrow.* Boston: Harvard Business Press.

Kayany, J. (1998). Contexts of uninhibited online behavior: Flaming in social news-groups on usenet. *Journal of the American Society for Information Science, 49*(12), 1135–1141.

Keashley, L., & Jagatic, K. (2002). By any other name: American perspectives on workplace bullying. In C. Cooper, S. Einarsen, H. Hoel, & D. Zapf (Eds.), *Bullying and emotional abuse in the workplace: International perspectives in research and practice* (pp. 31–61). New York: Routledge.

Kelloway, E. K., Barling, J., Kelley, E., Comtois, J., & Gatien, B. (2003). Remote transformational leadership. *Leadership and Organizational Development Quarterly, 24*(3), 163.

Klein, E. E., Clark, C. C., & Herskovitz, P. J. (2003). Philosophical dimensions of anonymity in group support systems: Ethical implications of social psychological consequences. *Computers in Human Behavior, 19*, 355–382.

Kersten, G. E., Koeszegi, S. T., & Vetschera, R. (2003). The effects of culture in computer-mediated negotiations. *Journal of Information Technology Theory and Application, 5*(2), 1+.

Kiesler, S., Siegel, J., & McGuire, T. W. (1984). Social psychological aspects of computer-mediated communication. *American Psychologist, 39*(10), 1123–1134.

Kock, N. (2002, May). *Evolution and media naturalness: A look at e-communication through a Darwinian theoretical lens.* Paper presented at the International Conference on Information Systems, Toronto.

Kuzmits, F., Sussman, L., Adams, A., & Raho, L. (2002). Using information and e-mail for political gain. *Information Management Journal, 36*(5), 76.

Lang, M. (2003, December 17). Software piracy runs rampant across Canada: Alberta firms pay $77,000 to settle claims. *Calgary Herald,* p. A3.

Leavitt, H. J., & Whisler, T. L. (1958, November–December). Management in the 1980s. *Harvard Business Review, 36,* 41–48.

Lemos. (2002). *Ex-IT worker charged with sabotage.* Retrieved January 15, 2004, from http://news.com.com/2100-1001-978386.html

Levitt, H. (2003). Why you need a policy on worker email: Misconduct not always obvious from observation. *National Post,* p. FP10.

Lim, V. K. G. (2002). The IT way of loafing on the job: Cyberloafing, neutralizing and organizational justice. *Journal of Organizational Behavior, 23*(5), 675+.

Luengo, M. A., Carillo-de-la-Pena, M. T., Otero, J. M., & Romero, E. (1994). A short-term longitudinal study of impulsivity and antisocial behavior. *Journal of Personality and Social Psychology, 66*(3), 542–548.

Lyytinen, K., & Yoo, Y. (2002). Research commentary: The next wave of nomadic computing. *Information Systems Research, 13*(4), 377–388.

MacGregor, K. (2000, November 24). Email campaign leaves don facing the sack. (London) *Times,* p. 15.

Makris, S. (2004, February 25). Piracy on wireless Internet raises legal challenges. (Montreal) *Gazette,* p. B12.

Manross, G., Rice, R. E. (1986). Don't hang up: Organizational diffusion of the intelligent telephone. *Information & Management, 10*(3), 161.

March, S., Hevner, A., & Ram, S. (2000). Research commentary: An agenda for information technology research in heterogeneous and distributed environments. *Information Systems Research, 11*(4), 327–341.

Markus, M. L. (1994a). Electronic mail as the medium of managerial choice. *Organization Science, 5*(4), 502–527.

Markus, M. L. (1994b). Finding a happy medium: Explaining the negative side effects of electronic communication on social life at work. *ACM Transactions on Information Systems, 12*(2), 119–149.

Martin, M. M., Hiesel, A. D., & Valencic, J. (2001). Verbal aggression in computer-mediated decision making. *Psychological Reports, 89*(1), 24.

McBride, S. (2004, March 18). News Corp.'s Fox fears piracy ring began internally, *Wall Street Journal,* p. B7.

Mearian, L. (2002). Security: An internal affair. *Computerworld, 36*(32), 44.

Miceli, M. P., & Near, J. P. (1985). Characteristics of organizational climate and perceived wrongdoing associated with whistle-blowing decisions. *Personnel Psychology, 38,* 525–542.

Miceli, M. P., & Near, J. P. (1988). Individual and situational correlates of whistle-blowing. *Personnel Psychology, 41*(2), 267–281.

Miceli, M. P., Near, J. P., & Schwenk, C. R. (1991). Who blows the whistle and why. *Industrial and Labor Relations Review, 45*(1), 113–130.

Middelton, J. (2001). *Worktime e-flirtation costs industry dear.* Retrieved August 15, 2005, from www.vnunet.com/vnunet/news/2115862/worktime-flirtation-costs-industry-dear

Mirchandani, D., & Motwani, J. (2003). Reducing Internet abuse in the workplace. *S.A.M. Advanced Management Journal, 68*(1), 22–28.

Morris, F. C. (2003). The electronic platform: E-mail and other privacy issues in the workplace. *Computers and Internet Lawyer, 20*(8), 1.

Morris, M. G., & Venkatesh, V. (2000). Age differences in technology adoption decisions: Implications for a changing workforce. *Personnel Psychology, 53*(2), 375–403.

Muhl, C. J. (2003). Workplace e-mail and Internet use: Employees and employers beware. *Monthly Labor Review, 126*(2), 36–45.

Near, J. P., Dworkin, T. M., & Miceli, M. P. (1993). Explaining the whistle-blowing process: Suggestions from power theory and justice theory. *Organization Science, 4*(3), 392–411.

Near, J. P., & Miceli, M. P. (1986). Retaliation against whistle blowers: Predictors and effects. *Journal of Applied Psychology, 71*(1), 137–145.

Near, J. P., & Miceli, M. P. (1987). Whistle-blowers in organizations: Dissidents or reformers? In M. S. Barry & L. L. Cummings (Eds.), *Research in organizational behavior* (Vol. 9, pp. 321–368). Greenwich, CT: JAI.

Negroponte, N. (1995). *Being digital.* New York: Knopf.

Neumann, P. G., & Baron, R. A. (1997). Aggression in the workplace. In R. A. Giacalone & J. Greenburg (Eds.), *Antisocial behavior in organizations* (pp. 37–67). Thousand Oaks, CA: Sage.

Nonaka, I. (1994). A dynamic theory of organizational knowledge creation. *Organization Science, 5*(1), 14–37.

O'Leary-Kelly, A. M., Griffin, R. W., & Glew, D. J. (1996). Organization-motivated aggression: A research framework. *Academy of Management Review, 21*(1), 225–253.

Orlikowski, W. J. (2000). Using technology and constituting structures: A practice lens for studying technology in organizations. *Organization Science, 11*(4), 404–428.

Orlikowski, W. J., & Barley, S. R. (2001). Technology and institutions: What can research on information technology and research on organizations learn from each other? *MIS Quarterly, 25*(2), 145–156.

Orlikowski, W. J., & Iacono, C. S. (2001). Research commentary: Desperately seeking the "IT" in IT research: A call to theorizing the "IT" artifact. *Information Systems Research, 12*(2), 121–134.

O'Sullivan, P. B., & Flanagan, A. J. (2003). Reconceptualizing "flaming" and other problematic messages. *New Media & Society, 5*(1), 69–95.

Patten, T. G., & Woods, D. J. (1978). Victim attributions regarding the source of verbal aggression. *Journal of Psychology, 100*(2), 293–297.

Peirce, E., Smolinski, C. A., & Rosen, B. (1998). Why sexual harassment complaints fall on deaf ears. *Academy of Management Executive, 12*(3), 41.

Peterson, D. K. (2002). Deviant workplace behavior and the organization's ethical climate. *Journal of Business and Psychology, 17*(1), 47–61.

Post, D., & Brown, B. C. (2003, September 8). Court's right: No cybertresspassing here. *InformationWeek, 954,* 78.

Rafaeli, S., & Noy, A. (2002). Online auctions, messaging, communication and social facilitation: A simulation and experimental evidence. *European Journal of Information Systems, 11*(3), 196–207.

Raphael, J. (2003). *Man arrested for capturing lewd images at mall.* Retrieved February 16, 2004, from www.firstcoastnews.com/

Reddy Randazzo, M., Keeney, M. M., Kowalski, E. F., Cappelli, D. M., & Moore, A. P. (2004). *Insider threat study: Illicit cyber activity in the banking and finance sector: 25.* National Threat Assessment Center, United States Secret Service and CERT Coordination Center Software Engineering Institute, Carnegie Mellon University.

Reed, E. M. (2004). Electronic blackmail. *Smart Computing in Plain English, 15*(6), 49.

Reinig, B., Briggs, R., & Nunamker, J. (1998). Flaming in the electronic classroom. *Journal of Management Information Systems, 14*(3), 45–59.

Rice, R. E. (1984). *The new media: Communication, research, and technology.* Beverly Hills, CA: Sage.

Rice, R. E. (1992). Task analyzability, use of new media, and effectiveness: A multi-site exploration of media richness. *Organization Science, 3*(4), 475–500.

Rice, R. E., D'Ambra, J., & More, E. (1998). Cross-cultural comparison of organizational media evaluation. *Journal of Communication, 48*(3), 3–26.

Rice, R. E., & Gattiker, U. E. (2001). New media and organizational structuring. In F. M. Jablin & L. L. Putnam (Eds.), *The new handbook of organizational communication* (pp. 544–581). Thousand Oaks, CA: Sage.

Rich, R. (1992). Taxonomy: Definition and design. *Academy of Management Review, 17*(4), 758–781.

Riva, G. (2002). The sociocognitive psychology of computer-mediated communication: The present and future of technology-based interactions. *CyberPsychology and Behaviour, 5*(6), 581–598.

Roberts, K. H., & Grabowski, M. (1996). Organizations, technology and structuring. In S. Clegg, C. Hardy, & W. Nord (Eds.), *Handbook of organizational studies* (pp. 409–423). London: Sage.

Robinson, S. L., & Bennett, R. J. (1995). A typology of deviant workplace behaviors: A multidimensional scaling study. *Academy of Management Journal, 38*(2), 555–572.

Robinson, S. L., & Greenberg, J. (1998). Employees behaving badly: Dimensions, determinants and dilemmas in the study of workplace deviance. *Journal of Organizational Behavior, 5*(6), 1.

Robinson, S. L., & Greenberg, J. (1999). Employees behaving badly: Dimensions, determinants and dilemmas in the study of workplace deviance. In D. M. Rosseau & C. Cooper (Eds.), *Trends in organizational behavior* (Vol. 5, pp. 1–23). New York: Wiley.

Robinson, S. L., & O'Leary-Kelly, A. M. (1998). Monkey see, monkey do: The influence of work groups on the antisocial behavior of employees. *Academy of Management Journal, 41*(6), 658.

Rogers, K. A., & Kelloway, E. K. (1997). Violence at work: Personal and organizational outcomes. *Journal of Occupational Health Psychology, 2*(1), 63–71.

Romm, C. T., & Pliskin, N. (1997). Toward a virtual politicking model. *Communications of the ACM, 40*(11), 95–102.

Romm, C. T., & Pliskin, N. (1999). The office tyrant: Social control through e-mail. *Information Technology and People, 12*(1), 27.

Rosenwald, M., & Allen, L. (2004). Every step you take . . . Every move you make . . . My GPS unit will be watching you. *Popular Science, 265*(5), 88.

Rosman, K. (2002, December 1). They got mail: Not-so-fond farewells. *New York Times*, p. 1.

Rothman, J. B., & Taffae, P. R. (2003). E-mail: Corporate tool or business risk? *National Underwriter, 107*(45), 56.

Sackett, P. R., & DeVore, C. J. (2001). Counterproductive behaviors at work. In D. S. Ones, H. K. Sinangil, & V. Viswesvaran (Eds.), *International handbook of work psychology* (pp. 145–164). London: Sage.

Salkever, A. (2000, September 18). Cyber-extortion deserves no quarter. *BusinessWeek*, 94.

Sankar, Y. (1988). Organizational culture and new technologies. *Journal of Systems Management, 39*(4), 10.

Saunders, D. G. (1991). Procedures for adjusting self-reports of violence for social desirability bias. *Journal of Interpersonal Violence, 6*(3), 336–344.

Savicki, V., & Kelley, M. (2000). Computer mediated communication: Gender and group composition. *CyberPsychology and Behaviour, 3*(5), 817–826.

Schat, A. C. H., & Kelloway, E. K. (2005). Workplace aggression. In J. Barling, E. K. Kelloway & M. R. Frone (Eds.), *Handbook of workplace stress* (pp. 189–218). Thousand Oaks, CA: Sage.

Schroeder, B. M. (2002, November 12). SEC worker quits amid accusations of data misuse. *Wall Street Journal,* p. A6.

Short, J., Williams, E., & Christie, B. (1976). *The social psychology of telecommunications.* New York: Wiley.

Sia, C. L., Tan, B. C. Y., & Wei, K. K. (2002). Group polarization and computer-mediated communication: Effects of communication cues, social presence, and anonymity. *Information Systems Research, 13*(1), 70–90.

Siegel, J., Dubrovsky, V., Kiesler, S. B., & McGuire, T. W. (1986). Group processes in computer-mediated communication. *Organizational and Human Decision Processes, 37*(2), 157–187.

Skarlicki, D. P., & Folger, R. (1997). Retaliation in the workplace: The roles of distributive, procedural, and interactional justice. *Journal of Applied Psychology, 82*(3), 434–443.

Smola, K. W., & Sutton, C. D. (2002). Generational differences: Revisiting generational work values for the new millennium. *Journal of Organizational Behavior, 23,* 363–382.

Solomon, H. (1999, December 17). Employee abuse of e-mail grows. *Computing Canada, 25,* 19–21.

Somers, M. J., & Casal, J. C. (1994). Organizational commitment and whistleblowing. *Group & Organization Management, 19*(3), 270–284.

Sommers, J. A., Schell, T. L., & Vodanovich, S. J. (2002). Developing a measure of individual differences in organizational revenge. *Journal of Business and Psychology, 17*(2), 207.

Sophos. (2004, April 2). *Businessman sentenced after sending virus to competitor.* Retrieved August 7, 2005, from www.sophos.com/virusinfo/articles/comserve .html

Sorkin, A. R. (2001, May 22). An e-mail boast to friends puts executive out of work. *New York Times,* p. 2.

Spector, P. E. (1997). The role of frustration in antisocial behavior. In R. A. Giacalone & J. Greenburg (Eds.), *Antisocial behavior in organizations* (pp. 1–17). Thousand Oaks, CA: Sage.

Sproull, L., & Kiesler, S. (1986). Reducing social context cues: Electronic mail in organizational communication. *Management Science, 32*(11), 1492–1512.

Sproull, L., & Kiesler, S. (1994). *Connections: New ways of working in the networked organization.* Cambridge: MIT Press.

Sproull, R. F. (1994). Appendix: A lesson in electronic mail. In L. Sproull & S. Kiesler (Eds.), *Connections: New ways of working in the networked organization* (pp. 177–184). Cambridge: MIT Press.

Stafford, T. F., & Urbaczewski, A. (2004). Spyware: The ghost in the machine. *Communications of the Association for Information Systems, 14,* 291.

Stahl, S. (2004). When extortion threats go cyber. *InformationWeek, 1005,* 8.

Straub, D. W., & Watson, R. T. (2001). Research commentary: Transformational issues in researching IS and Net-enabled organizations. *Information Systems Research, 12*(4), 337–345.

Sundararajan, A. (2004). Managing digital piracy: Pricing and protection. *Information Systems Research, 15*(3), 287.

Survey, E. C. (2003). *E-mail communication survey*. Brisbane: Australian Psychological Society.

Sussman, S. W., & Siegal, W. S. (2003). Informational influence in organizations: An integrated approach to knowledge adoption. *Information Systems Research, 14*(1), 47.

Sussman, S. W., & Sproull, L. (1999). Straight talk: Delivering bad news through electronic communication. *Information Systems Research, 10*(2), 150–166.

Swartz, N. (2004). Cyber extortion targets office workers. *Information Management Journal, 38*(2), 12.

Tan, J. C. (2003). *Viruses caused $55b damage, anitvirus firm says*. Retrieved March 2, 2004, from www.computerworld.com/securitytopics/security

Tepper, B. J. (2000). Consequences of abusive supervision. *Academy of Management Journal, 43*(2), 178–190.

Towns, D. M., & Johnson, M. S. (2003). Sexual harassment in the 21st century: E-harassment in the workplace. *Employee Relations Law Journal, 29*(1), 7.

Trembly, A. C. (2004). E-mails nail wrongdoers. *National Underwriter, Property & Casualty, 108*(41), 5.

Trombly, M., & Holohan, M. (2000). Dow to fire up to 40 more employees for e-mail abuse. *Computerworld, 34*, 22–23.

Turnage, J. J. (1990). The challenge of the new workplace technology for psychology. *American Psychologist, 45*(2), 171–178.

Ulrich, W. (2001). A philosophical staircase for information systems definition, design, and development: A discursive approach to reflective practice in ISD (Part 1). *Journal of Information Technology Theory and Application, 3*(3), 55–84.

Valacich, J., Nunamker, J., & Vogel, D. (1994). Physical proximity effects on computer-mediated group idea generation. *Small Group Research, 25*(1), 83–104.

Vandekerckhove, W., & Commers, M. S. R. (2003). Downward workplace mobbing: A sign of the times? *Journal of Business Ethics, 45*(1), 41–50.

Varchaver, N., & Bonamici, K. (2003, February 17). *The perils of email*. Retrieved August 22, 2005, from www.fortune.com/fortune/print/0,15935,418678,00. html?

Venkatesh, V. (2000). Determinants of perceived ease of use: Integrating control, intrinsic motivation, and emotion into the technology acceptance model. *Information Systems Research, 11*(4), 342–365.

Verespej, M. A. (1998). Electronic evidence. *Industry Week, 247*, 12–16.

von Krogh, G. (2002). The communal resource and information systems. *Journal of Strategic Information Systems, 11*(2), 85–107.

Walker, R. (2001, June 3). And they told two friends . . . *New York Times*, p. 17.

Weatherbee, T. G. (2004, June). *Techno-stress: An exploratory study of the Canadian working population*. Paper presented at the Administrative Sciences Association of Canada, Quebec City, Quebec.

Weisband, S. P., & Schneider, S. K. (1995). Computer-mediated communication and social information: Status salience and status differences. *Academy of Management Journal, 38*(4), 1124–1152.

Wheelwright, G. (2003, August 25). Are you watching your workers? *National Post*, p. FE.1.Fr.

White, G. W., & Pearson, S. J. (2001). Controlling corporate e-mail, PC use and computer security. *Management & Computer Security, 9*(2/3), 88–93.

Whitty, M. T. (2003). Cyber-flirting. *Theory and Psychology, 13*(3), 339–356.

Williams, F., & Rice, R. E. (1983). Communication research and the new media technologies. In R. Bostrom (Ed.), *Communication yearbook* (Vol. 7, pp. 200–224). Beverly Hills, CA: Sage.

Yates, J., Orlikowski, W. J., & Okamura, K. (1999). Explicit and implicit structuring of genres in electronic communication: Reinforcement and change of social interaction. *Organization Science, 10*(1), 83–103.

Yates, J., & VanMaanen, J. (1996). Information technology and organizational transformation: Editorial note. *Information Systems Research, 7*(1), 1–4.

Yukon's computer porn scandal. (2004, March 8). *Canadian HR Reporter, 17,* p. G4.

Zack, M. H., & McKenney, J. L. (1995). Social-context and interaction in ongoing computer-supported management groups. *Organization Science, 6*(4), 394–422.

Zall, M. (2001). Do you know how your employees are using your computers? *Office Solutions, 18*(3), 38.

Zellars, K. L., Tepper, B. J., & Duffy, M. K. (2002). Abusive supervision and subordinates' organizational citizenship behavior. *Journal of Applied Psychology, 87*(6), 1068–1076.

Zyglidopoulos, S. (1999). Initial environmental conditions and technological change. *Journal of Management Studies, 36*(2), 241–262.

PART III

Prevention and Intervention

20 Editors' Introduction to Part III

I n the first sections of this handbook, we exposed readers to the prevalence and diverse nature of workplace violence. The chapters in this section provide a perspective on workplace violence prevention and intervention. As one might expect, given the enormous complexity of the problem and the relatively recent academic interest in the topic, very little is known regarding best practices for prevention and intervention. Indeed, the body of empirical research on how to prevent or intervene in workplace violence is at best scant; however, it is quite clear that workplace violence involves a complex interaction between an individual worker and the work (and home) environment. Thus, prevention and intervention must be viewed from both an individual and environmental perspective. The chapters contained in this section examine both perspectives. They further address prevention and intervention from a public health viewpoint that categorizes prevention-intervention efforts as primary, secondary, or tertiary in nature. *Primary prevention* is aimed at preventing aggressive and violent acts from occurring; *secondary intervention* seeks to lessen the consequences of aggressive and violent acts once they have occurred; and *tertiary intervention* focuses on treating those who are already suffering often debilitating consequences.

The section begins with a chapter by Kelley and Mullen that emphasizes the importance of organizational context in the occurrence of workplace violence and suggests possible organizational level primary prevention efforts. Organizational factors discussed include recruitment, selection, performance appraisal, and disciplinary policies and practices. These authors also explore the organizational responses to violence, noting the paucity of research in the area.

The chapter by Glomb and Cortina explores abuses and the role of chronic and traumatic work stress in their occurrence. Suggestions for both primary and secondary interventions are offered. A common—and highly debilitating—individual consequence of exposure to extreme workplace violence is post-traumatic stress disorder (PTSD). In his chapter, Hurrell examines the efficacy of critical incident stress debriefing (CISD), a widely accepted secondary intervention for the prevention of PTSD. Day and Catano discuss the role of individual and organizational variables in the etiology of workplace violence and examine the efficacy of primary prevention through employee screening. Schat and Kelloway carefully consider the role of training as a primary prevention strategy for workplace aggression and violence. Finally, Hershcovis and Barling consider means of preventing insider-initiated workplace violence.

21 Organizational Response to Workplace Violence

Elizabeth Kelley
Jane Mullen

Workplace aggression and violence now occur with such frequency that no organization can afford to ignore them. In 1992, the Centers for Disease Control and Prevention declared workplace violence a national epidemic (Resnick & Kausch, 1995). Approximately 1 million workers are victims of violent crime each year in the United States, and annual costs to organizations have been estimated to be as high as $4.2 billion per year (Howard, 2001; Howard & Voss, 1996; LeBlanc & Kelloway, 2002; Neuman & Baron, 1998; Peek-Asa, Runyan, & Zwerling, 2001; Robinson & Greenberg, 1998).

Specifically, organizations need to be concerned about the prevention of and response to workplace violence because of its well-documented negative impacts on employees (both victims and observers), other stakeholders, and the organization itself, as well as because of an increasing legal emphasis (Hashemi & Webster, 1999; Johnson, Lewis, & Gardner, 1995; LeBlanc & Kelloway, 2002; Paul & Townsend, 1998; Smart & Vertinsky, 1984; Vu, 2003). For example, LeBlanc and Kelloway (2002) have demonstrated that there are direct links between public-initiated violence and turnover intention and coworker-initiated aggression and decreased affective commitment. Howard's (2001) findings are consistent with this: Acts of violence committed by employees had a significantly greater impact on the firm than the acts committed by outsiders. Pauchant and Mitroff (1992) have observed that employees in "crisis prone" organizations are seven times as likely to use defense mechanisms such as denial, disavowal, fixation, and projection as are employees in "crisis prepared" organizations.

On a more general level, victims may seek a revision of the social order, and dissatisfaction with existing roles or leadership may result (Habermas, 1975). In terms of legal compliance, the California Occupational Safety and Health Administration, for example, requires all businesses in California to implement an injury and illness prevention program (Peek-Asa et al., 2001), and other jurisdictions are enacting similar legislation (Vu, 2003). It has been said that no longer do employers simply have a duty to provide employees with a safe workplace; now employers must be concerned with providing society with safe workers. The torts of negligent hiring, negligent retention, and negligent training must be addressed by employers (Johnson & Gardner, 1999; Johnson et al., 1995).

Despite the overwhelming evidence of the prevalence and negative impact of workplace violence, as well as the increasing legal obligation of employers to provide a safe workplace (Johnson et al., 1995), most organizations are prepared neither to prevent nor to respond appropriately. Howard (2001) found that only 8.75% of organizations surveyed had a workplace violence policy. The majority of organizations queried responded that as they had not experienced workplace violence, they did not require a policy (Howard, 2001). This research parallels a study conducted on crisis management in small businesses, the scene for a significant proportion of outsider violence (Neuman & Baron, 1998). Spillan and Hough (2003) found that crisis planning receives little attention in small businesses, and concern for crisis preparation becomes significant only after the organization experiences an event. Further, most small businesses that have actually experienced crises did not have a structure, such as a crisis response team, in place.

Clearly, there is a lag between the requirement for workplace violence preparedness and the extent of response in industry. Pearson and Clair (1998) theorize that this is caused by a sense of false security on the part of managers who have taken some limited steps such as instituting a grievance procedure and/or who have had previous successes at managing problems with only limited crisis preparation. This gap, however, is not evident in the number of articles and books dealing with the topic, which has grown exponentially in recent years (Neuman & Baron, 1998). The majority of these publications are prescriptive. To date, there has been little integrated empirical research on either immediate organizational responses to workplace violence or longer term prevention-as-response strategies (Allen & Lucero, 1998; Howard, 2001; O'Leary-Kelly, Griffin, & Glew, 1996; Pearson & Clair, 1998; Robinson & Greenberg, 1998). Some authors have speculated on the reasons for this significant gap, attributing it to methodological, data availability, and ethical issues associated with the sensitive nature of the topic; the problems inherent in self-reports; and the infrequent and small samples (Peek-Asa et al., 2001; Robinson & Greenberg, 1998). Whatever the reason, there has been little progress in empirically demonstrating which, if any, specific organizational responses to workplace violence are most effective in mitigating its effects and preventing its recurrence (Howard, 2001).

Definitional Issues

Different scholars have defined the term *workplace violence* in different ways. These have been organized into eight categories by Robinson and Greenberg (1998). There are two components, the differing meanings of which have significant implications for the types and ranges of organizational responses. The areas requiring clarification relate to perpetrators, the act itself, and the target: More simply, what constitutes *violence* and what makes it *workplace*?

Some authors distinguish between *aggression* and *violence* as being act and consequence, respectively (O'Leary-Kelly et al., 1996). Others consider them positions on a continuum of undesirable behavior (Neuman & Baron, 1998). The violence that the popular press reports constitutes only a small percentage of the total amount of workplace violence. The physical assaults and homicides are merely the most visible and dramatic examples that draw the attention; for example, in 1994, only 1 in 650 workplace crimes of violence in the United States involved homicide. In reality, it is the often unreported commission of other forms of abuse that constitutes the more significant hazard to the organization and its workforce (Neuman & Baron, 1998). Therefore, some authors prefer the term *aggression,* as it is less likely to evoke dramatic and erroneous images, and it is the broader term, which can subsume *violence.*

Neuman and Baron (1998) observed that *aggression* in this context is consistent with its use in the substantial literature on human aggression and implies any efforts by individuals to harm others. These researchers specifically exclude acts of domestic violence in the workplace, robbery, and acts of terrorism. This definition, however, essentially restricts the study of workplace aggression to acts committed by insiders. Much of the extant scholarly literature employs this limitation (O'Leary-Kelly et al., 1996; Robinson & Greenberg, 1998). One response to this definition is that it does not address the majority of workplace violence, which is committed by outsiders in the exponentially growing service sector (Howard & Voss, 1996). An additional consideration is that providing a workplace free of hazard is a requirement of the Occupational Safety and Health Administration (OSHA) (Howard, 2001; Johnson & Gardner, 1999). With over 50% of workplace violence committed by outsiders (Howard, 2001; Neuman & Baron, 1998), legislative compliance becomes problematic if the focus is limited to violence committed only by organizational insiders (Peek-Asa et al., 2001). This definitional limitation may also be contributing to the paucity of empirical findings that organizations can use to prepare for, prevent, and reduce the impact of the majority of workplace violence. A further complication involves the issue of where the act is committed; for example, if an employee is assaulted while traveling on business, should this be considered workplace violence (Howard & Voss, 1996)? Most scholars have focused only on acts that occur on the organization's premises.

Merchant and Lundell (2001) report on a categorization that encompasses a wide range of acts and allows for different categories of perpetrators and locations. The four types of workplace aggression are Type I, Criminal intent; Type II, Customer/client; Type III, Worker on worker; and Type IV, Personal relationship. This scheme resolves the issues raised above and effectively encompasses a full range of acts, perpetrators, and locations. The categories can be very helpful when designing strategies to prevent workplace violence because each type of violence may require a different approach, and some workplaces may be at higher risk for certain types of violence (Merchant & Lundell, 2001).

Given the wide range encompassed by this typology, it is clear that no one strategy can be effective to prepare for all incidents; however, there appears to be a consensus in both the academic and practitioner literature that the best response is prevention. This has been the focus of the limited research that has been conducted on this topic (Peek-Asa et al., 2001). Although intervention programs must be designed to fit the specific work environment, a comprehensive approach should involve several components. These general components apply to all types of violence, but specific modifications will be required to address the type of hazard identified in the business. This approach usually takes the form of organizational level, behavioral, and environmental actions, the specific sequence and selection of which vary, depending on the perspective of the author (Blythe, 2002; Braverman, 1999; Denenberg & Braverman, 1999; Franklin, 1991; Johnson & Gardner, 1999; Labig, 1995; Resnick & Kausch, 1995; Wilkinson, 1998). The literature of the security industry, for example, tends to focus on physical environmental measures, such as extra lighting and access control (Franklin, 1991).

Drawing from the crisis management literature, Pearson and colleagues have outlined a general five-stage crisis management process that generates specific strategies at each stage and which can be applied effectively to workplace violence (Pearson, Clair, Misra, & Mitroff, 1997).

The first step, *signal detection,* is clearly targeted at prevention. Pearson et al. (1997) observed that cues are generally available but are often ignored. The next step, *preparation,* involves the senior management adoption of a crisis management mind-set, the creation of a structure, and introduction of response training. The practitioner workplace violence and crisis management literatures focus extensively on activities at this stage (Blythe, 2002; Braverman, 1999; Denenberg & Braverman, 1999; Johnson & Gardner, 1999; Johnson et al., 1995; Labig, 1995; Pauchant & Mitroff, 1992; Wilkinson, 1998). The third stage, *damage containment,* contains the majority of an organization's crisis management resources. The literature on organizational communication, organizational support, employee assistance programs (EAPs), and stress interventions largely focuses on activities in this stage (Franklin, 1991; LeBlanc & Kelloway, 2002; Merchant & Lundell, 2001; Miller-Burke, Attridge, & Fass, 1999; Nalla, 1996; Rogers & Kelloway, 1997; Schat & Kelloway, 2000, 2003; Smart & Vertinsky, 1984; Wilkinson, 1998). The fourth stage, *recovery,* involves the development of short- and long-term plans to resume normal business. There is little relevant literature on this stage, other than isolated chapters in practitioner-oriented texts (e.g., Blythe, 2002). The final stage is *learning,* in which the focus is on assessing and reflecting on the incident with a view to improving operations and procedures (Pearson et al., 1997). Research that integrated the findings addressing the previous stages would assist organizations in this process; however, the research on the efficacy of organizational, behavioral, and environmental efforts to prevent workplace violence in these individual stages is fragmented and preliminary, and points to no single, effective strategy (Merchant & Lundell, 2001; Peek-Asa et al., 2001; Robinson & Greenberg, 1998; Runyan, Zakocs, & Zwerling, 2000).

Organizational Level Variables

Contrary to the well-known benefits associated with a proactive management approach to crisis (Pearson & Clair, 1998), it is not unusual for organizations to manage to workplace violence in a reactive manner. In fact, many organizations implement few, if any, crisis preparations (Mitroff, Pearson, & Harrigan, 1996). Reasons for this vary, although Starbuck and Milliken (1988) suggest that leaders who experience a repeated success at managing crises with limited preparations may become overconfident of their decisions and believe that investing time and energy in preparing for problems is unnecessary. Others believe that organizational crises will ultimately become resolved because they always have been in the past (Kets de Vries, 1991). This argument is similar to Weick's (1995) notion of ongoing sense making and suggests that in order to reduce ambiguity or uncertainty in the environment, individuals pay attention to specific moments from their ongoing experiences and extract cues from them in order to make sense of their environment. This creates a habitual and continuous, ongoing sense of a situation. It is when individuals begin to rely on these habitual behaviors that vulnerability occurs, such that managers tend to rely on solutions to crises that have worked in the past and fail to effectively prepare for events that may occur in the future, including workplace violence.

Blame is often the organizing principle for crisis response and research. Typically, investigators are interested in who or what is to blame as they seek out cause and effect. On some occasions, including incidences of workplace violence, blame is attached to an individual or individuals (Hofmann & Stetzer, 1996) who are cited for some level of criminal intent. When violence occurs in the workplace, investigations are conducted to determine the underlying causes. Hofmann and Stetzer (1996) suggest that investigators seem to focus on attributing blame to an individual most proximal to the incident rather than conducting an investigation to determine the underlying factors that may have contributed to the situation. This suggests that important organizational factors may be overlooked when identifying the root causes of workplace violence and may directly impair the organization's ability to respond to such events. In the following discussion, we identify various organizational factors that must be examined, along with their respective implications for violence, to further our understanding of how organizations may effectively manage and respond to violence in the workplace.

Leadership

Response strategies begin with organizational leaders (e.g., see Blythe, 2002). Leaders are responsible for minimizing the potential risks before the violent event occurs and responding to the behavioral and emotional responses aimed at recovery and readjustment (Pearson & Clair, 1998) once the violent event has occurred. Thus, independent of whether or not violence is an immediate issue for organizations, there is an increasing need for leaders in general to respond to the increase in violence that is occurring in the broader organizational and environmental context.

Despite the vast amount of research that has been conducted using numerous leadership theories (e.g., Barling, Weber, & Kelloway, 1996; Howell & Hall-Merenda, 1999; Judge & Bono, 2000; Kirkpatrick & Locke, 1996; Pillai, 1995; Zohar, 2002), few studies, if any, have been conducted that examine the effects of leadership and its role in the response to workplace violence. Drawing from organizational crisis literature, however, cognitive views of leadership suggest that the increased perception of a crisis in organizations creates the need for charismatic leadership (Pillai, 1995). Charismatic leaders provide a vision of the future and a sense of mission. These leaders enact behaviors such as setting a personal example and demonstrating high ethical standards (Bass & Avolio, 1993). In one of the few empirical investigations of the effects of crisis on leadership, Pillai (1995) found that an increased sense of crisis among followers was associated with reduced perceptions of leader charisma and that leaders lose charismatic appeal; however, competing empirical evidence (House, 1971; Pillai & Meindl, 1998) suggests a positive correlation between crisis and charismatic leadership, such that there is an increased need for charismatic leadership when a crisis occurs. Thus, this perspective would suggest that the stress and uncertainty that result when violence occurs lead followers to affiliate with others and seek strong leaders. These contradictory findings offer weak insights into the parallel notion that leadership is a critical factor in organizational response to violence and crisis, and they suggest the need for a major research initiative aimed at understanding the relationship between various leadership theories and response to workplace violence.

It has been argued that leaders play an important role in shaping the perceived climate within a workplace (e.g., (Hofmann & Morgeson, 1999; Zohar, 1980). For example, in the safety literature, perceptions of climate are generally described as "shared perceptions of managerial policies, procedures, and practices as indicators of concern for employees" (Zohar, 2002, p. 75; Zohar, 1980). Climate perceptions may also encompass shared perceptions of managerial concern for providing employees with a workplace free from violence. These shared perceptions then influence the employees' actions and behavior in the workplace (Hofmann & Stetzer, 1996). For example, previous studies on accidents in the workplace have shown that a transformational leadership style that includes charismatic behaviors directly affects the perceived climate and is significantly associated with fewer accidents (Barling, Loughlin, & Kelloway, 2002).

Transformational leadership has been defined as influencing subordinates by "broadening and elevating followers' goals and providing them with confidence to perform beyond the expectations specified in the implicit or explicit exchange agreement" (Dvir, Eden, Avolio, & Shamir, 2002; Shin & Zhou, 2003). Burns's (1978) transformational leadership theory suggests that transformational leadership is composed of four dimensions: idealized influence, inspirational motivation, individualized consideration, and intellectual stimulation. Although the constructs *charisma* and *transformational leadership* have been used synonymously, Bass has included charisma as one of the dimensions of transformational leadership known as idealized influence. *Idealized influence* is defined as providing a vision of the future and a sense of mission. It includes behaviors such as setting a personal example and demonstrating high ethical standards. In the context of workplace violence, managers' actions may directly affect individuals' perception of the climate, such that if management is committed to providing a safe environment free from violence, then it is more likely that the workers will exhibit the same commitment that could directly predict reduced violence in the workplace. This has yet to be empirically examined, however.

In a similar vein, using Bandura's (1977) social learning theory, researchers have examined various environmental factors that encourage antisocial behavior at work (e.g., Robinson & O'Leary-Kelly, 1998). This research argues that individuals are more likely to behave in antisocial ways if the individuals with whom they work behave in antisocial ways and therefore serve as models for such types of behaviors. Individuals often look to their leaders in particular for information regarding appropriate behaviors, attitudes, and beliefs. For example, it has been found that when leaders emphasize the importance of safety through their own personal commitment and become role models of safety, individuals will model such behavior and their perceptions of safety climate will also be improved (Barling et al., 2002). Thus, in the case of workplace violence, followers may also look to their leaders for information regarding behaviors and attitudes associated with violence. If leaders are committed to nonviolence in the workplace, it is also likely that followers will model similar behaviors and beliefs. Again, this is an area in need of empirical investigation.

Finally, coworkers are usually the first to recognize that an individual may become potentially violent within the workplace; however, when employees raise their concerns, managers all too often fail to respond in an effective manner or to respond at all (Braverman, 2003). Past theory and research suggest that an individual's perceived probability of successfully raising an issue with management will be related to his or her willingness to raise an issue (Dutton & Ashford, 1993; Mullen, 2002; Mullen & Kelloway, 2003). Thus, the degree of effort an individual exerts to identify a workplace violence concern should also be affected by the individual's perceived probability that management will respond appropriately. If individuals perceive a favorable context (e.g., managers taking action in response to a violence-related concern), they are more likely to believe that issues will be treated seriously by management. This is critical to the investigation process, given that individuals are often reluctant to report even minor violent events (Johnson et al., 1995).

Overall, the research drawn from various bodies of literature suggests that organizations must not overlook the role of effective leadership when responding to an event of workplace violence. In fact, Braverman (2003) recently suggested that the largest mistake organizations can make in response to violence is to only "focus on systems, operations, infrastructures and public relations and ignore the people. . . . They [employees] need to be assured of their safety and have their trust in leadership reinforced" (p. 10).

Recruitment

The recruitment literature offers interesting findings that provide us with a sense of how organizational response to violence may affect potential applicants. For example, recent research on recruitment has examined issues such as recruitment image (Cable, Aiman-Smith, Mulvey, & Edwards, 2000) and employer attractiveness (Highhouse, Stierwalt, Bachiochi, Elder, & Fisher, 1999). Similarly, Cable et al. (2000) examined the beliefs that job applicants develop about organizational culture during the anticipatory stage of socialization. The results suggest that job applicants' beliefs about organizational culture can be managed by organizations. The results build on existing literature on employer attractiveness by suggesting that organizational information has a significant impact on job applicant beliefs.

These findings are of particular importance when considering the impact that information about an organization's response to violence has on potential employees. Organizational crisis literature shows that employees may develop retributive intentions toward an organization if the crisis response is handled unfairly (Skarlicki, Ellard, & Kelln, 1998), which leads employees to disseminate negative information about the organization to prospective applicants (Mullen, 2001). In turn, on receiving negative information, potential applicants have also been shown to develop retributive intentions toward an organization and have expressed the intention not to consider future employment with the organization (Mullen, 2001). Furthermore, during the process of organizational socialization, which is defined as "the process by which an individual acquires the social knowledge and skills necessary to assume an organizational role" (Van Maanen & Schein, 1979), potential employees experience conversations with coworkers and observe coworker behavior and the rewards and punishments given by coworkers for certain behaviors. As Cable et al. (2000) have shown, beliefs are developed about organizational culture during the anticipatory stage of socialization. If the applicant receives negative information from organizational members (e.g., potential coworkers) about the organization's response to a violent event during this socialization phase or observes that aggressive behaviors are ineffectively managed, the applicant may form negative beliefs about the organization's image and attractiveness as a potential employer. Given that organizational activities have such an impact on job applicant beliefs and behavioral intentions associated with becoming an organizational member, it is likely that an organization's response to violence has significant implications and warrants research attention.

Selection

A substantial body of research demonstrates that individuals differ in their propensity to engage in aggressive behavior in the workplace (Neuman & Baron, 1998). Dispositional variables such as type A behavior pattern, self-monitoring behavior, hostile attributional bias, negative affectivity, locus of control, and impulse control; information processing differences, such as tolerance for ambiguity and equity sensitivity; and attitudinal variables, such as organizational frustration, have been posited as potential antecedents for workplace violence (Neuman & Baron, 1998; O'Leary-Kelly et al., 1996). For example, Douglas and Martinko (2001) found that a combination of individual attributes accounted for 62% of the variance in the participants' self-reported incidence of workplace aggression. Generally, this research into describing the perpetrator of workplace violence is limited because it is descriptive rather than predictive (Barling, 1996; Braverman, 1999).

Selecting out those candidates with a propensity for workplace violence is subject to several complications. First, this is only effective in combating violent acts committed by organizational insiders; as previously observed, this constitutes a small part of the problem. Second, some of the best predictors of criminal violence are demographic variables, such as age, gender, and previous aggression (O'Leary-Kelly et al., 1996); there is a body of employment law that prohibits organizations from using these variables as selection screens. Additionally, the profile of the perpetrator varies depending on the type of workplace violence under consideration. Perpetrators of nonlethal violence are typically men under 30 years of age with a history of violence or substance abuse. Perpetrators of workplace homicides, however, are generally middle aged, with no history of violence or substance abuse—in other words, a profile that may represent a majority of an employer's workforce

(Resnick & Kausch, 1995). Further, work by Greenberg and Barling (1999) suggests that demographic variables do not predict violence against a coworker. Third, the measurement instruments are often imprecise; however, after an in-depth review of the instruments available and the studies in which they have been used, Slora, Joy, Jones, and Terris (1991) concluded that on-the-job violence can be predicted when problems such as sample choice, design, and model selection are addressed. On this basis, Neuman and Baron (1998) subsequently suggest that personnel screening, preemployment testing, and carefully structured job interviews may assist in preventing workplace violence by identifying potential offenders before they enter an organization. In a more recent review of the extant literature on deviant behavior at work, however, Robinson and Greenberg (1998) noted that when aggregate findings are considered, "no clear picture emerges of the 'deviant personality type' in organizations," and that personality variables alone accounted for a small portion of the variance in predicting deviant workplace behavior (p. 13). They, along with other researchers, have postulated that the interaction of the environment and the individual accounts for more variance than either set of factors independently (Greenberg & Barling, 1999; O'Leary-Kelly et al., 1996; Robinson & Greenberg, 1998).

Training

Employees at all organizational levels should be trained in organizational policies and response to workplace violence (Braverman, 2003). In a quasi-experiment, Klein and Weaver (2000) showed that employees who completed a new-hire orientation program were significantly more socialized with respect to goals, values, history, and people than those who did not participate in the orientation program. Thus, it is expected that orientation programs serve as a useful mechanism for employees to become exposed to the organizational policies, values, and beliefs about violence.

Schat and Kelloway (2003) examined the effects of control perceptions on the relationships between workplace violence and stress and strain. The results show that control perceptions can have a positive impact on individuals who experience violence at work. The authors provide empirical evidence that interventions targeted at enhancing individuals' perceptions of control at work reduce levels of stress and strain. Furthermore, the findings of their study suggest that training aimed at increasing perceived control should not be limited to those who face direct violence in their jobs but also to individuals who may experience vicarious violence, as they would also benefit directly from such training. In sum, they argue that whether as a preventative strategy or a corrective intervention response, organizations should provide violence-related training to all employees, as it has been shown to improve their emotional and somatic well-being.

Interaction of Individual
and Organizational Attributes

This theoretical approach is consistent with social learning theory, which suggests that an individual's behavior is often influenced by social cues in his or her environment (Bandura, 1977). One set of cues that appears to be related to aggressive behavior in organizations is perceptions of fairness (Allen & Lucero, 1998; Barling, 1996; Chen & Spector, 1992; Douglas & Martinko, 2001; Greenberg & Alge, 1998; Greenberg & Barling, 1999; Howard & Voss, 1996; Martinko & Zellars, 1996; Neuman & Baron, 1998; O'Leary-Kelly et al., 1996; Skarlicki, Folger, & Tesler, 1999; Sommers, Schell, & Vodanovich, 2002; Tyler & Bies, 1990). Perceptions of procedural justice are formed in part by the existence of formal procedures in an organization and in part by interactional justice, or specifically how a manager carries out the procedures and explains decisions to employees (Greenberg & Barling, 1999). There is conflicting evidence on the role of procedural justice in workplace violence, however. Consistent with the interaction explanation proposed by Robinson and Greenberg (1998), some research suggests that the relationship between perceptions of justice and deviant or aggressive behavior may be affected by personality variables. Skarlicki and colleagues (1999), for example, provide evidence that person-by-situation interactions explain more variance in retaliation behaviors than is explained by perceptions of fairness alone. Specifically, agreeableness and negative affectivity were found to be moderators of this relationship. Sommers and colleagues (2002) developed a scale to be used in selection that measures an individual's propensity to endorse aggressive reactions to unjust organizational behavior. Dietz, Robinson, Folger, Baron, and Schulz (2003), however, found that violent crime rates in the community where a plant was located predicted workplace aggression in that plant, whereas the plant's procedural justice climate did not. Clearly, more research is required in this area to specify the variables involved and the relationships among them, particularly to identify the internal mediators between conditions in organizational settings and acts of aggression (Neuman & Baron, 1998). Enough research demonstrates that aggression is frequently associated with perceptions of intentional provocation and with feelings of exploitation so that any prevention-response strategy should seek to minimize these perceptions (Neuman & Baron, 1998; O'Leary-Kelly et al., 1996).

Distributive justice reflects the perceived fairness of the rewards employees receive for their inputs (Greenberg & Barling, 1999); however, these perceptions are not determined by absolute reward level. A preliminary study by Beugre and Baron, discussed by Neuman and Baron (1998), suggests that when employees perceive procedural justice to exist in their organizations, they tend to view the distribution of outcomes as fair also. Robinson and

Greenberg (1998) similarly refer to a 1997 study by Giacalone and Greenberg that suggests that the more intensely deviant reactions to injustice are likely to occur in reaction to a situation in which underpayment is accompanied by insensitive and uncaring treatment. Robinson and Greenberg further suggest that there is nothing inherent in a compensation system that causes deviant behavior; it is the reaction to the system that triggers such behavior, leading them to suggest that an important prevention technique for workplace violence is the "management of impressions of unfairness."

Performance Appraisal

One of the key methods of developing perceptions about organizational fairness is the performance appraisal process, which generally influences both compensation and promotion outcomes for employees. In a discussion of workplace violence from the social learning perspective, O'Leary-Kelly et al. (1996) note that aversive treatment is a trigger for aggressive behavior. Using Bandura's (1973) view, this trigger may include the removal of rewards or interference with goals, as in the performance appraisal process (Neuman & Baron, 1998). A model proposed by Allen and Lucero (1998) suggests that aggression against managers is immediately preceded by a triggering event (such as an appraisal interview) that can be perceived by the individual as another example of aversive treatment. This kind of reaction generates a recursive cycle in which hostility and frustration increase with each iteration. It is clear that the appraisal process has potential for inciting aggressive behavior (O'Leary-Kelly et al., 1996). Given the importance of managing perceptions of unfairness, the appropriate actions and attitudes of managers throughout the appraisal process can be tools in the prevention of workplace aggression. It has been suggested that training can mitigate some of these effects. For example, training employees to critically examine the outcomes of their behavior in terms of understanding how they can control and improve their performance may reduce the incidence of workplace violence (Martinko & Zellars, 1996). The efficacy of training managers in the conduct of appraisal interviews has been well documented (Neuman & Baron, 1998); specific instruction in the design and conduct of evaluations may reduce perceptions of unfair treatment and its associated feelings of frustration and hostility.

Discipline

The related issue of discipline has even more potential to incite workplace violence on the part of organizational members; interestingly, both discipline and the lack of it are contributing factors. The administration of discipline, like the appraisal process, can act as a trigger for violence. Overly close supervision may be considered a disciplinary measure, which takes on more importance in this era of increasingly complete electronic surveillance. Some research suggests that this type of supervision and monitoring has negative outcomes for the individual and the organization, one of which may be increased frustration, hostility, and ultimately aggression. For example, overly close supervision led to verbal aggression against a supervisor in one older empirical study (Day & Hamblin, 1969). More recent studies, reviewed by Neuman and Baron (1998), provide support for the link between monitoring and increased levels of stress.

The role of discipline in responding to workplace aggression has been the subject of substantial theorizing but little research. One aspect that has received some attention is the role played by normative pressures and behavioral modeling. Robinson and Greenberg (1998) suggest that the effects of social norms on deviant workplace behavior, especially workplace aggression, have been established in previous research (Greenberg & Alge, 1998). Neuman and Baron (1998) noted two ways in which aggression-related norms, which do not result in disciplinary action, encourage the existence and spread of workplace aggression. First, there may be a widespread belief that aggression is just a normal part of the job. One survey they examined found that high percentages of workers in certain occupations, such as health care and corrections, viewed verbal abuse as job-related and did not report such episodes. Lack of disciplinary response associated with these episodes indirectly reinforces the norms (Neuman & Baron, 1998; O'Leary-Kelly et al., 1996). Certain organizational cultures may encourage an aggressive climate and celebrate rather than punish those who behave aggressively, thereby directly reinforcing the norms (Neuman & Baron, 1998; O'Leary-Kelly et al., 1996).

Some theorists suggest that because behavioral modeling plays a role in the development and maintenance of norms of aggressive behavior, organizations should adopt policies to counter its effects (Allen & Lucero, 1998; Greenberg, 1988; Howard, 2001; O'Leary-Kelly et al., 1996; Robinson & Greenberg, 1998). This is particularly important, given theories (Bandura, 1973, 1977) and preliminary findings that suggest that unpunished acts of aggression escalate into more serious varieties and are modeled by others in the environment. For example, Allen and Lucero (1998) found that individuals who were aggressive in the past and were not disciplined were more likely to engage in physical than verbal abuse. Social learning theory suggests that watching others being aggressive can trigger aggression in the observer (Bandura, 1973; O'Leary-Kelly et al., 1996). Robinson and O'Leary-Kelly (1998) found that employees modeled aggressive behavior when coworkers acted aggressively, especially when coworkers were similar in age, gender, and education. The effect was also intensified the longer they worked for the company and the closer they worked together. These researchers concluded that aggressive behavior is "socially contagious" (Goulet, 1997; Robinson & O'Leary-Kelly, 1998). Interestingly, surveillance did not mitigate the effect, suggesting that selection may be the more effective preventive measure.

Some theorists have suggested that a zero-tolerance policy against workplace violence would prevent these outcomes (Howard, 2001; Nalla, 1996; Neuman & Baron, 1998; O'Leary-Kelly et al., 1996). Implementation of such a policy should include clear definitions of unacceptable behavior and sanctions for policy violations, as well as procedures for reporting inappropriate behavior (Neuman & Baron, 1998). There has been little research into the efficacy of zero-tolerance policies, however, and some recent preliminary findings suggest that they may have undesirable effects and do little to address the negative effects violence may have on the victims or observers in the workplace (J. Haiven, personal communication, February 2004).

Discipline itself is one of the more common triggers for aggression by subordinates (Allen & Lucero, 1998). Organizations can minimize this outcome by working to ensure that employees perceive that procedural and interactional justice are part of the organizational climate (Howard, 2001). Frustration encountered in the disciplinary process can be addressed through referral to an EAP (Chen & Spector, 1992; Denenberg & Braverman, 1999; Greenberg, 1988; Howard, 2001; Nalla, 1996; Neuman & Baron, 1998; Paul & Townsend, 1998). Organizations can provide training to supervisors on the appropriate use and communication of disciplinary procedures. Some employees may perceive that they have lost control through the disciplinary process and therefore resort to violent means to regain it (Barling, 1996). The existence of a grievance procedure that may allow for the correction of perceived injustice may reduce the incidence of workplace violence resulting from feelings of loss of control (Howard, 2001).

Environmental Variables

One of the environmental factors that has been postulated to increase workplace aggression is the economic climate and its accompanying trend toward downsizing the permanent workforce completely or in favor of an increased number of contingent workers (Neuman & Baron, 1998).

A substantial body of research suggests that after downsizing, victims, survivors, and executioners all experience increased levels of stress, frustration, depression, and feelings of unfair treatment (Allen, Freeman, Russell, Reizenstein, & Rentz, 2001; Bennett, Martin, Bies, & Brockner, 1995; Brockner, 1988; Brockner, Davy, & Carter, 1985; Brockner, Grover, Reed, & DeWitt, 1992; Brockner & Tyler, 1992; Kinicki, Prussia, & McKee-Ryan, 2000; O'Neill, Lenn, & Caimano, 1995; Wanberg, Bunce, & Gavin, 1999; Wright & Barling, 1998). All of these have been implicated as triggers for workplace aggression (Denenberg & Braverman, 1999; Neuman & Baron, 1998). A trend closely related to downsizing is the use of contingent workers in place of long-term employment relationships. This may be considered a violation of important social norms on the job and as such may be viewed as an injustice requiring retaliation (Neuman & Baron, 1998). Organizations that take steps to increase the perception of procedural and interactional justice in a workforce reduction initiative may prevent related workplace aggression (Howard, 2001). These steps may include outplacement and other counseling, a transparent decision-making process, delivery of the message by managers trained in conflict resolution and anger management, and possibly proactive intervention by security personnel (Howard, 2001; Johnson et al., 1995; Nalla, 1996; Neuman & Baron, 1998). A transparent decision-making process includes worker participation, as well as an explanation of the outcome (the *what* and *why*) and the process (the *how*) (Greenberg, 1988). Catalano, Novaco, and McConnell (1997) suggest that augmenting coping skills among victims of downsizing may be the best strategy for preventing incidents of workplace violence. This suggested initiative is broader than outplacement counseling and includes training in job search skills, stress inoculation, and social support (Catalano et al., 1997).

The increasing diversity of the contemporary workforce has also been suggested as a contributor to workplace aggression. Cultural differences heighten tension and interpersonal conflict in the workplace (Johnson et al., 1995; Neuman & Baron, 1998). There is a substantial literature that deals with the organizational consequences of differences in the workplace (Ashforth & Mael, 1989). To the extent that differences are perceived by individual employees, decreased levels of attraction may result, and there may be an increased potential for aggressive behavior (Neuman & Baron, 1998). In two recent studies, Baron and Neuman (1998) found that greater workforce diversity significantly correlated with greater experience of workplace aggression. Cross-cultural and diversity-training initiatives may mitigate the undesirable outcomes of increased diversity (Linnehan & Konrad, 1999).

The workplace itself may contribute to the incidence of aggression. Poor air quality, high noise levels, crowding, poor lighting, uncomfortably low or high temperatures, high humidity, and even shift work have been suggested as causes of negative affect, increased stress levels, and aggression (Neuman & Baron, 1998). Organizations have a legal obligation to provide a workplace free of hazard and health risks (Howard, 2001; Johnson & Gardner, 1999; Johnson et al., 1995), but there are clearly situations in which conditions are less than optimal. In these cases, organizations may be able to prevent environment-related aggression through such simple measures as providing protective clothing and equipment and rest breaks (Neuman & Baron, 1998), but there has been little research to demonstrate these relationships.

There has been minimal investigation into the effect of external factors on workplace violence due in part to the narrow definition used by some researchers. Dietz and colleagues (2003), however, have demonstrated that levels of workplace aggression are affected by external factors such as violent crime rates in the community where a plant is located, even when other factors, such as economic deprivation and family disruption, are controlled for. This was not community violence taking place in the organization but rather the level of workplace aggression actually affected by it. This is consistent with the behavior-modeling research outlined above and suggests that failing to consider external factors may be an important oversight in determining the causes and ultimately preventing workplace violence.

Many of the variables discussed above are significant only when organizational insiders commit workplace aggression; however, the majority of incidents of workplace aggression are committed by organizational outsiders (Howard, 2001; Johnson & Gardner, 1999). Therefore, a focus on developing a profile of violence-prone employees or workplaces may be ineffective. Instead, it may be more fruitful to focus on identifying job characteristics that increase the risk for violence (LeBlanc & Kelloway, 2002). LeBlanc and Kelloway (2002) developed and tested a measure of risk for violence using 28 items designed to assess employee risk for workplace violence on the basis of job characteristics. With further research, this instrument could be used to assist organizations in identifying employees at risk and developing strategies to address workplace violence.

The factors that cause externally motivated workplace violence are largely beyond the control of an organization. Prevention strategies then largely revolve around physical security and facility design measures, including control of entries and exits, lighting, and general maintenance (Johnson et al., 1995; Peek-Asa et al., 2001). Lighting in particular has been cited as an important part of reducing events involving aggression by customers, as has control of facility access and physical space to avoid isolated areas. An approach defined in the 1970s called crime prevention through environmental design has been applied and evaluated only in limited settings. Despite the limitations, the evidence clearly suggests that these programs are highly effective in reducing robbery and related injury (Peek-Asa et al., 2001). The practitioner literature is full of recommendations in this area, although few have the backing of empirical data. One benchmarking study conducted by Nalla (1996) provides insight into environmentally related prevention and control strategies from a best practices perspective.

Implications for Future Research and Conclusion

Interest in workplace violence is growing among researchers and practitioners as the impact of violence on organizations is becoming stronger. Despite this growing interest, however, the need for extensive research that informs those who manage workplace violence is critical. Although the response to workplace violence literature is replete with prescriptive advice for violence response, there have been few studies (e.g., Schat & Kelloway, 2003) that empirically evaluate the effectiveness of these guiding principles; thus, the potential for research in the area is limitless. We offer some suggestive points of research to redress this situation.

First, the role of leadership is a critical and interesting area that is worthy of further examination. Specific research questions designed to examine various leadership styles and approaches that are most effective for responding to workplace violence are essential. For example, research has shown that charismatic leadership style is associated with positive organizational outcomes, such as employee perceptions of climate and productive work behaviors. As discussed earlier, future research might be aimed at empirically evaluating such relationships with respect to workplace violence. Another interesting question might explore whether leadership styles adopted under normal operations have similar effects during violence-response operations. Gaining the perspective of both leaders and followers would provide useful insights into the effectiveness of response strategies.

Researchers may also examine the impact that violence-response strategies such as training and counseling have on the physical and emotional well-being of employees at all organizational levels. Schat and Kelloway (2003) have provided support for the effectiveness of violence-related training for all employees, as it has been shown to improve their emotional and somatic well-being. They suggest that future research should be aimed at examining training program content in order to further our understanding of the types of training programs that are most effective for responding to the various forms of workplace violence. For example, little is known about various dimensions of perceived control, including involvement in the decision-making process and its impact on stress and strain. Thus, the effects of training aimed at increasing employee involvement in the decision-making process, along with other dimensions of perceived control, may ameliorate the negative outcomes associated with violence. Furthermore, longitudinal research aimed at determining the causal effect of training on violence outcomes is necessary for assisting organizations with developing effective response strategies.

Research aimed at understanding the effectiveness of response polices and procedures is also a critical area that calls for immediate attention. For example, much of the prescriptive literature on organizational crisis provides guidelines for developing effective response procedures such as mobilizing crisis response teams, delivering effective communication, and establishing zero-tolerance polices for employee aggression, threats, and other inappropriate aggressive behaviors (Distasio, 1995). There are also recommendations for developing selection policies and procedures aimed at assessing the degree of potential risk an employee poses to coworkers and customers; however, implementing selection practices that have not undergone rigorous testing to establish validity will likely result in discriminatory practices. To our knowledge, there are no studies that examine the effectiveness of workplace violence response policies and procedures, and research in the area is essential, as organizations are increasingly depending on the accuracy of the assumptions presented in the literature.

The importance of perceived fairness, as previously discussed, requires further research. There are few findings on the role of each kind of workplace justice in preventing and/or minimizing aggression. As the trend toward electronic employee monitoring accelerates, understanding these relationships becomes increasingly important to the prevention of aggression. The efficacy of zero-tolerance policies in response to the violence as "socially contagious" theory has not been explored and is a pressing issue.

The role of environmental variables, with the exception of economically motivated downsizing, has been the topic of very little investigation. The effect of the contingent workforce has not been explored. The effectiveness of diversity training on the reduction of conflict and aggression in the workplace has similarly been discussed but not empirically tested.

The part played by physical variables in triggering workplace violence has been the topic of much trade literature but almost no research. The popular business press is replete with discussions of physical preventive and response measures that can be taken, but few studies have tested their effectiveness. Some preliminary benchmarking studies have been conducted (Nalla, 1996), but there have been, to our knowledge, no studies that have incorporated a controlled design. The methodological difficulties may in part be to blame for this.

Measurement of workplace aggression and violence, especially as more widely defined, poses challenges for researchers. Moving toward a consensus on the definition may prove beneficial. Many instances of workplace aggression go unreported, exacerbating the research design issues identified above. In fact, unless the violence borders on criminal and is committed by outsiders, there may be no record of it whatsoever (Neuman & Baron, 1998). In some occupations, the risk of workplace violence is higher than in others (LeBlanc & Kelloway, 2002). As previously observed, however, many employees consider it all part of the job and do not recognize and report it (Howard, 2001). These factors make it difficult to appropriately size the issue and hence impress organizations with the need for preparedness (Howard, 2001). Future research might focus on more accurately determining the scope of the problem.

A further challenge that faces researchers is the frequency with which events occur in organizations. Although workplace violence is becoming a growing concern for many organizations, by definition violent events typically occur infrequently within organizations (Pearson & Clair, 1998). This places restraints on the type of research designs investigators may use to empirically test their hypotheses. Furthermore, gaining access to organizations that have experienced violence also challenges researchers, as organizations tend to be reluctant to undergo examination of their response strategies. Thus, it is essential for researchers to establish themselves as trustworthy partners in order to negotiate ongoing research relationships with organizations.

References

Allen, R. E., & Lucero, M. A. (1998). Subordinate aggression against managers: Empirical analyses of published arbitration decisions. *International Journal of Conflict Management, 9*(3), 234–258.

Allen, T. D., Freeman, D. M., Russell, J. E. A., Reizenstein, R. C., & Rentz, J. O. (2001). Survivor reactions to organizational downsizing: Does time ease the pain? *Journal of Occupational and Organizational Psychology, 74*(2), 145–164.

Ashforth, B. E., & Mael, F. (1989). Social identity theory and the organization. *Academy of Management Review, 14,* 20–39.

Bandura, A. (1973). *Aggression: A social learning analysis.* Englewood Cliffs, NJ: Prentice Hall.

Bandura, A. (1977). *Social learning theory.* Englewood Cliffs, NJ: Prentice Hall.

Barling, J. (1996). The prediction, experience and consequences of workplace violence. In E. Q. Bulatao (Ed.), *Violence on the job: Identifying risks and developing solutions* (pp. 29–49). Washington, DC: American Psychological Association.

Barling, J., Loughlin, C., & Kelloway, E. K. (2002). Development and test of a model linking safety-specific transformational leadership and occupational safety. *Journal of Applied Psychology, 87,* 488–496.

Barling, J., Weber, T., & Kelloway, E. K. (1996). Effects of transformational leadership training on attitudinal and financial outcomes: A field experiment. *Journal of Applied Psychology, 81*(6), 827–832.

Baron, R. A., & Neuman, J. H. (1998). Workplace aggression—the iceberg beneath the tip of workplace violence: Evidence of its forms, frequency, and targets. *Public Administration Quarterly, 21*(4), 446–465.

Bass, B. M., & Avolio, B. J. (1993). *Manual: The Multifactor Leadership Questionnaire.* Palo Alto, CA: CPP.

Bennett, N., Martin, C. L., Bies, R. J., & Brockner, J. (1995). Coping with a layoff: A longitudinal study of victims. *Journal of Management, 21,* 1025–1040.

Blythe, B. T. (2002). *Blindsided: A manager's guide to catastrophic incidents in the workplace.* New York: Portfolio.

Braverman, M. (1999). *Preventing workplace violence: A guide for employers and practitioners.* Thousand Oaks, CA: Sage.

Braverman, M. (2003). Managing the human impact of crisis. *Risk Management, 50*(5), 10–14.

Brockner, J. (1988). The effects of work layoffs on survivors: Research, theory and practice. In L. L. Cummings (Ed.), *Research in organizational behaviour* (Vol. 10, pp. 213–255). Greenwich, CT: JAI.

Brockner, J., Davy, J., & Carter, C. (1985). Layoffs, self-esteem and survivor guilt: Motivational, affective and attitudinal consequences. *Organizational Behaviour and Human Decision Processes, 36,* 229–244.

Brockner, J., Grover, S., Reed, T. E., & DeWitt, R. L. (1992). Layoffs, job insecurity, and survivors' work effort: Evidence of an inverted-U relationship. *Academy of Management Journal, 38,* 113–151.

Brockner, J., & Tyler, T. R. (1992). The influence of prior commitment to an institution on reactions to perceived unfairness: The higher they are, the harder they fall. *Administrative Science Quarterly, 37,* 241–261.

Burns, J. M. (1978). *Leadership.* New York: Harper & Row.

Cable, D. M., Aiman-Smith, L., Mulvey, P. W., & Edwards, J. R. (2000). The sources and accuracy of job applicants' beliefs about organizational culture. *Academy of Management Journal, 42,* 1076–1085.

Catalano, R., Novaco, R., & McConnell, W. (1997). A model of the net effect of job loss on violence. *Journal of Personality and Social Psychology, 72,* 1440–1447.

Chen, P. Y., & Spector, P. E. (1992). Relationships of work stressors with aggression, withdrawal, theft and substance use: An exploratory study. *Journal of Occupational and Organizational Psychology, 65*(3), 177–185.

Day, R. C., & Hamblin, R. L. (1969). Some effects of close and punitive styles of supervision. *American Journal of Sociology, 69,* 499–510.

Denenberg, R. V., & Braverman, M. (1999). *The violence-prone workplace: A new approach to dealing with hostile, threatening and uncivil behavior.* Ithaca, NY: Cornell University Press.

Dietz, J., Robinson, S. L., Folger, R., Baron, R. A., & Schulz, M. (2003). The impact of community violence and an organization's procedural justice climate on workplace aggression. *Academy of Management Journal, 48*(3), 317–326.

Distasio, C. (1995). Employee violence in health care: Guidelines for health care managers. *Health Care Supervisor, 13*(3), 1–15.

Douglas, S. C., & Martinko, M. J. (2001). Exploring the role of individual differences in the prediction of workplace aggression. *Journal of Applied Psychology, 86*(4), 547–559.

Dutton, J. E., & Ashford, S. J. (1993). Selling issues to top management. *Academy of Management Review, 18*(3), 397–423.

Dvir, T., Eden, D., Avolio, B. J., & Shamir, B. (2002). Impact of transformational leadership on follower development and performance: A field experiment. *Academy of Management Journal, 45*(4), 735–744.

Franklin, F. P. (1991). Over the edge: Managing violent episodes. *Security Management, 35*(9), 138–142.

Goulet, L. R. (1997). Modeling aggression in the workplace: The role of role models. *Academy of Management Executive, 11*(2), 84–85.

Greenberg, J. (1988). Cultivating an image of justice: Looking fair on the job. *Academy of Management Executive, 2*, 155–158.

Greenberg, J., & Alge, B. J. (1998). Violence behaviors in organizations. In J. Collins (Ed.), *Dysfunctional behavior in organizations* (pp. 43–81). Greenwich, CT: JAI.

Greenberg, L., & Barling, J. (1999). Predicting employee aggression against coworkers, subordinates and supervisors: The roles of person behaviors and perceived workplace factors. *Journal of Organizational Behavior, 20*(6), 897.

Habermas, J. (1975). *Legitimation crisis.* Boston: Beacon Press.

Hashemi, L., & Webster, B. S. (1999). Non-fatal workplace violence workers' compensation claims (1993–1996). *Journal of Occupational and Environmental Medicine, 41*, 561–567.

Highhouse, S., Stierwalt, S. L., Bachiochi, P., Elder, A. E., & Fisher, G. (1999). Effects of advertised human resource management practices on attraction of African-American applicants. *Personnel Psychology, 52*, 425–442.

Hofmann, D. A. & Morgeson, F. P. (1999) Safety-related behavior as a social exchange: The role of perceived organizational support and leader-member exchange. *Journal of Applied Psychology, 84*, 286–296.

Hofmann, D. A., & Stetzer, A. (1996). A cross-level investigation of factors influencing unsafe behaviors and accidents. *Personnel Psychology, 49*, 307–339.

House, R. J. (1971). A path-goal theory of leader effectiveness. *Administrative Sciences Quarterly, 16*, 321–338.

Howard, J. L. (2001). Workplace violence in organizations: An exploratory study of organizational prevention techniques. *Employee Responsibilities and Rights Journal, 13*(2), 57–76.

Howard, J. L., & Voss, R. B. (1996). Workplace violence and the sector ignored: A response to O'Leary-Kelly, Griffin and Glew. *Academy of Management Review, 21*, 920–922.

Howell, J. M., & Hall-Merenda, K. E. (1999). The ties that bind the impact of leader: Member exchange, transformational and transactional leadership, and distance on predicting follower performance. *Journal of Applied Psychology, 84*(5), 680–694.

Johnson, P. R., & Gardner, S. (1999). Domestic violence and the workplace: Developing company responses. *Journal of Management Development, 18*(7), 590.

Johnson, P. R., Lewis, K., & Gardner, S. (1995). Fire me? Bang! Bang! You're dead! *Journal of Managerial Psychology, 10*(7), 28.

Judge, T., & Bono, J. E. (2000). Five-factor model of personality and transformational leadership. *Journal of Applied Psychology, 85*(5), 751–765.

Kets de Vries, M. (1991). *Organizations on the couch.* San Francisco: Jossey-Bass.

Kinicki, A. J., Prussia, G. E., & McKee-Ryan, F. M. (2000). A panel study of coping with involuntary job loss. *Academy of Management Journal, 43*(1), 90–100.

Kirkpatrick, S. A., & Locke, E. A. (1996). Direct and indirect effects of three core charismatic leadership components on performance and attitudes. *Journal of Applied Psychology, 81*(1), 36–51.

Klein, H. J., & Weaver, N. A. (2000). The effectiveness of an organizational-level orientation training program in the socialization of new hires. *Personnel Psychology, 53*(1), 47– 66.

Labig, C. E. (1995). Forming a violence response team. *HR Focus, 72*(8), 15–16.

LeBlanc, M. M., & Kelloway, E. K. (2002). Predictors and outcomes of workplace violence and aggression. *Journal of Applied Psychology, 87*(3), 444–453.

Linnehan, F., & Konrad, A. M. (1999, December). Diluting diversity: Implications for intergroup inequality in organizations. *Journal of Management Inquiry, 8*, 399–414.

Martinko, M. J., & Zellars, K. L. (1996, August). *Toward a theory of workplace violence: A social learning and attributional perspective.* Paper presented at the Academy of Management Conference, Cincinnati, OH.

Merchant, J. A., & Lundell, J. A. (2001). Workplace violence intervention research workshop: Background, rationale and summary. *American Journal of Preventive Medicine, 20*(2), 135–140.

Miller-Burke, J., Attridge, M., & Fass, P. M. (1999). Impact of traumatic events and organizational response: A study of bank robberies. *Journal of Occupational and Environmental Medicine, 41*, 73–83.

Mitroff, I. I., Pearson, C. M., & Harrigan, L. K. (1996). *The essential guide to managing corporate crises.* New York: Oxford University Press.

Mullen, J. E. (2001, August). *Downsizing: Victim and observer perceptions of procedural justice and retributive intentions.* Paper presented at the Tenth European Conference of the Congress on Work and Organizational Psychology, Prague.

Mullen, J. E. (2002, October). *Investigating factors that influence safety behaviour.* Paper presented at the Petroleum Research Atlantic Canada Conference, St. John's, NL.

Mullen, J. E., & Kelloway, E. K. (2003). *Testing a model of employee willingness to raise safety issues.* Revised manuscript submitted for publication.

Nalla, M. K. (1996). Benchmarking study of workplace violence prevention and response: Forty-two components from leading edge programs. *Security Journal, 7*, 89–99.

Neuman, J. H., & Baron, R. A. (1998). Workplace violence and workplace aggression: Evidence concerning specific forms, potential causes and preferred targets. *Journal of Management, 24*(3), 391–419.

O'Leary-Kelly, A. M., Griffin, R. W., & Glew, D. J. (1996). Organization-motivated aggression: A research framework. *Academy of Management Review, 21*(1), 225–254.

O'Neill, H. M., Lenn, D. J., & Caimano, V. F. (1995). Voices of survivors: Words that downsizing CEOs should hear. *Academy of Management Executive, 9*(4), 23.

Pauchant, R. C., & Mitroff, I. I. (1992). *Transforming the crisis prone organization.* San Francisco: Jossey-Bass.

Paul, R. J., & Townsend, J. B. (1998). Violence in the workplace: A review with recommendations. *Employee Responsibilities and Rights Journal, 11*(1), 1–14.

Pearson, C. M., & Clair, J. A. (1998). Reframing crisis management. *Academy of Management Review, 23*(1), 59–76.

Pearson, C. M., Clair, J. A., Misra, S. K., & Mitroff, I. I. (1997). Managing the unthinkable. *Organizational Dynamics, 26,* 51–64.

Peek-Asa, C., Runyan, C. W., & Zwerling, C. (2001). The role of surveillance and evaluation research in the reduction of violence against workers. *American Journal of Preventive Medicine, 20*(2), 141–148.

Pillai, R. (1995). Context and charisma: The role of organic structure, collectivism, and crisis in the emergence of charismatic leadership. *Academy of Management Journal,* 332.

Pillai, R., & Meindl, J. R. (1998). Context and charisma: A "meso" level examination of the relationship of organic structure, collectivism, and crisis to charismatic leadership. *Journal of Management, 24*(5), 643.

Resnick, P. J., & Kausch, O. (1995). Violence in the workplace: Role of the consultant. *Consulting Psychology Journal: Practice and Research, 47*(4), 213–222.

Robinson, S. L., & Greenberg, J. (1998). Employees behaving badly: Dimensions, determinants and dilemmas in the study of workplace deviance. In C. L. Cooper & D. M. Rousseau (Eds.), *Trends in organizational behavior* (Vol. 5, pp. 1–30). New York: Wiley.

Robinson, S. L., & O'Leary-Kelly, A. M. (1998). Monkey see, monkey do: The influence of work groups on the antisocial behavior of employees. *Academy of Management Journal, 41*(6), 658–673.

Rogers, K. A., & Kelloway, E. K. (1997). Violence at work: Personal and organizational outcomes. *Journal of Occupational Health Psychology, 2*(1), 63–71.

Runyan, C. W., Zakocs, R. C., & Zwerling, C. (2000). Administrative and behavioral interventions for workplace violence prevention. *American Journal of Preventive Medicine, 18,* 116–127.

Schat, A. C. H., & Kelloway, E. K. (2000). Effects of perceived control on the outcomes of workplace aggression and violence. *Journal of Occupational Health Psychology, 5*(3), 386–402.

Schat, A. C. H., & Kelloway, E. K. (2003). Reducing the adverse consequences of workplace aggression and violence: The buffering effects of organizational support. *Journal of Occupational Health Psychology, 8*(2), 110–122.

Shin, S. J., & Zhou, J. (2003). Transformational leadership, conservation, and creativity: Evidence from Korea. *Academy of Management Journal, 46*(6), 703–714.

Skarlicki, D. P., Ellard, J. H., & Kelln, B. R. (1998). Third-party perceptions of a layoff: Procedural, derogation and retributive aspects of justice. *Journal of Applied Psychology, 83*(1), 19–27.

Skarlicki, D. P., Folger, R., & Tesler, P. (1999). Personality as a moderator in the relationship between fairness and retaliation. *Academy of Management Journal, 42*(1), 100–108.

Slora, K. B., Joy, D. S., Jones, J. W., & Terris, W. (1991). The prediction of on-the-job violence. In J. W. Jones (Ed.), *Preemployment honesty testing* (pp. 171–184). Westport, CT: Quorum Books.

Smart, C., & Vertinsky, I. (1984). Strategy and the environment: A study of corporate response to crises. *Strategic Management Journal, 5*(3), 199–214.

Sommers, J. A., Schell, T. A., & Vodanovich, S. J. (2002). Developing a measure of individual differences in organizational revenge. *Journal of Business and Psychology, 17*(2), 207–223.

Spillan, J., & Hough, M. (2003). Crisis planning in small businesses: Importance, impetus and indifference. *European Management Journal, 21*(3), 398.

Starbuck, W. H., & Milliken, F. J. (1988). Challenger: Fine-tuning the odds until something breaks. *Journal of Management Studies, 25,* 319–340.

Tyler, T. R., & Bies, R. J. (1990). Beyond formal procedures: The interpersonal context of procedural justice. In J. S. Carroll (Ed.), *Applied social psychology in business settings* (pp. 77–98). Hillsdale, NJ: Erlbaum.

Van Maanen, J. V., & Schein, E. H. (1979). Toward a theory of organizational socialization. In B. M. Staw (Ed.), *Research in organizational behavior* (Vol. 1, pp. 209–264). Greenwich, CT: JAI.

Vu, U. (2003, October 6). New rules to prevent violence. *Canadian HR Reporter, 16,* p. 1.

Wanberg, C. R., Bunce, L. W., & Gavin, M. B. (1999). Perceived fairness of layoffs among individuals who have been laid off: A longitudinal study. *Personnel Psychology, 52,* 59–84.

Weick, K. (1995). *Sensemaking in organizations.* London: Sage.

Wilkinson, C. W. (1998). *Violence in the workplace: Preventing, assessing and managing threats at work.* Rockville, MD: Government Institutes.

Wright, B., & Barling, J. (1998). "The Executioners' Song": Listening to downsizers reflect on their experiences. *Canadian Journal of Administrative Studies, 15*(4), 339–355.

Zohar, D. (1980). Safety climate in industrial organizations: Theoretical and applied implications. *Journal of Applied Psychology, 65,* 96–102.

Zohar, D. (2002). The effects of leadership dimensions, safety climate, and assigned priorities on minor injuries in work groups. *Journal of Organizational Behaviour, 23,* 75–92.

22

The Experience of Victims

Using Theories of Traumatic and Chronic Stress to Understand Individual Outcomes of Workplace Abuse

Theresa M. Glomb
Lilia M. Cortina

E mpirical work on the outcomes of workplace aggression and violence (hereafter collectively termed "workplace abuse") has accumulated in recent years, suggesting that this abuse has a detrimental impact on a variety of psychological, job-related, and physical outcomes. Despite the research attention to these victim outcomes, this body of literature would benefit from additional theorizing about processes linking abusive workplace events to outcomes. Although theoretical models of workplace violence and aggression have been proposed, many theories focus on the organizational and individual antecedents of the abuse, without sufficient attention to its outcomes; the abusive behavior is the outcome of interest (see for exception Barling, 1996). In this chapter, we turn to the literatures on traumatic and chronic stress to build a theoretical understanding of outcomes of workplace abuse.

Before we begin, we outline the boundary conditions and foci of this chapter. First, the focus of the chapter is on the *outcomes* of workplace abuse. There is little attention to antecedents of workplace abuse, as this material is covered in other chapters of this volume. We recognize that antecedents may influence the attributions for the abusive experience (e.g., the hostile personality of a coworker, the job stress of a situation) and in turn influence the nature of the outcomes; however, for our purposes, we assume these antecedents and attributions will contribute to the variability in the type and intensity of the outcomes felt.

Second, our chapter addresses a broad spectrum of workplace abuses, ranging from high-intensity, extreme examples of workplace violence (e.g., physical and sexual assault) to less intense but more frequent instances of workplace aggression, harassment, and bullying (e.g., psychological aggression, gender harassment). Our goal is to be more inclusive of the work experiences of a greater number of employees. Further, given the low base rate of extreme violent incidents, the research on such incidents is somewhat smaller than that on workplace aggression and sexual harassment more broadly defined. Inferences from research specifically on workplace violence would be more circumscribed than those inferences from a broader workplace aggression focus. Our focus is also primarily on abuse that emanates from within the workplace context (e.g., at the hands of coworkers or customers) rather than abuse emanating from the community or home. Throughout the chapter, we will use the term *workplace abuse* to denote this set of different types of violence, aggression, and harassment that occurs as a result of one's employment (except in discussing empirical work when we adopt the original terms used by authors).

Third, throughout the chapter, our perspective will be that of the direct victims of workplace abuse. Although research has suggested that witnessing workplace abuse can have deleterious effects (Glomb et al., 1997; Glomb & Liao, 2003; Miner-Rubino & Cortina, 2004; Rogers & Kelloway, 1997; Schat & Kelloway, 2000; Schneider, 1996) and in certain occupations (e.g., police officers) witnessing violence is a frequent antecedent of negative outcomes, our discussion focuses on the processes explaining outcomes for direct victims. That being said, many of the theoretical processes resulting in these outcomes would likely apply to witnessing abusive or violent acts, and thus generalizability to alternative forms of exposure may be reasonable.

The chapter will be structured as follows: First, we will discuss a select number of empirical studies of the outcomes of workplace violence, aggression, and sexual harassment. This will provide a sense of the myriad outcomes that occur as a result of workplace abuse. Next, we will discuss the literatures on traumatic and chronic stress to provide theoretical explanations for these outcomes. Finally, we will discuss avenues for future research and implications for practice.

Selected Empirical Studies of Outcomes

In an effort to describe the outcomes for victims of workplace abuse, we review briefly selected empirical scholarship on outcomes of workplace violence, aggression, and harassment. This is in no way meant to be a comprehensive review; rather, in selecting studies, we attempted to include research focusing on different types of workplace abuse (e.g., physical violence, psychological aggression, sexual harassment, bullying) from different sources (the public, coworkers, and supervisors) with multiple outcome types (psychological, job, and health related). The studies described below illustrate the diverse panoply of outcomes for victims of workplace abuse.

In a program of research on the outcomes of workplace violence, Kelloway and colleagues developed and tested a model of the outcomes of workplace violence and aggression in several contexts. Rogers and Kelloway (1997) demonstrated that exposure to workplace violence had detrimental effects on employees' psychological well-being, physical symptoms, and turnover intentions; these effects were mediated by fear of future violence. Building on this model, LeBlanc and Kelloway (2002) found differential effects on outcomes for public-initiated violence, public-initiated aggression, and coworker aggression. Specifically, public-initiated violence and aggression predicted perceptions of the likelihood of future violence, which in turn predicted fear of violence. Public-initiated violence directly predicted turnover intent. A different pattern emerged for coworker aggression; coworker aggression did not predict perceptions of the likelihood of future violence but had direct effects on emotional and psychosomatic well-being as well as affective commitment. This work is noteworthy in parsing the outcomes by the source of the violence.

Schat and Kelloway (2000, 2003) investigated important moderators of the relationships between workplace violence and aggression, fear of future violence, and outcomes. In two studies, they demonstrated the moderating impact of perceived control (2000) and organizational support (2003). Specifically, organizational support moderated the effects of violence and aggression on emotional well-being, physical health, and job affect. Perceived control also influenced outcomes, although its role was through its impact on emotional well-being. This program of research provides insight into a variety of outcomes of both direct and indirect exposure to violence and aggression from both coworkers and members of the public.

In a sample of 598 employees from a variety of occupations, Budd, Arvey, and Lawless (1996) found that being victimized at work was related to a variety of job-related outcomes including heightened worry about being victimized, lower job satisfaction, and increased likelihood of considering bringing a gun, mace, or other weapon to work. These authors also examined the outcomes of fear of harassment or violence and found that victimization was related to increased fear, resulting in considerations of job change, absenteeism, psychological distress, and self-reported productivity declines. This study is significant in the variety of job-related outcomes that are examined, including behavioral outcomes such as bringing weapons to work and considering a job change.

Unlike much of the research on workplace abuse that examines the effects of aggregate frequency of abuse, Glomb (2002) conducted a qualitative and quantitative examination of the antecedents and outcomes of specific aggressive incidents. This study found that the specific aggressive experiences had effects predominantly on job-related (e.g., job satisfaction, job stress) rather than personal outcomes. Results also suggested that the effects of the experience on outcomes generally increased as the severity of the incident increased.

In their examination of aggression among 338 university employees, Björkqvist, Österman, and Hjelt-Bäck (1994) found that victims of workplace harassment reported higher levels of depression, anxiety, and aggressiveness than nonvictims. In follow-up interviews with individuals who considered themselves to be harassed severely, victims claimed without exception that these outcomes were a direct consequence of the harassment. Thus, in addition to shedding light on outcomes for employees who are moderately harassed, this study provides insight into the experiences of those who have faced workplace "bullying," or "long-term aggression directed toward a person who is not able to defend him/herself, leading to victimization of that individual" (p. 175). Recent reviews of bullying (Hoel, Rayner, & Cooper, 1999; Keashley & Jagatic, 2003; Rayner & Cooper, Chapter 7, this volume), as well as a special issue devoted to bullying (Zapf & Einarsen, 2001), suggest detrimental outcomes similar to those discussed here.

In a longitudinal examination of abuse at the hands of a particular perpetrator (one's supervisor), Tepper (2000) found that subordinates in a number of occupations who perceived their supervisors to be abusive were more likely to quit their jobs; however, for those who retained their jobs, abusive supervision was related to both job outcomes (including lower job satisfaction and lower commitment) and nonwork outcomes (including lower life satisfaction; greater conflict between work and family; and greater psychological distress, i.e., depression, anxiety, emotional exhaustion). For many of the relationships between abusive supervision and outcomes, perceptions of organizational justice had a mediating effect, and job mobility had a moderating effect. The role of job mobility is particularly noteworthy, as those subordinates who felt they did not have alternative employment opportunities experienced more negative outcomes, presumably because changing jobs was not a plausible means of coping with the abuse.

Sexual harassment has also been recognized as a form of workplace abuse with detrimental outcomes. In their test of an integrated model of sexual harassment, Fitzgerald, Drasgow, Hulin, Gelfand, and Magley (1997) provided theoretical and empirical support for the job, psychological, and health outcomes resulting from sexual harassment. In their study of women at a large public utility company, sexual harassment was related to lower job satisfaction, psychological health, and physical health; these outcomes in turn led to work and job withdrawal. These results persisted after controlling for general job stress. Similar outcomes were investigated in Schneider, Swan, and Fitzgerald (1997), who demonstrated through discriminant function analyses that women who had and had not been harassed could be differentiated on the basis of job (e.g., satisfaction, withdrawal, commitment) and psychological (e.g., mental health, PTSD symptoms) outcomes.

These results could not be attributed to differences in respondents' negative disposition, general job stress, or attitudes about sexual harassment.

As evident from the description of the empirical research, the outcomes for victims of workplace abuse are multifaceted. Outcomes can be categorized as organizational or job-related such as attitudinal outcomes (job satisfaction, commitment, job stress) and behavioral outcomes (work withdrawal, turnover and turnover intentions, impaired performance) as well as personal outcomes such as psychological (depression, anxiety, negative affect/mood) and health outcomes (somatic complaints, sleeplessness).

Much of this abuse would be consistent with clinical definitions of trauma, and as Leymann (1990) notes, many targets of workplace abuse show symptoms of traumatic stress. In the next section, we draw on theories of trauma to better understand outcomes of acute workplace abuse. We then turn to theories of chronic stress to explain outcomes of chronic workplace abuses (e.g., harassment, bullying), which often do not qualify as trauma.

Theoretical Explanations for Outcomes of Workplace Abuse

As reviewed above, research on victims of workplace abuse has focused heavily on cataloguing the outcomes of this behavior, with less attention to theoretical mechanisms driving these outcomes. In other words, we know that experiences of workplace abuse can be harmful to employee victims, but we know little about the process by which these harms unfold. To build theoretical accounts for the multitude of negative outcomes that can follow these experiences, we turn to the clinical and social-personality literatures on stress.

Generally speaking, *stress* comes in (at least) two varieties: acute and chronic. Likewise, the events (or "stressors") that trigger stress responses can also be considered either acute or chronic. These two types of events differ in their duration (brief vs. extended), onset (specific vs. ambiguous), and offset (predictable or clear vs. open-ended; Hepburn, Loughlin, & Barling, 1997; Wheaton, 1997). Applied to the domain of workplace abuses, events qualifying as *acute* are typically time-limited, sudden, isolated events, for example, workplace shootings, physical and sexual assault, and armed robbery. *Chronic* workplace abuses, by contrast, would be enduring and repetitive (often to the point of appearing to have no end), and their time of onset is often difficult to pinpoint; examples from this category include many manifestations of gender harassment, psychological abuse, and (nonphysical) bullying. Different theories have emerged to explain the harms of the two types of stressors. We begin by reviewing theories of traumatic stress, which may account for outcomes of acute workplace violence, and then we turn to the literature on chronic stress to understand how everyday workplace abuses can also trigger negative consequences for victims.

Theories of Traumatic Stress

Multiple theoretical models have emerged to account for the variety of symptoms reported by victims of acute stressors and trauma. It is impossible to identify one model that would be most applicable to victims of workplace abuse, given that this abuse takes many behavioral forms, stems from different perpetrators, and varies in its degree of psychological, physical, and occupational threat. Moreover, employees demonstrate great interindividual variability in their reactions to workplace abuse. For these reasons, different theoretical frameworks may be useful for capturing different victim outcomes. Below we present four such frameworks that could help us understand the experience of workplace abuse victims. This is not intended to represent an exhaustive review of traumatic stress research; rather, we present several prominent trauma theories to illustrate how this literature could inform the understanding of victim outcomes of acute workplace abuse.

First, a brief comment on *posttraumatic stress disorder* (PTSD) is warranted, as many theories of traumatic stress specifically address PTSD in victims. The *Diagnostic and Statistical Manual of Mental Disorders* (4th ed., text revision [*DSM-IV-TR*]; American Psychiatric Association [APA], 2000) classifies PTSD as an anxiety disorder that results from exposure to "an event or events that involved actual or threatened death or serious injury, or a threat to the physical integrity of self or others" (p. 467). During this event, the person must have experienced "intense fear, helplessness, or horror" (APA, 2000, p. 467). The more extreme varieties of workplace abuse would qualify as trauma under these criteria. PTSD then manifests itself with symptoms falling into three domains: reexperiencing (e.g., intrusive thoughts, flashbacks), avoidance or numbing (e.g., avoidance of people or places that arouse memories of the trauma, emotional detachment), and hyperarousal (e.g., irritability, anger, impaired concentration). It is important to understand that for such symptoms to qualify as PTSD, they must cause "clinically significant distress or impairment in social, *occupational,* or other important areas of functioning" (APA, 2000, p. 468; italics added). This inclusion of occupational dysfunction in the PTSD diagnosis identifies the workplace as a key setting where PTSD can take its toll (Penk, Drebing, & Schutt, 2002). Lifetime prevalence of PTSD in the United States ranges from 8% (Kessler, Sonnega, Bromet, Hughes, & Nelson, 1995) to 12% (Resnick, Kilpatrick, Dansky, Saunders, & Best, 1993), and Penk and colleagues (2002) speculate that rates could be even higher within the workforce, owing to the stress that accompanies many occupations. The disorder tends to be more severe when the stressor is of human design (e.g., intentional violence), as opposed to nonhuman-induced stressors such as natural disasters and accidents (Green, 1990; Herman, 1992). Although PTSD does not capture the full range of outcomes reported by victims of workplace abuse, it provides a useful framework within which to understand many of these outcomes.

Learning Theory

Following Mowrer's (1960) two-factor learning theory, both *classical* and *operant conditioning* can explain the development of fear, anxiety, and avoidance among victims of trauma (e.g., Keane, Zimmerling, & Caddell, 1985; Kilpatrick, Veronen, & Best, 1985). First, due to classical conditioning, fear and anxiety experienced during a traumatic event become associated with stimuli that are present during the event, such that these previously neutral stimuli develop fear-eliciting properties. Through *stimulus generalization* and *higher-order conditioning*, a variety of associated stimuli can also become fear- and anxiety-arousing. For example, an employee who is assaulted by a disgruntled male customer may become conditioned to fear the office where the assault took place, disgruntled customers, or even male customers. In other words, the traumatized employee becomes highly anxious in the presence of these stimuli.

Because the experience of fear and anxiety is unpleasant, the victim attempts to reduce anxiety by avoiding the feared stimuli. This avoidance can take a number of forms such as distraction, blocking of memories, and avoidance of specific people and places. As a result, the victim feels less fear and anxiety (temporarily). Thus, through principles of operant conditioning, this avoidance behavior functions as a form of *negative reinforcement*: It is highly rewarding because it removes an aversive emotional state.

For victims of workplace abuse, learning theory can explain a number of outcomes, particularly anxiety and PTSD. The avoidance component of PTSD also helps us to understand organizational withdrawal behavior. Employees may engage in work withdrawal (e.g., absenteeism, tardiness, substance use) as a way of distancing themselves from the workplace situation that now arouses fear and anxiety. They may also become less committed to the organization, as a means of putting further psychological or emotional distance between themselves and the feared context. To achieve more complete avoidance, they could turn to job withdrawal in the form of turnover or turnover intentions. In addition, the hyperarousal aspect of PTSD could explain irritability, angry outbursts, and concentration difficulties among employee victims of abuse. Concentration problems and high distractibility could also result from intrusive cognitions, the reexperiencing component of PTSD. Of course, a secondary effect of work withdrawal (e.g., low commitment, concentration problems, distractibility) could be performance decline.

Learning theory has been highly influential in the field of traumatic stress, and it can explain many of the prominent symptoms of workplace abuse victims; however, this theory does not account for the full range of cognitive and emotional reactions that many victims experience. For this reason, we turn to more cognitively oriented theories to understand additional victim outcomes.

Theory of Shattered Assumptions

Janoff-Bulman (1995; Janoff-Bulman & Frieze, 1983) proposed an important theory that takes a more cognitive than behavioral approach to understanding trauma reactions. According to this theory, traumatic experiences, especially those that involve violent victimization, seriously challenge very basic assumptions and expectations about the self and the world. Three types of assumptions are especially vulnerable to violation during trauma, entailing beliefs that (a) the self is invulnerable to serious harm, (b) the self is worthwhile and good, and (c) the world is meaningful and just. These assumptions are critical to psychological well-being because they serve as guides for how to navigate the world, thus fostering psychological stability or equilibrium.

Victimization calls into question these three core beliefs that constitute peoples' "assumptive world" (Janoff-Bulman, 1995, p. 75), throwing them into a state of psychological disequilibrium or crisis. When the assumption of personal invulnerability is violated, the victim feels unsafe and apprehensive in a malevolent world; the problem is exacerbated when the victimization is human-induced because then the victim feels unsafe in a world of malevolent people. The trauma of victimization can also challenge the assumption of personal worth, leading victims to view themselves as weak, helpless, needy, and perhaps even guilty. Finally, victims of abuse often find that they can no longer endorse assumptions that the world is meaningful and just; instead they begin to believe that life is uncontrollable and unpredictable, negative events occur for no reason, and being a "good person" does not offer protection from misfortune. Disruption of these three fundamental assumptions results in intense anxiety.

Applied to victims of workplace abuse, this cognitive theory accounts primarily for psychological outcomes such as anxiety, depression, and PTSD. For example, the sense that people are malevolent and the world is no longer predictable could produce intense feelings of fear and anxiety in the workplace abuse victim. Negative self-appraisals such as feeling vulnerable, helpless, and insecure could also contribute to depression. Attempts to reconcile the disconnect between the abuse experience and the assumptive world could fuel the intrusive cognitions that characterize reexperiencing symptoms of PTSD (e.g., Horowitz, 1986). This theory of shattered assumptions can also explain certain job outcomes. For example, intense perceptions of vulnerability could lead the victimized employee to be preoccupied with fear that the victimizing event could reoccur, detracting from concentration and performance on the job. Moreover, the abuse experience could violate previously held assumptions that the workplace is safe and people within it are just; the result could be lowered satisfaction with and commitment to the organization and its members.

Emotional Processing Theory

Foa and colleagues (e.g., Foa & Kozak, 1986; Foa & Rothbaum, 1998; Tolin & Foa, 2003) advanced another cognitive theory to account for outcomes (particularly PTSD) among trauma victims, focusing on the architecture of fear. According to their *emotional processing theory*, all fear is a memory-based cognitive structure containing information about (a) the feared event (including details such as its location and perpetrator), (b) emotional, behavioral, and physiological responses during and after that event, and (c) the interpretation or meaning of that event and those responses. These different elements or "nodes" of the fear network are interconnected. In the case of pathological fear, the connections are particularly numerous and strong, and the response elements are "disruptively intense" (Tolin & Foa, 2003, p. 79). The threshold for activating a pathological fear structure is low; various internal and external events can activate a component of the network, and activation then spreads to other components.

Using workplace robbery as an example, a bank manager who is held at gunpoint at her desk by a robber would form associations in memory between desk and gun nodes (elements of the event), fear and hypervigilance nodes (her responses during and after the event), and a threat-to-life node (her interpretation of the event). These connections would be much stronger than connections between the desk node and other response and meaning nodes formed on other workdays when no threatening events took place and the manager was in a neutral or positive mood. Now, sitting behind the desk may trigger unwanted and intrusive thoughts about the gun and other aspects of the robbery (reexperiencing symptoms of PTSD), which then activate intense feelings of danger, fear, and hypervigilance (hyperarousal symptoms). It could even be that sitting behind the desk is sufficient to activate hypervigilance. In an effort to prevent the intrusive thoughts and escape the aversive anxiety, the manager may arrive to work late, neglect tasks that require work at the desk, or resign her job altogether (avoidance symptoms); however, these attempts at anxiety reduction may be unsuccessful because the pathological fear structure remains intact and may become activated again by various environmental or physiological cues (e.g., the sight of a similar desk or another branch of the same bank).

Emotional processing theory is a useful framework for understanding anxious and avoidant reactions to workplace abuse, especially as manifested in the context of PTSD. These symptoms can clearly interfere with job satisfaction, commitment, and performance; however, this theory does not attempt to explain other common emotional reactions to trauma, such as sadness, guilt, shame, betrayal, and humiliation, all of which could give rise to major depressive disorder. Next we turn to learned helplessness theory to better understand connections between workplace abuse and depression.

Learned Helplessness

According to *learned helplessness theory* (e.g., Burns & Seligman, 1991; Peterson & Seligman, 1983), during inescapable, unpredictable, aversive events, some people learn that they have no control over the onset and termination of the events; in other words, responses and outcomes become noncontingent in their minds. This belief that any response would be futile fosters numbness, passivity, and helplessness, and the individuals demonstrate the characteristic deficits of depression. For example, they report feeling hopeless that things will change for the better in the future; express sadness, crying, and anhedonia; and appear unmotivated. Not all victims of uncontrollable negative events, however, develop these same helplessness and depressive reactions. Thus, a cognitive component was added to the model to account for variations in victim response.

The cognitive component of this theory argues that people seek explanations for negative events unfolding around them. These explanations have three dimensions: internal versus external cause, stable versus unstable timecourse (i.e., persistent vs. time-limited), and global versus specific generality across situations. Individuals who tend to generate internal, stable, global explanations for negative events are more likely to become depressed in the face of such events. For example, if a female employee who experiences sexual harassment makes internal attributions for the harassment ("I must have done something to lead him on"), her self-esteem would likely drop. If she sees the harassment as stable ("this will never end"), then she may develop chronic depressive symptoms. Finally, if she believes that she will encounter similar harassment across different contexts (e.g., "even if I requested a transfer, he would still pursue me"), then she could develop helplessness deficits that generalize across situations.

Learned helplessness theory articulates cognitive mechanisms by which workplace abuse can trigger depression in victims. Symptoms of depression have implications for other victim outcomes as well. For example, key symptoms (according to the *DSM-IV-TR*) include concentration problems and indecisiveness, which could interfere with job performance. Physical symptoms such as fatigue, psychomotor retardation, and insomnia could also impair performance and increase errors, particularly in technical, skilled, and unskilled labor occupations. Finally, employees suffering from severe depression may experience difficulty getting out of bed and initiating activities, eventually requiring hospitalization; the result would be increased absenteeism, use of sick leave, and/or prolonged leaves of absence. Significantly, the learned helplessness model also specifies a cognitive variable (explanatory style) that can account for employees' individual differences in depressive responses, explaining why many employees do *not* become depressed following workplace abuse.

Theories of Chronic Stress

Whereas theories of traumatic stress can help us to understand victim outcomes of acute workplace violence, they are less applicable to chronic manifestations of psychological abuse at work, which often would not qualify as trauma, per se. To explain outcomes of chronic workplace abuse, we now turn to the literature on chronic stress. This literature is much less developed than that addressing major life events and traumatic stress, but important theory has emerged to account for how enduring, everyday stressors can interfere with the health and well-being of victims.

To begin with basic definitions, Wheaton (1994, p. 82) defines *chronic stressors* as "problems and issues that are either so regular in the enactment of daily roles or activities, or so defined by the nature of daily role enactments or activities, that they behave as if they are continuous for the individual." Likewise, Gottlieb (1997, p. 10) characterizes chronic stressors as "persistent demands" that are "woven into the tapestry of life." As noted earlier in this chapter, chronic stressors generally distinguish themselves from traumatic events in that they have an extended duration, an onset that is difficult to identify, and no clear or predictable offset. Lazarus (1999) and his colleagues term these experiences *daily hassles,* that is, insidious frustrations that become fixed and ongoing in everyday settings, including settings of work (e.g., DeLongis, Coyne, Dakof, Folkman, & Lazarus, 1982; DeLongis, Folkman, & Lazarus, 1988; Lazarus & Folkman, 1984). Certain forms of workplace abuse would qualify as chronic stressors or hassles, especially persistent psychological and sexual aggression, as well as bullying (which, by definition, is persistent). These stressors would create "socially noxious environments" (Gottlieb, 1997, p. 5) for the employee-victims, which could give rise to negative outcomes.

Although they lack the drama and intensity of acute stressors, chronic stressors or hassles should not be dismissed as inconsequential. In fact, these stressors can have a greater impact on certain psychological and health outcomes than major, exceptional life events (e.g., DeLongis et al., 1982; DeLongis et al., 1988; Jandorf, Deblinger, Neale, & Stone, 1986; McGonagle & Kessler, 1990). Such outcomes include negative emotions, mood disturbance, energy problems (e.g., fatigue, sleep difficulty), somatic symptoms (e.g., headaches, back pain), and health conditions (e.g., hypertension).

In theorizing about why and how chronic stressors or hassles undermine health and well-being, Lazarus and Folkman (1984; Lazarus, 1999) suggest two possible alternatives. One is that hassles simply have an additive effect, accumulating over time to add to the total "wear and tear" experienced; however, their more complex, preferred explanation emphasizes the mediating role of *cognitive appraisal.* This refers to an evaluation of whether a situation involves harm or loss, threat, or challenge for the individual (or, conversely, is irrelevant or benign). A *harm or loss appraisal* occurs when the person perceives that physical or psychological damage has already been sustained. When the harm or loss has not yet occurred but is anticipated, then a *threat appraisal* ensues. These two types of appraisals then trigger negative emotions, such as fear, anxiety, and sadness. By contrast, a *challenge appraisal* takes place when the individual sees potential for growth or gain in a demanding situation, often resulting in positive emotions (e.g., hopefulness, eagerness, confidence). In sum, this theory holds that it is not simply the objective, observable characteristics of the stressor that trigger particular outcomes; instead, outcomes (both negative and positive) result from the individual's subjective evaluation of the situation. Simply put, "how a person construes an event shapes the emotional and behavioral response" (Lazarus & Folkman, 1984, p. 24).

These theories of chronic stressors or hassles can help us understand how seemingly minor but chronic workplace abuses (e.g., ongoing and repeated derisive comments, disparagement toward one's gender, sexual teasing) can trigger negative psychological and health outcomes in employee-victims. According to this literature, cognitive appraisals (especially harm or loss, and threat appraisals) are the key mechanisms that drive victims' negative affect or mood, depression, anxiety, and somatic complaints. For example, a workplace bullying victim might manifest depression as a result of perceiving damage to personal or social esteem (a harm appraisal), and the victim may also experience anxiety due to anticipation of future psychological attacks and damage (a threat appraisal). Although these general theories of chronic stress or hassles do not address occupational outcomes in any detail, it seems logical that an eventual consequence of appraising long-term, seemingly never-ending workplace events as harmful or threatening could be disengagement from that workplace as a means of coping; this disengagement could manifest either psychologically (e.g., lowered commitment, greater burnout) or behaviorally (e.g., substance abuse, work and job withdrawal). Finally, the literature on chronic stress or hassles also gives insight into individual differences in victim outcomes, explaining, for example, why gender harassment triggers intense psychological distress in some employees (who may appraise the situation as threatening) yet barely fazes others (who may evaluate the situation as trivial).

Future Research

With respect to future empirical work on workplace abuse, research should consider approaches for tapping into the motives of workplace abuse behaviors. Although a focus on behavioral constructs is advantageous in that it defines the construct space, these behaviors do not take into account the motive or perceived motive of the perpetrator. As is evident from learned helplessness theory, the attribution or motive may be important in determining victim outcomes. Victims who ascribe workplace abuse to a criminal motive, situational factors (e.g., stress or frustration), a personal vendetta (i.e., someone is out to get me), or individual difference factors in the perpetrator (e.g., hostile attribution bias; aggressiveness) may all react differently. Given the same behavior, the motive may play a role in how workplace abuse is perceived and the type of outcomes that ensue. For example, health care professionals working in populations of mentally unstable individuals may report being the frequent target of verbal abuse; however, these employees may ascribe a nonaggressive or nonthreatening motive to the behavior if this is common in their patients' behavioral repertoires. By contrast, a target of verbal abuse from a supervisor may ascribe an aggressive or threatening motive to this behavior. Equivalent behaviors with different motives are likely to have different outcomes. Consideration of the motive behind behaviors would provide a fuller picture of the workplace abuse experience.

Future research might also investigate the influence of traumas in the non-work environment on work outcomes. For example, the role of domestic violence or childhood trauma on work outcomes for the individual, coworker group, or organization has not been well explored. Take for example the issue of domestic violence. At present, there is a general sense that domestic violence has a detrimental influence on the work life of the victims, as well as the work group and larger organization; however, the nature of these deleterious effects, the mechanisms by which these effects occur, and intervention options have not been well explored in the literature (for exceptions, see Mighty, 1997; Rothman & Perry, 2004; Swanberg & Logan, 2005). The pathways by which domestic violence may have an impact on the work environment are multifold. For example, the spouse or partner is the number one cause of homicide for women at work; thus, domestic violence clearly spills over into the workplace. The effects of domestic violence, however, are likely to be much more insidious. For example, domestic violence may result in increased absenteeism, strained relationships with coworkers, decreased job performance, increased benefits utilization, and so forth. The spillover may also go the other way; conditions in the work environment (e.g., stressful work environment, burnout) may exacerbate family violence. In sum, there are a variety of relationships and points of integration that may be explored.

Although we chose to focus on the direct targets of workplace abuse, it is clear that the effects of such abuse go well beyond the target. Indeed, in several of the studies mentioned above, outcomes for employees witnessing workplace abuse were similar to and in some cases approximated the level of outcomes reported by direct victims. Given that the literature on trauma and PTSD covers events that are both directly experienced and witnessed, it is not surprising that the effects are similar, so we anticipate that much of the theoretical processes suggested here would generalize. There may be boundary conditions or differences, however, in the theoretical mechanisms that underlie outcomes of witnessed workplace abuse. The applicability of these models to bystanders would be an interesting avenue for future research.

Despite a growing body of literature on workplace abuse, much of the research is self-report and cross-sectional in nature, limiting its ability to capture adequately the complexities of the abusive experiences and their effects. Studies typically use retrospective, aggregated self-reports of abuse to test what are typically conceived of as a dynamic set of antecedents, behaviors, and consequences. Future research should strive to incorporate alternative methodologies to capture the dynamic complexities of abusive experiences, such as longitudinal research, experience sampling methods, reports from others in the work environment, in-depth qualitative reports on specific incidents, and case studies. As noted by McGrath (1981), "multiple methods is not just a desirable approach but rather is the *sine qua non* for the knowledge accrual process" (p. 129). Additional methods will allow triangulation on relationships within the workplace abuse experience.

Implications for Policy, Practice, and Intervention

Because our chapter addresses negative outcomes of workplace abuse, we focus on interventions that may mitigate these outcomes. Clearly, primary prevention is critical, and interventions should be aimed at reducing workplace abuse; however despite the best efforts of employers, policymakers, and researchers, workplace abuse is not likely to dissipate fully, and thus secondary and tertiary prevention efforts are needed. Therefore, we focus on those implications for practice that deal squarely with ways to mitigate the detrimental effects of workplace abuse.

It is critical that employers recognize the severe impact of a range of workplace abuses on employees. Although headline-grabbing violence is what comes to mind for most employers, the quotidian abuses and slights have negative consequences as well. Employers should be made aware of the potential sources and harms of various types of abuse, particularly those that are most likely for occupational groups in their purview. For example, the stressors of dealing with clients, patients, and coworkers, stressful work environments, and threat of criminal activity should all be considered and recognized in the totality of work demands.

Employers should also be aware of the potential outcomes of workplace abuse so that assistance and/or referrals can be provided. Employee assistance programs (EAPs) or outside mental health resources can be utilized to provide diagnosis and counseling as indicated. Counselors of these victims should be aware of the manifestations of workplace abuse, as clients may present with depression, anxiety, PTSD, and other symptoms that may not be immediately attributed to a workplace source (Lewis, Coursol, & Herting Wall, 2002). The theories of trauma and chronic stress described above have treatment plans associated with them that would be helpful for victims of workplace abuse.

In some of the empirical studies discussed above, important moderators were found for the workplace abuse–outcome relationships. These moderators may provide potential ideas for buffering conditions of workplace abuse. Infusing the work environment with conditions shown to be helpful in reducing the negative outcomes from workplace abuse (e.g., perceived control, organizational support, coping strategies) may be one avenue for mitigating its effects. Future research to extend work on possible buffers, particularly those suggested by the literatures on traumatic and chronic stress, would provide insight into the situational and individual factors that play a role in the workplace abuse–outcome relationship.

For some occupations, interventions might be developed that deal with the most likely source of workplace abuse. As discussed in LeBlanc and Kelloway (2002), the California Occupational Safety and Health Administration (Cal/OSHA; 1995) categorized workplace abuse as coming from three primary sources: criminals, clients, and coworkers. This framework might be appropriate for developing interventions for people who are the likely victims of particular types of workplace abuse. For example, employees in many service occupations often bear the brunt of abuse at the hands of customers or clients of an organization. Allowing employees to exercise some coping strategies to deal with harassing customers may help to diminish negative outcomes for employees who are targeted with abuse. For example, empowering employees to cease communication with abusive customers may not adhere to a "the-customer-is-always-right" philosophy, but it does provides a tool for coping with workplace abuse on the spot and may deflect some of the negative outcomes. In high-risk occupations, organizations might also provide employees with information about workplace abuse. In a form of bibliotherapy, such information would assist employees in normalizing their experiences and equip them with strategies for dealing with workplace abuse (Lewis et al., 2002). These organizational interventions may have the added benefit of signaling organizational support, an important moderator of the abuse-outcomes relationships (Leather, Lawrence, Beale, Cox, & Dickson, 1998; Schat & Kelloway, 2005).

The importance of arresting workplace abuses immediately cannot be underestimated. As noted by Andersson and Pearson (1999) in their theoretical exploration of the incivility spiral, aggression begets aggression. Thus, even seemingly minor abuses should be handled so that they do not escalate into additional, potentially more extreme abuses. Peer support and a zero-tolerance normative climate are likely to be helpful in this regard. Developing a climate that is intolerant of such abuse and providing employees with tools and outlets for handling workplace abuses may help ensure that workplace aggression does not deteriorate into more extreme workplace violence and may ultimately reduce multiple forms of workplace abuse.

References

American Psychiatric Association. (2000). *Diagnostic and statistical manual of mental disorders* (4th ed., text revision). Washington, DC: Author.

Andersson, L. M., & Pearson, C. M. (1999). Tit for tat? The spiraling effect of incivility in the workplace. *Academy of Management Review, 24,* 452–471.

Barling, J. (1996). The prediction, experience, and consequences of workplace violence. In E. Q. Bulatao & G. R. VandenBos (Eds.), *Violence on the job: Identifying risks and developing solutions* (pp. 29–49). Washington, DC: American Psychological Association.

Björkqvist, K., Österman, K., & Hjelt-Bäck, M. (1994). Aggression among university employees. *Aggressive Behaviors, 20,* 173–184.

Budd, J. W., Arvey, R. D., & Lawless, P. (1996). Correlates and consequences of workplace violence. *Journal of Occupational Health Psychology, 1,* 197–210.

Burns, M. O., & Seligman, M. E. P. (1991). Explanatory style, helplessness, and depression. In C. R. Snyder & D. R. Forsyth (Eds.), *Handbook of social and clinical psychology: The health perspective* (pp. 267–284). Elmsford, NY: Pergamon Press.

California Occupational Safety and Health Administration. (1995). *Guidelines for workplace security.* Sacramento, CA: Author.

DeLongis, A., Coyne, J. C., Dakof, G., Folkman, S., & Lazarus, R. S. (1982). Relationships of daily hassles, uplifts, and major life events to health status. *Health Psychology, 1,* 119–136.

DeLongis, A., Folkman, S., & Lazarus, R. S. (1988). The impact of daily stress on health and mood: Psychological and social resources as mediators. *Journal of Personality and Social Psychology, 54,* 486–495.

Fitzgerald, L. F., Drasgow, F., Hulin, C. L., Gelfand, M. J., & Magley, V. J. (1997). The antecedents and consequences of sexual harassment in organizations: A test of an integrated model. *Journal of Applied Psychology, 82,* 578–589.

Foa, E. B., & Kozak, J. J. (1986). Emotional processing of fear: Exposure to corrective information. *Psychological Bulletin, 99,* 20–35.

Foa, E. B., & Rothbaum, B. O. (1998). *Treating the trauma of rape: Cognitive-behavioral therapy for PTSD.* New York: Guilford Press.

Glomb, T. M. (2002). Workplace anger and aggression: Informing conceptual models with data from specific encounters. *Journal of Occupational Health Psychology, 7,* 20–36.

Glomb, T. M., & Liao, H. (2003). Interpersonal aggression in work groups: Social influence, reciprocal, and individual effects. *Academy of Management Journal, 46,* 486–496.

Glomb, T. M., Richman, W. L., Hulin, C. L., Drasgow, F., Schneider, K. T., & Fitzgerald, L. F. (1997). Ambient sexual harassment: An integrated model of antecedents and consequences. *Organizational Behavior and Human Decision Processes, 71,* 309–328.

Gottlieb, B. H. (1997). Conceptual and measurement issues in the study of coping with chronic stress. In B. H. Gottlieb (Ed.), *Coping with chronic stress* (pp. 3–42). New York: Plenum.

Green, B. L. (1990). Defining trauma: Terminology and generic stressor dimensions. *Journal of Applied Social Psychology, 20,* 1632–1642.

Hepburn, C. G., Loughlin, C. A., & Barling, J. (1997). Coping with chronic work stress. In B. H. Gottlieb (Ed.), *Coping with chronic stress* (pp. 343–366). New York: Plenum.

Herman, J. (1992). *Trauma and recovery: The aftermath of violence from domestic abuse to political terror.* New York: Basic Books.

Hoel, H., Rayner, C., & Cooper, C. L. (1999). Workplace bullying. In C. L. Cooper & I. T. Robertson (Eds.), *International review of industrial and organizational psychology* (Vol. 14, pp. 195–230). New York: John Wiley.

Horowitz, M. J. (1986). *Stress response syndromes.* New York: Jason Aronson.

Jandorf, L., Deblinger, E., Neale, J. M., & Stone, A. A. (1986). Daily versus major life events as predictors of symptom frequency: A replication study. *Journal of General Psychology, 113,* 205–218.

Janoff-Bulman, R. (1995). Victims of violence. In G. S. Everly & J. M. Lating (Eds.), *Psychotraumatology: Key papers and core concepts in post-traumatic stress* (pp. 73–86). New York: Plenum.

Janoff-Bulman, R., & Frieze, I. H. (1983). A theoretical perspective for understanding reactions to victimization. *Journal of Social Issues, 39,* 1–17.

Keane, T. M., Zimmerling, R. T., & Caddell, J. M. (1985). A behavioral formulation of posttraumatic stress disorder in Vietnam veterans. *Behavior Therapist, 8,* 9–12.

Keashley, L., & Jagatic, K. (2003). By any other name: American perspectives on workplace bullying. In S. Einarsen, H. Hoel, D. Zapf, & C. Cooper (Eds.), *Bullying and emotional abuse in the workplace: International research and practice perspectives* (pp. 31–61). London: Taylor Francis.

Kessler, R., Sonnega, A., Bromet, E., Hughes, M., & Nelson, C. (1995). Posttraumatic stress disorder in the national comorbidity survey. *Archives of General Psychiatry, 52,* 1048–1060.

Kilpatrick, D. G., Veronen, L. J., & Best, C. L. (1985). Factors predicting psychological distress among rape victims. In C. R. Figley (Ed.), *Trauma and its wake* (pp. 113–141). New York: Brunner/Mazel.

Lazarus, R. S. (1999). *Stress and emotion: A new synthesis.* New York: Springer.

Lazarus, R. S., & Folkman, S. (1984). *Stress, appraisal, and coping.* New York: Springer.

Leather, P., Lawrence, C., Beale, D., Cox, T., & Dickson, R. (1998). Exposure to occupational violence and the buffering effects of intra-organizational support. *Work & Stress, 12*(2), 161–178.

LeBlanc, M., & Kelloway, E. K. (2002). Predictors and outcomes of workplace violence and aggression. *Journal of Applied Psychology, 87,* 444–453.

Lewis, J., Coursol, D., & Herting Wall, K. (2002). Addressing issues of workplace harassment: Counseling the targets. *Journal of Employment Counseling, 39,* 109–116.

Leymann, H. (1990). Mobbing and psychological terror at workplaces. *Violence and Victims, 5,* 119–126.

McGonagle, K. A., & Kessler, R. C. (1990). Chronic stress, acute stress, and depressive symptoms. *American Journal of Community Psychology, 18,* 681–706.

McGrath, J. E. (1981). Introduction. *American Behavioral Scientist, 25,* 127–130.

Mighty, E. J. (1997). Conceptualizing family violence as a workplace issue: A framework for research and practice. *Employee Responsibilities & Rights Journal, 10*(4), 249–262.

Miner-Rubino, K., & Cortina, L. M. (2004). Working in a context of hostility toward women: Implications for employees' well-being. *Journal of Occupational Health Psychology, 9,* 107–122.

Mowrer, O. H. (1960). *Learning theory and behavior.* New York: John Wiley.

Penk, W., Drebing, C., & Schutt, R. (2002). PTSD in the workplace. In J. C. Thomas & M. Hersen (Eds.), *Handbook of mental health in the workplace* (pp. 215–248). Thousand Oaks, CA: Sage.

Peterson, C., & Seligman, M. E. P. (1983). Learned helplessness and victimization. *Journal of Social Issues, 2,* 103–116.

Resnick, H. S., Kilpatrick, D. G., Dansky, B. S., Saunders, B. E., & Best, C. L. (1993). Prevalence of civilian trauma and posttraumatic stress disorder in a representative national sample of women. *Journal of Counseling and Clinical Psychology, 61,* 984–991.

Rogers, K., & Kelloway, E. K. (1997). Violence at work: Personal and organizational outcomes. *Journal of Occupational Health Psychology, 2,* 63–71.

Rothman, E. F., & Perry, M. J. (2004). Intimate partner abuse perpetrated by employees. *Journal of Occupational Health Psychology, 9,* 238–246.

Schat, A., & Kelloway, E. K. (2000). Effects of perceived control on the outcomes of workplace aggression and violence. *Journal of Occupational Health Psychology, 5,* 386–402.

Schat, A., & Kelloway, E. K. (2003). Reducing the adverse consequences of workplace aggression and violence: The buffering effects of organizational support. *Journal of Occupational Health Psychology, 8,* 110–122.

Schneider, K. T. (1996, August). *Bystander stress: The effect of organizational tolerance of sexual harassment on victims' coworkers.* Paper presented at the meeting of the American Psychological Association, Toronto.

Schneider, K. T., Swan, S., & Fitzgerald, L. F. (1997). Job related and psychological effects of sexual harassment in the workplace: Empirical evidence from two organizations. *Journal of Applied Psychology, 82,* 401–415.

Swanberg, J. E., & Logan, T. K. (2005). Domestic violence and employment: A qualitative study. *Journal of Occupational Health Psychology, 10,* 3–17.

Tepper, B. J. (2000). Consequences of abusive supervision. *Academy of Management Journal, 43,* 178–190.

Tolin, D. F., & Foa, E. B. (2003). Gender and PTSD: A cognitive model. In R. Kimerling, P. Ouimette, & J. Wolfe (Eds.), *Gender and PTSD* (pp. 76–97). New York: Guilford Press.

Wheaton, B. (1994). Sampling the stress universe. In W. R. Avison & I. H. Gottlieb (Eds.), *Stress and mental health* (pp. 77–114). New York: Plenum.

Wheaton, B. (1997). The nature of chronic stress. In B. H. Gottlieb (Ed.), *Coping with chronic stress* (pp. 43–74). New York: Plenum.

Zapf, D., & Einarsen, S. (Eds.). (2001). Bullying in the workplace: Recent trends in research and practice [Special issue]. *European Journal of Work and Organizational Psychology, 10*(4).

23

Critical Incident Stress Debriefing and Workplace Violence

Joseph J. Hurrell Jr.

As discussed in various chapters in this handbook, workplace violence, regardless of its type, can have both organizational and individual consequences. Although an emerging body of evidence suggests that various types of preventative efforts may help reduce the frequency of aggressive acts, relatively little is currently known regarding how best to deal with the individual psychological consequences of workers who are directly or indirectly exposed to them. Many people experience transient stress-related symptoms in the aftermath of traumatic events; however, for some people, the trauma inherent in workplace violence can have debilitating psychological consequences. The most common of these debilitating consequences are thought to be posttraumatic stress disorder (PTSD) and acute stress disorder (ASD).

PTSD was first recognized as a psychiatric disorder in the third edition of the *Diagnostic and Statistical Manual of Mental Disorders* of the American Psychiatric Association (APA; 1980). The more recent fourth edition of this manual (*DSM-IV*; APA, 1994) defines PTSD as a syndrome comprising three clusters of symptoms or signs: (a) repeated reexperience of the trauma (e.g., intrusive recollections of the events, nightmares); (b) emotional numbing (e.g., difficulty in expressing positive affect) and avoidance of activities reminiscent of the trauma; and (c) heightened arousal (e.g., exaggerated startle reflex and insomnia). A diagnosis of PTSD requires that the symptoms be present at least 1 month after trauma exposure and cause impairment or clinically significant distress. Significantly, *DSM-IV* recognizes that the subjective perception of threat qualifies as traumatic stressor, and individuals need not be direct victims to be considered trauma exposed. Recognized traumatic events include but are not limited to military combat, violent personal assault (sexual assault, physical attack, robbery, mugging), being kidnapped, being taken hostage, terrorist attack, torture, incarceration as a prisoner of war or in a concentration camp, natural or man-made disasters, severe automobile accidents, or being diagnosed with a life-threatening illness (*DSM-IV*; APA, 1994).

The traumatic event itself is generally believed to have overriding causal significance in producing PTSD, and personal vulnerability factors have generally been minimized (McNally, Bryant, & Ehlers, 2003); however, epidemiologic data seem to suggest that individual factors may play a role. For example, Breslau, Davis, Andreski, and Peterson (1991) found that among adults living in metropolitan Detroit, 89.6% reported exposure to *DSM*-defined traumatic stressors, yet only 20.4% of the women and 6.2% of the men developed PTSD. It is noteworthy that intentional acts of violence seem to be especially likely to produce PTSD (Yehuda, 2002). For example, in the Breslau et al. (1991) study, only 11.6% of the respondents who had been exposed to sudden injury developed PTSD, but 22.6% of those who experienced physical assault and 80% of female rape victims developed the disorder.

ASD, first officially recognized in *DSM-IV*, results from the same type of traumatic stressors thought to be capable of producing PTSD and is characterized by many of the same symptoms. According to *DSM-IV*, ASD is diagnosed if an individual manifests at least three dissociative symptoms, reexperiencing of the traumatic events, marked avoidance, and marked hyperarousal. ASD differs from PTSD in two ways. First, the problem must last at least 2 days and no more than 4 weeks (after which time a diagnosis of PTSD could be made). Second, the ASD criteria emphasize dissociative reactions. That is, the diagnosis requires at least three of the following symptoms: a sense of emotional numbing or detachment, reduced awareness of one's surroundings, derealization, depersonalization, and amnesia for aspects of the traumatic event. The diagnosis of PTSD, by contrast, does not require individuals to display dissociative symptoms. The rates of ASD, like those of PTSD, seem to be greater for those who have been exposed to human-caused trauma, as opposed to other traumatic events, with rates following mass shootings and violent assaults having been found to be 33% and 19% respectively (Bryant, 2000). Although it is widely believed that a large percentage of individuals with ASD will ultimately develop PTSD, the diagnosis of ASD does not appear to be a reliable or sensitive predictor of a subsequent PTSD diagnosis (McNally et al., 2003).

Though lacking empirical support, the belief is extremely common that exposure to traumatic events, if not contravened through focused immediate intervention, will lead to ASD and/or PTSD and other psychiatric maladies (Gist & Woodall, 2000). In this regard, psychological debriefing, which aims to reduce the risk for psychopathological sequelae of traumatic experiences, has become a widely adopted psychological intervention technique (Braverman, 1991). Psychological debriefing had its origins in great world wars of this century when after major battles commanders would meet with their troops to boost morale by sharing stories about what happened during the engagement (Everly & Mitchell, 1995; Litz, Gray, Bryant, & Alder, 2002). Such debriefings provided an opportunity for individuals to talk about the experience of combat and to receive psychological support and were thought to have made the participants better prepared to return to combat (Everly & Mitchell, 1995). Noting these historical roots and drawing on his experiences with firefighting and emergency medical services workers, Mitchell (1983) developed a particular type of psychological debriefing known as Critical Incident Stress Debriefing (CISD). CISD is a semistructured, small-group, seven-phase intervention process involving both psychological and educational elements (Mitchell & Everly, 1993). It was designed to mitigate the adverse psychological consequences of traumatic events by attenuating the intensity of the acute stress symptoms. A typical debriefing takes place within approximately 3 to 5 days after the critical incident and consists of one group meeting that lasts approximately 2 to 3 hours, although shorter or longer meetings may be determined by the circumstances (Everly & Mitchell, 1995). In this structured group meeting, participants are given the opportunity to discuss their thoughts and emotions about the distressing event in a controlled and highly structured manner. The debriefing process is designed to move in a nonthreatening manner from the usual cognitively oriented processing of human experience through a more emotional processing of the same material (Everly & Mitchell, 1995). Mitchell (1983) believed that CISD would alleviate acute stress responses (such as those associated with ASD) and eliminate or inhibit delayed stress responses (such as those associated with PTSD). CISD is thought to be particularly useful for the prevention of posttraumatic stress and PTSD among occupational groups that are routinely exposed to violence such as firefighters, law enforcement officers, emergency medical workers, and disaster response personnel (Everly & Mitchell, 1995; Mitchell, 1983, 1988a, 1988b).

Since its inception, CISD has been widely adopted by the military, law enforcement agencies, and fire departments and appears to be the most widely used group intervention technique in the world for the prevention of work-related PTSD among high-risk emergency response personnel (Everly, Flannery, & Mitchell, 2000; Everly & Mitchell, 1995). Approximately 40,000 people are trained in the use of Mitchell's method each year (McNally et al., 2003), and its use and acceptance has become so pervasive that some believe that CISD ought to be routinely conducted after all traumatic events (Kenardy & Carr, 2000). Others (e.g., Hokanson & Wirth, 2000) have recommended that it be made mandatory or automatic. CISD has also been commonly utilized by employee assistance programs (EAPs) in a wide range of workplace settings in response to workplace violence (Plaggemars, 2000). Indeed, the EAP at one of the world's largest employers, the United States Postal Service, provides CISD in response to traumatic violence (Kurutz, Johnson, & Sugden, 1996). CISD is also an integral part of the increasingly recognized and adopted assaulted staff action program (ASAP; Flannery, Fulton, Tausch, & DeLoffi, 1991; Flannery, Penk, Hanson, & Flannery, 1996), specifically developed for addressing the psychological sequelae of patient assaults on staff in mental health care settings.

Despite its widespread use, until very recently little empirical data were available to gauge its efficacy; however, because of concerns for a potential upsurge in the incidence of PTSD following the terrorist attack on the World Trade Center and the widespread use of CISD following this disaster, considerable attention has been focused on whether CISD or other psychological secondary prevention efforts are efficacious.

The Efficacy of CISD

Although there is considerable evidence of satisfaction among psychological debriefing (PD), and specifically CISD recipients (Arendt & Elklit, 2001; Carlier, Lamberts, Van Uchelen, & Gersons, 1998), clearly interventions should be evaluated with more stringent criteria (Bass, 1983). In response to concerns regarding the ability of PD, and CISD in particular, to prevent subsequent psychopathology (see, for example, Raphael, Meldrum, & McFarlane, 1995), beginning in the mid-1990s, investigators began to take a much more critical look at the efficacy of PD and CISD. Consistent findings, however, do not emerge when using more objective outcome criteria. Wessley, Rose, and Bisson (1998), for example, reviewed eight randomized trials and found no evidence that debriefing had any impact on psychological morbidity. Likewise, in a comprehensive review of 67 studies (including randomized controlled studies) of the effects of various PD methods, Arendt and Elklit (2001) concluded that although PD may have some benefits as a screening procedure, it does not *prevent* psychiatric disorders or mitigate the effects of traumatic stress. More specifically, a recent meta-analysis of single-session debriefing following psychological trauma found that non-CISD interventions and no interventions at all improved PTSD symptoms more than CISD (van Emmerik, Kamphuis, Hulsbosch, & Emmelkamp, 2002). Finally, a recent review by McNally and colleagues (2003) concludes that because of their many serious methodological limitations—including small sample sizes, no control groups, nonrandom treatment group assignment, and the use of nonstandardized CISD procedures—studies of CISD fail to provide a convincing case for the efficacy of debriefing to mitigate distress and prevent future psychopathology.

Despite such evidence, CISD proponents (e.g., Deahl, Srinivasan, Jones, Neblett, & Jolly, 2001) have suggested that it is premature to conclude that debriefing is ineffective. They argue that many negative studies have relied principally on outcome measures of PTSD and fail to incorporate a broader range of outcomes, such as measures of comorbid psychopathology and behavioral and social dysfunction. In a study of British soldiers returning from Bosina, for example, Deahl, Srinivasan, Jones, Neblett, and Jolly (2000) found that CISD reduced alcohol misuse. This study, however, was not without methodological limitations, including the administration of

CISD to study participants on returning from their missions, as apposed to immediately following a specific traumatic event. Although it is possible that CISD may have beneficial effects on outcomes other than PTSD—as McNally et al. (2003) have noted—if CISD is a form of secondary prevention, it should be expected to prevent the development of PTSD.

In response to criticism of CISD, Everly and Mitchell (2000) have acknowledged that considerable confusion has arisen because of ambiguity about the term *CISD*. According to Everly and Mitchell, the term was used by Mitchell at various times to denote (a) the overarching framework for Mitchell's crisis intervention system; (b) a specific six-phase, small-group discussion process (*formal* CISD); and (c) an optional follow-up intervention (*follow-up* CISD). As a result, according to these authors, the literature is "plagued" with the erroneous notion that CISD group discussion was intended to be a "stand-alone" (meaning administered in a single session) intervention; however, as many observers (e.g., Rose, Berwin, Andrews, & Kirk, 1999) have noted, CISD is almost always administered in a single session, as opposed to being part of a larger intervention program. Moreover, Mitchell's original work (Mitchell, 1983) suggests that a single session will often reduce or eliminate delayed stress responses.

To reduce some of the confusion and rectify the situation, Everly and Mitchell (2000) have chosen the term *Critical Incident Stress Management* (CISM) "to denote the overarching multi-component approach to crisis intervention, thus replacing the term CISD as it was originally used in that context" (p. 213). The term *CISM* is now used to characterize a group crisis intervention process with seven core components. One of the core components is the seven-phase CISD. Other components include pre-incident preparation; defusing (small-group discussion for triage and symptom mitigation administered within 12 hours of the incident); family CISM; and follow-up or referral. In a recent clarification, Mitchell (2004) has stated that CISD should never be provided outside of "an integrated package of interventions within the Critical Incident Stress Management (CISM) program" (p. 4). Moreover, according to Mitchell (2004), CISM does not focus on primary victims of violence, but rather the primary focus is "to *support staff members of organizations* or members of communities which have experienced a traumatic event" (p. 5).

Everly and Mitchell (2000) and Everly, Flannery, and Eyler (2002) have attempted to provide support for the effectiveness of the integrated CISM model through the use of both qualitative and quantitative (meta-analysis) information; however, as the integrated CISM model did not appear until the mid-1990s, much of the "support" cited comes from studies that utilized CISD but did not explicitly follow the CISM model. Moreover, many of the quantitative studies cited by Everly et al. (2002) in a statistical analysis of the literature involve outcomes other than the emergence of PTSD and thus limit the validity of the analysis (Devilly & Cotton, 2003).

Although Mitchell (2004) has offered a defense of CISM that cites the success of more comprehensive interventions generally built around CISD, no comprehensive studies could be found that critically evaluate the specific merits of CISM relative to other interventions and CISD offered alone; however, a study of victims of armed robberies (Richards, 1999, 2001) is often cited (e.g., Everly & Mitchell, 2000; Mitchell, 2002, 2004) as being supportive of the CISM model. This prospective trial compared the efficacy of CISD (as a stand-alone group intervention) and integrated CISM delivered to two groups of British bank employees who had witnessed robberies. The banks involved had both been offering single-session CISDs for their employees following robberies and later switched to the more comprehensive CISM program. Richards (1999, 2001) compared the experiences of employees getting only CISD with those who received CISM. Morbidity was assessed using two measures of stress and a general health index at 3 days, 1 month, and 3 to 12 months postrobbery. Morbidity in both groups was equivalent at 3 days and 1 month postrobbery; however, the CISM group had significantly less morbidity at the 3 to 12 month follow-up. Unfortunately, the methodological limitations inherent in the study prevent firm conclusions. For example, individuals were not randomly assigned to the treatment groups, there was no control group, and the CISM treatment followed the CISD treatment.

Is CISD Harmful?

One of the premises of underlying PD is that repressing thoughts and feelings about the trauma will impede recovery, and conversely, expressing them will hasten it. In support of this premise, various authors (e.g., Ehlers, Mayou, & Bryant, 1998) have noted that attempts to avoid thinking about traumatic events and avoiding reminders of the events themselves are associated with PTSD symptoms; however, professionals dealing with the aftermath of violence may have wrongly concluded that the unwillingness of traumatized individuals to discuss their trauma is a form of avoidance that will impede recovery (McNally et al., 2003). Indeed, concern has been raised that PD may actually cause harm by limiting the distancing that is needed in the aftermath of traumatic events (Gist & Woodall, 2000). Also, it seems possible that participation (particularly mandatory participation) in PD could exacerbate any feelings of loss of control, thereby raising the subjective experience of stress and further impeding the recovery process. Likewise, individual group members, even if relatively unaffected, could be vicariously traumatized by listening to group members recount their experiences with the traumatic event.

Some limited evidence of potentially harmful effects of PD (including CISD) can indeed be found. For example, two studies of debriefing to prevent postpartum maternal depression (Kenardy, 2001; Small, Lumley, Donohue, Potter, & Waldenstroem, 2001) found worsening psychological health in those given the intervention. Likewise, Hobbs, Mayou, Harrison, and Worlock (1996) randomly assigned 106 victims of road traffic accidents to either a single PD session or an assessment-only control group. The treatment group received a single, 1-hour, individual debriefing (not a group debriefing) at 24 to 48 hours after the accident. At baseline, the groups showed no difference in symptom reporting. At a 4-month assessment, neither group showed a decrease in symptoms, but the treatment group was found to have significantly poorer scores on two symptom measures. In a 3-year follow-up of these individuals (Mayou, Ehlers, & Hobbs, 2000), those who had been debriefed experienced significantly more general psychiatric symptoms, travel anxiety, pain, physical problems, problems in functioning, and financial problems. Likewise, in a randomized controlled study, acute burn trauma victims who received PD were significantly more likely to show high levels of depression and anxiety and higher PTSD rates at a 13-month follow-up (Bisson, Jenkins, Alexander, & Bannister, 1997). Last, in a study involving CISD among police officers who responded to a plane crash and had received CISD, Carlier et al. (1998) reported that those who had undergone debriefing exhibited significantly more disaster-related hyperarousal symptoms 18 months after the disaster. Clearly, these studies challenge the maxim that interventions do no harm, and there is a tremendous need for well-controlled outcome studies.

In defense of CISM, Mitchell (2004) correctly notes that debriefings used in the studies purporting to show that PD may be harmful involved *individual debriefing* and not group debriefing called for in CISM. He argues that "there has never been a study that indicates that harm has been done by any CISM service if the following two conditions are met: personnel have been properly trained in CISM; providers are adhering to well published and internationally accepted standards of CISM practice" (p. 43). He maintains that CISM teams should never engage in a stand-alone intervention and need to commit themselves to involvement in a comprehensive, systematic, multi-component program of crisis intervention. In Mitchell's view, more research is clearly indicated, but the research needs to address what interventions should be implemented, when they should be implemented, and who should implement them.

What Should and Shouldn't Be Done?

It seems quite obvious from the literature reviewed above that little evidence exists to support the efficacy of individual and/or stand-alone CISD interventions for preventing the psychological sequelae of exposure to traumatic workplace violence. Despite this accumulation of evidence, individual and stand-alone CISD efforts continue to be offered on a seemingly routine and unending basis. This may occur because of an employer's genuine (though ill-informed) desire to help and provide support for employees in the wake of violent workplace events. Others (e.g., Devilly & Cotton, 2003) have suggested a less altruistic motive involving the desire to avoid litigation for not providing a safe and healthy work environment. Regardless of the nature of the motivation, given the evidence of the potential for harm, there appears to be no justification for providing individual and/or stand-alone CISD, either to direct victims of workplace violence or to those who have indirectly experienced the violent events. Whether or not CISM (involving CISD as a part of a more comprehensive program) is an effective intervention for preventing long-term negative psychological consequences among those who have been exposed to workplace violence is an open research question. To date, however, there is no truly convincing empirical evidence of its efficacy for the prevention of PTSD.

Given these circumstances, what *should* be done? Social support in the workplace appears to be highly important for employee health and well-being. A tremendous amount of research has examined the nature and effects of four different types of social support (emotional, informational, instrumental, and appraisal) from both coworkers and supervisors over the past three decades (Cobb, 1976; Cohen & Wills, 1985; House, Landis, & Umberson, 1988). The evidence is overwhelming that social support has beneficial effects, exerting main effects on psychological and physical health and buffering the negative effects of work stress on strain (e.g., Dormann & Zapf, 1999; Frese, 1999).

There are strong indications that social support may exert equally important effects following violent and traumatic events. First, a meta-analysis by Berwin, Andrews, and Valentine (2000) found that perceived absence of social support was linked to the risk of future PTSD. Second, Chisholm, Kasl, and Mueller (1986) studied employees who were assigned to the Three Mile Island power plant on March 28, 1979, the date of a serious accident. Their results showed that emotional social support served as a main effect and as a buffer on several health-related outcomes during the crisis. Third, Schat and Kelloway (2003) found that instrumental and informational support moderated the relationship between workplace aggression and violence and emotional well-being. Their findings on workplace aggression and violence may be especially salient in understanding the role of social support in coping with the violent events.

Informational support in the immediate aftermath of traumatic violence seems to be especially important. For employees in crisis, factual information is essential (particularly as it pertains to their safety) and helps provide both comfort and a sense of control (Braverman, 1991). Employers should be cognizant of potential constraints (including legal and privacy constraints) on specific information that is conveyed, but generally speaking, information on what has happened, who has been hurt, how to access help, and what is being done and by whom can be enormously helpful. There should be a consistent, coordinated process for conveying this information, and it should be conveyed in ways that are easily accessible by employees (e.g., e-mail, group meetings, hard-copy distributions).

The role of instrumental support immediately after violent events for short- and long-term employee well-being has received little research attention and needs to be investigated explicitly. Indeed, Raphael, Wilson, Meldrum, and McFarlane (1996) have suggested that practical help is so important that it may ultimately be viewed by those affected as more helpful than the specific psychological care offered. The types of instrumental support that may be needed clearly vary depending on the nature and circumstances of the violent events. Such support could include things such as financial assistance, time away from work, medical assistance, food, housing, child care, transportation, and communications assistance. Providing access to an EAP and/or qualified professional mental health providers to those employees who request it clearly falls within the domain of potentially beneficial instrumental support.

As noted in the introduction, most people who are exposed to traumatic stressors will experience transient symptoms that will resolve within a relatively short time. An important function of mental health, EAP, and human resource professionals in the immediate aftermath of traumatic violence is to try to determine who may be particularly affected by the events and thus may be at greater risk for developing a chronic disorder. Individuals may be disproportionately affected because of their connection to the event, their closeness to the victim(s), or individual risk factors that include recent losses or tragedies and health problems (Braverman, 1991). Monitoring at-risk individuals in the days and weeks immediately following the trauma is especially important. Monitoring provides the opportunity to screen for symptoms of ASD, PTSD, and depression, which may be particularly predictive of PTSD. Indeed PTSD symptom severity (particularly 1–2 weeks posttrauma) is thought to be a good predictor of the risk of chronic PTSD (McNally et al., 2003).

Even Mitchell (2004) acknowledges that neither CISD nor CISM is a substitute for psychotherapy, and employee screening provides an opportunity to identify individuals who are not likely to recover on their own and offer them access to treatment. Apart from any secondary prevention efforts, a variety of psychological treatments (tertiary prevention) are available for those experiencing ASD and PTSD symptoms. These include cognitive therapy, anxiety management, and exposure therapy (Foa, Keane, & Friedman, 2000). Unfortunately, however, there is yet little consensus regarding the relative superiority of any of these treatments. Results of randomized clinical trials demonstrate that certain medications (selective serotonin reuptake inhibitors, tricyclic antidepressants, and monoamine oxidase inhibitors) mitigate PTSD symptoms and are useful in improving psychological functioning. At the same time, results from randomized clinical trials also indicate that extreme caution should be used before using other medications as a treatment for PTSD (e.g., benzodiazepines, alprazolam, clonazepam) (Foa et al., 1999; Yehuda, 2002). Irrespective of their effectiveness, however, like other tertiary prevention strategies, psychological and pharmacological treatments are only offered once PTSD has developed.

Primary Prevention?

A number of the chapters in this handbook suggest that there are opportunities for preventing violence in the workplace. If effective, such efforts obviously function as primary prevention for PTSD and other potential adverse psychological consequences; however, beyond specific efforts aimed at preventing workplace violence, other (though perhaps less direct) approaches to the primary prevention of PTSD are possible. For example, Corneil, Beaton, Murphy, Johnson, and Pike (1999), in a study of more than 800 firefighters in Canada and the United States, found that frequency of exposure to traumatic events does not necessarily predict PTSD and that the exposure outcome relationship may be mediated by both social support and chronic stress levels. Thus, a comprehensive workplace approach to the prevention of PTSD could involve ongoing efforts to bolster social support and identify and eliminate chronic job and organizational stressors.

A number of systematic approaches on how to cope with violence in the workplace are illustrative of the kinds of primary and secondary intervention discussed above. For example, recognizing that corporate downsizing often results in workplace violence, Root and Ziska (1996) developed a systematic primary workplace violence prevention approach. This approach, involving a variety of organizational resources (e.g., human resources, EAPs, health services), begins well in advance of the actual downsizing and involves providing a variety of types of social support to potentially affected employees. Although CISD is provided to employees who request it, unlike the CISM approach, CISD does not serve as a centerpiece for the model. Braverman (1991) has developed a secondary prevention approach aimed at limiting both individual and organizational dysfunction following the occurrence of workplace violence. The intervention (generally starting within 12 hours of the violence) relies on a collaborative effort between trauma specialists (usually from outside the company), management, and other key company personnel. The process involves first establishing communication within the organization, then determining the circle of impact and convening affected groups to provide information and education. Crisis counseling for individual employees is offered, and primary victims and witnesses are specifically contacted to assure that the counseling services are offered. The model also includes a follow-up phase that allows for recommendations on how to have better primary and secondary prevention for future violence. It is noteworthy that in both of these models, planning and crisis readiness are stressed. Both rely strongly on developing communications within the organization and providing extensive social support.

References

American Psychiatric Association. (1980). *Diagnostic and statistical manual of mental disorders* (3rd ed.). Washington, DC: Author.

American Psychiatric Association. (1994). *Diagnostic and statistical manual of mental disorders* (4th ed.). Washington, DC: Author.

Arendt, M., & Elklit, A. (2001). Effectiveness of psychological debriefing. *Acta Psychiatry Scandanavia, 104,* 423–437.

Bass, B. M. (1983). Issues involved in relations between methodological rigor and reported outcomes in evaluations of organizational development. *Journal of Applied Psychology, 68*, 197–199.

Berwin, C. R., Andrews, B., & Valentine, J. D. (2000). Meta-analysis of risk factors for posttraumatic stress disorder in trauma-exposed adults. *Journal of Consulting and Clinical Psychology, 68*, 748–766.

Bisson, J. I., Jenkins, P. L., Alexander, J., & Bannister, C. (1997). Randomized controlled trial of psychological debriefing for victims of acute burn trauma. *British Journal of Psychiatry, 171*, 78–81.

Braverman, M. (1991). Post trauma crisis intervention in the workplace. In J. C. Quick, L. R. Murphy, & J. J. Hurrell Jr. (Eds.), *Stress and well-being at work: Assessments and interventions for occupational mental health* (pp. 299–316). Washington, DC: American Psychological Association.

Breslau, N., Davis, G. C., Andreski, P., & Peterson, E. (1991). Traumatic events and posttraumatic stress disorder in an urban population of young adults. *Archives of General Psychiatry, 48*, 216–222.

Bryant, R. A. (2000). Cognitive behavior therapy of violence-related post traumatic stress disorder. *Aggression and Violent Behavior, 5*, 79–97.

Carlier, I. V., Lamberts, R. D., Van Uchelen, A. J., & Gersons, B. P. (1998). Disaster-related post-traumatic stress in police officers: A field study of the impact of debriefing. *Stress Medicine, 14*, 143–148.

Chisholm, R. F., Kasl, S. V., & Mueller, L. (1986). The effects of social support on nuclear worker responses to the Three Mile Island incident. *Journal of Occupational Behaviour, 7*, 179–193.

Cobb, S. (1976). Social support as a mediator of life stress. *Psychosomatic Medicine, 38*, 300–314.

Cohen, S., & Wills, T. A. (1985). Stress, social support and the buffering hypothesis. *Psychological Bulletin, 98*, 310–357.

Corneil, W., Beaton, R., Murphy, S., Johnson, C., & Pike, K. (1999). Exposure to traumatic incidents and prevalence of posttraumatic stress symptomology in urban fire fighters in two countries. *Journal of Occupational Health Psychology, 4*, 131–141.

Deahl, M. P., Srinivasan, M., Jones, N., Neblett, C., & Jolly, A. (2000). Preventing psychological trauma in soldiers: The role of operational stress training and psychological debriefing. *British Journal of Medical Psychology, 73*, 77–85.

Deahl, M. P., Srinivasan, M., Jones, N., Neblett, C., & Jolly, A. (2001). Evaluating psychological debriefing: Are we measuring the right outcomes? *Journal of Traumatic Stress, 14*, 527–529.

Devilly, G. T., & Cotton, P. (2003). Psychological debriefing and the workplace: Defining a concept, controversies and guidelines, for intervention. *Australian Psychologist, 38*, 144–150.

Dormann, C., & Zapf, D. (1999). Social support, stressors at work and depressive symptoms: Testing for main and moderating effects with structural equations in a three-wave longitudinal study. *Journal of Applied Psychology, 84*, 874–884.

Ehlers, A., Mayou, R. A., & Bryant, B. (1998). Psychological predictors of chronic posttraumatic stress disorder after motor vehicle accidents. *Journal of Abnormal Psychology, 107*, 508–518.

Everly, G. S., Jr., Flannery, R. B., & Eyler, E. A. (2002). Critical incident stress management (CISM): A statistical review of the literature. *Psychiatric Quarterly, 73*, 171–182.

Everly, G. S., Flannery, R. B., & Mitchell, J. T. (2000). Critical incident stress management (CISM): A review of the literature. *Aggression and Violent Behavior, 5,* 23–40.

Everly, G. S., Jr., & Mitchell, J. T. (1995). Prevention of work-related posttraumatic stress: The critical incident stress debriefing process. In L. Murphy, J. Hurrell, S. Sauter, & G. Keita (Eds.), *Job stress interventions* (pp. 173–183). Washington, DC: American Psychological Association.

Everly, G. S., Jr., & Mitchell, J. T. (2000). The debriefing "controversy" and crisis intervention: A review of lexical and substantive issues. *Journal of Emergency Mental Health, 2*(4), 211–225.

Flannery, R. B., Jr., Fulton, P., Tausch, J., & DeLoffi, A. Y. (1991). A program to help staff cope with psychological sequelae of assaults by patients. *Hospital and Community Psychiatry, 42,* 935–938.

Flannery, R. B., Jr., Penk, W. E., Hanson, M. A., & Flannery, G. J. (1996). The assaulted staff action program: Guidelines for fielding a team. In G. VandenBos & E. Q. Bulatao (Eds.), *Violence on the job: Identifying risks and developing solutions* (pp. 327–341). Washington, DC: American Psychological Association.

Foa, E. B., Davidson, J. R. T., Frances, A., Culpepper, L., Ross, R., & Ross, D. (1999). Expert consensus guidelines series: Treatment of posttraumatic stress disorder. *Journal of Clinical Psychiatry, 60*(16), 4–76.

Foa, E. B., Keane, T. M., & Friedman, M. J. (2000). *Effective treatments for PTSD: Practice guidelines from the International Society for Traumatic Stress Studies.* New York: Guilford Press.

Frese, M. (1999). Social support as a moderator of the relationship between work stressors and psychological dysfunction: A longitudinal study with objective measures. *Journal of Occupational Health Psychology, 4,* 179–192.

Gist, R., & Woodall, S. J. (2000). There are no simple solutions to complex problems. In J. Violanti & D. Patton (Eds.), *Posttraumatic stress intervention: Challenges, issues and perspectives* (pp. 81–95). Springfield, IL: Charles C Thomas.

Hobbs, M., Mayou, R., Harrison, B., & Worlock, P. (1996). A randomized controlled trial of psychological debriefing for victims of road traffic accidents. *British Medical Journal, 313,* 1438–1439.

Hokanson, M., & Wirth, M. (2000). The Critical Incident Stress Debriefing process for the Los Angeles County Fire Department: Automatic and effective. *International Journal of Emergency Mental Health, 2,* 249–257.

House, J. S., Landis, K. R., & Umberson, D. (1988). Social relationships and health. *Science, 241,* 540–545.

Kenardy, J. (2001). Posttraumatic stress prevention: How do we move forward? *Advances in Mind-Body Medicine, 17*(3), 183–186.

Kenardy, J. A., & Carr, V. J. (2000). Debriefing post disaster: Follow-up after a major earthquake. In B. Raphael & J. P. Wilson (Eds.), *Psychological debriefing: Theory, practice, and evidence* (pp. 174–181). New York: Cambridge University Press.

Kurutz, J. G., Johnson, D. L., & Sugden, B. W. (1996). The United States Postal Service employee assistance program: A multifaceted approach to workplace violence prevention. In G. VandenBos & E. Bulatao (Eds.), *Violence on the job: Identifying risks and developing solutions* (pp. 343–352). Washington, DC: American Psychological Association.

Litz, B. T., Gray, M. J., Bryant, R. A., & Alder, A. B. (2002). Early intervention for trauma: Current status and future directions. *Clinical Psychology: Science and Practice, 9,* 112–134.

Mayou, R. A., Ehlers, A., & Hobbs, M. (2000). Psychological debriefing for road accident victims: Three-year follow up of randomized control trial. *British Journal of Psychiatry, 176,* 589–593.

McNally, R. J., Bryant, R. A., & Ehlers, A. (2003). Does early psychological intervention promote recovery from posttraumatic stress? *Psychological Science in the Public Interest, 4,* 45–79.

Mitchell, J. T. (1983). When disaster strikes: The critical incident stress debriefing process. *Journal of Emergency Medical Services, 8,* 36–39.

Mitchell, J. T. (1988a). Development and functions of critical incident stress debriefing team. *Journal of Emergency Medial Services, 13,* 43–46.

Mitchell, J. T. (1988b). History, status and future of CISD. *Journal of Emergency Medical Services, 13,* 49–52.

Mitchell, J. T. (2002). *Crisis intervention and CISM: A research summary.* Retrieved August 19, 2005, from www.icisf.org/articles/cism_research_summary.pdf

Mitchell, J. T. (2004). *Crisis intervention and Critical Incident Stress Management: A defense of the field.* Retrieved August 19, 2005, from www.icisf.org/articles/Acrobat%20Documents/CISM_Defense_of_Field.pdf

Mitchell, J. T., & Everly, G. S. (1993). *Critical Incident Stress Debriefing: An operations manual for the prevention of trauma among emergency service disaster workers.* Baltimore: Chevron.

Plaggemars, D. (2000). EAPs and Critical Incident Stress Debriefing: A look ahead. *Employee Assistance Quarterly, 16,* 77–95.

Raphael, B., Meldrum, L., & McFarlane, A. (1995). Does debriefing after psychological trauma work? *British Medical Journal, 310,* 1479–1480.

Raphael, B., Wilson, J., Meldrum, L., & McFarlane, A. C. (1996). Acute preventive interventions. In B. A. van der Kolk, A. C. McFarlane, & L. Weisaeth (Eds.), *Traumatic stress: The effects of overwhelming experience on mind, body and society* (pp. 463–479). New York: Guilford Press.

Richards, D. (1999, April). *A field study of CISD vs CISM.* Paper presented to the 5th World Congress on Stress, Trauma, and Coping Resources in the Emergency Services Professions, Baltimore.

Richards, D. (2001). A field study of Critical Incident Stress Debriefing versus Critical Incident Stress Management. *Journal of Mental Health, 10,* 351–362.

Root, D. A., & Ziska, M. D. (1996). Violence prevention during corporate downsizing: The use of a people team as context for the critical incident team. In G. VandenBos & E. Bulatao (Eds.), *Violence on the job: Identifying risks and developing solutions* (pp. 353–365). Washington, DC: American Psychological Association.

Rose, S., Berwin, C. R., Andrews, B., & Kirk, M. (1999). A randomized controlled trial of individual psychological debriefing for victims of violent crime. *Psychological Medicine, 29,* 793–799.

Schat, A. C. H., & Kelloway, E. K. (2003). Reducing the adverse consequences of workplace aggression and violence: The buffering effects of organizational support. *Journal of Occupational Health Psychology, 8,* 110–122.

Small, R., Lumley, J., Donohue, L., Potter, A., & Waldenstroem, U. (2001). Randomized controlled trial of midwife led debriefing to reduce maternal depression after operative childbirth. *British Medical Journal, 321,* 1043–1047.

Van Emmerik, A. A. P., Kamphuis, J. H., Hulsbosch, A. M., & Emmelkamp, P. M. G. (2002). Single-session debriefing after psychological trauma: A meta-analysis. *Lancet, 340,* 768–771.

Wessley, S., Rose, S., & Bisson J. (1998). *A systematic review of brief psychological interventions (debriefing) for the treatment of immediate trauma-related symptoms and the prevention of post-traumatic stress disorder* (Cochrane Review, Cochrane Library, Vol. 4). Oxford, UK: Updated Software.

Yehuda, R. (2002). Current concepts: Post-traumatic stress disorder. *New England Journal of Medicine, 346*(2), 108–114.

24

Screening and Selecting Out Violent Employees

Arla L. Day
Victor M. Catano

Predicting and Screening for Workplace Aggression

Workplace violence almost always happens after a predictable sequence of events.

(Nicoletti & Spooner, 1996, p. 268)

Red flags that warn of violence do not always exist.

(Thornburg, 1993, p. 42)

There are simply no legally recognized methods of predicting which individuals are likely to engage in violence.

(Paetzold, 1998, p. 162)

Whether as a function of nature or nurture, some individuals are more predisposed to aggression than others. . . . Our point is not to suggest that these predispositions lead inexorably to aggression but rather that antecedents to aggression are associated with individuals as well as situations and environmental conditions.

(Neuman & Baron, 1997, p. 55)

Violence and aggression in the workplace are hot topics for the media. The media around the world report extreme examples of workplace violence. Although workplace homicide or assault causing bodily harm is by far the most visible type of aggression in the workplace, its occurrence is relatively rare (Neuman & Baron, 1998). Nonetheless, these rare, extreme acts of violence may be only the tip of the iceberg of workplace aggression (Folger & Baron, 1996; Neuman & Baron, 1998). Many of the less severe and more prevalent forms of aggression such as verbal abuse may go unreported (Folger & Baron, 1996; Neuman & Baron, 1998).

Increasingly, researchers have turned their attention to the problem of workplace aggression, which may affect not only the psychological and physical health of employees but also the health and functioning of the organization; there are high financial costs associated with workplace aggression (Anfuso, 1994). These costs include not only those associated with the pain, suffering, or loss of life of the victims of workplace violence but also costs to the organization in terms of lost productivity and need to deal with the fallout from the violence. This fallout may include legal liability for employees' aggressive and violent behaviors at work, as well as charges of negligence in hiring violent employees (Gatewood & Feild, 2001; Nicoletti & Spooner, 1996; Paetzold, 1998). These concerns raise the question of whether we know enough about violent and aggressive work behavior to allow us to predict in advance which employees might resort to workplace aggression.

Screening out potentially aggressive employees may be one way to reduce workplace aggression (Paetzold, 1998). As indicated by the quotes at the start of this chapter, opinions are divided as to whether individual factors play a role and whether workplace aggression and violence even can be validly *predicted*, let alone be *prevented* by screening out the potentially aggressive individual. Screening may be problematic for other reasons: Employers face the dual legal responsibilities of not only ensuring a safe work environment for employees but also respecting applicants' civil or privacy rights (Paetzold, 1998).

Our goal in this chapter is to review the relevant research on the prediction and prevention of employee aggression, focusing on the validity of methods of screening out individuals who are prone to aggressive and violent behaviors. Therefore, we first will briefly outline our definition of aggression and violence. We will then review the aggression literature and examine the predictors of aggression, as well as the various screening techniques. Finally, we will examine some of the potential methodological and legal problems with screening and provide a framework for future research in this area.

Defining Aggression and Violence

There are multiple definitions of *workplace aggression* and *violence,* as well as a multitude of related concepts (see Schat and Kelloway, Chapter 25, this volume, for an overview of these definitions). We base our definition of *workplace aggression* on previous work, which defines it as any employee behavior (in the context of work) that is intended to physically or psychologically injure or hurt another individual, who is normally another employee (Jenkins,

1996; Schat & Kelloway, Chapter 25, this volume). We focus our definition primarily on aggression of one employee toward another and to a lesser degree toward other third parties such as clients, although we recognize that much of our discussion may be relevant to this latter type of situation. We will also examine research pertaining to related constructs, such as counterproductive work behaviors or antisocial behaviors (which often subsume violence and aggression), bullying, harassment, and revenge.

Although the terms *aggression* and *violence* occasionally are used interchangeably in the organizational literature (Baron, Neuman, & Geddes, 1999), we will differentiate between these terms: *Violence* is limited to direct and physical assaults (Baron et al., 1999; Neuman & Baron, 1998), whereas *aggression* is a more general term that tends to encompass all behaviors that are meant to harm other individuals (Baron & Neuman, 1996; Neuman & Baron, 1998).

Predictors of Workplace Aggression and Violence: Person Versus Environment

Both situational factors and individual differences are antecedents of workplace aggression (Martinko, Gundlach, & Douglas, 2002). Some researchers argue that individual factors are the best predictors of counterproductive behavior such as aggression (Hogan & Hogan, 1989; Ones, Viswesvaran, & Schmidt, 1993). Others argue that the exclusive study of individual behavior is misguided without examining the context of the organizational factors leading to workplace aggression (e.g., O'Leary-Kelly, Griffin, & Glew, 1996).

Individual and organizational factors can be further separated into (a) biological antecedents (e.g., gender, drugs), (b) cognitive interpretations of events, (c) stable individual factors (e.g., personality traits), (d) the situation and environment, and (e) social issues (i.e., norms and expectations; Folger & Baron, 1996). Based on these antecedents, there are several possible routes to take to reduce workplace aggression: screening out aggressive applicants, punishing employees' aggressive behaviors, and changing organizational factors (Neuman & Baron, 1998).

If the primary antecedents of workplace aggression are individual characteristics, then strategies can be devised to screen out applicants with those characteristics, punish employees who exhibit the aggressive behaviors, train employees to control negative aggressive-prone traits, and/or train employees to prevent workplace aggression from occurring by recognizing warning signs. If aggression is more a factor of the environment and situation, then those organizational factors that lead to aggression can be modified to help minimize aggression. The effectiveness of any of these strategies will depend on the degree to which either individual characteristics or organizational factors are truly predictive of workplace aggression. Folger and Baron (1996) concluded, however, that there are multiple causes of aggression that include both factors. For example, revenge is a function of both situation and individual factors (Bies, Tripp, & Kramer, 1997); it involves a precipitating event and is followed by individual reactions (i.e., cognitions and emotions) to that event, which may include attributing others' behaviors to malicious motives (Bies et al., 1997). Similarly, perceived reasons for bullying involve both situational factors (e.g., weak leadership) and individual factors (e.g., envy; Einarsen, 1999).

Folger and Skarlicki (1998) argued that they initially developed their "popcorn" model of workplace aggression to ensure that organizational and situational influences were taken into consideration. They believed that previous research had overemphasized "a 'profile' approach to workplace aggression" in an attempt to identify the "disgruntled employee [who] might be most likely to 'explode'" (p. 75). They concluded, however, that workplace aggression was best understood by examining how the individual characteristics and situations *interact* to create aggressive behaviors. Therefore, individual factors that may predict workplace aggression should be examined not only in terms of their direct relationship with aggression but also in terms of how these individual characteristics may interact with situational factors. Any attempt to screen employees for aggressive behavior must be examined both in terms of the efficacy of using individual characteristics and also in terms of the context in which the screening will take place.

Regardless of the predictors or the criteria, there can be four potential outcomes in any selection decision. As illustrated in Figure 24.1, B and C quadrants (true positives and true negatives) are correct decisions: With respect to screening for violence, the selected applicants are deemed to be "nonviolent" and the nonselected applicants are deemed "violence-prone individuals." The problems, however, appear in quadrants A and D (false negatives and false positives). Quadrant A contains the individuals who *would have been* nonviolent employees if given a chance, but they were not hired. Quadrant D contains the individuals who *were* selected but were actually violence-prone workers. These last two incorrect outcomes have different consequences for the organization. A false negative has little organizational impact unless a nonhired applicant sues the company or makes a public issue of the use of the screening procedure. False positives are more serious because the organization must deal with the potential violence from an employee who was thought to be nonviolent.

Therefore, employers must focus on maximizing true positives and true negatives and minimizing errors based on false negatives and false positives. One of the main ways to maximize correct decisions (quadrants B and C) and minimize errors (quadrants A and D) is to ensure that the methods of selection are valid and accurately assess the criterion (in this case, violent tendencies), the more valid the measure (the elliptic *E* in Figure 24.1 represents validity), the fewer the misclassifications that will occur. Conversely, less valid measures (as illustrated by the circle *F* in Figure 24.1) will have more classifications errors.

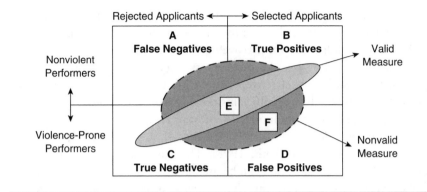

Rejected Applicants ←——→ Selected Applicants

	A False Negatives	B True Positives	Valid Measure
Nonviolent Performers			
Violence-Prone Performers	C True Negatives	D False Positives	Nonvalid Measure

Figure 24.1   Decision Chart When Screening Individuals on the Basis of Violent Tendencies

Several methods have been proposed to screen out potentially aggressive employees:

1. Background screening, including the following:
   a. Demographic and background factors (Stokes, Mumford, & Owens, 1994)
   b. Background checks of violent behaviors (Paetzold, 1998)
   c. Screening for current and past alcohol and drug use (Bennett & Lehman, 1996)

2. Psychological testing (including both clinical and nonclinical methods; Ones et al., 1993), including the use of actuarial methods and profiling (Baron, 1993)

3. Structured employment interviews (Mantell, 1994)

Background Screening

Demographics

Background data, such as specific demographics or biographical data, have been used over the years to screen employees (see, for example, Stokes et al., 1994). Biographical data, also known as biographical information blanks (BIBs), ask job applicants to provide information on their personal background and life experiences by answering a series of multiple-choice or short-answer questions (Catano, Wiesner, Hackett, & Methot, 2004). The BIB produces a total overall score and factor scores derived from specific sets of items. Either the total score or a profile based on the derived factors provides a prediction about the applicant's future work-related behavior. The BIB is based on the premise that past behavior is the best predictor of future behavior. Understanding how an applicant behaved in the past through examination of items on the BIB is thought to provide an understanding of how the individual will behave in the future (Stokes et al., 1994).

Validation studies suggest that well-developed BIBs can be very effective in predicting certain types of job behaviors (e.g., absenteeism, turnover, job proficiency, supervisory effectiveness, and job training) in a wide range of occupations, with validity coefficients ranging from .30 to .40 (Asher, 1972; Ghiselli, 1966; Hunter & Hunter, 1984; Maertz, 1999; Rothstein, Schmidt, Erwin, Owens, & Sparks, 1990; Stokes & Cooper, 1994; Vinchur, Schippmann, Switzer, & Roth, 1998). There is some evidence that BIBs developed in one organization can be used in other contexts. For example, a BIB developed to predict the rate of managerial progress in one organization successfully predicted managerial progression in 24 other organizations (Carlson, Scullen, Schmidt, Rothstein, & Erwin, 1999). Biodata forms used by the insurance industry to select insurance agents remained stable across applicant pools from the United States, the UK, and Ireland (Dalessio, Crosby, & McManus, 1996).

More recently, researchers have examined the efficacy of using biodata information to screen out applicants who may be prone to violence (Baron, 1993; Mantell, 1994). There is some evidence to suggest that factors such as a history of family violence, child abuse, and substance abuse tend to be related to criminal behavior (see Loucks & Zamble, 2000, for a review); however, there has been little work to create structured BIBs specifically for the purpose of screening out potentially aggressive employees. Furthermore, before BIBs can be developed as aggression-screening measures, we first need to establish the demographic correlates of workplace aggression. To date, research related to these correlates has been mixed.

Research on general aggression indicates that men are more likely to engage in overt, aggressive behaviors than are women (Eagly & Steffean, 1986), especially when they are unprovoked (Bettencourt & Miller, 1996), and that younger individuals tend to be more aggressive (Baron et al., 1999). Conversely, Douglas and Martinko (2001) found that there were no age or gender differences in self-reported aggression at work. Similarly, Greenberg and Barling (1999) found that age, education, and income did not account for a significant amount of variance in self-reported aggression toward coworkers, supervisors, and subordinates. Some of these differences may be a factor of the type of aggression being studied; that is, men may engage in more overt, physical displays of aggression and violence, whereas women may engage in more covert, nonphysical displays of aggression.

Nicoletti and Spooner (1996) recommended using detailed background checks (regarding past employment, military service, credit history, criminal record, workers' compensation history, driving records, and general character and reputation) to screen out individuals who are at risk for violent behaviors. Nicoletti and Spooner, however, did not specify what to do with this information and the extent to which these factors indicated a "violence-prone individual." As Nicolletti and Spooner noted, some of this information is protected under state and federal laws, like much of the best predictive information obtained from biodata (see Stokes et al., 1994, for a list of items excluded in various state jurisdictions). Having applicants sign a release to obtain this information may not stand up in court challenges unless employers can show that this information is job-related (Gatewood & Feild, 2001).

Aggression History

Past violence may be the best predictor of future violence (Kausch & Resnick, 2001). Greenberg and Barling (1999) found that a history of aggression, measured by the frequency of self-reported physical and verbal aggressions made against friends and family during and after high school, predicted aggression toward coworkers but not toward subordinates or supervisors. History of aggression, however, interacted with both job insecurity and procedural injustice to predict aggression toward subordinates; employees who had an aggressive background and who are experiencing high job insecurity or low procedural justice tended to be aggressive toward their subordinates. At low levels of job insecurity and procedural justice, aggressive history was unrelated to current aggression (Greenberg & Barling, 1999). In addition to being the perpetrator of aggression, a "history of aggression" also can be defined in terms of being an observer or being the victim. Previous exposure to aggressive behaviors within one's home and neighborhood tends to be associated with self-reported workplace aggression, including verbal and behavioral aggression (Douglas & Martinko, 2001).

It may be possible to use measures such as Bennett and Robinson's (2000) Organizational Deviance and Interpersonal Deviance Scales to assess self-report instances of past deviant behavior (including aggression) to predict future instances of deviant behavior. Respondents, however, may minimize past instances of such behavior in efforts to appear positive to the organization. Even Bennett and Robinson (2000) stressed that in order to minimize response distortion, the respondents must remain anonymous; therefore, the utility of this type of measure for screening purposes is questionable.

In addition to violence per se, interests and hobbies may be linked to workplace aggression. For example, an interest in and preoccupation with weapons may be characteristic of a violence-prone individual (Baron, 1993). Questions relating to interests and hobbies that predict workplace violence could be incorporated into a BIB, but only if there is solid empirical evidence indicating a link.

Alcohol and Drug Use

Many employees believe that alcohol or drug abuse is a contributing cause of workplace violence (Northwestern National Life, 1993). The relationship between alcohol use and aggression, however, is not as straightforward as it may first appear. Although many studies have found a relationship between alcohol and aggression, the exact nature of this relationship is unclear and may be somewhat complex (Bennett & Lehman, 1996). Self-reports of the amount of alcohol consumption have been positively related to aggression against coworkers but not to aggression toward subordinates or supervisors (Greenberg & Barling, 1999). Alcohol consumption tends to interact with perceptions of procedural justice to predict aggression toward coworkers and subordinates. That is, alcohol consumption tends to predict aggression only when the employees perceive low levels of procedural justice (Greenberg & Barling, 1999). Alcohol consumption may also interact with job insecurity to predict aggression toward subordinates; there is a positive relationship between alcohol consumption and aggression toward subordinates when job insecurity is high, but alcohol consumption is unrelated to aggression at low levels of job insecurity (Greenberg & Barling, 1999).

Instead of a direct relationship with aggression, alcohol may increase the propensity for aggression in individuals who are at high risk for aggression (British Medical Association, 1995, cited in Bennett & Lehman, 1996). When alcohol use is an outcome of stress, it may serve as an indication of future violence (Mantell, 1994) because it may exacerbate the stress reactions. Alcohol abuse also may create more stress or interact with stress and strain to predict aggression. Bennett and Lehman (1996) noted that aggression may be due to several personal and situational factors and that when "any of these factors are simultaneously present, alcohol increases the likelihood of aggression" (p. 111).

To complicate matters further, Pernanen (1991) suggested that the effect of alcohol goes beyond a basic physiological reaction to alcohol and also may be affected by the context and individual expectations (based on cultural attributions) about alcohol. For example, individual expectations can interact with the pharmacological effect of alcohol to lead to aggression (Bushman & Cooper, 1990). Bennett and Lehman (1996) found support for this theory, in that feelings of alienation and an organizational climate that supported drinking were associated with more violence and antagonistic behaviors over and above individual alcohol use. They concluded that because alcohol use is only one of many risk factors associated with workplace aggression, screening solely on this individual factor is not justified.

Psychological Testing

Psychological testing to screen out potentially aggressive employees is based on the premise that individuals have a predisposition for aggression and that we can measure this tendency using valid testing practices (Paetzold, 1998). Psychological testing can be divided into clinical and nonclinical testing. Therefore, we first will review some general trait or personality characteristics that tend to be associated with aggression. We then review psychological and integrity testing, followed by clinical and statistical methods.

Personality Characteristics

Several personality factors, such as a lack of conscientiousness, agreeableness, and emotional stability, predict general counterproductive work behaviors, including aggressive behaviors (Ones et al., 1993; Viswesvaran, 1998). Several personality traits correlate with different aspects of workplace violence: Self-monitoring ability correlates significantly with *obstructionism,* which is defined as "actions that are designed to impede an individual's ability to perform his or her job" and tend to include passive types of aggression (Neuman & Baron, 1998, p. 398); trait anger, attitudes toward revenge, negative affectivity, and self-control all correlate with self-reported incidence of workplace aggression (Douglas & Martinko, 2001). As well, type A behavior pattern (TABP) positively predicts aggression, although the degree of relationship is low (Baron et al., 1999; Neuman & Baron, 1998). It is also correlated with hostility and obstructionism (Neuman & Baron, 1998); however, neither of the noted TABP studies examined the specific facet of Impatience/Irritability, which may be more strongly related to aggression than the overall TABP scores. Finally, negative affectivity and agreeableness moderate the relationship between organizational injustice perceptions and retaliatory behaviors (Skarlicki, Folger, & Tesluk, 1999).

Emotions, perceptions, and attributions can all influence aggressive behaviors. Several emotions, such as anger (Fox & Spector, 1999) and frustration (Baron, 1993; Spector, 1997) contribute to aggression. According to Martinko et al.'s (2002) theoretical two-stage model of aggression, if employees perceive some type of "disequilibrium" (e.g., injustice) in the workplace and if they attribute this injustice to being caused by external, stable, and intentionally hostile behaviors, there is an increased risk of aggression. Similarly, the manner in which individuals perceive and make sense of their environment may influence aggressive behaviors. For example, attributional style (Martinko, Henry, & Zmud, 1996) and attributions may contribute to aggression. Similarly, externalization of blame tends to be associated with increased aggressive behaviors (Baron, 1993), and hostile attribution style (i.e., attributing failures to external hostile and stable factors) is associated with workplace aggression (Douglas & Martinko, 2001). Hostile attribution error (i.e., a tendency to view other people as having hostile intentions behind their behaviors) also tends to be associated with increased aggression (Folger & Baron, 1996). Moreover, perception of fairness, social sensitivity, and sinister attribution may be associated with aggression (Greenberg & Alge, 1998).

In other research, Marcus, Schuler, Quell, and Humpfner (2002) measured a lack of self-control through a self-report measure that assessed behaviors such as traffic violations and school problems from respondents' childhood, adolescence, and adulthood. A lack of self-control was related to higher aggression for both a manufacturing sample and a retail sample.

Integrity and Personality Testing

Based on this research, work on individual differences and aggression has specifically focused on the use of integrity and personality testing. Counterproductive behaviors, including aggressive behaviors, have tended to be assessed through personality and integrity tests (e.g., Hogan & Hogan, 1989). There are several published integrity tests that are marketed to identify counterproductive work behaviors, including aggression: Inwald Personality Inventory (Inwald, 1992); London House Personnel Selection Inventory (London House, 1980); The Reid Report (Reid Psychological Systems, 1996); and the Reliability Scale of the Hogan Personality Inventory (Hogan & Hogan, 1995).

The proponents of integrity tests argue that these tests predict counterproductive behaviors, such as aggression, violence, and/or sabotage (Brown, Jones, Terris, & Steffy, 1987; Hogan & Brinkmeyer, 1997; Hogan & Hogan, 1989; Spector, 1997). There is some evidence to support these arguments. Marcus et al. (2002) found that both overt and personality-based integrity tests predicted self-reported workplace aggression for both retail and manufacturing employees. Similarly, based on several meta-analyses, Ones and Viswesvaran (2001) reported that violence scales tend to predict violent behaviors at work, general counterproductive work behaviors, and overall job performance, with operational validities ranging from .41 to .48. They concluded that the use of integrity tests should lead to a decrease in counterproductive work behaviors (Ones & Viswesvaran, 2001); however, they also noted that "if personality testing is being considered as part of a selection system for the purpose of reducing counterproductivity only, there may not be a clear advantage to integrity tests and other [criterion-oriented personality scales] over conscientiousness measures" (p. 37). Conscientiousness, along with openness to experience, agreeableness, extroversion, and emotional stability (also known as neuroticism), are collectively referenced as the Big Five personality factors. Recent studies have shown that the many hundreds of personality traits could be categorized under these five major categories (Digman, 1990), which have become an important classification scheme in summarizing relationships between personality and job performance variables (Hough & Furnham, 2003). The evidence for personality tests to predict aggressiveness, however, may not be as conclusive as suggested by Ones and Viswesvaran (Baity & Hilsenroth, 1999).

Several studies have examined the ability of both clinical and nonclinical personality tests to predict aggression and related criteria. Sharpe (2001) found that the NEO-PI-R (Costa & McCrae, 1992) accounted for incremental variance in aggression above the variance accounted for by the MMPI-2 PSY-5 (Harkness, McNulty, & Ben-Porath, 1995). The Antisocial Personality Questionnaire (including its aggression factor) was correlated with criminal career data (Blackburn & Fawcett, 1999). Baity and Hilsenroth (1999) examined several aggression-related variables on the Rorschach: aggressive movement, morbid content, aggressive content, aggressive past, aggressive potential, primary process aggression, and secondary process aggression. They found that Rorschach Aggressive Past was related to an anger subscale of the MMPI-2 and that the Rorschach Aggressive Content was related to the MMPI-2 antisocial practices. Overcontrolled Hostility scores on the MMPI-2 differentiated among women who were classified as being nonviolent or being repeat offenders from women who had engaged in one violent act (Verona & Carbonell, 2000).

Several psychological tests have also been used as part of preemployment screening processes (Blau, 1994; Detrick, 2002). The driving violations, family conflicts, and guardedness scales from the Inwald Personality Inventory (Inwald, 1992) are correlated with police officer performance (Detrick, 2002). An MMPI index, which is composed of the *F* scale, Psychopathic Deviance, and Hypomania, was associated with disciplinary suspensions in a sample of 107 police officers (Costello, 1996); however, there is a lack of research with measures such as the MMPI-2 in police officer applicants, making comparisons difficult (Detrick, Chibnall, & Rosso, 2001). Moreover, research specifically examining the relationship of these measures and subscales with aggression is lacking.

In conclusion, personality and integrity testing shows promise as indicators of aggressive workplace behavior. Unfortunately, the existing data is such that it would be problematic to base a systematic selection program on the use, at this time, of these types of tests to exclude violence-prone individuals.

Clinical Assessment, Actuarial Models, and Profiling

Forensic and clinical psychologists use both clinical and actuarial methods for assessing risk for aggression and violence; however, there is a disconnect between the research conducted on violence in organizations and that conducted in clinical situations. The clinical judgment approach is primarily based on the clinician's professional judgment (de Vogel, de Ruiter, van Beek, & Mead, 2004). Clinicians also use statistical and actuarial methods to help assess individuals' potential risk for violence (Monahan et al., 2000). The focus of statistical and actuarial methods is on the *prediction* of aggression, without necessarily *understanding* why aggression occurs. These methods examine individual factors (e.g., age, gender, marital status, history of abuse) that have been shown to predict aggression both individually and collectively. Profiling involves creating a description of the typical aggressive employee (Paetzold, 1998). Profiling, clinical assessment, and actuarial methods tend to examine the individual factors discussed above (e.g., personality, history of aggression, gender) and create a picture of the typical aggressive-prone individual. For the most part, these methods fail to examine the organizational context in which the violence occurs.

The reasons for this apparent disconnect between the forensic assessment of potential violence and assessment of violent behavior at work may be legitimate. Clinical methods may not be applicable to the organizational setting or they may be impractical for use as part of a selection system. The forensic literature tends to deal solely with clinical and criminal populations, which rarely overlap with a typical job applicant population. As well, forensic and clinical methods tend to be extremely time-consuming and difficult to use (Gardner, Lidz, Mulvey, & Shaw, 1996). Nevertheless, forensic and clinical methods have improved over the past three decades, producing increased levels of accurate assessments of risk of violence (Douglas & Webster, 1999; Nicholls, Ogloff, & Douglas, 2004). Furthermore, although profiling is not an entirely accurate predictor of violence, it can help employers identify some of the red flags associated with potentially aggressive applicants and employees (Baron, 1993).

There are several forensic or clinical measures that can be used to screen for violence risk, including the Psychopathy Checklist (PCL-R; Hare, 2003); PCL–Screening Version (PCL-SV; Hart, Cox, & Hare, 1995); HCR-20 (Webster, Douglas, Eaves, & Hart, 1997); McNiel-Binder Violence Screening Checklist (VSC; McNiel & Binder, 1994); and the VRAG (Rice & Harris, 1995; Quinsey, Harris, Rice, & Cormier, 1998). The effectiveness of these measures in predicting recidivism and violent behaviors is mixed. For example, the VRAG predicted violent behaviors over a 10-year period (Rice & Harris, 1995); Part 2 of the HCR-20, the PCL-SV, and the VSC predicted a broad category of aggressive behaviors (including physical violence and threatening behaviors) against women (Nicholls et al., 2004); and the Hare PCL-SV (Hart et al., 1995) distinguished between high- and low-violence risk groups (Steadman et al., 2000). The PCL-SV also illustrates the problems with clinical assessments: Although it can statistically distinguish between these groups, it is a time-consuming process, and it must be administered and scored by an experienced clinician.

In an effort to reduce the amount of time spent on clinical evaluations of violence, Monahan et al. (2000) suggested using an "Iterative Classification Tree" (p. 312) to assess various combinations of 15 risk factors that included personal factors (e.g., age, gender), historical factors (e.g., abuse as a child, father's drug use, employment history, fights with parents while growing up, recent violence, seriousness of prior arrests), and psychological and emotional factors (impulsiveness, anger, violent fantasies, and clinical symptoms such as delusions, presence of schizophrenia, or major psychological disorder). These factors are similar to items that might be found on a biodata questionnaire. Using these 15 risk factors, Monahan et al. (2000) successfully classified 72.6% of the clinical sample as either high risk (50.9%) or low risk (21.7%). Despite this high success rate, 27.4% of the sample was misclassified; that is, they were either false negatives (i.e., classified as violence-prone and high risk when they were not high risk) or false positives (i.e., classified as non-violence-prone and low risk when they were high risk). Misclassifications are undesirable when trying to screen out employees with a potential for violence in the workplace. As discussed earlier in this chapter, decision errors falling in quadrant A of Figure 24.1 (false negatives) may have fewer consequences for the organization and may be more tolerable for an organization than those falling in quadrant D, in which the mistaken hiring of a violence-prone applicant may lead to violence in the workplace and negative fallout for the organization.

There may be a relationship between the characteristics of people who commit nonlethal violence and those who commit more serious forms of aggression in the future, such that clinical psychologists might draw on these more serious cases when evaluating employees' potential for violence (Kausch & Resnick, 2001). There may be significant differences, however, between individuals who engage in nonlethal and lethal forms of violence. Individuals who commit nonlethal violence are typically men who are under 30 years of age and who have a history of drug and/or alcohol abuse and past violence; conversely, individuals who commit lethal violence are typically over the age of 30 with no history of past violence or drug or alcohol abuse (Filipczak, 1993). Nevertheless, characteristics of those who commit lethal violence may still be relevant to workplace aggression.

Hempel, Meloy, and Richards (1999) identified individual characteristics of 30 individuals who committed mass murder between 1949 and 1998; half of these murders were job-related. All of the 30 mass murderers were men, 77% were White, 63% had a preoccupation with weapons, and 94% were described as loners. About half had antisocial personality traits, had served in the military, had a documented psychiatric history, and/or had a history of violence. Forty percent had narcissistic personality traits, and 37% had paranoid personality traits. The risk profiles of these perpetrators may be relevant to developing a profile of employees who are prone to workplace aggression, based on depression, paranoia, delusions, preoccupation with weapons, paramilitary lifestyle, history of past violence, inability to control anger, and narcissistic or antisocial personality (Kausch & Resnick, 2001).

Kausch and Resnick (2001) suggested that clinicians who are assessing potentially violent employees collect collateral information from a variety of sources. They recommended that these clinicians have ongoing sessions with the employee; review the violence risk factors; conduct a review of past violence (including types, severity, and frequency of violence) and check for patterns in the behaviors; assess current and past relationships with peers, family members, and authority figures; assess the presence of clinical disorders (e.g., antisocial personality, narcissism, paranoia); assess personality traits, such as impulsivity and low tolerance for criticism and frustration (see Reid & Balis, 1987); ask about past grievances (and about probable reactions to a failed grievance); inquire about alcohol and drug use; ask about hobbies and interests; and assess past and current ownership and use of weapons (Kausch & Resnick, 2001). In addition to these individual characteristics, Kausch and Resnick recommended examining the workplace factors that may play a role in aggression and violence at work.

Despite the similarity in profiles for perpetrators of lethal and nonlethal violence, Kausch and Resnick (2001) recognized that "there is no one risk factor or combination of factors which accurately predicts violence" (p. 17) and concluded that "actuarial approaches developed for general violence risk assessment are not likely to be as helpful in decision making about workplace violence risk" (p. 18). Nonetheless, they still suggested that clinicians take actuarial information into consideration. Combining actuarial tools with clinical approaches may be most effective in predicting potential for violence (Webster et al., 1997).

Kinney (1995) argued that although there are warning signs for the potential aggressive behaviors in the workplace, using profiles is ineffective because of the complexity of this type of approach. Kinney also cautioned that only a small proportion of individuals who have these warning signs will actually engage in violent behaviors. That is, employers must be cautious because many individuals who have these signs will not engage in violent behaviors, and other individuals who do not have these signs may engage in violent behaviors. The legal implications are evident on both accounts: Both of these types of erroneous classification (i.e., incorrectly targeting individuals who do not have a proclivity toward violence based on these warning signs [i.e., false positives] and incorrectly ignoring individuals without these warning signs who will become violent [i.e., false negatives]) should be avoided. Finally, although there any many suggestions about profiles and clinical factors that may be associated with workplace aggression, there is no specific information on how to use such information in a screening process that would satisfy legal and psychometric requirements.

Structured Employment Interviews

Interviews are one of the most prevalent selection methods used in organizations (Catano et al., 2004), and they tend to be valid predictors of job performance if they are structured (Wiesner & Cronshaw, 1988) and if the interview questions are job-related. Structured interview questions are normally developed through the use of job-analytic procedures that identify critical incidents in the workplace and then transform those incidents into interview questions. These critical incidents are examples of both effective and ineffective work-related behaviors, and they are used to develop scoring keys for the structured interviews (Catano et al., 2004; Gatewood & Feild, 2001).

Mantell (1994) believed that employers could use structured interviews to ask potential employees about their experience with respect to organizational injustice and their reactions to it. Job applicants' reported reactions to unfair situations they have encountered in the past as well as their intended reactions to hypothetical situations presented in interviews could identify "violent tendencies while remaining well within legal boundaries" (Bush & O'Shea, 1996, p. 290). Perceptions of continuous unfair treatment or aggressive and hostile responses to perceived injustice may indicate potentially violent individuals (Mantell, 1994).

Mantell's (1994) assumptions, although intriguing, need to be tested empirically. If structured interviews are to be used to identify individuals with a propensity for violent or aggressive behavior, critical incidents related to aggressive acts would have to be identified along with aggressive and nonaggressive responses to the incident in an attempt to construct interview questions that focus on aggressive behavior. The validity and reliability of this type of interview would next have to be established before it was used as a screen for potentially violent job applicants.

Psychometric Issues

Before any of the methods we have discussed can be used as screening methods, they must first demonstrate strong psychometric properties (i.e., reliability, validity, generalizability) and must meet the legal requirements of the jurisdiction in which they will be used. From a psychometric perspective, little has been done to ensure that these processes and measures can be used in an employment situation to screen out violence-prone job applicants.

Reliability and Validity

Although "the past decade has seen a proliferation of instruments designed to predict violence" (Harris, Rice, & Camilleri, 2004, p. 1063), there is a lack of *valid* measures available to screen potentially aggressive job applicants. Most of the measures are for use with criminal "offenders" (Harris et al., 2004). No psychological test has effectively demonstrated its validity as a screening process for workplace violence and aggression (Paetzold, 1998).

Clinical and actuarial measures are inconsistent in their prediction of recidivism and violent behaviors. Profiling may be too broad and impractical for effective use in organizations (Braverman, 1999). Clinical judgments tend to have low reliability and validity (Monahan, 1981; Quinsey et al., 1998), be subject to systematic biases (de Vogel et al., 2004), and demonstrate differential validity for women and minorities. For example, the PCL-R is a poor predictor of adjustment and recidivism among female inmates (Salekin, Rogers, Ustad, & Sewell, 1998), whereas unstructured violence risk assessments are not very accurate predictors of violent behavior for women (Nicholls et al., 2004).

Most of the personality and integrity scales, as well as the profiles and actuarial analyses, have not been examined in other cultures; therefore, their generalizability outside of the context in which they were developed is unknown. Ones and Viswesvaran (2001) suggested that future research should examine the cross-cultural equivalence of criterion-oriented personality scales (which assess violence along with other behaviors), in terms of their language and cultural equivalence and their factor structure across cultures.

We can use reference checks to collect information about a job applicant's past employment history (and potential aggressive behaviors). The available data, however, tend to indicate that reference checks have low to moderate validity when predicting job performance measured by supervisor ratings

(Gatewood & Feild, 2001). To date, the validity and reliability of these procedures as predictors of violent behavior have not been determined.

The predictive validity for any one BIB is typically established for a fairly large and specific pool of individuals applying for a specific job. With very few exceptions, there are no commercially available BIBs that screen for aggression. An organization will need to develop and validate its own BIB, which will require a large applicant pool; this requirement may explain why very few North American corporations use BIBs as part of any type of selection process (Catano et al., 2004).

Although the use of iterative classification trees (ICTs) may be beneficial in a clinical setting, they are difficult to use in an employment situation for several reasons. First, the ICT model was developed on individuals hospitalized for acute psychiatric disorders (e.g., schizophrenia, mania, personality disorder). Therefore, its generalizability to a general population (or even to other clinical settings) is unknown (Monahan et al., 2000). Second, findings with the ICT are based on reporting only the most serious, violent acts. Monahan et al. defined violence as including "acts of battery that resulted in physical injury; sexual assaults; assaultive acts that involved the use of a weapon; or threats made with a weapon in hand" (p. 315). Many of the less serious forms of violence, which may be more likely to occur in the workplace, were excluded in their study. Finally, Monahan et al. were unable to classify a relatively large group of their participants (27.1% of the sample); and the violence rate for this unclassified group was sufficiently large (24.1%) to be disturbing.

Even in situations in which the tests are valid and testing is based on legally acceptable factors, we still must be concerned about applicant perceptions of the test (Gilliland, 1994; Whitney, Diaz, Mineghino, & Powers, 1999). Although face validity is not a true type of validity, applicants' perceptions of tests in terms of their perceived validity and job relevance may influence their test-taking motivation (Whitney et al., 1999) and thus the test's ability to accurately predict aggressive behaviors.

Faking

Personality tests can be faked when respondents are motivated to do so (Mueller-Hanson, Heggestad, & Thornton, 2003). Self-report measures of current workplace aggression or prior aggressive acts also may be subject to socially desirable responding (or "faking good"; Bennett & Robinson, 2000). Hershcovis and Barling (Chapter 26) argued that it is very difficult to assess such personal characteristics and that individuals may not admit to possessing negative characteristics or a negative past history. In advising clinicians on how to assess employees for a predisposition for violence, Kausch and Resnick (2001) noted that the employees may be motivated to lie and that information from employees should be supplemented with "collateral information, such as police reports, hospital charts and school or military records" (p. 11).

Collection of this type of supplementary information may be impractical or prohibited by law for employment situations.

Faking is also an issue in the use of BIBs, particularly when applicants are asked to report negative life events. When applicants believe that their answers on a BIB will be verified, they tend to be more honest than when there is no verification. Unfortunately, little research has examined the accuracy of information provided on BIBs. Studies that have examined the truthfulness of information provided on traditional application blanks suggest that as much as 25% of that information is inaccurate (Goldstein, 1971). There is no reason to believe that the rate of inaccuracy on a BIB, whether intentional or not, differs from accuracy rates on application blanks.

Proponents of integrity testing, however, argue that respondents do answer honestly (Ones et al., 1993). Moreover, Ones et al. argued that self-report integrity measures may be more valid than other measures: That is, because many employees may engage in covert aggression and try to hide their aggressive or deviant behaviors, employers may not directly observe or detect these examples of aggression.

Legal Issues

In addition to the predictive and psychometric issues associated with screening, we will examine the legal implications of screening and failing to screen applicants and failing to deal with violence-prone employees. Both violence in the workplace and screening for this violence have important and sometimes paradoxical legal implications for employers. On one hand, employers can be held liable for the aggressive actions of their employees (Roher & Gervais, 2004). One the other hand, screening out potentially aggressive applicants can be very problematic from a legal standpoint (Bush & O'Shea, 1996) and may result in costly litigation and liability for the employer who used the screen (Paetzold, 1998). That is, an employer may be sued (a) if an employee harms another employee or client or (b) if an applicant is not selected based on screening measures designed to prevent violence in the workplace (Bush & O'Shea, 1996; Di Lorenzo & Carroll, 1995).

A charge of negligence may be brought against an employer by an employee or another third party (e.g., customer) if harm, damage, or loss has occurred and if the employer has somehow failed in its duties. In an employment situation, the plaintiff must demonstrate that (a) the employer owes a duty of care to its employees, and (b) the level of care was breached leading to the employee's harm, loss, or damage (Roher & Gervais, 2004). Similarly, Paetzold (1998) argued that negligence requires several standards to be met before an employer will be held liable for the employee's violent acts: (a) The employee had a propensity for the aggressive behavior; (b) the employer knew, or should have known, about this propensity; (c) the employee engaged in aggressive behavior that harmed another individual; and (d) the employer's negligence in employment caused the harm to happen.

Employers may be held liable for several reasons, including a failure of duty of care, a failure to warn of violence, a failure to provide a safe workplace, negligent hiring, negligent retention, and negligent supervision (Roher & Gervais, 2004). That is, employers have a duty of care because they have "sufficient proximity" with employees to assume that their actions will affect employees and vice versa (Roher & Gervais, 2004, p. 12). Moreover, this duty of care may extend to third parties outside of the organization.

Employers also have a responsibility to warn employees and other third parties of violence; however, it is the responsibility of the plaintiff to show that the act was reasonably *foreseeable* by the employer and that harm would not have occurred without the employer's negligence (Roher & Gervais, 2004). More generally, employers are also responsible to provide a safe workplace, "which can lead to potential liability from acts of violence" (Roher & Gervais, 2004, p. 16). Employers, however, must also be careful in their efforts to warn third parties. Any disclosure of information must be "accurate and limited to avoid a claim of defamation" (Roher & Gervais, 2004, p. 14).

Employers can be found negligent in employment, in terms of hiring, retention, and supervision. That is, they are negligent in hiring if they have knowledge that an applicant poses a risk for violence or they should have knowledge about this potential violence but have failed to take reasonable action to identify or screen (Paetzold, 1998; Roher & Gervais, 2004). That is, Roher and Gervais (2004) argued that employers must engage in "reasonable investigation" (p. 17) of applicants. Moreover, "the screening for potential employees who will have access to restricted areas should go beyond the following up of references provided by the candidate" (Roher & Gervais, 2004, pp. 18–19). Therefore, they recommend that employers use a detailed application form, check with references and past employers, and conduct an in-depth interview; however, as illustrated by our review on the reliability and validity of reference checks and interviews, the content of these interviews and reference checks may not always be valid. The paradoxical side of negligent employment is that employers can be held liable, not only for damages caused by violent employees but also for their own "overzealous attempts" to screen out "applicants or current employees who are judged to be likely to commit violence in the workplace" (Paetzold, 1998, p. 144; i.e., false negatives). Therefore, not only must employers ensure their screening methods are valid and legally defensible to select out violence-prone applicants; there must be evidence of harm (or potential harm) to another individual in order to avoid charges of unfair screening out of nonviolent employees.

Negligent retention is the second form of negligent employment and may occur if an employer continues to employ an aggression-prone individual, even after the employer knows (or should have known) about the individual's aggressive propensity (Roher & Gervais, 2004). The employer, however, also has a responsibility in many jurisdictions under the law to this aggressive (or potentially aggressive) employee, such that the employer may not be able to fire the individual and may have to accommodate the employee. Finally, negligence in supervision may occur if a lack of proper supervision leads to employee aggressive behavior, which leads to an incident involving harm, loss, or damage (Roher & Gervais, 2004).

Background Checks

Although checks of past employers and references are recommended to minimize legal liability (Roher & Gervais, 2004), use of background checks can be problematic because they violate applicants' right to privacy, because of their disparate impact, and because of the belief that offenders deserve a second chance (Paetzold, 1998). Many jurisdictions do not allow employers to select out based on past criminal convictions, except for some high-risk occupations. Therefore, in many jurisdictions, questions related to criminal convictions may not be included in the screening process (Bush & O'Shea, 1996). Arrest records may have an adverse impact, making them ineligible for inclusion as screens (Paetzold, 1998). In addition, background checks for criminal records may not be foolproof. Bushway (cited in Smallwood, 2004) sent a list of 120 people who were on parole or probation in Virginia to the FBI for criminal background checks. The bureau only reported that 87 of these people had criminal records, a hit rate of 72.5%. A private company that did background checks performed worse: They reported that only 56 of the people on the list (46.6%) had criminal records.

When asked to provide a reference, past employers have a legal obligation "not to misrepresent facts regarding the qualifications and character of former employees, particularly when those misrepresentations would present a substantial and foreseeable risk of physical injury to either the prospective employer or third persons" (Paetzold, 1998, p. 152); however, the references may not be accurate for two reasons. First, applicants typically select their references based on the probability of receiving a favorable recommendation. Second, because of "privacy of information statutes and the heightened awareness of defamation suits . . . it is often difficult to find out a good deal of information about a potential job applicant's violent tendencies" (Bush & O'Shea, 1996, p. 289). Because they fear that giving former employees a negative reference may lead to a lawsuit, many employers state only that a person worked for them or not and provide no other information.

BIBs

Although BIBs have good predictive validity, many organizations refuse to use them out of fear that their use will lead to human rights complaints. These concerns arise from the fact that BIBs may request personally sensitive information on family background and experiences that may violate local human rights and privacy legislation. These issues are similar to issues that arise with background checks. In the United States, each item on a BIB must be shown not to have an adverse impact on members of protected groups (Catano et al., 2004). Before such items can be used, an employer must establish that they are indicators of bona fide job requirements and have value as predictors. Despite the fact that BIB items may screen out violence-prone applicants, they may be perceived as discriminatory or unfair by all job applicants and have the unintended effect of turning away highly qualified, nonaggressive candidates (Saks, Leck, & Saunders, 1995).

Drug and Alcohol Testing

There is a legal consideration that must be taken into account when considering screening out individuals on the basis of drug or alcohol use. In many jurisdictions (e.g., Canada), drug and alcohol problems are considered to be medical issues that must be accommodated in the workplace. Employees cannot be terminated simply because they have a drug or alcohol problem as long as they are making an effort to recover from the problem. Courts and labor arbitrators recognize that it may take time to overcome such problems. Employees can be terminated, however, for insubordination and violence to others in the workplace regardless of their recovering status from substance abuse. In the United States, the Americans With Disabilities Act of 1990 (ADA) specifies that preemployment alcohol testing can only take place after a conditional offer of employment has been made and in accordance with ADA regulations. The ADA regulations allow a preemployment drug test to be made *before* a conditional offer of employment if (a) the test accurately identifies only the use of drugs, (b) the test is not given as part of a preemployment physical, and (c) the test does not require the applicant to disclose information about prescription drug use, unless a positive test result may be explained by use of a prescription drug. These legal issues, together with the lack of solid empirical data, make it difficult if not impossible to use a history of drug or alcohol abuse to screen out potentially violent employees.

Testing

Paetzold (1998) suggested that the use of any type of clinical or personality test may violate applicants' rights to privacy, subjecting employers to statutory violation claims. In addition to the limits imposed by the ADA on the use of psychological tests, some states have prohibited the use of honesty tests and other psychological testing (Paetzold, 1998). Because aggression and violence may be a product of the interaction of individual characteristics and situational organizational factors, screening solely based on psychological factors is controversial and may perpetuate the myth of aggression stemming solely from clinically distressed employees (Paetzold, 1998).

Because tests used to determine psychiatric or mental health are considered to be a medical exam under the ADA, they should only be given *after* a conditional offer of employment has been made (Paetzold, 1998). That is, employers should not ask applicants about any psychological problems before a conditional job offer has been made. Moreover, because the use of these types of tests in employment situations is regulated under the ADA, even if testing indicates a predisposition toward aggression, the employer may be responsible to accommodate the applicant and must hire the individual unless there is "a direct threat to the health or safety of others" (Paetzold, 1998, p. 153).

Profiling

Several legal and ethical issues surround the use of profiling to identify potentially violent employees. Profiling is based on retrospectives of behaviors of individuals who have been violent. Profiling involves all characteristics that are associated with aggression; however, many of these characteristics are not legitimate employment selection criteria (e.g., union involvement; DiLorenzo & Carroll, 1995). O'Leary-Kelly et al. (1996) argued that although demographic variables tend to be the best predictors of "criminal violence," organizations are limited in their use of such variables to screen employees because of Title VII of the U.S. Civil Rights Act of 1964. Moreover, many of the profile characteristics can only be assessed through clinical means. As previously mentioned, the use of some types of clinical testing is covered under both state law and the ADA, which severely limits its use for screening. Finally, although the profiling characteristics may help identify people with aggressive tendencies, it also incorrectly labels a large number of individuals as being potentially violent. This problem of false positives, along with the other legal ramifications, underscores the problems of profiling leading Paetzold (1998) to conclude that profiling should not be used.

Implications for Practice

Employers have a legal obligation to provide a workplace that is free from violence and aggression. One method of accomplishing this objective is to screen out potential employees who may have a propensity for violence. To successfully screen out aggression-prone employees, we need reliable and valid measures that assess an individual's likelihood of committing violence in the workplace without violating the individual's legal rights. As our review suggests, however, it is premature to try to screen based on violence propensity. No measure at this time meets our criteria for being psychometrically sound, respecting a job applicant's civil rights, and being efficient and cost-effective in its administration. There are still too few studies on workplace aggression to allow us to understand the individual factors that contribute to aggression and violence in the workplace (Douglas & Martinko, 2001; Neuman & Baron, 1998). We cannot identify "the deviant personality type in organizations" (Robinson & Greenberg, 1998, p. 13). We agree with Paetzold (1998) that "preemptive screening . . . appears to be unfounded and dangerous" (p. 158). In the meantime, until we know more about the specific individual characteristics in the workplace that would allow us to develop effective, valid, and legally defensible screens, a better approach may be to focus on strategies that prevent workplace aggression from occurring. Failing that, employers should monitor problematic workplace behaviors carefully and take immediate and decisive action when needed (Paetzold, 1998).

Alternative Individual Based Methods for Preventing Workplace Aggression

Workplace aggression appears to be a function of the environment, the individual, and the organization. Although many employers focus their attention on screening potentially aggressive employees (Bush & O'Shea, 1996), there are other methods of reducing violence, such as implementing workplace violence policies, training supervisors, creating crisis management teams to deal with violence, fostering a supportive work environment, providing personal counseling, and establishing fair grievance procedures (Johnson & Indvik, 1994; Northwestern National Life, 1993; see Chapter 21, this volume for an overview). Interestingly, although these methods tend to focus on organizational factors, there is an implicit assumption that individual employees may react differently to potential stressors and thus must be accommodated accordingly. For example, training programs can be developed for employees and supervisors to identify the red flags or "profile" of aggression-prone employees (Baron, 1993). Therefore, even when the focus is on organizational programs, individual variables should not be ignored.

Summary

Like most organizational issues, it is too simplistic to view aggression as an outcome of solely individual characteristics or solely situational characteristics. Aggression must be examined from both individual and situational perspectives (Barling, 1996). "It is usually a combination and sequence of factors and events that leads to violence, especially explosive violence (Kausch & Resnick, 2001, p. 19). These interactions can help us predict the occurrence of workplace aggression. Our review, however, leads to the conclusion that screening out applicants who may be prone to engaging in aggressive behaviors is still problematic for the following reasons:

- No selection process is perfect; selection decisions always produce two types of errors: false negatives and false positives. Both types of errors may have negative consequences for an organization screening job applicants for potential violent behavior.
- To meet legal and professional standards, any screening device must meet acceptable standards of reliability and validity. With respect to workplace violence, there is simply inadequate information about the antecedents of workplace violence at this time that would allow the development of valid predictors.
- Background checks, including information on demographics, criminal and violent past behavior, and alcohol and drug use; psychological tests, including both clinical and nonclinical tests as well as actuarial and profiling methods; and structured interviews have all been suggested as screening tools for potential workplace violence. There is insufficient empirical data to support the use of any of these devices to screen out employees that would overcome legal objections to their use.
- Workplace violence does not appear to be a simple function of individual differences that can be measured; organizational factors appear to interact with or set the stage for the occurrence of the violent behavior. Insufficient information is known about such predisposing organizational factors to allow development of complete models that examined how such factors interacted with individual characteristics.

The lack of valid and reliable measures that assess an employee's likelihood of committing violence in the workplace (without violating the employee's legal rights) means that there is no acceptable way to screen potential job applicants based on these criteria. Until additional research produces the empirical evidence needed to develop effective, valid, and legally defensible screens, employers must focus on strategies that prevent workplace aggression from occurring; when these strategies fail, employers most monitor problematic workplace behaviors carefully and take immediate and decisive action as part of their obligation to ensure a workplace that is free of violence, yet respectful of the rights of all employees. In the absence of effective screening programs, employers should focus on organizational strategies and methods for reducing violence, such as implementing workplace violence policies, training supervisors, creating crisis management teams to deal with violence, fostering a supportive work environment, providing personal counseling, and establishing fair grievance procedures.

References

Anfuso, D. (1994). Deflecting workplace violence. *Personnel Journal, 73*(10), 66–77.

Asher, J. J. (1972). The biographical item: Can it be improved? *Personnel Psychology, 25,* 251–269.

Baity, M. R., & Hilsenroth, M. J. (1999). Rorschach aggression variables: A study of reliability and validity. *Journal of Personality Assessment, 72*(1), 93–110.

Barling, J. (1996). The prediction, experience, and consequences of workplace violence. In G. R. VandenBos & E. Q. Bulatao (Eds.), *Violence on the job: Identifying risks and developing solutions*. Washington, DC: American Psychological Association.

Baron, R. A. (1993). *Violence in the workplace: A prevention and management guide for business*. Ventura, CA: Pathfinder.

Baron, R. A., & Neuman, J. H. (1996). Workplace violence and workplace aggression: Evidence on their relative frequency and potential causes. *Aggressive Behavior, 22*(3), 161–173.

Baron, R. A., Neuman, J. H., & Geddes, D. (1999). Social and personal determinants of workplace aggression: Evidence for the impact of perceived injustice and the Type A behavior pattern. *Aggressive Behavior, 25*, 281–296.

Bennett, J. B., & Lehman, W. E. K. (1996). Alcohol, antagonism, and witnessing violence in the workplace: Drinking climates and social alienation-integration. In G. R. VandenBos & E. Q. Bulatao (Eds.), *Violence on the job: Identifying risks and developing solutions*. Washington, DC: American Psychological Association.

Bennett, R. J., & Robinson, S. L. (2000). Development of a measure of workplace deviance. *Journal of Applied Psychology, 85*(3), 349–360.

Bettencourt, B. A., & Miller, N. (1996). Gender differences in aggression as a function of provocation: A meta-analysis. *Psychological Bulletin, 119*(3), 422–447.

Bies, R. J., Tripp, T. M., & Kramer, R. M. (1997). At the breaking point: Cognitive and social dynamics of revenge in organizations. In R. A. Giacalone & J. Greenberg (Eds.), *Antisocial behavior in organizations* (pp. 18–36). London: Sage.

Blackburn, R., & Fawcett, D. (1999). The Antisocial Personality Questionnaire: An inventory for assessing personality deviation in offender populations. *European Journal of Psychological Assessment, 15*(1), 14–24.

Blau, T. H. (1994). *Psychological services for law enforcement*. New York: Wiley.

Braverman, M. (1999). *Preventing workplace violence: A guide for employers and practitioners*. Thousand Oaks, CA: Sage.

Brown, T. S., Jones, J. W., Terris, W., & Steffy, B. D. (1987). The impact of pre-employment integrity testing on employee turnover and inventory shrinkage losses. *Journal of Business and Psychology, 2*, 136–149.

Bush, D. F., & O'Shea, P. G. (1996). Workplace violence: Comparative use of prevention practices and policies. In G. R. VandenBos & E. Q. Bulatao (Eds.), *Violence on the job: Identifying risks and developing solutions*. Washington, DC: American Psychological Association.

Bushman, B. J., & Cooper, H. M. (1990). Effects of alcohol on aggression: An integrative research review. *Psychological Bulletin, 107*, 341–354.

Carlson, K. D., Scullen, S. E., Schmidt, F. L., Rothstein, H., & Erwin, F. (1999). Generalizable biographical data validity can be achieved without multi-organizational development and keying. *Personnel Psychology, 52*, 731–755.

Catano, V. M., Wiesner, W. H., Hackett, R. D., & Methot, L. M. (2004). *Recruitment and selection in Canada* (3rd ed.). Toronto: ITP Nelson.

Costa, P. T., & McCrae, R. R. (1992). *Revised NEO Personality Inventory (NEO-PI-R) and NEO Five-Factor Inventory (NEO-FFI) professional manual*. Odessa, FL: Psychological Assessment Resources.

Costello, R. M. (1996). Validation of a preemployment MMPI index correlated with disciplinary suspension days of police officers. *Psychology, Crime, & Law, 2*(4), 299–306.

Dalessio, A. T., Crosby, M. M., & McManus, M. A. (1996). Stability of biodata keys and dimensions across English-speaking countries: A test of the cross-situational hypothesis. *Journal of Business and Psychology, 10,* 289–296.

Detrick, P. (2002). Prediction of police officer performance with the Inwald Personality Inventory. *Journal of Police and Criminal Psychology, 17*(2), 9–17.

Detrick, P., Chibnall, J. T., & Rosso, M. (2001). Minnesota Multiphasic Personality Inventory–2 in police officer selection: Normative data and relation to the Inwald Personality Inventory. *Professional Psychology: Research and Practice, 32*(5), 484–490.

de Vogel, V., de Ruiter, C., van Beek, D., & Mead, G. (2004). Predictive validity of the SVR-20 and Static-99 in a Dutch sample of treated sex offenders. *Law and Human Behavior, 28*(3), 235–251.

Digman, J. M. (1990). Personality structure: Emergence of the Five-Factor Model. In M. Rosenzweig & L. W. Porter (Eds.), *Annual Review of Psychology.* Palo Alto, CA: Annual Reviews.

DiLorenzo, L. P., & Carroll, D. J. (1995). Screening applicants for a safer workplace. *HR Magazine, 40*(3), 55–58.

Douglas, K. S., & Webster, C. D. (1999). Predicting violence in mentally and personality disordered individuals. In R. Roesch, S. D. Hart, & J. R. P. Ogloff (Eds.), *Psychology and law: The state of the discipline* (pp. 176–239). New York: Plenum.

Douglas, S. C., & Martinko, M. J. (2001). Exploring the role of individual differences in the prediction of workplace aggression. *Journal of Applied Psychology, 86*(4), 547–559.

Eagly, A., & Steffen, V. J. (1986). Gender and aggressive behavior: A meta-analytical review of the social psychological literature. *Psychological Bulletin, 100,* 309–330.

Einarsen, S. (1999). The nature and causes of bullying at work. *International Journal of Manpower, 20*(1/2), 16–27.

Filipczak, B. (1993). Armed and dangerous at work. *Training, 30,* 39–43.

Folger, R., & Baron, R. A. (1996). Violence and hostility at work: A model of reactions to perceived injustice. In G. R. VandenBos & E. Q. Bulatao (Eds.), *Violence on the job: Identifying risks and developing solutions.* Washington, DC: American Psychological Association.

Folger, R., & Skarlicki, D. P. (1998). A popcorn metaphor for employee aggression. In R. W. Griffin, A. O'Leary-Kelly, & J. M. Collins (Eds.), *Dysfunctional behavior in organizations: Violent and deviant behavior* (pp. 43–81). Stamford, CT: JAI.

Fox, S., & Spector, P. E. (1999). A model of work frustration-aggression. *Journal of Organizational Behavior, 20*(6), 915–931.

Gardner, W., Lidz, C. W., Mulvey, E. P., & Shaw, E. C. (1996). A comparison of actuarial methods for identifying repetitively violent patients with mental illness. *Law and Human Behavior, 20,* 35–48.

Gatewood, R. D., & Feild, H. S. (2001). *Human resource selection.* Toronto: Harcourt College.

Ghiselli, E. E. (1966). *The validity of occupational aptitude tests.* New York: Wiley.

Gilliland, S. W. (1994). Effects of procedural and distributive justice on reactions to a selection system. *Journal of Applied Psychology, 79,* 691–701.

Goldstein, I. L. (1971). The application blank: How honest are the responses? *Journal of Applied Psychology, 71,* 3–8.

Greenberg, J., & Alge, B. J. (1998). Aggressive reaction to workplace injustice. In R. W. Griffin, A. O'Leary-Kelly, & J. M. Collins (Eds.), *Dysfunctional behavior in organizations: Violent and deviant behavior*. Stamford, CT: JAI.

Greenberg, L., & Barling, J. (1999). Predicting employee aggression against coworkers, subordinates and supervisors: The roles of person behaviors and perceived workplace factors. *Journal of Organizational Behavior, 20*(6), 897–913.

Hare, R. D. (2003). *Hare Psychopathy Checklist–Revised*. Toronto: Multi-Health Systems.

Harkness, A. R., McNulty, J. L., & Ben-Porath, Y. S. (1995). The Personality Psychopathology Five (PSY-5): Constructs and MMPI-2 scales. *Psychological Assessment, 7*(1), 104–114.

Harris, G. T., Rice, M. E., & Camilleri, J. A. (2004). Applying a forensic actuarial assessment (the violence risk appraisal guide) to nonforensic patients. *Journal of International Violence, 19*(9), 1063–1074.

Hart, S., Cox, D., & Hare, R. (1995). *The Hare Psychopathy Checklist: Screening Version*. Toronto: Multi-Health Systems.

Hempel, A. G., Meloy, J. R., & Richards, T. C. (1999). Offender and offense characteristics of a nonrandom sample of mass murderers. *Journal of the American Academy of Psychiatry and the Law, 27*, 213–225.

Hogan, J., & Brinkmeyer, K. (1997). Bridging the gap between overt and personality-based integrity test. *Personnel Psychology, 50*, 587–599.

Hogan, J., & Hogan, R. (1989). How to measure employee reliability. *Journal of Applied Psychology, 74*, 273–280.

Hogan, R., & Hogan, J. (1995). *Hogan Personality Inventory manual* (2nd ed.). Tulsa, OK: Hogan Assessment Systems.

Hough, L. M., & Furnham, A. (2003). Use of personality variables in work settings. In W. C. Borman, D. R. Ilgen, & R. Klimoski (Eds.), *Handbook of psychology: Industrial and organizational psychology* (Vol. 12, pp. 131–169). New York: Wiley.

Hunter, J. E., & Hunter, R. F. (1984). Validity and utility of alternative predictors of job performance. *Psychological Bulletin, 96*, 72–98.

Inwald, R. (1992). *Inwald Personality Inventory technical manual* (Rev. ed.). New York: Hilson Research.

Jenkins, E. L. (1996). *Violence in the workplace: Risk factors and prevention strategies* (DHHS-NIOSH Publication No. 96-100). Washington, DC: U.S. Government Printing Office.

Johnson, P. R., & Indvik, J. (1994). Workplace violence: An issue of the nineties. *Public Personnel Management, 23*(4), 515–523.

Kausch, O., & Resnick, P. J. (2001). Assessment of employees for workplace violence. *Journal of Forensic Psychology Practice, 1*(4), 1–22.

Kinney, J. A. (1995). *Essentials of managing workplace violence*. Charlotte, NC: Pinkerton Services Group.

London House. (1980). *Personnel Selection Inventory*. Park Ridge, IL: Author.

Loucks, A. D., & Zamble, E. (2000). Predictors of criminal behavior and prison misconduct in serious female offenders. *Empirical and Applied Criminal Justice Review, 1*, 1–47.

Maertz, C. P., Jr. (1999). Biographical predictors of turnover among Mexican workers: An empirical study. *International Journal of Management, 16*, 112–119.

Mantell, M. R. (1994). *Ticking bombs: Defusing violence in the workplace*. Burr Ridge, IL: Irwin.

Marcus, B., Schuler, H., Quell, P., & Humpfner, G. (2002). Measuring counterproductivity: Development and initial validation of a German self-report questionnaire. *International Journal of Selection and Assessment, 10,* 1–2, 18–35.

Martinko, M. J., Gundlach, M. J., & Douglas, S. C. (2002). Toward an integrative
theory of counterproductive workplace behavior: A causal reasoning perspective. *International Journal of Selection and Assessment, 10*(1/2), 36–50.

Martinko, M. J., Henry, J. W., & Zmud, R. W. (1996). An attributional explanation
of individual resistance to information technologies in the workplace. *Behavior
and Information Technology, 15,* 313–330.

McNiel, D. E., & Binder, R. L. (1994). Screening for risk of inpatient violence:
Validation of an actuarial tool. *Law and Human Behavior, 18,* 579–586.

Monahan, J. (1981). *The clinical prediction of violent behavior.* Rockville, MD:
National Institute of Mental Health.

Monahan, J., Steadman, H. J., Appelbaum, P. S., Robbins, P. C., Mulvey, E. P.,
Silver, E., et al. (2000). Developing a clinically useful actuarial tool for assessing
violence risk. *British Journal of Psychiatry, 176,* 312–319.

Mueller-Hanson, R., Heggestad, E. D., & Thornton, G. C. (2003). Faking and selection: Considering the use of personality from select-in and select-out perspectives. *Journal of Applied Psychology, 88,* 348–355.

Neuman, J. H., & Baron, R. A. (1997). Aggression in the workplace. In
R. A. Giacalone & J. Greenberg (Eds.), *Antisocial behavior in organizations*
(pp. 37–67). London: Sage.

Neuman, J. H., & Baron, R. A. (1998). Workplace violence and workplace aggression: Evidence concerning specific forms, potential causes, and preferred targets.
Journal of Management, 24(3), 391–419.

Nicholls, T. L., Ogloff, J. R. P., & Douglas, K. S. (2004). Assessing risk for violence
among male and female civil psychiatric patients: The HCR-20, PCL: SV, and
VSC. *Behavioral Sciences and the Law, 22,* 127–158.

Nicoletti, J., & Spooner, K. (1996). Violence in the workplace: Response and intervention strategies. In G. R. VandenBos & E. Q. Bulatao (Eds.), *Violence on the
job: Identifying risks and developing solutions.* Washington, DC: American
Psychological Association.

Northwestern National Life. (1993). Fear and violence in the workplace: A survey
documenting the experience of American workers. Reprinted as Appendix A in
G. R. VandenBos & E. Q. Bulatao (Eds.), *Violence on the job: Identifying risks
and developing solutions.* Washington, DC: American Psychological Association.

O'Leary-Kelly, A. M., Griffin, R. W., & Glew, D. J. (1996). Organization-motivated
aggression: A research framework. *Academy of Management Review, 21,*
225–253.

Ones, D. S., & Viswesvaran, C. (2001). Integrity tests and other criterion-focused
occupational personality scales (COPS) used in personnel selection. *International Journal of Selection and Assessment, 9,* 1–2, 31–39.

Ones, D. S., Viswesvaran, C., & Schmidt, F. L. (1993). Comprehensive meta-analysis
of integrity test validities: Findings and implications for personnel selection and
theories of job performance. *Journal of Applied Psychology, 78*(4), 679–703.

Paetzold, R. L. (1998). Workplace violence and employer liability: Implications for
organizations. In R. W. Griffin, A. O'Leary-Kelly, & J. M. Collins (Eds.),
Dysfunctional behavior in organizations: Violent and deviant behavior
(pp. 1–42). Stamford, CT: JAI.

Pernanen, K. (1991). *Alcohol in human violence.* New York: Guilford.

Quinsey, V. L., Harris, G. T., Rice, M. E., & Cormier, C. A. (1998). *Violent offenders: Appraising and managing risk*. Washington, DC: American Psychological Association.

Reid Psychological Systems. (1996). *The abbreviated Reid report*. Chicago: Author.

Reid, W. H., & Balis, G. U. (1987). Evaluation of the violent patient. *American Psychiatric Association Annual Review, 6*, 491–509.

Rice, M. E., & Harris, G. T. (1995). Violent recidivism: Assessing predictive validity. *Journal of Consulting and Clinical Psychology, 63*, 737–748.

Robinson, S. L., & Greenberg, J. (1998). Employees behaving badly: Dimensions, determinants and dilemmas in the study of workplace deviance. *Journal of Organizational Behavior, 5*, 1–30.

Roher, E. M., & Gervais, B. L. (2004). *Violence in the workplace* (2nd ed.). Toronto: Thomson Carswell.

Rothstein, H. R., Schmidt, F. L., Erwin, F. W., Owens, W. ., & Sparks, C. P. (1990). Biographical data in employment selection: Can validities be made generalizable? *Journal of Applied Psychology, 75*, 175–184.

Saks, A. M., Leck, J. D., & Saunders, D. M. (1995). Effects of application blanks and employment equity on applicant reactions and job pursuit intentions. *Journal of Organizational Behavior, 16*, 415–430.

Salekin, R. T., Rogers, R., Ustad, K. L., & Sewell, K. W. (1998). Psychopathy and recidivism among female inmates. *Law and Human Behavior, 22*(1), 109–128.

Sharpe, J. P. (2001). The revised Neo Personality Inventory and the MMPI-2 Psychology Five in the prediction of aggression. *Personality and Individual Differences, 31*(4), 505–518.

Skarlicki, D. P., Folger, R., & Tesluk, P. (1999). Personality as a moderator in the relationship between fairness and retaliation. *Academy of Management Journal, 42*(1), 100–108.

Smallwood, S. (2004, July 30). No surprises please. *Chronicle of Higher Education*, pp. A8–9.

Spector, P. (1997). The role of frustration in antisocial behavior at work. In R. A. Giacalone & J. Greenberg (Eds.), *Antisocial behavior in organizations* (pp. 1–17). London: Sage.

Steadman, H. J., Silver, E., Monahan, J., Appelbaum, P. S., Clark Robbins, P., Mulvey, E. P., et al. (2000). A classification tree approach to the development of actuarial violent risk assessment tools. *Law and Human Behavior, 24*, 83–100.

Stokes, G. S., & Cooper, L. A. (1994). Selection using biodata: Old notions revisited. In G. S. Stokes, M. D. Mumford, & W. A. Owens (Eds.), *Biodata handbook* (pp. 103–138). Mahwah, NJ: Erlbaum.

Stokes, G. S., Mumford, M. D., & Owens, W. A. (Eds.). (1994). *Biodata handbook*. Mahwah, NJ: Erlbaum.

Thornburg, L. (1993, July). When violence hits business. *HR Magazine*, 40–45.

Verona, E., & Carbonell, J. L. (2000). Female violence and personality: Evidence for a pattern of overcontrolled hostility among one-time violent female offenders. *Criminal Justice and Behavior, 27*(2), 176–195.

Vinchur, A. J., Schippmann, J. S., Switzer, F. S., III, & Roth, P. L. (1998). A meta-analytic review of predictors of job performance for salespeople. *Journal of Applied Psychology, 83*, 586–597.

Viswesvaran, C. (1998). Handbook of personality psychology. *Personnel Psychology,* *51*(3), 764–767.

Webster, C. D., Douglas, K. S., Eaves, D., & Hart, S. D. (1997). *HCR-20: Assessing* *risk for violence* (Version 2). Vancouver, BC: Mental Health, Law, and Policy Institute, Simon Fraser University.

Whitney, D. J., Diaz, J., Mineghino, M. E., & Powers, K. (1999). Perceptions of overt and personality-based integrity tests. *International Journal of Selection* *and Assessment,* *7*(1), 35–45.

Wiesner, W. H., & Cronshaw, S. F. (1988). A meta-analytic investigation of the impact of interview format and degree of structure on the validity of the employment interview. *Journal of Occupational Psychology,* *61*(4), 275–290.

25

Training as a Workplace Aggression Intervention Strategy

Aaron C. H. Schat
E. Kevin Kelloway

The growing literature on workplace aggression and related constructs (e.g., bullying, emotional abuse, harassment) suggests that exposure to such behavior is associated with a wide range of negative consequences for individuals and organizations (for reviews, see Keashly & Jagatic, 2003; Schat & Kelloway, 2005). The depth and breadth of these consequences—which include negative work attitudes, reduced well-being, and, in cases of physical violence, bodily injury or death—demonstrate the need for interventions that prevent the occurrence and negative effects of workplace aggression. Included among the potential forms of intervention is training, which is the focus of the present chapter.

Despite the increased attention that workplace aggression has received in the organizational behavior, industrial-organizational psychology, and management literatures over the past several years, very few studies of training or other forms of workplace aggression intervention have been reported. Although training has been suggested as a possible means of addressing workplace aggression in these literatures (e.g., Glomb, Steel, & Arvey, 2002;

Authors' Note: Preparation of this chapter was supported by research grants from the DeGroote School of Business at McMaster University to the first author and both the Social Sciences and Humanities Research Council and the Nova Scotia Health Research Foundation to the second author.

Schat & Kelloway, 2005) and there is preliminary evidence of its effectiveness (e.g., Schat & Kelloway, 2003), most of the research on training has appeared in the health care literature where the focus has been on training health care workers to manage patient aggression (e.g., Infantino & Musingo, 1985; Rice, Harris, Varney, & Quinsey, 1989). Despite the greater attention paid to training in this literature, there are very few rigorous scientific evaluations of its effectiveness (Runyan, Zakocs, & Zwerling, 2000). Several studies report beneficial effects of training (e.g., Rasmussen & Levander, 1996; Rice et al., 1989). However, the extent to which these findings generalize to the management of aggressive behavior in different work-related contexts (e.g., retail or office settings) and from different sources (e.g., customers, clients, coworkers) remains to be examined.

Another gap in the literature is the development and assessment of training programs that are intended to help people manage their emotions and behavioral tendencies that, if unmanaged, may lead to aggressive behavior at work. Therefore, in this chapter, we integrate research findings from the psychology of aggression and emotion regulation literatures—which deal with emotional antecedents of aggressive behavior (e.g., anger) and strategies that help people manage their emotional and behavioral reactions to aversive events—with findings from the workplace aggression literature and propose a framework for the application and evaluation of training that aims to address workplace aggression.

Defining Workplace Aggression and Violence _____

We define *workplace aggression* as "behavior by an individual or individuals within or outside an organization that is intended to physically or psychologically harm a worker or workers and occurs in a work-related context" (Schat & Kelloway, 2005, p. 191). This definition encompasses a wide range of aggressive behaviors that may be enacted by individuals in a work-related context (e.g., peers, bosses, customers, clients). Whereas *workplace aggression* represents a general construct that includes a variety of behaviors that are intended to cause harm, *workplace violence* is a specific form of workplace aggression that involves physical behavior intended to cause physical and psychological harm to the target(s). This would include behavior such as hitting, kicking, biting, using a weapon or object, or other assaultive behavior. *Workplace psychological aggression* is another form of workplace aggression that includes nonphysical acts—verbal and nonverbal—that are intended to cause psychological harm to the target(s). Examples include yelling, cursing, or spreading rumors. This distinction between *psychological aggression* and *violence* has been made before in the workplace aggression literature (e.g., Neuman & Baron, 1997; Schat & Kelloway, 2005) and is consistent with the general human aggression literature (e.g., Anderson & Bushman, 2002).

Prevalence and Consequences
of Workplace Aggression and Violence

Elsewhere in this volume, Schat, Frone, and Kelloway (see Chapter 4) review the existing literature regarding the prevalence of employee exposure to workplace aggression and report the results of a national survey of its prevalence in U.S. wage and salary workers. According to data available from the Bureau of Labor Statistics (2004) Census of Fatal Occupational Injuries (CFOI), in the year 2003, workplace homicide—acts of workplace violence that cause death—represented the third leading cause of work-related death and accounted for 631 deaths. This number is up slightly from the year before (in which there were 609 work-related homicides) but represents a decrease of about 40% since 1994 (when there were 1,080 work-related homicides). Despite the stereotype that such acts are often carried out by "disgruntled" employees, most work-related homicides are perpetrated by organizational outsiders during armed robberies or other crimes (Sygnatur & Toscano, 2000).

Physical assault represents another serious form of workplace violence that can cause serious injury to the target. Published estimates of the percentage of workers experiencing physical assaults vary widely, ranging from 5% (National Center on Addiction and Substance Abuse at Columbia University, 2000) to 30% (Pizzino, 1993, as cited in Pizzino, 2002). According to the survey results reported by Schat et al. (Chapter 4), 6% of U.S. workers experienced acts of assault during the previous year. They also found that members of the public (e.g., customers, clients, patients) were more likely to be the perpetrator of assault than coworkers or supervisors and that the risk of exposure to assault was influenced by a number of demographic variables (e.g., occupation type).

Nonphysical acts of workplace aggression (i.e., psychological aggression)—including swearing, yelling, spreading rumors, public ridicule—are more common than acts of physical violence. The survey results reported by Schat et al. (Chapter 4) demonstrate that 41.4% of U.S. workers experienced psychological aggression during the previous year and that members of the public were more likely to be the source of such aggression than coworkers or supervisors. As with physical assault, the degree of exposure to psychological aggression was associated with a number of demographic characteristics.

Although the harm caused by acts of psychological aggression may not be as tangible as the harm caused by physical violence, research suggests its consequences can be serious for both individuals and organizations. In fact, in a recent study, health care staff rated verbal aggression as more distressing than physical aggression (Walsh & Clarke, 2003). The available empirical evidence (e.g., Glomb, 2002; Keashly, 1998; Rogers & Kelloway, 1997; Schat & Kelloway, 2000, 2003; Tepper, 2000) suggests that exposure to aggression is associated with affective reactions (e.g., fear, anger), psychological symptoms (e.g., depressive, anxiety, and somatic symptoms), negative work attitudes (e.g., job dissatisfaction, reduced affective commitment to the organization), behavioral intentions, and behaviors (e.g., turnover intentions, substance abuse; see Keashly & Jagatic, 2003, and Schat & Kelloway, 2005, for reviews). There is also evidence suggesting that a target of aggression may respond to aggression with aggression and that this reciprocation can result in psychological aggression escalating into more serious acts of violence (Glomb, 2002). The breadth and seriousness of these consequences for individuals and organizations suggest the importance of interventions such as training aimed at preventing the occurrence and mitigating the consequences of workplace aggression.

Workplace Aggression Interventions

Occupational health interventions have traditionally been classified into three types: primary, secondary, and tertiary (Quick, Murphy, Hurrell, & Orman, 1992). *Primary interventions* seek to reduce or eliminate the occurrence of a given stressor. Related to workplace aggression, such interventions would involve efforts to prevent aggression from occurring. *Secondary interventions* assume that the stressor has occurred or will occur and are directed at modifying how individuals respond to the stressor. Applied to workplace aggression, secondary interventions would involve efforts to reduce targets' negative reactions immediately following exposure to aggressive behavior. *Tertiary interventions* assume that individuals have been harmed by exposure to a given stressor and seek to ameliorate the harm that has taken place. Applied to workplace aggression, tertiary interventions would involve efforts that are intended to remediate the psychological, physical, or behavioral symptoms associated with exposure to aggression. Although the boundaries between these three types of interventions are not always clear, this classification provides a useful framework for identifying occupational health interventions such as workplace aggression training.

Primary interventions can be generally classified into three categories: environmental, organizational, and behavioral (University of Iowa Injury Prevention Research Center, 2001). *Environmental* approaches involve modifying aspects of the work environment that may increase or reduce the occurrence of aggressive behavior and could include installing security hardware or making adjustments to entrances and exits. *Organizational* approaches involve developing policies, procedures, and work practices to reduce the likelihood of aggression, such as the use of selection assessment instruments to assist in the identification and screening out of potentially aggressive individuals (e.g., Glomb et al., 2002; see also Day & Catano, Chapter 24, this volume). *Behavioral* approaches involve efforts to prevent aggression by modifying people's behavior in workplaces. Workplace aggression training would fall into this category of intervention.

The potential importance of training as a means of preventing workplace aggression has been suggested in a number of outlets, including the publications of institutes concerned with health and safety (e.g., National Institute for Occupational Safety and Health [NIOSH], 2002; University of Iowa Injury Prevention Research Center, 2001) and the theoretical and empirical research literature (e.g., Hatch-Maillette & Scalora, 2002; Mack, Shannon, Quick, & Quick, 1998; Neuman & Baron, 1997; Schat & Kelloway, 2000). Despite these suggestions, and the survey evidence indicating that a number of organizations have implemented training programs to address workplace aggression (Society for Human Resource Management, 1999), very little research has been carried out to evaluate systematically the effectiveness of workplace aggression training (Runyan et al., 2000).

Types of Workplace Aggression Training

Workplace aggression training is best viewed as a broad class of intervention strategies rather than a singular strategy. Workplace aggression training can be generally classified into a two-by-two matrix, with the timing of intervention on one axis and the recipient of the training on the other. With respect to the former, training can be prevention-focused (i.e., a primary intervention) or consequence-focused (i.e., a secondary or tertiary intervention). With respect to the latter, training can be target-directed (i.e., training potential targets of aggression to avoid experiencing aggression) or assailant-directed (i.e., training potential aggressors to control their own aggressive behavior). Target-directed, prevention-focused training is defined as training that seeks to provide potential targets with knowledge and skills they can use to understand, anticipate, and effectively respond to potential aggressors and aggressive situations to prevent the occurrence of aggressive behavior. Assailant-directed, prevention-focused training is defined as training that seeks to provide potential aggressors with knowledge and skills they can use to understand, anticipate, and manage their emotional and behavioral responses to potentially provocative events to prevent an aggressive response. Consequence-focused workplace aggression training would represent a secondary intervention, aimed at providing targets of aggressive behavior with knowledge and skills they can use to manage their reactions following exposure to workplace aggression to prevent or mitigate the negative consequences that may result from such exposure.

Determining what specific type of training intervention is most appropriate for a given situation must begin with a thorough training needs analysis (McGehee & Thayer, 1961) that would consider, among other things, the organizational context, those who will receive the training, and the type(s) and source(s) of aggressive behavior the training will seek to address. Although the distinction between prevention- and consequence-focused training many not always be clear (e.g., the knowledge and skills learned in prevention-focused training could help employees to manage their reactions to an episode of aggression that occurs) and consequence-focused training is likely useful in its own right, the focus of the present chapter is on prevention-focused training.

Whether workplace aggression training is prevention- or consequence-focused, to effectively prevent workplace aggression, the development of such programs should be guided by sound theoretical understanding of, and empirical research findings related to, the causes of workplace aggression. A number of situational, organizational (e.g., O'Leary-Kelly, Griffin, & Glew, 1996), and individual difference (e.g., Douglas & Martinko, 2001; Greenberg & Barling, 1999) variables have been suggested and found to predict workplace aggression (see Glomb et al., 2002, for a review). Although many of these variables could be addressed by intervention strategies that aim to prevent workplace aggression, in this chapter, we focus on antecedents of aggressive behavior that may be amenable to training. For target-directed, prevention-focused training, it is important to consider both job-related and individual level predictors of aggression and include knowledge and skill development related to both of these in training programs. For assailant-directed, prevention-focused training, the focus is on facilitating awareness of negative affect-provoking events that may occur and developing skills to managing one's emotional and behavioral reactions to these events. Accordingly, before describing the characteristics of workplace aggression training programs, we briefly review the literature to identify potential job-related, affective, and cognitive antecedents of workplace aggression.

Occupational and Employee-Related Antecedents of Workplace Aggression

LeBlanc and Kelloway (2002) conducted a study to examine the extent to which various job characteristics are associated with exposure to public- and coworker-initiated aggression. Job characteristics that emerged as the strongest predictors of public-initiated violence included exercising physical control over others; handling weapons; having contact with individuals under the influence of medication, alcohol, or illegal drugs; exercising security functions; providing physical care for others; making decisions that influence people's lives; and disciplining others. Other risk factors included going to a clients' home, working alone, working at night, and handling or guarding money or valuables.

Extrapolating these risk factors to occupations that comprise these job characteristics suggests some occupations are characterized by a number of these risk factors, including, for example, the work of taxi drivers (who often work alone, at night, and handle money), nurses (who provide for the physical care of others and have contact with patients who may be on medication or other substances), and police and security officers (who exercise security functions, may work at night, and may have to exercise physical control over others). Also, many occupations, some of which are not typically considered at risk for aggression, are characterized by at least some degree of risk. For example, nonnursing hospital staff (e.g., orderlies), teachers, professors, psychologists, counselors, managers, manufacturing employees, and bartenders have some degree of risk and reported experiencing aggression from members of the public or coworkers and, in some cases, both (LeBlanc & Kelloway, 2002). Employees working in the retail and service sectors are also at risk of exposure to workplace aggression (NIOSH, 1995; see also Howard & Voss, 1996). These results suggest that workplace aggression training (and other interventions) should be (a) considered for a variety of occupations in a variety of organizational contexts, and (b) tailored to suit the particular characteristics (e.g., risk factors, types and sources of aggression) of the occupations and organizations to which they are being applied.

Researchers have also investigated risk factors of violence in mental health institutions. Although much of this research is more descriptive than predictive (Quinsey, 2000), a number of aggression correlates have been identified including psychiatric diagnoses and patient-staff conflict. Cunningham, Connor, Miller, and Melloni (2003) found that patient psychiatric diagnoses were correlated with the frequency of assaults on staff in a mental health setting. This may be due, in part, to the finding that psychiatric illness is associated with negative affective states (e.g., depression, fear, irritability, anger) and low impulse control that are predictors of aggression (Berkowitz, 1993). An important caveat needs to be considered with respect to the association between psychiatric diagnosis and aggression in mental health hospitals. As Quinsey (2000) states, because discharge from psychiatric hospitals is associated with symptom improvement, patients who remain hospitalized are often still symptomatic (which may include aggressive behavior) and may be less treatable than those who are discharged. Therefore, research carried out in these settings is more likely to find an inflated relationship between patient characteristics such as psychiatric diagnosis and aggressive behavior. This does not attenuate the concern with aggression in these settings, but the association between psychiatric condition and aggressive behavior needs to be considered in this light and should not be taken to support the popular assumption that psychiatric symptoms necessarily cause aggressive behavior.

Another important finding is that in mental health institutions, staff are more likely to be assaulted than other patients (Harris & Varney, 1986; Quinsey & Varney, 1977), suggesting there is something unique about staff-patient interactions that contributes to aggression. The research evidence suggests that assaults are more likely to occur during interactions involving staff setting limits on patient behavior (Chou, Lu, & Mao, 2002; Harris & Varney, 1986; Quinsey & Varney, 1977). Whether patients respond aggressively out of frustration (i.e., when their behavior is thwarted) or due to the manner in which the limit setting is done is important to consider. Research examining the attributions that patients and staff make for assaultive behavior suggests that staff tend to attribute assaults to patients' psychopathology, whereas patients attribute them to teasing and staff giving orders in an adversarial manner (Harris & Varney, 1986; Quinsey & Varney, 1977). These results suggest that patients perceive behaviors of the targets (i.e., staff members) as provoking assaults (Quinsey, 2000).

More direct evidence for the importance of training comes from research examining the influence of staff experience and training on assault and injury rates. A survey of mental health staff conducted by Cunningham and colleagues (2003) showed that younger and less experienced staff reported more assaults and injuries than older and more experienced staff. Similarly, Blair and New (1991) found that nursing assistants and student nurses reported higher incidences of assault than more experienced nurses. Rasmussen and Levander (1996) investigated training in particular and found that staff who were trained to manage assault were less likely to be assaulted than untrained staff. Chou et al. (2002) found similar results in their study of psychiatric hospital staff in Taiwan. They suggested that when staff set limits on patient behavior in an adversarial manner, they are more likely to elicit a violent reaction. Thus, training staff to set limits using problem-solving and conflict resolution strategies should reduce their exposure to incidents of assault.

That staff with more experience and training report experiencing less aggression suggests that they possess skills that make them more effective at avoiding or preventing aggressive behavior. Research investigating what specific dimensions of experience (Quinones, Ford, & Teachout, 1995) are relevant and whether training incrementally improves the skills of experienced employees would be helpful. In addition, research examining the association between training, experience, and exposure to aggression in work settings other than health care is also needed.

Theoretical Foundations of Workplace Aggression Training

In order to develop interventions that have the potential to prevent workplace aggression, it is important to understand the factors both that cause people to behave aggressively and that contribute to the escalation of work interactions into aggression (Beale, Lawrence, Smewing, & Cox, 1999). In this chapter, we draw on affective events theory (AET; Weiss & Cropanzano, 1996) and emotion regulation theory (ERT; e.g., Gross, 1998a, 1998b) to theoretically situate our discussion of training as a strategy for preventing workplace aggression. Both AET and ERT consider the processes by which events act as proximal causes of emotion and by which emotion leads to behavioral responses (e.g., aggression). As such, they provide the theoretical context for considering the potential foci of training that seeks to prevent workplace aggression. One potential focus of training may be to influence the nature and extent of an individual's reaction to a negative workplace event (e.g., unjust performance evaluation, public humiliation). Of particular concern here would be trying to reduce the occurrence or strength of the negative affective reactions that may lead to affect-driven behavior such as violence. The other potential focus of training would be to influence the relationship between the affective reaction and affect-driven

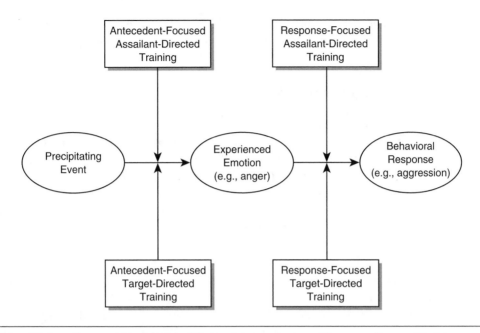

Figure 25.1   Proposed Model of the Effects of Antecedent- and Response-Focused Training on Workplace Aggression

behavior. This might include, for example, strategies aimed at defusing anger to reduce the likelihood that it would lead to aggressive behavior. Consistent with ERT, these two foci of training are referred to as antecedent-focused and response-focused, respectively. A model integrating AET and ERT and applying them to workplace aggression (see Glomb et al., 2002, for a model of AET applied to workplace aggression) that incorporates the proposed influences of workplace aggression training is provided in Figure 25.1.

Affective and Cognitive Antecedents of Workplace Aggression

Training that seeks to prevent aggressive behavior is designed to focus on helping people manage the emotions and cognitions that may lead them to behave aggressively. Although there has been research on predictors of workplace aggression, much of this research deals with general individual difference and situational characteristics rather than specific emotions or cognitions and is based on cross-sectional rather than longitudinal data. As a result, it does not directly address the temporal sequence of affect, cognitions, and behaviors that immediately precede and cause acts of workplace aggression; however, this research does provide some insight into such variables. Taken together with the findings of basic research on human aggression, there are several antecedent variables that seem to be particularly relevant and on which training could focus. These include anger, frustration, hostile attribution style, and rumination.

Anger and Frustration

In general, the aggression literature suggests that anger represents an affective response to a particular event that in turn may lead to aggressive behavior (e.g., Berkowitz, 1993). Spielberger (1996) has distinguished between state anger and trait anger. *State anger* is an emotional response to a specific event and *trait anger* involves a general disposition to experience state anger in various situations. Douglas and Martinko (2001) found that trait anger was a significant predictor of self-reported aggressive behavior. By implication, training people to manage their own or others' anger should reduce the likelihood of aggressive behavior.

Frustration, the thwarting of one's goal-directed behavior, is often believed to be a predictor of aggressive behavior. The frustration-aggression hypothesis (Dollard, Doob, Miller, Mowrer, & Sears, 1939) was based on this supposition. Baron and Richardson's (1994) review of the literature suggests that there is mixed support for the proposed effect of frustration on aggression. They identify a number of variables that intervene in the relationship between frustration and aggression, suggesting that frustration is more likely to lead to aggression when the frustration is particularly intense, arbitrary, or unexpected; other aggressive cues are present; or the frustration results in negative affect (e.g., anger or fear). This latter element is particularly relevant, as it suggests that it is not frustration per se that leads to aggressive behavior but an individual's reaction to frustration. Here again, the research on aggression points to the centrality of people's affective reaction to events—rather than events themselves—that are the more proximal causes of aggression. Although prevention of frustrating events is certainly desirable and should be considered as part of a broader aggression-prevention strategy, training is perhaps better aimed at helping people manage how they respond to—and, more specifically, how they manage their emotions in response to—frustrating or otherwise aversive events.

Hostile Attribution Style

In addition to affect, evidence suggests that cognition is also associated with aggressive behavior. In particular, when people experience an aversive behavior or event, they seek to understand why the person behaved as he of she did or why the event occurred. This cognitive appraisal of the cause of a behavior or event is referred to as *attribution*. Basic research in aggression demonstrates that the type of attribution one makes can influence the likelihood that one will respond with aggressive behavior (e.g., Weiner, 1995). These attributional influences have also been included in a number of theoretical contributions to the workplace aggression literature (e.g., Folger & Skarlicki, 1998; Martinko & Zellars, 1998). Empirical evidence for these influences on workplace aggression was provided by Douglas and Martinko (2001), who found the *hostile attribution style*—the tendency for people to attribute negative events to external, stable, intentional, and controllable causes—was a significant predictor of aggressive behavior. Based on this work, if training is able to reduce people's tendencies toward negative attributions, it should help to reduce the aggressive behavior that may emerge from such attributions.

Rumination

Rumination involves directing attention toward oneself and particularly one's negative mood (Lyubomirsky & Nolan-Hoeksema, 1994). Despite the position of catharsis theory, which suggests that focusing on and venting one's anger helps to reduce feelings of anger and aggression, research suggests that rumination does not reduce aggression but, in fact, tends to increase it (e.g., Bushman, Baumeister, & Stack, 1999). For example, Rusting and Nolen-Hoeksema (1998) examined the mood regulation strategies used by people following an anger induction task in a laboratory setting. Participants who used a rumination strategy were more likely to experience an increase in anger, whereas those who adopted a *distraction strategy*—in which individuals focus attention away from the mood and onto pleasant or neutral stimuli—were more likely to experience lower or unchanged levels of anger. Similar results were found in a study by Bushman (2002) in which angered participants who vented their anger by hitting a punching bag and thought about the person who angered them felt angrier and exhibited higher levels of aggressive behavior than participants in distraction and control conditions. This evidence suggests that training aimed at reducing people's focus on the source of their anger (e.g., reducing rumination) and changing their focus to something else (e.g., distraction) should help to mitigate work-related anger and aggression. These issues will be elaborated on later in the chapter when we discuss emotion regulation training.

Target-Directed, Prevention-Focused Workplace Aggression Training

In a publication addressing occupational hazards in hospitals, the Department of Health and Human Services of NIOSH (2002) suggests providing all workers with training to recognize impending violence, resolve conflicts, and maintain awareness of potentially violent situations. With respect to recognizing potential violence, this publication refers to several signals of impending violence: verbally expressed anger, threatening body language, signs of substance use, and the presence of a weapon.

With respect to resolving conflicts, it offers several suggestions that may help to defuse anger: present a calm, caring attitude; acknowledge a person's feelings; and avoid behavior that may be interpreted as aggressive (e.g., speaking loudly, moving quickly).

Although the focus of most training programs is on the development of skills, the development of knowledge is also important, as it provides the context and basis for skill development. For workplace aggression training, knowledge related to understanding why aggressive behavior occurs and recognizing potential risk factors to facilitate response preparation would be particularly important. This is highlighted by the results of a study by Walsh and Clarke (2003), who found that half of the participants in their study who experienced aggression reported that they did not expect and were not prepared for it, although they had experienced similar incidents in the past.

Sutton and Kahn (1987) suggested that workers who are able to understand, predict, and influence their experience of work-related stress would be less negatively influenced by exposure to it. In a recent study (Schat and Kelloway, 2000), we conceptualized understanding, prediction, and influence as three dimensions of perceived control and empirically investigated Sutton and Kahn's suggestions in a study of workplace aggression. The results showed that perceived control—which included employees' perceived ability to (a) understand why aggressive behavior occurred (i.e., understanding), (b) predict the timing and nature of workplace aggression (i.e., prediction), and (c) take action when aggression occurs (i.e., influence)—was associated with reduced fear and fewer negative psychological consequences of aggression. Furthermore, those who had received training to deal with workplace aggression reported higher levels of the three dimensions of perceived control than those who had not received training. These results suggest that training may be effective at increasing employees' understanding of the causes of aggression and their ability to predict it and respond when it occurs.

Evidence from the risk assessment literature shows the importance of providing accurate, empirically based information regarding potential workplace aggression risk factors. Research on risk assessment—which involves assessing the dangerousness of patients or clients to others (e.g., Werner, Rose, & Yesavage, 1983, 1990)—has shown that the variables used by evaluators to determine risk of future violence are not always consistent with the variables that are known predictors of such behavior (e.g., Cooper & Werner, 1990; Werner et al., 1983, 1990). Arkes, Dawes, and Christensen (1986) suggest that staff tend to be overconfident in their expertise and rely on it rather than empirically based decision rules, leading to less accurate judgments of likelihood of violence. As a result, potential predictors of violent behavior may be overlooked and the opportunity for corrective action missed, resulting in increased risk of violence and injury. These risks will be reduced to the extent that training provides information on known predictors of violence, increases evaluators' ability to accurately identify factors that precipitate violence, and develops their skill in taking appropriate corrective action.

Conflict Management and De-escalation

Research suggesting that serious acts of workplace violence are often the culmination of a series of interactions of increasing intensity has led to suggestions that employees should be provided with training that improves their skills in responding to situations involving individuals who are angry or agitated and who may become increasingly aggressive if not responded to appropriately (Beale et al., 1999; Fox, Polkey, & Boatman, 2002; NIOSH, 1995). A number of interventions, including conflict management, nonviolent intervention, and de-escalation, seek to develop these skills. Although there may be differences in these interventions, they all emphasize techniques that workers can use to respond to and manage their own and other people's emotions and behavior during potentially threatening situations with the goal of preventing the situation from escalating into violence. These techniques include monitoring one's own levels of arousal to the situation (Nunno, Holden, & Leidy, 2003), responding with calmness (e.g., Cox & Leather, 1994; NIOSH, 2002) and empathy (Beale et al., 1999; NIOSH, 2002), avoiding power struggles and counteraggressive responses (Nunno et al., 2003) or responses that may be perceived as aggressive (NIOSH, 2002), and trying to deal with the situation in private (Beale et al., 1999).

Cunningham et al. (2003) suggest that the higher rates of assault and injury faced by less experienced workers compared with rates for more experienced workers may be due to differences in the way they respond to aggressive behavior. Specifically, they suggest that experienced staff may be more likely to de-escalate potentially aggressive behavior before it occurs, whereas inexperienced staff may be less prepared for and more likely to respond in a reactive manner to aggression when it occurs. If their suggestion is correct, then training workers in the use of de-escalation strategies should reduce the likelihood that violent behavior will occur.

Nunno and colleagues (2003) studied the effectiveness of a crisis intervention strategy called *therapeutic crisis intervention* (TCI), which was implemented in a residential child care facility. The TCI method is based on crisis management and de-escalation theory (e.g., Parad & Parad, 1990) and teaches residential care staff to interpret children's aggressive behavior as an expression of their needs (rather than defiance directed at the staff themselves), to monitor their own levels of arousal to aggression, and to exercise behaviors that reduce the potential for a counteraggressive response. Evaluation of the TCI program showed that it resulted in enhanced staff knowledge about and confidence in crisis intervention, increased staff skill in handling children's aggressive behavior (as rated by supervisors), and fewer critical incidents of children's aggressive behavior. Additional evidence comes from Dubin, Wilson, and Mercer (1988), who found that when psychiatrists were confronted by a patient with a weapon, those who verbally calmed their patients experienced less bodily injury and property damage than those who responded with verbal or physical aggression.

Restraints, Self-Defense, and the Use of Physical Force

In certain occupations and organizations that have an increased risk of exposure to physical violence, it may be appropriate to train employees in physical restraint methods, self-defense techniques, and the use of reasonable force to facilitate the control of violent individuals. The use of physical force as a violence-management strategy is controversial (Lewis, 2002; Stanton-Greenwood, 1999) and introduces a number of challenges. A review of the topic is beyond the scope of the present chapter (for a review, see Wright, 1999). We note, however, that because of the difficulties associated with defining appropriate levels of physical force or restraint, the potential for increased risk of injury associated with physical interventions (e.g., Parkes, 1996), and the potential health-related, legal, and other ramifications of the inappropriate use of same, it is imperative that due attention be given to alternative means of addressing violence. If physical responses such as restraint techniques are deemed necessary, then the training in these techniques must be thorough to ensure that those using these strategies have the ability to use them safely and effectively (Beale et al., 1999).

Multifaceted Target-Directed, Prevention-Focused Training Interventions

Training to address workplace aggression should be designed and implemented to address the specific needs of an organization or a specific segment of the organization. In some cases, this may lead to a training program that addresses a narrowly defined problem by providing training in a very specific set of skills. In other cases, however, the problem may be more general, involving the presence of a number of situational, occupational, and personal antecedents of workplace aggression. In these cases, training should be multifaceted to develop a variety of the skills that are needed. There are few examples of such programs being evaluated in the literature.

In one study, Infantino and Musingo (1985) examined the effect of a number of aggression control techniques on the rates of physical assault and injury reported by staff in a psychiatric hospital. The techniques included verbal intervention procedures to defuse potentially violent situations and physical intervention techniques (e.g., instruction on restraining and controlling violent individuals). Ninety-six staff were followed for 9 to 24 months. Of the 65 staff who were not trained, 37% were assaulted (19 were injured). Of the 31 staff who were trained, only one (3%) was assaulted (and not injured).

A study by Weitlauf, Smith, and Cervone (2000), though not aimed specifically at addressing workplace aggression, is illustrative of a comprehensive, multifaceted training program that could be applied to addressing workplace aggression. Weitlauf et al.'s program involved training women to develop a variety of skills to help them to emotionally, verbally, and physically defend themselves against sexual assault. A rigorous evaluation methodology demonstrated that the program increased women's self-defense efficacy, general self-efficacy beliefs, and self-reported assertiveness. The results also showed posttraining decreases in hostility and aggression, demonstrating that the training did not result in the disinhibition of aggressive behavior.

Perhaps the most comprehensive workplace violence training program was developed and evaluated by Rice and colleagues (1989), who conducted a 10-year study of violence in psychiatric institutions. They developed a 5-day training program that included instructing frontline psychiatric institution staff in security measures, calming interventions, de-escalation techniques, conflict resolution, manual restraint, and self-defense. Outcome measures included knowledge and skills displayed in simulated crisis situations, measures of program acceptance, measures of patient affect and morale, and incidence of assault and injury. Program acceptance was high, patient affect and morale increased in the training wards compared with that in the control wards, and both the incidence of assault and assault-related injuries declined. Adapting and investigating the efficacy of such a comprehensive and multifaceted workplace aggression training program in other organizational settings besides psychiatric institutions would make a significant contribution to the workplace aggression literature and have significant practical implications.

Assailant-Directed, Prevention-Focused Workplace Aggression Training

As we stated earlier, the purpose of assailant-directed, prevention-focused workplace aggression training is to prevent aggressive behavior by developing employees' knowledge and skills to help them manage the emotions and cognitions that may lead them to behave aggressively, including anger, rumination, and hostile attributions. This type of training essentially amounts to training in emotion regulation.

Kanfer and Kantrowitz (2002) define *emotion regulation* as "the psychological and behavioral processes involved in the (self) management of affective response tendencies" (p. 437). Gross (1998b) offers a more specific definition of *emotion regulation*, describing it as "the process by which individuals influence which emotions they have, when they have them, and how they experience and express these emotions" (p. 275). Gross (1998a) further distinguishes between antecedent-focused and response-focused emotion regulation. *Antecedent-focused emotion regulation* occurs before an emotion is generated and involves manipulating or appraising one's experience of emotion in response to an affective cue or event. *Response-focused emotion regulation* occurs after the emotion is generated and involves regulating the observable manifestations of one's emotions (e.g., behavioral reactions). In effect, the former focuses on reducing the affective precursors of aggressive behavior and the latter focuses on reducing the likelihood that aggressive behavior occurs in the presence of the affective precursors.

Training in both antecedent- and response-focused emotion regulation represents a promising approach to preventing workplace aggression. Below we consider a number of emotion regulation strategies that have appeared in the literature and discuss their potential applicability to preventing workplace aggression and, in turn, their appropriateness for training. Before we consider these, we note that our review of training interventions for potential emotion regulation is not exhaustive. Researchers have identified hundreds of different emotion regulation strategies (Kanfer & Kantrowitz, 2002); therefore, we limit our discussion to those that have received the most attention in the literature and that focus specifically on addressing anger and aggressive behavior. We also note that we were not able to locate published empirical studies that have examined the effectiveness of emotion regulation interventions in preventing workplace anger and aggression. Therefore, we draw on the evidence available in the basic aggression and emotion regulation literatures to suggest interventions that may be effective for reducing workplace anger and aggression and urge researchers to empirically investigate the effectiveness of such interventions.

Antecedent-Focused Emotion Regulation

As defined earlier, antecedent-focused emotion regulation occurs before an emotion is generated and involves modifying one's experience of emotions following exposure to an affective cue or event. Gross (1998b) describes four forms of this type of emotion regulation: situation selection, situation modification, attentional deployment, and cognitive change. We discuss each of these forms of emotion regulation as they might relate to workplace aggression.

Situation Selection

For most people, there are certain circumstances that are more likely to elicit emotions than others. Awareness of these circumstances and the emotions they are likely to elicit provides people with the opportunity to control emotion elicitation by controlling their exposure to the circumstances. When people control their exposure to these circumstances, they are exercising *situation selection,* defined by Gross as "approaching or avoiding certain people, places, or objects in order to regulate emotions" (1998b, p. 283). Applying the concept of situation selection to workplace aggression would involve people's awareness of elements of their workplace—people, places, or things—that are likely to elicit negative affective reactions such as anger. For example, consider the following scenario. John has a particular coworker,

Joe, with whom he has had a number of previous angry exchanges. Situation selection would suggest that John could forestall experiencing anger by avoiding interactions with this coworker. In this case, training that fosters awareness of workplace situations that may elicit negative emotional reactions and encourages appropriate decision making to avoid these situations should lead to reductions in the negative emotional precursors of aggressive behavior and, in turn, reductions in aggressive behavior.

Situation Modification

Not all potentially emotion-eliciting situations can be avoided. However, even when people are exposed to potentially emotion-eliciting situations, it does not guarantee that emotion is elicited. Attempts to modify the situation to influence the degree of emotion elicitation constitute the emotion regulation strategy of *situation modification* (Gross, 1998b). Drawing on our previous example, let's assume that a work-related project requires John to interact with Joe. John could exercise situation modification in various ways, including, for example, by behaving amicably and keeping the interaction with Joe task-focused. Training in situation modification would involve developing problem-solving and related strategies to help people modify situations that they know have the potential to elicit negative emotions.

Attentional Deployment

Attentional deployment involves focusing one's attention toward or away from something and includes strategies such as distraction and rumination (Gross, 1998b). *Distraction* includes efforts to focus attention away from the immediate situation and onto pleasant or neutral stimuli. In the workplace, this could include focusing one's attention away from a potentially emotional situation and onto a job-related task or other stimulus that is not emotion-laden. *Rumination* involves directing attention toward an emotion, its causes and consequences, and self-evaluations related to it (e.g., Rusting & Nolan-Hoeksema, 1998). In light of our current discussion, these strategies are most likely to be employed following the elicitation of emotion; therefore, we discuss them in the section on response-focused emotion regulation strategies below.

Cognitive Change

When confronted with a potentially emotion-eliciting situation, one can evaluate the situation or one's ability to manage it, thereby influencing one's emotions. This process is referred to as *cognitive change*. *Reappraisal* is a cognitive change strategy that involves cognitively reframing how one experiences a situation to reduce its emotional impact and has been shown to be effective at reducing a number of indicators of emotional arousal in response to a film shown to elicit disgust (Gross, 1998a). Consider our example of John and Joe again. Let's assume that Joe publicly criticizes John's job performance during a meeting. John's attempts to modify his view of the event by trying not to take the criticism personally would reflect reappraisal. This modification should reduce the degree of anger he experiences and, indirectly, the likelihood of an aggressive response. A study by Grandey, Dickter, and Sin (2004) found that call center employees who used a reappraisal strategy, compared with those who used suppression, faking, or venting strategies, were less likely to appraise customer aggression as highly stressful. Although more research is needed to evaluate the effectiveness of this strategy in the reduction of workplace anger and aggression, a comprehensive emotion regulation training program should include instruction in the use of cognitive change strategies, such as reappraisal.

Response-Focused Emotion Regulation

As defined earlier, response-focused emotion regulation occurs after an emotion is generated but before an emotional response (i.e., behavior) has been generated in response to an affective cue or event (Gross, 1998b). Strategies include attentional deployment that occurs after an emotion such as anger has been experienced, emotional suppression, and anger management interventions.

Response-Focused Attentional Deployment

Two attentional deployment strategies we introduced earlier are self-focused rumination and distraction. Studies by Rusting and Nolen-Hoeksema (1998) and Bushman (2002) suggest that rumination "fuels the fire" of anger rather than purges it as would be suggested by catharsis theory (Bushman, 2002). Although research is needed to examine whether these results would generalize to work settings, they suggest that training aimed at developing people's ability to respond to anger by self-distraction or reappraisal rather than rumination should reduce (or at least prevent the exacerbation of) anger and, in turn, reduce the likelihood of an aggressive response.

Emotional Suppression

Emotional *suppression* is a form of response-focused emotion regulation that involves the inhibition of emotionally expressive behavior during emotional arousal (Gross & Levenson, 1993). Gross (1998a) conducted a study in which he experimentally elicited disgust in participants (by having them view a film clip) and then evaluated the effects of two different emotion regulation strategies: reappraisal and suppression. Compared with participants in the control condition, participants in the reappraisal condition showed decreases in behavioral, subjective, and physiological indicators of emotion. Participants in the suppression condition showed reductions in emotionally expressive behavior but increases in several indicators of physiological response (e.g., finger pulse amplitude, skin conductance). These results suggest that suppression may be effective at reducing emotionally expressive behavior but not reducing one's emotional experience. In their study, Grandey et al. (2004) found that call center employees who appraised aggressive customers as highly stressful tended to report using suppression and faking strategies. As Gross (1998a) suggests, because different types of emotion regulation have different consequences, "no one strategy is likely to prove uniformly superior to all others across all contexts" (p. 232). Therefore, it is important to consider the relative benefits or drawbacks of various strategies in various situations and ensure that the intervention strategies match the demands of the situation. In light of the many different types of aggressive workplace behavior and their individual and situational predictors, the need to ensure a match between the emotional regulation intervention and situational characteristics seems particularly important to consider. Continued investigation of these issues would facilitate the tailoring of emotion regulation training and related interventions to the needs of particular situations.

Anger Management

Anger management is a term that represents a broad range of interventions that can be used to reduce the experience and expression of anger. Techniques include relaxation therapy, meditation, progressive muscle relaxation, cognitive-behavioral therapy, and others (DiGiuseppe & Tafrate, 2003). These techniques are often included as elements of multimodal stress management programs (Cartwright & Whatmore, 2003). A recent meta-analysis of the effectiveness of anger treatment programs for adults by DiGiuseppe and Tafrate (2003) suggests that participants who received treatment showed large improvements—reductions in angry affect, reductions in aggressive behaviors, and increases in positive behaviors—compared with their pretest levels and moderate improvements compared with untreated participants, and that these improvements were maintained over time.

It is important to note that the studies included in this meta-analysis were based on data from clinical populations and, in many cases, included psychotherapeutic anger management treatment. Therefore, although the results demonstrate that anger treatment may result in reductions in anger and aggression, the extent to which such treatment would also reduce work-related anger and aggressive behavior needs to be investigated. In addition, the most appropriate design of work-related anger treatment must be considered. For example, should anger treatment programs be adapted to deal specifically with work-related anger and affect or would general anger treatment programs be appropriate for—and their effects generalize to—workplace anger? Also, in multimodel stress management programs, what elements are effective or ineffective, and what individual differences influence their (in)effectiveness (Cartwright & Cooper, 2004)? Data from studies examining these questions could inform the development of training programs that aim to address the management of workplace anger.

Design, Development, and Implementation of Workplace Aggression Training

Work-related situations that involve aggressive behavior can be highly stressful, and it is important that the training approach used to address workplace aggression recognizes its inherent stressfulness. Driskell, Salas, and Johnston (2001) argue that skills acquired through traditional training methods (e.g., classroom-based training) are unlikely to transfer to high-stress situations that include time pressure, distractions, and high work load. They go on to suggest that for training to effectively transfer to such situations, it must provide some form of preexposure to the high-stress conditions and incorporate instruction in the use of specialized skills required for the situation. *Stress training* is a term that represents training programs that have as their purpose "to prepare the individual to maintain effective performance in a high-stress environment" (Driskell et al., 2001, p. 58). The stress training approach developed by Driskell and Johnston (1998), called *stress exposure training* (SET), provides a useful framework for structuring the design, development, and implementation of workplace aggression training. Their approach consists of three phases: information provision, skill acquisition, and application and practice.

The *information provision* phase involves providing trainees with information about stress and its consequences. Applied to workplace aggression, this would entail providing information regarding the types of behavior that constitute workplace aggression and its causes and consequences. Because of the wide range of behaviors that constitute workplace aggression, the information provided during this phase should reflect the behaviors that are identified through training needs analysis as being the focus of the training program. For example, a training program developed to address physically violent behaviors should focus on the nature, predictors, and consequences of such behaviors.

According to Driskell and Johnston (1998), the *skill acquisition* phase involves teaching and giving trainees the opportunity to practice the cognitive and behavioral skills that they require to perform effectively in a stressful environment. In their framework, the purpose of the training is not to prevent the stressor from occurring but rather to perform the required tasks in spite of its occurrence and the stress it may elicit. Although this focus on maintaining effective performance under stress would be important in contexts involving aggression (e.g., a nurse effectively performing a medical procedure while being verbally abused by a patient), the primary focus of this phase of workplace aggression training would be on developing trainees' skills that help to reduce the occurrence of workplace aggression. If the training is aimed at potential aggressors, the focus would be on skills they could use to reduce the likelihood that they would behave aggressively in a provocative situation. If the training is aimed at potential targets, the focus would be on skills they could use to prevent another person from behaving aggressively in a provocative situation.

The *application and practice* phase involves providing trainees with the opportunity to apply and practice their skills in a graduated manner in a simulated stress environment. The way in which this phase would be applied to workplace aggression training would depend on the particular focus of the training program (e.g., physical violence, nonphysical aggression). In general, however, this phase would involve trainees responding to simulated aggression-provoking scenarios of increasing intensity, the goal of which would be to increase the likelihood that the learned skills transfer to actual aggression-provoking situations and result in the prevention of aggressive behavior.

Evaluation of Workplace Aggression Training

There are numerous references to training programs in the workplace aggression (e.g., National Center on Addiction and Substance Abuse at Columbia University, 2000) and sexual harassment (e.g., Williams, Fitzgerald, & Drasgow, 1999) literatures, and workers generally report that these programs are effective. For example, Pryor and Fitzgerald (2003) cite the results of a survey of federal employees in the United States, 63% of which reported that the training provided by their agencies reduces or prevents sexual harassment. Similarly, a focus group evaluation of the U.S. Postal Service violence awareness training programs showed that participants found it to be effective in increasing awareness of potential warning signs and responses to violence (National Center on Addiction and Substance Abuse at Columbia University, 2000). However, no evidence of a more systematic evaluation of the training was presented. As Pryor and Fitzgerald note, surveys of this nature are more reflective of participant reactions to the training programs than scientific evaluations of their effectiveness. Indeed, there are very limited data available that represent rigorous evaluations of the effectiveness of training programs that aim to address workplace aggression (Runyan et al., 2000). As we have pointed out elsewhere (Schat & Kelloway, 2005), "systematic assessment of the characteristics and effectiveness of training programs targeting workplace aggression . . . represents a significant research need in this area" (p. 213).

Epilogue

The research evidence regarding the negative consequences of workplace aggression—for individuals, organizations, and society as a whole—continues to accumulate, demonstrating the need for interventions to prevent its occurrence and mitigate its negative consequences. In this chapter, we have focused on training as one category of intervention. In light of the lack of rigorous empirical attention this topic has thus far received, our goal was to review the available literature related to workplace aggression training and draw on other relevant literatures to identify a number of training interventions that have the potential to contribute to the prevention of workplace aggression and violence. For several of the training interventions we describe, there is evidence available to indicate their effectiveness in reducing workplace aggression and violence (e.g., Rice et al.'s [1989] program addressing violence in psychiatric institutions). Others appear promising but their effectiveness in preventing aggression remains to be investigated (e.g., emotion regulation training). We encourage both researchers and practitioners concerned with workplace aggression to develop and rigorously evaluate the effectiveness of workplace aggression training and other interventions with the hope that these interventions will contribute not only to the reduction of workplace aggression but to the enhancement of the health of organizations, their individual members, and society as a whole.

References

Anderson, C. A., & Bushman, B. J. (2002). Human aggression. *Annual Review of Psychology, 53,* 27–51.

Arkes, H. R., Dawes, R. M., & Christensen, C. (1986). Factors influencing the use of a decision rule in a probabilistic task. *Organizational Behavior and Human Decision Processes, 37,* 93–110.

Baron, R. A., & Richardson, D. R. (1994). *Human aggression* (2nd ed.). New York: Plenum.

Beale, D., Lawrence, C., Smewing, C., & Cox, T. (1999). Organisational and environmental measures for reducing and managing work-related violence. In P. Leather, C. Brady, C. Lawrence, D. Beale, & T. Cox (Eds.), *Work-related violence: Assessment and intervention* (pp. 87–105). London: Routledge.

Berkowitz, L. (1993). *Aggression: Its causes, consequences, and control.* Philadelphia: Temple University Press.

Blair, D. T., & New, S. A. (1991). Assaultive behavior: Know the risk. *Journal of Psychosocial Nursing, 29,* 25–29.

Bureau of Labor Statistics. (2004). *National census of fatal occupational injuries in 2003.* Washington, DC: Author.

Bushman, B. J. (2002). Does venting anger feed or extinguish the flame? Catharsis, rumination, distraction, anger, and aggressive responding. *Personality and Social Psychology Bulletin, 28,* 724–731.

Bushman, B. J., Baumeister, R. F., & Stack, A. D. (1999). Catharsis, aggression, and persuasive influence: Self-fulfilling or self-defeating prophecies? *Journal of Personality and Social Psychology, 76,* 367–376.

Cartwright, S., & Cooper, C. (2004). Individually targeted interventions. In J. Barling, M. Frone, & E. K. Kelloway (Eds.), *Handbook of work stress* (pp. 607–622). Thousand Oaks, CA: Sage.

Cartwright, S., & Whatmore, L. (2003). Stress and individual differences: Implications for stress management. In A. Antoniou & C. L. Cooper (Eds.), *New perspectives in the area of occupational health*. London: John Wiley.

Chou, K., Lu, R., & Mao, W. (2002). Factors relevant to patient assaultive behavior and assault in acute inpatient psychiatric units in Taiwan. *Archives of Psychiatric Nursing, 16,* 187–195.

Cooper, R. P., & Werner, P. D. (1990). Predicting violence in newly admitted inmates: A lens model analysis of staff decision making. *Criminal Justice and Behavior, 17,* 431–447.

Cox, T., & Leather, P. (1994). The prevention of violence at work: Application of a cognitive behavioral theory. In C. L. Cooper & I. T. Robertson (Eds.), *International review of industrial and organizational psychology* (Vol. 9, pp. 213–245). Chichester, UK: John Wiley.

Cunningham, J., Connor, D. F., Miller, K., & Melloni, R. H. (2003). Staff survey results and characteristics that predict assault and injury to personnel working in mental health care facilities. *Aggressive Behavior, 29,* 31–40.

DiGuiseppe, R., & Tafrate, R. C. (2003). Anger treatment for adults: A meta-analytic review. *Clinical Psychology: Science and Practice, 10,* 70–84.

Dollard, J., Doob, L. W., Miller, N. E., Mowrer, O. H., & Sears, R. R. (1939). *Frustration and aggression*. New Haven, CT: Yale University Press.

Douglas, S. C., & Martinko, M. J. (2001). Exploring the role of individual differences in the prediction of workplace aggression. *Journal of Applied Psychology, 86,* 547–559.

Driskell, J. E., & Johnston, J. (1998). Stress exposure training. In J. A. Cannon-Bowers & E. Salas (Eds.), *Making decisions under stress: Implications for individual and team training* (pp. 191–217). Washington, DC: American Psychological Association.

Driskell, J. E., Salas, E., & Johnston, J. (2001). Stress management: Individual and team training. In E. Salas, C. A. Bowers, & E. Edens (Eds.), *Improving teamwork in organizations: Applications of resource management training* (pp. 55–72). Mahwah, NJ: Lawrence Erlbaum.

Dubin, W. R., Wilson, S. J., & Mercer, C. (1988). Assaults against psychiatrists in outpatient settings. *Journal of Clinical Psychiatry, 49,* 338–345.

Folger, R., & Skarlicki, D. P. (1998). A popcorn metaphor for employee aggression. In R. W. Griffin, A. O'Leary-Kelly, & J. M. Collins (Eds.), *Dysfunctional behavior in organizations: Violent and deviant behavior* (pp. 43–81). Stanford, CT: JAI.

Fox, B., Polkey, C., & Boatman, P. (2002). *Managing violence in the workplace*. Croydon, UK: Reed Elsevier.

Glomb, T. M. (2002). Workplace anger and aggression: Informing conceptual models with data from specific encounters. *Journal of Occupational Health Psychology, 7,* 20–36.

Glomb, T. M., Steel, P. D. G., & Arvey, R. D. (2002). Office sneers, snipes, and stab wounds: Antecedents, consequences, and implications of workplace violence and aggression. In R. G. Lord, R. Klimoski, & R. Kanfer (Eds.), *Emotions at work* (pp. 227–259). San Francisco: Jossey-Bass.

Grandey, A. A., Dickter, D. N., & Sin, H. P. (2004). The customer is not always right: Customer aggression and emotion regulation of service employees. *Journal of Organizational Behavior, 25,* 397–418.

Greenberg, L., & Barling, J. (1999). Predicting employee aggression against co-workers, subordinates and supervisors: The roles of person behaviors and perceived workplace factors. *Journal of Organizational Behavior, 20,* 897–913.

Gross, J. J. (1998a). Antecedent- and response-focused emotion regulation: Divergent consequences for experience, expression, and physiology. *Journal of Personality and Social Psychology, 74,* 224–237.

Gross, J. J. (1998b). The emerging field of emotion regulation: An integrative review. *Review of General Psychology, 2,* 271–299.

Gross, J. J., & Levenson, R. W. (1993). Emotional suppression: Physiology, self-report, and expressive behavior. *Journal of Personality and Social Psychology, 64,* 970–986.

Harris, G. T., & Varney, G. W. (1986). A ten-year study of assaults and assaulters in a maximum security psychiatric unit. *Journal of Interpersonal Violence, 1,* 173–191.

Hatch-Maillette, M. A., & Scalora, M. J. (2002). Gender, sexual harassment, workplace violence, and risk assessment: Convergence around psychiatric staff's perceptions of personal safety. *Aggression and Violent Behavior, 7,* 271–291.

Howard, J. L., & Voss, R. B. (1996). Workplace violence and the sector ignored: A response to O'Leary-Kelly, Griffin, & Glew. *Academy of Management Review, 21,* 920–922.

Infantino, J. A., & Musingo, S. Y. (1985). Assaults and injuries among staff with and without training in aggression control techniques. *Hospital and Community Psychiatry, 36,* 1312–1314.

Kanfer, R., & Kantrowitz, T. M. (2002). Emotion regulation: Command and control of emotion in work life. In R. G. Lord, R. Klimoski, & R. Kanfer (Eds.), *Emotions at work* (pp. 433–472). San Francisco: Jossey-Bass.

Keashly, L. (1998). Emotional abuse in the workplace: Conceptual and empirical issues. *Journal of Emotional Abuse, 1,* 85–115.

Keashly, L., & Jagatic, K. (2003). By any other name: American perspectives on workplace bullying. In S. Einarsen, H. Hoel, D. Zapf, & C. Cooper (Eds.), *Bullying and emotional abuse in the workplace: International perspectives in research and practice.* London: Taylor Francis.

LeBlanc, M. M., & Kelloway, E. K. (2002). Predictors and outcomes of workplace violence and aggression. *Journal of Applied Psychology, 87,* 444–453.

Lewis, D. M. (2002). Responding to a violent incident: Physical restraint or anger management as therapeutic interventions. *Journal of Psychiatric and Mental Health Nursing, 9,* 57–63.

Lyubomirsky, S., & Nolan-Hoeksema, S. (1994). Effects of self-focused rumination on negative thinking and interpersonal problem-solving. *Journal of Personality and Social Psychology, 69,* 176–190.

Mack, D. A., Shannon, C., Quick, J. D., & Quick, J. C. (1998). Stress and the preventive management of workplace violence. In R. W. Griffin, A. O'Leary-Kelly, & J. M. Collins (Eds.), *Dysfunctional behavior in organizations: Violent and deviant behavior* (pp. 119–141). Stanford, CT: JAI.

Martinko, M. J., & Zellars, K. L. (1998). Toward a theory of workplace violence: A cognitive appraisal perspective. In R. W. Griffin, A. O'Leary-Kelly, & J. M. Collins (Eds.), *Dysfunctional behavior in organizations: Violent and deviant behavior* (pp. 1–42). Stanford, CT: JAI.

McGehee, W., & Thayer, P. W. (1961). *Training in business and industry.* New York: John Wiley.

National Center on Addiction and Substance Abuse at Columbia University. (2000). *Report of the United States Postal Service Commission on a Safe and Secure Workplace*. New York: Author.

National Institute for Occupational Safety and Health. (1995). *Preventing homicide in the workplace* (DHHS Publication No. 93-109). Washington, DC: U.S. Government Printing Office.

National Institute for Occupational Safety and Health. (2002). *Violence: Occupational hazards in hospitals* (DHHS Publication No. 2002-101). Washington, DC: U.S. Government Printing Office.

Neuman, J. H., & Baron, R. A. (1997). Aggression in the workplace. In R. A. Giacalone & J. Greenberg (Eds.), *Antisocial behavior in organizations* (pp. 37–67). Thousand Oaks, CA: Sage.

NIOSH. (2002). *Violence: Occupational hazards in hospitals* (DHHS Publication No. 2002-101). Washington, DC: U.S. Government Printing Office.

Nunno, M. A., Holden, M. J., & Leidy, B. (2003). Evaluating and monitoring the impact of a crisis intervention system on a residential child care facility. *Child and Youth Services Review, 25,* 295–315.

O'Leary-Kelly, A. M., Griffin, R. W., & Glew, D. J. (1996). Organization-motivated aggression: A research framework. *Academy of Management Review, 21,* 225–253.

Parad, H. J., & Parad, L. G. (Eds.). (1990). *Crisis intervention, Book 2: The practitioner's sourcebook for brief therapy*. Milwaukee, WI: Family Services of America.

Parkes, J. (1996). Control and restraint training: A study of its effectiveness in a medium secure psychiatric unit. *Journal of Forensic Psychiatry, 7,* 525–534.

Pizzino, A. (2002). Dealing with violence in the workplace: The experience of Canadian unions. In M. Gill, B. Fisher, & V. Bowie (Eds.), *Violence at work: Causes, patterns, and prevention* (pp. 165–179). Cullompton, UK: Willan.

Pryor, J. B., & Fitzgerald, L. F. (2003). Sexual harassment research in the United States. In S. Einarsen, H. Hoel, D. Zapf, & C. Cooper (Eds.), *Bullying and emotional abuse in the workplace: International perspectives in research and practice* (pp. 79–100). London: Taylor Francis.

Quick, J. C., Murphy, L. R., Hurrell, J. J., & Orman, D. (1992). The value of work, the risk of distress, and the power of prevention. In J. C. Quick, L. R. Murphy, & J. J. Hurrell Jr. (Eds.), *Stress and well-being at work: Assessment and interventions for occupational mental health* (pp. 3–13). Washington, DC: American Psychological Association.

Quinones, M. A., Ford, K. J., & Teachout, M. S. (1995). The relationship between work experience and job performance: A conceptual and meta-analytic review. *Personnel Psychology, 48,* 887–910.

Quinsey, V. L. (2000). Institutional violence among the mentally ill. In S. Hodgins (Ed.), *Violence among the mentally ill: Effective treatments and management strategies* (pp. 213–235). Dordrecht, The Netherlands: Kluwer.

Quinsey, V. L., & Varney, G. W. (1977). Characteristics of assaults and assaulters in a maximum security psychiatric unit. *Crime and Justice, 5,* 212–220.

Rasmussen, K., & Levander, S. (1996). Individual rather than situation characteristics predict violence in a maximum security hospital. *Journal of Interpersonal Violence, 11,* 376–390.

Rice, M. E., Harris, G. T., Varney, G. W., & Quinsey, V. L. (1989). *Violence in institutions: Understanding, prevention, and control*. Toronto: Hogrefe & Huber.

Rogers, K., & Kelloway, E. K. (1997). Violence at work: Personal and organizational outcomes. *Journal of Occupational Health Psychology, 2,* 63–71.

Runyan, C. W., Zakocs, R. C., & Zwerling, C. (2000). Administrative and behavioral interventions for workplace violence prevention. *American Journal of Preventive Medicine, 18,* 116–127.

Rusting, C. L., & Nolan-Hoeksema, S. (1998). Regulating responses to anger: Effects of rumination and distraction on angry mood. *Journal of Personality and Social Psychology, 74,* 790–803.

Schat, A. C. H., & Kelloway, E. K. (2000). The effects of perceived control on the outcomes of workplace aggression and violence. *Journal of Occupational Health Psychology, 4,* 386–402.

Schat, A. C. H., & Kelloway, E. K. (2003). Reducing the adverse consequences of workplace aggression and violence: The buffering effects of organizational support. *Journal of Occupational Health Psychology, 8,* 110–122.

Schat, A. C. H., & Kelloway, E. K. (2005). Workplace aggression. In J. Barling, M. Frone, & E. K. Kelloway (Eds.), *Handbook of work stress* (pp. 189–218). Thousand Oaks, CA: Sage.

Society for Human Resource Management. (1999). *Workplace violence survey.* Alexandria, VA: Author.

Spielberger, C. D. (1996). *State-Trait Anger Expression Inventory, research edition: Professional manual.* Odessa, FL: Psychological Assessment Resources.

Stanton-Greenwood, A. (1999). Managing violence in residential settings. In H. Kemshall & J. Pritchard (Eds.), *Good practice in working with violence.* London: Jessica Kingsley.

Sutton, R. I., & Kahn, R. L. (1987). Prediction, understanding, and control as antidotes to organizational stress. In J. W. Lorsch (Ed.), *Handbook of organizational behavior* (pp. 272–285). Englewood Cliffs, NJ: Prentice Hall.

Sygnatur, E. F., & Toscano, G. A. (2000, Spring). Work-related homicides: The facts. *Compensation and Working Conditions,* 3–8.

Tepper, B. J. (2000). Consequences of abusive supervision. *Academy of Management Journal, 43,* 178–190.

University of Iowa Injury Prevention Research Center. (2001). *Workplace violence: A report to the nation.* Iowa City, IA: Author.

Walsh, B. R., & Clarke, E. (2003). Post-trauma symptoms in health workers following physical and verbal aggression. *Work & Stress, 17,* 170–181.

Weiner, B. (1995). *Judgments of responsibility: A foundation of a theory of social conduct.* New York: Guilford Press.

Weiss, H. M., & Cropanzano, R. (1996). Affective events theory: A theoretical discussion of the structure, causes and consequences of affective experiences at work. In B. M. Staw & L. L. Cummings (Eds.), *Research in organizational behavior* (Vol. 18, pp. 10–74). Greenwich, CT: JAI.

Weitlauf, J. C., Smith, R. E., & Cervone, D. (2000). Generalization effects of coping-skills training: Influence of self-defense training on women's efficacy beliefs, assertiveness, and aggression. *Journal of Applied Psychology, 85,* 625–633.

Werner, P. D., Rose, T. L., & Yesavage, J. A. (1983). Reliability, accuracy, and decision-making strategy in clinical predictions of imminent dangerousness. *Journal of Consulting and Clinical Psychology, 51,* 815–825.

Werner, P. D., Rose, T. L., & Yesavage, J. A. (1990). Aspects of consensus in clinical predictions of imminent violence. *Journal of Clinical Psychology, 46,* 534–538.

Williams, J. H., Fitzgerald, L. F., & Drasgow, F. (1999). The effects of organizational practices on sexual harassment and individual outcomes in the military. *Military Psychology, 11,* 303–328.

Wright, S. (1999). Physical restraint in the management of violence and aggression in in-patient settings: A review of the issues. *Journal of Mental Health, 8,* 459–472.

26 Preventing Insider-Initiated Workplace Violence

M. Sandy Hershcovis
Julian Barling

August 27, 2003, Chicago, Illinois:

> *Gunman Kills 6 Co-workers, Dies In Shootout With Police: A man killed six employees at the Chicago auto parts supply warehouse, where he had been fired six months ago, before he was killed in a shootout with police as they stormed the building. . . . One employee escaped with his hands tied behind his back. Another arrived at work as the crime was being committed and was able to escape. (Retrieved on August 27, 2003, from www.cnn.com/2003/US/Midwest/08/27/chicago.shooting/ index.html)*

Workplace aggression and violence is a growing concern for organizations. Given the serious nature of aggression and violence in the workplace, organizations need to act proactively to prevent workplace aggression. What can organizations do to ensure that aggression does not occur? Are there steps that organizations can take to prevent violent actions and reactions from employees? This chapter will examine such questions and attempt to provide some suggestions and strategies to help organizations prevent insider-initiated aggression (hereafter, *insider aggression*).

Violence is defined in a number of different ways. In its strictest sense, it is a physical act against another human being (e.g., pushing, hitting, and killing); however, *psychological aggression*, such as threatening behavior, may also produce similar stress-related outcomes. *Aggression* is more broadly defined as a behavior performed by an individual that harms (physically or psychologically) another individual (Jenkins, 1996). Therefore, this chapter uses a definition of *aggression* that includes both physical and psychological aggression (Jenkins, 1996; LeBlanc & Kelloway, 2002).

As noted in an earlier chapter, aggression has been categorized into four types, depending on the assailant's relationship to the workplace (Injury Prevention Research Center [IPRC], 2001). In the first type of aggression, the assailant has no formal relationship to the organization and only enters the workplace to commit a crime (e.g., robbery). With the second type of aggression, the assailant is the recipient of current or past services provided by the organization. For instance, the assailant may be a patient at a mental institution, a prisoner at a penitentiary, or a customer at a clothing store. In the third type, the assailant has a legitimate employment relationship with the organization. This type of aggression consists of aggression between employees, from an employee toward a subordinate, or from an employee toward a supervisor. Finally, in the last type of aggression, the assailant has some relationship with an employee of the company. For instance, the assailant may be a spouse or partner, and he or she enters the work environment to commit the violent act against his or her partner.

Aggression perpetrated by a criminal or by a client or customer is associated with certain occupations and industries (California Occupational Safety and Health Administration [Cal/OSHA], 1995). Criminal acts resulting in aggression are prevalent in organizations that carry cash on hand, such as banks, and organizations that have minimal staff and operate late at night, such as convenience stores, and the taxi industry (Castillo & Jenkins, 1994). To deter such aggression, organizations should ensure that they have good internal controls and security measures that are visible to potential assailants. They should keep a minimum amount of cash on hand, use safes that are time-lock controlled, display a video surveillance camera, and ensure that at least two people are scheduled to work at any given time whenever possible. Additionally, managers and staff must be trained on what to do when faced with a violent situation. The organization should ensure that the safety of the employee is the top priority when training managers on how to deal with potentially violent situations (see Chapter 12).

Aggression from organizational outsiders such as customers and patients is often also associated with particular industries. Because such aggression is initiated by recipients of services offered by the organization, any organization that serves dangerous or unstable individuals may be at higher risk. Some of these organizations include the police force, mental institutions, medical care providers, and alcohol and drug treatment providers (Cal/OSHA, 1995). Although this type of aggression may be more predictable, it is difficult to control, given the nature of the businesses in question. In many outsider aggression situations, dealing with potentially violent people is part of regular job responsibilities, and workers are aware of the risks; however, it is important to note that violence is not restricted to such industries. Customers and other members of the public may also become verbally or physically aggressive when dissatisfied with organizational products or services. To help prevent this type of aggression, organizations must take similar security measures and ensure that they have a safety program with well-defined procedures. In addition, conflict resolution and self-defense training programs are particularly important for this type of aggression because employees may hold high-risk jobs and therefore have higher exposure to potentially violent individuals. Police officers, for example, tend to have fewer injuries than people in most other occupations because of their extensive training in dealing with such situations. The type of safety program and security plan will vary depending on the industry. In Chapter 12, LeBlanc, Dupré, and Barling discuss some strategies for preventing these first two types of aggression.

Aggression perpetrated by an individual who is associated with an employee, such as a disgruntled spouse, is not associated with a particular type of industry. With this type of aggression, a spouse or partner enters the workplace to commit an act of aggression against a partner, and as such, it can occur in any industry. Threats of violence in this category have the highest risk of being carried out (Braverman, 1999). All employees in a work environment are in danger when one employee is threatened; therefore, it is the responsibility of the employer to take action to protect them. Managers must make employees aware that such threats affect the safety of all employees, and any employee facing such threats should immediately make management aware of the situation. Organizations can then address the threats by increasing security measures, applying for restraining orders, and enforcing them (Braverman, 1999).

Although outsider-initiated aggression is of obvious importance, this chapter focuses on insider aggression or aggression initiated by employees and managers of the organization. Insider aggression is the least prevalent of the four types; however, in this form of aggression, the organizational setting or a particular work-related situation, such as organizational injustice, may be a key contributing factor to the act (e.g., Barling, 1996; Braverman, 1999; Martinko & Zellars, 1998). Such situations are at least to some degree within the control of the organization (O'Leary-Kelly, Griffin, & Glew, 1996); therefore, it is important to consider the situations that may lead to such aggression in order to understand how to take proactive measures to prevent it.

Prevalence and Incidents of Workplace Aggression

Although there is a relationship between the type of service provided and aggression perpetrated by a customer, client, or criminal, insider aggression is not believed to be associated with a specific type of organization or industry (Cal/OSHA, 1995). This type of aggression can occur in any organization for a number of reasons, some of which will be discussed in the next section. Due to the sometimes shocking nature of this type of aggression, insider aggression receives a great deal of media attention. Headlines like the one in the opening quote sensationalize these acts of aggression, creating the false perception that such aggression occurs more often than it does. Estimates vary across different studies and across time; however, according to the National Institute for Occupational Safety and Health (NIOSH), aggression perpetrated in the act of committing a crime is the most prevalent, with deaths caused by this form of aggression representing approximately 75% of total workplace homicides in 1992. The Injury Prevention Research Centre (IPRC) at the University of Iowa suggests the current percentage of such homicides may be as high as 85% (Bureau of Labor Statistics, 1998, as cited in IPRC, 2001), and Sygnatur and Toscano (2000) suggest that it may be as low as 60%. In contrast, estimates of insider aggression range from only 6% to 15% of total workplace homicides (see Braverman, 1999; Sygnatur & Toscano, 2000). Although insider aggression may be the least prevalent cause of workplace deaths, when psychological aggression is taken into account, vastly larger numbers of employees are probably affected by insider aggression (Baron & Neuman, 1998).

Although these data suggest that insider aggression should be the least of our concerns, four important factors suggest otherwise. First, recent changes in the workplace, such as downsizing and increased workforce diversity, have led to an increase in insider workplace aggression (Baron & Neuman, 1998). Second, these data reflect violent forms of aggression only, whereas psychological aggression is a much more frequent occurrence. Third, research suggests that insider aggression is often caused by an interaction between individual characteristics of the aggressor (e.g., trait anger) (Douglas & Martinko, 2001) and workplace factors (Braverman, 1999; Inness, Barling, & Turner, 2005), such as workplace injustice, abusive supervision, and overcontrol. Indeed, Chapters 3 and 6 outline several workplace predictors of insider aggression, suggesting that there may be a number of actions the organization can take to prevent this type of workplace aggression. Fourth, there are data (LeBlanc & Kelloway, 2002) that suggest that insider aggression has direct (rather than mediated) effects on personal outcomes, so the prevention of this form of aggression may be particularly salient for individuals.

In the next section, we address the three factors that interact to predict workplace aggression: the individual, the situation, and the organizational context (Braverman, 1999). We do so to draw attention to the specific options the organization can undertake. The remaining sections will propose a model for the prevention of workplace aggression, suggesting specific points of intervention and tactics for proactively preventing workplace aggression.

The Individual, the Situation, and the Setting

Workplace aggression is the result of an interaction between three factors: the individual, the situation, and the setting (Braverman, 1999).

The Individual

Researchers have attempted to provide a profile of the potentially dangerous worker; however, several issues plague the use of profiles in aggression prevention. First, the brevity of the selection process makes it very difficult to assess whether an individual possesses the characteristics of a typical profile. Such factors as alcohol consumption, previous exposure to aggression (Greenberg & Barling, 1999), self-esteem (Inness et al., 2005), trait anger, attribution style, negative affectivity, attitudes toward revenge, and self-control (Douglas & Martinko, 2001) are related to workplace aggression; however, it is difficult for organizations to determine whether potential employees possess many of these characteristics. Although many selection processes are rigorous, the likelihood that a potential job candidate will admit to possessing these characteristics is very low, given that such characteristics are not perceived to be socially acceptable. In addition, just because potential employees possess some of these characteristics, it does not necessarily follow that they will become violent. Therefore, even if an organization were able to determine whether prospective employees hold some of these characteristics, they might well be excluding potentially good employees based on an improbable outcome.

Second, the privacy rights of each individual make it difficult for organizations to determine whether potential employees may be predisposed to violent tendencies. Although organizations would be prudent to conduct a thorough reference check on employees and to look for indirect cues (i.e., what the reference is not saying) to determine potential problems, it is often difficult to obtain references from past employers. Fear of lawsuits has left employers reluctant to provide negative references for employees (Howard, 2001; Sovereign, 1994).

In summary, profiles are too vague and difficult to obtain to be a useful tool for aggression prevention. Given that profiling decisions derive from assumptions about possible future behaviors based on individual characteristics and limited information, they are simply a poor organizational policy that potentially violates the privacy rights of applicants. Given the severe limitations involved with profiling, an organization has little control over the individual predictors of workplace aggression.

The Situation

Although the organization has little control over the individual attributes that may predict aggression, it has a great deal of control over the situational factors that may lead to workplace aggression. Situational factors refer to specific occurrences that lead to loss, humiliation, or exclusion from others (Braverman, 1999) within the organization. These situational factors are *stressors,* or objective environmental characteristics that may lead to the subjective state known as *stress* (Pratt & Barling, 1988). For instance, when layoffs are imminent, job insecurity is likely to increase. In a situation in which an employee who is predisposed to violent tendencies experiences heightened stressors, an aggressive outcome could result.

Situational factors that have been demonstrated to lead to aggressive behavior include job-related stressors (e.g., Chen & Spector, 1992; Fox &

Spector, 1999; Glomb, 2002), surveillance (Greenberg & Barling, 1999), abusive supervision (Inness et al., 2005), supervisory overcontrol (Dupré, 2004), and organizational injustice (Baron, Neuman, & Geddes, 1999). Subsequent sections will briefly describe each of these and consider possible actions and strategies for prevention.

The Organizational Context (Setting)

Although certain individuals may be predisposed to aggressive behavior and may find themselves in situations that cause higher levels of stress, aggression cannot occur unless the organization permits it to occur (Braverman, 1999). Employees often give repeated warnings that they will commit a violent act; they often voice their concerns or feelings of perceived unfairness before they engage in such acts; and they ask for restitution before they commit violent acts. Only after their attempts to achieve a favorable outcome fail do they fulfill their promise of aggression. Indeed, some research (e.g., Dupré, 2004) suggests that aggression may be the result of escalating forms of aggression. As such, organizations have repeated opportunities to disarm the employee before he or she carries out a threat of violence. Organizations should therefore ensure that policies are in place to deal with grievances as well as threats of aggression when they occur.

Research has also shown that perceived organizational sanctions are negatively associated with sexual harassment (Drekker & Barling, 1998) and aggression (Dupré, 2004; Fox & Spector, 1999). Organizations may be able to discourage aggression by outlining a formal policy that is associated with sanctions for aggressive behavior (Dupré, 2004). The next section will address in more detail how organizations can ensure that their organizational setting is not conducive to aggression.

Situational Predictors of Workplace Aggression _____

Although there is still a paucity of research on the causes of aggression in the workplace, some interesting recent evidence suggests that different organization-specific predictors may lead to different targets within insider aggression. For instance, a study by Greenberg and Barling (1999) found that employee-on-supervisor aggression was predicted by procedural injustice and workplace surveillance. Those who felt that they were being watched by various monitoring devices (e.g., punch cards, timed lunches) were more likely to act aggressively toward a supervisor. In addition, employees who held perceptions of procedural injustice were more likely to aggress against their supervisor. Similarly, in a study that attempted to compare individual and workplace predictors of aggression, Inness et al. (2005) found that abusive supervision predicted aggression against the supervisor only in the job in which it occurred (i.e., it was highly situation specific). In contrast, person-specific behaviors such as history of aggression and alcohol consumption predict employee-on-employee aggression (Greenberg & Barling, 1999). Finally, in a meta-analysis of the predictors of workplace aggression, Hershcovis et al. (in press) found that abusive supervision and interactional injustice were much stronger predictors of supervisor-targeted aggression than coworker-targeted aggression, and trait anger was a stronger predictor of interpersonal aggression than organizational aggression.

Organizational Injustice

Organizational injustice is concerned with the lack of fairness of outcomes, processes, and interactions within the organization. At least three types of justice have been studied in relation to aggression: distributive, procedural, and interactional. Research has found that *distributive justice,* which is concerned with the fairness of outcomes, has some relationship (albeit weak) with workplace aggression (Greenberg & Barling, 1999; Hershcovis et al., 2004). Interestingly, Hershcovis et al. (2004) found that distributive injustice was related to coworker-targeted, but not supervisor-targeted, workplace aggression. This finding suggests that through social comparison, employees may become envious of coworkers whose input/output ratio is higher than their own, leading them to become aggressive toward their coworkers. Previous research has found that envy associated with unfavorable work outcomes is positively related to aggression (Cohen-Charash, Mueller, & Goldman, 2004).

Procedural justice is defined as the individual's perception of the fairness of the process that leads to decisions about how to allocate various organizational outcomes (Leventhal, 1980). There is some evidence to suggest that procedural justice predicts aggression. A number of individual studies (Bennett & Robinson, 2000; Greenberg & Barling, 1999; Skarlicki, Folger, & Tesluck, 1999) have found that procedural justice is associated with workplace aggression; however, in a meta-analysis of the predictors of aggression, Hershcovis et al. (in press) found that after controlling for other predictor variables the main effect between procedural injustice and workplace aggression became insignificant. Hershcovis et al. (in press) suggest that existing operationalizations of workplace aggression may confound results. In particular, studies often include multiple targets (supervisor, coworker, and organization) in their measures of aggression (e.g., Skarlicki et al., 1999) or do not specify the target at all (e.g., Bennett & Robinson, 2000). Because aggression is likely to be target-specific, ambiguous operationalization may lead to incorrect conclusions for both distributive and procedural injustice.

Of the three types of injustice studied, by far the strongest predictor of aggression is interactional injustice (Hershcovis et al., in press). *Interactional injustice* is concerned with the quality of interactional treatment received during the enactment of procedures (Bies & Moag, 1986).

Research in retaliatory behavior found that when interactional justice was high, the interaction between procedural and distributive justice did not predict retaliation (Skarlicki & Folger, 1997). That is, high interactional justice counteracted the negative effects of low procedural and distributive justice; however, when interactional justice was low, the interaction between distributive and procedural injustice produced strong retaliatory outcomes. Other researchers have also shown that interactional injustice leads to negative behaviors such as employee theft (Greenberg, 1993), which may be considered a form of organization-targeted aggression. In addition, although Skarlicki and Folger (1997) measured covert forms of retaliation such as taking supplies home, damaging equipment, and spreading rumors, they argue that these behaviors may lead to more direct forms of retaliation such as aggression. This is consistent with the *escalation of aggression hypothesis,* which suggests that aggression may start with relatively minor behaviors but subsequently develop into more serious forms of aggression or violence (Dupré, 2004).

Abusive Supervision, Surveillance, and Control

Preliminary evidence suggests that the manner in which leaders supervise their employees may contribute to aggressive responses, and this has critical implications for prevention. Dupré (2004) found that employees are more likely to aggress against supervisors who tend to overcontrol their employees through pressures to work at a certain pace or in a certain way. Similarly, Greenberg and Barling (1999) found that surveillance predicted aggression against supervisors. The marital aggression literature similarly finds that overcontrol may lead to violent responses. Ehrensaft, Langhinrichsen-Rohling, Heyman, O'Leary, and Lawrence (1999) found that spouses in unhappy aggressive marriages felt more controlled than spouses in unhappy nonaggressive marriages.

Tepper (2000) defined abusive supervision as a sustained display of hostile verbal and nonverbal behaviors toward employees. Abusive supervision also predicts aggression against the supervisor (Hershcovis et al., in press; Inness et al., 2005). In a study that examined moonlighters, or individuals who worked in two different jobs, Inness et al. (2005) investigated whether individuals who were aggressive in one organization were also aggressive in the other. The study was an attempt to disentangle individual and organizational predictors of aggression. They found that among people who had more than one supervisor, abusive supervision predicted more variance in aggression only against the abusive supervisor.

Role Stressors

Role stressors also significantly predict workplace aggression (Beehr & Glazer, 2004). Role stressors include environmental demands, constraints, and events that affect the ability of individuals to meet their roles (Beehr & Glazer, 2004). Three role stressors have been studied in relation to aggression, namely role ambiguity, role overload, and role conflict.

Role ambiguity is the lack of specificity and predictability regarding an employee's job functions and responsibilities (Kahn, Wolfe, Quinn, Snoek, & Rosenthal, 1964). In a study of 2,117 employees working in various industries, Einarsen, Raknes, and Matthiesen (1994) found that role ambiguity was positively associated with workplace bullying. Other researchers (e.g., Bedeian, Armenakis, & Curran, 1980; Chen & Spector, 1992) also found that role ambiguity was positively associated with aggression.

Role overload reflects the inability to fulfill work expectations in the time available (Kahn, 1980). The evidence is mixed regarding the relationship between role overload and aggression. Einarsen et al. (1994) found a significant positive relationship between role overload and bullying, whereas Chen and Spector (1992) found no relationship between aggression and work overload.

Role conflict is defined as two or more sets of incompatible demands concerning an employee's work (Beehr, 1995; Beehr & Glazer, 2004). Of the three role stressors, role conflict has the strongest association with workplace aggression (Hershcovis et al., 2004). Chen and Spector (1992) found that role conflict was positively related to sabotage and interpersonal aggression, as well as hostility and complaints; and Einarsen et al. (1994) found a positive relationship between bullying and role conflict.

Job Insecurity

A final situational predictor of workplace aggression is job insecurity. Studies have found that job insecurity is positively associated with aggression (e.g., Baron & Neuman, 1998); however, Greenberg and Barling (1999) argued and found that job insecurity should predict aggression against the supervisor but not the subordinate, because the supervisor is responsible for the job security of an employee.

The research on situational predictors suggests that individuals do not tend to act aggressively; rather, they *react* aggressively. That is, aggression is target-specific (Greenberg & Barling, 1999; Hershcovis et al., in press), such that employees attribute a perceived transgression to a particular target and aggress against that target as a retaliatory act. Given this knowledge, certain steps can be taken to limit and prevent workplace aggression and violence.

_____ Escalation of Aggression: Points of Prevention

As noted in the preceding sections, organizations have limited control over the individual predictors of aggression but can control situations that may trigger aggression and the settings that enable it. It bears repeating that insider aggression is very infrequent. In general, there are at least three points at which the organization can act proactively to prevent a violent outcome.

There is some limited evidence to show that aggression escalates. In a study that investigated aggression against supervisors, Dupré (2004) found strong support for the notion that over time less serious forms of aggression escalate to more serious forms, such as violence. Research from the marital aggression literature (e.g., Murphy & O'Leary, 1989) also suggests that aggression does not occur immediately. Rather, a series of exchanges lead to an escalation process that ultimately results in aggression.

Figure 26.1 suggests a model for understanding the progression and prevention of workplace aggression. The model suggests an escalation effect that begins with a situational predictor, which leads to an expression of discontent and a request for restitution and ends with an act of violence. The left side of the model indicates the opportunities for primary prevention whereas the right side of the model indicates opportunities for secondary prevention designed to respond to possible threats of aggression. Organizations can take three key proactive measures to prevent violence: (a) eliminate the situational predictor, (b) create a transparent and nonthreatening environment, and (c) prevent aggressive acts. Reactive responses include (a) investigating

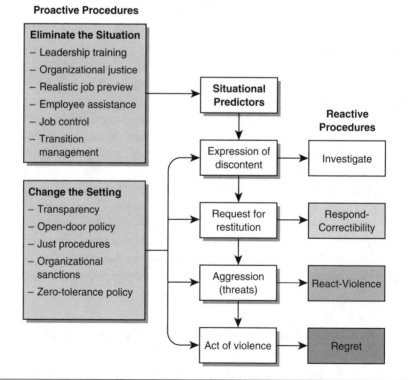

Figure 26.1   Preventing Escalation of Aggression

expressions of discontent, (b) responding to requests for restitution, (c) reacting to aggression, and (d) regretting the outcome.

_____ Proactive Procedures: Eliminating the Situation

The most proactive measure that an organization can take to prevent aggression involves eliminating the situational predictors that lead to aggression. This section will discuss strategies for increasing perceptions of justice, improving leadership skills, reducing role stressors, and minimizing job insecurity.

Enhancing Organizational Justice

Although interactional injustice has the strongest relationship with workplace aggression, both distributive and procedural injustice have main effects with workplace aggression. In addition, as noted earlier, the interaction between distributive and procedural injustice is strongly associated with workplace aggression when interactional injustice is low (Skarlicki & Folger, 1997). Therefore, to prevent workplace aggression and violence, it is important to pay attention to all forms of injustice.

Distributive Justice

Distributive justice is a comparative process in which employees compare their inputs and outcomes with a comparable other. Organizations that ensure fair procedures are more likely to arrive at organizational outcomes that are distributively just. Because procedures that are applied consistently, ethically, and without bias are likely to result in distributions that are fair across people, ensuring procedural justice is an effective way to also ensure distributive justice; however, comparative information is not always available; therefore, employees may form their own expectations about distributions such as wage increases based on knowledge using their own inputs. Mueller, Iverson, and Jo (1999) argued that people will be more likely to perceive the organization as distributively fair when expectations regarding desired outcomes are met. They found that met expectations were positively related to perceptions of distributive justice.

Based on these findings, managers may wish to manage the expectations of employees by ensuring transparent communication regarding potential outcomes. For instance, employees who received a 5% wage increases in past years may expect the same increase in future years, assuming the same level of inputs (e.g., effort, time, and skill); however, external factors beyond the control of the individual may result in reduced earnings for the organization in a given year. When such contingencies occur, requiring the organization to cut costs, it would be important to communicate potential reductions in annual wage reviews. Such information allows employees to revise their expectations, thereby mitigating negative responses; and Shaw, Wild, and Colquitt (2003) have shown that providing adequate explanations can limit retribution by 43%.

Procedural Justice

Leventhal (1980) argued that *procedural justice* comprises six factors. The first is *accuracy,* or basing decisions on accurate information. The second is *bias-suppression,* which requires that managers remain impartial when making organizational decisions. The third factor is *consistency,* which requires that organizations treat employees the same across people and across time. The fourth factor is *voice,* or the ability of employees to participate in important decisions that affect them. Voice has been identified as one of the most crucial aspects of procedural justice (Lind, Kanfer, & Earley, 1990) because employees who are given the opportunity to participate are more likely to feel a part of the decision process and are therefore more likely to buy into the process (Leventhal, 1980). Fifth is the *ethicality principle,* which suggests that all decisions should be based on prevailing ethical principles (e.g., equity, need, or equality). Sixth and finally, a fair system must *allow for the correction of mistakes.*

These factors of procedural justice are particularly important when an organization is making decisions of importance to employees (e.g., performance appraisals, promotions). Allowing employee participation in the evaluation process, for example, will help employees recognize their weaknesses and show them where they need to improve in order to achieve valued outcomes. In addition, organizations should ensure that policies for making decisions that affect employees are transparent. *Internal transparency,* defined as the visibility of organizational processes and procedures that affect employees, ensures that employees are aware of what they need to do in order to achieve a certain outcome. Because greater transparency will lead to fewer surprises regarding decisions that relate to employees, transparency should help mitigate aggressive responses.

Interactional Justice

Interactional justice is concerned with the content of interactions between employees and supervisors (Bies & Moag, 1986) and is the strongest predictor of the three types of justice studied in the aggression literature (Hershcovis et al., in press; Skarlicki & Folger, 1997). There are two components of interactional justice: explanation and communication. The *explanation* component, known as *informational justice* (Colquitt, 2001), requires that managers provide employees with adequate explanations for decisions that affect them. Jones (2004) found that informational justice was negatively related to both retaliatory intent and aggression against the supervisor. As such, one way to reduce aggression is for managers to provide reasonable and complete explanations for decisions that affect employees. If an employee does not get a wage increase, for example, managers should ensure that they provide reasons why. The explanation should include adequate information and data to support the decision (e.g., employee evaluations and expectations), as well as a plan to help the employee achieve a wage increase next year.

Simply providing an explanation is insufficient, however. The manner in which the explanation is *communicated* is equally important. Jones (2004) examined the communication content (interpersonal justice) and explanation (informational justice) components of interactional justice separately and found that interpersonal justice accounted for more variance than informational justice (though both were significant) in explaining aggression against the supervisor. Therefore, managers should ensure that they treat employees with respect and dignity, particularly when communicating bad news.

Finally, because there is a strong positive correlation between procedural justice and interactional justice (Colquitt, Conlon, Wesson, Porter, & Ng, 2001), improving procedural justice will also improve interactional injustice and vice versa. For instance, when managers encourage participation in the decision processes that affect employees (procedural justice), they also communicate to employees that they respect and value employee input (interactional justice).

Often, interactional justice is a function of good leadership. Good leaders treat employees with respect and dignity and encourage participation because such treatment generally encourages more positive responses from employees. Therefore, another way to improve justice perceptions is to improve organizational leadership through leadership training programs.

Leadership

The situational predictors outlined earlier suggest a common theme, namely poor leadership, which includes procedural, distributive, and interactional injustice, overcontrol, abusive supervision, job insecurity, and role stressors (Barling, Kelloway, & Frone, 2004). All these predictors are indicators of poor leadership skills and suggest that leadership training may be a critical proactive step to deterring aggression. Research has shown that leadership is amenable to training (Barling, Weber, & Kelloway, 1996; Kelloway, Barling, & Helleur, 2000).

There are a number of different theories of leadership in the organizational behavior literature. A discussion of the virtues of different definitions of leadership is beyond the scope of this chapter; therefore, the chapter will focus on two theories of leadership. The first, *leader-member exchange (LMX) theory*, emphasizes the reciprocal nature of the leadership relationship. The reason for the focus on LMX is that the quality of the exchange relationship seems to manifest itself in the situational predictors of aggression. For instance, abusive, disrespectful, or unfair treatment may characterize low-quality leadership, with aggression becoming the reciprocal response. The second, *transformational leadership*, focuses on managing change by the leader within an organization. Some of the most serious decisions that managers make are with regard to change, and the communication of such change is critical to how subordinates deal with such change.

Leader-Member Exchange: Managing Relationships

LMX theory is concerned with the quality of the dyadic leader/follower relationship. LMX suggests that leaders develop a unique, individualized relationship with subordinates and that the quality of the relationship will have important implications for attitudinal and behavioral outcomes (Graen & Uhl-Bien, 1995). Dienesch and Liden (1986) proposed three dimensions of LMX: contribution, loyalty, and affect. They defined *contribution* as the perception of the amount and quality of work each party contributes toward the common goal. *Loyalty* reflects the extent to which the leader and subordinate are loyal to one another, and *affect* refers to the mutual affection the leader and follower feel for each other. Liden and Maslyn (1998) found that a fourth factor emerged from their model, which they identified as *professional respect* or the perception of the degree to which each member of the dyad is respected within or outside the organization.

Although no research has been conducted on LMX and aggression in particular, some research has examined the relationship between LMX and retaliation (Townsend, Phillips, & Elkins, 2000). This study found that LMX was negatively related to retaliation, which included some aggressive acts such as damaging company property, such that high-quality relationships led to lower levels of retaliation. Wayne, Shore, and Liden (1997) found that high LMX employees perceive their organizations as more supportive than do low LMX employees. This suggests that training managers to maintain high-quality relationships with their employees may well be important.

Although the dimensions of high-quality leadership have been proposed, LMX says little about the specific steps needed to promote a high-quality relationship. Indeed, the notion of *quality* is difficult to define and therefore may be difficult to train. Some key characteristics of high-quality relationships may include fostering mutual support, mutual respect, mutual trust, and mutual loyalty. The key term in LMX leadership is *mutual*, which emphasizes the mutuality of leader/subordinate relationships. Managers who are learning to supervise employees must be trained early on that leadership is in fact an exchange relationship. To gain respect, support, trust, and loyalty, managers must act accordingly with their employees. Managers who are abusive or unjust do not demonstrate the respect and support required for high-quality relationships and thus do not gain trust or loyalty from their employees.

Transformational Leadership: Managing Change

Transformational leadership also emphasizes the reciprocal role of leaders and is characterized by four key components: inspirational motivation, idealized influence, individual consideration, and intellectual stimulation. *Inspirational motivation* involves charismatic communication of a vision for the organization, using symbols and emotion to gain employee confidence and buy-in to the vision (Bass, 1985; Kark, Shamir, & Chen, 2003). *Idealized influence* includes behaviors such as leading by example and demonstrating high ethical standards. *Individualized consideration* is concerned with providing support and encouragement to employees and coaching them in an effort to develop their skills and to help them succeed. Finally, *intellectual stimulation* is intended to challenge problem-solving skills and encourage subordinates to perceive problems and solutions in different ways. A number of studies have shown that transformational leadership leads to higher satisfaction with the supervisor (Koh, Steers, & Terborg, 1995), higher organizational commitment (Bycio, Hackett, & Allen, 1995; Koh et al., 1995), and performance (Howell & Avolio, 1993). Research also shows that training managers on transformational leadership effectively leads to higher organizational commitment, leader perceptions, and performance (Barling et al., 1996).

Transformational leadership has a potentially important role in managing change because such leadership, when successful, engenders support from organizational members. Organizational change, which often includes increased diversity, restructuring, layoffs, job insecurity, and new technology, has been associated with aggression (Baron & Neuman, 1998). Managers who receive transformational leadership training may develop better communication skills that help employees understand the reasons for change and, ultimately, generate support for such change.

Although studies have not directly examined the relationship between transformational leadership and aggression, Pillai, Schriesheim, and Williams (1999) showed a main effect of transformational leadership on justice perceptions. They found that transformational leadership was positively associated with both distributive and procedural justice and that procedural justice mediated the relationship between transformational leadership and organizational citizenship behaviors. Because both procedural and distributive *in*justice have been positively associated with aggression against the supervisor (Greenberg & Barling, 1999), it is reasonable to suggest that transformational leadership will negatively relate to aggression against the supervisor.

Training in either LMX or transformational leadership may also help address issues of interactional fairness because both theories of leadership emphasize the mutuality of the leader/follower relationship. The loyalty and affect components of LMX and the individualized consideration component of transformational leadership are concerned with providing support to employees. Such support implicitly suggests that high-quality interpersonal treatment, characterized by respect and integrity, are necessary components of high-quality leadership.

Reducing Role Stressors

Role stressors derive from poor leadership; therefore, many of the same strategies would be relevant for reducing role stressors. Individuals may also have different tolerances for role stressors and abusive supervision. What one employee may perceive as a stressor, another employee may consider a challenge; however, there are certain actions an organization can take to prevent employees from experiencing role stress. As suggested by the International Labour Organization (ILO), work design is important for reducing tension and avoiding workplace aggression. Organizations can reduce role overload by ensuring that staffing levels are appropriate and working hours are not excessive ILO, 2000). Role ambiguity and conflict can be reduced by ensuring tasks are clearly defined and employees receive the same information from all supervisors.

The degree of control employees have over their work may also reduce role stressors. Dupré (2004) showed that overcontrol by a supervisor is positively associated with workplace aggression, suggesting that greater job control may also be negatively related to workplace aggression. Job control has been suggested as a moderator between role stressors and job strain (Spector, 2002). Karasek's (1979) job demands-control theory predicts that people who do not have job control will be less able to cope with job stress. There has been mixed support for the ability of job control to moderate the stressor/strain relationship (Beehr & Glazer, 2004). Beehr (1976) found that autonomy over one's work moderates the relationship between role ambiguity and depression; however, other researchers have found that job control does not moderate the stressor/strain relationship (e.g., O'Driscoll & Beehr, 2000).

Schaubroeck and Merritt (1997) tested the three-way interaction between self-efficacy, job control, and job demands to determine whether employees with higher self-efficacy are better able to use job control to cope with job demands. They found support for this prediction, suggesting that organizations that provide greater autonomy to employees should work to enhance their self-efficacy. When employees believe they can do a good job, having control over their job mitigates the effects of high job demands on stress outcomes.

Job Insecurity: Managing Transition

Job loss is an extremely traumatic experience for employees. Jahoda (1979) argued that work fills a variety of functions for employees that are critical to their identity and well-being. Work provides a shared experience with others, allows contact with people outside the family, defines a meta-goal in life, suggests aspects of status, and imposes a time structure for employees. In a study of workers who had lost their jobs, Fineman (1983) similarly found that the loss of a job meant far more than just the loss of remuneration; it resulted in personal disorientation that challenged the individuals' understanding of their own identity. As such, it is critical for organizations to recognize the magnitude of loss such an experience has for employees and take proactive measures to help employees through the process, whatever the reason for the termination.

In terms of the decision to lay off, it is critical to implement such decisions with dignity and respect, consistent with the discussion of interactional justice mentioned previously. Similarly, the decision to lay off employees should be made using transparent and procedurally just decision criteria. Hemingway and Conte (2003) found that consistency of implementing layoffs and an unbiased layoff policy were key predictors of perceived fairness in layoff policies. Similarly, the size of the severance package was positively associated with justice perceptions (Hemingway & Conte, 2003). Procedural justice and transparency in the layoff process is critical, as it enables employees to gauge whether they should begin preparing for the possibility of job loss. Advance warning allows employees an opportunity to maintain control over their transition, enabling them to cope better with imminent unemployment.

A second important step is for organizations to ease the layoff process as much as possible for the employee. Waxman (1995) recommends several specific steps to help make the layoff process as dignified as possible. He suggest that although some companies immediately confiscate keys and have a security guard escort employees out due to security concerns, this process is demeaning and is likely to increase the likelihood of a hostile reaction. Waxman (1995) argues that organizations should instead allow employees the time to say good-bye to coworkers and to take their time clearing out their belongings. More important, he suggests that the manager who is terminating the employment relationship should provide specific details about the severance package, the procedures for termination, unemployment benefits, and outplacement services. Such information communicates to the employees that the organization cares about their well-being and also provides the employee with some guidance on how to take action rather than leaving them at a loss about how to proceed.

Finally, it is likely that employees who are provided with a reasonable explanation for the layoff are less likely to become aggressive, although no research exists on the effects of explanation on perceptions of justice among employees being laid off. *Informational justice* is defined as the accuracy and quality of explanations employees receive regarding procedures (Kernan & Hanges, 2002). Kernan and Hanges examined the effects of informational justice on *survivors* of layoffs and found that explanations increased trust in management. Shaw et al. (2003) found that employees who were provided with an adequate explanation for a negative outcome held higher justice perceptions than those who did not receive an adequate explanation. Waxman (1995) emphasizes that explanations should focus on the behavioral aspects of the employees' performance and avoid personal issues.

Proactive Prevention: Changing the Setting

Despite efforts to prevent them, some of the situational predictors outlined above may occur despite organizational efforts to prevent them. In addition, as we outlined earlier, situational predictors are not the only antecedents to aggression; individual predictors also contribute to aggressive acts. As such, organizations must consider the aspects of the organizational context (or setting) that could help prevent aggression.

Transparent Policies and Organizational Sanctions

A number of researchers have recommended that organizations implement an organizational policy on aggression as one potential preventative technique (Braverman, 1999; Fitzgerald, 1993; Howard, 2001). Recent research has demonstrated that organizational tolerance of aggression and organizational policies on aggression are related to workplace aggression (Schat, 2004). In particular, Schat found that employees report lower levels of supervisor aggression in organizations that communicate and enforce a workplace aggression policy. Schat also found a positive relationship between supervisor tolerance for aggression and employee reports of aggressive behavior. This suggests that the attitude of the supervisor is critical in setting the example for acceptable behavior. Therefore, a clearly communicated policy of workplace aggression is an important first step for proactive prevention of workplace aggression.

Such a policy, if transparent, would ensure that employees are aware of the organization's position regarding aggression and the process that should be taken if a threat of aggression occurs. A transparent aggression policy should include a *clear* and *visible*

definition of aggression,

statement about the organization's policy regarding aggression,

set of guidelines for how policy violations are to be reported,

set of procedures about how reports of violations will be handled,

process for investigated charges of policy violation, and

set of specific sanctions that will follow if the policy is violated.

The most important aspect of transparency is clear and visible communication. Clarity is important as it ensures that there can be no misunderstanding of the meaning of the definition of aggression, the policy, the process, or the sanctions; however, clarity alone is insufficient, because clear policies that employees never see will be ineffective. The visibility of the definition, policy, sanctions, and process is also necessary.

In order for employees to understand and adhere to a policy on aggression, they must understand what *aggression* means. The academic literature is fraught with definitional inconsistencies and disagreements (O'Leary-Kelly et al., 1996), so an organization should not assume that the meaning of *aggression* is obvious to employees. Management of the organization must decide what definition of *aggression* they deem to be appropriate and communicate this definition clearly to employees, ensuring that all aspects of the definition are addressed (i.e., physical and sexual harassment, psychological harassment). Once a definition is agreed on, a zero-tolerance policy should be devised and a process for investigation articulated (Braverman, 1999). This policy should include specific sanctions that are agreed on by management.

To ensure greater visibility, organizations should include a discussion about the aggression policy in their training program and policy manual for all new employees. Managers should also ensure that they provide reasonable explanations about why they are setting a particular policy. Greenberg (1994) found that when managers provided lots of information related to a new smoking ban policy, employees who were smokers were more accepting of the ban than when they were not given adequate information. In addition, managers should receive aggression and violence training that deals in particular with the process of addressing a complaint about aggression. Informed managers who are properly trained will help ensure a coordinated response that serves to mitigate escalation and protect employees (Braverman, 1999).

A key difficulty with the implementation of aggression policies is that managers may be reluctant to take action against employees who they believe might become aggressive or violent (Braverman, 1999). Managers often fear that taking action will instigate an aggressive act. Neglecting to take action threatens the safety of employees and exacerbates the situation because distraught employees usually want to see that some action is being taken to address their concerns.

Reactive Prevention

Expression of Discontent and Requests for Restitution

As noted earlier, employees often indicate that they are unhappy with a process or a situation before they take action (Braverman, 1999). As such, an organization can mitigate acts of aggression by ensuring that they have fair procedures in place for investigating, addressing, and correcting the conditions that fostered the expressions of discontent. Kuzmits (2001) warns never to ignore employee grievances. Such expressions of discontent are a possible warning that a situational predictor has occurred, and the organization can still take action to address the issue.

On occasion, managers may mistakenly violate one or more of the first five factors of procedural justice discussed earlier. Such a violation may be one situational predictor that leads to an expression of discontent, which may escalate to aggression. The final factor suggested by Leventhal (1980) is *correctibility,* which enables biased, inaccurate, unethical, or inconsistent decisions to be investigated and corrected if they are determined to be errors. When employees express discontent over a decision or a process, organizations must have a process in place whereby the situation can be investigated and corrected. Such a system should involve the participation of the employee and should be completely transparent to the employee so that he or she is aware of the process that will be used to investigate their complaint.

The employee must be told what is being done, how it is being done, and how long it will take for the management to arrive at a decision. When employees perceive that the organization is taking their complaints seriously, they will be more likely to perceive the process as fair and will be less likely to escalate toward aggression.

Aggression: Reacting to Threats

If the preventative measures outlined in the previous sections are adhered to, organizations should not have to react to acts of aggression because such acts are unlikely to occur. Unfortunately, many organizations, particularly those that have never been faced with aggression in the workplace, do not proactively implement policies and training because the possibility of aggression or violence is not even on the horizon. Acts of aggression, including verbal threats to carry out violence, yelling, and other nonphysical threatening behavior are strong signals that the organization *must* take seriously. Management must immediately react to reports of such threats according to the training they received. In particular, it is crucial that the offender be directly confronted, told about the threat, and told exactly what will be done to investigate this threat.

Braverman (1999) suggests that reactions to threats are often ignored either because managers believe the threats will not be carried through or because of fear that reacting to the threats will instigate a violent response. Ignoring threats is likely to lead an organization to the final reactive procedure for dealing with aggression, *regret*. Once a violent action has occurred, a different set of procedures, discussed in Chapter 21, must be taken. Organizations can avoid such negative outcomes by taking a proactive stance on violence prevention to ensure a safe environment for all organizational members.

Future Research

The study of any infrequent occurrence (e.g., injuries, workplace violence) creates difficulties for research, and this is particularly so when examining how to prevent such occurrences. As noted in this chapter, however, the organization has a strong hand in contributing to acts of workplace aggression; therefore, it is the responsibility of organizational behavior researchers to determine the best strategies for preventing such aggression. Future research should specifically focus on proactive measures to determine whether they help mitigate workplace aggression. We argued that transparent organizational policies, adequate explanations for layoffs, realistic job previews, increased workplace control, fair procedures, and training on transformational and transactional leadership would help eliminate situational predictors. Many of these strategies have not been empirically examined. In addition, although limited exploratory work has been conducted (Howard, 2001), we do not yet know whether workplace aggression training and policies mitigate aggressive acts. Past research has focused on understanding the key predictors of aggression. Such research has revealed that preventable situational factors that are under the control of the organization predict aggression. The more important question of how to eliminate such predictors has yet to receive research attention.

Epilogue

Prevention of workplace aggression is an understudied topic. This chapter provided many suggestions on how an organization can go about preventing workplace aggression; however, research in this area is needed in order to determine which strategies for aggression prevention are most effective. This chapter provided a number of avenues for future research. First, researchers should examine which proactive strategies are most effective in preventing the situational predictors of workplace aggression. There is some evidence that leadership training improves subordinate perceptions of the leader (e.g., Barling et al., 1996); however, there have been no studies that examine whether realistic job previews reduce the experience of role stressors. Similarly, the research on job control and the reduction of role stressors is contradictory. Further research should examine whether greater autonomy leads to lower levels of stress and ultimately lower levels of workplace aggression. Second, researchers should examine whether the use of transparent policies are effective in mitigating workplace aggression. Third, although much research has examined the effects of layoffs on survivors, few studies examine how layoffs affect those being laid off. Research should examine the effects of transition programs to determine whether such programs are associated with higher perceptions of fairness. Do employees who are provided with information related to social assistance and job placement programs have more positive feelings toward the organization after being laid off? Finally, researchers should try to understand which damage control (reactive) procedures are effective in mitigating workplace aggression after a situational predictor has occurred. After identifying injustice or poor leadership, how should managers react to correct the problem? Do fair procedures and the provision for correctibility stem the escalation of aggression? Research addressing these important questions would help managers determine which strategies work best for the prevention of workplace aggression.

References

Barling, J. (1996). The prediction, experience, and consequences of workplace violence. In G. R. VandenBos & E. Q. Bulatao (Eds.), *Violence on the job: Identifying risks and developing solutions* (pp. 29–49). Washington, DC: American Psychological Association.

Barling, J., Kelloway, E. K., & Frone, M. R. (Eds.). (2004). *Handbook of work stress.* Thousand Oaks, CA: Sage.

Barling, J., Weber, T., & Kelloway, E. K. (1996). Effects of transformational leadership training on attitudinal and financial outcomes: A field experiment. *Journal of Applied Psychology, 81,* 827–832.

Baron, R. A., & Neuman, J. H. (1998). Workplace aggression: The iceberg beneath the tip of workplace violence: Evidence on its forms, frequency, and targets. *Public Administration Quarterly, 21,* 446–464.

Baron, R. A., Neuman, J. H., & Geddes, D. (1999). Social and personal determinants of workplace aggression: Evidence for the impact of perceived injustice and the type A behavior pattern. *Aggressive Behavior, 25,* 281–296.

Bass, B. M. (1985). *Leadership and performance beyond expectations.* New York: Free Press.

Bedeian, A. G., Armenakis, A. A., & Curran, S. M. (1980). Personality correlates of role stress. *Psychological Reports, 46,* 627–632.

Beehr, T. A. (1976). Perceived situational moderators of the relationship between subjective role ambiguity and role strain. *Journal of Applied Psychology, 61,* 35–40.

Beehr, T. A. (1995). *Psychological stress in the workplace.* London: Routledge.

Beehr, T. A., & Glazer, S. (2004). Organizational role stress. In J. Barling, K. Kelloway, & M. R. Frone (Eds.), *Handbook of work stress* (pp. 7–33). Thousand Oaks, CA: Sage.

Bennett, R. J., & Robinson, S. L. (2000). Development of a measure of workplace deviance. *Journal of Applied Psychology, 85,* 349–360.

Bies, R. J., & Moag, J. F. (1986). Interactional justice: Communication criteria for fairness. In R. J. Lewicki, B. H. Sheppard, & M. H. Bazerman (Eds.), *Research on negotiations in organizations, 1,* 43–55.

Braverman, M. (1999). *Preventing workplace violence: A guide for employers and practitioners.* Thousand Oaks, CA: Sage.

Bycio, P., Hackett, R. D., & Allen, J. S. (1995). Further assessment of Bass's (1985) conceptualization of transactional and transformational leadership. *Journal of Applied Psychology, 80,* 469–478.

California Occupational Safety and Health Administration. (1995). *Guidelines for workplace security.* Sacramento, CA: Author.

Castillo, D. N., & Jenkins, E. L. (1994). Industries and occupations at high risk for work-related homicide. *Journal of Occupational Medicine, 36,* 125–132.

Chen, P. Y., & Spector, P. E. (1992). Relationships of work stressors with aggression, withdrawal, theft and substance use: An exploratory study. *Journal of Occupational and Organizational Psychology, 65,* 177–184.

Cohen-Charash, Y., Mueller, J. S., & Goldman, M. (2004, August). *When do we help and when do we harm? Effects of outcome favorability and procedural fairness on envy and behavior.* Paper presented at the 2004 Academy of Management Meetings in New Orleans.

Colquitt, J. A. (2001). On the dimensionality of organizational justice: A construct validation of a measure. *Journal of Applied Psychology, 86*, 386–400.

Colquitt, J. A., Conlon, D. E., Wesson, J. M., Porter, C. O. L. H., & Ng, K. Y. (2001). Justice at the millennium: A meta-analytic review of 25 years of organizational justice research. *Journal of Applied Psychology, 86*, 425–445.

Dienesch, R. M., & Liden, R. C. (1986). Leader-member exchange model of leadership: A critique and further development. *Academy of Management Review, 11*, 618–634.

Douglas, S. C., & Martinko, M. J. (2001). Exploring the role of individual differences in the prediction of workplace aggression. *Journal of Applied Psychology, 4*, 547–559.

Drekker, I., & Barling, J. (1998). Personal and organizational predictors of sexual harassment of women by men. *Journal of Occupational Health Psychology, 3*, 7–18.

Dupré, K. E. (2004). *Beating up the boss: The prediction and prevention of interpersonal aggression targeting workplace supervisors.* Unpublished doctoral dissertation. Queen's University, Kingston, Ontario, Canada.

Ehrensaft, M. K., Langhinrichsen-Rohling, J., Heyman, R. E., O'Leary, K. D., & Lawrence, E. (1999). Feeling controlled in marriage: A phenomenon specific to physically aggressive couples? *Journal of Family Psychology, 13*, 20–32.

Einarsen, S., Raknes, B. I., & Matthiesen, S. B. (1994). Bullying and harassment at work and their relationships to work environment quality: An exploratory study. *European Work and Organizational Psychologist, 4*, 381–401.

Fineman, S. (1983). Work meanings, non-work, and the taken-for-granted. *Journal of Management Studies, 20*, 143–155.

Fitzgerald, L. F. (1993). Sexual harrassment: Violence against women in the workplace, *American Psychologist, 48*, 1070–1076.

Fox, S., & Spector, P. E. (1999). A model of work frustration-aggression. *Journal of Organizational Behavior, 20*, 915–931.

Glomb, T. M. (2002). Workplace anger and aggression: Informing conceptual models with data from specific encounters. *Journal of Occupational Health Psychology, 7*, 20–36.

Graen, G. B., & Uhl-Bien, M. (1995). Relationship-based approach to leadership: Development of leader-member exchange (LMX) theory of leadership of 25 years: Applying a multi-level, multi-domain perspective. *Leadership Quarterly, 6*, 219–247.

Greenberg, J. (1993). Stealing in the name of justice: Informational and interpersonal moderators of theft reactions to underpayment inequity. *Organizational Behavior and Human Decision Processes, 54*, 81–103.

Greenberg, J. (1994). Using socially fair treatment to promote acceptance of a work site smoking ban. *Journal of Applied Psychology, 79*, 288–297.

Greenberg, L., & Barling, J. (1999). Predicting employee aggression against coworkers, subordinates and supervisors: The roles of person behaviors and perceived workplace factors. *Journal of Organizational Behavior, 20*, 897–913.

Hemingway, M. A., & Conte, J. M. (2003). The perceived fairness of layoff practices. *Journal of Applied Social Psychology, 33*, 1588–1617.

Hershcovis, M. S., Turner, N., Barling, J., Arnold, K. A., Dupré, K. E., Inness, M., et al. (2004, August). *Right on target: A meta-analysis of the predictors of insider-initiated workplace aggression.* Paper presented at the Annual Academy of Management Conference, New Orleans, LA.

Hershcovis, M. S., Turner, N., Barling, J., Arnold, K. A., Dupré, K. E., Inness, M., et al. (in press). Predicting workplace aggression: A meta-analysis. *Journal of Applied Psychology.*

Howard, J. (2001). Workplace violence in organizations: An exploratory study of organizational prevention techniques. *Employee Responsibilities and Rights Journal, 13,* 57–75.

Howell, J. M., & Avolio, B. J. (1993). Transformational leadership, transactional leadership, locus of control, support for innovation: Key predictors of consolidated-business-unit performance. *Journal of Applied Psychology, 78,* 891–902.

Injury Prevention Research Center. (2001, February). *Workplace violence: A report to the nation.* Iowa City: Injury Prevention Research Center, University of Iowa. Retrieved September 9, 2005, from http://www.public-health.uiowa.edu/iprc/NATION.PDF

Inness, M., Barling, J., & Turner, N. (2005). Understanding supervisor-targeted aggression: A within-person, between-jobs design. *Journal of Applied Psychology, 90,* 731–739.

International Labour Oranization. (2000). *Safework: What can be done about violence at work?* Retrieved December 30, 2004, from www.ilo.org/public/english/protection/safework/violence/canbe.htm

Jahoda, M. (1979). The impact of unemployment in the 1930s and the 1970s. *Bulletin of the British Psychological Society, 32,* 309–314.

Jenkins, E. L. (1996). *Violence in the workplace: Risk factors and prevention strategies* (DHHS Publication No. 96-100). Washington, DC: Government Printing Office.

Jones, D. (2004, August). *Counterproductive work behavior toward supervisors and organizations: Injustice, revenge, and context.* Paper presented at the best paper proceedings of the 64th Annual Meeting of the Academy of Management, New Orleans, LA.

Kahn, R. (1980). Conflict, ambiguity, and overload: Three elements in job stress. In D. Katz, R. Kahn, & J. Adams (Eds.), *The study of organizations* (pp. 418–428). San Francisco: Jossey-Bass.

Kahn, R. L., Wolfe, D. M., Quinn, R. P., Snoek, J. D., & Rosenthal, R. A. (1964). *Organizational stress: Studies in role conflict and ambiguity.* New York: John Wiley.

Karasek, R. A. (1979). Job demands, job decision latitude, and mental strain: Implications for job redesign. *Administrative Science Quarterly, 24,* 285–308.

Kark, R., Shamir, B., & Chen, G. (2003). The two faces of transformational leadership: Empowerment and dependency. *Journal of Applied Psychology, 88,* 246–255.

Kelloway, E. K., Barling, J., & Helleur, J. (2000). Enhancing transformational leadership: The roles of training and feedback. *Leadership and Organizational Development Journal, 21,* 145–149.

Kernan, M. C., & Hanges, P. J. (2002). Survivor reactions to reorganization: Antecedents and consequences of procedural, interpersonal and informational justice. *Journal of Applied Psychology, 87,* 916–928.

Koh, W. L., Steers, R. M., & Terborg, J. R. (1995). The effects of transformational leadership on teacher attitudes and student performance in Singapore. *Journal of Organizational Behavior, 16,* 319–333.

Kuzmits, F. E. (2001, Spring). Workplace homicide: Prediction or prevention. *SAM Advanced Management Journal,* 4–7.

LeBlanc, M. M., & Kelloway, E. K. (2002). Predictors and outcomes of workplace violence and aggression. *Journal of Applied Psychology, 87,* 444–453.

Leventhal, G. S. (1980). What should be done with equity theory? New approaches to the study of fairness in social relationships. In K. Gergen, M. Greenberg, & R. Willis (Eds.), *Social exchange: Advances in theory and research* (pp. 27–55). New York: Plenum.

Liden, R. C., & Maslyn, J. M. (1998). Multidimensionality of leader-member exchange: An empirical assessment through scale development. *Journal of Management, 24,* 43–72.

Lind, A. E., Kanfer, R., & Earley, C. P. (1990). Voice, control, and procedural justice: Instrumental and non-instrumental concerns in fairness judgments. *Journal of Personality and Social Psychology, 59,* 952–959.

Martinko, M. J., & Zellars, K. L. (1998). Toward a theory of workplace violence and aggression: A cognitive appraisal perspective. In R. W. Griffin & A. O'Leary-Kelly (Eds.), *Dysfunctional behavior in organizations: Violent and deviant behavior* (Monographs in Organizational Behavior and Industrial Relations, Vol. 23, pp. 1–42). Stamford, CT: Elsevier Science/JAI Press.

Mueller, C. W., Iverson, R. D., & Jo, D. G. (1999). Distributive justice evaluations in two cultural contexts: A comparison of U.S. and South Korean teachers. *Human Relations, 52,* 869–893.

Murphy, C. M., & O'Leary, K. D. (1989). Psychological aggression predicts physical aggression in early marriage. *Journal of Consulting and Clinical Psychology, 57,* 579–582.

O'Driscoll, M. P., & Beehr, T. A. (2000). Moderating effects of perceived control and need for clarity on the relationship between role stressors and employee affective reactions. *Journal of Social Psychology, 140,* 151–159.

O'Leary-Kelly, A. M., Griffin, R. W., & Glew, D. J. (1996). Organization-motivated aggression: A research framework. *Academy of Management Review, 21,* 225–253.

Pillai, R., Schriesheim, C. A., & Williams, E. S. (1999). Fairness perceptions and trust as mediators for transformational and transactional leadership: A two-sample study. *Journal of Management, 25,* 897–933.

Pratt, L., & Barling, J. (1988). Differentiating daily hassles, acute and chronic stressors: A framework and its implications. In J. R. Hurrell, L. R. Murphy, S. L. Sauter, & C. L. Cooper (Eds.), *Occupational stress: Issues and developments in research* (pp. 41–53). London: Taylor Francis.

Schat, A. C. H. (2004). *In praise of intolerance: Investigating the effects of organizational tolerance on the incidence and consequences of workplace aggression.* Unpublished dissertation. University of Guelph, Ontario, Canada.

Schaubroeck, J., & Merritt, D. E. (1997). Divergent effects of job control on coping with work stressors: The key of role self-efficacy. *Academy of Management Journal, 40,* 738–754.

Shaw, J. C., Wild, E., & Colquitt, J. A. (2003). To justify or excuse? A meta-analytic review of the effects of explanations. *Journal of Applied Psychology, 88,* 444–458.

Skarlicki, D. P., & Folger, R. (1997). Retaliation in the workplace: The roles of distributive, procedural and interactional justice. *Journal of Applied Psychology, 82,* 434–443.

Skarlicki, D. P., Folger, R., & Tesluk, P. (1999). Personality as a moderator in the relationship between fairness and retaliation. *Academy of Management Journal, 42,* 100–108.

Sovereign, K. L. (1994). *Personnel law* (3rd ed.). Englewood Cliffs, NJ: Prentice Hall.

Spector, P. E. (2002). Employee control and occupational stress. *Current Directions in Psychological Science, 11,* 133–136.

Sygnatur, E. F., & Toscano, G. A. (2000, Spring). Work-related homicides: The facts. *Compensation and Working Conditions, 5*(1). Retrieved September 9, 2005, from http://www.bls.gov/opub/cwc/archive/spring2000art1.pdf

Tepper, B. J. (2000). Consequences of abusive supervision. *Academy of Management Journal, 43,* 178–190.

Townsend, J., Phillips, J. S., & Elkins, T. J. (2000). Employee retaliation: The neglected consequence of poor leader-member exchange relations. *Journal of Occupational Health Psychology, 5,* 457–463.

Waxman, H. S. (1995). Putting workplace violence in perspective. *Security Management, 39,* 123–126.

Wayne, S. J., Shore, L. M., & Liden, R. C. (1997). Perceived organizational support and leader-member exchange: A social exchange perspective. *Academy of Management Journal, 40,* 82–111.

Name Index _____

Subject Index _____

About the Editors _____

E. Kevin Kelloway holds an appointment as Professor of Management and Psychology in the Sobey School of Business, Saint Mary's University. He is a prolific researcher having published over 100 articles, book chapters, and technical reports. His research interests include occupational health psychology, leadership, the development and measurement of work attitudes and values, unionization, and the management of knowledge workers. He is coauthor of *The Union and Its Members: A Psychological Approach* (Oxford University Press, 1992), *Using Flexible Work Arrangements to Combat Job Stress* (John Wiley, 1998), and *Management of Occupational Health and Safety* (3rd ed., Nelson, 2005) and the author of *Using LISREL for Structural Equation Modeling: A Researcher's Guide* (Sage, 1998). With Dr. Julian Barling (Queen's University), he edited a book series, *Advanced Topics in Organizational Psychology* (Sage) and has coedited the volume *Young Workers: Varieties of Experience* (APA, 1999). Most recently he coedited *The Handbook of Work Stress* (Sage Publications, 2004). He serves on the editorial boards of both the *Canadian Journal of Behavioral Science* and the *Journal of Occupational Health Psychology*. As a consultant, he maintains an active practice consulting to private and public sector organizations on issues related to leadership, performance management, and measurement of employee attitudes and performance.

Julian Barling, PhD, is Professor and Associate Dean, Queen's School of Business, a Fellow of the Royal Society of Canada, and Queen's Research Chair at Queen's University. He is the author of several books, including *Employment, Stress and Family Functioning* (John Wiley, 1990) and *The Union and Its Members: A Psychological Approach* (with Clive Fullagar and Kevin Kelloway, Oxford University Press, 1992). He coedited *The Psychology of Workplace Safety* (APA, 2003) and was senior editor of *The Handbook of Work Stress* (Sage, 2004). In addition, he is the author or editor of well over 125 research articles and book chapters and serves on the editorial boards of the *Journal of Applied Psychology, Leadership and Organizational Development Journal,* and *Stress Medicine*. He was the editor of the *Journal of Occupational Health Psychology* and chair of the American Psychological Association's Task Force on Workplace Violence.

From 1989 to 1991, he was the chairperson of the Advisory Council on Occupational Health and Safety to the Ontario Minister of Labour.

Joseph J. Hurrell Jr., PhD, is currently a consultant in the area of occupational health and safety and was formerly a researcher at the National Institute for Occupational Safety and Health (NIOSH). Before leaving NIOSH in January of 2005, he served as the Associate Director for Science for the Division of Surveillance, Hazard Evaluations and Field Studies. In this position, he was responsible for the scientific quality of research generated by over 180 occupational health researchers. He received his PhD from Miami University in 1982 and was an adjunct faculty member at Xavier University. He has had a long-standing research interest in the health and safety consequences of occupational stress and has published numerous scientific articles and edited six books on the topic. He is a cofounder of the *Journal of Occupational Health Psychology* and served as its coeditor for 6 years. He currently serves as a member of the American Psychological Association's National Task Force on Occupational Violence.

About the Contributors

Collette Arens Bates is currently finishing her PhD in the Sam M. Walton College of Business at the University of Arkansas. Her research interests include work-family conflict, social support, sexual harassment, and gender diversity and differences.

Lynn Bowes-Sperry is Associate Professor of Management at Western New England College. Her research, which focuses on the areas of sexual harassment, ethical decision making, and organizational justice, has been published in journals such as *Academy of Management Review, Journal of Management, Human Resources Management Review, Small Group Research,* and *Group and Organization Management.* Her work also appears in several edited books such as *The Handbook of Gender and Work* and *Misbehavior and Dysfunctional Attitudes in Organizations.* She has held several leadership roles in the Gender and Diversity Division of the Academy of Management. She received her PhD in business administration from the University of Connecticut.

James E. Cameron is Associate Professor in the Department of Psychology at Saint Mary's University in Halifax, Nova Scotia, where he has taught since 1999. He received a PhD degree in social-personality psychology from York University in Toronto. Most of his previous and current research is concerned with social identity, or the contribution of various group memberships— including gender, nation, and organization—to the self. He is particularly interested in the nature and consequences of social identification with respect to intergroup attitudes, collective action, psychological well-being, and globalization. His article "A Three Factor Model of Social Identity" was recently published in *Self and Identity.*

Victor M. Catano is Professor and Chairperson of Psychology at Saint Mary's University, Halifax, Nova Scotia. He is the first author of *Recruitment and Selection in Canada,* one of the leading texts in the field of human resource management. He served for 8 years as Editor of *Canadian Psychology,* the flagship journal of the Canadian Psychological Association. In recognition of his contributions to the science and practice of psychology in Canada, he was elected a Fellow by the Canadian Psychological

Association and an Honorary Member by Canadian Forces Personnel Selection Officers Association. He was recently awarded the Canadian Psychology Association's Award for Distinguished Contributions to Education and Training and the Canadian Society for Industrial and Organizational Psychology's Award for Distinguished Contributions to Industrial and Organizational Psychology.

Cary L. Cooper, CBE, is Professor of Organizational Psychology and Health at Lancaster University, England. He is President of the British Academy of Management, Founding Editor of the Journal of Organizational Behavior, and an Academician of the Academy for the Social Sciences. He is a Fellow of the British Psychological Society, Royal Society of Medicine, Royal Society of Health, Royal Society of Arts, and the Academy of Management. He was awarded the Commander of the Most Excellent Order of the British Empire by the Queen in June 2001 for his contribution to occupational safety and health. He is the author or editor of over 100 books and several hundred scholarly articles.

Lilia M. Cortina is Assistant Professor of Psychology and Women's Studies at the University of Michigan. She received her PhD in clinical-community psychology from the University of Illinois at Urbana-Champaign in 1999. Her research addresses sexual harassment, incivility, and gender in organizations, focusing in particular on factors that mitigate or exacerbate the impact of victimization on employees' psychological and occupational health. Her work has appeared in such journals as the *Journal of Applied Psychology, Journal of Personality and Social Psychology, Journal of Consulting and Clinical Psychology, Journal of Occupational Health Psychology,* and *Psychology of Women Quarterly.* She currently serves on the editorial boards of the *Journal of Applied Psychology, Journal of Occupational Health Psychology,* and *Psychology of Women Quarterly.*

Arla L. Day, PhD, is an Associate Psychology professor at Saint Mary's University. She received her BA in Psychology from the University of Manitoba, and her MASc and PhD in industrial/organizational psychology from the University of Waterloo. She is a founding member of both the CN Centre for Occupational Health and Safety and the Centre for Leadership Excellence. Her current research activities involve the areas of organizational and employee health and well-being (in terms of workplace aggression, stress, coping, and work-family balance), selection practices, emotional intelligence, and leadership, and she is a reviewer for several scholarly journals. Her teaching activities involve psychometrics and assessment, organizational psychology, human resources management, and statistics. She has extensive consulting experience for several private and public organizations, in terms of developing and administering organizational surveys, conducting structured selection interviews, administering and validating employment tests, providing performance feedback, conducting job analyses, reviewing and developing employment equity plans, and evaluating selection procedures.

Joerg Dietz is Associate Professor in the Richard Ivey School of Business at the University of Western Ontario. He earned his PhD in organizational behavior at Tulane University's A. B. Freeman School of Business. His current research interests include employee-customer linkages in service organizations, contextual models of workplace aggression, and prejudice and discrimination in the workplace. He has published articles in journals such as the *Academy of Management Journal, Journal of Applied Psychology,* and *Organizational Behavior and Human Decision Processes.*

Theresa Domagalski is Associate Professor of Management in the College of Business at the Florida Institute of Technology in Melbourne, Florida. She received her PhD from the University of South Florida in management and organizational behavior. Her current research interests include emotions in organizations, the relationship between gender and status, and the use of film and literary genres as methodological and pedagogical tools for understanding organizations. Her work is published in *Human Relations, Organizational Analysis, Organization & Environment,* and *Journal of Management Inquiry.*

Kathryne E. Dupré received her PhD in organizational behaviour from Queen's University (Kingston, Ontario). She joined the faculty of business administration at Memorial University of Newfoundland in 2003 where she teaches in the areas of organizational behavior and human resource management. She received her MSc in industrial/organizational psychology from Saint Mary's University (Halifax, Nova Scotia) and her honors BA in psychology from Queen's University. Her research interests include workplace aggression, employee safety, occupational stress, and young employees' experiences in the workplace. Her recent research involves investigating the prediction and spillover of workplace aggression within and across contexts, as well as the escalation of workplace aggression. Her work has been published in the *Journal of Applied Psychology* and *Handbook of Stress, Medicine and Health* and presented at several national and international conferences.

LCol Kelly M. J. Farley earned his PhD in social psychology from Carleton University and is a researcher and analyst in the Shape Army Culture Project located at the National Defence Headquarters in Ottawa. He is the author of several papers in the area of stress in operations and the human dimension of operational readiness. His current research interests include military organizational culture issues such as the right of association, the "social contract," and the role of the regimental system in the development of army culture.

Richard B. Felson is Professor of Crime, Law, and Justice and of Sociology at Pennsylvania State University. His is currently doing research on domestic violence, race differences in assault, alcohol use by offenders and victims, and the response of the criminal justice system to different types of assault. His articles have appeared in *Criminology, Journal of Marriage and Family, Social Psychology Quarterly,* and *Journal of Personality and Social Psychology.* His books, including *Violence and Gender Reexamined* and

Violence, Aggression, and Coercive Actions (with J. Tedeschi) were published by the American Psychological Association.

Suzy Fox is Associate Professor in the Institute of Human Resources and Industrial Relations, Graduate School of Business, Loyola University Chicago, where she teaches organizational behavior, global human resource management, and ethics of employment and diversity. She received her PhD in industrial/organizational psychology and MBA from the University of South Florida. Current research projects include studies of emotional and behavioral responses to job stress, counterproductive work behavior, relations between subtle/symbolic/modern racism and workplace bullying (racial/ethnic bullying), and international comparisons of professionally successful women. With Paul Spector, she coedited *Counterproductive Work Behavior: Investigations of Actors and Targets*. She has published in the *Journal of Vocational Behavior, Journal of Organizational Behavior, Organizational Dynamics, Journal of Occupational and Organizational Psychology, Journal of Occupational Health Psychology, Human Resource Management Review, International Review of Selection and Assessment, Personnel Psychology,* and *Handbook of Organization Studies*. She just completed 3 years as associate editor of *Human Relations*.

Lori Francis is currently Assistant Professor in the Department of Psychology at Saint Mary's University in Halifax, Nova Scotia. She received a PhD in industrial/organizational psychology from the University of Guelph, Ontario, Canada. She has broad research interests in organizational psychology, including occupational health and safety and workplace fairness. She is a member of Saint Mary's University's Centre for Leadership Excellence as well as the CN Centre for Occupational Health and Safety.

Michael R. Frone, PhD, is a Senior Research Scientist at the Research Institute on Addictions and Research and Associate Professor of Psychology, State University of New York at Buffalo. He has published extensively in leading journals on work-family dynamics; the work-related predictors and outcomes of employee mental health, physical health, and substance use; and the developmental outcomes of youth employment. He is coeditor of *The Psychology of Workplace Safety* (APA, 2004) and *The Handbook of Work Stress* (Sage, 2004). He is associate editor of the *Journal of Occupational Health Psychology* and has served on the editorial boards of the *Journal of Applied Psychology, Journal of Occupational Health Psychology, Journal of Organizational Behavior, Organizational Behavior and Human Decision Processes,* and *Organizational Research Methods*. With funding from the National Institutes of Health, he recently completed a large national telephone survey of workplace health and safety.

Harjinder Gill is Assistant Professor in the Psychology Department at the University of Guelph. She completed her graduate studies in industrial and organizational psychology at the University of Western Ontario. Her research focuses on issues of fairness and aggression in the workplace. She has presented her work at peer-reviewed conferences and in journals.

Theresa M. Glomb is the Carlson Professor of Human Resources and Industrial Relations in the Carlson School of Management at the University of Minnesota. She received her PhD in industrial/organizational psychology from the University of Illinois in 1998 and her BA in psychology from DePaul University in 1993. She has conducted research and published in the areas of anger and aggressive behaviors in organizations, emotional labor, emotional expression in organizations, sexual harassment, and job attitudes and behaviors. She has published in outlets such as the *Journal of Applied Psychology, Organizational Behavior and Human Decision Processes, Academy of Management Journal,* and *Journal of Occupational Health Psychology.* She has been teaching masters and doctoral students in the human resources and industrial relations program at the University of Minnesota in the areas of staffing, training and development, motivation, and organizational behavior.

M. Steve Harvey is Professor and Department Chair at the Williams School of Business, Bishop's University in Lennoxville, Quebec. In addition, he is an adjunct graduate faculty member with the Department of Psychology at the Université de Sherbrooke where he serves as adviser to students in the doctoral program. He earned his PhD in industrial and organizational psychology from the University of Guelph in 1996. His research interests span various domains of organizational psychology including occupational stress, health and well-being, young workers' experiences, organizational leadership, and psychological harassment and violence in the workplace. His academic work, both in English and in French, has been published as book chapters, conference proceedings, and in several journals including, among others, *Canadian Psychology, Journal of Business and Psychology, Work & Stress,* and the *Journal of Occupational Health Psychology.*

M. Sandy Hershcovis is a PhD candidate in management, specializing in organizational behavior, at Queen's University. Her research examines the predictors, outcomes, and prevention of workplace aggression. She has conducted two meta-analytic reviews of the field of workplace aggression. The first meta-analysis examines the situational and individual predictors of insider-initiated aggression and the target-specific nature of such aggression. The second meta-analysis examines the attitudinal, health, and behavioral outcomes of experienced aggression from insiders and outsiders of the organization. Her work has appeared in book chapters as well as peer-reviewed journals, including the *Journal of Applied Psychology.*

Michelle Inness is Assistant Professor at the University of Alberta, School of Business. She is currently completing her PhD at Queen's University School of Business with a specialization in organizational behavior. Her research interests include a wide range of topics related to employee well-being, such as workplace aggression, occupational health and safety, job attitudes, and unique groups of workers such as peacekeepers. Her work has appeared in the *Journal of Applied Psychology* and the *British Journal of Social Psychology*.

Loraleigh Keashly is a Social–Organizational Psychologist and Associate Professor at Wayne State University. She is currently Academic Director, MA in Dispute. For the past 20 years, her research and practice has focused on conflict and conflict resolution at the interpersonal, group, and intergroup levels. Her current research focus is the nature of, and the personal and organizational effects of, emotionally abusive behaviors in the workplace. She has published a number of articles in the past 11 years on this topic that have appeared in venues such as *Violence and Victims, Work & Stress, Journal of Emotional Abuse, Journal of Healthcare Management, Employee Rights and Employment Policy Journal*, and several edited volumes. She has a particular interest in the role of organizational structure and culture in the facilitation or mitigation of emotionally abusive behavior among employees with an eye to developing and evaluating prevention and intervention efforts. She also has extensive experience as a consultant and trainer in conflict analysis and resolution.

Elizabeth Kelley is Assistant Professor of Management at the School of Business Administration, Dalhousie University, Halifax, Nova Scotia. Her primary research focus is leadership, particularly in the remote environment. Her most recent research has examined the effect of context on remote leader-member relationships. Secondarily, she has published in the area of the role of context in the development of management theory.

Marilyn Lanza is a Nurse Researcher and Psychotherapist. She has done extensive research, writing, and lecturing on assaultive patients. She was the first researcher to document staff reactions to being assaulted. Many hospitals now offer counseling to their assaulted staff based upon her work. Her current research includes factors contributing to blame placement, simulation methodologies to study assault, development of clinical pathways for use of the community meeting as a prevention of or intervention to assaultive behavior, and a treatment model for psychodynamic group psychotherapy as an intervention for assaultive men and batterers. She has developed, psychometrically validated, and published four instruments: The Assault Response Questionnaire (ARQ), Assault Rating Scale (ARS), Patient Assault Vignettes, and Aggression Observation Scale for Group Psychotherapy (AOSGP). She is a member of the American Psychiatric Association Task Force on Clinician Safety, is the 1994 recipient of Massachusetts Nurses' Association Research Award and the Distinguished Nurse Research Award, and the AHEC Nursing Research Award, 2000. She served on the Massachusetts Governor's Commission on Quality Improvement and Violence Task Forces, both locally and nationally. In her current position as Nurse Researcher, she is responsible for a national VA study: *Violence Assessment, Mitigation, and Prevention*.

Manon Mireille LeBlanc teaches Organizational Behavior and Human Resource Management in the Williams School of Business at Bishop's University (Lennoxville, Quebec). She is also pursuing a PhD in organizational behavior from Queen's University (Kingston, Ontario). She received her honors BA in psychology from Concordia University (Montreal, Quebec) and her MA in industrial/organizational psychology from the University of Guelph (Guelph, Ontario). Her research interests include employee safety, occupational stress, and workplace violence. Her dissertation is focused on the effects of intimate partner violence on women's employment. She has coauthored three book chapters, and she has published in peer-reviewed journals, including the *Journal of Applied Psychology*.

TK Logan is currently an Associate Professor in the Department of Behavioral Science at the University of Kentucky with an appointment in the Center on Drug and Alcohol Research. She has been funded by the National Institute on Drug Abuse (NIDA) and by the National Institute on Alcohol Abuse and Alcoholism (NIAAA) and has completed several drug court program evaluations as well as studies focused on intimate partner violence and divorce; intimate partner violence and custody outcomes; stalking victimization and perpetration; health and mental health status, barriers, and service use among women; HIV risk behavior; and health, mental health, substance use, and victimization among rural and urban women. She is senior author on several books focused on victimization, mental health, and substance abuse among women and is also coauthoring an evaluation text.

Catherine Loughlin was recently appointed Canada Research Chair in Management at the Sobey School of Business. She completed her PhD in industrial/organizational psychology at Queen's University and held a Social Sciences and Humanities Research Council of Canada (SSHRC) Post-doctoral Fellowship there in the Business School before teaching in management at the University of Toronto. She has published papers in the *Journal of Experimental Psychology, Journal of Organizational Behavior,* and *Journal of Applied Psychology* and coauthored book chapters on work stress, workplace health and safety, and the quality of youth employment. She is a reviewer for journals including the *Journal of Applied Psychology* and the *Journal of Occupational Health Psychology*. She has consulted for the government of Canada and private industry on leadership, work stress, occupational health, and the future workforce. Her latest SSHRC grant supports leadership research on women in management (with Dr. K. Arnold, 2005–2008).

Caroline Macke, MSW, is pursuing a doctoral degree in social work at the University of Kentucky. While working as a research assistant for Dr. Jennifer E. Swanberg, her research activities have focused predominantly on domestic violence and employment. In addition, she is interested in attachment theory, particularly as it pertains to violent relationships. Before earning her MSW at the University of Kentucky, she was awarded a bachelor's degree in economics, business, and international studies, as well as an associate's degree in political science at Thomas More College.

Jane Mullen is an Assistant Professor of Organizational Behaviour and Human Resource Management at Mount Allison University, New Brunswick, Canada. She received her PhD in Business Administration (Management) from Saint Mary's University. Her research interests include transformational leadership, occupational health and safety, and workplace violence.

Anne M. O'Leary-Kelly is the William R. and Cacilia Howard Chair in Management in the Department of Management at the University of Arkansas. She received her PhD in organizational behavior from Michigan State University in 1990. Her research interests include the study of aggressive work behavior (violence, sexual harassment) and individual attachments to organizations (psychological contracts, identification). Her work has appeared in, among others, the *Academy of Management Review, Academy of Management Journal, Journal of Applied Psychology, Journal of Management,* and *Journal of Organizational Behavior.* She has been a corecipient of the Outstanding Publication in Organizational Behavior Award and the Dorothy Harlow Outstanding Paper Award given by the Academy of Management; a corecipient of the Richard A. Swanson Award for Excellence in Research from the American Society for Training and Development; and a corecipient of the Ralph C. Hoeber Award for Excellence in Research for work in the *American Business Law Journal.* She currently serves on the Executive Committee of the Organizational Behavior Division of the Academy of Management.

Stephen B. Perrott is Associate Professor of Psychology at Mount Saint Vincent University in Halifax, Nova Scotia. He served as a constable in the Halifax Police Department from 1976 to 1986 and completed his doctorate in clinical psychology at McGill University in Montreal in 1992. His research focuses at the interface of clinical, social, and criminal justice psychology with a special focus on policing issues. While maintaining a part-time clinical practice, he has increasingly focused upon international development, including a sex tourism project in the Philippines and a peer health program in the Gambia. He is currently project director of a 6-year, $1 million project funded by the Canadian International Development Agency promoting community-based policing and restorative justice with the Gambia Police Force.

Charlotte Rayner is Professor of Human Resource Management at Portsmouth Business School, UK. She has been involved in research into bullying at work since the mid-1990s, when she completed the first major UK survey for the BBC. She has continued to research this topic, including a set of surveys for Britain's largest trade union, UNISON, in 1997 and 2000. She has recently published a book, *Workplace Bullying: What We Know, Who Is to Blame and What Can We Do?* with Cary Cooper and Helge Hoel. She has a PhD from Manchester, an MBA from City University Business

School, and a first degree in psychology from Newcastle, and she is a Fellow of the RSA. She writes on the topic of bullying at work and negative behavior generally for professional and academic publications. She is particularly interested in prevention strategies. (Email: charlotte.rayner@port.ac.uk)

Aaron C. H. Schat is Assistant Professor of Organizational Behavior and Human Resource Management at the DeGroote School of Business at McMaster University. He received his BA from Redeemer University College and his MA and PhD in industrial-organizational psychology from the University of Guelph. His research interests include the nature, antecedents, and consequences of aggressive behavior at work and workplace aggression and violence intervention strategies. He is a member of the Academy of Management, Canadian Psychological Association, American Psychological Association, Canadian Society for Industrial and Organizational Psychology, and the Society for Industrial and Organizational Psychology.

Irvin Sam Schonfeld is Professor of Psychology and Education at the City University of New York and a Lecturer in Psychiatry at Columbia University. He completed his doctoral degree at the CUNY Graduate Center and completed a postdoctoral degree in epidemiology at Columbia. He has published in *Developmental Psychology, Child Development, Journal of Occupational Health Psychology,* and *Genetic, Social, and General Psychology Monographs.* His current interests include impact of working conditions on the health and morale of teachers, antisocial conduct in youth, and methodological issues in research.

Paul E. Spector is Professor of Industrial-Organizational Psychology and the Industrial-Organizational Psychology Doctoral Program Director at the University of South Florida. His work has appeared in many journals, including *Academy of Management Journal, Journal of Applied Psychology, Journal of Management, Journal of Organizational Behavior, Journal of Occupational and Organizational Psychology, Journal of Vocational Behavior, Organizational Behavior and Human Decision Processes, Personnel Psychology,* and *Psychological Bulletin.* At present he is the Point/Counterpoint editor for *Journal of Organizational Behavior* and is on the editorial boards of *Journal of Occupational and Organizational Psychology, Organizational Research Methods,* and *Personnel Psychology.* In 1991, the Institute for Scientific Information listed him as one of the 50 highest-impact contemporary researchers (of over 102,000) in psychology worldwide.

Jennifer E. Swanberg is Assistant Professor at the College of Social Work, University of Kentucky. Her research focuses on the relationships between work, family, and organizational effectiveness, especially among understudied populations, including low-wage workers, victims of intimate partner violence, informal caregivers, and workers employed in nonprofit public organizations. She has published in journals such as *Work, Family and Community, Nonprofit Management & Leadership, Journal of Economic* *and Family Issues, Trauma, Violence & Abuse,* and *Journal of Occupational Health Psychology.* She has been funded by the Ford Foundation and the Alfred P. Sloan Foundation.

Sean Tucker is a PhD candidate in the Queen's School of Business at Queen's University. His research interests include workplace safety, workplace aggression, apologies, shared leadership, and labor history.

Terrance Weatherbee currently teaches at the F. C. Manning School of Business at Acadia University and is a PhD candidate in the midst of completing his dissertation. Before entering the academy, he had 24 years of experience as a manager in both private and public sector organizations, the majority of which were in the area of corporate training and organizational change or restructuring, usually driven by the introduction of new technologies. Consequently, his research interests primarily focus on the uses of technology with specific concentration on the emergent, and often organizationally unforeseen, negative postintroduction effects, such as "technostress" or "cyberaggression." Additional areas of research include the historical evolution of business schools and business education from both institutional and critical perspectives. He has held positions in both the Sobey School of Business at Saint Mary's University and the F. C. Manning School of Business at Acadia University.